THE THEORY AND PRACTICE
OF
SEAMANSHIP

THE THEORY
AND PRACTICE OF
SEAMANSHIP

BY

GRAHAM DANTON
EXTRA MASTER MARINER
ROYAL SOCIETY OF ARTS SILVER MEDALLIST 1950 AND 1957
GRIFFITHS AWARD 1957
SENIOR LECTURER IN SEAMANSHIP
PLYMOUTH POLYTECHNIC

LONDON, BOSTON AND HENLEY

ROUTLEDGE & KEGAN PAUL

First published in 1962
Second edition (revised) 1966
Third edition 1969
Fourth edition (revised and metricated) 1972
Fifth edition (with minor revisions) 1974
Sixth edition (revised) 1976
Seventh edition (revised) 1978
Eighth edition (with minor revisions) 1980
by Routledge & Kegan Paul Ltd
39 Store Street
London WC1E 7DD
Broadway House, Newtown Road
Henley-on-Thames, Oxon RG9 1EN and
9 Park Street, Boston, Mass. 02108, USA

Reprinted by photolithography in Great Britain
by Unwin Brothers Limited
The Gresham Press Old Woking Surrey England
A member of the Staples Printing Group

ISBN 0 7100 0502 4

CONTENTS

AUTHOR'S NOTE   *page* xiii

ACKNOWLEDGMENTS   xiv

TABLE OF CONVERSIONS   xv

I.   THE ANCHOR   1

II.   MOORING   35

III. THE PRINCIPLES OF SHIP HANDLING   51

IV.   PRACTICAL SHIP HANDLING   75

V.   ICE   108

VI.   LIFE-SAVING AND DISTRESS   118

VII. DAMAGE CONTROL   141

VIII. STRANDING AND BEACHING   159

IX.   EMERGENCIES   182

X.   TOWING   214

XI.   FIRE   231

XII. DRYDOCKING AND LOADLINES   256

XIII. THE OFFICER OF THE WATCH   280

XIV. THE SAFETY OF NAVIGATION   291

XV.   LIFTING GEAR   373

XVI. ROPE AND CANVAS   407

XVII. DECK APPLIANCES   446

XVIII. THE SHIP'S BOAT   469

XIX. THE DEPARTMENT OF TRADE (D.O.T) ORAL EXAMINATION
      —FOREIGN-GOING   495

      INDEX   499

FIGURES

1.1   Hall's patent stockless anchor—common anchor   *page* 3
1.2   Admiralty cast anchor, Type A.C.14   5
1.3   Chain cable and its components   7
1.4   Lugless joining shackle   8
1.5   Markings on anchors and cables   11
1.6   Devil's claws—Blake's stopper—patent slips   15
1.7   Yaw of a ship at single anchor   21
1.8   Anchoring on a shoal   25
1.9   Pointing ship   25
1.10   Anchoring on a steep-to beach   26
1.11   Weighing anchor without a windlass   31
1.12   Lifting a bower anchor on deck   34

2.1   Stresses when at open moor   35
2.2   Executing an open moor   36
2.3   Mooring with an anchor each way   37
2.4   Fouling a hawse   38
2.5   Anchoring near a shoal   39
2.6   Executing a standing moor   40
2.7   Executing a running moor   41
2.8   Correcting leeway when mooring   42
2.9   The Baltic moor   43
2.10   Clearing a berth when Baltic-moored   44
2.11–15   Clearing a foul hawse   46–9

3.1   Transverse effect of a propeller   52
3.2   Forces exerted by twin screws   54
3.3   Thruster units   56
3.4   The turning circle   58
3.5   The effect of wind on a vessel   63
3.6   Effect of wind when stopping and reversing a vessel   65
3.7   Turning in a current, ahead and astern   66
3.8   Canal effect   67
3.9   Effect of inequalities of the sea-bed   68
3.10   Sheering effects of a river stream   70

FIGURES

3.11	Entering a dock	*page* 71
3.12	Girding a tug	73
3.13	Effect of passing a moored ship	74
4.1–17	Manœuvring to and from buoys	76–84
4.18	The ship's hawsers	85
4.19–27	Manœuvring to the berth in calms, and currents. Clearing the berth	86–90
4.28–51	Manœuvring to the berth in a wind. Clearing the berth	90–103
4.52	Turning a vessel short round	104
4.53	Turning in a river stream	104
4.54	Turning in a river stream	105
4.55	Entering a dock from a cross-stream	105
4.56	Leaving a dock into a cross-stream	106
4.57–59	Turning a vessel in a wind	106–7
6.1	Rigging the breeches buoy	130
6.2	Firing a rocket in a cross-wind	131
6.3	The R.F.D. Automatic release hook for life-rafts	137
6.4	The Welin–Maclachlan Single-point suspension davit	139
7.1	Patching a hole in ship's side plating	145
7.2	Alternative method of patching	146
7.3	Plan view of the patch	147
7.4	Makeshift fish-bolt	150
7.5	Patent rivet stopper	150
7.6	Shoring a bulkhead	151
7.7–11	Jury rudders	154–7
7.12	Steering by drags	157
8.1	Carrying out a kedge anchor in a lifeboat	161
8.2	Alternative method	162
8.3	Laying out anchors in tandem	163
8.4	Carrying out a bower anchor between two boats	165
8.5	Securing a purchase to ground-tackle hawser	166
8.6	Anchors in tandem	167
8.7	Ungrounding when broadside on to sea	175
8.8	Ungrounding when stern-on to sea	175
8.9	Beaching a vessel	178
8.10	Securing lines ashore	179
9.1	The drift directions of a wreck	191
9.2	Manœuvres for recovery of a man overboard	197
10.1	Practical towing—layout before towing	226
10.2	Practical towing—layout during towing	227

FIGURES

10.3	Securing the messenger to the hawser	*page* 228
10.4	Fairlead chafing sleeve	230
11.1	Kidde Zone detecting system	247
11.2	Kidde smoke-detector layout	250
11.3	Kidde visual smoke-detector	251
11.4	Kidde audible smoke-detector	252
12.1	Stability of a ship in a floating dock	266
12.2	Loadlines for a steamer	270
12.3	Loadlines for a timber-carrying vessel	270
12.4	Loadlines for a sailing ship	272
12.5	Calculation for the dock allowance	273
14.1	Conventional direction of buoyage in the United Kingdom	293
14.2	Lateral marks, system 'A'	295
14.3	Cardinal marks, system 'A'	296
14.4	Isolated danger and safe water marks	297
14.5	Special marks	298
14.6	Light characteristics	300
14.7	Specimen routes, system 'A'	301
14.8	Action of sailing ships when collision is imminent	316
14.9	Action of powered ships when collision is imminent	318
14.10	Determining the direction of a vessel's heading	326
14.10A	The compass card	331
14.11	The International Code Flags	350
15.1	Reeving a three-fold purchase	374
15.2	Purchases	376
15.3	Hallen derrick	388
15.4	Velle derrick	389
15.5	Stuelcken derricks	391
15.6	Rigging sheers	392
15.7	Rigging a gyn	394
15.8	Telescopic and fitted topmasts	396
15.9	The union purchase	397
15.10	Doubling gear	398
15.11	Yo-yo gear	398
15.12	The wing-lead derrick	399
15.13	The backweight rig	400
15.14	The Liverpool rig	401
15.15	The heavy derrick	402
15.16	The swinging derrick	404

ix

FIGURES

16.1 The construction of fibre rope *page* 408

16.2 Overhand knot—sheet bend—figure-of-eight knot—clove-hitch—timber hitch 416

16.3 Reef knot—bowline—rolling hitch—half hitch—marline spike hitch 418

16.4 Carrick bend—cow hitch—Blackwall hitch—marling hitch—awning hitch 419

16.5 Clove hitch on the bight—bowline on the bight—sheep-shank 421

16.6 Passing rope and chain stoppers 422

16.7 Stage hitches and chair hitches 423

16.8 Whippings 424

16.9 Worming, parcelling, and serving 425

16.10 Flat, round, and racking seizings 427

16.11 Chain, cut, and eye splices 429

16.12 Long splice 430

16.13 Coiling a 'Frenchman'—Eye splice—Bulldog grips 438

16.14 Sewing canvas 444

17.1 Electromagnetic Log Sensor assembly 455

17.2 Chernikeeff Electronic log 457

18.1 Half-section and side elevation of wooden lifeboat 475

18.2 Belaying falls on a staghorn bollard 481

18.3 A lifeboat, fully rigged 488

18.4 The theory of sailing 490

PLATES

Between pages 460 and 461

1. Schermuly line-throwing rocket. Detail and firing operation
2. Schermuly buoyant head. Lifebuoy lights and smokefloats
3. Inflatable rubber liferaft—sectional view
4. Single-point suspension raft
5. Single-sheave cargo blocks
6. Multiple blocks and fittings
7. Commodore Log equipment
8. Commodore Log Rotator
9. Chernikeeff Log—Impeller assembly
10. Chernikeeff Log—Indicator
11. Chernikeeff Log—Tube assembly
12. Desk-mounted 'Synchrostep' telegraphs
13. Single-speed quadrantal davits
14. Overhead-type quadrant davits
15. Welin gravity davits (*Saxonia*)
16. Welin gravity davits (B.T.C. Vessel)
17. Underdeck davits—top picture shows boat stowed, lower picture shows boat swung out
18. Underdeck davits handling glass-fibre lifeboats
19. Clarke Chapman electric windlass—fore side
20. Clarke Chapman steam windlass—aft side
21. Clarke Chapman splash-lubricated steam windlass—aft side
22. Clarke Chapman electric mooring capstan
23. Clarke Chapman splash-lubricated electric cargo winch
24. Kelvin electrically-driven sounding machine

AUTHOR'S NOTE

AFTER lecturing to Officers of the Merchant Navy for twenty years, I am more than ever convinced that there is no such thing as the perfect seamanship textbook. As it stands, the profession may lead an Officer to serve on ships built at any time during the last fifty years. A textbook must therefore blend techniques both ancient and modern with equipment which may be new or even obsolescent. At the same time, it must cope with ever-changing statutory rules and regulations.

This book is aimed primarily at Officers and Cadets studying for British Certificates of Competency. I hope it will be of interest also to everyone connected with the profession and a source of reference for experienced seafarers.

Since it was first published in 1962 it has been continually revised, culminating to date with this fully metricated edition which now includes details of Hallen, Velle and Stuelcken derricks.

For obvious reasons, colour has not been used in diagrams. Colour keys have been provided however, and some careful crayoning by the reader will enhance the usefulness of these diagrams.

The book should be studied in conjunction with the latest and inexpensive Statutory Instruments, in particular those relating to Life-Saving Appliances, Fire Appliances, Oil Pollution, Dangerous Goods, Docks Regulations, Construction Rules and Musters.

I am indebted to my readers for their support and encouragement and also to my publishers for their continued help and guidance.

GRAHAM DANTON

ACKNOWLEDGMENTS

I WISH to extend my gratitude to the following for their assistance in supplying photographs and information:

Messrs. Brown, Lennox and Company Ltd. (Anchors)

The Secretary of the Institute of Naval Architects for permission to quote from a paper by Mr. H. Pope

The Department of Trade

Pains Wessex Schermuly Ltd.

The R.F.D. Company Ltd. (Liferafts)

Beaufort Air-Sea Rescue Ltd.

Welin Maclachlan Davits Ltd.

Shell Tankers Ltd.

The Walter Kidde Company Ltd.

The Comptroller, Her Majesty's Stationery Office

The Gourock Ropework Company Ltd.

Thomas Walker and Sons Ltd.

Chernikeeff Instruments Ltd.

Messrs. Chadburns (Telegraphs) Ltd.

Messrs. Clarke, Chapman Ltd.

Kelvin Hughes Ltd.

TABLE OF CONVERSIONS
(WITH BS ABBREVIATIONS)

Length	1 inch	=	2·54 centimetres (cm)
	1 foot	=	0·3048 metres (m)
	1 fathom	=	1·83 m
	1 metre	=	3·28 feet (ft)
		=	39·37 inches (in)
Weight	1 pound	=	0·4536 kilogrammes (kg)
	1 ton	=	1 016 kg
	1 kg	=	2·205 lb
	1 000 kg	=	0·985 ton
		=	1 metric ton or tonne (t)
Pressure	1 lb/in^2	=	70·31 g/cm^2
	1 atmosphere (atm)	=	14·7 lb/in^2
		=	76 cm of mercury (cm Hg)
Volume	1 gallon	=	4·546 litres (1)
	1 litre	=	0·22 gallon (gal)
	1 m^3	=	35·314 ft^3
Power	1 horsepower	=	746 watts (W)
	1 000 W	=	1 kilowatt (kW)
		=	1·34 horsepower (hp)
Frequency	1 hertz (Hz)	=	1 cycle per second (c/s)

Various   Diameter of a rope in millimetres (mm) equals circumference in inches (in) multiplied by 8
1 tonne of sea water occupies roughly 1 m^3

As not all readers are familiar with the metric system, imperial equivalents have been put where appropriate in the margin. These imperial quantities are not identical with the metric quantities but are approximately of the same order, and arithmetical calculations with imperial quantities will be self consistent.

CHAPTER I

THE ANCHOR

THE ADMIRALTY PATTERN, STOCKED OR COMMON ANCHOR

THIS anchor is illustrated in Fig. 1.1 together with the names of the various parts. It is fitted with a stock, which should be of an approved design and weigh one-quarter of the specified weight of the remainder of the anchor. It is renowned for its excellent holding qualities, and even today most designs of patent stockless anchors are no more efficient, so far as holding properties are concerned, than the common anchor of one hundred years ago, assuming anchors equal in weight.

When the anchor strikes the sea-bed the stock, being longer and heavier than the arms, assumes the horizontal position as soon as the anchor is stressed, thus causing the lower arm and fluke to become embedded. The stock gives the anchor great stability, i.e. it prevents it from rotating under heavy load or a stress applied other than in line with the shank. The anchor will turn in a horizontal plane quite easily as a ship swings with the tidal stream or wind. There are no moving parts to become choked with sea-bed material, so that should the anchor be accidentally broken out of its holding position it remains efficient for re-anchoring.

The upper fluke, which protrudes from the sea-bed, contributes no holding power and may become fouled by the cable as the ship swings. Further, in very shallow water, or where the sea-bed dries out, small craft may become impaled on this fluke. The common anchor is difficult to stow with the stock in position. In merchant ships it is usually found as a light (non-compulsory) kedge anchor with the stock stowed parallel with the shank, or as a lifeboat anchor. As a kedge anchor it is likely to weigh up to 2 tonnes, dimensions for this weight being roughly 3·9 m overall length; 3·7 m length of stock, and 2·5 m width of arms.

The steel common anchor of today has a holding power of roughly three to four times its weight, depending upon the sea-bed. It is of surprising historical interest to note that Admiral Lord Nelson's anchor

2 tons
12 ft 6 in
12 ft
8 ft

1

(H.M.S. *Victory*), with its buoyant oak stock, had a holding power of 2·8 times its weight. Efficiency improvements have therefore been small since then, and are only just developing.

The spheres or enlargements at the stock extremities serve two purposes: they assist rotation of the anchor when biting, and prevent, to a certain extent, sinking of the stock into the sea-bed when it is providing stability under load.

THE PATENT STOCKLESS ANCHOR

This anchor is also illustrated in Fig. 1.1. It has no stock, and can therefore be hove right home into the hawse pipe, quickly secured, and is ready for instant letting go. The entire head, including the arms and flukes, is able to pivot about the end of the shank. Its angle of rotation is limited by stops to 45 degrees from the axis of the shank. In some designs this angle is as low as 30 degrees. The head must weigh at least 60% of the total weight of the anchor.

If it strikes the sea-bed with the flukes vertical, their tripping palms chafe the surface and start rotation of the arms. The anchor has good holding power, in the region of three to four times its weight in efficient holding ground, but has a moving part which can become choked with sea-bed material. This may well cause the flukes to fail to re-trip should the anchor be broken out of its holding position. For this reason, when anchoring for some time, it is a good practice to regularly weigh the anchor and *sight it*. This applies particularly on sandy and muddy sea-beds, and an opportunity is afforded to hose the anchor using a high-pressure water jet. Some shipping companies insist upon this being done.

Having no stock this type of anchor is unstable, and when dragging under heavy load is liable to rotate through 180 degrees. If the flukes fail to re-trip, any holding power remaining is due entirely to weight and, in turn, friction. The size of the flukes is a direct measure of the holding properties.

Disadvantages such as are noted above are generally overlooked in the light of its easy stowage. It is an ideal (non-compulsory) stream anchor for vessels fitted with stern hawse pipes.

Both the stocked and the stockless anchor may have a ring secured to the shank at the anchor's centre of gravity. This is the *gravity band*.

The most common types found in the Merchant Service are the Byer's, Hall's, and Taylor's patent stockless anchors. Two are carried as bower anchors in the hawse pipes and a third is carried as a spare or *sheet anchor*. Typical dimensions of a 5-tonne anchor would be 3·5 m overall length; 2·1 m extreme length of head; 1 m measured in side elevation

5 ton 11·3 ft
7 ft 3 ft

2

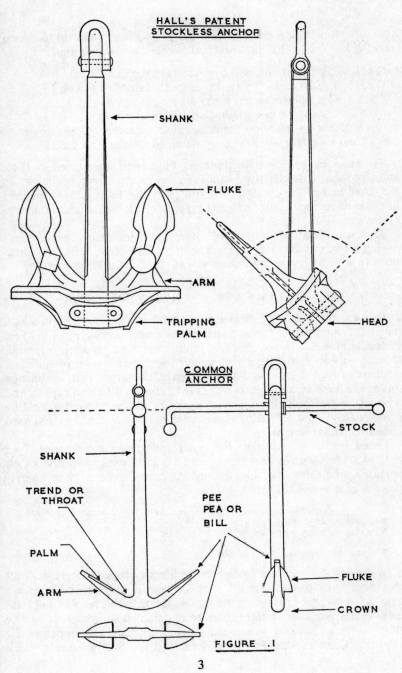

HALL'S PATENT STOCKLESS ANCHOR

SHANK

FLUKE

ARM

TRIPPING PALM

HEAD

COMMON ANCHOR

STOCK

SHANK

TREND OR THROAT

PEE PEA OR BILL

PALM

ARM

FLUKE

CROWN

FIGURE .1

3

5 ft 8 in across tripping palms of one fluke and 1·7 m from fluke tip to crown. Tests at the Admiralty Experimental Works have shown that:

(1) Holding power is raised by increasing the fluke area.
(2) It is also increased by having smooth, unribbed flukes.
(3) A holding power of ten times the weight can be obtained.
(4) Stability can be effected by using stabilising fins.
(5) A dihedral surface on the flukes gives a greater holding power.
(6) Such a surface is more easily obtained with hollow flukes.

The stockless anchor with tumbling flukes was introduced in 1840, and since that date effective changes in design have been negligible. In the latter half of the nineteenth century the Admiralty conducted tests in order to select the most efficient type, but little was done to improve efficiency.

Tests were reintroduced in 1943 after much complaint by personnel during the war of the inefficiency of anchors. After four or five modifications to a prototype, a new design was effected and is known as the

ADMIRALTY CAST ANCHOR TYPE A.C.14

This anchor is fully illustrated in Fig. 1.2 and is now accepted as a merchant ship anchor. It was tested in practically every type of sea-bed, including blue clay (a poor holding ground for stockless anchors), sand, shingle, soft mud, and hard rock covered with a thin layer of silt.

These proved it to be an anchor of great stability, having stabilising fins at the head extremities. It was able to change direction rapidly and without loss of pull. In almost all types of sea-bed it had a holding power of two and a half to three times that of a stockless standard anchor of equal weight.

52-cwt Listed below are some of the test results using a 2·5-tonne Type
5¼-ton A.C.14 anchor with hollow flukes, and a 5·25-tonne standard stockless anchor in the same bed. The figures compared are maximum holding powers in terms of weight.

Sea-bed	A.C.14	Standard stockless
Red clay, sand, shingle, rocks	10·0	3·9
Blue clay, thin layer of mud, sand.	13·6	3·1
Soft mud	8·2	1·6
Flat, smooth rock, thin layer of silt	2·8	1·9

In the first three cases, the lighter anchor developed the greater pull in tonnes—one to two times that of the heavier anchor. In the fourth case, however, the heavier anchor was superior in this respect and indicates that a minimum weight must be maintained for anchors fitted to ships likely to have to attempt anchoring in practically impenetrable sea-beds. Danforth-Jackson have developed the Stokes anchor which

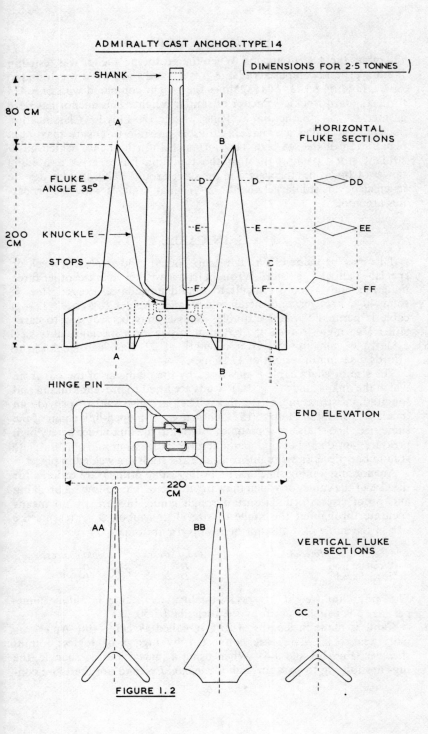

ADMIRALTY CAST ANCHOR. TYPE 14

(DIMENSIONS FOR 2·5 TONNES)

SHANK

80 CM

A

B

FLUKE ANGLE 35°

HORIZONTAL FLUKE SECTIONS

D — D — DD

200 CM

KNUCKLE

E — E — EE

STOPS

F — F — FF

A

B

HINGE PIN

END ELEVATION

220 CM

AA

BB

VERTICAL FLUKE SECTIONS

CC

FIGURE 1.2

resembles the A.C.14 anchor. When the prototype anchor was tested in holding ground composed of large gravel, sand and clay, it was found to have a holding power of 15·2 times the weight compared with only 4·4 for a standard stockless anchor of similar weight. This anchor has been granted a 25% reduction in Rule weight by Lloyd's Classification Society. The flukes are made as thin as possible to ensure maximum penetration of the sea-bed. The normal Danforth anchor which has a straight stock passing through the tumbling flukes gives a holding power of 14·2 times the weight in the same ground. This anchor, despite its efficiency, is still largely used only in small craft. Its stowage properties are good.

CHAIN CABLE

This may be made of wrought iron, forged mild steel, cast steel, or special-quality forged steel. Wrought iron is weaker than the other three materials and is more difficult to obtain nowadays. Forged steel is some 40% stronger, and therefore a smaller, lighter (by about 12½%) cable is permissible. For example, a vessel may be required to carry either a wrought-iron cable of 70 mm in size, or a special-quality steel cable of 61 mm in size. Over a length of 22 shackles of cable, this affords a saving in weight of 17 tonnes.

$2\frac{13}{16}$ in
$2\frac{7}{16}$ in
tons

The size of chain cable is measured by the diameter of the bar from which the link is made (Fig. 1.3). Studs are fitted to prevent kinking and longitudinal stretching of the links. They are also said to provide an increase in strength of up to 15%, compared with open-link chain of the same size. The studs are sometimes fitted into the link under a very high pressure (46t/cm²), but one manufacturer, at least, moulds his link and stud in one piece. In wrought-iron cable the studs are welded in place.

Anchor and joining shackles, and other cable fittings, are ordered for the size of the cable for which they are intended. The following breaking and proof stress formulae are a rough guide, but are by no means accurate throughout the range of size. The symbol D represents the size of the cable in mm, and the results are in tonnes.

Material				Proof stress	Breaking stress
Wrought iron	.	.	.	$D^2/36$	$D^2/26$
Special steel	.	.	.	$D^2/24$	$D^2/17$

The minimum weight of special-quality steel cable in kilogrammes per metre is roughly given by the formula $D^2/50$.

15 fathoms

Cable is made in lengths of 27·5 m called *shackles*—the Americans call them *shots*. They are connected by lugged or lugless joining shackles (Fig. 1.3 and 1.4). When using a lugged joining shackle, the lugs are too big to pass through a *common link* and are therefore con-

6

nected to an open link which is unstudded and known as the *end link*. Having no stud, it is weaker than the common links, and is therefore enlarged. This will not fit a common link either, and the two are therefore connected by an enlarged studded link called an *intermediate link*. Fig. 1.3 shows these links, and the joining shackle, together with their

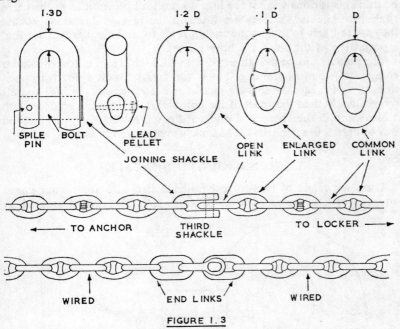

FIGURE 1.3

size relative to the common link. The sizes are approximate but near enough for practical purposes. The length of a link is $6D$ and its breadth $3.6D$.

LUGGED JOINING SHACKLES

These are closed by means of a *bolt*. This is secured in place by driving a brass or tinned-steel pin, having a taper of one in sixteen, through the bolt and one lug. When the pin is firmly home a lead pellet is hammered into the small, reverse-dovetailed chamber above the large end of the pin. The depth of this chamber is equal to the large diameter of the pin, and the total amount of dovetailing is equal to the half-depth.

The pin is called the *spile pin*, and in some cases, particularly in the first one or two joining shackles, is made of ash or male (solid) bamboo. This enables the bolt to be removed by hammering its unlipped end, thus shearing the wooden pin. If metal, the spile pin is removed by

7

punching its smaller end, the lead pellet being knocked out with the pin. Before fitting a new pellet, the remains of the old one must be reamed out of the dovetailing. Anchor shackles have a metal spile pin. Older ones may be found having a forelock.

These shackles are fitted to the cable with the bow end facing outboard. This is done so that the lugs do not foul projections as the cable runs out. Anchor shackles are fitted in the reverse direction because they are unlikely to foul as the anchor is let go, and the lugs will not foul a projection as the anchor is hove home.

The bolt should be well smeared with white lead and tallow or similar compound when assembling, otherwise it may become *frozen* in position. In such a case the shackle should be heated so that the lug expands more quickly than that part of the bolt within it. This can be done with a blowlamp in the absence of dockyard equipment. A very old method was to light a fire beneath the shackle using tar and oakum.

LUGLESS JOINING SHACKLES

These are made of non-corrosive nickel steel and are in four parts, one of which is the stud or chock (Fig. 1.4). The link is secured by

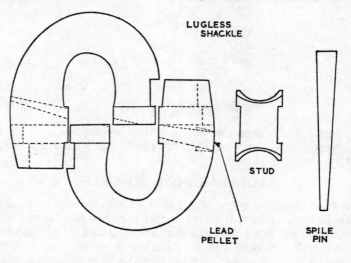

FIGURE 1.4

means of a metal spile pin and lead pellet, the pin being driven diagonally through the two sides of the link and the stud. These pins have a slow taper of about one in thirty-two. To part these shackles, the pin and pellet are driven out, the stud knocked clear, and the two sides of the shackle separated by means of a top swage available from the manufacturer. The use of this punch avoids damage to the accurately machined surfaces. The manufacturer also supplies a compound for coating these surfaces prior to assembly. Should the shackle be subjected to harsh treatment with a hammer, the machined surfaces may no longer fit together. Being similar to common links, though of larger maximum diameter ($1 \cdot 5D$), there is no question of fitting them to the cable, facing the wrong way. Their minimum diameter is the same as that of the chain cable to which they are fitted.

When using these shackles with forged-steel cables, no enlarged links are necessary, and they are therefore ideal for joining a broken cable. Anchor or end shackles are also made to this design, but are of a larger size for a given cable than joining shackles. They are slightly pear-shaped, with the tapered end having a size equal to $1 \cdot 25D$, the large end being roughly $1 \cdot 4D$ and the mid-section nearly $2D$. (D is the size of the chain cable.)

Lugless shackles made of nickel steel are not heat treated, only tested.

Both types of joining shackle, whether lugged or lugless, are larger than the common links, and may therefore jam in the sprocket or *snugs* of a cable holder. They should therefore be passed over the latter in the flat position. If used with a cable capstan, they should again lie flat against the holder, but this time they will be vertical. In other words, the spile pin of a lugged shackle must be perpendicular to the cable-holder surface, while the spile pin of a lugless shackle is parallel to the surface.

TESTS FOR ANCHORS

Under the Anchors and Chain Cables Act of 1967, all anchors which are to be used aboard United Kingdom registered ships are to be tested before being put into service. Anchors of 76 kilogrammes or less are 168 lb exempted. For the purposes of the Act, the weight of an anchor always includes the shackle, if any, and in the case of a stocked anchor it excludes the stock.

In the first instance, application must be made to a Certifying Authority, which may be the Department of Trade or the Authority appointed by them, such as the Classification Societies.

Anchors are tested to a proof tensile stress which varies from about twenty times the weight for a 1-tonne anchor, to just under five times the weight for a 30-tonne anchor. After the test is completed, the Supervisor must examine the anchor for flaws, weakness and material deformation.

Within one month of the test—if satisfactory—a certificate must be issued which contains a serial number, the name and mark of the testing establishment, the name and mark of the Certifying Authority and the name of the test Supervisor. In addition, it notes the type of anchor, weight in kilogrammes, weight of stock, length of shank in millimetres and length of arm. It must also show the diameter of the trend in millimetres (see Figure 1.1). The proof load is also revealed.

TESTS FOR CABLES

0·5 in   Under the same Act of 1967, chain cables are also required to be tested unless they are less than 12·5 mm diameter. The Testing Establishment considers the cable in lengths of 27·5 m (i.e. shackles of cable). Three links are taken from each length and tested to a tensile breaking stress. If this proves satisfactory, the length of cable is then subjected to a tensile proof stress. It is then inspected for flaws, weakness and material deformation. The manufacturer of the cable will thus provide each length for test with three extra links.

Certain grades of steel cable are then subjected to ultimate-stress, elongation and impact tests.

Shackles and other cable accessories are subject to the same tensile proof loads as the cable with which they are to be used. One sample in every batch of 25 is also subjected to the breaking stress (1 in 50 in the case of lugless shackles).

The chain cable is also awarded a certificate of test. This contains similar general information as in the anchor test certificate. It also shows the type and grade of chain, the diameter in millimetres, the total length in metres, the total weight in kilogrammes, the dimensions of the link in millimetres and the loads used in the tests. The formulae given on page 6 have been assessed from the official load table for cable of size 50 mm.

Some manufacturers like to carry out their own additional tests, such as those of Messrs. Brown, Lennox & Co., who recently achieved the following results:

2-in   A 50-mm studded link (breaking stress 141 tonnes) was subjected to an end-compression test and broke at the high stress of 137 tonnes.
0·625 in   The stud broke after the link had extended 16 mm.
1·625-in   A 41-mm open-link cable (breaking stress roughly 80 tonnes) remained unbroken after a tensile stress of 120 tonnes but was completely rigid.
4-in   A 100-mm studded cable (breaking stress 395 tonnes) remained unbroken at 700 tonnes tensile stress.

MARKINGS ON THE ANCHOR AND CABLE

Every anchor which has been officially tested under the Anchor and Chain Cables Rules, 1970 (made under provisions of the 1967 Act) must be marked.

A circle is to be marked in any conspicuous position on the anchor. Within this circle, two items of information appear. In Figure 1.5, the symbol x represents the Serial Number of the Test Certificate. The symbol YYY represents the letters of the Certifying Authority. It must not exceed three initials and one number (or four letters).

The chain cable is marked in a similar manner, as shown in Figure 1.5. The markings are to appear on every shackle, at each end of the cable, and every 30 m along its length.

These markings are much simplified compared with earlier requirements, much of which are now incorporated in the Certificates.

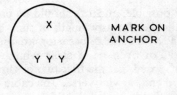

MARK ON
ANCHOR

MARK ON
CABLE

FIGURE 1.5
ANCHOR AND CABLE MARKS

Apart from official markings, the cable is also marked by crew or dockyard staff to show the number of the shackle. The number is reckoned from the anchor towards the chain locker. To indicate the third joining shackle, which will be 82·5 m from the anchor shackle, the third link on each side of the joining shackle is painted white and the stud is bound with seizing wire. When the cable is running out, even quite rapidly, the flashes of white may be seen providing the markings are well maintained.

If D-type shackles are fitted, the open link on each side of the shackle is ignored when arranging the marks. This is illustrated in Figure 1.3. In lugless joining shackles this is not necessary.

30 yd   It is a common practice to include an extra joining shackle somewhere within the first 27·5 m. This is most useful if it is necessary to trail the cable on the seabed, or to hang off the anchor. This extra shackle may be quite close to the anchor so that when the anchor is stowed in the hawse pipe, it is found just forward of the windlass. In other cases it may be at the 13·75 m mark, dividing the first shackle into halves. Seamen therefore sometimes refer to it as the half-shackle. It is obviously ignored when the cable is being marked for lengths.

If cable is rearranged (see next section) the marks require altering.

CARE OF ANCHORS AND CABLES

Whenever possible, anchors should be used alternately. Cable which lies idle in a locker for any length of time becomes brittle, and for this reason, whenever a suitable occasion arises, the cable should be ranged in a drydock, or even on a clear wharf or jetty, and two or three shackles transposed, i.e. the first two or three lengths should be placed at the inboard end, or vice versa. The cable will then need remarking.

When ranged, the cables should be examined for wear and renewed if necessary. Approximately 10% weardown in bar diameter (D) is allowed before replacement is required.

At a survey, joining shackles will be opened and all parts examined closely. These components will then be cleaned and well lubricated before assembly. Warm tallow is often used for the bolts and white lead for the spile pins. Every link will be sounded with a hammer to test for a clear ring. Loose studs in wrought-iron cable must be re-caulked or replaced. Wooden pins are renewed.

When links are replaced or repaired the cable is again tested to its statutory proof load. Cables benefit from regular heat treatment, but lugless shackles of nickel steel are exempted.

Anchors are not normally re-tested or given further heat treatment after their initial processing unless it is considered desirable. The anchors and cables benefit from a regular coating of Stockholm tar or special chain paint. The pivoting mechanism of a stockless anchor should be regularly lubricated with a thick grease.

When the cables are ranged the cable locker can be thoroughly cleaned out, scaled where necessary, and well coated with anti-corrosive paint. Cable-securing fittings should be thoroughly overhauled. In use, the lead pellets should be sighted whenever possible—faulty insertion often leads to their dropping out of the recess above the spile pin.

Anchors and cable must be well washed down after use. A thickly encrusted anchor can be trailed awash at slow speed (to avoid damage to hull plating), e.g. while navigating slowly out of an anchorage.

SECURING CABLE WITHIN THE LOCKER

In past times, the inboard part of a ship's cable was belayed on bitts, and the term *bitter end* is still used. Methods by which the bitter end is secured vary greatly from ship to ship. In some cases it has not been secured at all, presumably by accident, and the anchor and eleven shackles of cable have disappeared out through the hawse pipe. In some vessels the two bitter ends are shackled together, often with the intention of being able to use port cable on the starboard anchor and vice versa. It is generally thought to be a malpractice, since it can lead to complications when slipping the bitter end.

The end link is sometimes secured by several turns of wire rope, or small chain, or a cable clench which grips the cable and can be screwed tight, or a chain bridle incorporating a patent slip. The following are three efficient methods not including a patent slip in their components:

(1) The end link is placed between two steel lugs welded to the centreline bulkhead of the locker and a pin is driven through the lugs and link, being forelocked at one end. The forelock is removed, when the link is to be disconnected, and the pin knocked out.

(2) The end link is taken to the upper part of the chain locker, where it can be reached by a man standing in the lower forepeak storeroom, and is similarly secured to a strong bracket.

(3) The end link is placed through a slot cut in a stiffened area of plating so that it projects through the deck of the lower forepeak locker, or into one of the storerooms at the break of the forecastle. A pin secures it as before. This pin should either have a forelock— a flat, small piece of steel passed through a slot in the pin and chained to it to avoid loss—or else a portion of the end of the pin should be able to hinge about the pin axis. Either of these methods prevents the pin from slipping out accidentally.

The latter two methods avoid the necessity for a man having to enter the chain locker when slipping the bitter end. It is obviously an extremely good idea to become quickly acquainted with the method used in a particular ship, since the need to slip cable from the locker may be both unexpected and urgent. A prolonged search for the bitter end, only to find the securing means seized up, is not in keeping with the usual circumstances.

13

THE ANCHOR

EQUIPMENT

As an example, a cargo-passenger vessel of 165 m in length is required to carry two bower anchors of the stockless type, each weighing 5·4 tonnes, a spare bower stockless anchor weighing 4·5 tonnes and 22 shackles of special-quality steel cable of 61-mm link diameter. The vessel quoted also carries a non-compulsory kedge anchor of the stocked type, weighing 1·5 tonnes. She was originally required to carry wrought-iron cable of 70 mm.

ANCHORING TERMS

The following are a few of the expressions used in anchoring, and officers who may be in charge of the forecastle cable-party will do well to acquaint themselves with all of them, for a misunderstood order from the bridge may give rise to other spontaneous terms.

Windrode: A vessel is so described when she is riding head to wind.

Tiderode: A vessel is so described when she is riding head to tide.

Lee tide: A tidal stream which is setting to leeward or downwind. The water surface has a minimum of *chop* on it, but the combined forces of wind and tide are acting upon the ship.

Weather tide: A tidal stream which is setting to windward or upwind. The water surface is very choppy, but the forces of wind and tide are acting in opposition on the ship.

Shortening-in: The cable is shortened-in when some of it is hove inboard.

Growing: The way the cable is leading from the hawse pipe, e.g. a cable is growing aft when it leads aft.

Short stay: A cable is at short stay when it is taut and leading down to the water close to the vertical.

Long stay: A cable is at long stay when it is taut and leading down to the water close to the horizontal.

Come to, Brought up, Got her cable: These are used when a vessel is riding to her anchor and cable, and the former is holding.

Snub cable: To stop the cable running out by using the brake on the windlass.

Range cable: To lay out the cable on deck, or a wharf, or in a drydock, etc.

Veer cable, Walk back: To pay out cable under power, i.e. using the windlass motor.

Walking back the anchor: To lower the anchor under power.

Surge cable: To allow cable to run out freely, not using the brake or the windlass motor.

THE ANCHOR

A'cockbill: Used to describe the anchor when it has been lowered clear of the hawse pipe and is hanging vertically.

Foul anchor: Used to describe an anchor which is caught in an underwater cable, or which has brought old hawsers to the surface with it, or which is fouled by its own cable.

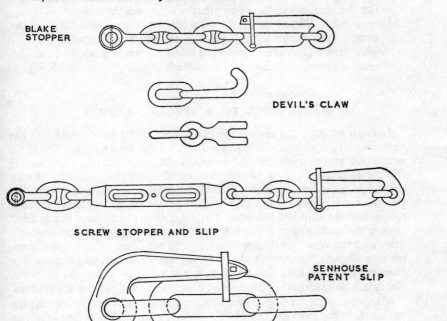

FIGURE 1.6

Up-and-down: The cable is up-and-down when it is leading vertically to the water.

Clear hawse: When both anchors are out and the cables are clear of one another.

Foul hawse: When both anchors are out and the cables are entwined or crossed.

Open hawse: When both anchors are out and the cables lead broad out on their own bows. A vessel lying moored to anchors ahead and astern is at open hawse when she lies across the line of her anchors.

Clearing anchors: Anchors and cables are cleared away when the securing gear on deck is removed. This may include chain bridles passed through cable and shackled to the deck, and *devil's claws*, which are metal bars hooked through the cable and screwed up

15

100 fathoms

tight by means of a rigging screw chained and shackled to the deck. Bow stoppers have their guillotines removed from the cable when it is cleared. Cables are cleared when the ship *strikes* soundings (i.e. she enters waters where depths are less than 200 m), when the visibility is poor in anchoring depths, and when nearing harbour. Fig. 1.6 shows various equipment used to secure cables.

Nipped cable: The cable is nipped when an obstruction, such as the stem or hawse-pipe lip, causes it to change direction sharply.

Render cable: The cable is rendered when the brake is applied slackly, so that as weight comes on the cable it is able to run out slowly.

ANCHORING TO A SINGLE ANCHOR

In calm weather the anchorage is approached at slow speed and the anchor is let go while the ship has either headway or sternway. The cable is laid out, and engines are used to relieve stresses in the cable just before the vessel brings-to. The officer who is anchoring his own ship usually prefers to stop his vessel at the anchorage by going astern. When the propeller wash reaches the ship abeam of the bridge he uses that as a guide that the ship has lost way. The engines are then kept going dead slow astern as the anchor is let go. Engines are stopped almost immediately and the vessel drifts astern laying out her cable, which grows continually ahead. Just before the required scope is out, the engines are *touched* ahead so that the vessel gets her cable as gently as possible. This method ensures the chain being clear of the hull plating at all times.

Many pilots prefer the simpler method of arriving at the anchorage with a little headway on the vessel, letting go the cable, laying it out as the vessel moves slowly ahead, and touching astern just before the required scope is out. With this practice, the cable grows continually astern while it is being rendered and will probably harm the paintwork on the hull. This is rather more serious than it may sound, because often the paint is removed to the bare metal and corrosion sets in rapidly. This is apparent when a vessel drydocks, since there is usually an occasion during a voyage when the cable does grow astern.

10 fathoms

In waters up to 20 m deep the anchor and cable should be let go on the run, allowing about double the depth (of cable) to run before checking it on the brake. If the cable is snubbed as soon as the anchor touches the bottom the anchor will be dragged along the sea-bed and will be unable to grip. Further, with the weight of the anchor off the cable, it sometimes happens that when the brake is released the cable will not render itself. This happens when there is a heavy weight of cable abaft the gypsy, leading down into the locker, and when the gypsy is in need of lubrication. By surging the cable initially, the anchor has a

16

chance to embed itself before the cable tightens. There is little risk of a stockless anchor being fouled in this way.

In water of over 20 m the anchor should first be walked back to within say 4 or 5 m from the sea-bed, and let go from there. This ensures that the anchor will not damage itself falling a considerable distance on to a hard bottom, and also that the cable will not *take charge* and run out so rapidly that it becomes extremely difficult to hold it on the brake. This practice therefore considerably lengthens the life of the brake linings.

10 fathoms
2 or 3 fathoms

In very deep anchoring depths, 100 m and over, the entire operation of anchoring should be done under power. The gypsy should not be taken out of gear at all, because the heavy weight of cable between sea-bed and hawse pipe will undoubtedly take charge.

50 fathoms

In a wind it is better to approach the anchorage heading upwind. The ship is more easily controlled and will make little leeway. If the wind cannot be brought ahead, however, the ship can let go the anchor in the usual way and, using her engines to relieve stresses on the cable, swing head to wind as she brings-to.

The weather anchor should be used so as to avoid nipping the cable round the stem. If the vessel is heading dead into the wind's eye she should have her head cast off one way or the other before letting go the weather anchor. The cast should not be excessive, because the ship will rapidly seek to lie across the wind and develop a sharp swing to leeward. Correcting helm and bold use of engines should be used if the cast develops into a swing.

In a tideway the vessel should stem the tide and again anchor with headway or sternway, as in calm weather or in a wind. Her helm will be of use even while making no way over the ground due to the tidal stream running past her. If the tidal stream cannot be stemmed the cable should be rapidly laid out slackly *across* the axis of the stream. As she brings-to in the stream, the bight of the cable dragging across the sea-bed will bring her up to her anchor very gently. When anchoring in a tideway floating objects overside are sometimes used to determine whether the ship still has headway. It should be noted that these objects indicate the ship's speed relative to the water, and a vessel stemming a stream with *stationary* floating objects beside her (i.e. pieces of wood, etc.) will have sternway over the ground equal to the rate of the stream. Only when these objects drift astern will the ship be stopped over the ground or have headway over it.

When anchoring stemming a stream and also having a wind abeam, the lee anchor should be let go first. As she gets her cable, her stem will then swing to the wind, causing the cable to grow clear. If she uses the weather anchor her cable will continually be foul of the bow plating.

17

DUTIES OF THE CABLE OFFICER

The anchors and cables will have already been cleared away. The selected anchor is now a'cockbilled by putting the appropriate gypsy in gear and walking the anchor back clear of the hawse pipe. We are assuming shallow water—if the water is over 20 m deep, then the anchor must be walked back close to the sea-bed or walked back under power all the way. This latter, of course, is done only when the ship has no headway, otherwise the trailing anchor will damage the forefoot. The brake is now screwed tight and the windlass taken out of gear ready for letting go.

10 fathoms

The anchor buoy will already be attached to the anchor by its wire pendant. The length of this pendant should preferably be equal to one and a half to two times the maximum depth of water at the anchorage so that the buoy is not *swamped* in a strong current and ceases to *watch*. The anchor buoy is streamed just before the anchor is let go. The windlass operator should be wearing goggles. The anchor should not be let go until the Officer has made sure that it is all clear below.

Cable is liable to be stowed in the locker with small stones wedged between the links and studs, and these pebbles are frequently projected at high speed as the cable runs over the windlass. Further, it is not unknown for the cable to part as it runs out. For this reason it is inadvisable to stand forward of the gypsy as the cable surges.

At the order to let go, the brake is released, usually by a blow from the carpenter's maul, and the cable is surged. It should be snubbed when twice the depth has run out. The brake is then slackened and the cable allowed to render. The bell is struck a number of times to indicate (by the number of strokes) the length of cable surged, i.e. three strokes as the third shackle runs out. The officer-in-charge must indicate to the bridge personnel how the cable is growing, particularly if it becomes nipped. If this happens, the brake is tightened and the bows allowed to swing towards the cable so that it grows clear. He indicates by pointing, and at night by swinging a lighted torch.

When the desired amount of cable is laid out the order will be given to *screw up*. The brake is then screwed tight and the handle struck with the carpenter's maul for good measure. The cable is then secured by placing the bow-stopper guillotine across the links, and if necessary, passing the devil's claws. The bow stopper relieves the windlass of much stress while at anchor. Sometimes, when the ship is pitching and the cable is tending to jerk, heavy coir springs (50% stretch) are secured to the cable and led well aft. When the springs have been made fast the cable is veered gradually until the springs share the stresses.

Having secured cable, it must now be carefully watched overside. It will grow to long stay as the ship brings-to her anchor and then slowly

18

slack down if the anchor is holding. Some officers prefer to watch a little longer before signalling that she has got her cable. It should be noted, however, that a regular cycle of coming to long stay, then slacking, then coming to long stay again, and so on, often indicates that a ship is dragging her anchor. Cross bearings or beam transit-bearings are more reliable. Strictly speaking, the anchor ball should not be hoisted nor anchor lights exchanged for steaming lights until the vessel is anchored, i.e. brought up. Before leaving the forecastle head, the officer should check the bow stopper and windlass brake.

AMOUNT OF CABLE TO USE

A term used here is *scope*. The length of cable laid out, measured from the hawse pipe to the anchor, divided by the distance measured vertically from the hawse pipe to the sea-bed, is called the scope of cable. The scope used depends upon several factors:

(1) The nature of the holding ground. Stiff clay, rock, shells, and stones are considered poor holding ground. Very soft mud can be a poor material in this respect.
(2) The amount of swinging-room available for the ship as the wind or stream changes in direction.
(3) The degree of exposure to bad weather at the anchorage.
(4) The strength of the wind or stream. As this strength increases so the ship moves astern, lifting her cable off the bottom so that it assumes long stay.
(5) The duration of stay at anchor.
(6) The type of anchor and cable.

If the cable leads from the anchor shackle in a direction 5 degrees above the shank axis the holding power of the anchor is reduced by one-quarter. If the angle becomes 15 degrees the loss of holding power is one-half. (This fact is repeated in Chapter VIII in view of the text contained therein.) For this reason, it is most important that a length of cable shall lead from the anchor shackle along the sea-bed before rising gently to the hawse pipe. Only a good scope will ensure this. Very often, when a ship drags her anchor, more cable is veered and the anchor holds. The action is correct, but the oft-resulting belief is a fallacy— that it is the resistance of the extra cable which has held the ship. The anchor was no doubt dragging because the angle between the cable and shank axis, at the shackle, was more than zero. The veering of cable removes this angle and the anchor holds once more.

A rough rule to lay out three to eight times the depth of water in cable length is haphazard. The Admiralty recommend the following lengths, which should be regarded as the minimum for calm weather and a 5-knot stream:

$45\sqrt{D}$ ft	For wrought iron cable, lay out $25\sqrt{D}$ of cable.
$50\sqrt{D}$ ft	For forged steel cable, lay out $28\sqrt{D}$ of cable.
$70\sqrt{D}$ ft	For special-steel cable, lay out $39\sqrt{D}$ of cable.
feet	(Where D is the depth of water in metres.)

It should be observed that more cable is laid in the case of the stronger chain. This represents a disadvantage of the special-steel in that it is roughly $12\frac{1}{2}\%$ lighter than wrought-iron cable, and therefore lifts from the sea-bed more easily. A heavy bight of cable must be used so that the cable partly lies on the sea-bed and its *catenary*, or curve, provides a spring which partially absorbs shocks due to pitching or yawing. The holding power of an anchor, i.e. the types sketched in this chapter (except the A.C.14), is roughly three to four times its weight. The resistance offered by cable is only about three-quarters of its weight, and there is thus no point in laying out more cable than is necessary. Further, the cable imparts a drag to the anchor, quite apart from the drag of the ship. Recent research has shown that a twin-screw ship, anchored in a 4-knot stream and a 55-knot wind, with locked propellers, imparts the following drag to her anchor:

tons	Screw drag	2 tonnes
tons	Tide drag on hull	4 tonnes
tons	Wind drag on hull	10 tonnes
tons	Cable drag	2 tonnes

DUTIES AT ANCHOR

Cross-bearings are usually taken as the anchor is let go (to get a rough position for the anchor itself) and again when the vessel is brought up. Anchor watches should be set and these bearings frequently checked. A rough circle of swing can be drawn on the chart. Beam transit-bearings, use of the echo sounder, and radar will all help to detect dragging. On a very rocky bottom the noise of the dragging anchor can often be heard quite clearly on deck.

The vessel will normally lie with the anchor and cable fine on its own bow, say a point to a point and a half. This angle is known as the vessel's *natural sheer*, because she lies sheered slightly across the stream or wind. In a strong wind the vessel will tend to yaw about as shown in Fig. 1.7. At the extremity of her yaw she surges ahead and then drops back on her anchor, jerking the cable. If during the yaw the wind catches her on the opposite side to that normally exposed by her natural sheer (i.e. catches her on the port side when using her starboard anchor), she may, at the extremity of her yaw, surge rapidly across her anchor to the other extremity of yaw, i.e. from position 6 to 8 in the figure, nipping her cable round the stem and breaking the anchor out of its holding position. This is called *breaking sheer*. If the anchor fails to re-trip the other anchor must be let go at once.

When initially bringing to, it is a good idea to arrange for a joining shackle to be situated on deck when the cables are secured. This will facilitate slipping the cable, and clearing a foul hawse should this become necessary.

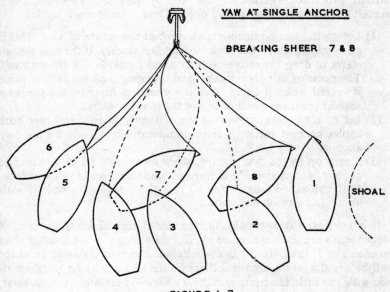

YAW AT SINGLE ANCHOR

BREAKING SHEER 7 & 8

SHOAL

FIGURE 1.7

At anchor it is desirable from the deck officer's point of view to have the main engines and steering-gear ready for immediate use. In a tideway the vessel may be steered by her rudder. It is, however, ineffective when there is no stream. A wind, blowing from one direction for some considerable time, will set up a surface drift current, but this is unlikely to be sufficiently strong for sensitive steering.

The shore signal-station should be watched at all times. Approaching and departing boats need vigilance, as do other vessels navigating in the vicinity. The officer of the watch should at all times have a rough idea of how his cable is lying, so that he can warn off other vessels which try to anchor across it.

DRAGGING ANCHOR

Generally speaking, once an anchor starts to drag, the vessel gathers sternway, and this may become excessive. Prompt action is necessary. However, there are exceptions, and a vessel riding out a gale has been known to drag slowly and steadily for some days at roughly a mile per day.

If the wind rises, extra cable should be laid out to ensure a bight lying on the sea-bed under conditions of yaw and pitch. Pitching can be partially prevented by trimming the ship by the head. Yawing is likely to start the anchor dragging, and one of three actions is advisable:

(1) Let go the second anchor underfoot at the centre of yaw. This is an excellent plan if the brake is held just slackly. If the first anchor starts to drag the second will bite and its cable will render itself. The noise of this gives warning of dragging, and the second cable is veered without delay. This is sometimes done by seamen as a regular practice, whether or not the weather is bad.

(2) Let go the second anchor at the extremity of yaw and veer both cables so that the ship rides comparatively quietly to her two anchors.

(3) Steam up to the first anchor, sheer away, and let go the second anchor. The first cable is hove in while approaching its anchor. Both cables are then veered so that the vessel rides quietly with an anchor fine on each bow.

If a hurricane is approaching, the vessel should leave harbour if other vessels are anchored close by, if the holding ground is other than excellent, or if the harbour is unsheltered. Departure should be made well before the storm arrives, otherwise the vessel may be caught outside with too little sea-room and drive ashore. If remaining in harbour, action (3) above should be taken and cables veered well away.

Once a vessel begins to drag, more cable should be veered. It should not be surged out slackly, otherwise the cable may part as the vessel brings-to. By veering it, the vessel may be brought up gently. The second anchor should be let go in good time, otherwise it may be found that so much cable has been veered on the first anchor (say 8 out of 11 shackles), that very little can be veered on the second (in this case only 2 to 3 shackles). Engines should be used to relieve stresses. If there is room it may be better to heave up and seek better holding ground.

WEIGHING ANCHOR

If, during heaving, the cable is subjected to a bad nip the windlass should be braked and the bows allowed to swing so that the cable grows clear. The cable should be well washed and stowed. The anchor, if fouled with sea-bed material, can be towed awash for a short distance at slow speed. The bell is again rung to indicate the number of the joining shackle appearing from the water's surface, and vigorously rung when the anchor is aweigh. It should be reported foul or clear as the case may be. The anchor ball, or lights, can now be lowered. The anchors should not be finally secured until deemed no longer necessary for immediate use. Heaving up is a good opportunity for checking spile-pin pellets and cable seizing-wire markings.

A windlass having an electric motor of 43 kilowatts can heave in slack cable at 4 minutes per shackle and tight cable at $5\frac{3}{4}$ minutes per shackle.

DROPPING DOWN

A vessel is said to *drop down* when she drifts with the tidal stream. A vessel at anchor wishing to do this will heave her anchor just clear of the sea-bed. Her speed through the water will be nil, but her speed over the ground will be equal to that of the stream. Her rudder will have no effect, because there is no water flowing past it. She cannot be controlled except by means of the engines or the anchors.

DREDGING DOWN

A vessel is said to *dredge* when she moves under the influence of the tidal stream but with her anchor held at short stay so that it drags along the bottom. Her speed over the ground is therefore retarded and is not so great as the rate of the stream. She therefore has headway through the water. Her rudder may be used to steer her. A strong tidal stream is necessary for her helm to be sensitive.

If a vessel, when dredging, puts her rudder to port, the vessel will remain parallel with the stream direction but will gradually move diagonally across it towards her port hand. She will dredge similarly to starboard. In each case the most efficient movement is achieved by using the anchor on the side opposite to that in which she wishes to dredge, i.e. it is preferable to use the starboard anchor if dredging to port under port helm. A vessel which is dragging, therefore, can, by putting her helm over, avoid other vessels, provided the stream is fast enough to make her steering sensitive. Also, the operation of dredging can be modified somewhat in the case of a ship at anchor which sees another dragging towards her. By surging her cable rapidly and using bold helm, she may be able to sheer away from the line of drag and bring-to on the other anchor. The first one is liable to be fouled, but this is of small moment in the circumstances. In both these latter cases there must, of course, be a stream.

23

ANCHORING AT HIGH SPEED

The anchors are the narrow-water navigator's stand-by in all cases of emergency. There is an old sea-saying, 'Never go ashore with an anchor in the pipe', and this should apply to most emergencies. A ship may fail to turn, take a sudden sheer, carry too much way, an engine may fail to go astern, a squall may catch the ship, the engine telegraph may jam, a collision may be imminent—in all cases the anchors are waiting to be used. *Both* anchors should be let go and allowed to run out their cable until sufficient is out to enable the anchors to hold. They are then snubbed and perhaps alternately veered and snubbed so that the ship gradually loses her way. Both cables will be growing astern throughout the operation, and both will be subject to bad nips. This means, however, that the hawse-pipe lips are relieving the windlass (although strongly bedded) of much of the stress. Further, both cables are taking an equal share. A ship with quite considerable headway may be brought up quite rapidly with two anchors used in this fashion. Needless to say, it will be wise later to have a survey made of the anchors, cables, hawse pipes, and windlass.

If a ship uses only one anchor she is likely to part the cable very quickly and then forge ahead into danger. This has happened all too frequently with the second anchor idle in the pipe. If there is insufficient room in which to pay out a good scope as above, the cables must be snubbed after, say, two shackles have run out and the anchors dragged along the bottom to reduce headway. This is highly dangerous, however, in harbours where there are submarine cables.

tons   A vessel weighing 27 000 tonnes when stopped in 30 m, travelling
tons initially at 4 knots, incurs a stress of 195 tonnes in a single cable. The
tons figure becomes 435 tonnes if the initial speed is 6 knots. The stresses are halved if two equally tensioned cables are used.

ANCHORING NEAR A DANGER

In Fig. 1.7 the vessel is riding to her starboard anchor. There is a danger to starboard. When she gets to the extremity of her yaw at position 5 and breaks her sheer she virtually sails across her anchor and may break it out. She is also headed towards the danger. For this reason, when anchoring near a danger, the offshore anchor should be used. If sheer is broken the vessel will be heading away from the danger.

ANCHORING ON A SHOAL

If this becomes necessary the vessel should head into the wind, cross the shoal, and take soundings. It is then decided in which depth the anchor is to be let go. The anchor is walked back to this depth and the vessel moves astern across the shoal. As soon as the cable grows ahead, showing that the anchor has touched bottom, cable is veered and laid out across the shoal, and the vessel will ride to her anchor in deep water beyond the shoal. This is a very good holding position, because it is

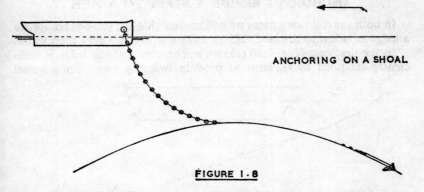

ANCHORING ON A SHOAL

<u>FIGURE I·8</u>

almost impossible to stress the cable at the anchor shackle in any way other than parallel with the shank (see Fig. 1.8).

POINTING SHIP

A ship riding to single anchor may require to create a lee on one side. An efficient method is to lead a wire, say 24 mm, from the after bitts, 3–3½ in along the ship's side clear of everything, and secure it to the cable close

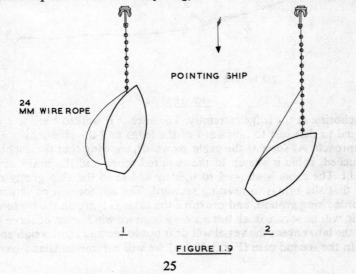

POINTING SHIP

24
MM WIRE ROPE

1   2

FIGURE I·9

to the hawse pipe. The wire is then belayed aft and the cable is gently veered. As the wire becomes stressed, the ship is *pointed* off the wind (see Fig. 1.9).

ANCHORING BESIDE A STEEP-TO BEACH

In both the following cases we will assume that the sea-bed comprises a ledge adjacent to the land, falling away sharply into very deep water.

In the first case (Fig. 1.10 (a)) we will assume that the ledge is sufficiently extended to seaward to provide swinging room for a vessel

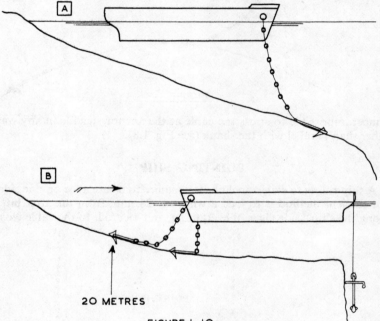

20 METRES

FIGURE 1.10

anchoring at the ledge extremity. The anchor is walked back to a depth equal to that just to landward of the ledge and the ship makes a slow approach. As soon as the cable grows aft, showing that the anchor has touched, cable is veered to the required scope and the brake screwed tight. The cable is allowed to tighten and snub the ship gently round so that she brings-to heading seaward. The anchor will be pulling towards rising ground, and provided the cable is lying on the bottom, the ship will be secure in all but a *strong* onshore wind or an offshore wind. In the latter event the vessel will drift out to sea and must weigh anchor.

In the second case (Fig. 1.10 (b)) we will assume an island having a

26

reef close inshore with typical depths as shown. The vessel must clearly anchor heading towards the land. The anchor should therefore be walked back to roughly 20–30 m and the vessel again headed in slowly. A sharp lookout must be kept for heads of isolated coral, etc. When the cable grows astern, and this should occur very gradually because the ship should have a minimum of headway, the engines are reversed and a bight of cable rendered. If only one anchor is used it is a good plan to lower the second one so that it bites, and screw up the brake slackly. If the vessel drags to seaward this second anchor will render further cable and give warning of the event. The operation can be carried out only in an offshore wind. If the wind blows onshore the vessel will drift to the reef and must weigh anchor and proceed before this occurs. A similar drift may occur in calms, but this may be prevented by lowering a heavy weight (such as the stream anchor) from aft to a depth well in excess of that at the ledge extremity. As the ship drifts onshore, this weight will foul the ledge and hold the ship.

10–15 fathoms

TURNING ON AN ANCHOR

When heading with the stream astern, the vessel may be quickly turned head to stream with the assistance of an anchor. The anchor, either one will do, should be let go and held at short stay. As the anchor drags it will snub the bows round and upstream. The headway should be simultaneously reduced by an astern movement. This is a simple manœuvre provided the anchor is kept at short stay. By dragging it along the bottom, heavy stresses are completely avoided.

If the sharp nip at the hawse pipe is considered undesirable it may be partially prevented by casting the ship slightly across the stream before letting go the upstream anchor. After swinging, the anchor may be quickly weighed.

In calm weather and no current the ship may be similarly turned, but with some modifications. The headway is reduced to a minimum and the anchor is let go on the run, allowing sufficient scope for the anchor to bite. If the cable is snubbed too quickly the anchor will be dragged and the manœuvre spoiled. When the brake is secure the vessel is brought up with the cable growing aft, and then steamed round the anchor on the taut cable at slow revolutions, with helm hard over towards the anchor. The vessel must be fully brought to her cable and the latter absolutely taut before using the engines in this fashion, otherwise the ship gathers headway and an undesirable sudden stress is imposed on the cable.

Sometimes a vessel is turned on her anchor before leaving an anchorage. Here the anchor cable is hove in until there is sufficient length out to enable the anchor to hold, and the ship moved ahead at slow revolutions until the cable grows astern. Before it tautens, the engines are stopped and the ship allowed to bring-to gently on the cable. When it is taut astern, the engines are moved ahead and the helm put hard over towards the anchor and the ship steamed round to the required direction. Twin-screw ships generally turn more rapidly in this manner than if they weigh anchor and work engines in opposite directions. The anchor is very effective for all turning manœuvres where there is insufficient room for rudder-controlled turns under headway.

CLEARING A FOUL ANCHOR

If the anchor is wedged in an underwater obstruction and cannot be weighed the vessel should be moved very slowly ahead, veering cable until it grows well astern. When the vessel is brought up and the cable is taut the engines are worked ahead very gently to see if the anchor will break out. The vessel can then slowly be steamed round in a circle with the cable taut (turning towards the anchor of course), to try to rotate the anchor and break it out by constant movement. If this fails, together with an attempt under sternway with the cable growing forward, then the cable must be slipped from the deck, buoying the end, and the anchor later recovered by divers.

If the anchor has fouled a cable, wire, or other similar underwater obstruction the anchor and fouling is hove well up to the hawse pipe. A strong fibre rope, such as a manila mooring line in the case of a heavy submarine cable, is passed round the obstruction and both ends are hove taut and made well fast on deck. In the case of an unimportant obstruction a wire rope can be used, but a fibre rope must be used in cases where the obstruction may be a telegraph cable or one carrying high-tension current. When the line is hove taut the anchor is walked back clear of the obstruction and then hove home into the pipe. Provided the *hanger* is secured at the forecastle deck in a region of maximum flare, the fouling will swing clear when the anchor is walked back. The hanger is then slipped from the deck to release the fouling.

If the obstruction is still partially lying on the sea-bed and offering resistance to the hanger, so that it does not swing to the flare of the bow, the ship should be gently sheered away so that the point of suspension of the fouling comes directly under the deck edge. The anchor can then be hove home.

On rare occasions it may happen that when the anchor is weighed it emerges from the water upside-down with the cable half-turned around the shank, close to the head. When this occurs the anchor must be hung off from the forecastle deck by means of a strong wire rope passed round the anchor head. When the wire is secure the cable may be veered until

28

the half-turn slides down and clear of the shank. The cable is then slowly hove-in until it takes the weight of the anchor, when the wire may be cast off.

HANGING OFF AN ANCHOR

If it is desired to have a free end of cable available for use, the anchor will have to be detached from the cable. Usually, the first shackle of cable includes a joining shackle 2–4 m from the anchor shackle, 1–2 fathoms so that when the anchor is stowed the joining shackle is between the gypsy and the hawse pipe. If the cable can be passed through a forward Panama Canal fairlead, then the anchor can simply be secured in the pipe using wire lashings and the bow stopper. The cable can then be eased off the gypsy and *broken*. It is then passed to the fairlead using chain hooks.

If the cable is to be passed through the hawse pipe the anchor must be removed from its housing and secured at the ship's side. First, the anchor is lowered clear of the pipe and a'cockbilled. With a 5-tonne 5-ton anchor, a 24-mm wire rope is then passed from bitts situated just abaft 3-in the hawse pipe, and preferably at maximum flare, through the anchor shackle and back on deck. Both parts are hove taut and belayed.

Another 24-mm wire rope, which we will call No. 2 wire, is passed 3-in from bitts, through the cable forward of the shackle and then led to the nearest winch warping barrel. The cable is eased to No. 2 wire and then broken. No. 2 wire is then veered slowly so that the anchor swings abaft the pipe. Both wires can be left taut (No. 2 wire will be stoppered off and belayed) so that the anchor is suspended equally by both, or else the whole of the weight can be transferred to the first wire. A man can then be sent overside to cast off No. 2 wire, which is hove inboard. This is advisable, because if this wire is left in the pipe it will be severely chafed by the cable.

Should the spare joining shackle be out of reach when the anchor is lowered clear of the pipe, No. 2 wire will have to be passed while the anchor is stowed. The cable is then eased, broken, and the anchor a'cockbilled by veering the wire. The other 24-mm hawser will then be 3-in passed overside as before.

Vessels which frequently engage in this operation use a specially made strop instead of the overside wire, and with this the anchor can be hung off in about 10 minutes. Other methods include taking the overside wire to a warping barrel and heaving the anchor up to the deck edge. The anchor is then either well clear of the plating due to the flare or else can be easily secured so that it does not swing.

HEAVING UP ANCHOR WITH NO WINDLASS POWER

Two efficient methods are employed in this instance. Fig. 1.11 shows one whereby a heavy purchase (15 tonnes S.W.L.) is secured to the cable and led well aft so as to get as much *drift* as possible. This avoids frequent overhauling. The purchase is attached to the cable by means of a long pendant of 24–32 mm wire. This avoids fouling the purchase in the many deck fittings adjacent to the windlass. The pendant is doubled so that the stress in each part is halved. A lighter, overhauling tackle is rigged as shown in the figure, to avoid delay and heavy work. As the cable is hove in, the gypsy should be free to revolve, so that the cable is stowed. The gypsies are fixed to the mainshafts, which revolve either when letting-go or when the main wheels are slid along and engaged with the driving pinions on the intermediate shaft, and also the sides of the gypsies. The intermediate shaft drives the warping barrels, so that in this particular case the main wheel is engaged with the gypsy and able to rotate the mainshaft. A friction drive is now set up by means of a heavy fibre mooring line run from the warping barrel to the drum of a winch. When the winch drum revolves it will drive the intermediate shaft of the windlass; this will drive the main wheel, and this will revolve the gypsy.

The brake must be screwed tight before the purchase is overhauled of course.

The second method is rather more simple. The topping lift from No. 1 derrick is unshackled from the derrick head and led forward. It is secured by a pendant to the cable. One topping lift only is necessary for one cable, provided it has a S.W.L. of at least 10 tonnes. The pendant must be doubled as before. The gypsy is placed in gear, the friction drive is set up, and the topping lift weighs the cable and anchor.

SLIPPING A CABLE

If caution is to be exercised, this work cannot be hurried. Usually the necessity for slipping arises when the anchor cannot be weighed.

(1) Slipping from the Deck

Veer cable, or heave, until a shackle is situated near to the hawse pipe upper lip. A 20–24-mm wire rope with any eyes frapped shut is passed through the cable forward of the shackle and both ends hove taut and made fast, preferably on separate bitts, i.e. a perfect slip-wire. The cable is eased to the wire hawser and then broken.

The problem now arises as to how to slip the wire. First, the engines should be worked ahead so that the cable is up and down and bearing the minimum of stress, only its own weight in fact. The wire can then

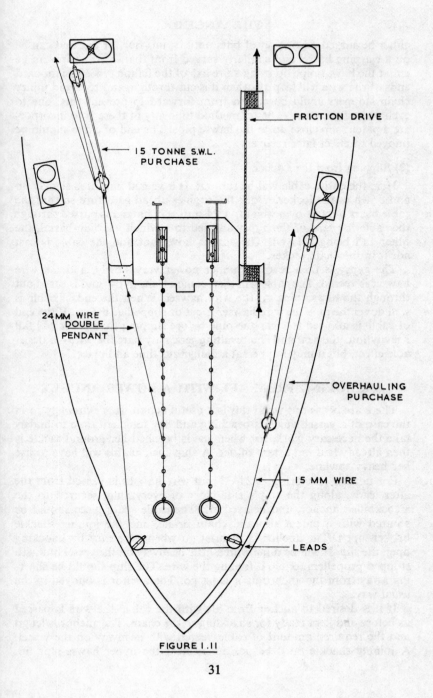

FRICTION DRIVE

15 TONNE S.W.L.
PURCHASE

24 MM WIRE
DOUBLE
PENDANT

OVERHAULING
PURCHASE

15 MM WIRE

LEADS

FIGURE 1.11

31

either be surged off one set of bitts until it runs free, or one end can be on a warping barrel and similarly surged from that, or the wire can be cut at the hawse-pipe lip using a fire axe of the felling type. The inboard ends of the wire will leap aft when it is cut through, and to avoid injury chain stoppers could be passed from forward to prevent this, one to each part of the wire. A better method than any of these is to incorporate a patent slip close up to the hawse pipe. The end of cable should be buoyed to effect later recovery.

(2) Slipping from the Locker

Here the entire cable will be run out. It is veered until it is slackly up and down in the locker. Work the engines ahead as before so that the cable bears only its own weight. A 24-mm wire hawser is passed through the cable forward of the gypsy and led to a winch warping-barrel, the other end being belayed. The wire is hove taut and the cable is cast adrift in the chain locker.

3-in

The gypsy is then revolved under power very slowly, and the wire hawser is veered. The cable will then come off the gypsy and is eased out through the hawse pipe on the wire hawser. When the end of cable is well down the pipe the wire hawser is cut or slipped as before. If the end of cable is allowed to clear the pipe before slipping the wire it will fall heavily into the sea, and the resulting jerk may part the wire—a desirable effect, but it may happen at a dangerous time and place.

ANCHORING FROM AFT WITH A BOWER ANCHOR

There are occasions when this is a useful action. It is extremely so in the case of a vessel which is beaching and has sufficient time to undertake the necessary work, for when she is beached her ground tackle is then already laid out astern of her. A ship such as this will have to use her heavy towline.

3-4-in

For normal anchoring, a 24–32-mm wire hawser is passed from the after leads, along the ship's side clear of everything, secured to the a'cockbilled anchor, and belayed aft. The cable spare piece should be secured with a patent slip and chain bridle, and the joining shackle broken open. The anchor is then let go when necessary by knocking open the slip. It will be done with a little headway on the vessel but with stopped propellers to avoid fouling the wire. The ship should be sheering away from the anchor as it is let go. The anchor is buoyed in the usual way.

If it is desired to anchor from aft with the cable, the wire is passed as before and kept ready for shackling to the chain. The anchor is let go and the required amount of cable veered with headway on the vessel. A joining shackle must be positioned near the upper hawse-pipe lip.

The ship is brought up gently on her cable, the latter growing astern. The wire is then rove upwards through the hawse pipe and secured to the cable forward of the joining shackle. A long, curved, specially made shackle is used for this called a *joggle* shackle. A chain stopper and patent slip is then rigged forward of the joining shackle, set tight, and the cable is *eased to the stopper*. The joining shackle is broken and the slip knocked off. The anchor is buoyed in the usual way. The ship is now moved slowly ahead while the wire hawser is hove-in aft. The ship is stopped when the wire is up and down over the stern. The wire is again hove-in and the cable brought aboard aft and secured around several pairs of bitts.

Another method is to ease out the cable from forward on a second wire as it is hove-in aft. This second wire will then have to be slipped.

CHANGING ANCHORS

If a bower anchor is to be unshipped from its cable and the spare bower installed into the hawse pipe the first anchor is lowered to the water's edge and the forecastle derrick swung overside. In Fig. 1.12 a 4-tonne anchor is being changed. In view of the bight of cable which the derrick will have to support, the latter should be at least of S.W.L. 5 tonnes. It is rigged with a 5-tonne S.W.L. lifting purchase. The purchase is led to the anchor and secured to it by means of a heavy strop.

The anchor is then lowered underwater to take advantage of the loss in weight due to its displacement. The cable is veered and the derrick fall hove-in until the anchor is directly below the derrick head. It may be kept underwater during this manœuvre. It is then lifted, together with the bight of slack cable, from (1) to (2) in the figure, and at this stage the cable must be secured at the ship's side. The derrick is swung inboard, the anchor landed, the shackle broken open, and the cable secured to the spare anchor. If the spare anchor is not directly below the derrick head it will have to be carefully guyed as it is *floated* off the deck to avoid a sudden swing. It may then be swung to the ship's side by guying the derrick.

The purchase is hove-on until, as before, the weight is off the ship's side cable lashing, which is then cast off. The anchor is lowered until submerged. By heaving on the cable and slacking on the derrick fall, the anchor is shipped and stowed into the hawse pipe.

In the figure the purchase blocks have been drawn much larger than the scale would permit, for the sake of clarity.

Sometimes the spare bower anchor is stowed forward of the forecastle-head breakwater, or washplate. In this case it must have a wire secured to it and led to the nearest forward warping barrel or bitts. This wire then becomes a *bullrope*. The purchase is led to the spare bower anchor, the bullrope set tight, and the purchase fall hove-in. This just floats the anchor clear of the deck and now, by placing heavy, greased planks of timber from the anchor to the top edge of the breakwater, the purchase can be further hove-on, slacking the bullrope, and the anchor will slide up the planks clear of the breakwater. The bullrope can then be used to guy the anchor until it is below the derrick head.

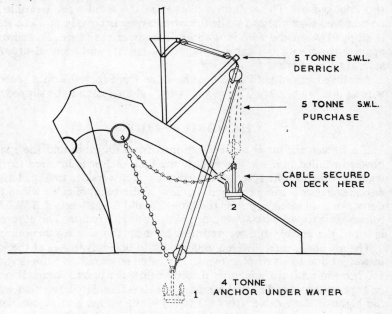

5 TONNE S.W.L. DERRICK

5 TONNE S.W.L. PURCHASE

CABLE SECURED ON DECK HERE

4 TONNE ANCHOR UNDER WATER

FIGURE 1.12

If the derricks on the forecastle are not of sufficiently high safe working load, suppose they are 3 tonnes each only, they should be rigged as a 'Yo-Yo' gear (see Chapter XV) so that each derrick has half the weight on it. Suitable purchases will have to be used, say 3 tonnes safe working load each.

The derrick on the side of the ship opposite to the anchor manœuvring will have to be lowered down dangerously close to the horizontal as the anchor is swung overside, and for this reason, extra guys should be used and the mast, or samson posts, stiffened with extra stays. Fortunately, the stresses are less when lowering than when hoisting, but precautions must be taken.

CHAPTER II

MOORING

WHEN a vessel is anchored with both anchors leading ahead, she is said to be on *open moor*. Supposing a vessel is lying to a single anchor dead ahead and with a stress in her cable of T tonnes. If she had two anchors leading dead ahead the stress in each would be $\frac{1}{2}T$ tonnes. When the angle between the cables becomes 120   tons   tons

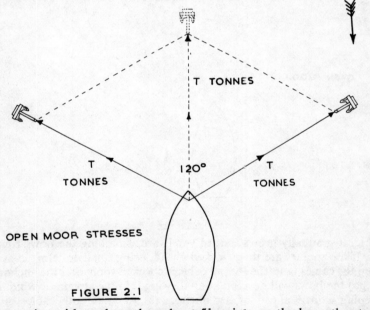

OPEN MOOR STRESSES

FIGURE 2.1

degrees, i.e. with each anchor about $5\frac{1}{2}$ points on the bow, the stress in each cable becomes T tonnes. This value increases to $2T$ and $3T$ as   tons the angle becomes 150 degrees and 160 degrees respectively.

When the angle exceeds the safe limit of 120 degrees she is commencing to ride to a *tight span*. Fig. 2.1 illustrates the parallelogram of forces for an angle of 120 degrees.

35

COMING TO OPEN MOOR

Fig. 2.2 shows the successive stages of this manœuvre. The vessel is headed into the anchorage with the wind or current on one bow in order to assist counteraction of lee drift. The weather anchor (or upstream anchor) is let go on the run (1), and headway continued for roughly one-third of the final length of cable. The second anchor is let go and the first one snubbed at the gypsy. As the vessel brings-to on her weather

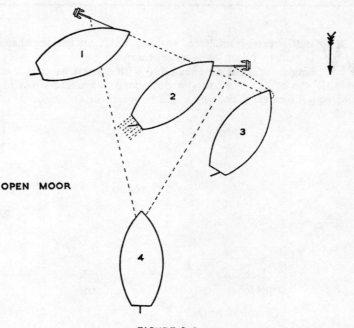

OPEN MOOR

FIGURE 2.2

cable, it gradually grows taut to windward, snubbing the bows round (2). If the engines are then worked ahead, using weather helm, so as to keep the cables taut (the second cable is checked soon after the anchor is let go) the bows will develop a rapid swing into the stream or wind. By keeping a little ahead of her anchors (3), so that both cables grow slightly aft, the manœuvre is hastened. When heading into the wind or stream, both cables are veered (the second one only, for a short while) and the vessel brings-to in position (4). The reason for veering the second one by itself while dropping back initially is to middle the ship between her anchors. By laying out one-third of the length between the anchors, each finally lies a point on the bow.

MOORING

Mooring is usually taken to mean securing the ship with two anchors, one ahead and one lying astern—a cable each way, as it was once called. The upwind or upstream anchor is known as the *riding anchor* and cable, the other being called the sleeping or *lee anchor* and cable (Fig. 2.3).

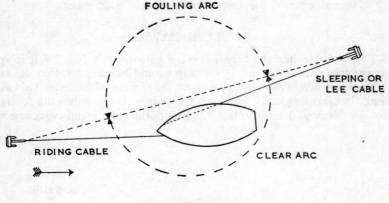

FIGURE 2.3

The advantages of mooring are:

(1) The vessel occupies little swinging room, turning almost in her own length about her stem.
(2) The scopes can be pre-adjusted for the prevailing strength of wind or stream. The scope of each cable is estimated in the same way as that for a single anchor (Chapter I).

The disadvantages are:

(1) The second, or lee, anchor lies astern and is of no value to the ship if a headwind increases or if the vessel begins to drag. In the latter event, if possible, it is better to drag the anchor down until the lee anchor is reached (heaving in the lee cable while dragging). The two cables can then be veered together. If cable is veered on the riding anchor initially and the vessel continues to drag, by the time the lee anchor is reached there may be so much cable out on the riding anchor that the other cable can be veered only a shackle or two.
(2) There is a risk of getting a foul hawse. To avoid this, the vessel must always be swung within the same arc at each consecutive tidal change (Fig. 2.3).
(3) Due to the fact that one cable leads aft, the vessel must be dropped down to it when leaving the anchorage, weigh it, and then heave

37

MOORING

herself back to the riding anchor. At 4–5 minutes per shackle, this will take a considerable time. At open moor, provided the anchors are close together, both cables can be hove simultaneously.

(4) In a beam wind the vessel will turn and lie at open hawse across the line of her anchors, creating a tight span. Both cables must be veered smartly, the vessel then riding to open moor.

FOULING HAWSE

This occurs when the cables become entwined. In Fig. 2.4 it is apparent that from position (1) the ship should be swung within the arc lying on the line of her anchors nearest the bottom of the page. This will result in clear hawse. If, however, she swings to (2) within the fouling arc she develops a cross in her cables. Another swing anti-clockwise to

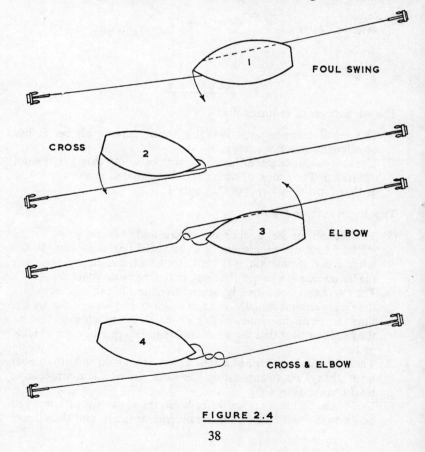

FIGURE 2.4

(3) results in an elbow, and a third similar swing produces a cross and an elbow, (4).

To avoid this, the vessel at (1) should have been given a broad sheer to starboard just before slack water so that the new stream catches her starboard quarter, swinging her within the clear arc. However, during calms or windy conditions at slack water this sheer may be cancelled and an adverse one develop. Engines will then have to be used as the new stream commences to run, in order to restore the correct sheer.

MOORED CLOSE TO A DANGER

In Fig. 2.5 a vessel is moored close to a shoal. This is hardly advisable, but the occasion may arise. In position (1) the vessel is initially moored

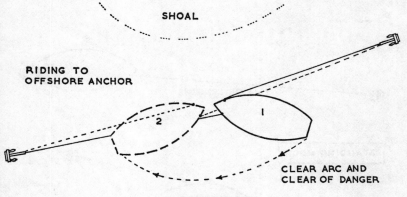

FIGURE 2.5

riding to her off-shore anchor. When she swings with the change of stream to position (2) she must do so to starboard, so avoiding running her stern close to the shoal. Because she is riding to the off-shore anchor, her hawse remains clear. In (2) she again rides to the off-shore anchor—the starboard one.

MOORING

There are two basic methods whereby a vessel may execute the moor.

(1) The Standing, Ordinary, Dropping, or Straight Moor

Let us assume the vessel is required to moor with her bridge along the line *AB* in Fig. 2.6. The stream is running from the left side of the page. Five shackles length is required on the port anchor and four on the starboard anchor. The vessel is headed into the stream (with a wind instead of a stream, the vessel is headed to windward, and when both are present the vessel heads the one which is having the stronger effect), with sufficient headway to take her to (1), which will be roughly five shackles plus a half ship's-length beyond the line *AB* (the vessel is to ride to her port anchor initially, let us say). At position (1) the port anchor is let go and the vessel drifts downstream, rendering her port cable to nine shackles, the sum of the two lengths. She is brought up

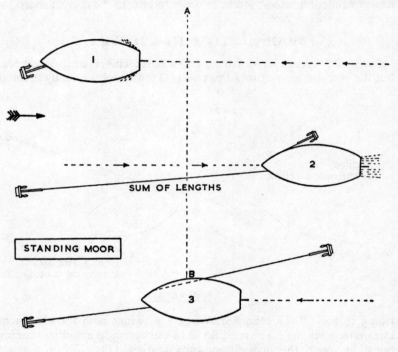

SUM OF LENGTHS

STANDING MOOR

FIGURE 2.6

gently on this cable and the starboard anchor is let go underfoot at (2). The vessel then middles herself between the anchors by veering or rendering four shackles on the starboard (lee) anchor cable and heaving in four shackles on the riding cable until she reaches position (3). During the middling, engines may be used to relieve the windlass of the stress on the taut riding cable.

The figure has been laid out in three sections to show the manœuvre with clarity, though, of course, the mooring is done along the first track of the ship. Notice that the vessel passes the bridge-position line twice during the manœuvre. To move from (2) to (3) will take approximately

16–23 minutes with a 48-kilowatt windlass, depending upon whether the riding cable is slack or taut.

(2) The Running, or Flying, Moor (Fig. 2.7)

Assuming the same conditions and requirements as before, the vessel again heads the tidal stream or wind. The starboard (lee) anchor is let go with headway on the vessel at a position distant from the line *AB* four shackles less a half ship's-length (1). The cable is rendered as the vessel moves upwind or upstream so that the bow is not checked round. The lee cable is laid out to a length of nine shackles, the sum of the two lengths, and the brake is screwed up. The cable is not allowed to tighten,

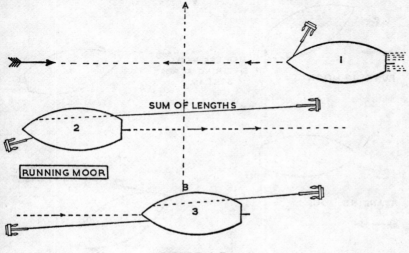

FIGURE 2.7

otherwise the bow will cross the stream and high engine revolutions will be necessary to correct this sheer.

At position (2) while the lee cable is still slack the port anchor is let go underfoot and the vessel moved astern. This riding cable can either be veered to its length or else alternately surged and snubbed. As the vessel moves down wind or stream, five shackles must be weighed on the lee cable (20 minutes) and five shackles veered on the riding cable. The vessel is then brought up on her riding cable at (3).

The figure is again laid out in three sections for the sake of clarity. The vessel passes the line *AB* only once in this manœuvre. Under certain conditions, this moor may take longer to execute, reckoning from the time the first anchor is let go. In the dropping moor, 9 shackles are rendered with the stream. In the running moor 9 shackles are rendered

41

against the stream. Again, in the dropping moor, only 4 shackles have to be weighed, against 5 in the running moor. Naturally, if the lengths had been reversed, this latter consideration would also be reversed.

In a cross wind the weather anchor is the first to be let go so that the vessel does not drift across her cable. If the lee anchor is let go the cable will grow under the ship, her bows will be snubbed up into the wind, and she will get across the stream. In the dropping moor slackening the riding cable at some stage between (1) and (2) and working the engines

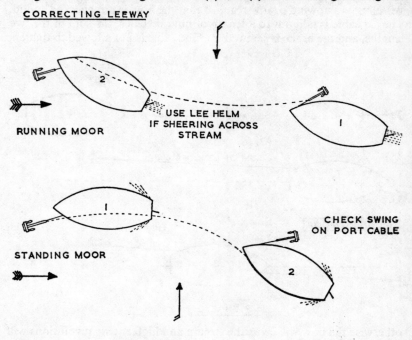

CORRECTING LEEWAY

RUNNING MOOR

USE LEE HELM
IF SHEERING ACROSS
STREAM

STANDING MOOR

CHECK SWING
ON PORT CABLE

FIGURE 2.8

astern under weather helm will help to counteract leeway, the swing of the bows across the stream being checked as necessary on the cable.

In the running moor leeway is checked by laying out the sleeping cable under engine power and steering upwind. Any sheer across the stream is then corrected with lee helm and also partially corrected by the vessel's tendency to pay off the wind under headway. Notice that in the dropping moor sheer across the stream due to astern movements is aggravated by this tendency. However, the cables provide a good checking action. Too much sternway should not be allowed (see Fig. 2.8).

In calm weather the port anchor is the better one to drop first in the standing moor, since any astern movements on the engine (right-handed single-screw ship) to reduce any remaining headway will cant the stem away from the anchor underfoot.

For similar reasons, in the running moor the port anchor is the better one dropped at (2). Further, in the event of the lee cable becoming jammed during the run from (1) to (2), an astern movement swings the vessel to starboard, the cable grows clear and avoids a bad nip.

The Baltic Moor

This method of mooring a ship is employed when a vessel is to lie alongside a quay, the construction of which is not sufficiently robust to permit ranging of the ship during bad weather. These days the naming of the moor is inappropriate, but there are no doubt such wharves in

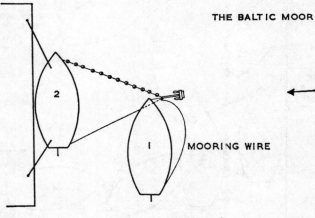

THE BALTIC MOOR

MOORING WIRE

FIGURE 2.9

various other parts of the world. It is a useful method of berthing a vessel in an onshore gale of wind, particularly when the vessel is expected to leave before the weather abates. It is a popular manœuvre in certain small classes of naval vessels.

If the manœuvre is to be executed in an average-sized merchant ship, a 25–30 mm wire is passed from the after leads on the poop, along the   3–3½-in
offshore side, outside and clear of everything. The offshore anchor is a'cockbilled and a man sent overside on a chair to secure the wire to the anchor, preferably at the shackle. The after end of the wire is sent to a warping barrel, ready for heaving in slack wire.

When the stem is abreast the position on the quay where the bridge will eventually be the anchor is let go, still with headway on the vessel.

43

About half a ship's length of cable is surged and then the cable is snubbed. The wire is hove-in aft.

The onshore wind will drift the vessel down on to her berth, and the scope of the cable, and the wire, is adjusted and slowly veered until the ship lands alongside. Fig. 2.9 shows the manœuvre. It is most important to let go the anchor having the best possible judgement of position, for if the anchor be let go too far off the quay the wire will be of insufficient length and the ship will fail to reach her berth. The anchor must then be 120 fathoms weighed and the manœuvre repeated. If the available wire is 240 m

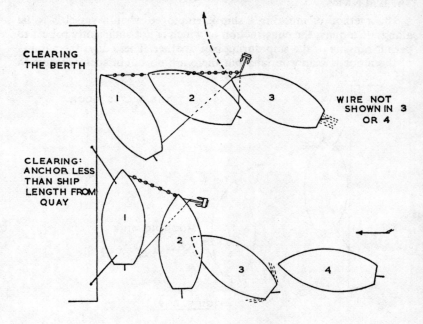

CLEARING THE BERTH

WIRE NOT SHOWN IN 3 OR 4

CLEARING: ANCHOR LESS THAN SHIP LENGTH FROM QUAY

FIGURE 2.10

110 fathoms in length and 220 m are to be veered, then roughly 7½ shackles of 500 ft 60 ft cable will also be veered. If the ship is 150 m long and 18 m in beam the anchor will then lie one-and-a-third ship-lengths off the quay.

If it is discovered, before too much cable is veered, that the anchor has been let go too far from the jetty the cable must be snubbed and the anchor dragged to the desired position.

If there is no wind at the time of berthing the cable and wire are kept slack and the vessel manœuvred to the berth under engine power and helm. Each time the propeller is moved the wire must be hove until it grows farther to long stay.

MOORING

In the event of the anchor lying more than a ship's length from the berth, clearing is comparatively easy: the vessel is hove out to her anchor by her cable, using the wire to make sure that the stern does not foul the berth. If desired, the reverse may be done and the vessel hove out to her anchor stern first, using the wire alone, picking up the slack cable as she goes. The anchor is weighed and the vessel swung to the desired direction (3). In an onshore wind, the anchor can be left at short stay and the vessel steamed round it, if she desires to head upwind (Fig. 2.10).

If the anchor is lying less than a ship's length from the quay the vessel can heave herself out to it, keeping parallel with the jetty. There is no room to swing head-to an onshore wind, so the anchor is weighed and the vessel bored up to windward stern-first under powerful revolutions. She will execute this swing rapidly. When sufficiently far from the quay, she can then swing to the fairway. If there is no wind it will be preferable to again heave out parallel with the quay, weigh anchor, and proceed to swing (if necessary, of course) under powerful headway (Fig. 2.10).

The Mediterranean Moor

This moor is used when wharf space is limited and there is deep water alongside the wharves. The vessel is moored stern on to the jetty with both her anchors lying ahead of her, fine on each bow. The manœuvre varies greatly according to the prevailing wind, and will therefore be fully discussed in Chapter IV after the reader has studied Chapter III.

CLEARING A FOUL HAWSE

The gear necessary for this operation should be made ready at slack water. It will include at least three 20–25-mm wires; a smaller wire, say 10 mm, or some lengths of 10–15-mm fibre rope; a boatswain's chair; and equipment necessary for breaking open a cable joining-shackle.

The operation may be started as soon as the ship is swung to a new stream, thus giving about 6 hours freedom. The clearing may take up most of this time if the hawse is badly fouled. Much will depend upon the men employed.

The hawse is cleared by unshackling the sleeping cable and passing the end around the riding cable.

In Fig. 2.11 the turns are hove above water and the cable lashed together below the turns, using the fibre rope. The naval method may be employed, by using the light wire as shown in the figure. The two ends of the wire are then belayed on deck. There should be no difficulty in bringing the cables together, since the sleeping cable will be reasonably slack. One of the bigger wires is then passed around the sleeping cable below the turns, hove tight, and belayed. This wire acts as a preventer in case the unshackled end of the cable is lost, and also relieves the turns

45

of some of the cable weight. A round turn may be used when passing this preventer around the cable. This enables the wire to be slipped later from the deck. The vessel is shown riding to her starboard cable.

In Fig. 2.12 a wire messenger has been passed down through the hawse pipe, dipped around the riding cable, following the run of the port cable, and returned to the forecastle deck. It is dipped only once, and only half a turn will be removed at any one time.

On deck (Fig. 2.13) the port cable has been veered until a joining shackle is forward of the gypsy. The third wire is secured to the cable just forward of the shackle, both parts are led to the bitts, belayed, and

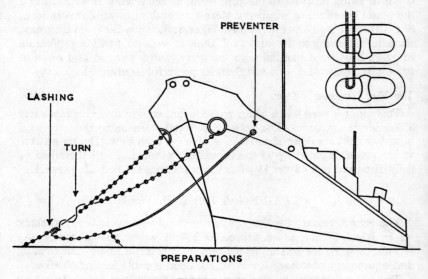

FIGURE 2.11

then the cable is eased to this wire. The shackle is broken open. When the cable is parted the shackle may be replaced and assembled. The easing wire should be capable of being slipped from the deck, and for this reason it is advisable to have it passing through the open end-link. Even when the stress of the cable is on the easing wire, the shackle should still be movable. If the shackle is jammed in position by this taut easing wire (through the end-link) it will not matter, because it can still be broken and reassembled in spite of this.

One inboard end of the messenger is now secured to the joining shackle, the other is taken, with as good a lead as possible, to a warping barrel, and set tight. The easing wire is shortly going to be surged on the bitts—if desired, one end of it can also be led to a warping barrel; it can

46

then be surged without risk of fouling the other end of the wire, or it can be veered under power.

In the case of a lugless joining shackle, where there are no end-links or enlarged common links, the cable is secured by chain stoppers or efficient bow stoppers, the cable shackle broken and then reassembled (when the cable has parted) fast to both the messenger and the easing wire. The easing wire is then hove, the weight taken off the stoppers, the latter cast off, and the situation is as before.

All is now ready for removing the first half-turn. The messenger is hove-in and the easing wire eased. The direction of movement of the messenger is as shown in Fig. 2.12. When the end of cable is about to be

MESSENGER

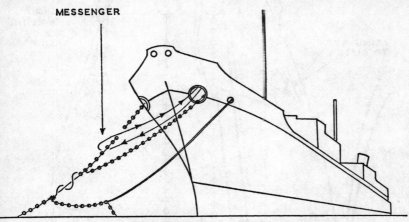

DIPPING THE MESSENGER

FIGURE 2.12

dipped the easing wire is slipped (Fig. 2.14), the messenger hove, and the end of cable dips around the starboard chain. It then continues on up to the hawse pipe and on to the forecastle deck.

On deck the easing wire is again set up, the weight is taken on it, the messenger cast off and re-dipped as before to remove the remaining half-turn.

When this has been achieved the situation is as shown in Fig. 2.15. The cable is re-joined, the preventer is cast off, and the fibre lashings are burned through. This is often done by sending a man overside on a chair. He swings himself along the cable, soaks the fibre rope in paraffin, and returns to the deck. A bucket is then lowered, containing burning paraffin rags, to set the rope alight. Many methods may be devised for this minor job. The cables will then part with very little whip, because the sleeping cable is still slack.

47

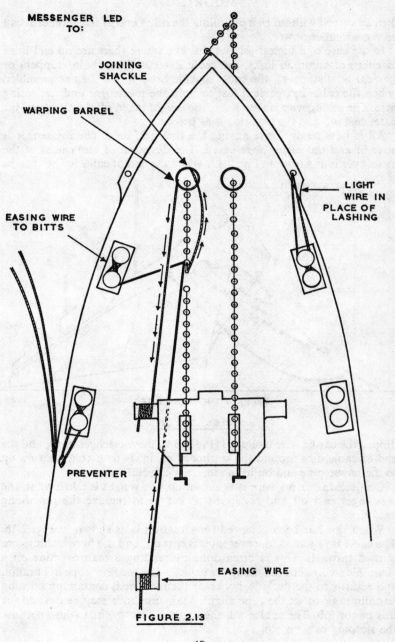

MESSENGER LED
TO:

JOINING
SHACKLE

WARPING BARREL

EASING WIRE
TO BITTS

LIGHT
WIRE IN
PLACE OF
LASHING

PREVENTER

EASING WIRE

FIGURE 2.13

48

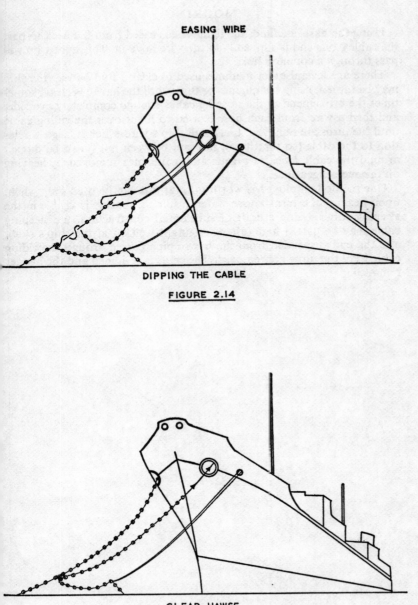

EASING WIRE

DIPPING THE CABLE

FIGURE 2.14

CLEAR HAWSE

FIGURE 2.15

49

Using the naval method, the light wire is eased from the deck to part the cables, one end is slipped, and the wire hove-in. This light wire will pass through a common link.

There are several other methods used to clear a foul hawse: the ship may be turned, using her engines or tugs, until the hawse is clear; sometimes the broken end of the sleeping cable is let go completely overside, and then a wire from each bow is used to lift it over the riding cable until the turns are removed. In a small ship a wire which is large in relation to the cable (so that it will not jam between links) can be dipped around the cable twice at a time and a full turn removed by heaving on this messenger once.

One method employed is worth noting; this can be used only when, upon heaving the turns above water, a joining shackle is visible in the sleeping cable. Using a craft of substantial construction, the sleeping cable may be parted here (after hanging it well off at the ship's side), and the end suspended from the hawse pipe passed around the riding cable until the turns are removed. The cable is re-joined and the hanger removed.

CHAPTER III

THE PRINCIPLES OF SHIP HANDLING

THE successful handling of ships is entirely dependent upon the handler having a wide knowledge of the many factors involved. Some of the factors are controllable by him, others are not, and he must quickly assess their effects so that he may make due allowance for them. Some factors, such as wind and current, may be used to great advantage, providing they are well understood. We shall discuss all the aspects involved, under separate headings, but they are not to be read as being in order of importance.

(1) THE ENGINES

The steam reciprocating engine is generally considered to be the best from the point of view of response. It is rapidly stopped and reversed, and may be relied upon to develop full power either way in a very few seconds.

The modern Diesel engine is started and stopped almost at once, and often develops power more quickly than the steam engine. However, the Diesel engine is difficult to start in a reverse direction while the vessel is making good way through the water. This is due to the resistance of the water stream on the propeller blades. Before ordering a change of engine direction, therefore, the way of the vessel is best allowed to reduce.

The turbine is slow to develop power—it must be given time to increase revolutions, and when stopped it must be allowed to run down. Therefore, when a turbine-equipped vessel is required to stop the turbines must be stopped a little in advance. The running-down of the turbine may take up to five minutes. A separate turbine provides astern power, and has usually only about two-thirds of the power of the ahead turbine. A great deal of foresight is necessary when handling such a ship.

All vessels, particularly Diesel-equipped ships, should be handled with as few starts and stops as possible.

51

THE PRINCIPLES OF SHIP HANDLING

(2) PROPELLERS

By convention, engines are designed to have clockwise-turning shafts when going ahead and when viewed from astern. For this reason, right-handed propellers are nearly universal in single-screw ships. Twin-screw ships invariably have outward-turning screws, i.e. the propeller on the right side of the ship is right-handed, and that on the left side is left-handed. When going astern, both propellers naturally turn inwards.

Triple-screw ships are usually manœuvred on the outer two screws, the central one being used to increase ahead or astern power.

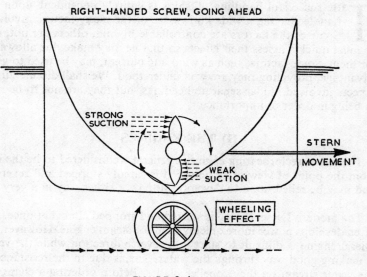

RIGHT-HANDED SCREW, GOING AHEAD

STRONG SUCTION

WEAK SUCTION

STERN MOVEMENT

WHEELING EFFECT

FIGURE 3·1

Quadruple-screw ships have a pair of propellers on each side, a right-handed pair on the starboard side and a left-handed pair on the port side. They are usually manœuvred on the outer screws only. A turbine-equipped ship with four screws generally has the outer pair only capable of going astern.

The thrust of the propeller blade is divided into two components, a fore-and-aft one and a very small athwartships one. The latter is called *transverse thrust*, *screwing effect*, or *starting bias*.

The result of this force may be deduced by considering the propeller to be a wheel, carrying the stern through the water at right angles to the vessel's line of motion. The cause, however, considering an immersed

52

propeller, is mainly due to the suction exerted upon the hull immediately behind the rotating blades. Since the hull is more full in way of the upper blades, the suction has its greater effect at this position and a bias is caused. This bias is very noticeable in full-sterned vessels, but is almost negligible in fine-lined destroyers. Density and aeration cannot be held responsible, since the specific gravity of salt water changes by only 0·000015 over a depth of 3 m, and the bias still occurs at depths where aeration is negligible. It is likely, however, that aeration may affect bias when the propeller is working close to the surface. When the propeller is partially emerged bias is undoubtedly very largely due to the paddling of the lower blades.

10 ft

In Fig. 3.1 a right-handed propeller is shown working ahead, together with the suction bias and the wheeling effect, swinging the bow to port. A starboard swing occurs when going astern, and the reverse is true when using a left-handed propeller. Readers should note that controllable-pitch screws will always produce the same bias, since they rotate in a constant direction, whether the vessel moves ahead or astern.

When the vessel moves ahead a belt of water called the *frictional wake* is drawn along by the hull. This provides a resistance to the upper blades, which reduces starting bias as the speed increases. In some cases an opposite bias may even develop. Under sternway there is very little wake strength at the propeller, and starting bias is maintained as speed increases. Considerable sternway may be necessary before the rudder will correct the bias, and sometimes stopping the engine provides the only correction.

Starting bias is naturally modified in conditions of wind, current, and when the ship's head is already swinging.

Summarising then, in a single-screw ship with a right-handed propeller:

> *When going ahead*, the bow cants to port, the swing decreasing as way is gathered and possibly changing in the opposite sense.
> *When going astern*, the bow cants strongly to starboard and will continue to do so until correcting helm is used.

In a twin-screw ship the propellers are offset from the centreline and a moment is created about the latter by the fore-and-aft thrust of the screw, turning the vessel to one side. If both engines are going ahead or astern, and at the same revolutions, the two transverse thrusts cancel each other. In any case, the port screw is left-handed, and both its transverse thrust and its *offset-effect* cant the bow to starboard when going ahead. Similarly, the starboard screw when going ahead cants the bow to port, both by its offset and its transverse-thrust effects. From this, it is obvious that a vessel fitted with outward-turning screws is more manœuvrable than one fitted with inward-turning screws. Consider the port propeller of such a ship; it is right-handed, and therefore when going ahead its transverse thrust cants the bow to port, while its offset-effect cants the bow to starboard. The net swing of the ship is the difference between these two effects. With outward-turning screws the swing is controlled by the *sum* of the effects.

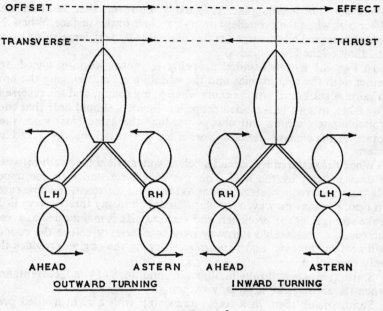

FIGURE 3.2

In narrow waters a vessel having inward-turning screws may become unmanageable. As far as handling it is concerned, engine movements are made as for any other twin-screw ship, but the behaviour may be unpredictable. The advantage of inward-turning screws will be discussed later, but it is vastly outweighed by the inferior manœuvring qualities.

To complete this discussion, imagine an outward-turning screw ship having its port engine going ahead, and its starboard engine going astern. This 'push-and-pull' turns the ship smartly to starboard. Both propellers are now turning left-handed. Consider them as one big left-hand propeller. The transverse thrust cants the bow to starboard, assisting the swing of the ship. Think of the inward-turning screw ship under similar conditions. Again the push-and-pull action turns the ship to starboard, but both propellers are now revolving right-handed and their transverse thrusts oppose the push-and-pull effect. Often the latter is opposed sufficiently to cant the ship in a reverse direction (Fig. 3.2).

When turning a twin-screw ship which is stopped or moving very slowly the transverse thrusts of her propellers is greater than the offset-effect, and the two combined are more effective than helm.

For freedom from vibration the propeller must turn in a smooth flow of water. This flow is restricted when the engines are reversed and also in shallow water, so that vibration occurs under these conditions.

Manœuvring Propellers

A device developed in 1950 is known as the Active Rudder. It consists of a submersible electric motor, water-filled and water-lubricated, installed in the trailing edge of the rudder. It can be supplied with ratings varying between 15 and 1200 kW. The rear end of the motor shaft carries a propeller which is capable of being reversed in the direction of rotation. Power can be supplied immediately to turn the ship in any direction. It is of particular use when the vessel is stopped. A side effect is that, in the event of a main engine failure, the active rudder gives sufficient power to propel the vessel to port.

Bow thruster units are increasingly in use. One of these, fitted to a coastal tanker, saved the initial expense of the unit in one year. These units (about 300 kW for a 9000-tonne deadweight vessel) enable a vessel to turn within her own length. Thruster units may also be fitted at the stern. Hull resistance is not increased if properly faired doors are fitted at each end of the thruster tunnel, the doors and the motor having interlock switching. In berthing or unberthing, the units are invaluable. By steaming ahead on a forward spring and thrusting towards the quay at the same time, a vessel can move sideways off the quay.

(3) THE WAKE CURRENT

If a beamy, rectangular barge is under headway a cavity will be created at its stern. Water will flow down the sides of the barge and swirl in to fill this cavity. Steering will be very adversely affected because the rudder will be working in what might loosely be termed a partial vacuum. Further, the propeller will be working in disturbed water, speed will be lost, and vibrations will be set up. This water, swirling into the cavity, is called the wake current. Both cavitation and wake current increase with speed.

If, however, a finely sterned yacht was under headway the cavitation

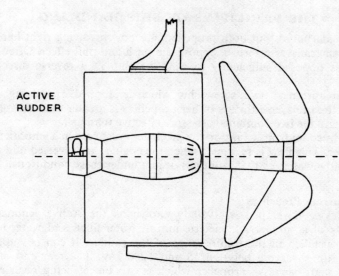

ACTIVE
RUDDER

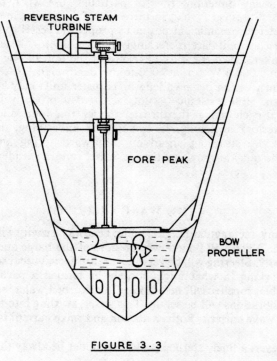

REVERSING STEAM
TURBINE

FORE PEAK

BOW
PROPELLER

FIGURE 3.3

56

and wake current would be very much smaller. Ships should therefore be constructed with as fine a form aft as possible. When the ship moves astern the cavitation and wake current exist at the stem and will be very small. In any case, it will not affect the propeller or steering.

(4) THE RUDDER

The turning properties of a ship depend largely upon the size, shape, and position of the rudder. Basically, there are two types: the older-fashioned rudder, which has all its area abaft the rudder post, and the balanced rudder, having about a third of its area forward of the post. When this type of rudder is turned water impinges upon the forward area and assists the rotation.

In a single-screw vessel the rudder is directly abaft the propeller and the slipstream strikes directly upon the rudder surface. In a twin-screw ship the rudder is situated midway between the two slipstreams and will have effect only when it is directed into either one, or when the ship has sufficient way upon her to cause a flow of water past the rudder.

It is for this reason that a single-screw ship is the more sensitive of the two types when the rudder is moved during very slow speeds or when the ship is stopped. We have already stated that the helm of a twin-screw ship, stopped or moving very slowly, is not as effective as the offset-effect of the two propellers.

It should be noted that despite the good steering qualities of a single-screw ship, the rudder is almost ineffective when the ship has her headway reduced by astern engine movements, due to the resulting turbulence.

In some twin-screw vessels twin rudders are fitted, one directly abaft each propeller, the steering qualities then closely approaching that of a single-screw ship. Vessels working upon the Canadian Great Lakes have their engines aft and their bridges right forward. This unusual distribution of weight adversely affects steering, even under full headway, and twin rudders are fitted to compensate for this.

Under sternway considerable way must be gathered in order for the rudder to be effective, and even then steering is likely to be unreliable. The best that can be hoped for is a trend in the right direction.

Vessels fitted with inward-turning twin-screws have a very much narrower screw stream, and hence better steering qualities than are found with outward-turning propellers. They also have a slightly improved speed. These factors are, however, greatly outweighed by their poor manoeuvrability at slow speeds. We have already stated how their transverse thrusts oppose the offset effect, and this will persist until the ship has sufficient way upon her for her rudder effect to predominate.

(5) SIDESLIP OR SKID

When a vessel turns under helm her ends skid about her pivoting point. There is also a bodily sideslip due to centrifugal force. When a vessel is light her sideslip, and skid, become more apparent because her reduced underwater volume has a less grip on the water. At high speeds the skidding has a marked effect in reducing headway.

(6) THE TURNING CIRCLE

When a vessel alters her course under helm through 360 degrees she moves on a roughly circular path called a *turning circle*. Throughout the turn her bow will be slightly inside the circle and her stern a little outside it. The circle will be the path traced out by her centre of gravity.

At any instant during the turn a line drawn from the centre of curvature of the path, perpendicular to the ship's fore-and-aft line, meets the latter at a point called the *pivoting point*. This is about one-third of the

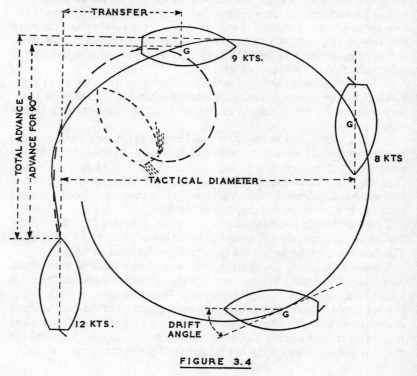

FIGURE 3.4

length from forward. For practical purposes, it may be taken as being just forward of the bridge. When the vessel moves under sternway the pivoting point moves aft, very close to the stern. Fig. 3.4 shows the starboard turning circle for a single-screw ship. The dotted track superimposed on the first circle is the turning circle of a similar vessel, but having twin-screws, one going astern and one going ahead, at equal revolutions.

The circle does not link up with the original course, due to some sideslip when the helm is first used. During the turn the vessel suffers some deceleration; after turning through 90 degrees she has lost about one-quarter of her original speed and after a further 90 degrees she has lost about one-third of her original speed. Thereafter the speed remains roughly constant.

With a right-handed propeller the circle to port will be slightly smaller in radius than the circle to starboard, due to the effect of transverse thrust.

Seamen usually refer to the turning circle as being the path traced out by the pivoting point, the definition given previously being that of naval architects. The two circles will be very close together, and concentric.

The *advance* is the distance travelled by the centre of gravity along the original course.

The *transfer* is the distance travelled by the centre of gravity, measured from the original track to the point where the vessel has altered her course by 90 degrees.

The *tactical diameter* is the transfer for 180 degrees.

The *drift angle* is the angle between the ship's fore-and-aft line and the tangent to the turning circle.

The average advance is about three to four ship-lengths, but may be considerably more at high speeds. The average tactical diameter for an easily turned ship is about four ship-lengths.

The time taken to complete a turning circle is roughly 7–8 minutes for a merchant ship.

(7) EFFECTS OF LOADING

When deeply laden a vessel will carry her way longer, cause greater damage under impact than if she were light, be slow to answer her helm, be sluggish in gathering way, be affected by wind to a minimum, have a turning circle generally unaffected by her speed, and will have a larger turning circle for a given speed than if she were light.

When light she will be lively to engine movements, sensitive to her helm, easily turned on her anchor, be affected by wind to a maximum, easily stopped, be more easily brought up by anchors or mooring lines, be subject to larger amounts of skid and sideslip, have a smaller turning circle for a given speed than if she were deeply laden, cause less damage under impact than if she were deeply laden, and will have a turning circle, the radius of which increases as the speed increases.

However, if the vessel is so light as to only partially immerse her propeller, her acceleration and deceleration will be small, making her slow to stop and start, though not so slow as if she were deeply laden.

A merchant ship handles best when she is a half to two-thirds loaded, and trimmed a little by the stern.

Generally speaking, the most awkward type of vessel to handle is one which is low powered, deeply laden, of large size, having a single screw, and poor steering qualities.

(8) EFFECT OF TRIM

A vessel trimmed by the stern has her pivoting point farther aft than if she were on even keel, has a larger turning circle, will develop maximum power, will steer well, and will turn more readily downwind.

A vessel trimmed by the head has her pivoting point farther forward than if she were on even keel, has a smaller turning circle, does not develop her full power, will be difficult to turn, and once swinging she will be difficult to check, will turn more readily into the wind, will be slow to seek the wind with her stern under sternway, and with the wind on the quarter may become unmanageable.

(9) EFFECT OF LIST

A vessel listed will turn more readily towards her high side, will have a smaller turning circle on that side, and in the case of a twin-screw ship the low-side engine will be more effective than the other. Low-side helm will be necessary to correct this.

(10) CARRYING WAY

A vessel will carry her way farthest when she is large, deeply loaded, smooth-hulled and non-fouled, and of fine form. When deeply laden she may carry her way up to three times as far as if she were light.

A ship usually reduces her headway quite quickly down to a speed where her wave-making is at a minimum, say 7 knots. Thereafter the loss of way occurs at a reduced rate.

720 ft
1·75 miles
1 mile

A tanker, 220m long, travelling at 16 knots, was stopped with full stern power in 2·8km (10 minutes). With the rudder hard over, the figures became 1·6km (9 minutes). This tanker had a deadweight of 66 000 tonnes.

tons
660 ft

The following figures relate to a twin-screw ship of 23 500 tonnes displacement, 26 000 kW, length 200 m, and speed 23·5 knots:

60

Under trials full speed was reached after 17½ minutes commencing from rest, during which time the vessel covered 9·3km. 5·8 miles
Upon reversing her engines, she came to rest in 4 minutes after carrying her way for 6½ ship lengths.

When handling a ship in narrow waters she should never have too much way upon her. This does not mean that full speed becomes a dangerous order; on the contrary, it is the most efficient when instant response from helm is desired, or for correcting or commencing a swing. It only becomes dangerous when too much way is allowed to be gathered.

(11) THE EFFECT OF SHALLOWS

As the hull moves through shallow water, that which it displaces is not so easily replaced by other water, and the propeller and rudder are working in what might again be loosely termed a partial vacuum. The vessel takes longer to answer her helm, and response to engine movements becomes sluggish.

In these circumstances vibration will be set up, and it will be extremely difficult to correct a yaw or sheer with any degree of rapidity.

At normal speed it is found that steering becomes erratic when the depth of water is equal to, or less than, one and a half times the deepest draught, i.e. a vessel drawing 8 m maximum draught will develop 24 ft
unsteady steering in water of depth 12 m or under. When a ship is 36 ft
nearing an extremely shallow depth of water, such as a shoal, she is likely to take a sudden sheer, first towards it and then violently away. This is called *smelling the ground*, and the movements of a sluggish ship may suddenly become astonishingly lively.

Due to the fact that the water displaced by a hull moving through shallow water is not easily replaced, the bow wave and stern wave of the vessel increase in height. Further, the trough which normally exists under the quarter becomes deeper and the after part of the ship is drawn downwards towards the bottom. By reducing speed, the wave heights and trough depth will be diminished, and the vessel will not therefore close the bottom, or *squat*.

The speed of a vessel moving in shallow water should always be moderate; if the speed is increased the keel will close with the ground and the ship will sheer about unpredictably. If the bow wave and stern wave are observed to be higher than is prudent speed should be reduced —but not suddenly. If the speed is taken off rapidly the stern wave will overtake the vessel and cause her to take a sheer, which in a narrow channel could be disastrous.

Further effects of shallows will be discussed later.

61

(12) THE EFFECT OF STERNWAY

A single-screw ship will answer her helm under these conditions provided she has good sternway, the conditions are calm, and her propeller is not revolving. In a wind steering under sternway is possible only, and then rather erratically, when the stern is run right into the wind's eye.

Despite the above, response to the rudder under sternway is generally poor unless it is desired to swing the vessel to starboard, when the rudder assists the transverse thrust. If the vessel is to be swung to port under sternway way must be gathered and the engines stopped before swinging, in order to avoid the adverse transverse thrust.

The twin-screw ship will steer quite well under sternway by varying the revolutions on each engine as appropriate. She will not, however, steer as well as she would under headway, and in a wind she will not steer under sternway.

(13) GENERAL EFFECT OF TWIN-SCREWS

Apart from what has already been discussed about these vessels, it should be noted that headway can be checked and a swing achieved simultaneously by reversing one engine. To achieve the maximum rate of swing in a twin-screw ship, she should be kept under headway. If space is restricted, however, the outside engine should be worked full ahead, the rudder is put hard over to make the turn, the inside engine is reversed full astern, and then the outer engine is slowed. By gathering sternway, and then slowing the inner engine and speeding the outer one, another run ahead can be made and the swing continued. The ship, in other words, swings in the same way as a car turns in a narrow road; the engines are never stopped, but accelerated or decelerated as required.

To turn a merchant ship, having twin-screws, in her own length by running the screws at equal but opposite revolutions is a very slow process.

As has been seen already, the twin-screw ship can make a very small turning circle by reversing the inner engine.

Twin-screws offer the further advantage of being more able to correct a sudden sheer than the single screw.

(14) THE EFFECT OF WIND

When a vessel is light, a gentle breeze can have the same effect upon her as a gale would have on a deeply laden ship.

When a vessel is stopped she adopts a position such that the wind is roughly on the beam.

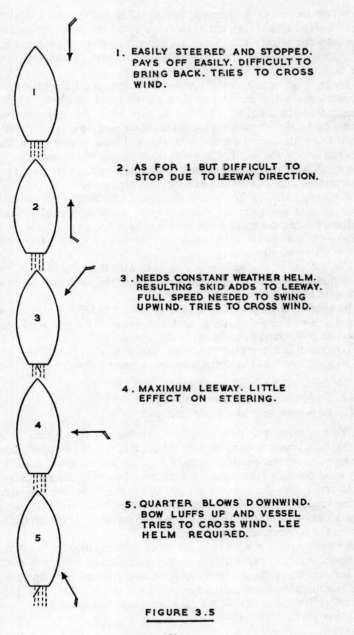

1. EASILY STEERED AND STOPPED. PAYS OFF EASILY. DIFFICULT TO BRING BACK. TRIES TO CROSS WIND.

2. AS FOR 1 BUT DIFFICULT TO STOP DUE TO LEEWAY DIRECTION.

3. NEEDS CONSTANT WEATHER HELM. RESULTING SKID ADDS TO LEEWAY. FULL SPEED NEEDED TO SWING UPWIND. TRIES TO CROSS WIND.

4. MAXIMUM LEEWAY. LITTLE EFFECT ON STEERING.

5. QUARTER BLOWS DOWNWIND. BOW LUFFS UP AND VESSEL TRIES TO CROSS WIND. LEE HELM REQUIRED.

FIGURE 3.5

63

When she is under sternway her pivoting point moves right aft, all her windage area is forward of this point, and she rapidly runs her stern up into the wind's eye. This is a general rule, and providing a vessel has appreciable sternway, she will do this even under full opposing helm.

Under headway, a vessel's movements in a wind are very much dependent upon the amount of windage forward or abaft her pivoting point, and the relative direction of the wind. Providing a vessel is trimmed by the stern, her greatest windage will be forward, and under headway with a wind on the bow, she will tend to pay off to leeward, i.e. run across the wind. The exceptions to this are vessels trimmed by the head, a deeply laden tanker whose funnel and superstructure aft act as a mizzen sail, and vessels having long, high poops.

A deeply laden tanker, although having an effective mizzen 'sail' aft, will still run her stern up into the wind under sternway. A tanker in ballast, having the usual large trim by the stern, pays off the wind and runs rapidly across it under headway, vigorously seeking the wind with her stern under sternway.

Fig. 3.5 shows a vessel under headway with the wind in all its relative directions. It should be studied carefully and the tendency to run across the wind noted.

In general, a wind is of great assistance provided it is not too strong for the condition of loading, and judgement does not need to be so exact as when manœuvring in a calm.

To appreciate the later work on practical ship handling, we must take careful note of the average vessel's three tendencies in a wind:

(1) To lie across it when stopped.
(2) To run across it under headway.
(3) To *sternbore* into it under sternway.

We can now anticipate a vessel's movements in a wind. Take, for example, a vessel under headway whose engines are stopped, and then reversed when she has lost way. In Fig. 3.6 she is shown running with the wind on the port quarter. As she loses headway she runs across the wind to (2). As she gathers her sternway, her bow develops a reverse swing to starboard and she bores her stern into the wind's eye as in (3). She does not, of course, reach her original position (1) due to the leeway which she is continually experiencing.

A twin-screw ship which is attempting to swing into the wind must do so under headway and not rely merely on the offset and push–pull effect of her screws. If she attempts to lie stationary and turn upwind using her engines ahead and astern her bows will pay off the wind. She must therefore turn into the wind under headway, full helm, and a reversed inside engine.

A twin-screw ship desirous of turning downwind will, as in the case of a single-screw ship, swing much more rapidly if sternway is gathered, so that the stern seeks the wind's eye.

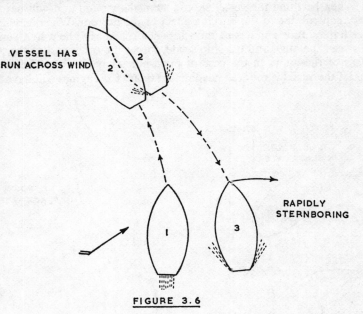

VESSEL HAS
RUN ACROSS WIND

RAPIDLY
STERNBORING

FIGURE 3.6

(15) THE EFFECT OF A CURRENT

Currents which are known, and not too strong, may be used to advantage. They do not affect a ship's handling qualities and affect all ships equally, regardless of trim or loading.

When handling a vessel in a current due allowance must be made for the downstream drift of the ship, the amount of which depends upon the strength of the stream and the period of time during which the ship is subjected to its influence.

When anchored or berthed in a current the rudder is effective due to the continual flow of water past it.

Slack water may be found close inshore, while reverse currents are often experienced off pierheads and similar projections into the stream.

A vessel stemming the stream at slow speed may complete the first part of her turning circle almost within her own length, as the stream runs against the vessel broadside.

A vessel running downstream may well develop double the speed over the ground normally attained in slack water by the existing engine revolutions, and if she is turned the radius of the first 90 degrees of turn is far in excess of her slack-water swing. These swings are shown in Fig. 3.7. Great care is necessary in handling a ship running downstream.

When berthing the vessel should stem the stream and will be under easy control due to the braking effect of the current. When leaving the berth the uptide end has its moorings slackened and the water, running between the quay and the ship's side, forces the other end of the vessel clear of the quay. In the case of open-pile wharves, this effect is lost, and if the vessel is moored heading upstream the engines will have to be

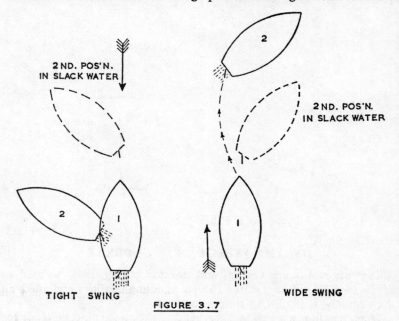

2ND. POS'N. IN SLACK WATER

2ND. POS'N. IN SLACK WATER

TIGHT SWING

WIDE SWING

FIGURE 3.7

worked ahead as soon as the bow is cast off across the stream, in order to prevent the stern fouling the piles. Heading downstream, this situation does not arise.

(16) THE EFFECT OF NARROW CANALS, RIVERS, AND RESTRICTED CHANNELS

In these localities all the effects of shallow water are present, together with others. The water displaced by a vessel moving ahead is restricted in movement by the proximity of banks. The general effect is a build-up in the water level ahead of the ship and a lowering in the level astern of her. This produces a surging effect which can part a moored ship's

hawsers up to 3 km ahead of the moving vessel, provided the same   2 miles
restricted conditions prevail all the way.

In addition, the moving vessel's bow wave, stern wave, and trough
increase in amplitude, and for this reason a vessel should proceed at
slow speed in such areas.

As the vessel moves through the restricted channel it is possible that
she may close one bank. In this event a streamlining or venturi effect
arises due to the restricted flow of water on one side of the ship. This

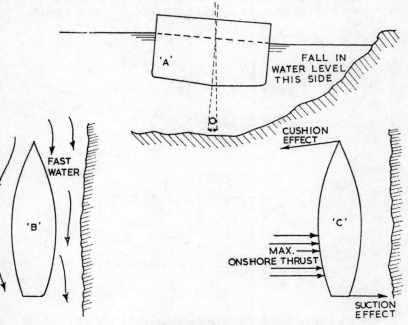

FIGURE 3. 8.

causes an increase in the velocity of the water on that side, together with
a loss of pressure head. The latter manifests itself as a drop in water
level at the nearer bank, and a thrust is set up towards it. The greater
fullness over the after body of the ship accentuates the thrust, and it thus
appears more strongly at the stern than at the bow. The stern moves
towards the bank and the bow away from it. American terms for these
sheers are *bank suction* and *bank cushion*, respectively; the terms are
useful in describing the effects, though there is no cushioning unless the
speed of the vessel is so high as to cause a build-up in water level at the
inshore bow. All these effects can be demonstrated easily in a simple

67

glass tank, and a person holding the ship-model can feel the suction at the stern. It should be noted that ships passing close to one another will also experience these venturi effects.

Fig. 3.8 illustrates canal effect, and it will be seen that the vessel heels towards the nearer bank so as to displace constant volume.

The drop in water level, and thus the canal effect, varies as the square of the speed. So a small change in speed will produce a large change in the canal effect. *Navigators using correcting helm when experiencing canal effect should be extremely alert to reduce this helm when slowing the ship.*

A ship wishing to make a right-hand turn in a river bend, i.e. to

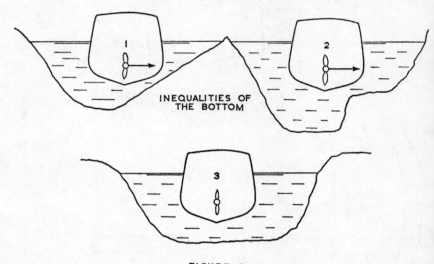

INEQUALITIES OF
THE BOTTOM

FIGURE 3.9

starboard, can, by keeping well into the port bank, use the effect of bank cushion forward to assist her turn. This is frequently resorted to in narrow channels, such as are present in the Panama Canal. There, a ship turning to starboard around a bend will be kept well into the port bank. She will turn quite easily with the rudder kept amidships. If the cushioning effect becomes excessive port helm may have to be used in spite of the fact that the turn is directed to starboard.

If the ship is kept in the true centre of the channel all these forces are equalised. Inequalities of the bottom can cause these forces to come into play despite the fact that the ship is equidistant from both banks. If the channel is deeper on one side than on the other, if the bank is steeper on one side, or if the vessel passes over a shoal suction and cushion will appear suddenly due to the river bed restricting the flow of water. This is similar to smelling the ground, and dangerous sheers may suddenly be taken.

For this reason, the ship should at all times be kept in the true centre of the channel, which, as shown in Fig. 3.9, is not necessarily the visual centre. In (1) she is taking a sheer to port because the starboard bank is less steep than the port bank and her stern is sucked towards the former. She should therefore have been kept closer to the port bank. In (2) she is taking a similar sheer because the starboard side of the channel is shallower than the port side. Again, her positioning should have been farther to port. In (3) the channel is of constant depth, the banks are of equal gradient, and the visual centre and true centre are the same. In all the drawings the vessel is shown heading away from the observer and positioned in the visual centre.

If the vessel is kept to the true centre the minimum amounts of helm are used. This is advantageous, because if the ship should suddenly take a sheer the maximum amount of correcting rudder is available. If the helm necessary to navigate the channel is consistently of half or full amount these sheering forces should be suspected and the ship's track examined on the chart.

Bank cushion and suction may be used to advantage under conditions when a cross wind is persistently causing a vessel to swing her bow downwind. By keeping farther towards the lee bank, the cushioning effect will correct this tendency. Similarly, if she is continually swinging upwind, such as might be the case with a deeply laden tanker, by keeping closer to the weather bank the sheering forces will steady her.

Due to the necessary slow speed of a vessel navigating in shallow, restricted waters, and the corresponding sluggishness of helm response, the rudder, when used, will have to be moved boldly. Further, for a given number of revolutions, her speed will be slower than that in deep water, due to the increased amplitude of her wave-making.

The ship should be navigated so that the maximum amount of correcting rudder is always available, together with as much manœuvring room as possible. A sheer should be instantly corrected by ordering full revolutions and full correcting helm, reducing both immediately the swing is checked. In an emergency the anchor on the side towards which the vessel is sheering should be let go and held at short stay.

(17) THE EFFECT OF BENDS

The use of bank cushion and suction in navigating bends has already been mentioned. For reasons which we are about to discuss, it is better, where possible, to avoid passing other vessels within a very narrow bend. Both are subjected to sheering.

In narrow waters the strength of stream varies greatly, and the vessel may well become out of control if her ends are subjected to opposing or differing currents. The water usually runs fastest in the middle of a straight run and in the concave bank of a bend. Off the convex bank, known as the point, slack water or even reverse currents may be found.

In Fig. 3.10 a vessel is shown rounding a bend to port against the stream. As she leaves the straight reach and enters the bend the current is flowing along her side aft, but on to her port bow forward. This, unless bold correcting helm is used, will cause her to take a sheer to starboard. When heading against the stream it is advisable to keep within the bend and as far away from the point as possible. Bank cushion will then assist in correcting the sheer, if any.

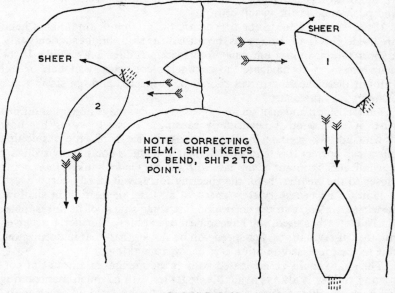

NOTE CORRECTING HELM. SHIP 1 KEEPS TO BEND, SHIP 2 TO POINT.

FIGURE 3·10

A vessel is also shown rounding a bend to port with the stream astern of her. As she changes her course, the stream aft catches her port quarter, causing her to sheer to port. When heading downstream it is advisable to keep close to the point, so that bank sheering forces assist in preventing a sheer.

The most dangerous situation arises when a vessel is heading downstream and executing a bend to starboard. The current catches her starboard quarter as she turns, sheering her to starboard. If now the engines are reversed (because the ship is perhaps out of control) the swing to starboard is aggravated and the ship will come athwart the stream.

(18) EFFECT OF NARROW ENTRANCES

A vessel entering a dock, lock, or pierheads off the river will, if there is a strong current, need tugs to control her entry. A small ship, however, can usually make the entrance unassisted, under bold headway. A larger vessel generally has not sufficient room in which to gather this headway.

As the bows come under the lee of the upstream pierhead her fore body is in slack water, while the stern is still under the influence of the stream. She will therefore tend to sheer towards this pierhead, and a

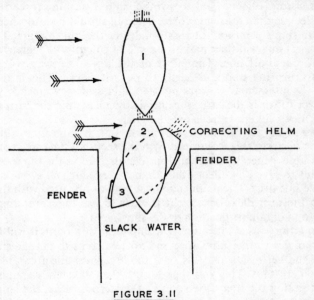

FIGURE 3.11

careful watch must be kept for the first sign of a cant. Bold correcting helm and a surge ahead on the engines will be necessary to counteract this. Since the approach may be made at right angles to the stream, due allowance must be made for downstream drift. Fenders should be rigged at the upstream bow and the downstream quarter (Fig. 3.11).

(19) THE EFFECT OF TUGS

In some localities the assistance of a tug is essential, particularly in conditions of strong current or wind. Elsewhere, the use of a tug or tugs will greatly add to the speed and safety of a manœuvre. In very restricted waters the tugs have almost complete control over the ship, the main engines being used to assist the vessel in gathering way or to complete a swing. Where there is plenty of manœuvring room, the ship is handled in the usual way, using the tugs to push or tow as required.

When using a tug to push, the force should be applied at the position of the centre of gravity. If this is done the vessel will move bodily, but if the tug's stem is a few metres out of position one end of the ship will swing rapidly while the other end remains practically stationary. When a strong wind is blowing on to the other side of the ship the tug's stem should be a little forward of the centre of gravity to correct for the swing of the ship's bow downwind.

When a tug is being used to swing a ship a pushing force is usually more effective than a towing force. The tug should position herself just abaft the ship's stem and at right angles to the hull plating. The tug's fore-and-aft line will then make an angle of roughly 70 degrees with the ship's fore-and-aft line. The effect of the tug's headway will then be partly to turn the ship and partly to push it astern. This latter movement is counteracted by working the engines at slow ahead; with the helm over towards the turn, the ship is then assisting the turn and it is often achieved in the vessel's own length.

If instead the tug is similarly positioned aft it cannot get sufficiently close to the stern; this, combined with the fact that the centre of gravity of the ship is generally abaft the mid-length, places the tug too close to this point to give any effect other than a very sluggish swing and considerable side drift. The main engines should not be used with the tug so close to the propellers. Even if it is clear to use them, the tug will be unable to maintain its position in the slipstream.

When a tug is used aft to heave a ship clear of a berth it will first tow at right angles to the ship's fore-and-aft line so as to get the stern well clear of the berth. During this time the headlines and forward springs must be kept taut. This will then ensure that the stem remains steady without raking the quay. As soon as the stern is clear, the ship works her engines astern for a moment, the tug swings round so that it leads out on the quarter, and the forward lines are let go.

When employing tugs, it should be borne in mind that a tug will have considerable difficulty in correcting a violent sheer. For this reason, the amount of way gathered should never be excessive.

When casting off an after tug, if the vessel has sternway on her, whether or not the engines are stopped, the line will be very liable to run in under the stern and foul the rudder or screws. The line should therefore be let go while the ship is carrying headway, and it will then stream astern, even more rapidly if the engines are working ahead due to the screw stream. There is no need to stop engines when letting go a tug while the ship has headway upon her.

Unfortunately it is not practical to secure a towline to a tug close by

72

its stern-rail. The line is usually secured very near the centre of flotation, and for this reason the tug may be *girded* or *girted*.

Fig. 3.12 shows a tug being girded. It occurs when a towline under stress is allowed to lead directly abeam from the tug. The craft is unable to turn, and may capsize, often with heavy loss of life. The list taken by the tug may be so acute and rapid that the crew may not be able to slip the hook. The men standing by the towline on board the towed vessel should therefore be instantly ready, at all times, to let go the line.

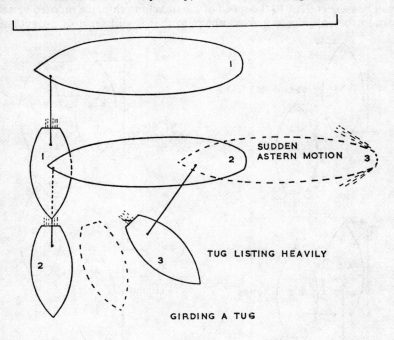

SUDDEN ASTERN MOTION

TUG LISTING HEAVILY

GIRDING A TUG

FIGURE 3 . 12

In the figure the ship has been towed broadside off the quay from (1) to (2). Without warning to the tug, she then moves ahead or astern; in the figure she has moved astern to (3). Her motion takes the tugmaster unawares, and before he can swing into line with the towrope the latter leads abeam and his craft is girded. Ample warning must be given to tugs if the ship is required to suddenly move ahead or astern. This is not so important if the towline is bowsed to the stern of the tug with a *gobline*.

(20) THE EFFECT OF PASSING A MOORED SHIP

Such a vessel will surge considerably, to and fro in the wash of a passing ship. The speed of the latter must therefore be reduced whenever a vessel is to be passed close by at, say, a river berth. The surging is due to the cushioning and suction effects existing at a travelling ship's bow and stern. There is also the fore-and-aft flow of water down her side to be considered. Fig. 3.13 shows the movements to which a moored ship will be subject. Due to the speed of the travelling ship, the moored vessel cannot be considered a fixed object in that it will repel or attract the

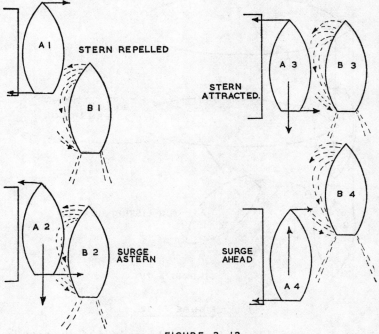

FIGURE 3.13

former's bow and stern. On the contrary, the moored vessel is regarded as a floating object which is subjected to these sheering forces. Strictly speaking, ship 'A' should have her lines tended during the passage of 'B', and the latter should proceed as slowly as possible in order to keep her wave-making to a minimum. Ship 'B' must also be kept well clear of the other bank so that she does not take a colliding sheer into 'A'.

CHAPTER IV

PRACTICAL SHIP HANDLING

WITHIN this chapter we shall make a comprehensive study of ship manœuvres. Each one will be illustrated and explained in the text. In some cases a mooring line or an anchor cable has been omitted from the drawing for the sake of clarity. A wind is indicated by means of an arrow feathered on one side only; current is shown by an arrow feathered on both sides.

All the examples feature a single-screw ship having a right-handed propeller. Twin-screw vessels have the advantage of being more easily handled in confined spaces, and their manœuvres are therefore not included.

A candidate who presents himself for a Department of Trade (D.o.T.) examination in oral seamanship will be required to demonstrate an ability to handle ships. Unless stated otherwise by the Examiner, the model ship is to be taken as having a single right-handed propeller. This model should be moved by the candidate as realistically as possible: generally, it should be handled slowly; the gathering and reduction of way must be demonstrated as being gradual, there being a slight delay between engine orders and response; the running-ashore of mooring lines must be indicated before the ship is required to be checked by them; the delay between a helm order and swing-response must be shown, together with a gradually increasing rate of swing.

In studying the next few pages, the reader is advised to concentrate on the drawings, taking careful note of each consecutive position of the ship before passing on to the next. The helm, engine movement, headway, sternway, mooring lines, and the growth of anchor cable, if any, should be studied for each position.

As the reader progresses, he will appreciate that only a very few basic principles are involved in each manœuvre, and these he will soon master.

Fig. 4.1. Securing to Two Buoys in Calm Weather

The approach should be made with the minimum of headway in order to avoid a swing developing when the engine is worked astern. In calms, with no wind braking-effect present, the risk of overshooting exists. For this reason, the vessel is headed for the headbuoy fine on the starboard bow. When the engine is working astern to reduce headway the swing is favourable.

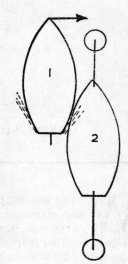

Fig. 4.2. Turning the Vessel before Securing to Two Buoys in Calms

The headbuoy is approached on the port bow and a line secured. The engine is then worked slow ahead on the taut line, with the helm hard over towards the buoy. The vessel is thus swung to (2), when a line to the sternbuoy is used to complete the swing.

By keeping the headbuoy to port, the transverse thrust effect is favourable.

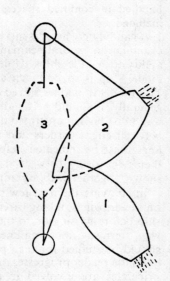

76

Fig. 4.3. Securing to Two Buoys with Current Ahead

The vessel approaches under slow headway over the ground with the headbuoy fine on the port bow (1). While the line is secured to the head-buoy, the engine must be worked slow ahead. With the buoy situated on the port bow, the effect of trans-verse thrust is favourable. The ves-sel is then allowed to drop down-stream so that the sternbuoy can be picked up.

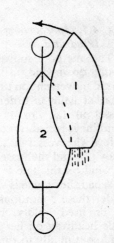

Fig. 4.4. Securing to Two Buoys with Current Astern

This is very similar to Fig. 4.2, since the vessel will secure to the first buoy on her port bow (1). She will then, having been given a slight cant to port, allow the current to carry her round to (2) and (3). Once she is beam-on to the stream, her engine should be worked slow ahead with port helm to relieve the stress on the headline.

In this instance the buoy could very well have been picked up on the starboard bow.

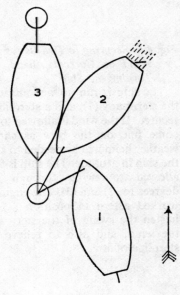

77

Fig. 4.5. Approaching a Buoy from Windward

The method shown is to drift bodily downwind, using occasional ahead movement on the engine with weather helm in order to keep the vessel in the correct attitude. A headline is run away to leeward well before the vessel has reached the buoy (2), and the vessel swung head to wind on this line.

When the engine is worked ahead under these conditions it will have to be used boldly, because with little headway on her the ship will tend continually to run beam-on to the wind.

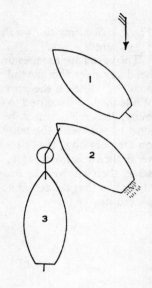

Fig. 4.6. Securing to Two Buoys with Wind or Current Ahead, and Turning the Ship

The ship is run up well ahead of the sternbuoy (1), and a sternline is secured. If the wind is allowed to become fine on the bow as shown weather helm will be needed to keep the ship in attitude. The ship is then allowed to swing through 180 degrees to (2) and (3). The engine is worked astern in position (2), to hasten the swing of the stern into the wind, and also to relieve the sternline of stress.

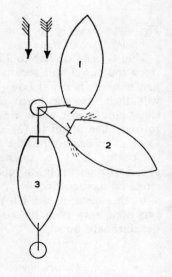

Fig. 4.7. Securing to Two Buoys in a Very Strong Wind

It will be extremely difficult to keep the vessel head to wind while securing to the headbuoy, for as soon as headway is lost the vessel will quickly pay off to one side.

Taking advantage of the fact that the vessel will keep her stern up to windward more easily when under sternway, the buoys are approached sternfirst (1). At (2), when the sternway has been run off, a headline is secured. It should be noted that if the vessel is allowed to have the wind on the starboard quarter as shown she will quickly drift athwart the line of buoys with the wind coming on to the starboard beam. It is therefore preferable in (2) to have the wind right aft or fine on the port quarter. This is difficult to achieve with adverse transverse thrust. At (2), then, the engine is worked ahead with port helm until the ship is swinging to (3), when she is allowed to drift further, to (4). Notice that at (1) the wind is on the port quarter —transverse thrust then assists the vessel to reach the wind's eye. Had the buoys initially been left to starboard, the headbuoy would probably have been missed altogether.

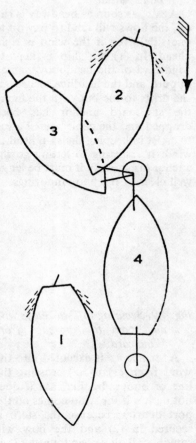

Fig. 4.8. Securing to a Buoy with a Wind Ahead

Again, as soon as headway is run off, the bows will tend to pay off to one side, even if the wind is right ahead. In (1) the ship is kept to windward of the headbuoy, canted to port, and the headline secured as she drifts to the buoy. In the figure the starboard anchor has been dropped and the cable veered away to assist in keeping the ship head to wind. If resorting to letting go the anchor (as shown), it must be let go well clear of the buoy moorings.

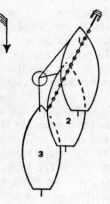

Fig. 4.9. Securing to Two Buoys with no Room to Approach from Windward

A *sternboard* is executed into the wind from (1) to (2) crossing the line of buoys. In this case it does not matter if the wind comes on the port quarter, because the stern is secured in (2) and the bow will rapidly fall downwind until (3) is reached. This should be compared with Fig. 4.7.

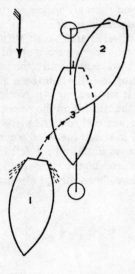

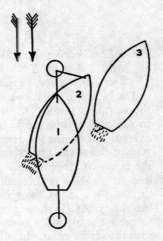

**Fig. 4.10. Clearing from Two Buoys
with Wind or Stream Ahead**

The sternline is let go and the vessel canted to starboard by slacking the headline. At the same instant the engine is worked ahead with weather helm (2), and as headway is gathered the headline is let go and the ship clears as in (3), still using weather helm to hold her in attitude.

**Fig. 4.11. Clearing from Two Buoys
with Wind or Stream Astern**

The vessel is canted as in (2) by easing the sternline. At the same instant, before the vessel overruns the headbuoy, the engine is worked astern. As way is gathered, the lines are let go and weather helm used to straighten the ship into the line of wind or stream.

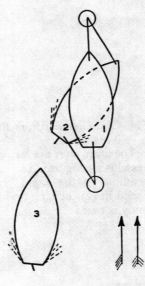

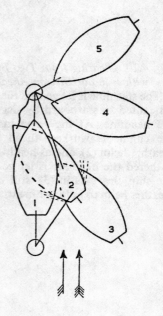

Fig. 4.12. Clearing from Two Buoys with Wind or Stream Astern, and Turning the Vessel

The headline is slacked down and the sternline eased. The ship cants to (2), and before the headbuoy is overrun, the engine is worked astern. As she clears the line of the buoys, the engine is stopped and the sternline let go. She is then allowed to drift to (4) and (5), swinging on the headbuoy. At (5) the engine can be worked ahead under port helm to ease the stress on the headbuoy.

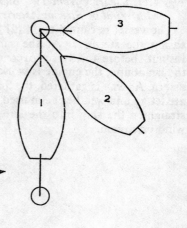

Fig. 4.13. Clearing from Buoys with Wind Abeam

The after lines are let go and the vessel is swung head to wind on the headline. If the engine is worked ahead in (2) the stress on the headbuoy is eased.

Fig. 4.14. Clearing from Buoys with Wind Abeam, to Head Down-wind

If desired, of course, the headline can be let go and the vessel swung downwind on the sternbuoy. In the figure, the sternline is let go and the vessel drifts to (2). Here the engine is worked astern under starboard or weather helm, and the headline is let go as way is gathered. The stern is rapidly bored upwind as in (3) and (4). This is a more satisfactory method if the fairway lies astern of the berth, because with the wind on the port quarter in some position (5) not shown, under ahead engine movement and port helm, the ship will swing very quickly to the fairway.

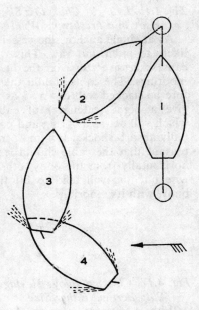

Fig. 4.15. Lying at Buoys with a Freshening Wind Abeam

The lines must be slacked down, however little room is available, so that the vessel lies at (2). In this attitude the lead of the lines enables them to more easily oppose the force of the wind.

If they are hove taut, as in (1), the two lines are working against each other to such an extent as may part them. They are expected to resist a force by acting at right angles to it.

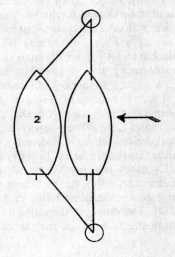

83

Fig. 4.16. Lying by Cable to a Single Buoy in a Freshening Wind

As at single anchor, the vessel is likely to pitch and yaw. This will cause excessive stress on the buoy moorings. The cable should therefore be slacked well down so as to give a bight (catenary) of cable which will act as a spring and partially absorb shocks. It is most important that the cable should lead horizontally from the buoy, otherwise pitching will tend to lift the buoy, with its moorings.

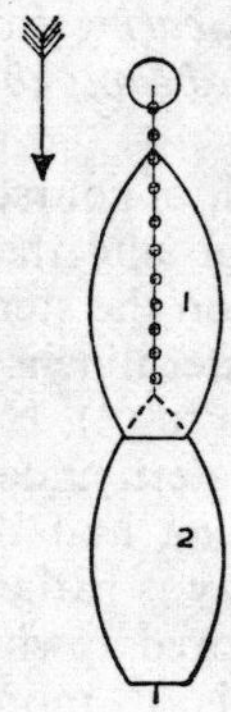

Fig. 4.17. Clearing Buoys Having a Ship Berthed Either Side

With a current running down from ahead, one of the outer ships, say (3B), slacks down her sternline until it sinks well to the bottom. A wire will do this easily, but in the case of a fibre line it may be advisable to let it go. (3B) then sheers away using port helm. The buoy now moves to a position midway between the sterns of (1B) and (2B). Ship (2C) now casts off the after line and also sheers away under port helm. Ship (1C) sheers away under starboard helm. Finally, ship (2C) eases her headline and, still under port helm, drops astern, letting go the headline when clear at (2D). The stronger the current, the more effective will be the sheers.

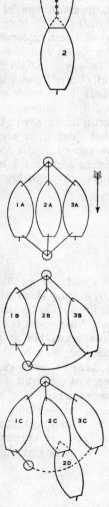

Before closing the work on buoys, we shall discuss the methods by which a ship may secure to them. When heading into the wind or stream, work is concentrated on securing the headbuoy, the sternlines being run in a more leisurely manner. Initially a wire is passed through the ring of the headbuoy and secured back on board; this bight is then used as a sliprope. A bight of fibre is similarly run to the buoy and the vessel can ride to this alone, with the sliprope slacked down.

When using bights of line it is the end which has been passed *down* through the ring of the buoy which is eventually let go from the ship. If the other end is cast off it may foul the buoy or its own part as it is unrove.

At the after end of the ship a bight of fibre will suffice unless it is expected that the final letting-go will occur from there, in which case a slipwire is also used. Sometimes fibre ropes have their eyes rove through the buoy-rings and secured to their own parts by means of heavy wooden toggles.

When clearing the buoys fibre ropes are slacked down and let go. When the ship is ready to leave, the slipwires are cast off.

If securing with the anchor cable, the anchor is hung off and the cable broken open. The end link is then shackled to the ring of the buoy. It can either be hove out to the buoy using a wire messenger rove through the ring, or else it can be slid down a single part of wire set up tightly between the ship and the ring and also passing through the enlarged link.

If desired the anchor can be secured in the pipe and the cable passed out through the forward Panama Canal leads.

Before heaving on any lines or cable, it should be ascertained that there are no boats lying across them, nor any men on the buoy.

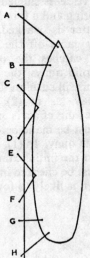

Fig. 4.18. Mooring Lines
    The following is the terminology used in the remainder of this chapter: 'A' Headline; 'B' Fore breastline; 'C' Fore backspring; 'D' Fore headspring; 'E' After backspring; 'F' After headspring; 'G' After breastline; 'H' Sternline. Beam winds produce five times as much stress as fore and aft winds. A 50-knot wind on a 250,000 tonner can cause stresses of 320 tonnes abeam and 60 tonnes fore and aft.

Fig. 4.19. Berthing in a Current

This method applies whichever side-to the ship is berthing. The current should always be stemmed, and there is then no danger of overrunning the berth. The ship is rounded-to under slow headway with perfect control. The stream will be setting the ship down during the approach and for this reason the ship can well be headed for the bow position when berthed. A broad angle of approach is permissible, but the quay should form a tangent to the turning circle. A broader angle of approach than in (1) will not fulfil this condition, and the ship will foul the quay.

Backsprings should be secured as soon as possible. The rudder will be effective even under conditions of no headway.

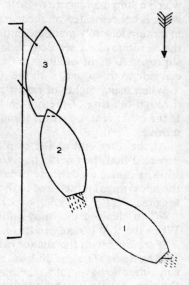

Fig. 4.20. Clearing a Berth with Stream Ahead

The vessel is singled up to an aft backspring and a fore breast. When the latter is slacked, the vessel quickly cants off the quay as the stream catches the inshore bow. With solid quays, the inshore flow of water will cushion the stern from the quay, as in (2). With open wharves, this effect is lost and headway must be made before the stern fouls the quay. In (1), helm is used to assist the initial cant. The breast line must be checked immediately if the stern is likely to foul the wharf.

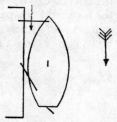

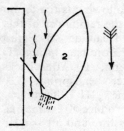

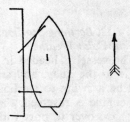

Fig. 4.21. *Clearing a Berth with Current Astern*

Again, the vessel is singled up as in (1), and offshore helm used to commence the cant in (2). The breast line can be let go quite soon, because even if the wharf is open and there is no cushioning forward, there is no likelihood of the stern fouling.

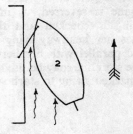

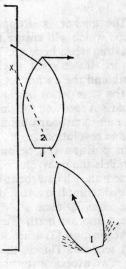

Fig. 4.22. *Berthing Port Side to in Calm Weather*

The vessel is headed in at an angle of about 1½ points with the quay, under slow headway and with steady head. As the engine is reversed, a swing to starboard develops and the vessel will arrive abreast of her berth with no way upon her and parallel to it. She will, however, be slowly swinging to starboard, and this must be checked with the headline.

Fig. 4.23. Berthing Starboard Side to in Calm Weather

The vessel is headed in at a fine angle to the quay, and since there will be a swing to starboard when the engine is reversed, the helm is put hard over to port with a burst ahead on the engine in (1). This starts a port swing, and when the engine is reversed, as in (2), the swing is checked and the vessel loses her headway lying close to, and parallel with her berth in (3). The sternline may be used to check a marked swing to starboard.

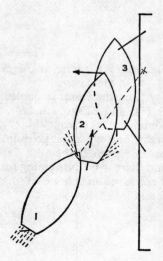

Fig. 4.24. Berthing Port Side to in Calms with the Offshore Anchor Away

The anchor is dropped with a scope which will ensure that it will not drag when hove on. The ship is headed in at right angles to the berth and the anchor let go abreast of the stem when berthed (1). The cable is surged and the ship rounded to under starboard helm and slow engine revolutions.

In position (2), before the ship parallels the quay, the engine is reversed and the starboard swing so caused completes the manœuvre. The ship is then slowly worked astern into her berth (3).

At position (2) a headline is run, and secured. This is then used to check an excessive starboard swing.

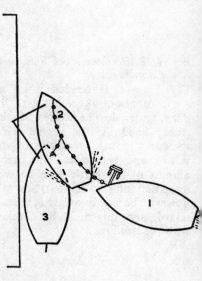

88

Fig. 4.25. Berthing Starboard Side to in Calms with the Offshore Anchor Away

Again the anchor is let go on sufficient scope, abreast of the stem when berthed. The ship is steamed round the anchor under full port helm, surging the cable as she does so. In position (2), when the ship has swung past the line parallel with the quay, the engine is reversed and the transverse thrust swings her parallel. A sternline is run at (2) and used to check an excessive starboard swing.

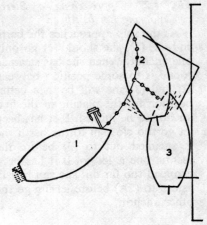

Fig. 4.26. Coming to Stern-moorings in Calms

In (1) the offshore anchor is let go on a slow run ahead. When about a third of the desired final length is veered the vessel is brought up to her cable, and as it grows taut aft, she is steamed round it under starboard helm on slow engine revolutions, letting go the port anchor as she does so, (2). While moving to (3), the port cable must be slack, otherwise it will impede the swing and may drag the anchor due to its, as yet, insufficient scope. In (3), when the ship's fore-and-aft line makes an angle of

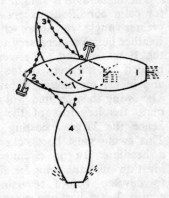

about 2 points with the line of berth, the cables are checked and the engine is reversed. The screw effect maintains the swing to starboard, but as she gathers sternway to (4), the cables grow on the port bow and will reduce any excessive starboard swing. The engine is stopped and the combined effect of the cables growing to port and the starboard swing brings the vessel into her line of berth with no side movement.

If berthing on the starboard hand instead of the port hand as shown, the vessel must be steamed around her port cable until she again adopts position (3), so that the screw effect will be used to straighten her up.

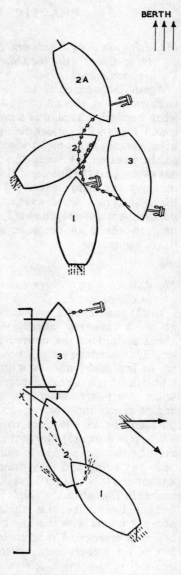

Fig. 4.27. Approaching a Stern-mooring Berth, Ahead

As the ship approaches the berth end-on, (1), she should let go only one anchor. When she has steamed round it to some position between (2) and (3) she will be in a better position for the placing of the first anchor to be judged. If it has been let go too close in to the berth she is steamed out to (3) before the second one is let go. If it has been dropped too far out she can be run astern to (2A) before letting go the other anchor.

Fig. 4.28. Berthing with Wind Offshore, on Beam or Bow

The manœuvre is similar to that for calm conditions except that a greater angle of approach (and weather helm) is necessary to hold the bows upwind. The vessel is headed for the stern of the berth, and in (2) the engine is reversed. The swing then created will accentuate the lee drift of the bows, hence the large accosting angle. This swing must be checked with a headline. In no circumstances must an offshore swing be allowed to develop before reversing the engine. When berthing on the starboard hand, the reversing of the engine keeps the bow upwind to some extent. With the wind on the bow (in the berthed position) the ship is headed into it on the approach, leeway is minimised, and there is a good braking effect. In both cases lines must be hove-in as soon as the ship parallels the berth. If an offshore anchor is required (as shown) it is better to let it go when the ship has drifted bodily off the quay with lines secure, rather than on the approach, when it may cause an offshore swing.

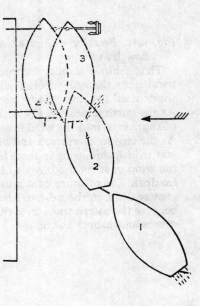

Fig. 4.29. Berthing with Wind On-shore and Abeam

The ship must be rounded-to, parallel, stopped, and clear of her berth in (3), and allowed to drift down to the quay using an offshore anchor if necessary to check the bow. The anchor will be necessary if too much headway exists, for a prolonged astern movement will tend to throw the stern upwind, particularly for a starboard hand berth when the transverse thrust will aggravate the swing.

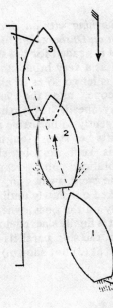

Fig. 4.30. Berthing Head to Wind

The ship is headed for the stem of the berth because of the braking effect available from the wind. In no circumstances must an onshore swing be allowed to develop in (1), because an astern movement will increase the tendency of the ship to run across the wind under reducing headway. The ship must maintain a slow offshore swing so that when the engine is reversed she is right in the wind's eye. A greater swing is allowed for a starboard-hand berth due to the astern transverse thrust producing an onshore swing.

91

Fig. 4.31. Berthing with an Onshore Bow Wind

The ship should approach parallel to the quay, being set towards it all the time due to leeway. As the berth is neared, (2), a slight offshore cant into the wind is given. As the engine is reversed and headway is lost, this swing is checked by the wind causing the bows to have lee drift. The offshore cant must be greater for a starboard-hand berth, because the astern transverse thrust causes an onshore swing.

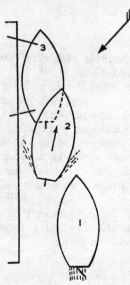

Fig. 4.32. Berthing with an Anchor Away in an Onshore Bow Wind

The vessel is headed for the stem of the berth at a very broad angle. The anchor is let go so as to allow sufficient scope, and the vessel moves slowly ahead. In (2), she is brought up gently to her cable and the wind drifts her stern alongside. The cable is kept taut by slow engine revolutions and weather helm. As the stern swings in, the chain is slacked out slowly until the bow is nearly on the quay, when it is checked. It is finally slacked down quickly when the ship parallels the berth. (Cable at (3) not shown.)

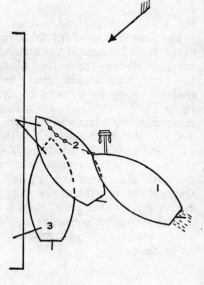

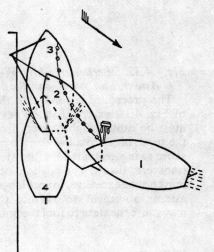

Fig. 4.33. Berthing with an Anchor Away in an Offshore Bow Wind

This time the ship is steamed round her anchor under full lee helm to (2), when a headline is run. The wind now blows the bow offshore, so the cable is slacked down and the vessel allowed to run ahead to (3). When she is parallel the engine is reversed and the offshore swing so produced is checked by the headline. The vessel then moves bodily into the quay as she tries to throw her stern upwind while under sternway from (2) to (3).

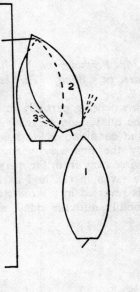

Fig. 4.34. Berthing with Wind Astern, Port-hand Berth

The leeway increases headway in this manœuvre, and the ship's behaviour under the necessary prolonged astern movement is unpredictable. The vessel is run dead before the wind (1), and canted slightly into the berth (2). The engine is reversed and the screw effect throws the stern back into the wind. As the vessel loses headway, she will parallel the berth in (3). The headline in (2) is used only to check an excessive offshore swing due to transverse thrust and the ship's tendency to seek the wind with her stern.

Fig. 4.35. Berthing with Wind Astern, Starboard-hand Berth

The procedure is similar to that of Fig. 4.34, except that the vessel must be canted slightly away from the berth in (2) to allow for the on-shore swing generated by the astern transverse thrust. The offshore cant must not be excessive, for prolonged astern movement to correct this may cause the stern to foul the quay.

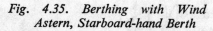

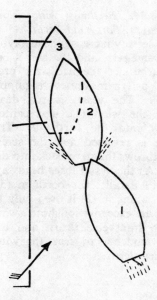

Fig. 4.36. Berthing in Offshore Quarterly Wind, Port-hand Berth

The bows, being partially in the lee of the quay, tend to swing inshore, the condition being aggravated by the quarterly wind. A slight swing away from the quay is therefore given in (1), and as the engine is reversed in (2) the stern moves bodily into the quay, and upwind.

94

Fig. 4.37. Berthing in Offshore Quarterly Wind, Starboard-hand Berth

Again, the approach is similar to Fig. 4.36, but a starboard swing must not be allowed to develop, because this will be aggravated by the astern transverse thrust. For this reason, a swing to port is generated at (1), which is corrected at (2) when the engine is reversed. A sternline is used to correct an excessive starboard swing.

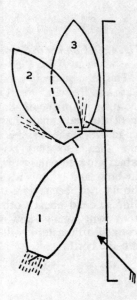

Fig. 4.38. Berthing in an Onshore Quarterly Wind

The vessel is headed into her berth with the wind aft, or on the offshore quarter. When the engine is reversed, the transverse thrust generates a starboard swing which, in the case of a port-hand berth, is aggravated by the starboard quarterly wind. This must be checked as the vessel loses headway in (2) by a headline. The angle of approach for a port-hand berth should therefore be as large as possible. For a starboard-hand berth the manœuvre is more simple, for the starboard swing due to the astern transverse thrust is counteracted by the lee drift of the stern. The angle of approach can therefore be finer.

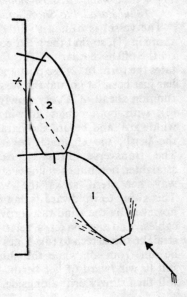

95

Fig. 4.39. Coming to Stern-moorings, with the Wind Onshore

The manœuvre is similar to Fig. 4.26, and the wind greatly facilitates the turning on the offshore anchor. In (2) the lee anchor has just been let go. In (3) the vessel is allowed to run ahead so that both anchor cables grow to windward, snubbing the bow rapidly upwind. The engine should not be reversed until the wind is dead ahead, otherwise the stern will swing upwind and a crooked run astern will be made into the berth.

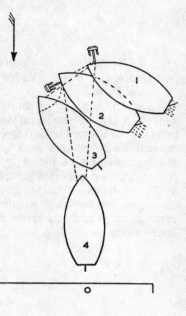

Fig. 4.40. Coming to Stern-moorings, Wind Parallel to Shore, and Aft

The vessel is canted slightly offshore in (1), so that the wind comes on the offshore quarter. This facilitates the turn. In (2) the port anchor has just been let go and the vessel is running ahead of it very slowly. In (3), with both cables growing to windward, and before she parallels the berth, the engine is reversed. The transverse thrust tends to straighten her, but then under sternway her stern seeks the wind. This swing to windward is damped, however, by the windward-growing cables, and she makes a relatively straight run astern to (4). Lines can be run from aft while the ship is still to windward of her berth. She will then slowly drift alongside.

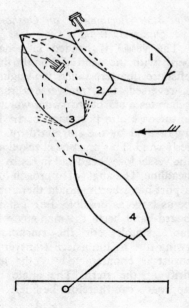

Fig. 4.41. Coming to Stern-moorings with Wind Parallel to Quay, and Ahead—Port-hand Berth

The vessel can be steamed round her anchors, (1), under bold helm and revolutions, and then run astern from (2) to (3), in which case she will arrive to windward of her berth, which is desirable. However, the manœuvre of turning is laborious and severely hampered by the fact that the bows drift to leeward of her cables, the latter then snubbing the bows upwind and resisting the desired turn. It is preferable, therefore, to swing the ship off the wind in (1), and then reverse the engine, which brings her rapidly to (2) as her stern seeks the wind. The anchors are then dropped on the run astern to (3). The swing of the bows to starboard is damped by the windward-growing cables.

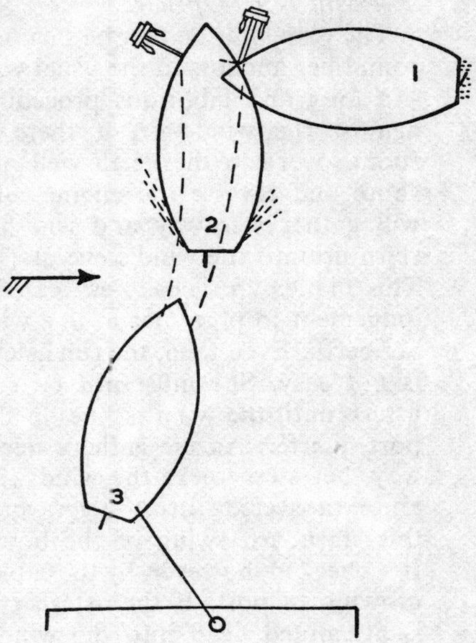

Fig. 4.42. Starboard-hand Berth

The manœuvre is performed as in Fig. 4.41, with the exception of position (2). Here, the stern is allowed to swing farther upwind before the run astern is made. (If this is not done the transverse thrust, which in this case partially resists a sternboard, may cause the ship to fail to reach the windward position (3).) In both figures the position (3) is identical.

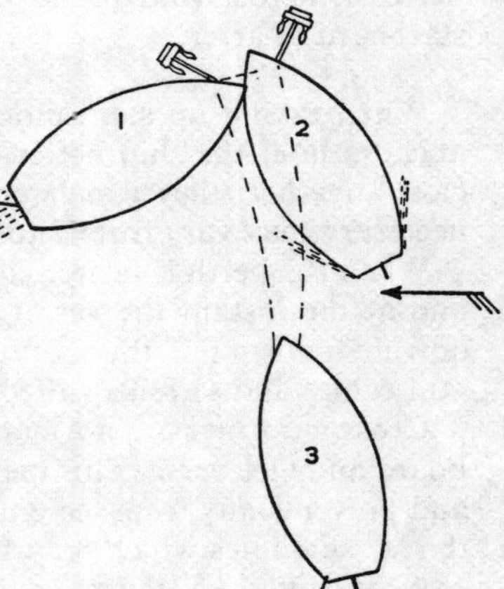

97

Fig. 4.43. Coming to Stern-moorings with Wind Offshore

The vessel must either be steamed round her anchors in the usual way —a long and laborious procedure against the wind—or, if there is room, over-run the berth well offshore and reverse the engine. She will gather sternway and run her stern up into the wind's eye at (1). This manœuvre needs very careful judgement to place her in line with her berth. Even then, the run astern is not easy. She must not be run astern until the wind is fine on the port quarter. As she gathers sternway, her stern seeks the wind, (2), and transverse thrust aggravates this starboard swing of the bows. It is checked, however, by the cables growing to port. If the astern run is attempted dead into the wind's eye she will run to leeward of her berth with the wind broad on the starboard quarter.

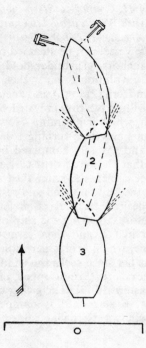

When taking up stern-moorings it should be remembered that two anchors hold the ship better than one alone. Provided they are let go close together, they can later be hove-in simultaneously. The lengths necessary may vary from 2 to 7 shackles.

When the berth is neared aft the sternway is checked with the cables, and at the instant the vessel loses way the cables are quickly slacked down 5 or 6 m. If this is not done the ship will surge ahead on her taut cables and seriously affect the running of the sternlines.

2 or 3 fathoms

Cross moorings are normally used aft, the port lines leading to starboard and vice versa. This method does hold the ship rigidly in position and prevents any transverse movements. In a beam wind however, it is the lee side lines which tend to take the stress.

As in Fig. 4.15, the moorings and cables must be slacked down as much as possible in a cross wind, so as to give them a more natural lead. In calm conditions the sternlines can always be tautened by heaving in a few links of cable.

When leaving, the sternlines are let go completely and not slacked out, as no useful purpose is served by so doing. The ship is then hove-out to her anchors. The engine is not used to check the momentum of the ship, since the bights of cable will do this quite effectively. The ship is then steamed around one anchor to face the fairway direction. In a wind the ship is allowed to swing head to it, the weather anchor being weighed last. When swung, the ship can conveniently be headed in any direction, for with the fairway abaft the beam, she will readily pay off to either side.

Fig. 4.44. Leaving Stern-moorings in a Very Strong Cross Wind

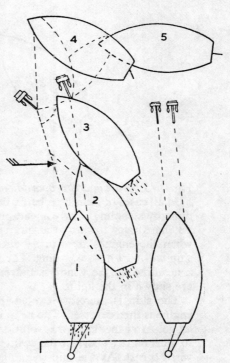

The sternlines are let go and the vessel steamed out to her anchors under bold engine movement and full weather helm. When the stern closely approaches the lee ship in (2) the helm is put amidships to momentarily check the swing. The ship is now under good headway, and when clear in (3), weather helm is again used. The ship may well overrun her anchors in (4), but the bights of cable will check this and snub her head to wind.

If the stern is not swung towards the lee obstruction and the ship heaves herself out to her anchors, or steams out to them with amidships helm, she will make rapid bodily leeway. As she drifts down on to the lee obstruction, her cables grow broad on the weather bow and drag the bow upwind. The stern is flung into the other ship and the application of lee helm increases the pull of the cables. The object at all times is to get upwind as quickly as possible.

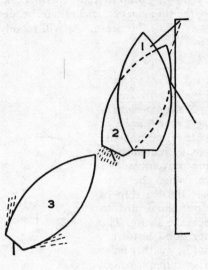

Fig. 4.45. Leaving a Starboard-hand Berth in Calms

In all cases of clearing a berth the stern must be canted clear. This is done by steaming slowly ahead on a fore headspring, while the helm is put hard over towards the quay. The spring must be absolutely tight when the engines are worked ahead, otherwise any momentum of the ship will part a slack spring. The spring may be made tight by putting a headline on the windlass barrel and heaving on it. These two lines are shown in the figure.

The ship is therefore canted in to the quay forward, (2), and the engine is then reversed. The helm is initially amidships and the lines are let go. After the first few revolutions astern the rudder is put hard over to starboard to correct the swing to starboard generated by the transverse thrust. As the slipstream flows in between the fore body and quay, the undesirable starboard swing is further damped, but as soon as she clears the quay the swing may tend to develop again, the transverse thrust overcoming the full rudder angle. In this case the engine must be stopped in order to have a straight run astern.

100

*Fig. 4.46. Leaving a Port-hand
      Berth in Calms*

Here, both the transverse thrust when reversing the engine in (2) and the cushioning slipstream between the forebody and quay cause the stern to swing rapidly back into the quay. The helm will be of no avail, because this will occur before sternway is gathered. However, the undesirable swing of the bow on to the quay in Fig. 4.45 does not exist here, and providing the manœuvre is correctly done, the clearing is, in many ways, more simple. The stern must be canted out to a very large angle as in (2) before the engine is reversed. By the time the stern has swung back parallel to the quay,

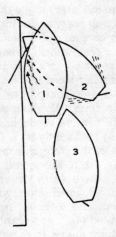

the ship will be under sternway and will be at (3). Starboard helm may then correct the swing of the stern inshore, but even so, a burst ahead on the engine with port helm will soon achieve this.

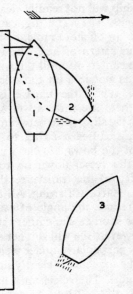

*Fig. 4.47. Clearing the Berth in an
      Offshore Wind*

This manœuvre is simple. The vessel can either be eased bodily off the quay on her fore and aft lines, or else as shown, her after lines are let go and she swings to (2). By reversing the engine and letting go, her stern will run back up into the wind to (3), when the swing is checked by a burst ahead on port helm. If desired, starboard helm can be used instead, continuing the swing under headway. This is useful for a fairway which lies astern of the berth.

Fig. 4.48. Leaving a Starboard-hand Berth in an Onshore Wind

The stern must be canted off the quay to a much larger angle than in calms. It is quite easy to do this even in a fresh breeze using full helm and bold engine revolutions. When the engine is reversed in (2) the ship rapidly runs her stern upwind and the bows swing sharply to starboard. The stem will damage the quay if the canting angle has not been initially sufficiently large. With a large angle, the stem will rapidly draw away from the quay. Full port helm is used when the engine is reversed. A small ship with a straight stem and a fender on her inshore bow will be able to cant herself off at right angles to the quay.

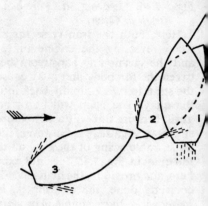

Fig. 4.49. Leaving a Port-hand Berth in an Onshore Wind

The ship will not readily clear her berth unless she has a tug, can run a line to an offshore mole, or has a clear run astern of her. The vessel must be canted off until the wind is as fine as possible on the offshore quarter. When the engine is reversed there are three adverse factors: (*a*) the slipstream between bow and quay causes a swing to starboard of the bows; (*b*) the wind is setting the vessel down on to the quay aft; (*c*) the transverse thrust creates a starboard swing. All these factors reduce the angle of cant at once. As soon as she gathers sternway, however, she will run her stern upwind, particularly under weather helm. The sequence is clearly shown

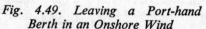

in the figure. The vessel must have good sternpower for this manœuvre and cant off to at least 45 degrees from the line of the berth.

Fig. 4.50. Leaving with an Onshore Quarterly Wind

For both port- and starboard-hand berths the ship must be sprung off to such an angle that the wind catches the inshore quarter, (2). This may be extremely difficult, for the stern tends to cling strongly to the quay in such a wind. A tug or a sternline to an offshore mole may have to be employed.

The wind on the inshore quarter then assists the canting-off of the stern. When the wind is in this relative position the engine can be worked astern, and the ship will

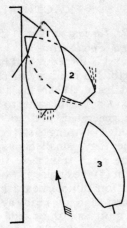

run easily clear of the quay into the wind's eye, (3). A slightly larger angle of cant must be made before reversing the engine for a port-hand berth, because the astern transverse thrust is adverse.

Fig. 4.51. Leaving a Berth with an Offshore Anchor Down, Offshore Wind

The sternlines are let go and the cable hove. The stem will tend to lead downwind more rapidly than the stern, and therefore the latter should be allowed to cant off before heaving cable, (2). A headline should be used to check the head, otherwise the bows may drift rapidly across the anchor and be snubbed sharply upwind. Alternatively, both fore and aft lines can be eased until the anchor is weighed; the lines are let go, and the engine is reversed to produce an offshore swing of the bows.

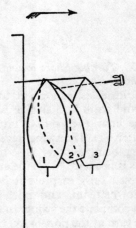

In calms the stern is canted off by slacking the cable a little and steaming ahead under full onshore helm

on a fore headspring. The lines are let go with the exception of a headline, and the cable is hove. The headline checks the bows and keeps the vessel parallel to the berth while heaving.

*Fig. 4.52. Turning a Vessel Short
Round, Single-screw*

The vessel is turned round in her
own length. No headway or sternway is gathered. When the engine
is reversed a powerful swing to starboard is generated, and so these
ships are always swung to starboard,
unless they have small high-speed
propellers, when transverse thrust
is small. In (1) the engine is worked
full ahead on full starboard helm.
At the first sign of headway the
helm is put amidships and the
engine reversed fully. The swing to
starboard continues, (2). The sequence is repeated in (3) and (4),
and so on, until the vessel is turned.
If the astern power is small the
watch for headway must be extremely diligent.

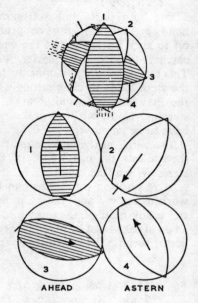

AHEAD   ASTERN

*Fig. 4.53. Turning Short Round in an
Ahead River-stream*

The vessel is run close to the
port-hand bank into slacker water,
and the bow given a cant into the
fast water, (1). The swing develops,
the stern being kept as close to the
bank as is prudent. In (3) the engine
is reversed fully to prevent bodily
drift downstream, and port helm
used to complete the swing. In making the turn at the port bank, transverse thrust is favourable throughout.

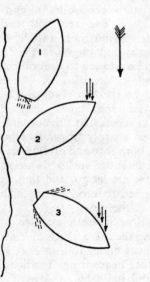

104

Fig. 4.54. Turning Short Round in an Astern River-stream

In (1) the bow is swung into the slacker water at the starboard bank and the engine is reversed. The helm is over to starboard for the cant inshore and is about to be placed amidships.

The reversed engine produces a favourable transverse thrust and also prevents excessive lee drift. In (2) the upstream anchor is let go and held at short stay. This rapidly snubs the bow round to (3), by which time the engine should be working ahead under starboard helm to complete the swing to (4). The anchor is held at short stay so that an excessive stress on the cable

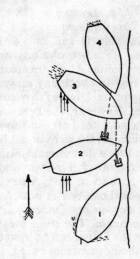

causes it to dredge rather than be strained. In (4) the cable appears to have been further veered, but this is only for the sake of clarity—actually the vessel swings very nearly in her own length at (3).

Fig. 4.55. Entering a Dock from a Stream Running Across the Entrance

The drawing needs little explanation. The ship is best secured to the lee pierhead, (1), while the upstream lines are run—these being labelled (1). Several inshore fenders are rigged overside and the vessel is hove ahead. The lines are moved without delay, as appropriate, to the positions labelled (2), and the ship is moved or *warped* into the entrance while pivoting on the lee knuckle. Engine ahead-revolutions and inshore helm assist the turn. The very long after backspring in

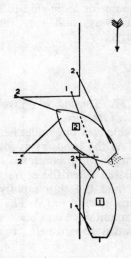

(2) takes a considerable stress while the stern is in fast water.

Had the entrance been made from the weather pier and a line parted, an impact might have been made on the lee knuckle.

Fig. 4.56. Leaving a Dock into a Cross Stream

The ship is run out with bold engine ahead-revolutions and upstream helm. At (2) upstream lines are used to check any downstream swing of the bows as they enter fast water. However, the headline soon has a poor lead aft, and too much checking on the stern breast line will aggravate a downstream swing. For this reason, full power and helm may have to be used. Alternatively, the vessel can be run out on the lee knuckle, using fenders to pivot downstream. The stern breast line, (3) in the figure, can be used to control the downstream swing.

In all cases of entering a dock direct, due allowance must be made for downstream set. A small ship can be run in under good headway, but there is not likely to be sufficient room for a big ship to gather this headway, and tugs may be necessary.

Fig. 4.57. Turning a Vessel with Wind Ahead

The ship is swung under headway to (2). As the headway is lost, the starboard swing continues. It is accentuated when the engine is reversed, and the ship rapidly runs her stern upwind to (3). The swing is then maintained on ahead-revolutions and starboard helm, to (4).

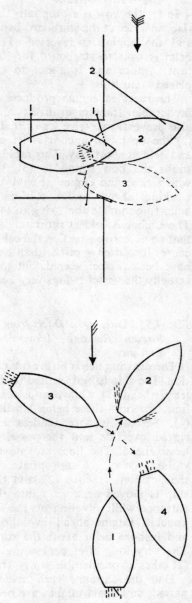

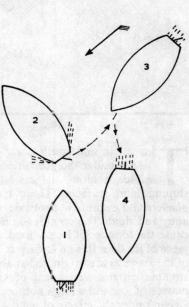

Fig. 4.58. *Turning in a Bow Wind*

The ship is swung off the wind to (2), and the swing is accentuated with a reversed engine and full weather helm to (3). If the sternway is continued sufficiently, when the engine is worked ahead under full port helm the ship will have made ground to windward at (4).

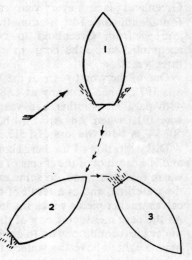

Fig. 4.59. *Turning in a Quarterly Wind*

A sternboard is executed into the wind to (2) and the swing is maintained to (3) under full power and starboard helm. If the wind is dead aft the ship must be turned under full power and helm through 16 points, maintaining good headway. In anchoring depths she can be turned on her anchor.

CHAPTER V

ICE

THE north and south polar ice caps are continually flowing outwards under the pressure of accumulated snows. The movement of ice is along the easiest routes, which are valleys and flat, sloping land surfaces. These moving masses of ice are known as *glaciers* and eventually protrude into the sea, where they acquire buoyancy and float. The combined effects of buoyancy, wind, and currents cause the tongues of ice to break away from the land, and every time a piece of ice does this an ice*berg* is *calved*. In the North Atlantic the bulk of the icebergs are originated at about twenty of the hundreds of glaciers situated on the west coast of Greenland. These bergs are irregular masses of ice, and a large number of them drift into the North Atlantic Ocean under the effects of wind and current. Every spring and summer they present a menace to shipping as far as, and occasionally south of, the 42nd parallel. It is estimated that about 7 500 bergs break away from Greenland glaciers every year, of which about 400 drift south of Newfoundland, some forty finding their way south of the 42nd parallel. This journey from Greenland to Newfoundland, roughly 2 880 km, is accomplished by the bergs in periods varying from a few months to three years.

1800 miles

One of the worst years in the North Atlantic from this point of view was 1972, when as many as 1 587 bergs found their way south of the 48th parallel. Another bad year, closely approaching these statistics, was 1912 when, on April 14th, the *Titanic* foundered in 41° 46′ N, 50° 14′ W with the loss of 1 517 lives.

Disintegration of the bergs commences immediately they are calved, and is a product of the effects of swell, heavy seas, wind, solar radiation, warm sea-water, and, to some extent, rain. Heavy erosion is caused at the waterline, and as a result of this and general deterioration, the berg calves smaller pieces which fall into the water with a loud roaring noise. As the berg melts, cracking of the ice occurs, and this is clearly audible under ideal conditions up to a mile away. In trade routes the bergs may have heights above the water of up to 80 m and lengths of 500 m.

270 ft 1700 ft

In the Antarctic temperatures are generally lower. Here, in addition to the formation of glacier ice and irregular bergs, the ice cap flows into

108

the sea and forms a vast barrier of floating ice around the continent, many hundreds of metres thick. A good example of this is the Ross Barrier. In the spring and summer the inequalities of air and sea temperature produce uneven rates of expansion, and vast pieces of the barrier break adrift and move northward. These bergs are known as *tabular* icebergs, and resemble floating islands with vertical sides and a level surface. These ice islands are usually about 50 m high, measured 180 ft from the waterline, and may be up to 110 km in length. Some are 70 miles reported as being up to 500 m in height. These bergs from the South 1 700 ft Polar cap drift up to the 55th parallel, but some have been reported as far north as 33° s in the Longitude of 50° w. Others have been seen along the 35th parallel in the vicinity of the Great Australian Bight and the Cape of Good Hope.

All icebergs have the bulk of their volume submerged. Usually about one-ninth only is visible, but this depends entirely upon the amount of rock, earth, or air which is trapped within the ice, and also upon the amount of loose snow lying upon the berg. Generally, the volume which is emerged lies between one-tenth and one-third. An iceberg south of the Grand Banks of Newfoundland may survive as a danger to navigation for up to a fortnight, but after June this decreases to about ten days. The bergs which are grounded upon the Banks seem to survive for long periods, possibly up to one month.

Off Newfoundland, the frequency of sea-fog, the density of fishing vessels, and the continuous flow of traffic add other dangers to the existing perils of ice. In 1898 the North Atlantic Track Agreement was devised, which laid down routes to be followed by east- and west-bound traffic, each route having a separate season. These seasons were varied from year to year depending upon the conditions. Many shipowners took part in this agreement, and naturally it left Masters and Officers more free to concentrate upon the hazards of ice. Collisions became less frequent, but ice tragedies continued, culminating in the loss of the *Titanic*. The following year (1913), an International Ice Patrol was set up to keep a vigilant watch on the most dangerous ice areas. Today the patrol is maintained by surface and air craft, and is managed by the United States Coastguard, while the cost is shared between the various maritime Governments.

During the ice season, the Patrol broadcasts in bulletins at 0000 and 1200 G.M.T. every day, commencing some time in March. After receiving the first bulletin, Masters are asked to transmit full weather reports every six hours while they are situated between the 40th and 50th parallels and the 42nd and 60th meridians of west longitude. This serves a dual purpose, for it assists the Ice Patrol and enables the latter to keep a close track on ships in the vicinity. The Ice Patrol may report vessels which are observed not to heed ice warnings.

Before sailing, Masters are advised to obtain all possible information regarding ice located in the vicinity of their intended course. On the voyage they should exercise the utmost vigilance in darkness or poor visibility, and make sure that every ice bulletin is received and brought to their notice immediately. The following are some of the many terms used in connection with ice navigation:

Beset: a vessel which is hemmed in and surrounded by ice. The ship cannot be controlled, but is not necessarily under pressure from the ice.

Boring: the operation of forcing a way through ice under the ship's motive power.

Calving: the breaking away of ice from a berg, glacier, or barrier.

Concentration of ice over the sea is measured in eighths of the sea surface. When one-eighth is ice covered the water is said to be open. *Close ice* refers to a coverage of six to eight-eighths, while a coverage of eight-eighths with no water visible is referred to as *consolidated ice.*

Crack: a small break in an ice field, which is unnavigable.

Fast ice: ice which is attached to the ground.

Field ice: a large area of sea ice driven closely together. It may have a vast surface area and is greatly influenced by wind and currents. It is mainly confined to the Arctic and coastal areas, and cannot survive for long far from the shore. It is of very shallow draught, but may be extremely hard, particularly if grey or green-coloured. Field ice is deceptively soft in appearance and is easily penetrated on the lee edge, which is ragged, while the weather edge is closely packed and well defined. Within a field, small pieces may prove to be dangerously large, thick, and heavy.

Floe: applies as a general term to all fragments of ice.

50 ft   *Floeberg:* a piece of thick ice having a hillocked or hummocked effect rather like a berg. It may exceed 15 m in height above sea-level.

Growler: a small floe calved from a berg. Often green in colour.

10 ft   *Heavy ice:* ice which is more than 3 m in thickness.

Hummock: a mound or hillock which is produced in ice under the pressure of surrounding ice.

16° F   *Ice crust:* is new, transparent ice which achieves no hardness or strength until it is cooled below about −9°C. It is almost pliable due to the entrapped layers of salt.

Lead: a long, narrow, navigable channel within an ice field.

1½ ft   *Lilypad ice:* small, round cakes of ice up to about 0·5 m in diameter.

Nipped: a ship which is beset and under pressure of ice.

ICE

Pack ice: otherwise called *sea ice* or field ice. When the pack has no lanes or leads visible it is referred to as close pack. When open, with many lanes visible, it may be called *loose, sailing,* or *drift ice,* and can sometimes be navigated at full speed.

Pancake ice: newly-formed pieces, circular in shape, and up to 2 m   6 ft in diameter. The rims are often raised.

Rafted ice: an effect achieved in close pack-ice when one cake of ice overrides another, under pressure.

Rotten ice: ice which is honeycombed due to thawing.

Screwing pack: is pack ice under constant rotation due to wind effects. The motion of the ice is dangerous to a ship's plating.

Shore ice: ice which has been cast ashore.

Slewing: the act of forcing a ship through close pack by working the engines ahead and the rudder from side to side. The floes are forced apart.

Slob: is dense, sludge ice.

Sludge: or *brash,* consists of small, soft ice and slush, and is usually the wreckage of pack ice.

Slush: ice crystals on the water's surface. It possesses no hardness, and is the first stage of surface freezing. The water appears oily and opaque.

Young ice: newly formed ice with no traces of hummocking. It is up to 20 cm thick.   8 in

Working: boring or slewing through the ice.

NAVIGATION IN ICE

(a) Preparation of the Vessel

When the vessel is expected to pass through pack ice, which in the North Pacific may be very prolific, the crew should equip themselves with clothing suitable for such a voyage. The deck machinery, and if possible the rigging too, should be covered with canvas. The heating systems throughout the vessel must be checked, pumping gear overhauled, and all drainage checked. Quantities of de-icing compound may be put aboard and the decks and superstructures coated with it just before encountering freezing temperatures and heavy weather. The compound may be applied by paint-brush or spray gun. Pickaxes and *ice mattocks* should be provided. A mattock resembles a pickaxe, but has only one spike, the end of which if flattened out into a 10–12-cm   4–5-in blade. The instrument is used similarly to a carpenter's adze, with the legs well apart, and employing a short chopping motion.

It is advisable to make sure that the ship is well equipped with damage control gear and leak-stopping equipment, including cement, sand, steel plates, shoring, collision mats, and patent rivet-stoppers. A quantity of

111

softwood wedges may prove to be of value. In freezing temperatures deck steam engines should be drained and the weather-deck fire main isolated and drained. Winter-grade oils should be used where recommended. Petrol engines, if water-cooled, should be drained or equipped with anti-freeze, and batteries cared for according to the maker's instructions. Some thought should be given to a suitable jury rudder for the particular vessel, and the necessary gear obtained.

This summary of precautions is by no means complete, but is intended to cover salient points.

(b) The Indications of Ice

One of the most reliable indications of the presence of field ice and of an extremely large berg, such as a tabular type, is *ice blink*. This is a whitish glare in the sky, on the horizon in the direction of the ice, and may extend to 15 degrees altitude. It is due to the intense reflection of light from the ice surface, and according to many experienced Arctic navigators is most marked in a clear, fine atmosphere when the sky is uniformly covered with cloud. The sea appears black beside the ice, and reflections from the sea produce a *water sky*. This effect is most marked within an ice blink, particularly when the ship is beset, and appears as black streaks or patches within the blink. It is useful in that it indicates open water and leads. If the ice blink is yellowish it may indicate an ice-covered land mass. If the ice is not snow-covered the same yellow haze may be encountered despite the absence of land. The ice blink is most brilliant after a fresh fall of snow upon the ice field.

Ice blink is often seen, fortunately, at night as well as by day, particularly if there is moonlight. The horizontal length, and to some extent the height, of the blink give a good indication of the field area. By day, under cloudless conditions, there may be no ice blink, but refraction may produce a mirage of the ice.

Other signs include an abrupt smoothing of the sea and swell, which may indicate ice to windward. Birds and seals sighted far from land may be in the vicinity of a pack. A sudden wall of fog may be experienced on the edge of an ice field and also large expanses of sea smoke, when the sea appears to be steaming. The sounds of disintegration and calving of growlers has already been discussed, this also being a warning.

Radar should detect a large berg in sufficient time but ice-echoes are one-sixtieth as efficient as ship echoes. Small ice and bergs may be lost in the *sea clutter*. The use of the whistle to return an echo from ice is unreliable, because the contours of the ice may prevent such an echo; further, a fog bank is likely to return a false echo.

Any sudden changes in sea or air temperature should not be relied upon as an indication that ice is near.

112

If growlers are sighted, several in a group, it may indicate that a berg is to windward, from which they have been calved. Since a growler may be sufficiently big to cause serious damage, a berg sighted at night or in poor visibility should be passed to *windward*.

All these warning signs are only supplementary to a good lookout, and this should be maintained in suspected waters from both forward and aloft, the men being provided with binoculars. In clear weather a berg may be sighted 20 miles away, depending upon the observer's height above sea-level, while in light mist or drizzle the distance is reduced to 1–3 miles. In a low haze the tops of large bergs may be detected at distances up to 10 miles. In fog the berg will appear as a white, luminous mass. On a clear night without moonlight it is unlikely that a sharp lookout will detect a berg at distances beyond about 500 metres, yds unless the bearing is known, and the sea may then be observed breaking against it, viewed through binoculars, at a range of up to a mile.

(c) Entering the Pack

The ice will have a deceptively quiet appearance, but is to be highly respected at all times. If the far boundaries of the field are visible it is better to detour the pack and avoid it altogether. If the far boundaries are not visible the hazards within the pack are unknown and the ship may be beset and nipped. In both cases, then, we arrive at the wisest conclusion of all, which is to avoid pack ice at all costs.

If entry is inevitable it should be made at right angles to the *lee edge*, where the ice is broken and loose. The vessel is entered very slowly, and speed is gradually increased to a safe level, endeavouring never to lose way, for then the floes will close in on the propeller and rudder. Lookouts should be posted high up to watch for leads, the latter possibly closing very soon after being sighted. The conning should be done from the bridge so that a better appreciation of the ice size is possible.

At all times, the stern must be cared for, bearing in mind that a rudder movement to avoid a floe will swing the stern towards it. Men should be posted aft, equipped with torches, whistles, or a telephone, so that the bridge can be informed immediately the propeller is endangered, particularly in the case of twin-screws.

It is unwise to enter hummocky or rafted ice where pressure exists and the vessel is likely to be nipped. The hummocks generally lie in a direction at right angles to the line of motion of the floes, and parallel to cracks and leads.

The navigation of pack ice requires patience, constant vigilance, preferably experience, and extremely good judgement. The ship will probably handle sluggishly at the low speeds, and a turn may require a burst ahead on the engines, using full helm. The shorter and beamier the ship, the better she will turn. Engine movements from ahead to astern, and vice versa, should be made carefully to avoid stressing the shafting in low temperatures, which are detrimental to steel and iron.

When the current is in the same direction as the wind the ice tends to open, but in the reverse conditions a close pack is formed. In such a pack the floes will have to be forced apart by slewing, and a thick fender should be rigged over the stem. When cleaving the ice the rudder will have little effect, and the ship will follow the crack.

Sharp alterations of course should be avoided, and the speed should be kept to steerage way in close pack, while up to 8 knots can be used in scattered pack ice. It is frequently necessary to work the engine astern in pack ice and gather sternway. When this is done the rudder should be kept amidships to afford some protection to a single screw. Twin-screws are very vulnerable when moving astern in ice, and the action of sternway should be accompanied by bursts ahead on the propeller(s) whenever ice approaches the screw(s). The resulting wash will tend to clear a channel in which to continue backing.

At night it is preferable to heave-to, since the lanes cannot be seen. The vessel should be stopped alongside the lee edge of the ice, where she will drift with the pack. If she is stopped along the weather edge the plating is likely to be seriously damaged by grinding between the hull and the ice. When hove-to at night a watch must be kept for large floes and bergs which may work through the field towards the ship. Such a watch should be aided by the use of powerful lights. During the night sea-water-lubricated tail-end shafts are in danger of freezing up, and in the case of single-screw vessels the after peak tank should be filled with water, kept warm by means of a steam-hose injection. In addition to this, the cast stern tube becomes excessively brittle at low temperatures. In twin-screw ships the stern tubes should be similarly kept warm. Modern practice is inclined to oil-lubricated tail-end shafts and provided the correct grade of oil is used, the danger of freezing up is small.

A twin-screw ship should preferably navigate field ice in the wake of an ice-breaker. When employing such a vessel it is desirable that the following ship should not have a beam greater than the breaker, because the leads created will be quite narrow. Following an ice-breaker may entail sharp turns on the edge of floes, and fenders should be liberally used.

When navigating in sludge the condenser inlets may become choked with ice particles, and a case is on record where a ship was able to combat this by connecting the fire main to the main sea injections. The fire main was kept supplied with warm water by coupling it to the condenser discharge, the water cooling sufficiently for the condenser to function. Hot water should be used to flush water closets in order to prevent soil pipes from freezing up. Any winches or deck machinery likely to be required for use should be kept slowly running if supplied by steam, once temperatures approach freezing point.

Sometimes, a vessel may navigate between the pack ice and the coast. In this case an offshore wind is desirable, and a grave danger exists if the wind changes to an onshore blow, for the ship will be beset and stranded.

(d) When Beset

The vessel will be out of control, and vessels with straight sides are especially vulnerable. A ship beset in early winter is in grave danger from a build-up of pressure within the pack, and from bergs working through the field. Frequent damage to the rudder and propeller(s) is likely when beset. Initially, action should be taken as for a nipped vessel.

(e) When Nipped

There is likely to be considerable damage to the hull, rudder, and propeller(s). The action usually taken, when nipped forward, is to order full speed and use full, swinging rudder. The action may be accompanied by bursts of full ahead and full astern in the case of a ship strengthened for ice navigation. If this fails, attempts should be made to trim and/or list the vessel, so that she frees herself. A ship beset and suffering increasing pressure from the pack may have her entire hull bottom nipped off, leaving her lying on the ice. When the ice parts in the spring, or before if winds and currents are suitable, the ship founders. If at any time a man descends to the ice and walks over it he should carry a boathook held horizontally across his chest so that if he falls between floes or through a crack in a floe, he has some means of support.

(f) Navigating Near Bergs

These are passed leaving them to leeward to avoid possible growlers. Due to erosion and melting at sea-level, it may appear that they are small, and close navigation is possible. Tongues or ledges of ice are likely to project outwards from them below water for distances *in excess of ten metres*, and they must therefore be given a wide berth.   35 ft

(g) Positioning the Ship

An artificial horizon may be used for sights when surrounded by pack ice. A bucket of oil is suitable. If a back-angle is possible, this should be used, i.e. the part of the horizon on a reciprocal bearing from the body is utilised if clear of ice. Every single course must be plotted on the chart and a thorough dead-reckoning check maintained throughout the passage.

(h) Towing in Ice

It has been found that a very short towline is desirable, but in the case of large vessels with high forecastles this entails a difficult lead. A bridle is generally preferable to a single towline. Towing is only possible through pancake ice or open pack, a concentration of up to five- or six-tenths being the maximum permissible for this manœuvre. If the towing vessel has to stop, a strong wash astern from the propeller(s) (i.e. engine(s) worked full ahead briefly) will prevent the tow from overriding.

(j) Anchoring and Mooring

A vessel should never be anchored near a glacier coast due to the risk from calving bergs. If forced to anchor in ice the chain should be kept at short stay. There is a great danger of such a vessel dragging, particularly if the pack bears on her weather side. If anchoring near fast ice the vessel should be ready to leave immediately the wind blows onshore, for with ice already cast ashore, it follows that more may approach from windward. The windlass engine, if steam-driven, should be kept running slowly while at anchor. In bays with drifting ice the shallowest, safe depths should be chosen for an anchorage, for then large bergs or floes will probably ground before striking the ship.

When hove-to at night it is not normally necessary to secure to the ice. It is better to stop near small floes rather than big ones, because the former, under pressure, will hummock and raft and relieve the ship of stress. If it is essential to secure, the vessel should lay alongside a floe having a concave bight in it with two projections, rather like an artificial dock. The hull is then clear of ice, except at the projections (where fenders can be used), which will protect the ship to some extent from drifting floes. Such a floe is sometimes called an *ice dock*. The vessel is secured either with a special ice anchor dropped on to the ice or else by cutting a shallow, flat-bottomed hole in the ice as far from the ship as possible and setting a baulk of timber in it called a *deadman*. Water is then poured into the hole to freeze the deadman into the ice. A heavy strop is attached to the timber. The mooring line may then be passed ashore to the deadman, where the eye of the line is secured to the strop by means of a wooden toggle.

(k) Ice Accretion

The addition of top-weight ice adversely affects the stability of the vessel and causes damage to gear, and injury to the crew, particularly in the case of ice falling from rigging and the masts, aerials, etc. Sea-water spray will freeze on to a cold superstructure when the air temperature is 20°F 30°F below $-6°C$ and the water temperature is below $-1°C$, the freezing

116

point of sea-water being $-2°C$. In a wind of twelve knots and above, 28½°F
under such conditions, the ice may build up on decks and structures
at a rate sometimes in excess of 5 cm per hour, particularly in a head- 2 in
wind.

Glazed frost is likely to occur on the vessel when rain falls on to the
freezing structures, and the build-up of this ice may be very rapid. Fresh-
water ice, such as this, is very brittle and easily broken away, unlike
salt-water ice. The formation of glazed frost on the decks will prevent
people from keeping on their feet, and salt should be sprinkled on it.

The danger of a list arises when spray is shipped on only one side of
the vessel. It is most important to clear the ice as quickly as possible,
and in this connection, all snow should be swept up and jettisoned at
once before it packs tight. If washed away with salt water by means of a
hose the air and sea temperatures should be checked beforehand, otherwise the water may freeze. The use of a de-icing compound will minimise the accretion of ice and facilitate its removal thereafter. The ice
should be chopped away with picks, shovels, and mattocks as quickly
as the men can work. The use of a steam hose to melt the ice may be
attempted, but it may be found that the steam is sublimating into hoar
frost, further aggravating matters. Sublimation refers to the transition
of a gas into a solid without passing through a liquid stage.

The loss of some vessels, particularly fishing craft, has been attributed
to a rapid build-up of ice and later capsizing. Sub-freezing temperatures
and ice accretion must be reported to all ships and local Authorities
immediately.

Ice accretion on wheelhouse windows can be minimized by the use
of electrically heated glass in conjunction with fresh-water sprays and
electric wipers. Some vessels have steam pipes fitted around exterior
metal doors so that the *dogs* do not freeze up, preventing them from
being opened.

The International Ice Patrol, previously mentioned, is paid for by
contributions from Belgium, Canada, the USA, the USSR, Spain,
Japan, Denmark, France, Italy, Holland, Norway, Sweden, and the
United Kingdom. Every year on 14 April, the Patrol drops a wreath at
the site of the sinking of the TITANIC.

CHAPTER VI

LIFE-SAVING AND DISTRESS

T HE importance of instantly recognising all distress signals and being fully conversant with their use, together with the procedure for rendering assistance, cannot be too strongly emphasised. For this reason a whole chapter is devoted to this section. The reader should thoroughly familiarise himself with the text, contents of current Notices to Mariners published by the Admiralty, and the excellent Merchant Shipping Notices published by the Department of Trade in the U.K. (D.o.T.). These publications are obtainable free by Masters from Mercantile Marine offices and Custom Houses.

Most maritime countries provide a life-saving service for persons in distress in their coastal areas. One of the biggest factors in providing assistance is the radio watch required to be maintained by vessels of 500 k/cs tons gross and upwards. The watch is kept on a frequency of 500 kHz k/cs if radio-telegraphy (W/T) is fitted, and on 2182 kHz with radio-telephony (R/T). The watch is to be maintained at all times except when the operator is performing other necessary duties, during which times he should endeavour to keep a loudspeaker watch. Silent periods are laid down from 15 to 18 and 45 to 48 minutes past each hour of G.M.T., k/cs during which the frequency of 500 kHz must not be used except for distress, urgency, or safety signals. In the case of R/T the silent periods k/cs for 2182 kHz are from 00 to 03 and 30 to 33 minutes past each hour of G.M.T. During all these silent periods even vessels which do not come under the Merchant Shipping (Radio) Rules requirements are asked to maintain a watch.

When an operator hears a distress call he must answer it, at the same time allowing a sufficient interval for ships to acknowledge it which are closer to the distressed vessel. He must then inform his Master of the call, whether other ships acknowledged it, and the positions of those ships. The Master may then instruct him to repeat the call on the distress frequency, particularly if his own ship is unable to render assistance or if other ships have not acknowledged the initial call. All relevant particulars must be entered into the Radio Logbook.

Many British ships have portable W/T equipment for use in lifeboats. k/cs These units are able to transmit on 500 and 8364 kHz and to receive on

118

LIFE-SAVING AND DISTRESS

500 kHz. They are also able to automatically transmit on 500 kHz, the k/cs k/cs
auto-alarm signal (12 dashes having one second intervals, all made
within a minute), followed by SOS sent three times, together with a
subsequent long dash, so that listeners can take a radio bearing of the
transmitter. On 8364 kHz the same signal is automatically keyed with k/cs
the exception of the auto-alarm signal. A manual key is also provided.

Private distress signals sent to a specific address are unwise, since in
the absence of a general distress call the public services are unable to
render assistance or to relay the call publicly. If the sender permits of
Lloyd's being informed, then and only then, the Coastguard will be
notified, who will alert rescue services where necessary.

VESSELS MISSING OR OVERDUE

By contacting Lloyd's Intelligence Department the latter will send
out a general message to shipping on the owner's behalf, via a Coast
Radio Station. Lloyd's will also alert appropriate Coastguard stations.

For fishing vessels, however, the Coastguards may be informed direct,
or preferably through the local Inspector of Fisheries (or similar officer),
who commence a search and rescue service on their own initiative.

PUBLIC DISTRESS SERVICES IN THE UNITED KINGDOM

In addition to vessels in the vicinity of the distress call, assistance may
be rendered by any of the following:

Coast Radio Stations (controlled by the British Post Office), who
keep watch on 500 and 2182 kHz and VHF Channel 16. A call is relayed k/cs
on all frequencies to ships at sea and also to shore Authorities by
other suitable communication. These stations are mostly able to take
radio bearings of the call on 500 kHz—some can also do it on 2182 k/cs
kHz. They keep H.M. Coastguard informed throughout. k/cs

The Royal National Lifeboat Institution is maintained by charity.
Each of the 132 off-shore boats has R/T operating on 2182 kHz. All k/cs
are fitted with VHF radio for communicating with service aircraft and
coastguards.

Her Majesty's Coastguard is a life-saving organisation which keeps a
radio watch on 2182 kHz and VHF Channel 16. Together with the
Coast Guard Auxiliary Service they also keep visual watch.

The Royal Navy provides search vessels, aircraft, and helicopters.

The Royal Air Force provides a similar service to the Royal Navy.
They are primarily responsible for service and civil aircraft casualties,
although they extend their service to all persons when able to do so.

Air traffic control centres, which assist in gathering and relaying
search data.

Lloyd's are notified of casualties by Coast Radio Stations, and are then responsible for informing ocean-going tugs.

Officers of the Fishery Departments, who contact the Coastguard when fishing vessels are overdue.

DUTIES OF MASTER

A Master, or person in charge of a vessel, must assist every person at sea in danger of being lost, even if that person is from an enemy State. He must do this so long as there is no serious danger to his own ship, passengers, or crew. As soon as he receives the distress call, he must proceed as quickly as possible to the distress area and indicate his intentions to the distressed person or persons. He may be exempted from going if:

(1) he is unable to do so; or
(2) he considers it unreasonable; or
(3) he considers it unnecessary; or
(4) he is released from the above statutory obligations.

The Master of a vessel in distress may *requisition* a ship which has answered his call. That ship must then proceed to him with all speed. Masters are released from their obligations to render assistance as soon as they hear of other ships being requisitioned (provided the latter are complying), or when they are officially informed that assistance is no longer necessary.

If the Master fails to abide by these statutory requirements he is guilty of a misdemeanour. If he does not render assistance, the Master of a British ship registered in the United Kingdom must enter his reasons in the Official Logbook. Every distress message received must be entered in this Logbook.

VESSELS IN DISTRESS

Signals to be used are:

(1) A gun or other explosive signal fired at intervals of about a minute.
(2) A continuous sounding with any fog signalling apparatus. (The D.T.I. suggests that this is unwise, and recommend that SOS should be made continuously on the apparatus.)
(3) Rockets or shells throwing red stars, fired one at a time at short intervals.
(4) SOS made in the Morse code on the W/T apparatus, or by any other signalling method.

(5) The spoken word 'Mayday' transmitted by R/T.

(6) The International Code flag signal 'NC'.

(7) A signal comprising a square flag having above it or below it a ball, or anything resembling a ball. (This is called the *distant signal*.)

(8) Flames on the vessel such as a burning tar barrel. (The D.T.I. advises that this may easily be confused with a flare-up light, which signal is often made with a paraffin-soaked rag. They therefore recommend that rockets or red flares are much more efficient.)

(9) A rocket producing a red flare on a parachute, or a red hand flare.

(10) The auto-alarm signal in W/T or R/T.

(11) An orange smoke-signal.

(12) A vertical motion of a person's extended arms.

Distress Rockets and Flares

Ships of Classes 1 and 7 are required to carry twelve rockets, each ejecting a red flare on a parachute. Vessels of certain other classes may instead carry red hand-flares, each throwing five red stars to 45 m 150 ft altitude.

Line-throwing and distress rockets, red flares and smoke signals should be renewed three years after manufacture. The condemned ones may be jettisoned in deep water well away from coasts to guard against the possibility of their being washed ashore.

Use of Distress Signals

No distress signal is to be used for any other purpose. The use of signals which are likely to be confused with distress signals is prohibited. Distress signals are to be used only upon the Master's orders, and then only if (*a*) his ship is in serious and imminent danger, or (*b*) another ship or aircraft is in similar danger and cannot itself use a signal, or (*c*) if assistance is required additional to that already available.

The signal must be revoked if assistance is no longer required. Failure to do this may cause unnecessary waste of time and anxiety to other persons.

Procedure for Transmitting Distress or Urgency Signals

Frequencies used are 500 kHz (W/T) and 2182 kHz (R/T). Any other k/cs k/cs frequency may be used, however, provided assistance will be summoned more quickly on that frequency. The W/T alarm signal is automatically keyed and sends twelve dashes in one minute. This operates the auto-alarms of other ships. It indicates to ships and coast radio stations that

121

a distress call is about to be transmitted. It is immediately followed by SOS sent three times to operate certain other auto-alarms. Then follows the W/T distress call after a period of 2 minutes which allows operators to stand by. The call consists of SOS sent three times, followed by the word 'DE', followed by the ship's call sign sent three times. Then follows the message, which consists of the ship's name, position, nature of distress, and assistance required. Included in this, for a vessel drifting, would be the estimated rate and direction of drift. Lastly, there should be sent two 10-second dashes to enable radio bearings to be taken. Other signals, visual and sound, should be used also, in darkness and poor visibility.

The R/T alarm signal consists of two tones transmitted alternately and automatically over a period of 30 seconds. After 2 minutes the R/T distress call should be sent consisting of the distress signal 'Mayday' spoken three times, followed by the words 'This is', followed by the ship's name spoken three times. The distress message is then sent as for W/T.

The W/T Urgency Signal

XXX in the Morse code, repeated three times, and the spoken word 'PAN' uttered three times on R/T, are used to indicate an urgent message regarding the safety of the ship or a person on board, or within sight. It does not necessarily indicate imminent danger or the need for immediate assistance.

This signal has priority over all signals other than distress signals. It is only used as a general signal (to no specific address), when a Master uses it to warn ships and stations that he may shortly have to use the distress signal. In such cases the signal must be revoked if precautionary action on the part of other persons becomes unnecessary.

ASSISTANCE AVAILABLE FROM AIRCRAFT

Aircraft can assist by dropping markers, smoke or flame floats, and survival equipment, consisting of a nine-person rubber dinghy and two bags of supplies. They can carry out an air search, locate a casualty, keep it under observation, and guide surface craft to it. Flying-boats may be able to alight and pick up survivors. Helicopters may also pick up survivors.

Use of Search and Rescue Helicopters

These can rescue 3 to 18 survivors depending on the type of machine. Some carry Decca Navigator equipment. They do not normally 270 miles operate more than 450 km from base, or in darkness, poor visibility or in winds above 45 knots. The ship approached by the helicopter should:

(a) Use an orange smoke signal to indicate herself, or alternatively
(b) use a daylight signalling lamp to give a steady light.
(c) Preferably head with the wind 30 degrees on the port bow. The helicopter will approach from leeward. The chosen area of deck should be marked with a white 'H'.
(d) Tow a man to be rescued, astern, in a boat on a long painter, if the ship cannot head into the wind.
(e) Never secure the winch wire or allow it to become fouled.
(f) If on fire, have the wind about 2 points on the bow.
(g) Indicate surface wind direction with flags, etc.
(h) Do not touch the winchwire until it is earthed.
(i) Clear all loose gear from the transfer area.

The helicopter will recover a man in the water by:

(1) Lowering a strop to him on the winchwire (if he is able to help himself), or
(2) lower a crew member from the helicopter to the man if he is helpless.

Helicopters are equipped with VHF/UHF/RT and signals are relayed to them via Coast Radio Stations, H.M. Coastguard, and thence finally to the R.A.F. All lifeboats belonging to the R.N.L.I. and an increasing number of Merchant vessels are also equipped with this type of radio.

AIRCRAFT

Radio is not carried by all civil aircraft. An aircraft distress call will normally be transmitted by radio on the frequency in use at the time between the aircraft and the appropriate Air Traffic Control Centre. If unable to make contact, the aircraft may use any other frequency to alert any D/F station. In addition, if possible, the call will be made on 500 kHz.

Distress Signals
(1) By W/T on 500 kHz 'SOS' sent three times, followed by 'DE', then the call sign sent three times, the position, nature of distress and type of assistance required.
(2) By R/T, the word 'MAYDAY' spoken three times, followed by the call sign sent three times and then the information as in (1) above.

(3) Visually, a red pyrotechnic light or lights, a red parachute flare, or the group 'SOS' on signalling apparatus.

Merchant ships will normally be informed of aircraft casualties at sea by Coast Radio Stations, broadcast on 500 kHz or 2182 kHz. Ships may instead become aware of the casualty by

(a) Picking up or intercepting calls made by the aircraft on 500 or 2182 kHz or
(b) by hearing and finding the direction of the 500 kHz transmission made from a survival craft or
(c) by picking up messages from Search and Rescue (SAR) aircraft.

An aircraft which has located a casualty, or ship or aircraft in distress, may notify ships in the area by passing a message in plain language on a signalling lamp prefixed by the group XXX. It may also to attract a ship's attention,

(a) Fire a succession of white pyrotechnic lights, and/or
(b) repeatedly switch the landing lights on and off, and/or
(c) repeatedly and irregularly flash its navigation lights.

If the aircraft wishes to guide the ship to the casualty or distress area, it may fly low around the ship, or cross ahead of her at low altitude, opening and closing the throttle or changing the propeller pitch. (To cancel any instructions, the aircraft may carry out this procedure astern of the ship.) The aircraft will then fly off in the direction in which the ship is to be led. British pilots will rock their wings when flying off towards the casualty. The ship should acknowledge all these messages by sending a series of 'T's in the Morse code. The ship will either follow the aircraft or indicate by visual means or radio that she cannot comply.

Search and Rescue aircraft, when searching for survivors, will fire green pyrotechnics. These will obviously be answered by distress flares (or other visual signals) from the survival craft.

Safety Signals

Aircraft may transmit messages concerning the safety of navigation as follows:

(a) By W/T, the call is prefixed by the group 'TTT' sent three times in the Morse code, followed by 'DE' sent once and then the call sign transmitted three times.
(b) By R/T, the call being prefixed by the word 'SAYCURITAY' spoken three times, followed by the call sign.
(c) By signalling lamp.

LIFE-SAVING AND DISTRESS

General Information on Aircraft

Navigation markers, or low flying, do not in themselves indicate distress signals. Aircraft survivors in rubber dinghies will indicate their predicament by using red-star pyrotechnics, heliographs, flashing SOS on a lamp or torch, using bright-green surface dye, or flying a yellow kite supporting the radio aerial.

Aircraft often sink rapidly a few minutes after ditching at sea, and rescue ships should make all speed to the area. Ships' Masters should discuss the best procedure as to rescue while on their way to the area. If the ship receives the distress signal direct from the aircraft she should take a radio bearing of it and send this, her position, and her intended action by radio to the nearest Coast Radio Station.

All rescued survivors should be questioned as follows, so that full information as to other possible survivors may be obtained:

(1) 'Did you bale out or ditch? What was the date and time?'
(2) 'At what altitude did you bale out?'
(3) 'How many others baled out?'
(4) 'How many persons were in the aircraft when she ditched?'
(5) 'How many people were present after ditching?'
(6) 'How many did you see in the water?'
(7) 'What buoyancy gear had they?'
(8) 'How many persons were originally in the aircraft?'
(9) 'What caused the casualty?'

If an aircraft is forced to ditch the Captain of the aircraft will be greatly assisted in locating a ship if she:

(1) Assists with homing bearings, or transmits a continuous signal so that the aircraft may use its radio direction finder, or
(2) makes black smoke by day, or
(3) directs a searchlight vertically upwards by night.
(4) Provides a lee; this is best done by steaming in a circle and spreading vegetable oil.
   (The aircraft will usually ditch—a dangerous and difficult operation—on the starboard side of a ship, since the Captain usually sits on the port side of the plane and has a better view from that side. He will ditch head to wind, but if seas are high he will probably land in the trough.)
(5) Illuminates the sea without dazzle.
(6) Streams six flares or battery-lights, in line astern, 180 m apart.   600 ft
(7) Informs the pilot of surface weather conditions.
(8) Has a boat ready for launching, boarding nets rigged, and some heaving lines ready.

125

SUBMARINES

A sunken submarine will try to indicate her plight and position by:

(1) Releasing an indicator buoy.
(2) By firing yellow, white or red smoke candles or pyrotechnics.
(3) By pumping oil to the surface.
(4) By blowing out air.

The Indicator Buoy

27 in 18½ in
6 in 3000 ft
of ½-in

1¾ miles

k/cs

Many submarines, particularly British ones, are fitted with two buoys, one at each end, which can be released from within the vessel. They are cylindrical, aluminium, 68 cm in diameter, 47 cm deep, and have a freeboard of 15 cm. A stirrup attached to the sides carries up to 915 m of 4-mm galvanised steel wire rope. A light on the top-centre flashes white, twice a second, for 40 hours and is visible in good visibility and darkness up to 3 km with the naked eye. A ring of cats-eye reflectors is mounted around the light. A whip aerial is fitted. Both buoys are painted with high-visibility orange paint. On each is painted a serial number and 'Finder inform Navy, Coastguard or Police. Do not secure to or touch.' It is painted in white on the forward buoy, and black on the after buoy. An automatic radio, operating on 4340 kHz transmits:

Serial Number (three figures) . . .	sent 3 times in 30 seconds
SOS	sent 6 times in 30 seconds
SUBSUNK	sent 3 times in 30 seconds
Long dash	lasting 30 seconds

The message is immediately repeated, the two occupying 4 minutes, followed by a 6-minute silence. An operator on a ship should report this signal at once, indicating signal strength, ship's position, and the bearing of the signal.

When finding the buoy the ship should report at once, and if possible give the submarine's name.

600 ft
If the depth of water exceeds 180 m the buoy will probably be adrift, but the report must still be made. The buoy may have broken adrift from a submarine which has *not* sunk. It should be weighed by hand to ascertain whether it is adrift, but a boat must not be secured to the buoy or wire.

¼ mile
A vessel finding a moored buoy must stand by, well clear and preferably down tide, with engines stopped and a boat lowered ready to pick up escaping survivors. To warn the crew of a sunken submarine that help is at hand, Naval vessels will drop small explosive charges at least half a kilometre away. Merchant vessels should run their echo-sounding machines, or hammer on the ship's plates below the waterline.

The submarine may then release a pyrotechnic float to indicate her position and to acknowledge these audio signals.

A new plastic indicator buoy has red and white vertical stripes. The white flashing light is visible for 9 000 metres (5 miles). The light, the automatic radio and a UHF beacon function for 180 hours. The attached 3 mm wire is 1830 metres long (6000 ft).

LIGHT-VESSELS AND LIGHTHOUSES

These are equipped with R/T for the purpose of transmitting distress calls concerning their crews or other persons in distress near by. They also make the following visual distress signals

(1) rocket(s) throwing red stars accompanied by a detonating signal, a sound rocket, or the firing of a gun; or
(2) the International Code group 'NC' by means of flags; or
(3) the distant signal, i.e. a square flag having either above or below it a ball, or anything resembling a ball; or
(4) a detonating signal, which by night, upon being fired reveals a small, yellow/white flash accompanied by a report. On reaching its ultimate height of about 100 m, a larger similar flash occurs 300 ft together with a loud, cracking report. By day, the effects are similar except that puffs of white smoke are visible both on being fired and at the zenith of trajectory, the latter volume of smoke being much larger and lingering for some considerable time.

The shore Authorities will reply to these signals,

By day, with an orange smoke signal or three 'Thunderlights' fired at minute intervals or, By night, with three white stars, fired at minute intervals.

These two signals will also be used by lighthouse and light-vessel crews to indicate to persons in distress near by that their plight has been observed.

Danger Signals

Light-vessels, and some lighthouses, may display, or make, any of the following signals:

The International Code flag group 'NF', the single Code flag 'U', or the flashing of the letter 'U' in Morse code on the signalling lamp, or the sounding of the letter 'U' in Morse code on the fog-horn. All these are used to indicate to a vessel 'You are standing into danger'. Attention may be drawn to the flag signals by means of a detonating signal, or the firing of a gun.

LIFE-SAVING AND DISTRESS

The International Code flag group 'PS1', which means 'You should not pass too close to me'.

Communication with Ships by the Crews of Light-vessels and Certain Lighthouses

This may be effected by hoisting the necessary Code flag groups, or by making the ship's call sign in Morse on the signalling lamp, or by flashing the letter 'K' in the Morse code. A light-vessel may also use a white flare, or make 'K' in the Morse code on the foghorn in fog. These signals are not distress signals.

USE OF ROCKET LINE-THROWING APPLIANCES AND LANDING SIGNALS

In the United Kingdom, shore life-saving stations will reply to a vessel's distress signal as follows:

By day, with an orange smoke signal or three 'Thunderlights' fired at minute intervals or, By night, with three white stars, fired at minute intervals.

These signals indicate that the vessel has been seen and that assistance will be given as soon as possible.

In the United Kingdom the following signals are used when small boats are landing survivors of wrecked vessels:

To mean 'THIS IS THE BEST PLACE TO LAND': by day, a vertical motion of a white flag or the arms, and by night the vertical motion of a white light. A second white light may indicate a direction. Alternatively, a green star rocket or 'K' in Morse.

To mean 'LANDING HERE IS HIGHLY DANGEROUS': by day, the horizontal motion of a white flag, or the arms extended horizontally. By night, the horizontal motion of a white light. Alternatively the letter 'S' may be used in Morse.

To mean 'LANDING HERE IS HIGHLY DANGEROUS. A MORE FAVOURABLE PLACE LIES IN THE DIRECTION INDICATED': by day, a white flag is moved horizontally and is then fixed in the ground. A second white flag is then carried in a certain direction. By night a similar procedure is carried out with white lights. Alternatively, a white star rocket in a certain direction or 'S' in Morse followed by 'L' or 'R' to mean alter course left or right.

Her Majesty's Coastguard Rocket Life-saving Apparatus

Signalling should be established by semaphore or lamp, but where this is not possible the following are used:

To mean '*Affirmative*', i.e. 'Rocket line is held'; 'Tail block is fast'; 'Hawser is fast'; 'Man is in buoy'; or 'Heave away':

A green star signal or, the vertical motion of a white flag or the arms or a white light (at night).

To mean '*Negative*', i.e. 'Slack away'; 'Avast hauling'; or 'Rocket line is not held', etc.:

A red star signal or, the horizontal motion of a white flag or white light (at night) or the arms extended horizontally.

When possible, the Coastguard will fire a rocket across the ship with a line attached, such as an 8-mm hemp line. If the crew of the ship fire a rocket ashore first, the Coastguard will get hold of this rocket-line and then attach a stronger line to it. When they signal affirmative, the crew should heave on their rocket line in order to get this stronger line aboard.   1-in

As soon as either the stronger line or the shore rocket-line is held, signal affirmative and then wait for a similar signal from ashore. As soon as it is seen, heave in on the line, and a tailed block with an endless fall rove through it will be hove on board. This is called the *whip* and may be 12-mm manila rope. Make the tailed block fast to the mast, or   1½-in other convenient position, where plenty of deck space is available. Leave space above the whip for the hawser or jackstay and unbend the rocket-line (or the stronger line) from the whip. Signal affirmative to those ashore.

As soon as this is seen, the men ashore will attach a hawser to the whip (24-mm manila), and will heave it out to the ship. Provided there   3-in are no obstructions between the ship and shore, the end of the hawser will have been passed round the whip and a bowline made with it. The bight of the whip will then have been clove-hitched to the hawser. When the hawser is aboard, cast off the bowline, bring the end of the hawser up between both parts of the whip, and make it fast to the same part of the ship as the tailed block, but just above it. (This will enable the outhaul of the whip to heave the breeches buoy as far out as possible.) The tally-board is made fast close by the hawser and tail block. Now unbend the whip from the hawser, see that the former runs clear and signal affirmative.

The men ashore will then set tight the hawser and haul off the breeches buoy to the ship, by means of the hawser, travelling-block, and the whip. The outhaul of the whip is called the *weather whip*, the inhaul being known as the *lee whip*.

The person in the buoy should sit well down and grasp the steadying line. When he is secure signal affirmative, and the Coastguard will haul him ashore and then return the buoy for the next person. Make a mark on the tally-board for each person landed. If conditions prevent the setting up of the hawser the buoy will be used on the whip alone. Women, children, and helpless persons must be landed first. The coolness of the crew and their strict attention to instructions will directly affect the success of the operation. The buoy is shown in Fig. 6.1.

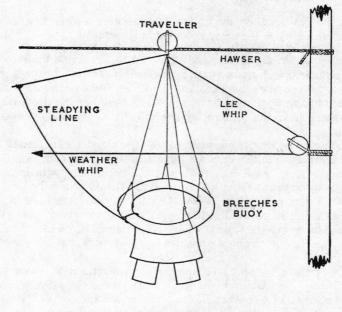

FIGURE 6.1

Use of Rockets for Tankers or Vessels with Flammable Spirit

It may be extremely dangerous to fire a rocket across such a vessel, due to the liability of flammable vapours being present. The rescue vessel should lie to windward of the tanker and fire a rocket only when it has been ascertained that it is safe to do so. When such a risk of ignition exists, the distressed tanker should hoist code flag 'B' at the masthead, use a red light in the same position by night, and supplement these signals in poor visibility by sounding the International Code group 'GU' on the fog-signalling apparatus, which means 'It is not safe to fire a rocket'.

The code group 'GT1' may be used by the rescue vessel since it means 'watch out for my rocket'.

When firing a rocket across the wind it is advisable to aim slightly downwind before igniting the rocket. The wind will then act on the bight of rocket line and deflect the rocket up into the wind. If a direct aim is used this deflection into the wind will probably cause the rocket to miss the target (Fig. 6.2).

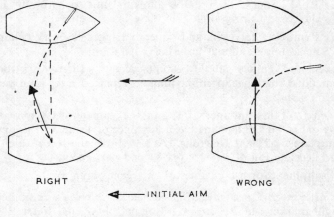

RIGHT   WRONG

 ◄——— INITIAL AIM

FIGURE 6.2

The Schermuly 'Speedline' International Rocket Apparatus

The Merchant Shipping (Life-saving appliances) Rules require that, among others, ships of Classes 1 and 7 shall carry a line-throwing appliance. These are passenger and non-passenger vessels engaged in long international voyages, and are generally the type of vessel considered in this book. The required range of the appliance is 230 m.   250 yds The Speedline gear is a completely self-contained unit with two important advantages over the older pistol type of apparatus:

(1) The set of four units normally carried by ships can be dispersed at strategic positions through the vessel.
(2) Each unit can be fired independently as required.

The unit consists of a plastic body/launcher incorporating the handle/ trigger assembly, and containing the rocket, igniter and 275 m of ready-   900 ft flaked line. The unit is weatherproof, being sealed at both ends by transparent, polythene caps. This enables the date of manufacture of the rocket and the igniter to be checked without removal. Full pictorial instructions are printed on both sides of the plastic body and can be read by either right or left-handed users.

Plate 1 shows the Speedline unit in relation to the size of an adult hand and also the unit being fired towards a life-raft. Notice that the optional buoyant head is being used in this example. Plate 2 shows the buoyant head about to be fitted.

The unit has been designed for maximum ease of operation as follows:

(1) Remove the front end cap and attach the free end of line to a strong-point.

(2) Hold handle horizontally, allowing unit to naturally assume the correct firing angle (see Plate 1).

(3) Remove safety pin and squeeze trigger lever. When rocket fires, hold container until line is paid out.

Rockets and igniters should be replaced every three years and it is recommended that the Speedline unit be replaced after nine years in service on a ship.

13 in 7·5 in
10 lbs
The length of the container is 330 mm, the diameter is 190 mm and the total weight is 4·6 kg. The line has a diameter of 4 mm and a minimum breaking stress of 2000 Newtons. (A Newton is the force which gives 1 kg an acceleration of 1 metre per second per second.)

Other equipment for use in times of emergency comprise:

The Pains Wessex Schermuly 'Manoverboard' which is a combined day and night marker, safe to use on oil or petrol-covered water. It is designed to be attached to lifebuoys by means of a lanyard, and when released it indicates its position by dense orange smoke and two water-activated lights at 3·5 candela. It can also be connected to a bulkhead-mounted lifebuoy and released manually. It produces orange smoke for 15 minutes and the two lights burn for 45 minutes (Plate 2).

The Pains Wessex Schermuly 'Buoysmoke' is similar to the *Manoverboard* signal but without the electric lights. It would be used where it is desired to install separate light and smoke signals. The mounting brackets fit both signals (Plate 2).

The Pains Wessex Schermuly 'Pinpoint' is a hand-held red distress flare for use in lifeboats or life-rafts. It burns for 60 seconds at 15,000 candela,
9 oz 10 in
weighs 260 grams and is 245 mm long. The flare is encased in a steel tube and is fitted with an integral twist-and-strike firing mechanism in the handle, which is simply rotated until two arrows align. The end of the handle is then struck a sharp blow with the palm or on a hard surface. The flare is held up, outboard and pointing downwind.

The Pains Wessex Schermuly 'Para Red' is a hand-held distress rocket which conforms to the requirements for both ship and lifeboat/raft
980 ft
rockets. It ejects a parachute-suspended red flare at a height of 300 metres when fired vertically and which burns for 40 seconds at 40,000
164 ft
candela. It burns out at 50 metres above sea level. Both end caps are

removed together with the safety pin. The signal is then held firmly, the trigger lever is squeezed and the signal is pointed slightly downwind. In low cloud conditions, the rocket should be fired at 45 degrees elevation to give maximum visibility.

The Pains Wessex Schermuly 'Lifesmoke' is safe to use on petrol or oil-covered water. It has a metal case and releases dense orange smoke for 3 minutes with a simple cord-pull ignition.

THE INFLATABLE RUBBER LIFE-RAFT (Plates 3 and 4)

On abandoning ship into this type of craft, the following actions should be taken but not necessarily in this order:

(1) Rescue survivors in water and take aboard if possible.
(2) Inflate the floor in cold weather and top up buoyancy chambers.
(3) Take charge of all sharp objects, especially belts with sharp buckles. Examine footwear for similar hazards.
(4) Bail dry and carry out repairs to chambers. Plug leaks.
(5) Connect up to other rafts which may otherwise drift away.
(6) Search for missing persons.
(7) Issue anti-seasickness pills.
(8) Distribute crews evenly and bunch together for warmth.
(9) Rig emergency transmitter if aboard.
(10) Give first aid and make casualties comfortable.
(11) Watch for frostbite and hypothermia.
(12) Collect useful flotsam.
(13) Identify bodies and cast adrift, having removed useful objects.
(14) Take charge of weapons, potential or otherwise.
(15) Post lookouts.
(16) Rig lights and close weather canopy.
(17) Take charge of pyrotechnics.
(18) Rig the sea anchors. Start collecting rainwater.
(19) Issue food and water on second day. Sick and injured may need water earlier.
(20) In a closed raft, people wearing wet clothing will soon find that the air becomes saturated and no further cooling of their bodies occurs. A heat balance is achieved. An experiment with seven men in a life-raft showed heat balance occurring after 15 minutes. In fact the temperature then began to rise and at no time, although in very cold conditions, did shivering take place.

These rafts are manufactured from rubberised, abrasion-resistant, cotton fabric, of high-visibility flame or orange colour. They are of three-ply material on the hull, two-ply being used for the self-erecting canopies, which are attached to the automatically-inflated arches or columns. The raft is inflated by carbon dioxide gas contained in a cylinder, or cylinders, attached to the underside of the hull. Inflation is commenced by a pull on the operating cord, which is thereafter used as a painter.

The raft has two main buoyancy chambers, independent of each other, and each capable of supporting the full load of equipment and persons in case of a puncture, so that if necessary the raft can be 100% over-loaded. An area of 0·37 m² is provided for each person that the raft is certified to carry.

4 ft²

The tent formed by the canopies, being of double thickness, provides insulation against extreme temperatures, protection from the weather, but is capable of being opened at each entrance to admit fresh air. At the initial inflation the canopy entrances are open to facilitate boarding. The floor is double-skinned, and inflatable by means of hand bellows. This not only provides extra buoyancy but also insulation from cold sea. In the tropics, by keeping it deflated, the interior of the raft may be kept cool. At each entrance a ladder or step is provided for boarding purposes.

In an emergency it is essential to make sure that the operating cord is well secured to a strong-point, and this should also be regularly checked while at sea. The raft, complete in its container, is then thrown over-board, the cord pulled out to its full length, whereupon a *further* sharp pull actuates the inflation process. The length of cord is 25 m, but shorter or longer cords are permitted, to suit the size of ship. Under no circumstances should cords be withdrawn and shortened by ships' personnel. The raft, after about 30 seconds, is sufficiently inflated for survivors to board it, either from the water or directly from the ship. It is quite safe to jump on to the canopy, provided it is not done from too great a height, which may cause injury to occupants. A raft which has inflated in the inverted position, may be righted by standing on the gas cylinder and heaving on the righting-line or straps.

80 ft

The raft may be manœuvred towards swimmers or other rafts by using the paddles, or else by repeatedly heaving the drogue in the required direction and pulling on it. Casting the drogue is easier if it is weighted, say with a shoe.

As soon as the occupants board the raft the person in charge should examine everybody's footwear to make sure that the soles and heels contain nothing which would damage the life-raft material.

After rescue, the raft should be recovered or else destroyed. If this is not done, the empty life-raft will attract rescuers and cause great trouble and anxiety.

Stowage

The rafts must be stowed so that not only can they be speedily launched but will also float clear if the ship founders before launching is possible. They must be fully protected from paint contamination, rats, heavy seas, salt-water accumulation, funnel-exhaust smoke and sparks, and icing conditions. Passengers and children should be warned of the danger which may arise if the rafts are tampered with. Life-rafts packed in canvas valises may be stored on perforated platforms, gratings, in suitably drained drop-side boxes, or in collapsible deck seats. These boxes should be sufficiently small to prevent chafe and preferably padded on their internal surfaces. The raft is stowed with the lifting handles freely accessible.

If desired, the valise may be stored on deck under a canvas cover and lightly lashed to the deck, but so that the lashing can be cast off by a single hand-movement. The entire success of the rafts is dependent upon their being released and jettisoned quickly. Some vessels incorporate ramps inclined at least 20 degrees to the deck, at the bulwark or rails, so that the rafts, which are stowed up to three in number on each ramp, can be rolled overside during conditions of adverse list up to 15 degrees. The ramps are fitted with rollers, and the rafts are secured by webbing belts. In some cases each of the three rafts is capable of being released separately. Again, the belts are released with one hand-movement.

The cylindrical glass-fibre container for a single raft is in halves bolted together, each bolt incorporating a shear-pin assembly so that the container bursts open on inflation. Other types use special joints of calculated bursting strengths. A steel carrier can be supplied, bolted to the deck, to which the container is secured by means of a webbing belt and Senhouse slip, with or without a hydrostatic release. With this type of container no further protection is necessary.

The raft should never be stowed vertically, for the gas cylinder will work its way to the bottom of the container and chafe the fabric. The operating cord must be kept secured to the ship, for then, if the vessel founders before the raft can be launched, the buoyancy of the container will pull the cord, actuate the inflation mechanism and, when inflated, the buoyancy of the raft will snap the cord. The cord is designed to snap under a stress of 900 kg, and even some eight-man rafts will have sufficient reserve buoyancy to achieve this. The raft can then float free of the ship. It is imperative that the lashings are cut or cast off (if no hydrostatic release is fitted) before the vessel founders. If this is not done the raft will probably sink with the ship, and still attached to it. 2000 lb

Inflatable rafts must be serviced by appointed agents about once a year. The crew should leave them strictly alone except for checking the lashings, the protection afforded, and the anchorage of the operating

135

cord. At boat drills the method of operation should be clearly explained to every member of the crew.

In the plates a raft is illustrated having a central column. This has the advantages of erecting a canopy having a lesser wind surface than the arch-type raft, providing a back support for persons sitting in the centre of the floor, a foot-brace for others, a virtual pneumatic jack if the raft is inverted, and a smaller stowage volume. This type of raft has an inflated entrance step. A type designed to accommodate twenty-five persons weighs 180 kg in a glass-fibre container or 163 kg in a canvas valise.

399 lb   365 lb

THE R.F.D. TYPE 20 MC, SINGLE-POINT SUSPENSION, INFLATABLE LIFE-RAFT FOR FULLY LADEN LAUNCHING

This raft has been introduced for use in passenger ships, especially those having a high freeboard. Criticism had been levelled at inflatable life-rafts in the past because survivors were required to descend ladders, or to leap from heights, before boarding. The 20 MC raft obviates these efforts, and it is therefore suitable for passengers of all ages and in all states of health.

The raft is inflated at deck level, and by the use of a single-arm davit, is lowered fully laden, by gravity, to the water. Here, it is released automatically. Boarding is facilitated by a flexible apron which serves the dual purpose of bowsing the raft firmly to the ship's side and providing a gangway. The suspension provides the means of recovering the raft, complete with survivors, by hoisting it aboard the rescue ship.

The design of the raft follows standard principles, but it incorporates a special design feature of a built-in, single-point suspension sling. The suspension is designed in the form of web straps, a number of which are secured to the outside of the buoyancy chamber and the remainder to the upper floor surface. The straps cross at the apex of the single column, at which point a single hoisting shackle is fitted. The normal method of launching is not precluded, for if necessary the raft can be jettisoned in its valise and inflated by pulling on the operating cord. The packed raft should be stowed near the davit gear in lockers, seats, or on ramps.

12 ft 6 ft
308 lb

This twenty-person raft has a diameter of 3·7 m, a height of 2m, and a weight, in a canvas valise, of 140 kg.

THE R.F.D. LIFE-RAFT RELEASE GEAR

This is shown in Fig. 6.3, and it will be seen that it consists basically of two side plates, a hook, and a locking lever. Since the gear is for use in unfavourable conditions, the operation has been kept as simple as

136

possible. The D.T.I. required a release which was instantaneous when the full weight of the raft was waterborne, but not so as to jeopardise the safety of the raft and its occupants in the early stages of boarding, should a wave reach the boarding station and take the weight of the raft.

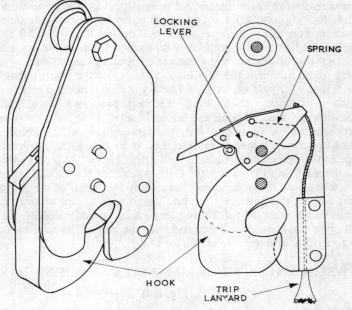

R.F.D AUTOMATIC RELEASE HOOK
SAFE WORKING LOAD 2270 KG

FIGURE 6.3

It was therefore necessary to have the release absolutely safe until boarding was completed and lowering commenced. This necessitated a safety-pin, or the equivalent, which would not be overlooked in an emergency. The release is noticeable in Plate 4.

Method of Operation

(1) The release gear is removed from its stowage adjacent to the davit pedestal, by pulling the lanyard which opens the hook.

(2) With the life-raft at the deck edge, the hook is closed on the suspension shackle protruding from the top of the valise. The action of closing the hook automatically springs over the locking lever and renders the release safe.

(3) The davit fall is raised, inflation of the life-raft follows, and the life-raft is boarded while suspended over the side. The shock of the inflating raft cannot cause the release to open, neither can a wave taking the full weight of the raft.

(4) When boarding is complete the bowsing lines are released and the raft is ready for lowering, and release as soon as it is waterborne. The safety locking lever must therefore be moved to the automatic release position, and this is achieved by a pull on the lanyard. This is easily carried out by the occupants. In a future development the hook will be 'cocked' to this position by an attachment at the davit head.

(5) At the moment the life-raft is waterborne the hook opens under the action of a pair of springs. These work in tandem, serving a dual function of holding the locking lever in its two positions of 'safe' and 'auto-release' and opening the hook. If one spring fails the other will carry out all the functions, but the release load will be halved. This release gear is a low-load release; that is to say, when the load is reduced to roughly 18 kg the hook will open. This slight load is necessary to overcome wind effect on the fall, or drift, of the raft. If the release fails to operate it can be opened manually by means of the lanyard. A hard pull on this can open the hook even with a load of 180 kg on it. Should a wave hit the raft during descent and take its weight, the hook will open and the raft will descend with the wave. The release is corrosion-resistant and has a safety factor of five.

40 lb

400 lb

WELIN–MACLACHLAN LIFE-RAFT LAUNCHING DAVIT
(Fig. 6.4)

This has been designed to launch life-rafts from passenger vessels, where speed, safety, and the minimum of operation requirements are of paramount importance.

The main feature is the automatic return of the fall from the water level, after the raft has been released. The automatic-release hook ensures that the operator will not be expected to observe the raft after it leaves the embarkation level for the water, which may be 15 m below. The automatic fall-recovery ensures that there is no chance of the hook thrashing after the raft is released, or remaining at the waterline, or on a downward course to damage the life-raft canopy, or other rafts.

40–50 ft

The recovery works on the spring-blind principle, the energy created by the lowering raft (at 20–30 m per minute) is used to recover the fall at a speed of 60–90 m per minute until it reaches a pre-arranged position where it is stopped automatically. During the entire loading and launching operation the davit head remains outboard, and only the hook is pulled inboard by a tricing line to attach the following raft.

60–90 ft
200–300 ft

138

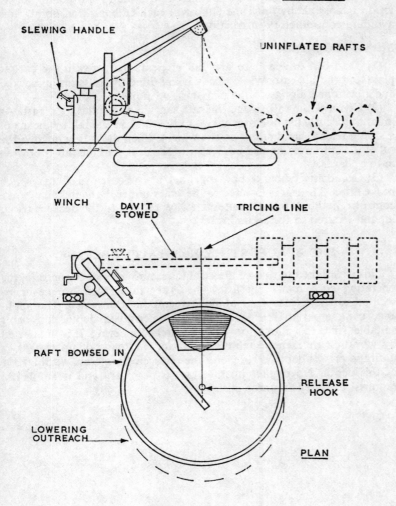

ELEVATION

SLEWING HANDLE

UNINFLATED RAFTS

WINCH

DAVIT
STOWED

TRICING LINE

RAFT BOWSED IN

RELEASE
HOOK

LOWERING
OUTREACH

PLAN

WELIN-MACLACHLAN LIFERAFT
DAVIT

FIGURE 6.4

139

Manual recovery is also allowed for, though at a slower speed. The winch has a centrifugal brake and also a dead-man main brake. Supervision is possible by only one Officer at each embarkation point, thus avoiding contradictory instructions.

Method of Operation

1 ft   (1) Turn out the davit to give 0·3 m clearance between the curtain plate and the life-raft. While this is being done the rafts are unpacked and positioned alongside the embarkation point.

(2) Connect the fall to the life-raft shackle and inflate the raft. As inflation occurs, the operator takes up the slack in the fall by means of a spring-release hand crank on the winch. When the raft is inflated the sill of the entrance flap will be level with the deck and the raft is bowsed in to bollards.

(3) Occupants embark, bowsing lines are released, and the winch brake lifted. The raft is lowered to the water under the centrifugal brake control. The hook releases automatically, returns to the deck, is triced in, and secured to the second raft.

THE BEAUFORT HYDROSTATIC RELEASE

This is designed to release the lashings securing a raft to the ship, the operating cord remaining fast. The latter must therefore never be secured to the release arm. Manual operation is provided. The appliance can be set to release at any pre-determined depth, 2m being suitable, since this allows for shallow water foundering. It is unaffected by vibration or extreme temperatures and by loads of up to 900 kg until the pre-set depth is reached. The release will operate within 0·3 m of this depth. No regular maintenance is necessary and no tools are required to re-set the mechanism.

1 fathom

2 000 lb
1 ft

CHAPTER VII

DAMAGE CONTROL

(1) COLLISION DAMAGE

(a) At Anchor or Moorings

When a vessel is anchored or secured to buoys there is very little that can be done in the event of an imminent collision except to veer away on the cable, or mooring wires, as rapidly as possible and use the rudder (if there is a current) to sheer the vessel away from the danger or to make the blow a glancing one. The question of slipping moorings or cable hardly arises, since the task requires valuable time, and further, engines must be available for instant use. Should it be possible, however, to slip the mooring wires from the bitts very rapidly or to release the windlass brake quickly, this may prove beneficial in that it will allow the vessel to move with the impact rather more than if she were still secure. Water-tight doors should be closed immediately the danger is realised and Emergency Stations should be signalled. The rapid use of fenders is of paramount importance.

(b) At Sea

Lookouts should be ordered to hail the Officer of the watch every half-hour or else communicate with him by telephone. They should report to him personally when relieved. In vessels where bells are made during the night the lookout is often instructed to repeat them either on the telephone or on the crow's-nest bell. The lookout should report every navigation mark, light, and unidentified object either by telephone or by indicating on a bell once, twice, and three times for objects sighted on the starboard bow, port bow, and dead ahead respectively. In low visibility extra lookouts should be posted forward and aloft—particularly the latter if the fog is low-lying.

In anchoring depths both anchors should be let go when collision is imminent. They may both be lost, but a collision may well be averted. It is better to lose both and *avoid* a collision than to lose one and *have* a collision. On the other hand, the Officer of the watch should bear in mind the fact that the use of one anchor may well cause a beneficial sheer away from the danger, resulting in a glancing blow. In narrow

141

waters it may also be preferable to run the vessel aground and so avoid damage to both ships. This should be done by driving ashore head-on to avoid damage to the bilges and after part of the ship, where damage is difficult to repair. Impact should be reduced by astern movement of the engines and the use of both anchors.

If collision is unavoidable the blow should be made a glancing one; bow to bow, quarter to quarter, or bow to quarter. If direct impact is inevitable the other vessel should if possible be struck forward of her collision bulkhead. The latter can then be shored up, the vessel trimmed by the stern, and slow headway resumed. If a vessel is struck amidships in the region of her largest compartments, serious and disastrous flooding may occur.

The Law

Under the Merchant Shipping Act the Master or person in charge of a vessel involved in a collision shall, provided there is no danger to his ship, crew and passengers render to the other vessel all possible assistance to save the ship and her complement from danger arising from the collision. He shall stand-by until such assistance is no longer necessary. The Masters, or persons in charge, shall also:

    (i) Exchange names of vessels.
    (ii) Notify each other of ports of registry, departure, and destination.
    (iii) Enter a witnessed statement in the Official Logbook.
    (iv) Notify the Department of Trade (D.o.T.) within 24 hours of arrival at the next port.

After Impact

It is to be hoped that in the event of a collision both vessels will have their engines going full astern. If a vessel strikes another head-on it is advisable to stop engines immediately on impact and remain embedded in the gash. This latter is only wise in conditions of smooth sea; in moderate or rough seas the action may lead to further extensive damage. Both vessels should have their boats swung out. In some cases of almost instantaneous foundering the effect of the *holing* vessel remaining in the gash and providing ladders over her bow has resulted in all persons on board the gashed vessel being saved before foundering.

Assuming the sea to be smooth and the above action taken by the holing vessel, it is then often possible for the crew of the other ship to ascertain the extent of damage and which compartments are liable to be flooded. Bulkheads can then be shored up, pumps started, and the ships slowly parted.

Officers should be aware of the rate of inflow of water through a gash. This rate is directly proportional to the area of the hole and the square root of its depth below sea-level, and may be found from the approximate formula:

$$\text{Rate} = 3A\sqrt{H} \text{ tonnes per second}$$

where A is the area of the hole in square metres and H is the depth below sea-level in metres.

Thus a hole of area 1 sq m, 4 m below sea-level, will produce an inrush of

$$6 \times 3600 \text{ tonnes per hour}$$
$$= 21600 \text{ tonnes per hour.}$$

Obviously it is virtually impossible to assess both A and H accurately enough to decide whether pumps can cope with this inrush. The formula serves, however, to demonstrate the severity of even the smallest hole. If the area of any hole is halved, then so also is the inrush so that makeshift plugging is always better than nothing. Not only can the area be reduced in this way, but by listing the ship, the quantity H can be changed. Unfortunately, the mechanics of flooding are such that H is usually likely to increase quickly as draught, trim and list change adversely. Flooding will only cease when the level within the ship reaches the outside level.

It should be decided quickly:

(a) whether the pumps can cope with the initial inrush;
(b) if they cannot, whether plugging is rapidly possible.

If in the latter case the decision is negative, then the vessel must be abandoned if it is considered that bulkheads are liable to collapse under the pressure of water in the flooding compartments. No dogmatic statement can be made with regard to the abandoning of ships—the matter is entirely in the hands of the Master or person in charge. The possibility of bulkheads holding and the ship remaining seaworthy should be considered however.

Collision Mats

These may be made of thick rope; they vary between 3 and 4 m 8 and 12 ft square, and have a cringle spliced into each corner to which bottom and top lines are secured. Some are made of several layers of canvas, plain on the outboard side and having *thrumbs* on the inboard side. Thrumbs are pieces of yarn pulled through the canvas so that their bights protrude to give a soft, cushioning effect. There are patent collision mats available of canvas construction with thrumbs, but having several galvanised-iron bars secured across their length, parallel to one another. These bars not only assist in the rigging and storing of the mats but also bear against the damaged plating, thus stiffening the mat.

143

A collision mat could be made from several thicknesses of canvas—such as tarpaulins—edged with rope, and having wire rope seized around the edge to give stiffening. The making of such a mat on board a damaged ship would be subsequent to at least partial plugging of the hole. The mats are primarily intended for below-water gashes, the idea being to rig the mat as rapidly as possible so as to bring the inflow of water under the control of the pumps. It is not suggested that their use will stop the inflow—there will be edge-leaks and also seepage to contend with even after the mat has been rigged as efficiently as possible. They are used on the assumption that the damaged plating has been turned inwards, the mat being unrolled over the outer plating. Long

$1\frac{1}{2}$–2-in lengths of 12–16-mm wire rope (*bottom lines*) are passed over the bow, under the forefoot, and dragged aft to the gash—let us assume the latter to be on the port side. The starboard ends of the lines are manned on deck and the port ends secured to the cringles on the bottom of the mat. Two similar *toplines* are secured to the cringles on the top of the mat and led well forward and aft, and belayed.

The mat, which has been kept rolled up, is now lowered over the side to the top of the gash (easing on the toplines), and is unrolled over the gash by heaving on the bottom lines from the starboard side. All lines are then set up very tight. It is absolutely essential to keep the bottom lines bar tight throughout the operation—a little imagination will assist the reader to visualise an underwater gash with water pouring through under great pressure—the slightest easing of the lines will cause the mat to be swept into the gash and ripped. Possibly the compartment has ceased to flood, so that pressures within and without are equal. The rigging of the mat is then simplified. However, as soon as the pumps begin to reduce the level within the compartment, a pressure on the outside of the mat will begin to form, increasing as the level is lowered in the compartment. The mat must be able to withstand this maximum pressure.

Temporary Repairs

When estimating the extent of damage it should be borne in mind that it is likely to occur at places quite remote from the area of impact; plates may be *set up*, rivets may be sheared, pipes may be fractured, and the pumping system damaged. Bilges and tanks should be sounded throughout the vessel after collision and repeated continuously until deemed no longer necessary.

A gash above the waterline will have to be closed either with a collision mat or with a *patch*. Salvage personnel use these patches on underwater damage, but this is not possible in the case of a vessel damaged at sea and with no divers available. It says much for the crew of one ship, however, who actually *made* a diving-suit from canvas, sufficiently ill-fitting to contain air for two or three minutes diving at a time, not to a very great depth of course.

A well-made patch is within the scope of most ships—it takes time to construct, but this will not matter, since the gash is above the water-level. Some of these patches have been so effectively made and fitted

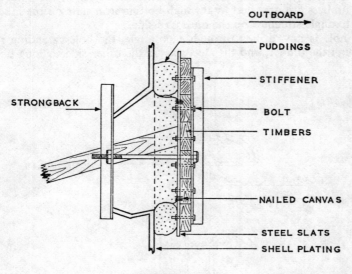

FIGURE 7. I

that a Certificate of Seaworthiness has been issued by Lloyd's surveyors. The materials necessary are now listed. (It is assumed that the Engineers can supply an electric drill and a few nuts, bolts, and a hacksaw with which to remove a few pieces of angle-iron from where they will not be missed for the time being.)

A large piece of strong canvas;
several lengths of uniform timber;
a quantity of oakum, cotton waste, or jute;
galvanised nails;
some steel slats;
nuts and bolts;
several pieces of angle.

The canvas is spread on the deck—the area of the canvas must be considerably larger than the area of the gash. The timbers are cut to size and laid on the canvas. The edges of the timber (all round the

145

rectangle) are now very thickly covered with the oakum or coir, etc., the canvas then being brought over this padding and nailed to the timbers. Better still, long canvas bolsters or *puddings* should be made. These resemble canvas tubes stuffed with oakum. The puddings are then laid along the edges of the timber and the canvas nailed down as before (see Fig. 7.3). The side covered with canvas will be the outer side. The timbers are now tied by through-bolting iron slats on the inboard side to angle stiffeners on the outboard side.

A hole is now drilled through each angle, the hole extending right through the timber, and the steel slat on the other side. A long bolt is

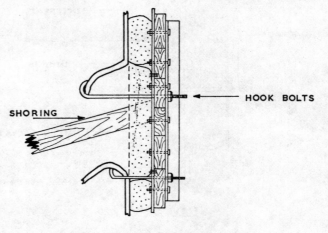

HOOK BOLTS

SHORING

FIGURE 7. 2

then procured, or made, to fit each of these holes. The patch is now ready for fitting.

It is placed over the outside of the gash, with the puddings resting on sound plating (see Fig. 7.1). The last piece of angle is now drilled to act as a *strongback* and through-bolted with the long bolts, as shown. The patch should be shored up from within.

If the hole is other than long and narrow, or if the plating is thin, the use of a strongback is not possible. In these circumstances the patch, or *pad* as it is sometimes called, is made in exactly the same way but is hook-bolted to the turned-in plating as shown in Fig. 7.2—again being shored from within the compartment.

The fitting of these patches below the waterline is a matter either for divers or subsequent to beaching. Pads fitted below the water-level will be subjected to severe external pressures when the compartment is pumped out, and for this reason the timber used must be extremely

146

strong and the patch well shored up from within. From the point of view of the seafarer, who will only be dealing with above-waterline patches, the use of shores is still advisable. Should he, however, find himself in the position of repairing his beached vessel, very careful regard should be paid to the strength of the materials used.

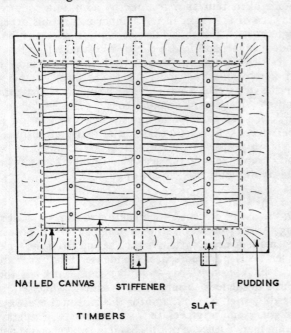

NAILED CANVAS   STIFFENER   PUDDING

SLAT

TIMBERS

FIGURE 7.3

Permeability

A compartment which is 90% filled with cargo is said to be 10% *permeable*. This is, of course, assuming that the cargo itself is not permeable by water.

A 300 m³ compartment which is 10% permeable will therefore admit a maximum of 30 m³ cubic feet of water, i.e. approximately 30 tonnes weight. Further, the presence of cargo will materially assist in preventing the setting-up of decks and tank tops due to water pressure below. It is unlikely that a general cargo, however well stowed, or for that matter any other cargo which normally requires vertical dunnage on the bulkheads, will prevent the collapse of a bulkhead. On the other hand, if the cargo was tightly stowed against the bulkhead and unable to move within itself, then a bulkhead may hold. This is an important

10 000 ft³
1 000 ft³
tons

147

factor when deciding upon emergency plugging of gashes prior to pumping.

Compressed Air

A flooded compartment which for any reason cannot be pumped out may have some of its buoyancy restored by admitting compressed air above the surface of the water in the compartment, thus expelling the water through the gash. Obviously these compartments must be capable of being made airtight, and in dry cargo vessels therefore this practice is normally restricted to tanks. Tankers lend themselves more freely to this method of regaining buoyancy, due to the large number of compartments in the ship which are capable of being made airtight. The air may be admitted through tank sounding or air pipes, and even through the steam-injection valves. In some cases pressures of as low as 0·8 of an atmosphere have sufficed (that is, a total of 1·8 atmospheres). The building-up of excessive pressures should be avoided in case the compartment is ruptured, e.g. the deckhead or tank top may be set up. These should be shored in any case, from above.

Cement

Generally, the use of cement by seamen for repair work is limited to leak-stopping. A leak should be stopped as efficiently as possible until the inflow is small. A drain system is then set up from the leak, to the bilges or other easily-pumped space. Condenser tubes are often used for this purpose. A *cement box*—a timber framework—is then built around the area of the leak to support the concrete while setting.

Cement used by itself is weak, and for this reason it is always mixed with an *aggregate* (sand or gravel) to form a concrete. Portland cement is slower setting than 'CIMENT FONDU'. Sand is known as fine aggregate, ½-in and 12-mm gravel is classed as coarse aggregate. The proportions used are: 1 part of cement, plus 2 parts of fine aggregate, to 4 parts of coarse aggregate, all parts by volume. A quicker-setting mixture is 1 part of cement to 1½ parts *each* of fine and coarse. The above mixtures are only a guide, many people having their own firm ideas on this matter, but the proportions submitted here are very effective. Both warm fresh water and washing soda are said to expedite the setting of the mixture. When the water is added to bring the mixture to a working consistency the volume will reduce by about one-third.

As soon as the drain is functioning satisfactorily, the concrete is poured into the box. Once set, the end of the drain tube can be plugged, or else withdrawn altogether, and the hole in the concrete plugged with a suitable piece of soft-wood.

The use of cement is not recommended for leaks in surfaces which are liable to move in a seaway, nor for oily, painted, or greasy surfaces.

Paintwork should be roughened, or else thoroughly cleaned with strong soda solutions. A rusty surface is ideal.

Leaks

For small leaks which do not warrant the use of a patch as described previously, the following equipment is useful:

(1) Cement boxes.
(2) Softwood plugs, tapered, and driven into small holes are very effective, since they quickly swell when wet.
(3) Pieces of steel plating may be placed over small, jagged fractures on the outer plating, cushioned with oakum, and tightened-up inboard using an angle strongback bolted through the plate. A stout piece of timber would suffice in place of the steel, provided it is of sufficient thickness to withstand external water pressures.
(4) A canvas mat may be made, plain on the inboard side and thrumbed on the outer side. It is then placed over the hole, from inboard, and shored up, using a piece of steel plating or timber between the mat and the end of a shore to act as a support or *padpiece*. This also distributes the thrust of the shore.

Sheared Rivets

A rivet hole may be plugged in any of the above ways and also by the following two methods:

(1) This is used by some salvage workers; a line is passed through the hole from inboard, on the outer end of which is a piece of steel rod such as a sounding rod. This enables the line to hang vertically. A surface craft then sweeps to recover the line and bring it to the surface. The rod is now detached and a large-headed bolt (drilled through close to the end of the thread) is secured to the line as shown in Fig. 7.4. The bolt is then hove in through the hole and screwed down tight with a nut. Sometimes a wooden peg is used to float the line to the surface, where sweeping is impractical. Some seafarers are highly amused by the above method, but it is often used, and is therefore submitted for the reader's consideration.
(2) A patent device can be used, called a *fish-bolt*, which is illustrated in Fig. 7.5.
   'A' is a metal tube having four cuts in its outboard end 'B', part of the tube being threaded and carrying a nut 'C'. Through the tube runs a rod, threaded, and carrying a nut at its inboard end 'D', having its outboard end conical and of increased cross-section. Its cross-section 'E' is greater than the inner cross-section area of the outer tube.

149

The bolt is passed through the plating 'F', and the small nut at 'D' tightened. The inner rod moves inboard, its conical end expanding the outer tube against the plating until the fit is watertight. Nut 'C' is then screwed tight.

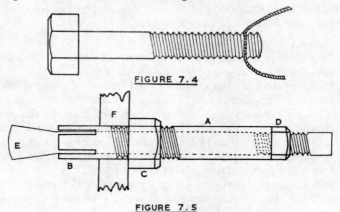

FIGURE 7.4

FIGURE 7.5

Shoring

Subsequent to collision damage, Officers should resort to shoring as soon as possible, if considered necessary. Shores are used for supporting damaged or weakened structures, watertight doors, hatches, plating, bulkheads and tanktops under pressure, patches and pads covering fractures, other leak-stopping devices, and for reinforcing decks.

Rectangular vertical areas under pressure, such as doors and bulkheads, should be shored up at a level of roughly one-third of the depth of the water causing the pressure, measured from the base of the structure, i.e. a door under 3 m of water pressure should be shored up 1 m from the base, on the other side. This is the centre of pressure. The shores should rest on padpieces, flat pieces of wood which distribute the thrust of the shores evenly over their area.

Shores should not normally be longer than thirty times their diameter. Wedges should not be used freely to tighten shores—the use of shores which are *proud* (i.e. longer than an exact fit) is considered a better practice. When resorted to, wedges are used in pairs and hammered towards each other simultaneously. Before rigging shores, oily surfaces should be sprinkled with sand. They are stepped against a rigid structure and not on unsupported plating; a deck should be shored up by stepping the heads and heels of the shores against the beams.

In the absence of rigid parts plenty of padpieces should be used. Shoring should be inspected frequently for signs of loosening. If possible a man should be in constant attendance. Shoring is illustrated in Fig. 7.6.

150

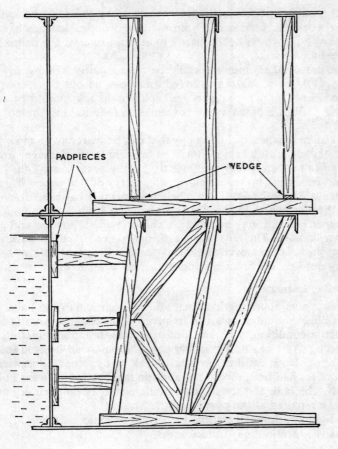

FIGURE 7. 6

(2) HEAVY WEATHER DAMAGE

Hatches

If hatches are stove-in during heavy weather tarpaulins will be ripped and wooden hatches smashed. The locking bars, if fitted, will probably remain intact and rigged. In order to prevent further inrush of water into the compartment, continued loss of buoyancy, and damage to cargo, the vessel should be swung off course so that she lies in as comfortable a position as possible with no water coming aboard at the damaged area. (For example, if No. 1 hatches had been stove-in the

151

vessel would probably have been swung stern to wind and sea while repair work was carried out.) Since strong wooden hatches have been smashed in, it would be foolhardy to attempt to clear the debris before the vessel is swung.

The damaged equipment should be cleared away, salving any whole hatches. Bilges should be sounded and pumped out if necessary; the cargo below, though probably well soaked already, should be covered with tarpaulins in case the new coverings on the hatchway are not watertight.

All spare hatches, including any that can be spared from other 'tween decks throughout the ship, should be brought to the damaged area and cut to fit the open hatchway. Once the hatchway is covered, the hatches should be shored up from below using plenty of padpieces. Three tarpaulins will then be fitted, stretched, and securely battened down. Now that the covers are shored, the vessel may be continued on course. On the other hand, it may be felt advisable to remain hove-to and risk no further damage. The tarpaulins, previously mentioned for covering the cargo, should be removed as soon as possible in order to allow the cargo to dry out—corner hatches removed in fine weather will assist this.

Pounding Damage

If excessive pounding has been allowed, particularly in ballast trim, No. 1 bilges should be sounded frequently. The case occurred of a vessel in such a condition, with her fore peak tank full, and suffering heavy pounding. As a result of this, her collision bulkhead became fractured in several places, causing the tank to leak badly. No. 1 bilges were full, the limbers had been forced up, and the tanktop in the lower hold was awash. The tank and the bilges were immediately pumped dry and the damage repaired at the port of destination.

In light conditions frequent inspections should be made aft, where excessive vibration may induce leaks.

Plating

If plating is leaking at lap joints the crevice may be securely caulked with oakum or similar material. The use of wooden plugs is inadvisable, since it may aggravate the situation. In some cases the lap joint has been drilled through—just as far as the *faying surfaces*, i.e. the plate surfaces which are together, and a stiff mixture of putty injected through the drilling to seal the crevice.

Ventilators

If these are sheared off by heavy weather a pad may be made and fitted as shown in Fig. 7.1, using the strongback in the deck below, tightened against the deckhead. A wooden plug may be used instead.

DAMAGE CONTROL

(3) LOSS OF RUDDER

Many attempts have been made at sea to rig up makeshift steering devices with varying degrees of success. Before discussing these, a preliminary word on rudder accidents is appropriate. Should the rudder fail to respond to wheel movements, it may be due to faulty steering-gear, or to a fractured rudder stock. In both cases the rudder should be brought under control before repairs are attempted. In the case of rod and chain steering-gear, if failure occurs in, say, the port steering linkage, then the wheel should be placed hard over to starboard, causing a similar action on the rudder, after which the quadrant can be secured.

In the case of a fractured rudder stock, the rudder cannot be controlled from inboard, and various methods are used to *catch* the rudder, including the lowering overside of knotted chains. These are used to catch the rudder trailing-edge and heave it to one side, after which it is secured while repairs proceed. If a kedge anchor is available it has proved more satisfactory to lower this over the side in a horizontal position, i.e. stock vertical, on wires, down to the level of the rudder. By careful handling of the wires, the fluke may be caught against the rudder arms, the rudder hove hard over, and then secured.

In all cases the vessel is stopped immediately. In addition, in heavy weather, the vessel must be manœuvred into a comfortable position while work proceeds. Without a rudder, the vessel will assume a position beam-on to wind, which may lead to disastrous *synchronous rolling*. Cargo may shift, and capsizing may occur. The ship should therefore be brought head to wind as quickly as possible. A makeshift mizzen sail may be rigged, a sea anchor may be streamed, but in some cases it has been successfully accomplished by simply lowering one anchor on a long scope of cable.

Occasionally, engineers have been able to cut into the rudder trunk and repair the fracture by ingenious use of clamps and circular steel bands. This method is generally limited to fractures which extend over a good length of stock. If the fracture occurs below the stuffing box the method cannot be used unless the vessel can be trimmed sufficiently by the head.

Jury Rudders

When steering with such a device, speeds should be slow, and as soon as the sea or weather conditions deteriorate, the vessel should be hove-to. This will avoid excessive stresses on the *steering machine*.

The basic idea of a rudder is that it shall provide resistance to the water on one side of the ship in order to turn the bow *towards* that side. For this reason, any contrivance which fulfils this function may be used as a jury rudder. It is most important to note, however, that what suits one vessel very well indeed, may prove quite valueless on another. Many of the well-known and successful jury rudders have been copied on other vessels and have proved useless. Rigs described for ships with counter sterns may be totally unsuited for cruiser-sterned ships. Again, some rudders can be quite satisfactorily made for small ships, but when copied on larger vessels may prove to be of inadequate strength despite the larger gear available.

In twin-screw ships the vessel may be steered by running one engine at constant revolutions and varying those on the other engine. On single-screw ships the seaman must try every method at his disposal. Some very long voyages have been made under jury rudder, but the gear must be constantly nursed, and the temptation to increase speed

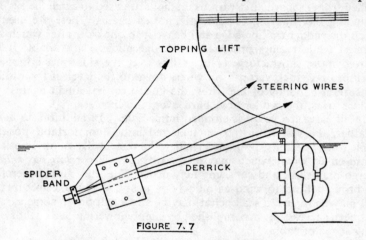

TOPPING LIFT

STEERING WIRES

SPIDER BAND

DERRICK

FIGURE 7. 7

in fair weather strongly resisted. Given the usual materials carried aboard a ship, and a number of enterprising men, a rudderless ship will soon be brought under control, provided the men are tireless and prepared to make two, or even three different rigs in order to find a satisfactory one.

The following methods are outlined briefly; they have all proved successful in their time on a particular ship, or perhaps on a small number of ships. The method of rigging must be left to the person doing the work—strength of gear available, layout of the vessel, fittings, and new ideas are his prerogative. For this reason, only the very basic ideas are included here. When actually undertaking the task the question of rigging will be rapidly solved.

(1) In the late 1920s a jury rudder was manufactured from a derrick and two steel doors, in the form of an oar having a box blade. The

154

doors were bolted to the derrick some distance from the derrick head, and the space between the doors was packed with timber, through-bolted to the doors. The 'oar' was hung overside with the doors vertical. The gooseneck was fitted to the top gudgeon under the counter stern, and the spider band at the derrick head was used for attaching port and starboard steering wires, and the topping lift. (A topping lift is necessary not only to control the depth at which the resistance to water occurs but also to heave the jury rudder clear of heavy seas when hove-to.) The method is illustrated in Fig. 7.7. In the case of a cruiser stern some thought might be devoted to using a similar rig, but with the

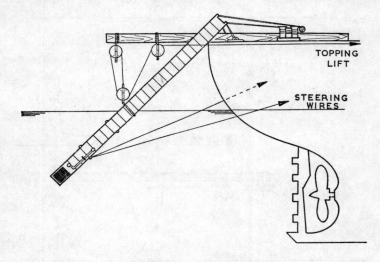

FIGURE 7.8

gooseneck passing through a hole made in the stern plating, the goose-neck being suitably secured inboard with a collar and pin.

(2) A gangway has been used by rigging the steps in the vertical plane and lashing one end securely at the poop deck-edge. This lashing needs careful thought, since the gangway must be very secure against movement both in the fore-and-aft line and the vertical plane, but it must be free to pivot from port to starboard about the poop deck-edge. The foot of the gangway will need to be weighted with, say, derrick span chains or the stock of a stream anchor. Steering wires and a topping lift are used (see Fig. 7.8). The tendency of these jury rudders to lift out of the water will be partly counteracted by weighting the lower end and partly by ensuring a long lead for the steering wires. The topping lift should be rigged either from the after derricks, the docking bridge, or perhaps

from a boom (such as a derrick—although the diagrams show a wooden spar) projecting over the stern as shown in Fig. 7.11. The topping lift must be secured to the gangway below its centre of gravity. A gangway may, instead, be streamed astern as a jury rudder.

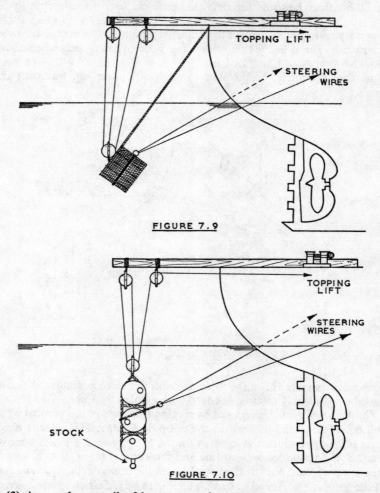

FIGURE 7.9

FIGURE 7.10

(3) A very large coil of heavy mooring rope, securely round-lashed, has been successfully towed on its own part. It becomes slowly water-logged and partially sinks, total sinkage being prevented by the speed of the ship (although slow) and a topping lift. Steering lines are again used to heave it to port or starboard. These steering wires are often led

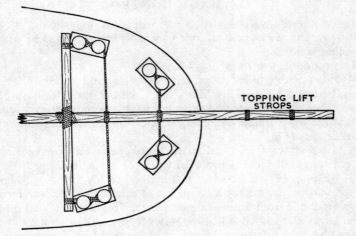

TOPPING LIFT
STROPS

FIGURE 7.11

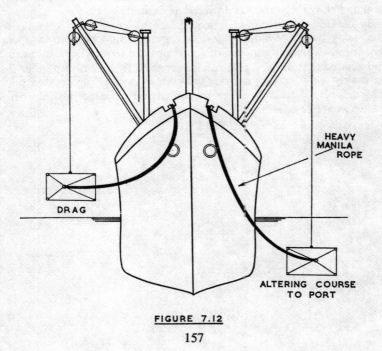

HEAVY
MANILA
ROPE

DRAG

ALTERING COURSE
TO PORT

FIGURE 7.12

to two connected warping drums and wound in opposite directions so that by means of one control, one wire is slacked at the same speed as the other is hove-in.

This rudder is shown in Fig. 7.9.

(4) It is possible to lash together several large oil drums. The drums are submerged by partially filling them with water. The base of the contrivance may be weighted in addition—say with an anchor stock—so that the rig is suitably submerged. Steering wires and a topping lift are necessary (Fig. 7.10).

With the above methods, due care should be taken to make sure that the gear does not foul the propeller when the vessel is stopped.

(5) *By drags* (Fig. 7.12). This is a method which is very well known indeed and is suitable for all ships. It is extremely effective. Two flat drags are made from timber or steel plates. They are weighted on their lower edges and suspended below water from derricks swung overside. In the absence of derricks, booms or spars could be rigged projecting horizontally over the side, to carry the hoisting tackles. Fore-and-aft motion is prevented by ropes running from the drag bridles to the forecastle-head leads. When it is desired to alter course to port the port drag is immersed and the starboard one lifted—and vice versa. If speed retardation is of no importance one could be kept immersed at a fixed level and the other raised or lowered as desired.

By making the bridles of unequal length, as shown, the drags will veer away from the ship's sides. One man should be able to operate the drags, even without remote-control on the winches. It must be appreciated that no jury gear can be expected to steer a ship other than on a very slow zig-zag course. Off-course yaws of up to two points ($22\frac{1}{2}$ degrees) should therefore be considered quite permissible before the drags are re-adjusted.

CHAPTER VIII

STRANDING AND BEACHING

W HEN a vessel is grounded intentionally she is said to be *beached*. If she is grounded accidentally she is *stranded*. A vessel is usually beached when she is damaged to such an extent that the pumps are unable to cope with the rate of flooding. There is therefore always an interval of time, however short, during which the action of beaching can be considered. Even if an emergency exists, the beaching can still often be controlled, and hence the problem of refloating the ship may resolve itself more easily than in the case of a stranded vessel. This is provided the person executing the manœuvre selects his beach, and method of approach, with a view to subsequent refloating. The wise seaman, however, will waste little time in considering such problems if danger of foundering is imminent.

A vessel which has stranded may be in contact with the ground at her bow, her stern, her mid-length, her entire length, or even all along one side, with the other side in deep water. Other shoals or rocks may exist close by, hampering the refloating; currents and weather may be adverse and there may be unfavourable silting-up as a result of these elements; adverse weather may cause her to drive farther aground, and she may also be damaged. All these problems may cause the refloating to be an extremely complicated operation calling for the use of ground-tackle, or tugs, or dredging craft, or even lighters into which to discharge cargo, or perhaps the hauling power of large vessels. Any combination, or perhaps all, of these forms of assistance may be required. We shall deal with them in detail commencing with:

GROUND-TACKLE

By this is meant the use of anchors, carefully placed at considerable distances from the ship, and connected to her by heavy wire hawsers, possibly using some lengths of her chain cable. Heavy purchases are then rigged, often one secured to the hauling part of the other to give greater mechanical advantage and lower stresses on the final hauling part, to impose a stress upon these anchors. This stress, which must be applied continuously, is beneficial in refloating the ship.

159

Salvage operators are generally agreed that the use of ground-tackle is the greatest single factor in refloating operations. The rigging of it by a ship's crew with the limited gear available calls for much ingenuity, improvisation, patience, and heavy work.

At some time during the operation anchors will have to be carried from the ship to selected sites. We will assume that the crew of a ship is required to lay ground-tackle and that a good variety of gear is available—if in a certain ship some piece of gear is not to hand, then the seaman must exercise his prerogative of improvisation for which he is well known.

Dispensing for the time being with the preliminaries of grounding, i.e. stranding, and the immediate action to be taken thereon, we will deal with the crew's problem in as much detail as possible. Initially, boats must be lowered. If a heavy bower anchor is to be slung across two boats, it may be advisable to tow the pair with a motor boat rather than use the latter as one of an echelon pair, which can pose heavy steering bias. Deck Officers will perform various emergency duties. As a guide, the Chief Officer may supervise internal tank soundings, damage control and ground tackle. The Second Officer could calculate the ship's position, estimated draught if afloat and the state of the tides. The Third Officer can read the actual overside draughts and, weather permitting, survey the area. In winds above force 4, ground tackle work in lifeboats is likely to be impossible.

Once afloat, all unnecessary gear should be removed from the boats and a rough survey of the bottom made to determine in which direction the vessel is best refloated. Then a survey of soundings and sea-bed material should be made at some distance from the ship, to decide upon the sites for the anchors. This distance will depend upon the length of hawsers available unless one is also prepared to carry out cable. In general, the distance should be as great as possible so that the stress is applied to the anchors in a direction parallel with the sea-bed. It is of interest here to note that if a stress be applied to an anchor such that the direction of stress is 5 degrees above the level of the sea-bed (or axis of the shank), then the holding power of the anchor is reduced by one-quarter. If the stress is applied at an angle of 15 degrees above the shank axis, then the holding power is reduced by one-half.

Having decided upon the direction of pull, and the anchor sites, the anchors must now be carried out. One anchor used by itself as a ground-tackle is not as efficient as one anchor *backed up* by another anchor a little farther away from the ship and in line with the proposed hawser. The two anchors are connected by a length of chain or wire, and the rig is known as *anchors in tandem*. There have been cases when ships have continually dragged their ground-tackle anchor home, only to find that this is prevented, or at least minimised, by backing it up. Since bower anchors are heavy objects, the work may be made lighter by backing up one bower anchor with a kedge anchor, if one is carried. Let us assume weights of 5 and $1\frac{1}{2}$ tonnes respectively. If a (non-compulsory) kedge anchor is not carried, then two bower anchors will have to be rigged in tandem. We have chosen to discuss the tandem rig, but there are no hard-and-fast rules about the rigging of ground-tackle—often both bower anchors are carried out and stressed on two separate hawsers— but the tandem method requires more complicated thought, and hence our choice.

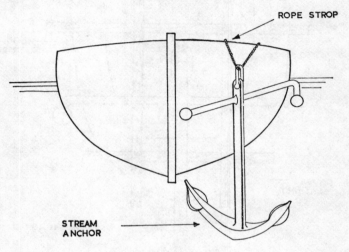

FIGURE 8.1

Owing to the fact that our stream (or kedge) anchor has a stock, it is not an easy one to carry between two boats. If it is decided to use two boats it will be carried in a similar manner to a bower anchor, or else by suspending it vertically from a spar lashed across the four padded gunwales. Fig. 8.1 shows a method of carrying the anchor by a single boat. With the lifeboat's whaler stern the anchor is slung over one quarter, close aft, and this produces a list as well as a large trim by the stern. This may be partly counteracted by stowing our heavy backing-up wire near the opposite bow. The rope strop is cut through when letting go the anchor; if a wire strop is used it will have to incorporate a patent slip.

Fig. 8.2 uses two heavy spars, probably greased on their upper surfaces, resting on the athwartships bearer spar and the quarter gunwales, which must be padded with wood. Due to the tendency for these spars

161

to slide along the gunwales, their after ends are tied together by using another spar lashed across, and below them. The anchor is secured during transit with a shank lashing and also a shackle lashing as shown. To unload the anchor, the forward ends of the fore-and-aft spars are raised and the anchor is slid over the stern. In the case of our 1½-tonne anchor, this may well prove to be an impossible piece of manhandling and make Fig. 8.1 a more attractive proposition. A steering oar will have to be used in Fig. 8.2 instead of a rudder.

ton

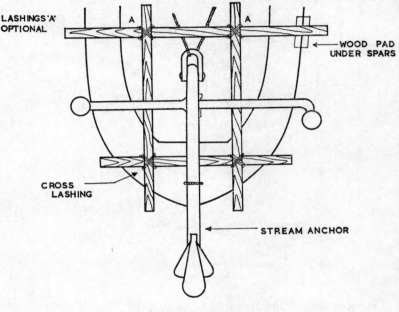

FIGURE 8.2

The anchor is lowered overside on a derrick fall and secured to the boat. A length of chain or heavy wire (at least 25-mm wire) is placed in the boat, and the first end to go in is secured to the anchor shackle. For reasons which will become apparent, the length of this wire should be equal to no less than twice the depth of water at the anchor site. If the depth of water is small, then the length of wire may be increased above this minimum limit in order to give a good drift between the two anchors. A light wire rope of length equal to at least one-and-a-half times the maximum depth of water at the *bower* anchor site should be secured close up to the free end of the heavy wire. A suitable buoy is attached to the end of the light wire. In the unfortunate event of a power-driven boat not being available, it will be wise to take out to the site a 25-mm

3-in

3-in

162

fibre rope, sufficiently long to reach between the anchor and the ship. It is a good idea to buoy this *warp* along its length, with sealed paint drums for example. The warp can later be used for heaving out the boats carrying the bower anchor. We shall assume a functioning, power-driven boat is available. A chain-check stopper can be placed in the boat for easing out the wire, if considered necessary.

The boat can now proceed to the anchorage. At a suitable distance from the anchor position the buoy is floated and its line paid overside, followed by the heavy wire as the boat slowly approaches the anchorage. The propeller must be kept clear. The chain-check stopper will be rigged by passing its end through a ringbolt in the bottom of the boat, or

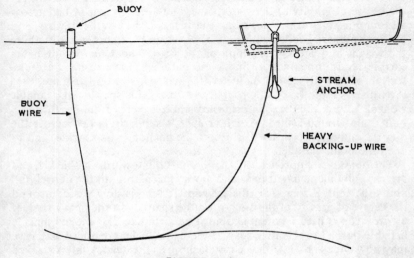

FIGURE 8.3

wherever else convenient, round the wire and back through the ring bolt. The wire is now passing through the bight of the chain. One end of the chain is made fast, and the other has a light purchase on the end of it. By heaving on this tackle the wire is bowsed close down to the ring bolt, checking its movement. This method will be invaluable later when paying out heavier wires.

When all is paid out the boat's crew prepare themselves for the sudden change of trim and the anchor is let go. Had we been using a warp, this would have been secured to the anchor before letting go and sufficient length paid out to prevent violent running. The remainder of the warp, with its buoys, would be paid out as the boat returns to the ship. It is immaterial at this stage how the anchor falls, since it will adjust itself and bite when the whole ground-tackle is finally stressed. Fig. 8.3

shows the method of laying out the backing-up wire—the warp is not shown.

Carrying out a Bower Anchor

For this it is advisable to use two boats. The anchor *may* be slung beneath one boat, but this will require a greater depth of water than may be available. The spare bower anchor can be broken out of its bed and hoisted overside. It will be slung at its centre of gravity and lowered until just awash—in the horizontal position.

The two boats should again be cleared of all unnecessary gear and manœuvred side by side, about a metre apart, and heading in the same direction. The centre of flotation of the boats should be estimated, i.e. the centre of gravity of the waterplane, and a heavy spar lashed across all four gunwales at this position. The spar is lashed to the thwarts, and the gunwales are padded with wide pieces of timber in order to distribute the weight and prevent crushing of the boat. The spar for our boats carrying a 5-tonne anchor, and 1 m apart, will have to have a cross-section of roughly 23 cm diameter. If the cross-section is square, then the square should be of side roughly 18 cm. If this spar is not available we shall have to build a spar, using any suitable pieces of timber through-bolted and round-lashed. A lighter spar is similarly lashed across the quarter gunwales in order to support the anchor at its shackle, and to keep the boats parallel.

The boats now approach the anchor, heading towards its shackle, and are carefully manœuvred over and along its length until the derrick fall abuts the central spar. An efficient rope lashing is now passed around the centre of gravity of the anchor on the shank, and the heavy spar. If a wire strop is used a patent slip must be included. The anchor shackle is lightly lashed to the after spar. If there is sufficient depth of water we may now choose to ease the central lashing as the derrick fall is slacked down in order to submerge the anchor. This will cause a displacement of water and a small but helpful upthrust on the anchor. If the anchor is correctly slung at its centre of gravity there should, in theory, be no weight on the after spar. If our lifeboats are 10 m long they will each have a tonnes-per-cm immersion of roughly 0·2, i.e. a weight of 0·2 tonne will submerge one boat 1 cm. Since the 5 tonnes is distributed between two boats, they will each sink about 12 cm.

The boats should be equipped with a chain check stopper, a sharp axe, and have a crew of about three men in each. Into the boats must now be loaded, and carefully flaked down, the big 40- or 50-mm wire which is to be finally hove-on. Half can be placed in each boat, making sure that it is clear to run. The end finally going into the boats should be passed clear of everything and shackled to the anchor ring. In order to avoid having to do this with the anchor just submerged, it could well be done

some 2–3 ft apart

ton 3 ft
9 in
7 in

32 ft

5- or 6-in

before easing away the derrick fall. At some stage the heavy bight of the wire will have to be dragged by the boats, either when paying it out as they return to the ship or when heading out to the anchorage if the ship is paying out the wire. In this latter case, only a few coils will be taken in the boats. Much will depend upon the prevailing wind and currents before deciding in which direction it will be easier for the boats to have this drag.

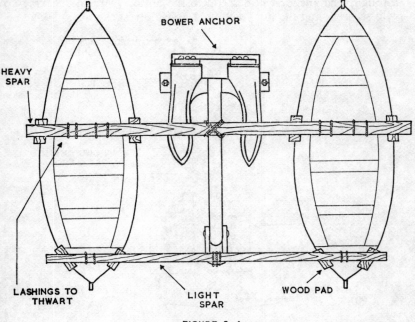

FIGURE 8.4

The boats can now head out to the stream-anchor buoy. Fig. 8.4 shows the two boats with the anchor slung in position. The boats are shown wider apart than in practice, for the sake of clarity.

The buoy is picked up and the buoy-wire hove inboard. Eventually the end of the 25-mm backing-up wire will be brought to the surface. 3-in The reader should now imagine himself to be in the boats and try to visualise the next step.

Pass the end of the 25-mm wire (having cast off the buoy-wire) under 3-in the spars, make a round turn on the anchor shank close to the head, and shackle the wire back on to its own part. The wire is now backed-up to the bower anchor and will slide down close to the head when stressed. Secure the buoy-wire to the bower anchor and pay out all the wire,

165

refloating the buoy. Making sure the heavy wire is clear of everything, pay out sufficient to at least reach the bottom, and pass the chain-check stopper *loosely*. We may find it difficult to estimate how much heavy wire we are paying out, and if we *under*-estimate it, and have a tight chain-check stopper, the falling anchor may assist in removing part of a boat. Cast off the lashing on the after spar and alert the boats' crews. Make a final check to see that all is clear, and cut the central lashing through. The anchor will descend to the bottom with the backing-up wire secured, and the buoy will float above the anchorage, making re-

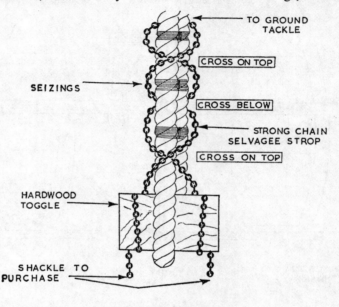

FIGURE 8. 5.

covery possible later if the ground-tackle has to be slipped and left behind.

Return to the ship, paying out the heavy wire (if carried) on the chain-check stopper. The end of wire is now taken on to the ship and rigged ready for heaving. Let us assume that the ship is aground forward and our ground-tackle has been laid leading right astern. Heavy purchases will be used for stressing the ground-tackle, and these may be rigged in many ways. Generally they are as heavy as possible and are often rigged with one purchase secured to the hauling part of the other. This gives a theoretical mechanical advantage equal to the *product* of the respective mechanical advantages. Also the stress necessary on the final hauling part is lowered.

166

This hauling part is led to the after winches or capstans. To distribute the stress more evenly, the hauling part is often turned round one warping drum and then similarly turned up on the next set of winches forward. Both winches are then run together. The lead of the hauling part should be kept as nearly as possible in one straight line. The purchases will be used to advantage, i.e. pulling in the direction of the moving blocks. If the end of the heavy wire has an eye in it this is most convenient for attachment to the purchases. But if the ship begins to move, and the heavy wire is slowly hove-in, how is the block now secured? Possibly by several chain stoppers—certainly not by one alone. A suc-

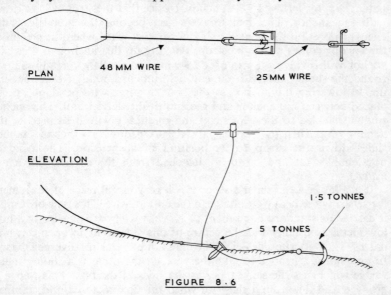

PLAN   48 MM WIRE   25 MM WIRE

ELEVATION

1·5 TONNES

5 TONNES

FIGURE 8·6

cessful method is to use a wooden toggle. This is a short cylindrical piece of hardwood, having a large end-diameter. The heavy wire is seized back on to its own part with many seizings, making as small an eye as possible. The toggle is placed through this eye and a chain selvagee strop is passed around the eye and toggle and shackled to the block (Fig. 8.5).

When overhauling the purchases, several chain stoppers should be passed on to the wire, and perhaps light tackles used similarly to the method shown in Chapter I for heaving up cable when the windlass is out of action.

The standing blocks of the purchases should be made fast round very strong points, such as hatch coamings and bitts. Winch beds are sometimes used. The same applies to chain stoppers—the ordinary deck fittings are often of inadequate strength. Bitts should be watched very closely for signs of lifting.

We have now rigged the gear ready for use and will change the subject for the time being. Fig. 8.6 shows how our tackle is lying.

(In passing, the method of carrying a bower anchor below one boat involves the use of a central spar lashed to the thwarts and resting on padded gunwales in way of the centre of flotation, as before. This time 10 in the sinkage of the boat will be 25 cm. The anchor is suspended vertically, or horizontally, from the bight of a wire strop passing right round the boat and spar. On the spar the strop eyes are joined by a patent slip, for letting go the anchor. Notice that the strop will go down with the anchor. The spar must project beyond the gunwales sufficiently to prevent the boat sides from being crushed when the weight of the anchor comes on to the strop. Backing up this anchor to a stream 3-in anchor will involve the use of a 25-mm wire pendant already secured round the shank, and with the end held inboard, ready for connecting up. In lowering the anchor to the boat, a short wire pendant will be placed between the anchor and the end of the derrick fall. The anchor ring is shackled to the wire strop and the heavy wire is secured to the anchor ring. Then the derrick fall is slacked down so that the anchor slides down the strop to its position of suspension. The pendant now enables the anchor to be detached from the derrick fall *above water*.)

If available, a carpenter's stopper is a very useful piece of equipment 6-in for securing the heavy purchases to the 50-mm wire. This type of stopper is carried as standard equipment in Naval vessels. It is basically a hollow metal box, hinged at the centre of one side so as to open out into halves. The opposite sides of the box are not parallel but diverge *inboard*. In one half is a groove to take the wire. In the other is a sliding metal wedge which has the same taper as the sides of the box. This wedge is grooved and fits around the wire when the box is closed and clamped shut. When the wire is stressed the wedge tends to be pulled in the direction of stress, its groove gripping the wire harder as the stress increases. The inboard end of the patent stopper has a chain bridle on it for securing to strong points on the deck—in our case the bridle may be shackled to the purchase block. A spare wedge is usually supplied with each stopper, having a different groove. By changing wedges, a different size of wire may be clamped in the stopper.

THE USE OF TUGS

In coast tidal waters it is generally wise to radio for tug assistance, since they are quickly available. These tugs will be able to assist the stranded vessel in several ways, but in all cases the Master should avoid any financial bargaining and insist upon signing Lloyd's Salvage Agreement on a 'no-cure, no-pay' basis before assistance is rendered.

Generally speaking, most tugs can exert a pull of from 5 to 15 tonnes, i.e. roughly 1 tonne pull for every 75 kW power of the engines, though some very powerful salvage tugs can exert up to 80 tonnes. The safe working load of a 50-mm flexible steel wire rope will be roughly 15–18 tonnes, so that in many cases ground-tackle is more effective than a tug's pull. Further, a tug will rise and fall in a seaway, and the stress in her towline will be continually changing. In the case of ground-tackle, a swell or sea can be very beneficial, since providing the gear is kept taut, the rising of the waterborne part of the ship in the swell produces surging, increased stresses in the tackle, which time and time again have resulted in moving a ship. It is for this reason that ground-tackle must comprise the heaviest gear available, since if kept tight there will be no spring in the lines to absorb sudden jerks, and stresses may become very high.

A tug cannot make use of these beneficial forces, and for this reason, salvage operators may suggest the use of ground-tackle in addition to their own pull. In this case, the tugs can be used to lay out the ship's anchors very speedily, and thus save considerable time and trouble. Once the ship is refloated, the gear may have to be slipped and left for later recovery—hence the use of buoys to mark the anchors.

A tug may also be employed in *scouring*, i.e. using the stream of water from her propeller or propellers, directed as far down as possible, to scour away the sea-bed which is silting up the stranded hull. It is often this silting which produces strong suction, holding the ship firmly in place. Scouring will be employed when a stranded ship cannot be moved by her own power, by ground-tackle, or by direct towing. It may be used to make a vessel settle deeper in the water and become waterborne, or to dredge a deep channel to seaward, or to dredge cavities beneath the keel. Any small craft having a suitable trim by the stern may be used, e.g. a trawler.

The area should be roughly surveyed before commencing, and the depths subsequently checked frequently in case undesirable banking is being caused by the scouring. It is quite possible for sand to be scoured from the ship's side and cause a shoal to form to seaward. If this is not carefully checked, she may strand again shortly after refloating. For dredging cavities beneath a keel, the tug should have no more than 2 m below her propeller. For freeing the area along her bilges, greater depths—up to 8 m total depth—are permissible. The tug is secured to the ship by a hawser from the towing hook, a manila hawser leading from each quarter for heaving the tug up and down the ship's length, and a headrope from each bow for altering the tug's inclination to the

169

Margin notes:
tons
tons
tons
6-in
tons

a fathom
4 fathoms

ship's fore-and-aft line. The tug should also have both her anchors out on open moor.

Assuming the use of two tugs, if tunnelling beneath the keel, both craft will be secured on one side of the ship and at about 70 degrees to the ship's side. This large angle prevents deflection of the stream of water by the bilge area. The craft are secured abreast of the masts, since cavities produced here will not unduly weaken the hull. Once the cavities are blown through, they are gradually widened—but not deepened unduly —by moving the tugs. If, on the other hand, the bilges are to be cleared of silt, then the tugs will be secured at a smaller angle to the ship's side —about 30 degrees—and will be continually worked from amidships towards both ends of the hull. Eventually the ship may be left resting on a ridge of sea-bed with deeper water on both sides. By heaving on bow or quarter and by using ship's engines and full alternating rudder, the ship may be slowly *rocked off* and become waterborne. Contrary to first thought, the engines are used *ahead*, otherwise the ship will become rebanked.

If scouring a channel to seaward, the tug is secured to the ship using a hawser made fast close up to the tug's pivoting point. The tug is also anchored to a single anchor leading ahead. As her engines are worked ahead she is slowly hove towards the stranded ship while veering her own cable, slewing her stern from side to side to widen the channel, and buoying and sounding the channel she is making.

Scouring is restricted to certain types of sea-bed—sand, shingle, and mud. Stiff clay is unsuitable. A rocky bottom may well be covered with a thin layer of loose silt, giving a false impression that scouring is possible.

As a matter of interest, the principle of scouring was first used in 1891 in Port Said, when a ship's engineers assembled a battery of pipes, lowered them overside until they were immersed in the banking around the hull, and pumped water at high pressure through them, the pipes being perforated. The silting was loosened and the ship hauled herself clear.

USE OF LIGHTERS—DISCHARGING CARGO

The discharge of cargo into lighters is very expensive and will delay refloating operations considerably. Further, there is the additional expense of arranging for the transhipment of the cargo, and in the case of perishables there may not be a suitable vessel available for some time. The problem of cold storage then arises. For obvious reasons, all other refloating methods should be attempted first. In the case of a tanker, however, it may be possible to quickly discharge cargo into other vessels, if available. Hoses and jackstays will be used in a similar manner to refuelling at sea. Whether the relief vessels are of large capacity or small, shallow-draught coastal tankers, their loaded draughts must be considered when their approach is made, i.e. they must be able to get to seaward when loaded.

ACTION ON STRANDING

The immediate and correct reaction on grounding is to stop engines. The engineers should be informed immediately of the situation. This will enable them to change over to the high-injection valves for the supply of salt water to machinery. If this is not done with the minimum of delay quantities of silt and sand are liable to be drawn into the machinery. This silt will have been stirred up by the impact of the vessel, and if astern movements of the engines are used the risks become even greater. The matter should never be overlooked, otherwise machinery will have to be stripped down and cleaned. Excessive astern movements may result in the ship becoming banked up by sand and silt. In tidal waters it is therefore better to confine astern movements to high-water times when refloating may be possible.

Generally, the most serious situation arises when a vessel strands at high water in an exposed position. Other dangerous situations are stranding at high water on a ledge with the other end of the ship in deep water, and on a midships bank at high water with both ends of the vessel in deep water. In both the latter cases the vessel is liable to become fractured as the tide runs out. In all cases of stranding the use of distress signals should be considered, both radio and visual. The owners and Lloyd's Agent should be informed as soon as possible. The owners are then in a position to get in touch with the Salvage Association, who are ready to assist and advise.

On a falling tide there is very little that can be done except to have everything ready and all possible assistance available at the next high water. One of the first things which should be done in most cases is to secure the vessel, e.g. with ground-tackle, so that she does not drive farther aground in heavy weather, remains *quiet* in a surf, and if initially end-on to the sea, does not become broadside on to it. A vessel which is stranded broadside on to the sea, i.e. aground along one side, cannot usually use her engines. In any case they may be of little use.

The vessel must be thoroughly inspected for damage, tanks and bilges being sounded round immediately and regularly thereafter. Damage causing flooding will have to be dealt with as described in Chapter VII.

As soon as a vessel strands and refuses to move off using her engines alone, a series of questions will have to be considered:

(1) *Are we in tidal waters?* If not, secure the ship with ground-tackle. Summon assistance if necessary.

171

(2) *What is the extent of the damage, if any?* If the damage is very severe and foundering is likely to occur on refloating it will be advisable to secure the ship and wait for the arrival of skilled salvage operators. If in tidal waters,

(3) *What is the state of the tide?* If rising, the problem is likely to be solved shortly. If falling, and there is the danger of fracture, make distress calls and lower boats. There is no point in using astern movements. Try to secure the ship with ground-tackle.

(4) *What is the tidal range?* Check the draught of the ship and compare it with the estimated draught prior to impact. The difference in cm multiplied by the tonnes per cm immersion indicates the amount of lost buoyancy. The tidal range may provide this required buoyancy at high water or even before. On the other hand, the tidal range may be almost negligible.

(5) *What can be discharged?* Water tanks may be discharged in order to provide the required buoyancy. If this action supplies only a part of the buoyancy the tidal range may produce the remainder. In a vessel having many lifeboats the lowering and floating of them should be considered. This will reduce the displacement of the ship to some beneficial extent. The discharging of oil fuel is a serious matter—it may severely hamper the laying of ground-tackle (using the ship's boats), and should normally be done only to save life. A vessel which is aground at one end and is being held by the suction of sand or silt should pump out water compartments (or discharge cargo if this is being done) from her *buoyant* end. This not only tends to break the suction at the other end, but also causes a smaller area of the wide, flat part of the bottom plating to be in contact with the sea-bed. This will enable the vessel to slide more easily when refloating. A ship end-fast on a ledge with her other end in deep water should try this. She may then slide clear under engine movements. On the other hand, ships end-fast on a rocky ledge have, from time to time, reversed the procedure, deepened their buoyant-end draughts and slid off without engine movements! The nature of the sea-bed must be taken into consideration on this point.

(6) *When are the next spring tides?* These will provide the best possible times for refloating if normal high waters give insufficient buoyancy. Unfortunately, excessively low waters also occur.

(7) *What is the nature of the bottom?* Ideally, a survey should be made of the surrounding sea-bed, noting depths and material. The sea-bed formation in some localities changes with every tide, making initial surveys unreliable. Some beaches are subject to strong cross-currents and scouring by surf. A survey will indicate the best possible direction for refloating.

172

If the bottom is rocky and the vessel is *lively*, i.e. she is moving persistently, it may be advisable to flood some compartments causing her to settle more deeply and become quieter. This matter should be considered also when the vessel is pounding on the beach under the action of surf, swell, or heavy weather. Although this action may set up the bottom plating, it is likely to prevent excessive tearing of the plates.

(8) *What is the legal situation?* The owners and Lloyd's Agent should be informed as soon as possible. The underwriters will then be notified. At the next port of call protest should be noted, and a survey of the hull and machinery carried out. A Certificate of Seaworthiness should be obtained before proceeding. The Department of Trade (D.o.T.) should be informed of the stranding as soon as possible. Full entries must be made in the Deck and Official Logbooks. General Average will have to be declared when discharging cargo.

The above questions are not to be taken as being in any specific order. Each is a separate matter, but the wise seaman will consider them all.

When a vessel is stranded along one side her engines are of little value in refloating her. Ground-tackle will have to be employed with or without towing assistance. Her seaward side must be surveyed to decide which end of her is to be slewed clear. Generally, she will be deeper aft, and the bow is chosen from which to lead the gear. The stern may require an anchor and hawser leading seaward, in order to prevent the after end from driving farther ashore as she is eventually slewed. Banking-up may be occurring all along the seaward side, calling for scouring craft. Fig. 8.7 shows a method whereby ground-tackle may be rigged for such a ship. She will need a considerable length of hawser on her ground-tackle, since if she were, for example, 150 m in length, by the time 500 ft she has pivoted on her stern a 200-m wire will leave little scope for 100-fathom further heaving. If the amount of wire available is not sufficient, then some chain-cable will have to be used, as shown in the figure. This will in any case be beneficial, because its weight will assist the applied stress to remain parallel to the anchor shank.

When carrying out a bower anchor with, say, a shackle of chain- 15 fathoms cable in addition to the heavy wire, great care will have to be used when paying out the cable from the boats. A good method is to stop it around the outside of the boats and cast off these stops when necessary. Cable hooks could be carried in the boats if desired. A shackle of 62-mm stud 2½-in cable will weigh roughly 2¼ tonnes, causing a sinkage of 5 cm in each 2¼-in boat ($D^2/50$ kg per m.)

The wire hawser in Fig. 8.7 is rove through a Panama Canal fairlead

173

and the purchase is fast to a heavy wire strop passed around a hatch coaming. The purchase should be anchored as far away from the fairlead as possible in order to avoid frequent overhauling, and therefore No. 2 coaming will be preferable to No. 1 coaming—depending, of course, upon the length of the purchase fall. The coaming corners are padded with timber to prevent cutting and chafing of the strop. Stoppers are anchored to the windlass or winch beds. The heavy wire hawser is sometimes buoyed along its length at frequent intervals, so that if it should part the ends may be quickly recovered.

A vessel stranded end-fast does not necessarily require such a great length of hawser, though in general it should always be as long as possible. Fig. 8.8 shows a suggested rig for such a ship. The purchases are anchored to a single strop, joining their standing blocks and passing around the padded No. 4 hatch coaming. Stoppers are again anchored to winch beds.

The above two examples are included as a guide only. The ways in which a ship may strand are numerous and cannot be dealt with individually in this chapter. The reader, however, should now have sufficient knowledge to devise a good hauling-rig for all cases.

As far as the gear used is concerned, the seaman has all too little choice. He will probably have only one really heavy wire (say 50 mm), and this may be in two parts. Its total length may be roughly 250 m. The warping power of his winches is also fixed, and he therefore has to select a purchase suitable for the wire and the winch. If he has no heavy purchases he will have to construct one by strapping together several single blocks of appropriate size.

As an example, suppose he has a winch with a warping power of 3 tonnes and a 45-mm heavy wire. The wire has a calculated safe working load of 15 tonnes. For his fall, he needs a wire having a safe working load in excess of the winch power, say a 25-mm wire with a safe working load of 4½ tonnes. If he reeves this wire fall in a three-fold purchase used to advantage his purchase will heave with a stress of roughly 13 tonnes, which is suitable for the heavy wire. His purchase blocks should have safe working loads of 15–20 tonnes.

If his big wire is 35-mm in circumference it will have a safe working load of 10 tonnes. Used with the same winch, a smaller purchase is necessary, e.g. a two-fold or double luff tackle rove with 20-mm wire as a fall. This wire has a safe working load of 3⅛ tonnes and is suitable for the winch. Used to advantage on this winch, the purchase will create a stress of roughly 10 tonnes, which suits the wire hawser. This purchase should have 15-tonne safe working load blocks. Such a purchase would be the guy of a 60-tonne heavy derrick.

The seaman changes his purchase out of respect for the safe working load of his main hawser. If he chooses to exceed the safe working load

174

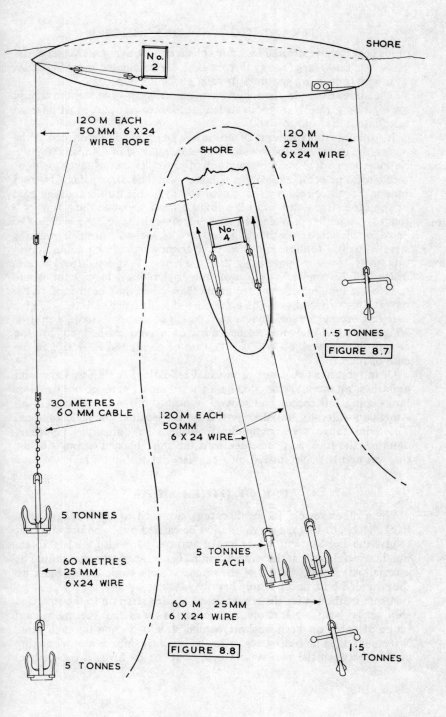

SHORE

No. 2

120 M EACH
50 MM 6 X 24
WIRE ROPE

120 M
25 MM
6 X 24 WIRE

SHORE

No. 4

30 METRES
60 MM CABLE

120 M EACH
50 MM
6 X 24 WIRE

1·5 TONNES

FIGURE 8.7

5 TONNES

5 TONNES
EACH

60 METRES
25 MM
6 X 24 WIRE

60 M 25MM
6 X 24 WIRE

FIGURE 8.8

1·5
TONNES

5 TONNES

of his gear it may part and lessen his chances of heaving the vessel clear. However, fairly large safety factors exist, the calculated breaking stress of a wire rope being six times its safe working load.

The above example, then, illustrates basically how the seaman should arrange his gear. Throughout its length the weakest part must have an adequate safe working load.

In the unfortunate event of no power being available on board the vessel, the use of man-power should not be ignored or dismissed lightly. Suppose we wish to maintain our pull of 13 tonnes on the hawser with no mechanical power available, i.e. winches, windlass, or capstan. If we set up another three-fold purchase used to advantage on the hauling part of the other, then this second purchase must produce the stress of 3 tonnes originally provided by the warping drum of the winch. To provide this stress, the hauling part of the second purchase must be stressed to 0·7 tonnes. Ten men of average weight 70 kg could supply this stress; if five men are used, then the hawser is stressed to $6\frac{1}{2}$ tonnes instead of 13 tonnes. The use of four-fold blocks throughout would reduce the number of men required. Man-power has been used in the past in this way and proved successful—if a little exhausting.

It has been estimated that a ship which is stranded needs a pull of 30% of her lost buoyancy to heave her off a sand sea-bed, 50% in the case of hard gravel, 60–80% in the case of coral, and 80–150% in the case of rock.

Of interest are two cases of unusual refloating. A ship was aground amidships on sand. She flooded her forward tanks, pumped out her after tanks, rang full speed, and moved smoothly off. Another vessel—an American—literally impaled herself on an isolated pinnacle of rock. The tidal range was negligible. Consider the difficulties! Nothing daunted, the rock was cemented into the ship, blasted through below the keel and the ship moved off—heavier, but without a leak.

USE OF OTHER SHIPS

When other vessels, larger than tugs, are used to heave a ship off a bank, beach, or ledge, a survey should be carried out as before, in order to give the assisting ship a safe line of approach and also the best direction in which to refloat the stranded ship. The sea-bed material should be ascertained; if soft, the use of the rescue vessel's engines may bank up the stranded hull, and possibly her own as well.

A safe method is for the rescue vessel to turn stern on to the stranded ship, let go both her anchors, and move slowly astern, veering a good scope of cable on both anchors, which should lie fine on each bow. Wires may then be passed across to the beached ship, either by making contact between the two vessels with boats or by firing a rocket line.

The wires are hove taut, made well secure, and the rescue vessel then begins heaving into short stay. The beached vessel may have to heave on her own ground-tackle as well. Should she not have any rigged and there is the possibility of her refloating with a rush—something which is the exception rather than the rule—then the towing wires must be capable of being instantly slipped. When making the towing wires fast around bitts a turn should be taken around the bollard nearest the fair-lead before belaying the wire. This avoids an undue stress on the farther bollard which might cause the bitts to lift from the deck.

A vessel of D.W. 10000 tonnes fitted with 70-mm special steel cable and an electric windlass of 48 kW power can, when heaving, exert a maximum stress of 29 tonnes on each cable, and therefore it is preferable to pass the towing hawsers around hatch coamings or deck houses (well padded with timber) rather than bitts. In the case of a ship stranded broadside-on, the towing wire was passed up one hawse pipe, down the other, round again, and finally shackled to its own part. This proved a secure arrangement. Again, the wire could be shackled to a stranded ship's cable if she were similarly beached.

If the assisting ship decides to use her engine power alone her Master must decide whether to tow from forward or from aft. If the beach shoals rapidly and is rocky it will be unwise to move in stern first for fear of damaging propellers and rudder. The ship should therefore approach the stranded ship bow-on, pass the towing wire or wires, and then use her astern power. There are two main advantages in that the Master has an excellent view of the towing hawser from the bridge and the ship is more easily kept in position while an onshore wind is blowing. The disadvantage is that stern power used over a soft bottom will probably lead to banking up and choking of machinery. The advantage of towing from aft, on the other hand, is that the ship will generally have a greater ahead thrust from her propeller than when reversed.

BEACHING

This does not form an entirely new section of this chapter, since everything which has already been discussed will be applicable when it comes to refloating the ship.

If a ship is in imminent danger of foundering any type of beach is welcome. Assuming the ideal, i.e. a certain amount of preparatory time and a choice of beach, the best type is one which has a firm surface, is free from rocks, has a gentle slope, is free from strong currents and scouring, is not subject to heavy surf, and is not too exposed to bad weather. Fortunate indeed is the seaman who can find such a beach at the right time. Tidal range is another factor; there should ideally be *some* so that overside or bottom damage can be repaired at low-water times without the aid of divers.

177

When beaching it is again ideal to do so at high water or on a falling tide so that the ship settles slowly, rather than to drive her hard ashore and strain the bottom plating. Further, it is possible to some extent to control the degree to which she is beached, by discreet use of the engines before her keel closes with the sea-bed. There is, of course, the danger of banking up and also drawing sand into the machinery, so much will depend upon the nature of the bottom.

A damaged ship losing buoyancy rapidly, if beached, may well be able to refloat at a later high water after repairs have been done, compartments pumped dry, and her buoyancy restored.

If beaching bow-on with a trim by the stern, a beach with a slope steeper than that of her keel will enable her stern to be kept buoyant

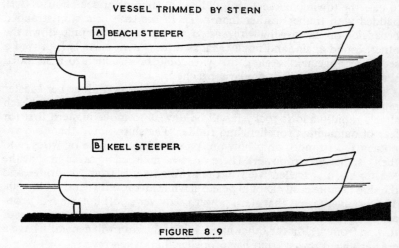

VESSEL TRIMMED BY STERN

A BEACH STEEPER

B KEEL STEEPER

FIGURE 8.9

while her fore end is grounded. Fig. 8.9 (*a*) shows this condition. If her keel has the steeper slope, then her stern will touch first, as shown in Fig. 8.9 (*b*). Trimmed by the head, she will, whatever the slope of the beach, take the ground forward. Similarly, if she beaches stern-on with a trim by the stern she will touch initially aft. If beaching stern-on with a trim by the head, then again the beach should have a steeper slope than the keel.

A vessel may be beached bow-on or stern-on. Whichever method is chosen, ground-tackle should be rigged to keep her seaward end steady, and to stop her from driving farther ashore. Equally, she should be secured to the shore to prevent her coming off unexpectedly. If beached stern-on she has the advantage of presenting her stronger, finer end to the forces of onshore sea and weather. Further, her anchors are ready for easy laying and later heaving; they can be carried out direct from

178

the hawse pipes and stressed by the windlass. In fact, her anchors and cables could well be laid out while making her approach to the beach. Provided the beach is firm and free from rocks, the propellers and rudder will be unharmed, but her impact, of course, must be as gentle as possible.

If beached bow-on her vulnerable, more buoyant, end is exposed to sea and weather. To keep the stern quiet, ground-tackle must be laid out from aft. This is laborious when done after beaching, but the vessel could well be anchored from aft as she makes her approach (see Chapter I).

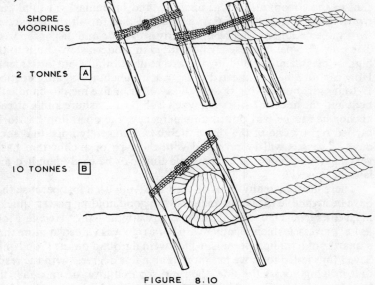

SHORE
MOORINGS

2 TONNES A

10 TONNES B

FIGURE 8.10

The seaman has a natural instinct by which he strongly avoids allowing his propeller and rudder to come into close proximity with objects such as wharves, piers, and other vessels. The suggestion that he should beach stern-on may well disgust him, but on close consideration the advantages are many.

Fig. 8.10 shows two methods whereby a vessel may secure her headlines to the shore to prevent unexpected refloating or being driven off shore by a gale.

The stakes may be of metal. If wooden, a timber having a natural elasticity is preferable, e.g. lifeboat oars made of ash. They should be driven to a depth of at least 1 m and at an angle of 20 degrees to the vertical. Fig. 8.10 (a) shows a combination of stakes suitable for a stress of up to 2 tonnes. Fig. 8.10 (b) shows a heavy spar (a light derrick would

3 ft

tons

179

be ideal) secured between pairs of stakes along its length. The stakes on
the seaward side must be exactly in line so that each bears a proportion
tons   of the stress, which can be up to 10 tonnes.

In closing this chapter I am including extracts from a discussion held
at the Institute of Naval Architects in 1950. This took place as the result
of a technical paper submitted by Mr. H. L. Dove, M.I.N.A., on model
anchor tests. I believe that the points made below will be of particular
practical importance to the serving Officer.

'Reference has been made by a previous speaker, Captain Thomson, to the stream and kedge anchors, and his remarks, I think, are
worthy of the closest attention. He stated that for all their practical
worth, they might as well be thrown over the side and dispensed with.
The present types of these anchors fitted in modern ships, built to the
highest classification of Lloyd's, are really nothing but ornaments.
How can anyone be expected to lay out an anchor weighing possibly
tons $1\frac{1}{2}$ tonnes from a rowing boat with say, four or five men to handle the
boat and the anchor? After all, when a ship runs ashore and a stream
anchor has to be laid out in an emergency, the operation has to be
carried out by one of the ship's lifeboats. I sincerely hope that some
day . . . vessels will be provided with the type of anchor that has a
very high efficiency and at the same time can be easily handled and
laid out quickly.

'There must be many cases of vessels having been lost because they
have been unable to lay out anchors with good holding power, quickly
in an emergency. Quoting one case as an example—the "Helena Modjeska", a vessel which together with her cargo was valued at more than
a quarter of a million pounds, which went aground on the Goodwins.
Seven tugs failed to move her more than a few degrees, with the result
that in lying across the tide, the sand scoured away from under the
bow and stern, after which she broke her back. I am assured by
friends at the Admiralty that half a dozen small but efficient anchors
tons   of a weight measured not in tonnes, but in kilogrammes would have
hundredweights   had far more effect than the seven tugs, and this vessel, being able to
maintain steam to all her cargo winches, could probably have hauled
herself off within a few hours.

'There is also another good example of the four-masted barque
"Archibald Russell". This vessel, laden with grain, was completing a
trip from Australia to Ipswich, and when entering Harwich harbour
in tow, with a south-east breeze and light ground swell, suddenly
took a very broad sheer and went ashore on Landguard Spit. Tugs
failed to move her, and it was evident that she was pretty well hard
and fast. Fortunately however, one of the Trinity House vessels, the
"Alert", under the command of Captain Guy Jarrett, happened to be

in the vicinity, and Captain Jarrett, quickly weighing up the position, laid out his two bower anchors to the extreme length of the cables, connected up his heavy towing hawser, and literally launched the "Archibald Russell" *which came off so quickly that she ran past the* "Alert", *which had to cut her towropes.*

'So long as vessels run the risk of grounding due to fog, or other causes, so will it be necessary to provide them with anchors with the highest possible holding power, but of the lowest weight for easy handling, and irrespective of whether or not they bury too deeply for subsequent lifting. It would be far better to lose two or three light-weight anchors . . . if there were any possible chance of saving a vessel and her cargo, than to have on board heavy kedge or stream anchors with very low efficiencies . . . but which, due to their weight could not, in any case, be laid out quickly in an emergency.

'. . . it would seem a matter of the utmost importance and the responsibility of the Classification Societies to see that ships in these modern times are sent to sea with stream and kedge anchors which are really efficient and designed primarily for use in an emergency' (Mr. S. T. Cope, ex-Principal Mooring Officer to the Air Ministry).

'In commercial vessels, particularly oil tankers, there is little suitable equipment for handling these anchors (present type stream and kedge) quickly and effectively in the case of an emergency.

'Unlike bower anchors, these types would only be required, we trust, on very rare occasions, and any extension of the experimental work on modified and possibly lighter types of kedge and stream anchors with suitable holding power would be warmly welcomed by officers serving in these vessels' (Mr. A. F. Walker, then A.I.N.A.).

It is ironical that soon after this interesting discussion took place, new British ships were no longer required to carry anything more than three heavy bower anchors. An additional requirement of two light anchors with great holding power, such as the A.C.14 or the Stokes–Danforth, would, I am sure, be welcomed by most Masters.

CHAPTER IX

EMERGENCIES

ABANDONING SHIP

IF all efforts to save a damaged vessel prove to be unsuccessful she
will be abandoned. This must be carried out in as orderly a manner
as possible, maintaining complete discipline, silence, strict adherence
to orders, and immediately controlling any evidence of panic or in-
subordination, using *force* if necessary. All members of the crew and
passengers will be required to exercise self-control, courage, and un-
selfishness. Failure to observe all these factors may result in unnecessary
loss of life. Public address systems should be fully utilised.

In all probability, the last persons to abandon the vessel will be those
engaged in last-minute damage control. When they leave their posts all
machinery should be stopped and watertight doors and hatches tightly
closed. On passenger ships, officers should be identifiable.

Boats should be lowered with as many people aboard as possible, and
should then quickly clear the ship's side and lie off ready to embark the
remaining complement from the water. This will avoid a dangerous
waiting period alongside the ship, during which the boat is liable to be
damaged and foul her falls.

Except in rough weather, the boats should secure themselves together
in groups, each group being towed well clear of the wreck area by a
power-driven boat. As soon as this is achieved, one or more of these
power craft should cruise the area to pick up swimming survivors. If
unable to carry any more persons the craft can provide the swimmers
with floating wreckage so that they can support themselves until such
time as the other boats can embark them. Swimmers should group themselves together and support each other. The group is then more easily
detected than individuals.

When leaving a ship directly into the water it is preferable to jump in
feet-first rather than to dive. When wearing a life-jacket, the height
from which the leap is made should be kept to a maximum of about
6 m, otherwise the impact of the jacket on the water is likely to cause
stunning or a broken neck. If a leap is unavoidable from a greater
height the arms should be crossed over the chest with the hands clamped
tightly down on the shoulders to keep the jacket in place. At all times

20ft.

182

the best method of entering the water is to lower oneself on a line or ladder.

In a strong wind it is preferable to leap from the weather side rather than the lee side, since in the latter case the rate of drift may well prevent the swimmer from getting clear and he may be overcome by the ship. On the weather side there are two possible hazards: the man may be hurled back against the ship by the sea, or he may find fuel oil extending well upwind. In such a case he has two alternative methods for negotiating the oil: He can swim underwater, surfacing now and then for air, but when he does so, he must spring from the water with his eyes tightly shut and use a rapid breast-stroke motion to thrust the oil away from his face. The second method entails swimming quickly through the oil on the surface with a rapid breast-stroke motion, the head being held high with the mouth closed. In the case of burning oil the former method is the only practical one. When about to commence such an underwater swim heavy clothing should be discarded, since it will remain buoyant for at least a quarter of an hour. A life-jacket should be similarly discarded.

A swimmer must move away from the ship as quickly as possible, since when it founders there is violent local suction, together with the surfacing, with great force, of air and wreckage.

When a ship is listed it is preferable to leap from the ends. If it is made from the high side the man is likely to strike underwater projections or the hull plating, while on the low side the man may be struck by masts, funnels, ventilators, or samson posts, etc., if the vessel capsizes before he is clear.

Procedure within the Boats; Preservation of Crew and Passengers

The importance of previous training cannot be too strongly emphasised, since this is a direct factor in reducing fear and shock. Even in the case of passengers, their regular attendance at previous boat drills will have given them a certain amount of confidence and familiarity which will materially assist in reducing panic. The passengers should not be mustered in such a way as to regard boat drill as an amusing weekly or fortnightly show. Their active participation will be of value to both themselves and the crew.

Occasionally in port, the crew should lower boats and pull clear of the ship. The same operation performed at an anchorage during a slight swell or moderate sea will do much to impress upon all concerned the difficulties of clearing a vessel in heavy weather. At boat drills a brief word on first aid, use and maintenance of lifeboat stores, and conduct in an open boat is most advisable, but regrettably rarely practised.

Ideally, a man should abandon ship dressed in warm clothing covered with oilskins and wearing boots or shoes. The clothing will not only keep him warm and dry but also provide protection against the sun's rays. His inner pockets should contain a change of underclothing and some spare pairs of socks. Clothing has the additional advantage of providing at least a quarter of an hour's buoyancy in the water. When space and time is available plenty of spare blankets should be stowed within the boat.

The officer in charge of the boat must be sympathetically strict, optimistic, cheerful, and confident. He should be provided, if possible, with a sextant, a watch set to G.M.T., a nautical almanac, details of the wreck's position, proximity of shipping lanes and land, and whether or not a distress call was transmitted and acknowledged. Each boat should preferably have a second officer to assist, and at least two able seamen.

If a call was sent out before the vessel was abandoned it is quite possible that it was received and not acknowledged before the wreck's operator closed down his equipment. For this reason, the survivors should at all times hope for rescue. If the call was acknowledged it will be unwise for the boats to move far from the area, but if no acknowledgement was received the near proximity of a coast may make a voyage in the boats a more attractive proposition than remaining stationary in the wreck area.

The officer in charge should arrange a daily routine within the boat, awarding each person a specific duty, however small, making sure that the work is carried out. He will take charge of distress signals to make sure that they are not used indiscriminately, all the rations, and all weapons potential or otherwise, including boat axes and spare crutches. The daily ration of food and water must be issued punctually to avoid grumbling and irritability, and each portion should be presented openly in full view of all hands so as to avoid bickering. Ideally, each person should have his own drinking vessel, however crude. The crew should be divided into three groups, one at each end with an officer, and the other amidships together with the ill and wounded. As soon as possible, the boat's stores and equipment should be checked and a logbook commenced.

If swimmers are found they should be hauled aboard (over the bows or quarters) only if it will not endanger the safety of the boat and the persons on board. Bodies should be stripped of clothing, putting personal effects aside, and the garments distributed among the boat's complement, particularly the ill and wounded. All useful flotsam should be recovered from the area, particularly pieces of canvas and tarpaulins, provided there is room available.

The boat should be kept dry and baled. Life-jackets may be removed if there is no danger of capsizing and used as cushions, or pillows for the helpless, to prevent sores and chafe. In hot weather it is most essential to keep cool. This is best achieved by rigging the protective cover across the gunwales with a current of air below it and keeping clothing damp all day. Bathing should not be allowed, because it consumes bodily energy. In the late afternoon clothing should be dried out ready for the cool night.

Duties should be kept to a minimum, and in this way, observing all these points, perspiring will be kept low. The head, eyes, mouth, nose, and neck must be kept shaded from the sun's rays—this applies particularly to those who are unable to shelter beneath the screen by virtue of their lookout or steering duties.

In cold weather a sail or tarpaulin should be similarly rigged to keep out rain, wind, and sea. All persons should huddle together for warmth and avoid removing wet clothing, as this action will induce frostbite and exposure. The arms, legs, feet, and hands should be exercised regularly to keep the circulation strong. The hands should be kept within the crutch, or thrust under the arms. To avoid frostbite to feet, the persons should be arranged in such a way that each one can place his feet on the bare abdomen of a neighbour within the latter's clothing.

The adult body normally contains about 45 litres of water. A man will lose 5 litres every 24 hours when resting in a temperature of 35°C. The maximum permissible loss before severe dehydration occurs is about 11 litres.   10 gal   1·1 gal   2·5 gal

Sea water must not be drunk. During World War Two, the mortality rate in lifeboats where salt water was drunk ranged between 700% and 800% higher than in boats where only fresh water was used.

Rain must be caught whenever possible in all available containers, such as tarpaulins, sails, and tins. They should be washed overside first to remove encrusted salt. Clothing can be spread out and later wrung into a container.

It is a good plan to organise sing-songs, story-telling, and reminiscences in order to keep up morale. Smoking is a great comfort, but it may tend to aggravate a thirst.

The food within a boat, biscuits, milk, and barley sugar or boiled sweets, is extremely nutritious and easily digested. It has a high content of fat, starch, and sugar, protein being avoided, since its digestion entails consumption of body water. For this reason, the stores should never be augmented with meat, fish, eggs, butter, or cheese, nor should fish or birds be eaten at sea, unless there is ample water available.

Water is given priority of boat space, because a man can exist without food for a month and longer, provided he is given sufficient water. Food, however, does provide energy, warmth, and helps to maintain good circulation of the blood. Generally, it is better to award a full daily ration rather than to reduce it so that the supplies last longer. A man should ideally have about 850 millilitres of water per day, with a minimum of about 425 millilitres. About 112 grammes of each food   1·5 pints   0·75 pint   3·5 oz

185

1·75 oz are desirable each day, with a minimum of 50 grammes of each per day. The minimum quantities quoted are those necessary to sustain life. Water should not be issued on the first day except to the ill or injured.

Seasickness wastes body water, and should be avoided if possible. Where a medical remedy is available, all persons must take it. It is essential to combat seasickness within the first two or three days.

A record should be kept of daily rations and existing supplies. All food should be eaten slowly and water kept in the mouth for as long as possible, finally gargling with it prior to swallowing.

As soon as possible after taking to the boats, the lifeboat radio transmitter should be used, if available. This should quickly guide rescue ships and aircraft to the scene of the wreck. If remaining within the area the sea anchor should be streamed in order to keep the boat head to sea and lessen her lee drift. If the seas are too heavy for this to be possible the boat should be run very slowly before the wind under her jibsail alone, streaming the sea anchor astern. In both cases the oil bag should be used. The effect may be augmented by pouring oil into punctured tins slung over the bows or quarters.

If the boat is to proceed to land she should be sailed on as comfortable a course as possible, bearing in mind that when close-hauled she is likely to ship plenty of water. The shortest distance may not necessarily be the most comfortable, and the health and well-being of the crew is of paramount importance. The boat will generally sail most comfortably with the wind aft or on the quarter. Should the wind fall light, the sails must be left hoisted, since they will be conspicuous to searchers. Oars should be used only to clear the ship, a danger, or to navigate into the path of a shower, and of course to land on a beach. Their use for voyaging is unwise, because the small distance made good is offset by the loss of energy from the oarsmen. In very cold weather, provided the crew is in good shape, their occasional use will do much to exercise the limbs. The sails will probably prove to be the most valuable parts of the boat's equipment, and should preferably be used for no other purpose, treating them with the utmost care. The boat cover, carried if space permits, will prove invaluable as an awning and rain collector.

A regular watch should be set, each having two helmsmen, one to support the other in case of weariness. If sharks or similar fish are in the area and come close to the boat they should not be annoyed, neither should blood nor raw meat be dumped overside in their vicinity.

A power-driven boat, as has already been mentioned, is used to tow the other craft clear of the wreckage and should remain with them at all times because its services will have to be returned when the fuel supply is exhausted, the boat having no mast or sails.

A good indication of the proximity of land is afforded by low-lying, stationary cloud in a clear sky, this being convectional or orographic cloud. The flight-direction of birds in the early evening is also a good indication of the bearing of the land.

The Recovery of Survivors

The rescue ship should bring the survivors aboard by any or several of the following methods:

(1) By hoisting the survivors' boats aboard together with their crews, using derricks. This is only possible if the boats are not too heavy and suitable lifting gear is available.

(2) Alternatively to (1), by lowering the vessel's own boats, transferring the survivors into these, and hoisting them inboard.

(3) Scrambling (cargo) nets and ladders may be rigged overside, and the survivors can climb these.

(4) In (3) the men may not have sufficient energy, and they must then be hoisted aboard in canvas slings, bosun's chairs, cargo baskets, or by means of whips rove through blocks on davit heads. It should be noted that in sea water of about 5°C a man can survive for about $\frac{1}{2}$–2 hours depending upon his fitness and build. To preserve heat, he should not swim or take off clothes, except to fill them with air. In freezing water, the fingers become frozen in about 4 minutes, consciousness is lost after about 7 minutes and death generally occurs within 20 minutes. These time intervals are all taken from the initial instant of immersion.

(5) A floating stretcher capable of being hoisted is useful for bringing injured men aboard.

(6) A cargo net can be slung overside between davits, with its lower end partly submerged. The davits are swung out and whips, passing through blocks attached to the davit heads, are secured to the lower cringles of the net. Swimming survivors can then manœuvre themselves across the submerged net and the whips are then used to heave the net, together with the men, up the ship's side. This is called *parbuckling*.

(7) Survivors in the water cannot necessarily be rescued together, and to make the waiting period more comfortable, the log boom or a derrick should be swung overside in the horizontal position having a net attached to it. The net must be partly submerged. The survivors can then cling to this net and await their turn.

(8) An isolated swimmer can be recovered by the use of line-throwing rockets. This is more fully discussed in Chapter VI.

(9) Inflatable rubber life-rafts may be dropped by aircraft or by ships which, for any reason, are unable to afford immediate rescue.

187

2-3-in 100 fathoms

(10) To pick up survivors in the water who are grouped together, a very long length of, say, 25-mm rope—up to 200 m—may be streamed by the rescue vessel. The last few metres should have several life-jackets attached to it, and the end should ideally be secured to a rubber life-raft, however small.

In the absence of such a raft, two or three life-buoys will be sufficient, in addition to the life-jackets. The ship is then headed across the wind, i.e. with the wind on the bow, making a wide turn while streaming the line. As the turn downwind is completed, the headway is checked and eventually the ship will come abreast of the survivors, making about 1 knot only, and with the line fully streamed abeam, across the wind and with the buoyant end close to the men in the water. The ship will now be heading downwind. Once the men are safely clinging to the jackets, the line may be hove-in, taking care not to use the propellers.

The recovery of survivors must be carried out well clear of propellers and overside discharges. At night searchlights, signalling lamps, and perhaps blue pyrotechnic flares may be used to augment the available lighting.

As soon as the persons are safely aboard they must be given first aid, a change of clothing, and warmth. Fuel oil is not particularly harmful to the skin, and is generally the least of a survivor's worries. It can be cleaned off with a detergent, but this treatment should not be used over burns, sores, or other wounds. A good drink will be the initial requirement of a survivor, and should be non-alcoholic. Both food and drink should be taken as slowly as possible, the food being light and readily digested. Exposure victims should be placed in boiler rooms, bathrooms having steam injection, or warm baths. Rapid heating may cause pain and injury. Frostbite should be thawed out in cold water, avoiding any type of massage. Future warming of the affected part must be very gradual, and re-cooling may be necessary for a while to reduce pain.

The officer or person in charge of the survivors must, as soon as possible, inform the owners of the wrecked vessel so that arrangements may be made for repatriating the crew and forwarding passengers to the original destination. On a British ship, the Department of Trade must be given a report of the accident. In all cases of wreck it is of great importance to salvage the Official and Deck Logbooks before final abandonment.

Rescuing the Crew and Passengers of a Disabled Ship at Sea

This operation depends upon several factors, namely the condition of wind and sea, the ability of the seamen to handle small boats, the urgency of required assistance, and whether any help is available from the persons on board the distressed vessel. From the commencement of the rescue it is important for the Master of the wreck to allow himself to be directed by the rescuing Master, since this will avoid unnecessary hesitation and confusion. Communication should be established by radio, code flags, or by signalling lamp, and both Masters fully acquainted with the conditions and system of rescue.

If boats are to be used the rescue vessel should cruise the area to ascertain whether there is heavy wreckage and flotsam about which will hamper and endanger boatwork. The rescue vessel should, ideally, manœuvre into the wake of the drifting wreck and stop her engines. It is then an easy matter to determine the relative drift of the two vessels.

If the rescue vessel arrives during the hours of darkness the Master of the wreck should endeavour to hold on until daylight. If, however, the weather is steadily deteriorating, such an action may be either impossible or unwise. Both vessels should spread low-viscosity oil freely. If the wreck is unable to do this the rescue vessel should steam around the area and spread copious oil in the form of a circular *slick* into which the wreck will drift.

The lifeboat selected for the rescue operation should have all gear removed which is irrelevant to the rescue procedure, and have it partially replaced with life-jackets and life-buoys. Oilbags filled with saturated oakum or cotton waste should be slung all around the gunwales.

Before lowering the boat (fully manned with the crew wearing life-jackets), the vessel should create as good a lee for it as possible, bringing the wind on the opposite bow. This action will also serve to reduce rolling, which is an adverse factor in the launching of a boat. Oil should be spread freely from both sides. The rescue vessel should at this stage be lying to windward of the wreck. Mattresses should be slung overside between the davits and secured at, and above the water-level in order to prevent the boat being stove-in during an adverse roll. A cargo net, also slung between the davits and trailing in the water, will be of great assistance to the crew if the boat should capsize alongside. The painter is rigged and kept tight throughout so as to keep the boat in position below the falls. The latter should be loosely frapped with lines, led to the deck and manned. These lines are then used to keep the falls and boat steady.

Just before the boat reaches the wave crests, the engine should be started and the plug checked. The fall-blocks are manned, and then in one rapid sequence the boat is launched, falls are released, the engine put into forward gear at full throttle, and the painter let go, using the tiller hard over towards the ship's side. Both lower fall-blocks must be released simultaneously, the men on board keeping the falls absolutely slack. If one block jams or cannot be released before the boat descends into a trough the engine must instantly be reversed to bring the boat under the davit heads again. Instead of the fast block heaving that end of the boat bodily out of the water, the weight of the boat will overhaul the fall because it is all slack on board. The crew must keep well down in order to avoid the suspended blocks as the boat clears the side. The operation is extremely tricky, and should preferably be carried out in absolute silence, with the officer in charge giving his orders clearly and concisely. If the vessel has very slight headway on at the time of launching the tight painter will enable the boat to take a very rapid sheer away from the side.

By now, a considerable slick will probably exist towards the wreck, and the boat may proceed downwind, spreading additional oil astern to prevent shipping seas in the sternsheets. The trim of the boat should be adjusted to suit the course relative to the sea. In a short sea the steering must be very competent, since the boat will tend to broach-to under the slightest provocation. If a big sea is approaching the temptation to take it on the bow should be resisted and the boat headed, as gently as possible, directly at it.

Generally, contact by boat with a wreck is to be avoided, but if it is inevitable the boat should on no account approach from the weather side of the wreck, where wave-battering will occur. Neither should she approach the lee side, where heavy wreckage will be accumulating and perhaps falling. Further, the drift of the wreck, which may be up to several knots, will usually prove to be a trap for the boat, and it will be extremely difficult to get clear. In addition to these problems, since the wreck will undoubtedly be lying with the wind and sea on the beam or slightly abaft it, she will be rolling, perhaps heavily.

Fig. 9.1 shows a wreck lying in four different positions relative to the wind, with her likely direction of drift in each case. The boat should approach at her lee end as shown for each position, for then trapping of the boat is unlikely.

The boat may secure to the wreck, end-on, by means of a line, ready to go astern at a moment's notice should signs of broaching-to appear. A man should stand by the line with an axe, ready to cut it adrift in such an emergency. Once fast, the survivors may lower themselves down the line to the boat as rapidly as possible.

To avoid actual contact with the wreck, the boat may lie off head to wind and sea, streaming oil, and will then pick up the survivors from the water. The rescued crew and passengers must unhesitatingly enter the water wearing life-jackets. Under these conditions, a life-buoy having two, strong, buoyant heaving lines attached can be useful for heaving persons from wreck to boat, one line being aboard each craft, the buoy being passed backwards and forwards.

Occasionally, it may be preferable to drop a boat downwind to the
3- or 4-in wreck on a 25–30-mm fibre hawser having only two or three men in

the boat. Plenty of spare line should be left in the boat so that its crew can control the boat to some extent should it suddenly become necessary to drop further downwind. A good method of signalling must be maintained between the boat and its parent ship. The boat is kept head to wind and sea by the hawser and steered with a steering oar. If the rescue ship is making a greater drift than the wreck she will have to use engines in order to maintain her distance. This calls for very efficient ship handling if the boat is not to be hampered.

Once the boat has been sent away to leeward, unless it is attached to

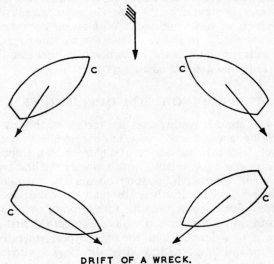

DRIFT OF A WRECK.
BOAT MAKES CONTACT
AT POSITION "C"

FIGURE 9.1

its parent ship the latter will steam to leeward of the wreck ready to pick up the boat again. This avoids any necessity for the boat having to make prolonged headway into the wind and sea.

When communication cannot be established by boat a raft may be towed across the line of drift of the wreck until the towline fouls that end of the wreck which would normally be approached by a boat. The survivors must then endeavour to get hold of the towline, and board the raft. For this purpose, an inflatable rubber life-raft is better than a decked, makeshift type, which will have a very small range of stability, and from aboard which survivors are easily washed off. A raft may be similarly dispatched after establishing communication by rocket-line.

191

Another method is for the rescue vessel to drift broadside on to the wreck (their fore-and-aft lines being parallel), but in such an attitude that they will pass clear and end-on. In this way, the ships may safely approach very closely for the purpose of establishing contact by line. If the rescue vessel is able to run slowly in the wake of the wreck the possibility of heaving survivors across on an endless whip should not be ignored.

Many other methods are possible, each depending upon the prevailing conditions. The above text applies equally well to vessels which are stranded. There is the advantage that one vessel is stationary, and therefore only the rate of drift of the rescue vessel need be considered. Boatwork is, however, hampered by the lack of water adjacent to the wreck and the proximity of rocks and reefs. With an onshore wind the boat should anchor to windward and veer down towards the wreck, maintaining a continuous sounding of the bottom with a boat lead-line. Again, the lee side should be avoided as an approach.

THE USE OF OIL FOR QUELLING SEAS

Oil floats and spreads readily over the surface of the sea. It reduces the crest-forming tendencies of waves, but has no effect upon a swell. It does, however, lessen the likelihood of a ship or boat shipping seas.

Low-viscosity animal, vegetable, or fish oils are the best types for this purpose. In their absence, lubricating oil may be used, but fuel oil should not be employed unless it is absolutely unavoidable. Petroleum is of very little value in preventing the formation of wave crests, but it may be used to thin a high-viscosity oil. Although the first-named oils are less harmful to swimmers than the other types, generally speaking, all oils used for quelling seas should be discharged with care and in 45 gal moderation. As a rough guide, it has been found that 200 litres of lubricating oil discharged slowly just above the level of the sea surface while steaming at slow revolutions has effectively reduced breaking 48 000 ft² seas over an area in excess of 4500 m². In terms of ship waterplanes, however, this is not as large an area as it would at first appear, for it amounts approximately to the area occupied by two vessels each of 500 ft 50 ft 150 m in length and 15 m abeam.

(In view of the deteriorating effect of oils upon the buoyancy of lifejackets, kapok is now required to be enclosed within sealed polyvinylchloride (P.V.C.) envelopes, and no other buoyancy materials are allowed to be used unless they are immune from this trouble.)

In cold weather oils should be warmed in order that their distribution may be made more easy, but it should be borne in mind that certain oils, including coconut oil and some fish oils, will congeal on the sea surface in low-temperature conditions, and they are then of no value.

The oil may be distributed in several ways as follows:

192

(1) By filling an old,.specially punctured hose with oil, sealing both ends, and trailing it overside in a position close to the horizontal in order to obtain as wide a coverage as possible.

(2) By filling large, punctured, and weighted canvas bags loosely with oakum, kapok, or cotton waste, filling the bags with oil, sealing, and trailing them overside.

(3) By placing a 5–10-litre tin filled with oil, and punctured at its base, into a wash-basin, bath, shower, or water-closet pan. The oil is then steadily flushed overside by means of water running through the soil-pipes. This method is most effective. In all cases the amount of puncturing of the oil container will regulate the flow. Often, the rate of flow desired is quite small, being in the region of 7 litres per hour.

1–2-gal

1½-gal

In (3) the tin may be sealed and trailed overside. When streaming oil from the bow under conditions of a head sea an oil bag is liable to be tossed well out of the water, and it should be heavily weighted. If forward soil-pipes are available they will provide a better means for distribution.

When running with the wind and sea astern or on the quarter, the oil should be streamed from right aft, the weather or *both* bows and the weather or *both* quarters. This provides protection from quarterly seas in the event of yawing.

When running with the wind and sea ahead, the oil is streamed from both bows, and when it is abeam, or when the vessel is hove-to or drifting, it is distributed from along most of the weather side, preferably at intervals of not more than 15 m. The vessel will make greater leeway than the oil, and the latter therefore appears to spread upwind, so providing protection from the right direction.

50 ft

When at anchor a block and endless whip is secured to the cable, the latter is veered and an oil bag hove out to the block and the water's edge, giving oil distribution from well ahead of the ship.

Oil may also be used to advantage when crossing a bar, manœuvring boats through surf (although the innermost surf will not be affected by oil), and when working boats alongside in heavy weather. Its use has already been mentioned in connection with wreck. American ships are compelled to carry an amount of storm oil, depending upon the gross tonnage of the ship. British ships are only required to carry such oil as part of lifeboat equipment.

THE MANUFACTURE OF RAFTS

In the absence of inflatable rubber life-rafts, an emergency may arise when rafts may have to be made quickly on board, such as when rescuing the crew of a wreck or when the vessel's own boats are destroyed.

Softwood is preferable to hardwood, it being lighter and having a higher freeboard when floating. Due to the generally low freeboard of a wooden-decked raft, it has a small range of stability, and survivors aboard are vulnerable to breaking seas.

A raft may be simply constructed by means of two heavy baulks of timber to form the fore-and-aft side stringers or boundaries. Across these are bolted timbers to form deck beams. They may be lashed if bolts are not available. The beams are finally close-decked by nailing planks across them in a fore-and-aft direction. It is desirable that the side stringers should be of length equal to at least twice the beam of the raft. Empty, sealed, oil, paint, or chemical drums are then lashed to and below the deck beams between the stringers. Awning spars and cargo hatches may be used in the absence of other suitable timber, the stringers being built up of several thicknesses of hatch. If this is done, the raft's dimensions will be governed by the size of hatch, and may be very small. The drums, if slung with their bungs or caps uppermost and accessible through the deck, can be pumped out by means of a portable lifeboat bilge-pump if they are found to be leaking. In very heavy weather smaller, punctured cans or bags filled with oil may be lashed around the perimeter to assist in quelling seas, for it is most important to reduce the breaking-aboard of seas, especially when the raft is manned. Ideally, the beams should project beyond the side stringers, and then a manila line can be clove-hitched and nailed to these ends around the entire perimeter to form a becketed grabline.

The raft can be controlled to some extent by means of two steering oars lashed at one end with lateral freedom of movement. Some form of simple drogue should be provided to keep the raft head to sea, and in the absence of anything more complex, a drum, wooden or metal buckets in a cluster, or a cargo basket can be streamed on a long line. Some thought might be given to the possibility of securing a cargo net across the deck of the raft, since this will not only provide a foothold while shipping water but also a handhold. Means should be provided for lashing helpless or unconscious people to the deck. When loading the raft it should be carried out symmetrically to prevent tilting and capsizing. As soon as the deck edge of the raft submerges the capsizing effect of deck-water pressure becomes evident.

When constructing the raft the reserve buoyancy of the materials, including the air canisters, must be sufficient to support the estimated load, while still possessing freeboard.

An alternative shape of raft is that of a triangular waterplane using the apex of the *isosceles* triangle as the bow.

Provided the raft is substantially constructed, there is no reason why it should not be jettisoned during a favourable roll, spreading oil beforehand. The use of derricks for lowering the raft is hardly practical in

194

heavy weather. If using boat falls from davit heads, the risk of men falling overside while handling such a cumbersome object must be borne in mind. Whichever method is used, means will have to be provided for slipping the purchase from the deck, if the raft is to be used as an unmanned float towed across a wreck. This might well be done by using a fibre rope fall and cutting it adrift when the raft is afloat. Once a raft having air canisters slung below it floats upside down it will prove very difficult to right.

An added advantage will be the addition of one or two self-igniting flares to the raft or, in the case of an unmanned raft used as a towed float, an automatic electric or water-activated light.

MAN OVERBOARD PROCEDURE

Assuming the accident to be observed, it is most important for the observer to cry, 'Man overboard to port (or starboard).' The officer of the watch should then carry out three simultaneous actions: he should stop engines, order the helm hard-over towards the side from which the man fell, and release a life-buoy to which is attached a self-igniting flare or a water-activated electric light. By day, the use of one also equipped with an orange-smoke float, burning for 15 minutes, will be to great advantage. Lookouts should be posted as high as possible, preferably supplied with binoculars, emergency stations sounded and a boat prepared for lowering, and a general urgency signal transmitted to all ships in the vicinity. In busy waters International Code flag 'O' is hoisted. The Master should be notified as quickly as possible, though doubtless the above procedure will already have alerted him.

The releasing of a second life-buoy is of questionable value, since the man may only sight the more distant one and become helpless before reaching it. Further, when the ship returns to the area it will be difficult to detect which buoy was initially released unless they are provided with different types of light.

The man, who initially sinks, loses the beneficial action of the bow-wave wash and comes under the immediate effect of propeller suction. If he is able to determine the direction of the ship's side upon becoming submerged he will instinctively strike out towards it, which will aggravate his danger. Whenever possible, he should swim rapidly away from the ship. A vessel of length 122 m travelling at 12 knots will travel its 400 ft own length in 20 seconds, and if the man falls over forward of amidships it will take between 10 and 20 seconds for him to reach the propellers. During this period, an alert engineer may be able to stop the appropriate propeller from revolving, but this will be out of the question in a ship equipped with turbine-driven shafting, which will take up to 5 minutes to run down, or in a Diesel equipped vessel.

Again, the stopping of engines and the use of immediate helm is of questionable value in protecting the man in the water, for so little time is available. However, if he rises to the surface before reaching the propeller, he will invariably float clear, even though he may pass directly over it. If the ship is rolling or pitching, causing the propeller to break surface or approach it very closely, then he is in grave danger.

If the engines are worked up to full revolutions as soon as the man is clear, maintaining full helm, the vessel will move through a turning circle taking up to 6 or 7 minutes to return to the area where the man is situated. If the ship is high-powered and quick-turning she will probably arrive within a ship's length of the man. The circular path will naturally be governed by the existing weather conditions, particularly in a heavy sea, when it will be necessary to reduce speed as the vessel heads up into the waves.

If recovery is to be made using a boat this may safely be done in most sea conditions while the ship has headway on her of up to about 3 knots. A lee should be made for the boat, and if the seas are breaking oil should be distributed in small quantities.

If the vessel is stopped under the action of reversed engines as soon as the man is clear, in moderate weather a boat may immediately be lowered and manœuvred to the victim, guided by semaphore signals from a lookout aloft. If the man is lost from sight the boat should proceed back along the ship's track on a compass course. In reversing her engines the ship will have made little lateral way over the ground, but any lee drift must be allowed for when using such a compass course.

There are, among others, three useful methods in which the ship may be handled so that she returns to the man in the water. Methods (*a*) and (*c*) have automatic-return features, and all are illustrated in Fig. 9.2.

(a) The Williamson Turn

This was devised and demonstrated by Commander J. A. Williamson of the United States Naval Reserve in 1942. A man in the water faces three hazards: drowning, mangling by the propellers, and abandonment due to non-location. This turn was originated in order to reduce these dangers to a minimum. In darkness, poor visibility, or bad weather, and when the time of the accident is unknown, the execution of this turn may be relied upon to bring the vessel as closely as possible back to her original track.

The helm is initially placed hard over towards the side from which the man fell, speed is not reduced, and the vessel is steadied when she has altered course 60 degrees from the original course. The angle varies for different ships, and should preferably be determined at sea trials. As soon as this deviation is attained the helm is placed hard-over the other way and the vessel brought rapidly round to the reciprocal of

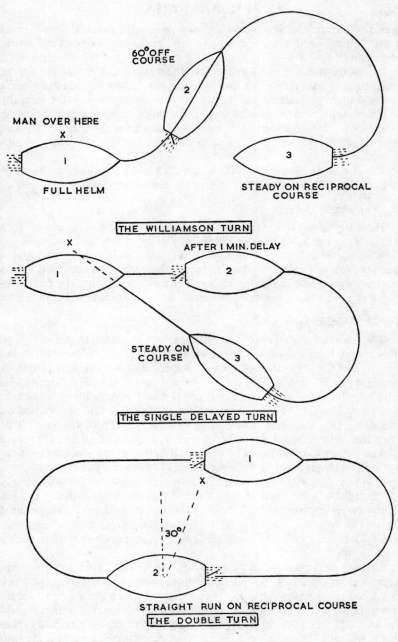

60° OFF COURSE

MAN OVER HERE
X

2

1

FULL HELM

3

STEADY ON RECIPROCAL COURSE

THE WILLIAMSON TURN

X

AFTER 1 MIN. DELAY

1

2

STEADY ON COURSE

3

THE SINGLE DELAYED TURN

1

X

30°

2

STRAIGHT RUN ON RECIPROCAL COURSE

THE DOUBLE TURN

FIGURE 9.2

her original course. She is steadied and the engine revolutions are carefully controlled, for the manœuvre will bring the victim very nearly dead ahead.

The Williamson turn takes the vessel farther from the man than most manœuvres, and may take up to 5 minutes longer to execute than a normal turning circle. It will be seen that at some stage in the turn the stern passes across the line of sight to the man, this, however, being no great disadvantage in view of the ultimate object of the turn. If the man can definitely be kept sighted an ordinary turning circle may be preferred.

In four cases where the Williamson turn has been used, the average time during which the victim was in the water was sixteen minutes.

(b) The Single Delayed Turn

Here the vessel is continued on course for about a minute and then the helm is put hard over to either side in calm weather, otherwise to windward. Speed is reduced during the latter half of the turn and a straight run is made towards the man. The course on this final run is entirely dependent upon the officer of the watch sighting the man continuously. The manœuvre is quick, but has no automatic-return feature.

(c) The Double Turn

The man in the water remains on the same side of the ship throughout this manœuvre. Initially, a turn is made under full helm towards the victim and the ship steadied on the reciprocal of her original course. A straight run is then made until the man is approximately three points abaft the beam, when another full turn is made using helm over towards the man. The ship is again brought round, but this time is steadied on the original course and placed slightly to windward of the man. This turn has automatic-return features only if the man's position is known.

The victim should always be recovered on the first approach, particularly in sea-water below 5°C when a man becomes numbed and helpless within a quarter of an hour. To achieve this, the ship should always be brought to windward of the man and allowed to drift down to him. If the vessel approaches to leeward he will be missed, and no time must be lost in heaving him another life-buoy. The Schermuly 'Speedline' Unit, fitted with the buoyant head to the rocket, may be useful in such a case.

40°F

Ladders and nets should be rigged on the lee side, attended by volunteers wearing life-jackets and safety lines secured to the ship, who are prepared to enter the water in order to help the man ascend or to secure a whip or safety belt to him. Astern movements close to the man should be avoided, since the propeller wash will tend to throw him away from the ship's side. When lowering a boat, or approaching a victim, the ship will invariably have lost headway when the propeller wash from the reversed propellers abreasts the bridge position.

In fog the Williamson turn is the most preferable manœuvre. If this is not used the vessel should be stopped quickly and a boat lowered. It should steer back along the ship's track using a compass course, and should be equipped with a megaphone, a foghorn, a radio and a radar reflector. The parent ship should make her fog signal frequently, and follow the boat's movement by radar. The megaphone, held to the ear instead of the mouth, provides a useful means of ascertaining the direction of sounds, particularly a man's cries.

For the victim, the best advice is to float rather than swim, in order to conserve energy; realise that the ship will rapidly disappear from view due to his negligible height of eye; never lose hope of rescue; remain as calm as humanly possible, and when reaching a life-buoy, strike it on one side only with both hands clenched. It will then tip over his head and he can support himself on it by his elbows. Professional life-savers advise swimmers to strike a persistent shark on what may be considered to be its nose, the resultant rapid retreat being his reward for such cool courage.

If the ship frequently sounds 'O' in Morse code on the siren it will do much to raise the victim's morale, even though the vessel is out of sight. Its use in foggy, traffic waters should preferably be avoided unless used in conjunction with a radio urgency message. When using a boat in poor visibility, the urgency signal should be followed by a warning of the boat's movements and approximate position.

Missing Persons

When a person is reported missing at sea, the Master may decide to search the ship before turning back. If the person is found to be aboard then of course no time has been lost on the voyage. On the other hand, if the person is not found, then the ship will have to be turned back. Because of this delay, the person will be in the water for a period of time equal to twice the duration of the search compared with a similar case where the ship is turned around at once. Clearly the latter action is to be preferred.

The ship should be searched by as many people as possible, looking in the most unlikely places. I once found a missing man in a cattle pen on the poop, another hiding in the chain locker, and a third crouched under gratings in the shaft tunnel over which the search party was walking! There can be no hard and fast rules on the subject. On a passenger ship the Officer on watch used the public address system at full power at 3 a.m. and located a missing boy asleep in a toilet. The sheer volume of sound awakened the boy.

When the person is missing in heavy weather, thick fog, darkness or freezing conditions or where many sharks are about, or where it is known that the person cannot swim, the Master is faced with a serious dilemma. However, people have survived for great lengths of time in the water regardless of their age. It is an occasion where the personality of the person virtually governs his survival. There is a report of an Australian naval seaman surviving for 17 days in the Pacific Ocean, having fallen overboard wearing a lifejacket. It must not be assumed of course, that because a person was last seen say 4 hours ago, that he or she fell overboard 4 hours ago.

HEAVY WEATHER

A wave which is breaking is more dangerous than one which is not, although the latter can become equally hazardous if it is unnaturally broken upon impact with the ship. A breaking wave is higher and steeper than one which remains unbroken, and while the motion within the latter is generally in the vertical plane only, the former wave projects a large volume of water downwards and ahead of itself, causing sudden horizontal motion of a buoyant object, such as a boat. In almost all sea conditions there tends to be a cycle of wave development and deterioration which is usually sufficiently regular to enable a seaman to predict a short period of moderating sea.

In open, deep waters where the wind has a long *fetch*, i.e. a large, smooth area over which it may blow without meeting obstructions, waves are higher and their successive crests are farther apart, the distance between two such adjacent crests being known as the *wavelength*. When the wavelength increases, so does the time interval between the passage of two successive crests past a fixed point, i.e. the true *period* of the waves. If the period remains constant, then the velocity of the waves must increase.

Large vessels behave best in a short sea, while smaller craft are more comfortable in a long sea, i.e. one having a large wavelength. A long vessel, supported only at her ends or amidships by wave crests, is subjected to severe bending stresses, and a shorter wavelength is therefore preferable. The seaman can estimate the wave characteristics once he has found the true period because: The velocity in knots is roughly equal to three times the period measured in seconds. The wavelength in metres is roughly equal to the square of the period (in seconds) multiplied by 1·5, e.g. a 5-second wave system has a velocity of 15 knots and a wavelength of 37 m. These very closely approach the observed characteristics.

feet

5
125 ft

The period of roll of a ship is the time taken to roll from, say, port over to starboard and back to port. It may similarly be described as the time interval between three successive transits of the mast through the vertical plane. This period is largely governed by the metacentric height, a short roll and an uncomfortable motion being associated with a centre of gravity positioned low down in the vessel. Such a vessel is described as being *stiff*, her counterpart with a long period of roll and high centre of gravity being known as *tender* or *crank*. The latter's motion is more easy, but both extremes are undesirable. The period of roll is increased by distributing weights farther away from the fore-and-aft line of the ship, the process being known as *winging-out* weights.

In a similar way the period of pitch of a ship is the time taken to ascend from the lowest position and return to it, or the time between three successive transits of a fixed point on the stem through a horizontal plane. The *apparent period* of the waves is the time interval between the passage of two successive crests relative to a shipborne observer. It is sometimes called the *period of encounter*. When a ship is running before a sea the apparent period exceeds the true period, and vice versa when the ship heads the sea. The period of encounter is the interval with which the seaman is most concerned.

Synchronism

When the roll period is equal to the apparent wave period each roll is boosted by the waves and a condition of synchronous rolling is set up. Within a minute or so the vessel rolls to large angles, which progressively increase. Shifting of the cargo may occur, but in cases where the range of stability is small the vessel may capsize. The condition must be recognised immediately and course altered rapidly in order to change the apparent wave period. The vessel is most vulnerable when the sea is abeam, and in this situation the true and apparent wave periods are equal. An increase in metacentric height (or lowering of the centre of gravity) will increase the amplitude of synchronous rolling.

Synchronous pitching occurs when the period of pitch is equal to the period of encounter and causes excessive racing of the engines as the propeller emerges from the water or approaches the surface, longitudinal straining of the hull, and heavy damage due to the shipping of seas. Alteration of speed will destroy the condition. The water resistance to pitching is greater than to rolling, and the pitching angle does not become abnormally large.

A vessel broken down and lying helpless in the wave trough is extremely vulnerable to synchronous rolling, and means should be adopted to bring the vessel head to wind and sea as soon as the engine failure occurs.

General Behaviour of the Ship

A vessel heading into a bow sea heels over towards advancing wave crests, and this part of her roll is damped. When running before a quarterly sea the reverse is true and she heels away from oncoming seas. In this condition the resistances to rolling are least and larger angles of roll are attained, in addition to which the waves traverse the ship's length more slowly than if they approach from ahead. The combination of these two factors renders the ship liable to ship heavy seas aft, a process known as *pooping*.

From the previous text, we now see that the ability of a ship to ride comfortably depends upon her course and speed relative to the waves, her strength, her range of stability, her weight distribution relative to the fore-and-aft line, her period of roll, and the period and wavelength of the seas.

When steaming head to sea the ship is subjected to pitching, racing of engines, longitudinal stresses, slamming and pounding at the fore end due to wave impact, and the shipping of water. Ideally, the ship should be trimmed a little by the stern so that the screws and the rudder are immersed to the maximum and the bow resists a tendency to bury itself. All the hazards of pitching are reduced by lowering the speed of the vessel. Occasionally, such a reduction in speed may adversely affect pitching, for it may cause the period of encounter to approach closely the period of pitch, setting up synchronism. From this, it follows that on rare occasions an increase in speed will reduce pitching, but this action will inevitably produce dangerous slamming of the forefoot.

The tendency of a vessel to pound her forefoot is most marked in light, flat-bottomed ships, particularly when the forefoot becomes emerged. It is decreased by reducing speed, but in very short waves extremely low speeds may prove a reverse effect. Certain slamming occurs even when the forefoot is buried deeply or ascending, and is due to the rapid variations of the pressure system which always surround a hull. These variations are caused by the ship's speed, and have been used in past hostilities to detonate certain types of mine.

When running before the sea a vessel usually experiences difficulty in steering, particularly one having a high counter stern which is easily lifted by the sea, producing an alarming yaw. Under these conditions with the sea astern, if the vessel is situated in the trough of a sea which is overtaking her and breaking she is likely to be pooped. If the ship and waves have equal velocities and the vessel is lying on an advancing wave slope, i.e. *surfing*, she is likely to be slewed violently, heeled over, and swamped. The process of slewing is known as *broaching-to*. The sudden addition of top-weight water when heeled over to a large inclination may reduce the angle at which positive stability disappears to the *existing* angle of heel, and capsizing is then likely.

If the sea has a wavelength considerably greater or less than the ship's length, i.e. a long or short sea, her motion will be safest, and it follows that the greatest danger from a quarterly or astern sea arises when the sea has: (a) a wavelength closely approaching the ship's length, and (b) a velocity equal to or greater than the ship's speed.

In these circumstances it is wise to reduce speed so that the seas overtake the vessel rather than run the risk of surfing and broaching-to. Ideally, the speed should be found at which the danger of pooping is also least.

With a sea abeam, allowance must be made for lee drift, which may have a rate in excess of 2 knots. If the wake is sighted and its direction compared with the course steered the angular difference will give a close approximation to the necessary upwind alteration of the ship's head. Alterations of speed will have little effect on behaviour in a beam sea, but course alterations will reduce the amplitude of rolling. Whether the alteration is made into or away from the sea will depend upon the wave characteristics relative to the ship's length and speed, and on her known preference for a bow or quarterly sea. The use of weather-side storm oil will produce a valuable slick spreading to windward, in which the breaking of seas is minimised.

Turning a Vessel in Heavy Weather

This requires the utmost accuracy of judgement and a knowledge of the ship's characteristics in answering helm and engine movements. The engine and catering departments of the ship should be informed and the decks cleared of men. Before turning, a study should be made of the wave-development cycles and the arrival of a moderating sea predicted.

When turning downwind away from a head sea it is desirable to experience the relative calm when the vessel is lying in the trough and commencing the last half of the turn, for this is the period when she is likely to be swamped. The latter half of the turn must be executed as rapidly as possible.

When running before a sea and wishing to turn upwind it is desirable to experience the relative calm during the latter half of the turn when the vessel is swinging up into the wind and sea. If this swing is executed in very heavy seas the ship may suffer extensive damage. For this reason the latter half of the turn should again be carried out as quickly as possible, so that the ship is fully prepared to meet oncoming seas while steady.

In both cases speed should be reduced before turning and bold helm used. The turns must be carried out with the minimum of headway, and the rudder is rendered operational by using short bursts of full-ahead revolutions. The ordering of full ahead and full helm has everything to recommend it providing: (a) the minimum of headway is gathered, and (b) the rate of swing kept low if misjudgement causes the arrival of heavy seas at a critical stage. In this event it may be preferable to resume course and make a second attempt. The use of storm oil is of great value in these manœuvres.

Heaving-to

A vessel heaves-to when, due to the stress of weather, the voyage is temporarily discontinued and the ship is manœuvred so as to ride out the storm in the most comfortable position. Generally, a ship will behave best in one of three positions: (a) with the sea on the bow and steaming at a reduced speed sufficient only for steering, (b) with the sea abaft the beam and at a similarly reduced speed, or (c) stopped and drifting to leeward.

In (a) the dangers of pitching and slamming are present, but the vessel will probably make little way over the ground, and the attitude is therefore a wise one when there is little sea room to leeward. It is a difficult position to hold when in light condition if the bow shows a tendency to pay off. In (b) considerable way is made to leeward and the danger of pooping exists. The attitude is therefore recommended only when a ship has plenty of leeward sea room and good steering qualities in such a condition of quarterly sea and low speed. In (c) a lesser amount of drift is made to leeward, but despite this a recent case showed a particular vessel, in light condition, to experience a rate of 5 knots lee drift in this attitude, so that again ample lee sea room is desirable. The vessel will probably roll heavily in this position, and synchronism may occur, so that at all times the vessel should be capable of being swung rapidly. The risk of a shifting cargo is present, and rolling may be very violent if the vessel is stiff. The method is often employed in low-powered vessels which are unmanageable in position (b) and which are incapable of turning head into the existing wind. This may be due either to a large wind surface forward or the inability to gather sufficient headway in the circumstances.

In all cases when hove-to the use of storm oil will do much to reduce hazards.

Preparing the Vessel for Heavy Weather

The vessel must be made as seaworthy as possible before the onset of bad weather, paying particular attention to the following points:

(1) The checking, and doubling-up if necessary, of all deck lashings.
(2) The tightening of boat gripes.
(3) The battening down of hatches. Locking bars, where fitted, should be tightly set up and consideration be given to the stretching of extra tarpaulins.
(4) Where the admission of continual fresh air to cargo holds is unnecessary or may be temporarily dispensed with, ventilators

should be covered to prevent the admission of sea-water. This applies particularly in the case of a cargo of wood pulp, where expansion due to wetting can be up to 50% and rupturing of the ship's side or deck can occur. Wet grain provides a similar danger, though not having such a great expansion.

(5) Lifelines of 25–30-mm fibre rope should be rigged and set up tightly throughout the exposed decks. Where a long unsupported span is inevitable the line should be stopped to the adjacent distant strong points by short lengths of line of preferably equal strength to the lifeline. **3–4-in manila**

(6) If time permits, unprotected accommodation storm doors should be hose-tested and any deficiency of watertightness made good with the use of waxed caulking felt.

(7) The securing of all derricks must be absolute.

(8) The existence of water or oil fuel which is loose, i.e. it is able to wash from side to side of the ship, produces a *free surface effect* reducing the stability of the ship. It should be reduced to a minimum, preferably by filling tanks, for this adds bottom weight and lowers the centre of gravity of the ship. Any flooding or pumping must be done well beforehand while the ship is steady, for the filling of an empty tank in itself produces a free surface effect in addition to any list which may be caused by off-centre loading. The deliberate introduction of free surfaces while the ship is in a seaway is a practice to be avoided, unless the vessel is light, in which case her margin of stability is usually high.

(9) If the stability of the ship is dangerously small due regard should be paid to the jettisoning of deck cargoes if the flooding of double-bottom tanks proves insufficient. The filling of a deep tank will have little effect in lowering the centre of gravity of the ship. Otherwise, the deck cargo should be securely lashed, and in the case of livestock, ample protection be given to the animals. A large supply of food and water should be provided in case men are unable to reach the animals at the height of the storm.

(10) The watertightness of the spurling pipes, leading to the chain locker, should be ensured and storm plates set in place over the upper ends of the hawse pipes to prevent the shipping of water through them.

(11) All loose gear, including ropes, should be cleared from the decks.

(12) Signal halliards may be slackened in anticipation of their tautening when wet.

(13) All doors on exposed decks should be tightly closed except for accommodation accesses.

(14) Deadlights (metal screens) should be fixed in place over portholes and scuttles.

(15) A swimming-bath should be drained, since this, when full, adds top-weight and free surface effects.

(16) A heavy weather routine should be adopted by the Chief Officer to ensure the minimum of men (if any at all) being on deck during the storm.

(17) All life-rafts and other buoyant apparatus should be checked for freedom of jettisoning.

(18) Oil bags, or other containers, should be filled with oil and lashed to the rails or placed in water closets ready for use.

(19) All spare hatches should be gathered by the carpenter and stored where they will be accessible in the event of hatches being stove-in (see Chapter VII).

(20) Awnings must be taken down, otherwise they will be ripped apart and the spars damaged.

Duties of the Officer of the Watch

He must avoid steaming too rapidly into a head sea, and reduce speed early in all attitudes where hazards are increasing despite the fear of being considered over-cautious. He must be satisfied that the ship is thoroughly seaworthy and at all times keep a close watch for synchronism. Only the best helmsmen should be employed during the storm, and if conditions arise where it is necessary to meet each wave with the helm he must consider the necessity of relieving the helmsman every $\frac{1}{2}$ hour to avoid weariness. The clear-view screens should be tested beforehand, together with the fog-signalling apparatus in anticipation of poor visibility. Distress rockets should be to hand.

HANDLING DISABLED VESSELS

A vessel which has shipped considerable water will be more deeply laden, and she may be both listed and trimmed by the head. Chapter III should be referred to at this stage, where the handling abilities of ships in these conditions are fully discussed.

A twin-screw ship will handle quite well with her rudder and one propeller. If both screws are available for use she can be steered, in the event of rudder loss or damage, by varying the port and starboard engine revolutions. A single-screw ship without the use of her rudder will be temporarily helpless unless a jury rudder is rigged (Chapter VII).

Any ship having no motive power is completely helpless unless a towing vessel is available. The vessel should be brought head to wind and sea as rapidly as possible in order that she may ride comfortably and with the minimum of lee drift. This necessitates the use of:

EMERGENCIES

Sea Anchors

In anchoring depths the easiest and quickest way of bringing a vessel head to wind is to trail a length of chain cable along the sea-bed. The anchor is detached from the cable to minimise the risk of it fouling. If one cable proves insufficient the other should also be used, but it is preferable to keep one anchor ready for use in the hawse pipe in case of an emergency. The cable should be ready for slipping and buoying should it foul an underwater obstruction, and this is best achieved by locating a joining shackle just abaft the upper end of the hawse pipe.

Since the weather entailing this procedure will be very bad, no attempt should be made to hang off the anchor, since this involves sending a man overside in a bosun's chair. The anchor is therefore lashed in its stowed position within the pipe and the cable is eased. The spare joining shackle just abaft the anchor shackle is broken, and the cable is man-handled out through a forward fairlead, the Panama Canal type being ideal. In the absence of such a lead, a mooring chock will have to be used, but any damage to it will be of small moment if the ship is saved from major damage or stranding. Three, or even more, shackles should be ranged along the sea-bed. The use of the weather cable, if only one is to be used, will prevent a continual bad nip at the stempost. This method of sea anchoring is used frequently by some Masters of short-sea traders when encountering bad weather in the North Sea.

In waters of all depths other methods are feasible, provided time and suitable gear is available. In past days a very effective sea anchor was made by lacing a trysail to a boom, weighting it at its lower apex—the tack of the sail—and streaming it ahead on a rope bridle. Nowadays, such an appliance would have to be made from spare canvas, or tarpulin, and a wooden spar. The latter is not always available. The canvas will take considerable time to prepare, and the strength of the finished appliance will be doubtful. The following are tried methods, but they may prove unsuitable for large vessels:

(1) The streaming, on a wire hawser, of several cargo baskets or empty oil drums rigged in a cluster, or even an empty container.
(2) The streaming of a wooden raft, weighted at its lower edge with spare chains.
(3) The streaming of a triangular-prism hatch tent having its apex removed and its base stretched open with two crossed awning spars. The strength of the spars will govern the life of the sea anchor.
(4) The streaming ahead of a waterlogged boat; the falls will probably have to be cut adrift and the boat may be non-recoverable. The use of life-saving appliances in this way may well be regretted at a later stage.

(5) The streaming of a wooden cargo slab hatch, i.e. five or six wooden hatches already strapped together with steel slats into a rectangle about 2·5 m square. It must be weighted at its lower edge so that it lies vertically in the water.

8 ft square

(6) The rigging of a makeshift mizzen sail to increase the wind surface aft.

All these methods take considerable time and trouble to rig, and their jettisoning involves danger to the crew in heavy weather. There are, however, cases reported where a vessel has been successfully turned head to wind by lowering one or both anchors to a considerable depth. The vessel makes leeway while her anchors tend to remain vertically above a fixed point. The bows are then slowly swung into the wind. The lower the depth to which the anchors are veered, the better will be the result, due to the increased water pressure. It is preferable therefore to attempt this method prior to commencing manufacture of an appliance of doubtful strength, life, and efficiency. The use of a drogue rocket has already been discussed for heaving life-rafts clear of a ship's side, and this acts as an excellent sea anchor for small boats. In all cases the use of storm oil is advised in conjunction with the sea anchor, the latter being extremely valuable in cases where a vessel is:

Running on to a Lee Shore

A *lee shore* is one towards which a strong wind is blowing. Occasions arise when a vessel is strongly set towards such a shore and is unable to turn head to wind in order to make favourable way out to seaward. This situation is most likely to occur in a low-powered vessel, particularly when in light condition. In addition to her leeway, the vessel comes under the influence of a surface drift current created by the wind, provided that the wind has blown unveeringly for more than 24 hours. In high latitudes this drift current is likely to have an average rate equal to 2% of the wind speed, and 4% in the case of low latitudes. It is therefore possible to predict, in low latitudes, a drift in miles per day roughly equal to the wind speed in knots, e.g. a 30-knot wind may produce an approximate drift of 30 miles in one day in low latitudes and 15 miles per day in high latitudes. Exceptions to these frequently occur, particularly within the Indian Ocean at the time of the south-west monsoon, where daily drifts of 160 miles can occur. The western coasts of the United Kingdom are renowned lee shores after a period of south-westerly gales, and cautionary notes are printed on the appropriate Admiralty charts to this effect. Despite this, a vessel grounded in recent years after being swept to leeward, with the loss of all hands together with the crew of the local Royal National Lifeboat Institution craft.

EMERGENCIES

There are four basic ways in which a vessel may attempt to clear a lee shore:

(1) By rapid use of a sea anchor to swing the vessel head to wind.

(2) By letting go both anchors, when in suitable depths, snubbing the bows head to wind, and steaming out to seaward, weighing her anchors as she does so. If the act of weighing anchors is likely to swing the bows off the wind, then preferably one anchor only should be used on a long scope and slipped from the deck while proceeding out.

(3) By turning through 270° downwind under full speed and helm until the vessel heads the wind. In sailing ships this is known as a wearing turn. The method is hazardous, because if it fails the vessel lies much closer to the coastline and, further, the momentum of her swing must be maintained in order for it to be successful, and this involves bringing the bows very rapidly into a heavy sea. This is likely to cause extensive damage.

(4) Apart from (2), the method most likely to succeed in deep water is as follows:

The engine is reversed and the vessel, which is allowed to gather only the minimum of sternway, runs her stern into the wind's eye. This position is then held while flooding of the after compartments is carried out. The flooding of the after hold alone will, though immersing the rudder and propeller further, create an awkward trim producing an increased wind surface forward and any benefit may be lost. If only one hold can be flooded, the one immediately abaft the engine-room will give the best results. It is desirable, however, to flood as many aft compartments as possible. The holds should be flooded to just below the level of the shaft-tunnel top. The tunnel then acts as a washplate, and free-surface effects are reduced to a quarter value.

This action, then, sinks the vessel bodily, and the greater thrust of the screw together with the increased rudder sensitivity offsets any adverse effect of trim. The flooding is carried out by means of hoses, removing non-return valves and pumping through the bilge line with limber boards (bilge covers) removed, and/or flooding up through the double-bottom tanks with manhole doors unshipped. Any other available means should be used in addition. If the double-bottom tanks contain fuel oil only the first two methods are used. If possible, all loose timber and gear should be taken into the 'tween deck, but in an emergency nothing should be allowed to interfere with the rapid flooding. A case on record shows the two after holds of a vessel of 6000 tonnes D.W., in light condition, to have been sufficiently flooded in forty minutes.

Once this is achieved, a turn into the wind is again attempted, preferably to port in a single-screw ship to make use of transverse thrust.

It is most undesirable to gather too much sternway into the sea for:

209

(*a*) the engines will race due to pitching, and (*b*) the rudder and propeller when under headway are protected to some extent from wave impact, but under sternway they are extremely vulnerable and are likely to be fractured. A case has occurred, however, of a vessel lying stern-to a heavy sea while maintaining her position off a lee shore, and with her screw turning over at very slow reversed revolutions for 36 hours. Oil was used to prevent breaking seas striking the blades, and no damage was suffered.

If the vessel has low astern-power, she may have little chance of avoiding stranding despite her following the above manœuvre. A war-time-built ship of 7000 tonnes D.W. was recently proceeded north off the coast of California, in light condition. At noon her position was fixed and conditions were calm. By 2000 hours the wind was gale force and freshening, with a heavy swell on the port beam. Her steering became difficult and at 2100 hours flooding of No. 5 hold was commenced, using four hoses. By 2200 hours the wind speed was about 55 knots and full helm had no effect. A wearing turn was attempted towards the land, to no avail. At 2300 hours the engine was reversed at full speed and the vessel ran her stern up into the wind. In this situation, due to low astern-power, she was unable to hold her position and virtually sailed before the wind. Visibility was approaching nil. At 0050 hours a reef was struck, tearing several bottom plates away adjacent to the forward engine-room bulkhead. At 0120 hours the bows struck and the vessel became fast on 150 yds ⟶ a rock 150 m offshore. Both anchors were let go.

At 0200 hours the 3rd Officer and one seaman went overside and managed to struggle ashore in the vessel's lee. At 0300 hours a rocket was fired from the ship to these two men, who then hove a $2\frac{1}{2}$-inch manila rope ashore and made it fast to a rock. At 0400 the remainder of the crew hauled themselves ashore.

The coastal country was desert, and the nearest village had been destroyed in the gale, the inhabitants taking to their fishing-boats in a sheltered bay. The men returned to the ship when the weather abated in order to get food and water. No electric power was available. Later the men were taken off by one of the fishing vessels.

The 3rd Officer of this vessel had, on another occasion, grounded near a Scottish lighthouse. Only a rocket line-throwing gun was avail-3-in ⟶ able ashore, and this was fired across the ship. A 25-mm manila line was hove ashore and made fast. The crew then managed to reach the shore one by one, in a bosun's chair travelling on the hawser by means of a shackle. An endless heaving line was used to haul them to the beach. By the time the last man was safely ashore the manila line, initially in good condition, was very badly worn. The slack in the hawser, necessary to allow for the rolling of the stranded ship, was so excessive that the men were partly submerged for most of the run ashore.

DANGERS TO NAVIGATION

A *derelict* is a vessel which has been completely abandoned but which remains afloat. Since their lights will usually be without power supply, collision is possible with them at night and will invariably be end-on at full speed. Extensive damage is likely. A derelict can be taken in tow and a claim made for a salvage award.

On sighting a dangerous derelict, the Master is bound to communicate the information to all ships in the vicinity and also to the nearest coastal Authority. It must be reported to the local Receiver of Wreck. The transmission will consist of a Safety signal and may be in plain language (preferably English) or in International Code. The message is free of charge to the ship concerned.

The same obligations apply to dangerous ice, any other direct danger to navigation, a tropical storm, severe ice accretion associated with gales and sub-freezing temperatures, and a wind of force 10 or above on the Beaufort scale for which no warning has been received.

The information transmitted should include, in the case of ice, derelicts and similar dangers:

(1) The kind of danger observed.
(2) The last observed position of the danger and the Greenwich Mean Time and date.

In the case of a tropical storm the transmission should include:

(1) A statement that the storm has been encountered, or that the Master believes one to exist or be developing in the area.
(2) The date and time (G.M.T.).
(3) The ship's position.
(4) The barometric pressure and whether it has been corrected.
(5) The barometer tendency, i.e. the change in the last 3 hours.
(6) The wind direction and Beaufort force.
(7) The state of sea and swell.
(8) The true course and speed of the ship.

The Master should then transmit further reports preferably every hour, and in any case at intervals of less than 3 hours for as long as he remains under the influence of the storm.

In the case of winds of force 10 and above for which no warning has been received the message should include all the above points with the exception of (7). Messages concerned with ice accretion should include:

(1) The position.
(2) The G.M.T.

(3) The air temperature and the sea temperature (if practicable).
(4) The wind force and direction.

The following are specimen messages:

TTT Ice. Extensive berg sighted 4600 N 5100 W 1200 GMT April 30.

TTT Derelict. Derelict sighted low in water heeled about 30 degrees. Name unknown. 3300 S 11014 E 0300 GMT Dec 20.

TTT Navigation. Mine sighted 5003 N 1023 W 0930 GMT June 15.

TTT Storm. Hurricane believed nearby due south. 1500 GMT July 22. 2002 N 4001 W. Corrected barometer 74 cm. Tendency down 5 mm. Wind E force 8 squally, Heavy southerly swell very rough sea. Course 252 speed 15 knots.

TTT Storm. Wind force 10 no warning received. 1400 GMT Feb 12. 5006 N 3005 W. Corrected barometer 74 cm. Tendency down 5 mm. Wind SW force 10 veering. Course 240 speed 9 knots.

TTT Severe icing occurring. 1100 GMT Feb 22. 70 N 12 W Air temp −10 Sea temp −1. Wind NNE force 9.

WRECK AND SALVAGE LEGAL ASPECTS

In the United Kingdom Officers of the Department of Trade supervise matters pertaining to wreck, and may appoint Receivers of Wreck, one to be situated in each wreck area of the country. They are often Customs Officers.

Wreck as a term also includes *flotsam*, i.e. goods which have been lost overboard or jettisoned and which are recovered because they remain afloat; *jetsam*, i.e. similar goods which are washed ashore; *ligan* or *lagan*, i.e. goods which are jettisoned and buoyed for later recovery; and derelict. All wreck must, if found by a person other than the owner, be delivered to the Receiver of Wreck. This applies to wreck found outside the United Kingdom waters and brought into the country. If found by an owner a full report must be made by him. Wreck is usually kept for a period up to one year, but smaller goods which are not of sufficient value to be stored may be sold. Unclaimed wreck will become the property of the Crown.

The Receiver of Wreck must proceed to any vessel which is stranded or in distress, on or near the United Kingdom coasts, and take charge of rescue operations. He can interfere between a Master and his crew only if the former so requests. The Master can prevent by force any person boarding his ship without his permission unless it is the Receiver of Wreck, or his representative.

212

Salvage

If a ship, lives, or cargo on board are saved from a danger, *voluntarily* and successfully, the person so doing carries out a salvage service and is entitled to a reward.

In spite of the fact that a Master must, by law, assist any vessel that collides with him or which is in distress, he is still regarded as a volunteer for the purposes of salvage. A passenger cannot claim salvage unless he chooses to remain aboard and assist, in spite of the offer of rescue. A member of the crew is bound by his agreement to preserve his ship, and can claim salvage only if he is ordered to abandon his ship (the order being given with no intention of returning), but later returns to it.

The Royal Navy may claim salvage; Coastguards may do so if they provide a greater service than that to which they are bound; members of a R.N.L.I. lifeboat may claim salvage if they find that their life-saving services are not required and they choose to save property.

Every salvor who contributes to the ultimate success may claim a share in the reward, but initially the Master of the salved ship may select his salvors if several arrive upon the scene. Others may assist later if he decides that their services are necessary, but only with his permission. In the case of derelict, the first salvor to arrive has complete control and sole rights; others may interfere only if he proves to be thoroughly incompetent.

The use of Lloyd's Standard Form of Salvage Agreement between the Master and his salvors saves time, bargaining, and refers all disputes directly to arbitration. No financial sum need be mentioned in the agreement, it being decided later by the Admiralty Courts. In the case of a salvage claim below £200 the Receiver of Wreck will probably deal with it himself.

Awards are usually paid for the salvage of lives only if property has been saved as well, because this then provides a source of finance. In United Kingdom waters life salvage in the absence of property salvage may be rewarded by the Department of Trade (D.o.T.) out of Treasury resources.

CHAPTER X

TOWING

THE type of towing discussed in this chapter is that employed in open waters by a vessel which is not a tug. In the text the vessel which is being towed will be referred to as the tow.

LEGAL ASPECTS

In certain circumstances a ship which requires to be towed may not necessarily be in distress, and for this reason, a Master proposing to tow her should ascertain that his Charter-party and/or Bills of Lading allow him to do so in such a case. If the vessel is in distress, then she must be towed to a place of safety, but the towing Master then has no right to continue towing for the purpose of completing a successful salvage operation unless the above documents permit him to do so.

Assuming that the towing Master is unrestricted, he should consider:

(*a*) The duration of the towing voyage.
(*b*) Any mail contract to which he may be a party.
(*c*) Whether he will be able to arrive at his original destination before the cancelling date of the Charter-party.
(*d*) Whether he has enough bunkers and a safe reserve.
(*e*) The effect of delay on his own cargo.
(*f*) The power of his engine(s).

In addition, he should:

(1) Notify his Owners, who will inform Lloyd's and the Underwriters, the latter possibly requiring a larger premium.
(2) Inform his charterer, if any.
(3) Enter into a Lloyd's Standard Form of Salvage Agreement.
(4) Preferably make for a port where the British law of salvage applies.

It has already been mentioned in Chapter IX that salvage claims are only admissible when a danger existed. The fact that a vessel may be disabled in calm weather does not detract from this, since as her stores are consumed, or the weather deteriorates, a peril arises.

214

TOWING

On arrival at the destination the offer of assistance from tugs should not be rejected under the impression that extra salvors are then involved. If required, they should definitely be employed, because the towing Master must conclude the operation successfully in order to submit a claim. The tugs may be engaged under an ordinary towage contract, and this does not entitle them to make any salvage claim unless a new peril arises and the tugs perform useful work over and above that which is demanded by the towage contract.

THE TOWLINE

Little can be laid down regarding the method of towing, since this depends upon the types of ships, the duration of the towing voyage, the weather, the route to be followed, and very largely upon the urgency with which the tow must be commenced.

In some cases, where the towing ship is of a suitable type, one of her anchor cables is ranged right along the deck to the stern rail, where it is shackled to the anchor cable of the tow. The anchor is left in the towing ship's hawse pipe, preferably with heavy wooden pads between the flukes and the bow plating, to act as a toggle. The cable must be well racked to bitts and other strong points throughout the vessel's length. Timber and canvas should be used copiously to minimise chafe.

Probably the ideal towline is one made of manila fibre, for this possesses great elasticity, which is very necessary in towing, when sudden stresses are likely to be applied to the line. Such a line, however, would be very bulky, cumbersome, and subject to rotting and exceptional chafe. If storm oil was used the manila would deteriorate in strength once it had been in contact with the oil. Wire rope of equal strength is less bulky, easily stowed and handled, and is less susceptible to rotting and wear. It possesses negligible elasticity, however, and will part under a sudden applied stress. In order to provide elasticity, a composite towline of wire and manila may be used, the manila being of cable lay (three left-handed ropes laid up together right-handed), which is more flexible and watertight than a hawser. A simple hawser-laid rope should not be used, since it tends to unlay when under stress and develop serious kinks when the stress is relieved. This can, however, be prevented by using swivels at each end of the hawser.

A towline can be made by securing two heavy wire pendants to each end of a special strop. This strop is made endless, of 70-mm manila, 9-in and the two parts are well seized together, leaving two thimbled eyes at the ends. Swivels are again recommended. The strop, forming the middle 20 m of the towline, provides valuable elasticity. ten fathoms

A very quickly rigged and frequently used towline is formed by securing the towing ship's towing wire to one anchor cable of the tow, the

215

latter vessel still retaining one anchor in the hawse pipe ready for an emergency. This necessitates those on board the tow disconnecting the anchor from the cable and preferably bringing the anchor on deck. Alternatively, the anchor may be hung off below the hawse pipe and secured by tackles leading from the deck. In an emergency consideration may be given to jettisoning the anchor in order to save time. The cable may now be led through the hawse pipe and shackled to the tow-wire. Naturally, the anchor could be lashed in the hawse pipe, and the cable led through a fairlead or mooring chock, but this may cause the cable to be badly nipped, quite apart from probable damage to the chock, which is not intended for cable use.

In such a composite towline the cable should be veered between three and, say, seven shackles. The weight of the chain causes the towline to lie in a shallow curve called a catenary, and this provides spring, for a sudden stress will be absorbed as the catenary becomes more shallow, and normally before the catenary disappears altogether the tow will be surged ahead, thus relieving the stress. In this way, two materials, neither of which possesses useful elasticity, may be combined to absorb shock. The longer the length of chain, the greater will be the shock-absorbing property of the towline. Using materials of equal strength, wire is about one-fifth of the weight of chain, the size of the wire (its diameter in mm) being roughly equal to the size of the chain (the diameter of the link bar in mm). To maintain a suitable catenary, the towline should never be allowed to close or break surface; on the other hand, it should never be so great as to foul the bottom, since the line may then part.

The towline is bound to be nipped at fairleads, and even if the leads are in fact fair, chafing will occur. The chafing part should be removed from the fairlead regularly either by veering or shortening the towline. This is called *freshening the nip*, and in this composite method is easily achieved by means of the tow's windlass, providing the tow is manned.

A minority are of the opinion that the use of the chain cable promotes link wear, but the weight of opinion is that the wear is considerably less than that caused by a ship yawing at a single anchor, and in any case the tow is more valuable than her cable.

590 ft

2 in
120–150 fathoms
5–8 in
in circumference

Vessels under 180 m in length, classed at Lloyds are required to carry a towline. As a guide, those ships which are equipped with special steel anchor chain cable of 50 mm and above are required to carry a flexible steel wire rope between 240 and 300 m in length, from 40 to 65 mm in diameter and having 6 strands, each strand containing 24 or 37 wires. All the figures, with the exception of the number of strands, vary with the size of ship. Vessels which are not classed might be considered unseaworthy under the Merchant Shipping Act if not equipped with a suitable towline.

216

TOWING

Other proved methods of towing include shackling the towing wire to both anchor cables of the tow, using the chains as a bridle. Sometimes, the towing ship provides a wire from each quarter, the ends being shackled to the towing wire about 10 m beyond the stern. This is a bridle and avoids the towline exerting a stress on only one side of the ship, or exactly amidships, both of which have been found to hamper steering. The same result may be achieved by shackling the tow-wire to several parts of wire loosely secured across the poop deck or around the stern of the towing vessel. It is virtually a bridle, but is known as a *span*. Such a span may also be achieved by leading a heavy wire out from one quarter of the towing vessel, while the main towline is led aboard through the other quarter leads. The wire is shackled to the towline and hove-in so that the latter is bowsed in towards the opposite quarter to its lead. This again appears as a bridle, but is termed a span. By letting go the wire, the span is instantly removed.

When the tow has full motive power but is rudderless a method sometimes used is for her to tow the assisting ship the latter sheering from side to side, as required, to steer the disabled vessel.

Nylon rope of equal size to top-grade manila is about twice as strong as the latter. For this reason, a manila rope can be replaced by a very much smaller nylon line to provide equal strength, a 50-mm manila being replaceable by a 35-mm nylon line. Since nylon possesses elasticity, it is ideal for towing purposes, but as yet is used for such a purpose only by tugs, and as a pendant secured to a wire towline in larger ships. It is light, easily handled, does not freeze when wet, and is, to a very large extent, rotproof.

Fittings

The strength of these must be in direct proportion to the towing pull, which in turn is directly related to the motive power of the towing vessel, the speed of towing, the tow's displacement, and the inclemency of the weather. If the security of bitts is doubtful the lines should be belayed to several pairs of bitts, all as nearly as possible in one straight line. By backing up the first pair of bitts in this way, provided the belaying is done evenly, the stress on the lines is evenly distributed.

Other strong points include winchbeds, the bases of cargo-hatch coamings, deckhouses, superstructures, masts, and samson posts. These are more easily made use of if the vessel is flush-decked aft. When using any strong point, particularly in the case of bitts, they should be well shored up and stayed, to provide added resistance in the direction of stress. If the deck is considered too weak to withstand the applied stresses of towing, the hull of the tow is sometimes completely girdled with wires frapped to the deck edges and shackled to the towing wire. If the tow's cable is being used as a component of the towline her windlass

217

will not be subjected to undue stresses provided an adequate catenary is maintained. The cable should be held firmly on the brake, using devil's claws, Blake stoppers, guillotines, and all other available means to act as preventers to protect the windlass.

With regard to the towline, its size should be sufficient to provide an ample factor of safety under the towing conditions. In practice, the average merchant ship usually carries only one towing wire, and therefore has no choice, unless several parts of a smaller wire are used. These towlines, carried under Classification Rules, are often known as *insurance wires*, the origin of the term being obscure, for Lloyd's Classification Society is not an insurance company. A classed vessel will, however, no doubt earn reduced insurance premiums from her underwriters.

It is estimated that a tug equipped with steam reciprocating motive power can, in calm weather, exert a pull of roughly 1 tonne for every 75 kW of engine power. The force required to tow a ship is naturally increased if the tow is damaged, yawing heavily, badly fouled on her underwater plating, or in bad weather. In the case of a cargo vessel of 10 000 tonnes displacement, in calm weather and with a fairly clean hull, a pull of very roughly 1 tonne per knot of towing speed is required up to speeds of 6 knots. Above this, the proportion disappears, and 11 tonnes are required to attain a speed of 8 knots. At this latter speed a 40-mm wire rope of 6 × 24 construction will provide a safety factor of approximately seven.

When connecting wires, lugless or lugged joining shackles should be used in preference to shackles fitted with screwed pins. Cable shackles are ideal for this purpose. If screwed shackles must be used the pins should be securely wired to the shackle jaws to prevent them loosening. This type of shackle is liable to foul in fairleads due to its projecting pin, the cable shackles, on the other hand, are designed to prevent such an occurrence. A swivel may be used where chain is connected to wire, and this, like all other fittings, must be of equivalent strength to the towline, for the towing pull must always be confined to the safe working load of the weakest component.

The Length of the Towline

This basically depends upon the depth of the water, the state of the sea and swell, and the sea room available. The greater the length, the more able is the line to absorb shocks, and for this reason the length must be increased when the factor of safety is low, when the tow has a large displacement, or when the towline is light in weight.

The length should not be excessive, otherwise the deep bight, i.e. the catenary, may foul the bottom and part, or at the very least it will provide an added resistance to towing. Generally, a short, heavy tow-

218

line is better than a long, light one in that it enables the ships to have greater manœuvrability. As a guide, the centre of the catenary is best kept about 6–9 m below sea-level, increasing this figure to 12 m in rough weather. 20–30 ft 40 ft

Wear

Throughout the towing voyage, chafe must be kept to a minimum by parcelling hawsers with canvas, lining fairleads with soft wood and canvas, and using liberal amounts of soft soap or grease. Cable passing through a fairlead need only be lubricated. Nips of hawsers should be freshened about four times a day in calm weather, and those of cable about once a day. To avoid bad nips, the fairleads should be padded with metal or pieces of hardwood in order to lessen the angle of lead. Bollards should be of adequate diameter for the hawser being belayed, ideally at least 12 times the size of the line. Cable should not be belayed to bitts, since to prevent a nip a 1 m diameter bollard is necessary for a 50 mm cable, and this size of bollard is not usually fitted to merchant ships. Instead, the cable is racked to several pairs of bitts or around strong points, using hardwood padding to round off any sharp corners. If chain can be used in fairleads in place of wire, the amount of wear will be diminished.

Propellers

The resistance to towing offered by locked screws may, particularly in twin or multiple-screw ships, exceed the underwater resistance of the hull. Shafting should be disconnected in order that the propeller(s) may trail and revolve freely.

SUPPLYING POWER TO THE TOW

If this vessel is equipped with electric pumps and has no power available the towing vessel can sometimes supply electricity, providing the current and voltage of the two ships is identical. This may prove invaluable, because the engine-room staff of the tow are then in a position to correct any list or adverse trim which may otherwise cause severe yawing. The power supply should be through one length of cable, because joints are unlikely to be watertight. A 16-mm wire rope should be rigged between the two ships as a jackstay, continually adjustable for conditions of roll and relative drift. The electric cable must be stopped in loose bights to the jackstay, parcelling both lines where seizings occur.

MESSENGERS

These are usually fibre ropes used to send a heavier and more cumbersome line to a distant point. They are of sufficient strength to support the larger line, but are sufficiently small in size to be easily used on a warping drum.

MAKING CONTACT

The method employed here must depend largely upon the types of ships involved and the weather conditions. If the weather is very bad and there is no immediate urgency to commence towing it is preferable to wait for a moderation, and in darkness it is wise to postpone contact attempts until daylight.

Much has already been discussed in Chapter IX regarding this aspect of seamanship. The engine(s) of the towing vessel should be stopped, her way run off, and her drift relative to the other vessel can then be estimated. This is probably best done while lying on the same heading as the other ship and with all masts in line. It must be remembered, however, that when manœuvring in the lee of a disabled ship one's own lee drift rate is slightly retarded due to the protection from wind afforded by the other vessel. Similarly, if manœuvring to windward of a drifting ship, her rate of lee drift is likely to be reduced. In these circumstances two ships having equal lee-drift rates when well separated may be caused to close each other. The manœuvring Master must therefore be prepared to use full revolutions and helm to correct any such tendency.

Methods used for making contact may include:

(1) Manœuvring close enough to the stern or bows of the tow in order to cast a heaving line. The end of the tow to be approached will be the same as that shown for a lifeboat in Fig. 9.1, since this will minimise risk of collision. If the vessels are tending to drift apart several linesmen should be standing by in case the first cast fails to establish contact.

(2) A buoyant line attached to a life-buoy may be streamed to leeward of the tow. The crew of the latter vessel can then grapple for the line as the ship drifts across it. In the absence of a grappling iron, a lifeboat anchor would prove a good substitute. The tow could similarly stream such a line to windward, as she drifts, and it can be picked up by the crew of the towing vessel, which will proceed past close to windward.

(3) If the weather is suitable, contact may be established using a lifeboat.

(4) The quickest method under all conditions will probably be to use the rocket line-throwing appliance from either vessel. The crew of the target vessel will greatly facilitate this operation if they lower the main radio aerials. The fouling of a rocket on such obstructions is an all too frequent occurrence, and valuable time is wasted. The rocket should be fired downwind.

In cases (1) and (4), if the rocket is fired, or the heaving line cast from the forecastle head, the Master will have better manœuvring control, since he will have a clear view of the attempts. Throughout the line-work between the two vessels, care must be exercised not to revolve the propeller(s) until the lines are clear of the water. The use of storm oil will greatly assist the manœuvring, particularly if a lifeboat is used, but lines which become oily will be difficult to handle.

When passing lines it is most desirable that neither ship should have any way on other than lee drift. Naturally, any dangerous closing of the two vessels must be instantly corrected, but nevertheless, the gathering of sternway or headway will considerably hamper line-work. Further, the development of sternway in conditions of wind will result in the vessel commencing a swing.

If, in case (1), the two vessels have differing rates of lee drift, they may be brought close enough for line-casting by using the principle shown on page 192. The towing vessel lies to windward or leeward of the tow according to whether the latter ship has a slower or faster lee drift rate. A vessel drifting is likely to have some headway or sternway due to her ability to sail through the water. This has already been shown in Fig. 9.1, to which the reader should refer, where the resultant motion is composed of leeway and sailing-way.

When casting a line, or firing a rocket from the towing ship, the line should be secured to a messenger, which in turn is led along the ship's side, clear of all obstructions, passed in through the towing fairlead and secured to the towline. This enables the towline to be passed between the two vessels extremely quickly.

Communication should be arranged between the two ships either by radio, semaphore, megaphone, loud-hailer, signalling lamp, or by the International Code of Signals. If the vessel is a derelict, it will be advisable to send the Chief Officer and Chief Engineer across by boat (weather permitting) in order to survey the possibilities of towing. Later a basic crew can be put aboard for steering and watchkeeping and tending navigation lights. A member of the Catering Department should be included.

SECURING THE TOWLINE

The heaving- or rocket-line will be secured to a carefully flaked messenger which will be passed to the tow as rapidly as possible. This is then led to a warping drum and the tow-wire, or a larger messenger, hove across. Ideally, when passing the messenger which is directly attached to the towline, an additional similar messenger should be sent across and kept secured to both vessels throughout the towing voyage. A situation may arise, such as the parting of a link, when this secondary line will save valuable time which would normally be lost in establishing fresh contact. The line must be kept very slack and attended throughout the voyage so that it can be instantly veered as soon as the towline parts. If this is not done the messenger itself will break.

If towing on a chain bridle from the tow the length of each bridle leg should be as long as possible so as to reduce uneven stresses, which are bound to arise except when the tow is situated in the towing ship's wake. Usually the tow rides at a steady angle of sheer away from the wake. Such a sheer should not be corrected by shortening one bridle-leg, for a bad nip is bound to occur.

If the tow's windlass is damaged the cable should be well frapped to several pairs of bitts, making use in addition of other forecastle-head strong points. On the other hand, the chain cable need not be used, in which case the tow may use a wire bridle; the absence of any chain in the towline will necessitate a greater length of hawser in order to attain a suitable catenary. A wire bridle is often used when the vessel has to be towed sternfirst. If the tow is not equipped with many strong points on her forecastle head, or if the existing points are considered too weak, the towing hawser may be passed through her hawse pipes several times and finally shackled to its own part. Both anchors will have to be shipped on deck or securely hung off.

In an emergency, such as towing a burning vessel clear of others, a method sometimes employed is to pass the eye in the towing hawser (making such an eye as rapidly as possible if the existing one is too small) over a fluke of the tow's bower anchor.

When securing a heavy wire hawser it may be belayed to two or more sets of bitts on the same side of the ship. An efficient method is to take a round turn on each of the first pair of bitts and belay the hawser to the succeeding pairs. Each turn on a bollard must be securely hove taut and lightly lashed to the underlying turn before passing the next. If this is not done the wire will quickly spring off the bitts and prove unmanageable. Chain stoppers (or carpenters' stoppers) should be secured to each pair of bitts, and a chain check-stopper is rigged just inboard of the fairlead, for use in controlling the wire when it is being surged around the bitts. Whenever a hawser is secured to the bitts a turn should be passed around the bollard nearest the fairlead before belaying commences. Failure to do this will result in the first turn occurring at the far bollard, and the set of bitts may then be lifted from the deck.

TAKING UP THE TOW

This is probably the most critical phase yet discussed, for the towline has to be stressed at a very slow, increasing rate, and a dead load of tons some 10 000–20 000 tonnes started into motion by this stress. The towing vessel should move slowly ahead and veer the towing hawser to the

222

required length, and at the same time the crew of the tow can veer the cable to the pre-determined scope. The vessel must be stopped dead in the water while the towline is secured, and when all is ready the engine is worked ahead in short bursts of slow revolutions, say five to ten. An officer is stationed on the poop to continually report the lead and state of the towline, for on no account must it be allowed to break surface. If it does, the use of astern revolutions may cause the line to foul the propeller. Great patience must be exercised until the tow begins to move, when speed may be gradually developed. Even at this stage of increasing revolutions, care is necessary to avoid losing the catenary and having to start all over again.

If the two vessels are on the same heading, as the tow is taken up, the stress on the line is used to move the tow bodily through the water. Some Masters, however, prefer to head about 90 degrees away from the tow's fore-and-aft line in order that the initial low stress is used to turn the tow, and full bodily motion is not achieved until the stress is sufficiently developed.

THE TOWING VOYAGE

The tow must be equipped with proper lights as laid down in the Regulations for Prevention of Collision at Sea, but if she is not manned and no power is available oil lamps will only burn for about 16 hours. The use of a searchlight, trained by the towing vessel to illuminate the tow, will be necessary in the vicinity of other shipping. The towing vessel must also be equipped with the proper lights, as laid down.

During the voyage the bight of the towline must be kept below the surface, and its length should be adjusted in a heavy swell so that the two ships are *in step*, i.e. they rise and fall simultaneously. The catenary must not be allowed to foul the sea-bed, particularly when towing across the wind and current, for if the ships are towing slowly and are brought up by the towline they will be set down wind or stream and will collide, unless the line can be quickly slipped. The nips should be freshened regularly, and grease applied to fairleads at least twice a watch. Any padding or canvas must be renewed as required.

If the towline tends to break surface speed should be reduced or the line lengthened. In heavy weather the tow (if using chain cable) may veer an extra shackle or so, in order to add weight to the towline. In heavy weather the forces necessary to heave-to, or steam head to wind, will be too great, and the ships should either temporarily run downwind or else the towline could be slipped and the vessels allowed to drift until the weather moderates sufficiently for the voyage to be continued. In shallow waters with a smooth sea-bed, if the towline is slipped from the towing ship the other vessel will have an admirable sea anchor.

Great care must be exercised in altering course, a swing being corrected at once. At the slow speeds of towing the effects of wind and current will be very noticeable, and for this reason the shortest route may not prove to be the quickest. Steering is likely to be difficult because the towline is not secured at the ship's pivoting point, and the stern is therefore reluctant to move away from the direction of the towline.

If the tow is unable to steer and her yaw is great, chafe, uneven stresses, and bad nips will arise. The effects of wind, sea, freeboard, trim, list, underwater projections caused by damage, draught, and superstructures all tend to cause yawing. Undoubtedly the greatest single factor is an adverse trim.

A deep-draught ship will yaw less than one which is lightly laden. The effects of wind and sea upon yawing can be partially diminished by altering course or speed. A vessel trimmed by the head will yaw very badly unless she is towed sternfirst. A listed vessel tends to sheer continually towards her high side, the tendency being corrected by a low-side wind. If the ship has underwater projections forward of the pivoting point the effect is that of a trim by the head; if they exist off the centre-line of the ship she will sheer towards that side.

Yawing may be corrected by trimming the vessel by the stern, and this should be done by transferring weights rather than by loading water ballast, which will increase the stress on the towline. An increase of speed tends to correct a yaw directly caused by list, while a decrease in speed often reduces a yaw produced by adverse trim. If the tow has a constant angle of sheer to one side of the towing ship's wake it may be corrected by setting the tow's rudder at a fixed angle. This has the disadvantage, however, of creating an additional drag on the towline. In a twin-screw ship a yaw to one side can be corrected by trailing only one propeller, and in all ships such a sheer can be reduced by rigging a large awning as a sail, either at the bow or stern.

In rough weather the use of storm oil by both ships will assist in making conditions more comfortable.

SLIPPING THE TOW

Arrangements must be made for slipping the towline in an emergency. Such an emergency might be the foundering of the tow. In shallow waters, if time permits, the line may be buoyed first, using a buoywire sufficiently heavy to recover the end of the hawser.

Letting go the Hawser at the Destination

This is almost as difficult as taking up the tow. Speed must be reduced very gradually so that the tow does not over-ride the other ship. This danger is partly avoided by allowing the towline to drag on the sea-bed (if smooth) for it will check the tow's headway, particularly if the line includes a length of chain. The crew of the tow should be prepared to let go an anchor immediately this danger arises and use it to check the headway as described in Chapter I (Anchoring at High Speed).

Once the way has been taken off both ships, the towline may be cast off, taking care not to revolve propellers while heaving the line aboard. If the tow has been using cable as part of the towline this is hove-in on the windlass and the wire cast off.

PRACTICAL TOWING

A typical example occurred in May 1959, when *Trochiscus*, 160 m in length overall, 16 500 tonnes deadweight, laden, and displacing some 21 500 tonnes, on passage from Singapore to Rotterdam, experienced a complete breakdown of the main propulsion unit when in the Indian Ocean. *Halia*, 170 m in length overall, 18 000 tonnes deadweight, in ballast, and bound for the Persian Gulf, proceeded to her assistance and successfully towed her, at an average speed of 6·5 knots, a total distance of 1 222 miles to Trincomalee, using 190 m of her own 50-mm wire towline connected to 210 m of anchor cable from *Trochiscus*.

525 ft
tons
tons

556 ft tons

95 fathoms 6-in
105 fathoms

While diverting to *Trochiscus*, *Halia* took on additional ballast to attain a full winter-ballast condition, so as to have a displacement similar to the vessel to be towed, and the following detailed preparations were put in hand to undertake the tow.

The 50-mm towing wire was laid out on deck on the starboard side, with the ends at the after end of the poop and the bight along the main deck. One end of this wire was secured with six turns round the 40-cm towing bitts, with backing turns to the capstans and 35-cm mooring bitts, and it is of interest to note that it took over 2 hours to complete the first part of this operation, each of the six turns having to be hove taut with the capstans, and lashed, before commencing the next turn. The capstans were then backed on to the forward mooring bitts on each side of the poop and the towing bitts securely shored from the roller fairleads, see Fig. 10.2. The Panama lead, through which the eye of the towline was led, was also shored from each side.

6-in

16-in
14-in

At the same time, a 30-mm wire mooring rope was flaked down on the port side of the poop deckhouse, once again with both ends at the after end of the poop, and a chain stopper rigged to control the wire while paying out, see Fig. 10.1. One end was then led through the port quarter fairlead to the Panama lead on the centre line, where it was shackled to the towing hawser, just clear of the additional serving. This method of securing the towing hawser enabled it to be shackled on to the anchor cable without first having to disconnect the 30-mm wire, see Fig. 10.3. The other end of the 30-mm wire was made fast to a 35-mm rope

3½-in

3½-in
3½-in 4-in

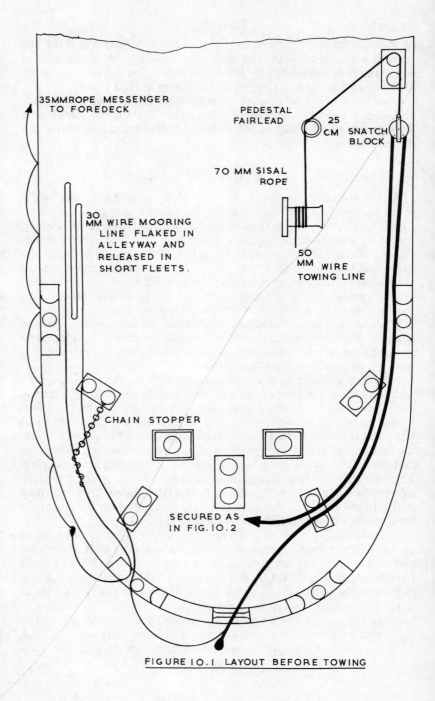

35MM ROPE MESSENGER TO FOREDECK

PEDESTAL FAIRLEAD

25 CM

SNATCH BLOCK

70 MM SISAL ROPE

30 MM WIRE MOORING LINE FLAKED IN ALLEYWAY AND RELEASED IN SHORT FLEETS.

50 MM WIRE TOWING LINE

CHAIN STOPPER

SECURED AS IN FIG. 10.2

FIGURE 10.1 LAYOUT BEFORE TOWING

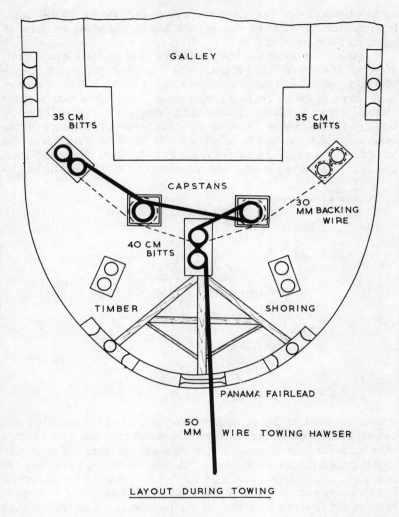

GALLEY

35 CM BITTS

35 CM BITTS

CAPSTANS

30 MM BACKING WIRE

40 CM BITTS

TIMBER

SHORING

PANAMA FAIRLEAD

50 MM WIRE TOWING HAWSER

LAYOUT DURING TOWING

FIGURE 10.2

messenger which had been made ready by hanging it along the port side in bights, clear of all obstructions, to the foredeck, where it was bent on to the end of the rocket-line.

In the meantime, *Trochiscus* had lifted her starboard anchor on deck and disconnected the cable, which was then hove-up through the hawse pipe, where a joining shackle was prepared for attaching the cable to

227

Halia's towing wire. A rope was made ready for heaving the messenger from the towing vessel up through the hawse pipe using the forward winch on the main deck.

Trochiscus was sighted on the morning of 23 May, and Captain R. R. Potter of *Halia* established contact with Captain J. Davison by radio-telephone, whereupon the procedure to be followed was fully discussed. *Halia* came in for an approach from some 3 miles dead astern of the disabled vessel, which was rolling and yawing beam-on to a long, low swell, and eased in close under her lee (starboard) side. During this run-in period, which was accomplished at a very slow speed, there was time to assess the handling qualities of *Halia* under the prevailing conditions, and also to observe the drift and movement of *Trochiscus*. In this in-

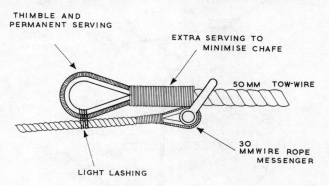

FIGURE 10.3

stance, it transpired that coming up from astern was the best approach course, but this cannot be taken as a hard-and-fast rule, as a different set of conditions may considerably influence the angle of approach. 70 ft *Halia*, in fact, passed about 20 m off the starboard side of the tow and 80 ft eventually came to rest about 25 m ahead of her. While passing, a line-throwing rocket was fired from *Halia* and connection was made between the two vessels. Here, the forethought that had been applied to the whole operation, and the care with which preparations had been made, became most creditably evident, and this will be readily appreciated in that 11 minutes after the rocket had been fired across the foredeck of *Trochiscus* the tow was shackled up.

As already mentioned, the towline was laid out along the starboard side of *Halia*'s main deck, and an ingenious method was devised of paying it out under complete control. The bight was rove through a 10-in 25-cm snatch block at the end of a mooring rope led to the winch on the

228

after deck, and it was thus possible to ease it out to the towing length of 190 m without fear of kinking or of taking charge, see Fig. 10.1.   **95 fathoms** (*Author's Note:* I have drawn Fig. 10.1 with clarity in mind, but it must be appreciated that two different decks are involved. Where the towline crosses the break of the poop, heavy wooden pads were used to prevent chafing of the wire on the plate edges.)

Although *Trochiscus* was loaded with high-flash cargo, suitable precautions were nevertheless taken against fire. fire-hoses being rigged, portable extinguishers placed in strategic positions, and all personnel not required on deck keeping under cover, there being an ever-present risk of the two vessels making physical contact. In as far as any danger may exist from the actual firing of the rocket line, it is desirable to point out that this may be considered negligible, provided the hulls of both vessels are intact and all tank openings properly closed.

As soon as *Trochiscus* had shackled on, her starboard cable was walked out to 7 shackles (193 m) and secured, and, in 38 minutes   **105 fathoms** from the time the rocket-line was fired across from *Halia*, the towing actually commenced. The method of securing the cable was by leaving it on the windlass, screwing up both brakes, putting on the devil's claws, and tightening up the bottle-screws. The commencement of the tow was a most critical period, when a rash engine movement or helm order would have completely undone hours of patient work and preparation, and might in fact have caused irreparable damage or loss. This risk was avoided in this case and, from being stopped, the first order was 5 revolutions per minute (0·75 knot) gradually building up by steps of 5 revolutions at 5-minute intervals, to 50 revolutions per minute, which gave an engine speed of 7·5 knots. Similarly, course was altered not more than 10 degrees at a time and the tow allowed to settle down before any additional alteration in course was made.

Slight trouble was experienced initially with the towline wearing through the chafing pad in the Panama lead, but this problem was overcome by the design and production of a patent multi-sleeved clamp, see Fig. 10.4. This consisted of three cup-shaped sections of 1·5-mm hard $\frac{1}{16}$-in copper sheet, one of 1·5-mm soft copper sheet, and an inner sheet of $\frac{1}{16}$-in 1·5-mm lead, with all friction surfaces thoroughly greased. The clamp $\frac{1}{16}$-in was first lightly secured round the towline on the inboard side, and the towline raised clear of the lower side of the fairlead by means of a 4-tonne   **ton** chain tackle secured to the hose-handling derrick pedestal. The sleeve was then slid into position and the packing pieces placed underneath. Clamped on the wire over a foundation of three coir doormats and eight thicknesses of canvas, this arrangement was found to be eminently effective in reducing chafe.

The initial tendency of *Trochiscus* to yaw, putting an added strain on the towline, was nullified by steering in the wake of *Halia*, and this proved satisfactory at a towing speed of 6·5 knots, until a fresh quarterly breeze was experienced towards the end of the voyage, when it was found that the tow automatically settled down a couple of points on the quarter. This same tendency to yaw was observed when speed was reduced approaching Trincomalee Harbour, when cable was shortened, and experience showed that all phases of altering course and reducing speed had to be cautiously achieved, step by step.

Off port, the services of a harbour tug were obtained to prevent the disabled vessel overrunning the tow while the cable was hove-up and

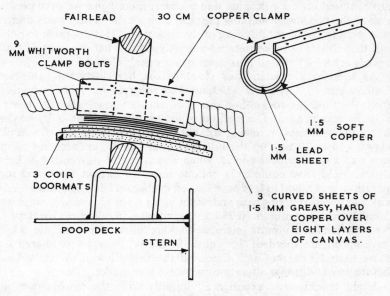

FIGURE 10.4

the towing wire disconnected. Slowing down a tow of this size requires considerable time and involves almost as much care as when getting under way. After slipping, *Halia*'s tow wire was recovered by adopting a similar procedure, but in reverse, to that used when connecting up, and it worked smoothly and efficiently.

It must, indeed, have been a relief to both Masters to see their ships safely in port, and it is no small tribute to the seamanship and ability of all concerned that the voyage was completed with so little trouble.

(The above example is from the *Shell Magazine*, and is based by Nautical Division, Shell Tankers Ltd., on reports from the vessels concerned and is reproduced here by the courtesy of the Company.)

230

CHAPTER XI

FIRE

A N outbreak of fire occurs when sufficient heat is applied to a flammable material within an atmosphere freely charged and supplied with oxygen. The fire will continue provided these three elements are present, and together they form what is known as the *fire triangle*. When one side or element is removed the triangle or fire can no longer exist. The process of fire-fighting involves eliminating one or more of these elements. Heat may be dissipated by cooling the area with water, flammable material may be physically removed and oxygen can be prevented from reaching the fire by placing a blanket of suitable material or gas between the burning substance and the atmosphere.

OXIDATION

All substances, when submitted to varying degrees of heat, emit gases from their surfaces as part of the slow chemical combustion known as oxidation. At a certain temperature, known as the *flash point*, gas is evolved in sufficient quantities which, when mixed with air in the correct combustible proportion, will flash when a naked light is introduced. Well above this temperature exists the *Spontaneous Ignition Temperature* (S.I.T.) at which, provided sufficient air is available, the substance will burst into flame without the introduction of a naked flame. The flash point of petrols is below −18°C. Because of this, petroleum is a highly dangerous substance even in Arctic conditions. The S.I.T. for most petroleum oils is between 260°C and 370°C. In the United Kingdom, substances with flash points below 23°C are deemed and must be labelled, *highly* flammable. If the flash point is between 23° and 60°C the substance is considered flammable.

500° and 700°F
73°F
73° and 141°F

All substances should be stowed in ships so that under normal conditions they cannot become heated to the flash point. In the case of highly flammable goods this is difficult to achieve other than by cold storage, and they should therefore be in airtight containers free from seepage. Provided air can be excluded from these substances, the vapour at their surfaces will be too rich for flashing to occur. If too much oxygen

231

is combined, such as at a considerable distance above the fluid level, the mixture will be too weak to flash. It is only at some small distance above the surface that flashing conditions are possible.

DESTRUCTION OF THE FIRE TRIANGLE

1. Removing the Heat by Means of Water

For several reasons, water is the ideal material to achieve this purpose. It has a high *specific heat*, i.e. it requires a great amount of heat to change its temperature one degree and needs a further input of 540 times as much heat to change it from boiling fluid into steam. Under normal atmospheric pressures it cannot be heated above 100°C and can in fact be boiled in a paper bag because the latter requires to be heated to nearly double this temperature before it will burn. Provided the bag is porous and remains wet, combustion cannot occur. When using water to extinguish a fire it is therefore imperative to keep the burning materials saturated. If they are poor absorbers of water, such as hardwood or rubber, or non-absorbers, such as metals, the saturation will occur at the surface only, and a continuous spray is necessary in order to dissipate the heat. Certain metals will burn if they come into contact with water, such as sodium and potassium, and these must be immersed in paraffin (kerosene) in order to exclude water vapour.

212°F

In addition to its cooling properties, water used for fire extinguishing is continuously vaporising into steam. The volume of steam created is about 1700 times as great as the original volume of water, and since it is an inert gas, the fire is starved of oxygen.

The use of sea-water should be avoided where possible, since it will quickly spoil goods surrounding the fire zone, particularly foodstuffs. Not only will it corrode steels, copper, and electrical machinery but it is also slow drying and finally leaves a corrosive residue of salts. The chemical action of sea-water on a molasses fire will rapidly produce toxic fumes.

The use of water in the vicinity of acids is dangerous. Acids are diluted by adding *them* slowly to water until the desired mixture is obtained. If, however, the water, and particularly sea-water, is admitted into a large quantity of concentrated acid, rapid heating, spluttering, and the evolution of toxic fumes occurs.

Carbides in contact with water will generate explosive and flammable acetylene gas in addition to heat.

If water is applied to burning coal or coke the generated steam, unless released quickly, will cause the emission of dangerous and highly combustible gases.

An oil fire may be extinguished by applying a water spray, but the use of a water *jet* will scatter the burning oil, which will float and cause isolated outbreaks of fire widely dispersed around the original fire zone. The use of water on an oil fire presents certain problems which are discussed in the subsequent treatment of liquid fuel fires.

When water is used to flood a compartment the following points should be borne in mind:

(1) Flooding high in the vessel reduces her stability.

(2) Flooding at the sides produces a list.

(3) Flooding low in the ship tends to increase her stability.

(4) All flooding, unless water is being transferred within the ship, reduces the freeboard and the reserve buoyancy, while it always creates a free surface effect which reduces stability.

(5) If the stability becomes zero or negative the ship will loll over to one side. If the fire zone is then situated on the high side of the ship it may become quite clear of the water level, enabling it to spread upwards throughout the ship on the high side. The high-side plating will then have to be cut open to admit further water and this, flowing to the low side, will further increase the list until capsizing may occur.

(6) If cutting holes in the ship's side to admit dock water, it should be remembered that the vessel can be flooded only up to the level of those holes. Once this is achieved, any further water applied by hose will level out with the dock water. The vessel is now in such a predicament that she may have to be flooded in other sound compartments in order to increase her displacement and immerse the holes.

(7) Any liquid fuels which are burning will float on the surface of the water and will gradually fire the upper compartments as the water level rises.

(8) If at sea, flooding may seriously impair the safety and manoeuvrability of the ship.

(9) The suctions are likely to be choked with debris, and once the fire is extinguished, the problem arises of how to pump the compartment dry. In this connection, a pump can only create a complete vacuum, and since air pressure can be measured by a water barometer 10·3 m in height, it follows that a pump can lift water to itself only if it is within 10·3 m of the water level. In practice, a high-efficiency pump may be able to develop a lift of 7·6 m while other pumps may achieve only 6·1 m. Thus, if the water level is more than 7·6 m below an efficient pump the latter will be of no value unless arrangements can be made to lower it and suspend it closer to the surface.

34 ft
34 ft
25 ft
20 ft
25 ft

Once the pump is able to develop a lift of water into its body, it may then be used to discharge water at some higher level, and in this connection it is interesting to note that a pressure of 100 grammes per cm^2 is necessary to raise the water 1 m in the discharge hose. If, for example, it is desired to deliver the water 10 m above the pump the pressure at the hose outlet will be 1 kg per cm^2 less than at the pump discharge.

(10) Water used to cool the bulkheads and boundary plating of a compartment, inside which a fire is being smothered by steam, will increase the rate at which the latter condenses on the inside of the plating. The steam, in condensing, will contract to one-seventeen-hundredth of its volume, and this original volume of occupation will tend to become a partial vacuum. The effect of this may be to induce air draughts through crevices which previously admitted no appreciable quantity of air. The fire may thus obtain a new oxygen feed.

Fire pumps, whether auxiliaries of the main propulsion unit or of independent Diesel type, are usually capable of supplying from 50 to 80 tonnes per hour. A hose, delivering water at a pressure of 3·5 kg per cm^2, may pass about 15 tonnes of water per hour through a jet nozzle and nearly double this amount through a spray nozzle due to the lower resistance in the latter case.

In a drydock full fire-fighting preparations should be made as soon as the vessel docks. Hoses are difficult to run from the dockside to the ship and the operation takes considerable time, so they should be kept permanently rigged. If pumps are under repair a supply of water should be arranged from ashore either through several rigged hoses or by means of one hose coupled to the ship's fire main or wash-deck line.

When flooding a fire in a drydocked vessel the effects of the added weight are very serious. The vessel is naturally unstable while on the blocks, and any flooding will aggravate this condition. In addition to this, high keel stresses are set up. The fact that the hull no longer has the cooling effect of surrounding sea-water means that a fire is likely to spread rapidly to adjacent compartments.

The fire main runs throughout the vessel, on both sides, and has hydrant outlets. The fire hoses, when required, are secured to the outlets by means of instantaneous couplings of 6·3 cm diameter. Two jets of water are capable of being directed to any one compartment by the fire main. The line is supplied by several pumps widely dispersed so that a fire will not render them all out of action. If the fire main is damaged the stop valves on either side of the fracture should be closed. The water is then by-passed by connecting a hose between two hydrants, each beyond the stop valves.

The hoses are fitted with jet or jet/spray nozzles of 12-mm outlet diameter. These should never be used for levering or hammering in an

234

---

1 lb/in^2 2 ft

30 ft
15 lb/in^2

tons 50 lb/in^2
tons

2½ in

½-in

emergency, and should be treated with respect at all times. The hoses are normally made of canvas, the use of rubber being prohibited. They are not to be used for any other purpose, must be drained and dried before stowage subsequent to firefighting or drill, and must not be left rolled up for long periods. They are drained by raising them to about shoulder height and then walking slowly forward, under-running the entire length. Walking on them will both drain and *damage* them very efficiently. They should not be painted, washed in strong cleansing fluids, or contaminated with oil or grease.

2. Smothering to Exclude Oxygen

The following are the substances normally used for this purpose:

(a) Steam. This gas is lighter than air, and will therefore seek to occupy the upper volume of the compartment. If the fire zone is situated at low level the steam will have to be injected for some considerable time before it will penetrate all the crevices within the fire. Its efficiency will be lowered if an air feed exists at low level, such as a damaged shaft-tunnel door.

In a fire area where packages are loosely stowed the steam may effectively control flame, but due to the high temperature, which will not be below 100°C, oxidation and slow combustion may continue, rendering the compartment liable to flashing when opened to the atmosphere. 212°F Some cargoes, such as grain and wood pulp, may swell extensively under the hot, moist conditions of steam smothering.

In the early stages of steam injection continuous condensation will occur, and any re-vaporisation of this moisture will assist in cooling the fire zone. With regard to the condensation, goods which are susceptible to water damage will be harmed by the application of steam.

It has already been mentioned that steam injection provides little or no cooling effect, and heat conductivity will continue freely to adjacent compartments, where further oxidation and flashing may occur. For this reason, flammable materials in adjacent compartments should be removed or kept sprayed with water while extinguishing a fire with steam injection.

The injection of steam into a burning stack of coal or coke produces an explosive and highly combustible water gas such as is produced in the retorts of a gas works.

(b) Carbon Dioxide. This gas is heavier than air and is a non-supporter of combustion, so it will effectively blanket a fire and exclude the oxygen from the burning material. It has the advantage of causing no damage to goods, but it will rapidly become heated and therefore conduct heat to adjacent compartments. The gas will settle at the bottom of a compartment, increasing in depth as the supply continues. As its level rises, air in the vicinity is driven to the top of the compartment. If the zone has been closed to the atmosphere it is possible that the pressure of the carbon dioxide in the bottom will become equal to that of the air layer, and should the fire exist at high level it will burn until the air is exhausted of oxygen, during which time the smothering gas is of no value, neither can more be injected. In the case of a very hot fire, however, there will be sufficient turbulence to mix the gas with the air, and as soon as the mixture has a 30–40% concentration of carbon dioxide the fire will be unable to continue.

It is not advisable to inject carbon dioxide and steam together since the cool gas ($-79°C$) will condense steam, producing vacuum and carbonic acid. The two gases are not compatible in fire-fighting. The normal level of carbon dioxide in air is 0·033% by volume.

Starvation of Air. Generally, the use of carbon dioxide or steam as a smothering gas calls for a sealed compartment to complete the control of oxygen, but unless the compartment is a tank the best that can be hoped for is a partial stifling effect and a retardation of oxygen inflow. When firefighters are working in a compartment the stifled air flow may at times have to be increased in order to dissipate heat and smoke.

In compartments adjacent to a fire ventilation should be maintained normally or even increased in order to dissipate heat and prevent oxidation and flashing. This does not apply to tanks containing liquid fuel, which should preferably be pressed full in order to exclude all air.

(c) **High-Expansion and Detergent Foams.** These are manufactured from waste protein matter. Shore fire-fighting brigades are equipped with machines which can inject this type of foam through powerful fans, filling a large space within minutes. The advantage of this material is that it is unlikely to cause damage to cargoes. Complete blanketing of the fire is achieved. On tankers, detergent foam can be made by drawing controlled amounts of the basic detergent concentrate into branch pipes fed with high pressure water.

(d) **Chemical Foam.** This is generated by solutions of sodium bicarbonate and aluminium sulphate in combined activity, and will effectively
2-gal blanket a fire. It may be supplied direct from a 9-litre portable extin-
10- or 30-gal guisher, by hose nozzle from 45- or 135-litre extinguishers, or in very large quantities from a permanently installed apparatus, via perforated pipes. When used on a burning liquid fuel it should be very lightly sprayed to avoid scattering the fire, or else directed at a nearby surface so that the stream disintegrates and flows gently over the fuel.

(e) **Solids.** Asbestos blankets or quantities of sand may be thrown over small fires, such as burning oils or fats, in order to exclude the atmosphere.

The use of all smothering materials, whether solid, liquid, or gaseous, provides little cooling effect, and it is therefore imperative to maintain the smothering until the fire zone has cooled sufficiently to prevent re-ignition when starvation ceases. Breathing apparatus should be worn when entering a blanketed compartment, even when high-expansion foam has been injected. If a face mask should break, the firefighter should instantly switch to continuous air feed and escape as soon as possible. The body is used to breathing 0.033% carbon dioxide and a concentration of only 10% will induce rapid unconsciousness.

Once a fire has been controlled with the use of smothering gas, the inflow should be maintained, at a reduced rate if necessary, until all dangers of re-ignition are past. If the fire is prematurely considered to be extinguished, or the zone sufficiently cool, and injection of gas is ceased, a renewed fire may be an extremely difficult one to bring under control, particularly when supplies of carbon dioxide are running low.

3. Removing Flammable Material

This entails clearing the edge of the fire zone of all combustible material. It is not, of course, suggested that blazing material should be moved, since this is safer left to burn out, even if of an explosive nature. Firefighting is concentrated at the fire zone, and any scattering by explosion is far more easily dealt with in that area rather than elsewhere, where a brave man, attempting to jettison blazing explosive material, may cause loss of life, new outbreaks of fire, and division of the firefighting strength.

Providing the outskirts of the fire can be starved of material food, control will be certain, but by outskirts is meant not only the immediate vicinity but all adjacent compartments. Gas cylinders are likely to explode due to the expansion of their contents under heat, and should be removed from the area or continually sprayed with water.

SOURCES OF FIRE

These are too numerous, and often completely unexpected, to list extensively, but a few of the more common sources are included:

(a) Leakage of Oils on to Hot Surfaces, Particularly within the Engine- and Boiler-rooms

This sometimes occurs when settling tanks overflow, oil hot-filters or oil supply lines leak on to exhaust uptakes or boiler surfaces. Suitable overflow alarm devices, overflow gutters, screens, and adequate lighting will prevent many of these fires, which have caused the loss of several ships and many lives. Any boiler-room supplied with an oil feed should have as much access as possible from the engine-room to enable fire-fighting to be effective. No woodwork should be permitted in boiler-rooms or engine-rooms supplied with oil, tank tops and floor plates should be scrupulously clean, any oil should be soaked up at once and the oily waste destroyed, bilges should be kept as free as possible from oil, and all combustible material kept well away from oil-feed lines. Fire appliances should be regularly examined, all personnel made familiar with their use and location, and foam appliances kept away from high temperatures, which may destroy the properties of the ingredients.

(b) Welding and Other Repairs

These produce sparking, and portable extinguishers should be kept at hand, both in the repair area and on the *opposite* side of the repair work (when possible) where a fire is likely to break out due to local heating. The compartment should be inspected regularly between work shifts for signs of smouldering.

(c) Seepage of Flammable Vapours or Fuels into Adjacent Compartments where Welding is in Progress or where Men are Smoking

(d) The Use of Radio or Radar Equipment

This can induce currents at very high electrical pressures, and should therefore not be worked when loading or discharging inflammable substances.

(e) Spontaneous Combustion

Many fires tend to be attributed to this phenomenon, since no person is then involved in blame. Probably in nine cases out of ten the fire originated from some other cause, often careless smoking, the dangers of which cannot be stressed too frequently. Certain fibrous substances, when impregnated with suitable oils, such as jute with colza oil, cotton waste with fuel oil, or canvas with paint, do become heated and may catch fire, particularly if the heating is accelerated by local unlagged steam pipes or other hot surfaces.

100°F   This type of combustion may occur when oxygen is absorbed at the surfaces of coal, particularly when bituminous and finely broken, and in such cases is accelerated at temperatures close to 38°C. The coal should be kept as cool as possible and all air supplies blocked off except for surface ventilators, which are used to remove the explosive methane gas. This gas is dangerous when concentrated 5% in air.

All materials which are liable to spontaneous combustion should be regularly tested for temperature, especially when carried as cargo. Risks are always minimised by local cooling.

(f) Electrical Fires

A short-circuit, the failure of an unscreened fuse, or overloading of wiring may result in a fire outbreak. Whenever a fire exists in a ship it is possible for insulation to become charred near the fire zone. The resulting short-circuit, i.e. a path of very low resistance for the current, results in a surge of excessive current which may overload the wiring and heat it sufficiently for it to burn. Such an outbreak may occur at the switchboard or even at places elsewhere and quite remote from the main fire zone.

While a fire exists, and for some considerable time after it has been extinguished, the switchboard should be closely watched for signs of overloading.

(g) Static Electricity

Many fires have started as a result of sparks caused by the discharge of static electricity at high voltage. An example occurs when friction within a filling hose produces static electricity, and the petrol or other fuel passing through it is ignited. Both the hose end and the filled tank should be securely earthed, as should all other equipment which is subject to static charging.

(h) Floating Oil or Petrol on the Surface of a Dock, the Sea, or a River

This may be ignited by a carelessly thrown cigarette end. The blazing fuel may be extinguished by means of a foam spray; or it can be driven clear of the ship either by powerful water jets or by the propeller wash of a small launch.

A vessel in collision may be surrounded by an area of burning fuel on the water surface. In a current the vessel may be brought quickly to anchor, and the stream will then carry the fuel clear of the ship. If no current exists, the vessel should, if possible, be moved rapidly clear of the fire zone.

(j) Steam Pipes

These should be regularly checked to make sure they are properly lagged. Such surfaces, if unprotected, may quickly start a fire among surrounding materials.

(k) Hot Bulkheads

These are equally dangerous if left uninsulated. A case occurred where a hot engine-room bulkhead ignited the cork insulation of an adjacent hold containing a full cargo of frozen butter. The only possible method of extinguishing was flooding of the entire compartment. Fortunately the permeability of the hold was very low, due to the compact block-stow of the butter, and the space existing for water was adjacent to the insulation. Only a small amount of water was needed to flood the hold, and the fire was quickly put out. The sea-water damage to the butter was less than 1 %, but the use of air sheathing on the engine-room side of the bulkhead, or fibre-glass insulation within the hold, would have greatly minimised the fire risk.

(l) Funnel Sparking

This can be avoided, or at least reduced, by regular cleaning of the exhaust uptakes. Burning of awnings, lifeboats, and other deck equipment is then less likely to occur.

(m) Timber

This is very combustible, and should be stowed well clear of hot surfaces and fuels.

(n) Galley Fires

These are not uncommon, and are frequently caused by the boiling-over on to hot-plates, or the ignition, of unattended cooking fats. Galley hoods should be cleaned regularly and not allowed to become caked with grease, which may be fired by heat uptake.

(o) Paint

This is very combustible, containing and evolving flammable substances. It should never be stowed other than in the official paint locker, which should be well away from heat areas. Isolated pots of paint left lying about the ship constitute a fire risk.

Ideally, painted surfaces should be maintained with the minimum of coats in order to reduce the amount of permanent combustible material. Paint will burn very rapidly indeed, and can quickly turn accommodation into an inferno. The use of heat-resistant plastic laminated materials is preferable to paint decoration.

(p) Batteries

These evolve an explosive and flammable gas and should be stowed in well-ventilated cool compartments containing a portable extinguisher.

(q) Leaky, Defective Packages Containing Flammable Materials

These are extremely dangerous, particularly when stowed in the holds on wooden dunnage. All such containers should be rejected.

(r) Smoking

This has caused the total loss of ships, and any regulations on board a vessel regarding this habit should be adhered to strictly. Cigarette ends must be properly extinguished and not thrown on to the deck or over the side. In both cases they may be blown through doors, portholes, or ventilators, causing a fire. Smoking in bunks has caused loss of life through the smoker prematurely falling asleep. In no circumstances should smoking be permitted in holds, for a burning cigarette end may smoulder beneath sawdust and similar material for many days before the smoke is detected. It is for this reason that many fires, discovered when several days out of port, are thought to be due to spontaneous combustion, since few people realise the length of time which can elapse before a carelessly thrown cigarette end will start a *detectable* fire.

FIRE PATROLS

These are required to be carried out regularly in Class 1 ships. Great care should be exercised in selecting patrolmen, for they should be physically and mentally suited to the task and well trained in modern firefighting techniques. Each man should be provided with a whistle or other portable alarm-signalling device. Every part of the ship should be visited at least once in every hour, and patrolmen should report at a place which is manned at all times, where all detection alarm bells ring, and which is provided with adequate fire appliances.

DISPERSAL OF GEAR

The fire appliances should be widely dispersed throughout the ship and in such a way that they may be easily found in conditions of smoke or darkness.

GENERAL ACTION IN THE EVENT OF FIRE OUTBREAK

The person first discovering the fire should instantly raise the alarm and commence fighting the flames. If it is rapidly and correctly attacked it may well be restricted to a small outbreak, rendering major measures unnecessary. Alarm bells should, if necessary, be rung throughout the ship, a continuous ringing being the usual signal, bearing in mind that too many persons at the scene of the fire may cause confusion. At sea emergency stations should be sounded and the boats swung out ready for lowering if it is thought that the fire is, or will be, of major proportions.

It is imperative to gain rapid access to a fire, but in many cases this may be possible only from above, where movements are hampered by rising smoke and heat. Every endeavour should be made to discover whether the fire has an air feed at low level. If this is so, and a means of access exists, the fire should be fought from this level, where a cool, fresh air supply will benefit the firefighters. If no means of access exists, the air feed should be blocked. A hose can be lowered from above, on lines, and directed at the seat of the fire.

Cutting holes in plating to gain access causes an air feed and destroys the ship's watertight integrity. In an accommodation fire access may be obtained by lowering a hose-handler over the side on a boatswain's chair so that he can direct a water jet through a porthole.

Generally, the Officer in charge of firefighting operations should not take part in the actual fighting, but should attend the entire perimeter of the fire zone and keep himself fully informed so that he is the ideal person to direct personnel.

He should:

(1) Make sure that the fire is stifled as efficiently as possible and that ventilating fans are switched off.
(2) Alter the course of the vessel so that the apparent wind force on board is nil, unless dense smoke is hampering operations.
(3) Discover what is burning, and also the seat of the fire.
(4) Muster appliances as necessary.
(5) Find all possible means of access.
(6) Ascertain that a sufficient water supply exists, using emergency pumps as required.
(7) Discover whether dangerous gases are present and equip firefighters with breathing apparatus.
(8) Ensure the safety of the firefighters.
(9) Always have a spare breathing apparatus available outside the fire zone, for rescue work.
(10) Spray all adjacent bulkheads and goods.
(11) Spray or flood any adjacent magazines containing dangerous goods.
(12) Muster extra firefighters and appliances as necessary.
(13) Watch for any complications that may arise.
(14) Continually watch for signs of the fire spreading.
(15) Remove any surrounding materials which are in danger of igniting.
(16) Make use of the ship's construction to prevent fire spread.
(17) Consider the ship's stability and pumping arrangements, if water is being used.
(18) Consider outbreaks of electrical fires.

In port, the local Fire Brigade should be called if the fire is beyond the control of the ship's staff, particularly in drydock. Liaison between the Chief Fire Officer and the ship's Officer in charge is most important, and the former must be acquainted with the following facts:

(a) When the fire was discovered.
(b) Where the seat of the fire is located.

(c) What cargo is burning and what materials are near by.
(d) Whether any fireproof bulkheads exist.
(e) Whether ventilators are closed and where they are located.
(f) The pumping capacity both on the fire-main and on the bilge discharges.
(g) The weight of water which is able to be pumped into the ship, bearing in mind her stability.
(h) Details of the ship's construction which may affect firefighting.
(j) Any lighting arrangements.
(k) When the compartment was last opened.
(l) Whether adjacent plating is becoming heated.

THE NECESSITY FOR, AND THE USE OF, BREATHING APPARATUS

It is most important to appreciate that a gas mask is designed to filter oxygen from a fouled atmosphere. If no oxygen is present the use of a gas mask will in no way prevent a person's asphyxiation. A breathing apparatus should therefore be used, and will usually be either one in which the wearer carries a bottle of oxygen or else one in which air is supplied through a long flexible hose, either by direct suction on the part of the wearer or by foot-operated bellows. In all cases the wearer uses a lifeline, and may signal to those at its other end by giving, say,

1 pull to mean 'More air required', or
2 pulls to mean 'Slack the lifeline', or
3 pulls to mean 'Get me out quickly'.

If the others give three pulls on the line this could be used to indicate. to the wearer, 'Come out at once.'

The lifeline is usually 10-mm hemp line with a wire heart and a breaking stress of 1 tonne. It is at least 3 m longer than the air hose. If the hose is more than 27·5 m long it must supply air by means of bellows.   1¼-in ton 10 ft 90 ft

Class 1 ships are required to carry one breathing apparatus for every 30 m of registered length, of which at least two must be the air-hose type. Class 7 ships are required to carry: 100 ft

1 air-hose type if the vessel is 500–2 500 tonnes.
2 appliances (one must be air-hose) if between 2 500 and 4 000 tonnes.
3 appliances (two must be air-hose) if over 4 000 tonnes.

The self-contained apparatus has the disadvantage of supplying a limited quantity of gas, and when the wearer is climbing out of a compartment his exertions will demand a larger amount of oxygen than the appliance may be able to provide.

It is most important for the wearer to avoid a circular path when groping in a smoky or dark atmosphere, for he may wind his lifeline around pillars, etc. If he crawls on all fours his visibility will be improved, since the smoke is continually rising. Further, he will avoid the risk of stumbling and injuring himself. He must always move very carefully and make sure that the surface ahead is quite firm.

If breathing apparatus is used by a person sporting anything larger than a small beard, water or grease should be applied to the beard to make sure that the face mask fits tightly.

A firefighter should bear in mind that when directing his water jet through crevices it may suddenly strike at the seat of the fire and there is likely to be a violent blow-back of hot gases and steam.

Carbon fuels, when burning in a plentiful supply of oxygen, evolve carbon dioxide gas, which, while not toxic, is unable to sustain life and when concentrated 9% in air is likely to prove fatal. If the same fuels burn in an atmosphere starved of oxygen, so that combustion is incomplete, odourless, tasteless, and highly toxic carbon monoxide gas is evolved; $\frac{1}{2}$% of this gas in air is fatal. Nearly all combustible materials contain carbon. If the fire is burning well with little smoke an abundant supply of oxygen is present, while the reverse is true when the fire burns badly, emitting much smoke. In this latter case fatal proportions of both carbon gases are probably present.

Petroleum fumes can be fatal when in a 0·1% concentration with air.

Oxygen will be in short supply both after an explosion and when entering a compartment which has been closed for some time, particularly if fresh paint exists, since this rapidly absorbs oxygen. The use of proper breathing apparatus is imperative, both when fire exists and *when entering a newly opened tank as part of normal ship routine*. In both cases unnecessary casualties are avoided which, in the instance of fire, will seriously hamper the efforts of the fighters.

A firefighter will find a spray nozzle useful for driving smoke ahead of him.

THE CONTROLLED FIRE

When this is believed to be true, the following points should be considered:

(1) Whether it is safe to open the compartment in order to ventilate and inspect.
(2) The breaking up and drenching with water of all smouldering debris.
(3) Steps to be taken to prevent re-ignition within the fire zone.
(4) Damage to cargo, the ship's structure, and electrical circuits.
(5) The removal of water from the compartment.

(6) The immediate servicing and recharging of all fire appliances in case there is a fresh outbreak.

(7) The treatment of all burns by first aid. Pain should be relieved by administering morphia. The burn should be protected from the air (which promotes pain) by means of clean dry dressings, making no attempt to clean or touch the burn, or to remove any clothing adhering to it. Victims of shock should be laid flat, kept warm, and given hot, sweet drinks.

FIRE TYPES

(1) Coal

A fire within bunker or cargo coal may be very slow-burning, and it may take several days to control by using carbon dioxide gas, steam being unsuitable. Often, it is of such major proportions that the fire cannot be extinguished, and it is therefore kept under control until the vessel reaches port, when the services of the local Fire Brigade are employed. Here, the danger of flashing exists when the compartment is opened. The adjacent plating must be kept cool and a constant watch kept on boundary temperatures.

If the fire cannot be controlled by carbon dioxide, flooding of the zone should be considered. If fighting a coal fire by means of hoses the coal should first be discharged in order to expose the seat of the fire, taking great care when walking on the surface of the coal in case it collapses. Surface ventilation should be maintained during this operation in order to clear away explosive gases.

(2) Liquid Fuels

Before these can be ignited, vapours must be emitted in sufficient proportions to form an explosive and combustible mixture with air. This occurs at the flash point, and in the case of petrol will be at sub-zero temperatures.

Petrol vapour is heavier than air, and at the surface of the fluid the mixture is too rich to burn. Just above the surface a combustible mixture of 2–7% of petrol vapour in air may be found, while above this level the mixture is too weak to burn. It is for this reason that it is usually perfectly safe to fire a rocket from the bridge of a tanker, even one in which a leak exists.

Once the combustible layer is ignited, the fire will continue due to convection and turbulence.

When loading or discharging petrols smoking is not permitted, galley fires are extinguished, and cooking may be continued by means of steam coils. The radio and radar installations must not be used, portholes should be closed adjacent to the hoses, and danger-signal flags must be flown. If working several fuels through one hose they are pumped in or out in *descending* order of flash point, so that the most highly flammable fuels move through the line last of all. In this way the less dangerous fuels are not contaminated.

A fire within a fuel tank may be stifled by closing the tank lids, in which case it will soon become extinguished due to the limited oxygen available. Other methods include the injection of carbon dioxide gas, detergent or chemical foam, inert gas, or steam. Fire brigades may use liquid nitrogen.

15 in   Within an oil-fuel fire, heating may spread downwards at the rate of 37 cm per hour, and if a base-layer of water exists it may boil over, causing the blazing oil to overflow. Again, if a water spray is used to extinguish burning oil it will be instantly turned to steam just below the surface of the oil as it sinks. This produces an oil froth at the surface having a high flash risk, and which is very combustible.

Petrol, adjacent to a fire, presents a problem in that although it will not necessarily ignite within its tank due to the very rich mixture above its surface, it will absorb heat from the hot surrounding bulkheads, expand, and probably slop over or seep into the fire zone. Such a tank should preferably be pumped dry. The greatest danger exists within a tank which is closed and partly filled, for here the hot, compressed gases are likely to explode. These should again be pressed full or pumped dry. Forced air is then used to clear the tank of vapours. The pressing-up of burning liquids in tankers may spread the fire to other tanks, through the gas lines.

(3) Magazines

These should either be flooded, if in imminent danger, or else continually sprayed to keep their contents cool. Explosives generate their own oxygen, and hence their burning can be prevented only by saturation or removal.

(4) Electrical Fires

This type of fire may be extinguished using a fresh-water spray, but not one of salt water, which is an excellent conductor. Water, however, should not be used where high voltages exist, such as in radio or radar installations. Here the use of carbon tetrachloride is advised, but the firefighters should wear breathing apparatus to avoid the toxic fumes and phosgene gas.

(5) Film

This has a highly flammable nitro-cellulose base, which on burning emits combustible toxic fumes. Ventilation should be provided to clear these fumes—it will assist the fire very little, since the burning film generates oxygen. The fire is best left to burn out, which it will do very quickly, but precautions must be taken to prevent spread.

MARINE FIREFIGHTING EQUIPMENT

The tables on pages 248–9 relating to fire extinguishers is reproduced by kind permission of the Walter Kidde Company Ltd.

FIRE DETECTING APPARATUS

(1) The Kidde Zone Type System

This gives warning of fire in passenger cabins, public spaces, crew quarters, storerooms and lockers, etc., by sounding an alarm in the wheelhouse or fire station and also in the engine-room and crew's quarters, which makes possible instant location of the zone in which the fire has started. The areas are divided into zones, each having a number of

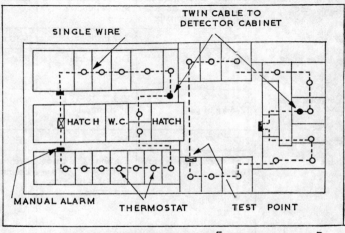

KIDDE ZONE DETECTING SYSTEM [TWO ZONES SHOWN]

FIGURE 11.1

bimetallic thermostats wired in series, and which are normally closed. A current of about 4 milliamps. is passed for continuous supervision of the circuit. Usually a key-operated test switch and a break-glass manual station are included in each zone.

When current ceases to pass through any circuit owing to a fire which operates a thermostat, or to breaking of glass at a manual station, the alarm bells are rung. The officer of the watch can then instantly locate the zone and take steps for extinguishing the fire. The manual alarm boxes are placed in full view of passengers, crew, and the fire patrol officer. Any person observing the first signs of fire is able to sound

		Carbon dioxide	Dry chemical	Foam
	CLASS 'A'. Paper, wood, cloth, general rubbish	Small surface fires only	Small surface fires only	YES — excell Has smothe and wetting ac
	CLASS 'B'. Flammable liquids: Petrol, Oil, etc.	YES—excellent. Carbon dioxide replaces oxygen, leaves no residue, does no damage	YES — excellent. Chemical smothers fire	YES — excell Foam floats top of liquid smothers fire
	CLASS 'C'. Live electrical hazards: motors, switches, etc.	YES—excellent. Carbon dioxide is a non-conductor. Leaves no residue, will not damage	YES — excellent. Dry chemical is a non-conductor	NO. Foam i conductor
5–10 ft 10–25 ft 25–35 ft	Range	2–3 m	3–7 m	7–10 m
	Extinguishing agent	Carbon dioxide	Dry chemical	Foam bubbles
5 lb 10 lb 15 lb 25 lb 5 lb 10 lb 20 lb 30 lb 2 gal	Most common sizes	2·5, 5, 7·5, 12·5 kg of gas	2·5, 5, 10, 15 kg of chemical	9 litres
	Subject to freezing	NO	NO	YES
	Propellant	Gas stored under pressure	Carbon dioxide cartridges. Pressurised with nitrogen or air	Pressure f chemical react
	Recommended maintenance	Weigh twice a year	Weigh twice a year. Check CO_2 cartridge or pressure gauge	Discharge anc charge annual

the alarm by the simple act of breaking the glass by means of a small chain-attached hammer.

Fig. 11.1 shows a typical layout of two zones in the Kidde system. A break in the circuit of either zone gives audible warning at the detecting cabinet, and operation of the control switches then indicates the zone in question. There is no limit to the number of circuits fitted in the ship and up to fifty spaces can be protected on each zone. Two electrical sources are used—normal ship's mains and a heavy-duty, nickel–iron

	Halogenated hydrocarbons	
oda acid, water/CO₂, pressurised water	Vaporising liquid *Chlorobromomethane*	Self-pressurised *Trifluoromonobromo-methane*
S—excellent. Water saturates materials prevents re-ignition	Small surface fires only	Small surface fires only
). Water will spread fire	YES. Heavy smothering gas is formed	YES. Heavy smothering gas is formed
). Water is a conductor	YES. Liquid is a non-conductor	YES. Gas is a non-conductor
–15 m	6–10 m	6 m
ater	Heavy vapour formed from liquid by heat of fire	Heavy smothering gas is discharged
itre	1 litre 4·5 litre	1 litre
ES—unless additive is used	NO	NO

30–50 ft 20–30 ft
20 ft

2 gal 1 quart
1 gal 1 quart

Soda acid	Water/CO₂	Pressurised water		
ressure from emical re-tion	CO₂ cartridge	Pressurised—with air or nitrogen	Hand pump—or pressurised with nitrogen	Liquid is self pressurised. Nitrogen is added normally
ischarge and charge an-ually	Weigh CO₂ cartridge twice a year	Check pressure gauge twice a year	Check pump by partially discharging twice a year, or check pressure gauge twice a year	Check pressure gauge and weigh twice a year

storage battery under trickle charge. Should the mains supply fail, the battery will automatically pick up the load and carry the system for more than a week. Visible and audible warning is immediately given of: (1) power failure; (2) earthing of the circuit; (3) any attempt to close the cabinet door when the system is not in normal operation; and (4) failure of the fire-alarm bells.

The system remains in operation as a fire detector even when either of the first two faults exist.

249

(2) The Kidde Marine Smoke-detector

This has proved to be one of the most satisfactory means for giving warning of fires in holds, and has been in service for some thirty years. Fig. 11.2 shows, diagrammatically, the piping layout for one hold when carbon dioxide extinguishing is used in conjunction with the smoke detector. Samples of the hold atmosphere are drawn continuously from each protected hold in the ship and passed through a dark chamber which is traversed by light from hidden sources. This light is not visible,

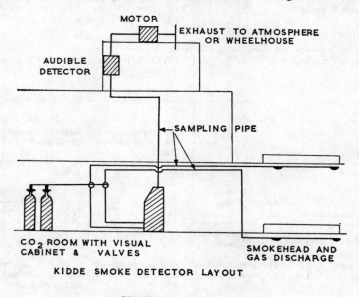

KIDDE SMOKE DETECTOR LAYOUT

FIGURE 11.2

but serves to strongly illuminate any smoke arising from the holds. Since each pipe-end is labelled, the smoking hold is quickly and surely identified. There is no possibility of false alarm; the observer knows with certainty that smoke is issuing from a particular hold and has a rough measure of the smoke density. Once it is detected, the fire is most effectively dealt with by the carbon dioxide flooding system. This consists of a battery of steel cylinders containing the gas, whose contents can be discharged as required along the sampling pipes to any hold, or holds. The gas is prevented from reaching the detecting cabinet by means of a three-way valve which is operated immediately the burning hold has been identified and before the gas is released.

The Visual Viewing-chamber. This has recently been improved so that

250

it greatly increases the visibility of small traces of smoke. The black interior of the chamber is normally quite dark, but has lamps so arranged that smoke issuing from any of the sampling pipes is made clearly visible. The hot-galvanised, solid-drawn, steel pipes from the holds enter the cabinet at the bottom, where they are connected to P.V.C. pipes leading up to the viewing chamber. These pipes terminate in 12-mm diameter glass tubes which pass through a brightly lit lamp box. ½-in Their ends protrude into the viewing chamber, where they are shielded by metal chimneys. This is shown in Fig. 11.3.

Light travels by multiple reflection and refraction along these tubes, irradiating the region near their ends with a diffuse light. This is in-

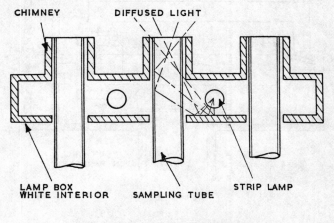

KIDDE VISUAL SMOKE DETECTOR

FIGURE II. 3

visible, but illuminates smoke issuing from any tube. The viewing-chamber window is angled from the vertical to prevent unwanted reflections from interfering with the view of the chimneys. By lifting a flap on the front of the viewing-chamber, the glass tubes can be examined a few inches below the lamp box. In this part of each tube is a small, moulded nylon, propeller-type draught-indicator whose rotation indicates that the line is not blocked.

The Audible Detector. This is fitted in the wheelhouse for additional protection. In some vessels the detecting cabinet with viewing-chamber may be installed in the wheelhouse, without employing the audible detector. The latter achieves high sensitivity by using both obscuration and reflection of light by smoke, to upset the balance of a photo-electric cell circuit. No thermionic valves are used, and a special arrangement

251

within the circuit avoids false alarms resulting from component failure. The layout of the instrument is shown in Fig. 11.4.

A concentrated filament lamp and lens form a parallel beam. After the beam has been reduced to square cross-section by a mask it passes through a slightly larger square of inward-facing, barrier-layer-type photo-cells. These are very stable, requiring no high-tension supply, and are normally illuminated by only a small amount of stray light, so that the output of the four in parallel is about 15 micro-amps. This current is balanced by the output of the end cell, which lies at a small angle to

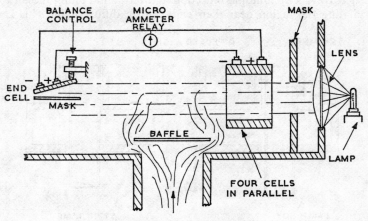

KIDDE AUDIBLE SMOKE DETECTOR

FIGURE 11. 4

the direction of the beam and therefore receives light obliquely. The orientation of this cell is adjustable in order to balance the circuit initially. The presence of smoke in the detector cuts off light from the end cell and reflects some on to the cells of the square. The difference in output currents thus caused passes through a relay which, on operation, causes the audible and visual alarms to function. Two foreseeable causes of false alarm in such a system are gradual deterioration of a photo-cell and slow distortion of the projector-lamp filament. The circuit is therefore arranged so that either of these events causes a fault indication instead of a false alarm.

Mounted above the wheelhouse are two independent electric motors driving the main sampling fan. Their use should be alternate, and a change-over switch is provided so that each motor functions only on alternate days. The exhaust valve may be set to discharge the sampled air to the atmosphere, or, as an additional detector, it can be set to exhaust into the wheelhouse. In this way the presence of smoke is also smelled. The visual-detector cabinet is connected to the audible-detector by a common pipe, and in this way the presence of fire within the ship is detected, while exact location is afforded by inspection of the visual-chamber. The layout in Fig. 11.2 avoids passing the sampling pipes all the way to the wheelhouse; this is a major advantage, particularly when the system is to be installed in a ship already constructed.

The alarm bells may be installed in the wheelhouse and engine-room, with additional bells fitted in the Officers' accommodation for use when in port. The same applies to the fault alarms, which emit a klaxon note.

Finally, the system gives several types of alarm which are here summarised:

(1) The ringing of alarm bells.
(2) The illumination of a coloured light within the wheelhouse.
(3) The odour of smoke in the wheelhouse.
(4) The view of smoke in the audible-detector cabinet.
(5) The ammeter on the front of the cabinet indicates an output current.

Once a fire is detected, the sampling pipe from that hold should be plugged, the end cell reset, and the system continues to detect other fires while fighting the initial one.

(3) The Kidde Lucas Inert Gas Generating Plant

Basic Principles. This equipment produces an unlimited supply of inert gas by burning Diesel oil in air, the oxygen being converted to carbon dioxide and water. After the produced gases have been cooled and washed they are directed to the fire zone. The generator can deliver 700–1 400 m^3 of gas per hour at an outlet pressure of 500 gr per cm^2. This meets the firefighting requirements of a ship, the largest hold of which has a grain capacity of 5 700 m^3.

25 000–50 000 ft^3
7–8 lb per in^2
200 000 ft^3

The analysis of the gas is as follows:

Nitrogen	85%
Carbon dioxide	14%
Oxygen	1%
Sulphur dioxide and carbon monoxide . .	Negligible

By adopting a technique of water cooling by direct contact with the gas, the cooling process is combined with a cleansing and scrubbing action, which removes the bulk of the soluble acidic gases which can result from the presence of sulphur or similar impurities within the fuel.

The Plant comprises (1) a blower driven by (2) an electric motor or

Diesel engine. The latter also drives an alternator to provide electrical power for (6) and (7). (3) A compact, combined, combustion and scrubbing unit. (4) Fuel pump, controls, instrumentation, safety interlocks, etc. (5) Piping system, control valves, suitable discharge fittings, etc. (6) A water pump driven by (7), an electric motor.

27 gal

The burner consumes roughly 120 litres of Diesel oil per hour. The burner is ignited by means of main and stand-by spark plugs powered from the ship's mains, via transformers or coils, or from the Diesel-driven alternator.

The inert gas is prevented from being contaminated with water droplets, after washing, by means of a baffle system within the delivery pipe. It is delivered to the fire zone at both deck and deckhead levels.

(4) The Use of Flue Gas for Inerting

tons
tons

All tankers over 100000 tonnes and combination carriers over 50000 tonnes ordered after July 1974 are required to be fitted with inert-gas systems. The most favoured and practical type is that which employs the flue gas from the funnel. The analysis of this gas is in the order of: oxygen $4 \cdot 2\%$, carbon dioxide $13 \cdot 5\%$, nitrogen 77%, sulphur dioxide $0 \cdot 3\%$ and water vapour 5%.

The flue gas is passed to a scrubbing tower where the gas is cleaned and cooled. A typical tower employs trays of sea-water, one above the other, with the water falling from top to bottom. The overflow from the bottom tray is piped overside through an effluent line and will contain sulphuric and sulphurous acid formed by a combination of sulphur dioxide and water. In cases of bad combustion, oily vapour may find its way into the tower and be condensed. As this passes overside the vessel may be committing a pollution offence. The gas bubbles up from the lower tray to the top, passes through a demister to remove moisture and is then piped to the tanks through a deck seal, which acts as a one-way valve and is designed to prevent cargo gas from passing back to the engine room. By this time the gas is about $2°C$ above the sea temperature.

The oxygen content of the gas must be kept below 5%—which also inhibits corrosion in the tanks. An alarm is usually fitted to give warning if the oxygen rises to 8%. The lowest oxygen concentration is found when boilers are working at full load.

Tank ullages are filled with inert gas for the loaded passage and will vent off in hot climates as the cargo expands. As the ambient temperature lowers, more gas will have to be injected.

When the cargo is discharged, the inert gas is driven in and this pressure aids pumping of the cargo overside. The empty tank can then either be left full of inert gas, or gas freed, or cleaned. Cleaning can be carried out with inert gas in the compartment. On the other hand, as soon as the tank is empty, it may be ballasted, in which case the inert gas will be vented off.

It should be noted that immediately after discharge of the cargo, the inert gas will be mixed with some hydrocarbon gas and the compartment will need to be purged with more inert gas before cleaning commences. This purging may take up to 28 hours and should eventually give an explosimeter reading of 1% or less.

(5) Halon Gas (1301)

This is the trade name for a compound chemically known as bromo-trifluoromethane, also known as BTM. Halon is colourless, odourless, non-conductive and 1·57 times heavier than air. It inhibits the chemical reaction of fuels with oxygen. Its great advantage is that it has low toxicity to humans and is safe for up to 4–5 minutes. It boils at −57°C   −71°F and freezes at −168°C. It is up to thirty times more expensive than   −271°F carbon dioxide but is an ideal substance for rapid injection into working spaces such as engine rooms. Only 5% of the space needs to be filled with halon in order to extinguish a fire.

(6) BCF or Halon 1211

The chemical name for this is bromochlorodifluoromethane. It is normally found in extinguishers and is a very effective smothering gas, which for short periods of exposure may be regarded as non-toxic.

CHAPTER XII

DRYDOCKING AND LOADLINES

THE STABILITY ASPECT
(EQUALLY APPLICABLE TO VESSELS AGROUND)

IT is desirable that a vessel entering a drydock shall be upright and have a small amount of trim by the stern, for then she will initially rest on the blocks at the aftermost point of her keel. She will then pivot about this point in a vertical plane as the water level falls and may also be pivoted laterally by means of her fore breast-lines so that her keel may be aligned with the blocks.

Until the water level falls below the keel the vessel's weight is supported partly by the blocks and partly by the water. The upward reaction of the keel blocks may be considered as a negative weight in a moment calculation, producing a decrease in the ship's stability, and it is most important that the vessel remains stable until she takes the blocks along the full length of her keel, i.e. when she is *sewed*, for until this moment the side shores cannot be successfully rigged. Once the vessel is laterally supported by shores, her stability condition is of no practical consequence.

A few moments' thought will make it apparent to the reader that the upward thrust of the keel blocks aft is that required to destroy the vessel's trim until she is sewed, and must therefore be in direct proportion to the trim value. The reader may prefer to consider the line of blocks moving upwards towards the keel; they make contact aft and exert a certain force which is a loss in displacement (if the blocks are supporting part of the ship's weight, then the water cannot also be doing this) and eventually make contact throughout the ship's length as she tilts about an athwartships axis.

Consider a vessel trimmed 25 cm by the stern and having a moment to change trim 1 cm (M.C.T.1 cm) of 25000 tonnes-cm. The after keel knuckle is 50 m from the tipping centre or centre of flotation.

The moment causing the initial trim is 25×25000 tonnes-cm.
The moment destroying this trim is a force $P \times 5000$ tonnes-cm.
They are equal and therefore,

$$25 \times 25000 = P \times 5000$$
From which $P = 125$ tonnes at the instant of sewing.

256

If her initial displacement was 10000 tonnes and her tonnes per cm immersion (T.P.I.) at that displacement was 25, then her displacement while being sewed becomes 9875 tonnes and she loses 5 cm of mean draught. At the same time the 125 tonnes upward thrust reduces her stability, and it is for this reason that the initial trim by the stern should be kept as low as possible.

Once the ship is flat on the blocks she loses roughly 25 tonnes of displacement for every cm loss of mean draught, i.e. an amount equal to her T.P.I. for the existing draught. This increasing thrust at the keel blocks steadily reduces the ship's stability by an amount equal to

$$\frac{P \times KG}{W\text{-}P}$$ cm, i.e. a rise in the position of the centre of gravity.

where P is the loss of displacement in tonnes, W is the initial displacement in tonnes and KG the distance of the centre of gravity above the keel measured in cm.

GENERAL PROCEDURE

Before entering a drydock, the following items should be given attention:

Repairs

A full and detailed list of repairs to be carried out while in dock should be prepared, duplicating at least six copies so that all interested parties, such as the Owners, the ship's Officers, the ship-repair Managers, the foremen, and the Dockmaster, can each be provided with a list. In dock, each item may be crossed off the list as soon as the repair is accomplished to the satisfaction of the Officer or Surveyor in charge.

Draught and Trim

In many cases these are stipulated by the Dock Authorities, who take into account the depth of water at the dock sill when the vessel is scheduled to enter, and also the *declivity*, i.e. the slope, of the blocks at the dock entrance. The Dockmaster should be informed of the draught and trim as soon as possible so that he may be able to give ample notice if he requires them to be altered.

Structural Features

The Dockmaster should be notified of the position of bilge keels, if any, the rake of the stem, the type and number of propellers, and the position of echo-sounder transmitter and receiver units. Any protruding logs (distance recorders) should be withdrawn into the hull.

257

Cargo

The Authorities should be informed of the existence and disposition of any cargo within the vessel. This subject will be dealt with in more detail at a later stage.

Movable Weights

These should be secured, since it is desirable that the vessel should be in the same condition of trim, preferably large stability, and zero list, both when entering and finally leaving the dock. Tanks should be either full or empty so that no free surfaces exist, which are detrimental to stability. The fore and after peak tanks should preferably be empty, since these are difficult areas to support with shores, and the vessel may become hogged. As soon as the vessel is sewed, the tanks and bilges should be sounded throughout the ship, and these readings are duplicated before refloating the vessel. A list of soundings may be given to the Dockmaster. If tanks are full there is the advantage of being able to rapidly observe leaks.

Derricks, Gangways, and Anchors

These should preferably be in the stowed positions both when entering and leaving the dock.

Inspecting the Dock

In ports of doubtful efficiency the Master should, if possible, view the dock when dry and ascertain that:

(a) suitable and efficient shoring arrangements are provided;
(b) the keel blocks have level top surfaces, are evenly dispersed, are substantially constructed, and are undamaged. They should naturally extend sufficiently to accommodate the vessel's keel; and
(c) whether bilge blocks or beds are provided.

The shoring of a vessel in a drydock is very necessary, since the upward pressure of the keel blocks tends to push the vessel out of shape, the bilges are inclined to sag, and the side plating tends to incline outwards. Wooden side (breast) shores are placed between the hull-side plating and the dock sides, which are stepped into *altars* to take the shore heels, making certain that the head of the shore rests on a frame, thus avoiding plate indentations. These shores are inclined slightly above the horizontal. A second layer of shores (bilge shores) are often rigged in a similar manner but just above the round of the bilge. In some docks these shores are hydraulically operated and are housed, when not in use, in the dock sides.

A line of bilge blocks, i.e. heavy baulks of timber built up into supports similarly to keel blocks, are often a permanent feature of the dock, and though more widely spaced than keel blocks, they are valuable in supporting the bilges, but they must be placed under a longitudinal side girder in order to avoid straining the plating. Once the dock is dry, these blocks are built up to the plating by means of extra wooden packing pieces and wedges. They are of particular importance when the vessel is partly or fully loaded.

Once the vessel has entered the dock, the caisson gate will be floated into place and locked. The vessel will be aligned over the keel blocks by the Dockmaster, using his docking-bobs forward and aft, and then the dock will be pumped dry. The following points should now be given attention:

Cleaning

As the water level falls, the ship's side will be scrubbed clean by men working from floating pontoons. If the water level falls too quickly the cleaning will be hasty and incomplete. Close liaison with the Dockmaster may result in a slowing of the pumping rate during this relatively important period. Care should be taken to see that no pontoons ground on the propellers or altars.

Shores

These cannot be secured in place until the vessel is sewed, but as soon as she has done this they will be swung into place by shore cranes and must be headed against frames, indicated by rivet lines. If the vessel is in a tender condition (low stability properties), the shores may be roughly rigged as soon as the vessel contacts the blocks aft, and the pumping may be completely stopped while they are being finally secured.

Once the dock is dry, the following items must be considered, the list not being in any chronological order:

Fore and Aft Shores should be rigged in place, particularly beneath the fore peak tank where the keel blocks do not give any support.

Tanks should have been sounded as soon as the vessel was flat on the blocks, or else done now without delay.

Discharges are opened overside for inspection. Baffle plates may be removed for cleaning and coating on their inner surfaces, after which they are welded back into place.

Water Closets should be locked and arrangements made for personnel to use toilets within the dock area. In ships fitted with septic tanks, arrangements may be made to drain this tank into the shore sewers. Alternatively it may be permissible to drain the tank directly into the dock outlet drain channels.

Fire

Arrangements should be made to provide the vessel with an adequate supply of firefighting water, and in addition, all fire appliances should be ready for instant use. Frequently the Dock Authorities provide a fire-patrol service whereby one or more watchmen visit every part of the ship each hour, their movements being recorded by suitably placed time clocks.

Telephone

This should be placed aboard the ship if possible, primarily for rapid summoning of fire or ambulance services.

Electricity

Electricity supplies, suitable for the vessel's equipment, should be provided if the Diesel generators are to be overhauled. Boilers will be allowed to burn down.

An earth return may be rigged by welding a suitable cable to a bared area of hull plating. The only other earthing routes available in a ship resting on wooden blocks are along the wire hawsers, which may not provide good contacts at their extremities.

Hot Water

This must be supplied for cooking and washing facilities, and if the vessel's domestic heating equipment is to be overhauled the Dock Authorities may provide electric water boilers.

Watchmen

Watchmen should be employed to prevent unauthorised persons from boarding, and to generally attend the gangway.

Draught Marks and Loadlines

These may be repainted, the former being checked by the shipwrights. Along the side plating there are often small spots of weld at a certain known waterline. These are joined by a chalk line and the draught marks are examined for accuracy, using this as a datum line. It is sometimes convenient to arrange for the loadline survey to coincide with a drydocking, these marks being examined at the same time.

Damage

The vessel will be carefully surveyed by the Officers, a Lloyd's Hull Surveyor, the Company's Engineer Superintendent, and also the Dockyard Manager. The Marine Superintendent is also present. Dented plates will be straightened (faired), bearing in mind that those removed for this purpose will have to be hose-tested on replacement. Weeping rivets and seams will be caulked, the tail end shaft(s) may be withdrawn for examination of liner wear-down, and the rudder examined for suspension wear. The propeller blades will be examined for tip damage and then polished on their surfaces. When listing areas of damage, or plates which require scaling, the shell plating plan will be used, bearing in mind that plates are numbered from aft and lettered from the garboard strake ('A') upwards towards the sheer strake.

Tanks

Any tanks which need draining will have their plugs removed from the shell plating, into which they are usually recessed if they have a protruding hexagonal head to prevent it shearing. These plugs must be placed in safe custody and replaced before the dock is flooded.

Cathodic Protection

Arrangements for this should be examined by the installing firm and anodes renewed where required. The zinc plates in way of the stern frame may need renewing if badly corroded. These represent the earliest method of cathodic protection, and it is of interest to note that when Sir Humphry Davy designed them, their purpose was understood so little that they were often fitted to wooden ships.

Anchors and Cables

These may be ranged in the dock bottom for greasing, testing for wear-down, changing the cable lengths, re-marking, renewal of lead pellets, and at the same time the chain locker can be cleaned and scaled/coated if necessary. (The reader is here referred to Chapter I.)

Painting

This will generally be commenced as soon as the vessel is dry and her bottom has been cleaned of all growths. These are particularly evident at plate lap-joints, and are likely to be ignored close to the keel, where headroom is limited for working. The lower sides of bilge keels are frequently thickly coated with marine growths. The deposits may need slicing off if very hard, and in some cases they are burned off, a process called *breaming*.

Where the hull paintwork is in good condition a fresh coat of antifouling is all that is necessary, applied over a quick-drying coat of antifouling *undercoat*, which seals and binds the surface of the old paint and makes it compatible with the antifouling composition. When the paint-work is grazed or pitted, as often occurs in way of the collision bulkhead due to anchor-cable chafe, the surface should be cleaned, smoothed, and coated with a metallic primer which is anticorrosive. This is finally covered with antifouling paint.

If the vessel has rested on the keel blocks in a different position from last time, patches of her keel will be bare or short of antifouling, and particular attention should be given to this area.

For new or bare plating (and often a few plates are scaled at each drydocking in order to keep the surface smooth), three to four coats of metallic primer should be applied, followed by one coat of antifouling. To make sure that the priming coats are properly applied, it is often convenient to use separate colours for each coat, say pink, brown, and yellow. In this way, any patches short of paint will be avoided, in addition to which the Officers and paint foremen can instantly assess the progress of the painters.

500 ft^2 per gal

As long as possible should be allowed between these coats, which dry in about four hours. The covering capacity is about 10 m^2 per litre. This primer has a very high resistance to water, and a surface which is compatible with antifouling, which is now applied direct.

Antifouling composition is applied in order that the slow and constant solution of the toxic substances which it contains will keep the ship's surface in an antiseptic condition, so that no marine growth can obtain a foothold; the paint is thus a store for poisonous materials, but the antiseptic condition is obtained only at the expense of a depletion of this store, in other words it is a wasting process. The composition of the paint must be such that it has a highly controlled rate of toxic depletion. These materials are derived from copper and mercury. Arsenic is occasionally used, but is far more effectively poisonous on higher biological orders.

£4 to £10 per gal

The composition varies in price from about £1 to £2 per litre, but should never be thinned, as this is a false economy. It is designed to be applied at a certain consistency, and any thinning will reduce its protective properties. The price is usually directly proportional to the strength and duration of this protection. If, in warm climates, the paint is found to be thin, two coats should be applied. The strongest and most expensive antifouling covers at the rate of about 6·5 m^2 per litre.

320 ft^2 per gal
500 ft^2 per gal

Antifouling undercoats cover at the rate of about 10 m^2 per litre and dry in about two hours. Antifouling paint should always be applied over the undercoat or final primer not later than twenty-four hours after the former has dried. It must never then be allowed to dry hard unless of polyurethane base. The dock must therefore be flooded between six and twenty-four hours after application of the composition.

The boot-topping should be coated either with enamel paint or else with antifouling composition, the latter being preferable, since weed growth is most evident at, and near, the water surface. Enamel paint, however, is far more easily cleaned of oil stains. A different coloured antifouling may be used if desired.

Flame Cleaning

Certain dockyards are using this method of paint removal in preference to the traditional scaling. The instrument is virtually a gas-supplied (oxy-acetylene) blowlamp, but the flame is emitted from a wide-angle fishtail aperture and quickly removes paint, however thick or old. The plating should then be wire-brushed by a man following the flame-operator. The method has the advantage that the metal is now dry and warm and thus ideal for painting. In damp conditions it is advisable to use teams of four men; one man burns off the paint, a second man follows close behind wire-brushing the plating clean, and the remaining two follow along with the first priming coat.

There is one point to be watched, however, which is most important. During surveys it may occur that there will be a Surveyor and Officers examining oil tanks under which flame cleaning is in progress. The oily residue on the inside bottom plating quickly vaporises into suffocating fumes. Shot blasting, sand blasting and ultra-sonic cleaning are safer methods in this respect.

Cleanliness

Every endeavour should be made to keep the ship as clean as possible, and while deck-washing may not be convenient, there is no reason why a regular daily sweeping should not be carried out. Arrangements should be made to have the ship's refuse removed at frequent intervals, particularly in hot weather.

Smoke-detecting Gear

If the ship is light, an admirable opportunity is afforded to carry out testing and cleaning of this system by means of compressed air.

When the vessel is ready to leave the drydock the following items will need attention:

Discharges

These should have all non-return valves replaced, and baffles fitted (where supplied).

Plugs

All tanks should have their underwater drain plugs in place, and in most drydocks the dock is not flooded until the Dockmaster is presented with a signed certificate stating that an Officer has inspected the hull and is satisfied on this count.

Times

The ship's log should be checked to see that it contains:

(1) The time at which the vessel entered the dock.
(2) The time at which the gate was closed.
(3) The time when pumping commenced.
(4) The times when the vessel was sewed and also when the dock was dry.

When leaving, the log should contain:

(1) The time when flooding commenced.
(2) The time when the vessel floated.
(3) The times when the gate was opened and when the vessel left the dock.

A report should be furnished to the owners, retaining a copy aboard, giving all the above times, details of the work done in dock, the quantities and types of paint used, the Marine Superintendent's opinion of the initial condition of the underwater paintwork, and all other relevant facts.

DOCKING METHODS

In past days there were two methods of exposing a ship's underwater surface, and they are worthy of mention purely from the points of view of interest and increasing the reader's sea vocabulary.

Careening

In this case the vessel was run close inshore over a suitable beach, at high water, so that she grounded at low water and heeled over. The time available for repair and maintenance work was necessarily very limited. The method is still widely used for small craft. It is, of course, essential that the sea-bed dries out completely at low water in the locality of the vessel.

Heaving Down

Here, a vessel was heeled over by means of tackles set up between her masts and another ship, hulk, or shore attachments. Her masts were rigged with extra preventer shrouds to distribute the stresses involved. The method was not so successful as careening, but since the hull was waterborne, there was little hull stress, unless, of course, it touched the sea-bed.

Nowadays, there are three basic methods for preparing a ship for underwater hull work:

(1) A Graving Dock

This is one which is excavated from the land and closed to the sea or river by means of a floating caisson gate. This is virtually a large, robustly-built, steel tank. The edge of the dock bottom beneath the gate is referred to as the sill. The sides of the dock are terraced into concrete steps or altars into which the shores are heeled. Along the centre line of the dock, huge baulks of timber are built up into keel blocks. In some cases another parallel line of bilge blocks or beds is built on each side of the centre line. The blocks are tied together to prevent them from toppling or being tripped as the vessel is sewed or refloated. The line of the blocks' upper surfaces is usually on a slight gradient relative to the horizontal, known as the declivity. The dock is filled from the river or sea, and the gate is opened when the levels of the water on both sides are coincident. The ship is then floated in and positioned over the keel blocks, the gate is closed, and the dock is pumped dry.

The top edge of the gate, along which persons may walk, is often 15 m above the dock bottom and the gate has to withstand, in this case, a maximum pressure of 12 tonnes/m² if the water outside the dock is of density 1 tonne/m³ and 3 m below the gate-edge.

50 ft
2 500 lb/ft²
64 lb/ft³ 10 ft

(2) A Floating Dock

This is virtually a huge, flat, subdivided steel tank rather like a ship's double bottom, on the upper centre-line of which is a line of keel blocks, with or without associated bilge beds. This forms the bottom of the dock, which has no ends but high narrow sides which are also tanks. These are constructed along the longer sides of the rectangular dock.

The tanks, both in the double bottom and the sides, are flooded so that the dock bottom is at a deeper draught than the ship's keel. The ship is then floated over the dock's centre-line and the latter is pumped dry until the ship is clear of the water. The docking Manager will require detailed data regarding the ship's stability, trim, and loading condition, and may require any of these to be changed. Each section of the dock must be capable of lifting that portion of the ship's length, and weight, which lies within it, and the ship must therefore be evenly loaded. If this is not arranged, the dock is subjected to severe bending stresses.

To keep the dock properly trimmed, the ship's centre of gravity must

265

be vertically above the dock's centre of buoyancy, and these points are marked, by means of paint, on the sides of both the ship and dock. The two eventually form one floating craft or system, the stability of which, like any craft, is directly proportional to the beam of the waterplane, i.e. the area of the craft's cross-section at, and parallel to, the water level. This, and therefore the stability of the system, is least when the water level is between the ship's keel and the dock bottom, for then the waterplane area is only that of the narrow side tanks. This may be referred to

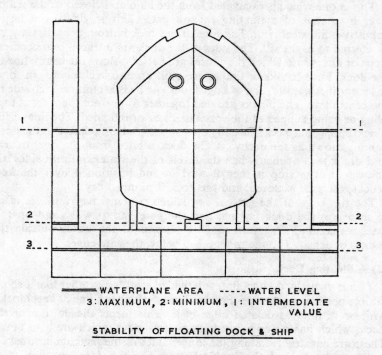

━━━ WATERPLANE AREA ----- WATER LEVEL
3: MAXIMUM, 2: MINIMUM, 1: INTERMEDIATE VALUE

STABILITY OF FLOATING DOCK & SHIP

FIGURE 12.1

as the *critical moment* of docking. (In the case of a graving dock, this occurs just before the vessel is sewed, for then the upthrust at the keel is at a maximum for the unshored condition.) In the floating dock the stability is greatest when the dock bottom is clear of the water surface. There is an intermediate value, varying with the draught of the ship, when the ship is still submerged, for then the waterplane area is that of the ship together with the side tanks' area. These conditions are illustrated in Fig. 12.1. Free surfaces in the dock's and ship's tanks will reduce the stability of the system.

266

(3) The Floating Cradle

This is used for small vessels, and consists of a reinforced slipway on which is built a railway carrying a heavy cradle. The latter is run down the slipway into the water under the ship's keel, and when the ship rests on the cradle the two are hove up the slipway.

DOCKING WITH CARGO ABOARD

In such cases the ship is likely to be subjected to severe stresses and be strained. Certain precautions must therefore be taken. The pressing-up of all double-bottom tanks, particularly beneath holds, will help to distribute the weight of cargo evenly over the inner bottom, and avoid local loading. As soon as the vessel is sewed, divers may be employed to build up the bilge blocks before further pumping is allowed. This makes sure that the vessel is well supported before too much of her weight is transferred to the keel blocks. In such a case, bilge blocks should be underneath a longitudinal side girder to avoid plate-buckling. Extra shores will have to be employed throughout the ship's length and at her ends. If the damage or repair work is in a suitable position it may be possible to pump out only some of the dock water, i.e. sufficient to expose the area in question, and leave the vessel partly waterborne. This reduces not only the reaction of the blocks but also any tendencies for the ends to droop (*hogging*), and also tendencies for the bottom plating to sag between the lines of blocks. The Dockmaster must initially be furnished with a detailed loading plan.

LOADLINES

The International Load Line Rules (1968) apply to all vessels whose Governments are parties to the Loadline Convention of 1966. All British ships, with the exception of:

(1) warships,
(2) vessels engaged solely in fishing, and
(3) pleasure yachts,

are required to use statutory loadlines to ensure that they do not become submerged more than is prudent, having regard to the latitudes and seasons in which they are sailing. They must not put to sea unless the ship has been surveyed, marked with loadlines, complies with assignment conditions and carries proper stability information.

These loadlines are awarded by Assigning Authorities, such as the Department of Trade but more often on behalf of the Government, Lloyd's Register of Shipping and the British Committee of the Bureau

Bureau Veritas. The vessels must be constructed and equipped as laid down in the Loadline Rules (obtainable from H.M. Stationery Office) to certain conditions of assignment, after which a summer loadline (in salt water) is computed, other freeboards are assigned, and the marks are cut in or painted on the ship's sides. A loadline certificate is presented to the Owners, and must be posted in a conspicuous position within the ship, while in force. The certificate is valid for five years, but an annual survey is held to ensure that the conditions of assignment are fulfilled and the loadline marks are unaltered. Before a Master can sign on a crew he must enter details of this certificate and his loadlines into the agreement. Every voyage, similar particulars must be recorded in the Official Logbook.

International loadline ships are those of 24 m and over. They will have an International Loadline Certificate (1966). Other vessels will have a United Kingdom Loadline Certificate. If a vessel is loaded so that in a condition of zero list, her loadline is submerged, her owner or Master shall be liable to a fine of £400 and in addition another £400 for every 2·54 cm (or fraction thereof) that she is overloaded. A further fine of £400 is likely if she is sent to sea in an overloaded condition. These are maximum fines in a court of summary jurisdiction. It is a defence to prove that the overloading was caused by deviation or delay beyond the Master's control. A vessel may be detained until she ceases to be overloaded.

Amidships means at the centre of the length of the summer load water-line.

Loadline Marks

These shall be painted in white or yellow on a dark ground or in black on a light ground, and shall be carefully cut in or centre-punched on the sides of iron or steel ships. On wooden ships they shall be cut in for at least 3 mm.

$\frac{1}{8}$ in

12 in × 1 in *The Deck Line* is a horizontal line measuring 300 mm × 25 mm marked amidships, with its upper edge passing through the point where the continuation of the upper surface of the freeboard deck (or its sheathing) intersects the outer surface of the shell plating. The *freeboard deck* is the uppermost complete deck having permanent means of closing all openings in weather sections, e.g. hatchways.

12 in 1 in *The Loadline Disc* is 300 mm in external diameter and 25 mm thick. Its centre is amidships and below the deckline. The disc is intersected by
18 in × 1 in a horizontal line measuring 450 mm × 25 mm whose upper edge passes through the centre of the disc. This line, at its upper edge, marks the summer salt waterline and is often referred to as the *Plimsoll line* after Samuel Plimsoll, a pioneer in the prevention of ship-overloading.

DRYDOCKING AND LOADLINES

The Loadlines. At a distance of 540 mm forward of the centre of the disc, there is a vertical line 25 mm wide, from which horizontal lines measuring 230 mm × 25 mm extend forward and aft, the upper surfaces of which indicate the maximum depths to which the ship may be submerged in differing circumstances and seasons.

21 in
1 in
9 in × 1 in

Types of Loadlines

(1) Steamers, Including Tankers (Fig. 12.2). The loadlines are shown for the *starboard* side of a ship. The following are marked:

Summer (*S*). This is level with the Plimsoll line and is the basic computed freeboard line. A separate table is used for computing the tanker summer loadline. Other loadlines are based on the summer mark.

Winter (*W*) is one forty-eighth of the summer draught below the summer line.

Tropical (*T*) is one forty-eighth of the summer draught above the summer line.

Winter North Atlantic (*WNA*) is marked on all vessels of 100 m or under in length. It applies to voyages within the North Atlantic north of the 36th parallel of latitude, during the winter months, as laid down in the Loadline Rules. It is marked at a distance of 50 mm below the winter loadline.

When the vessel is floating in fresh water, the freeboard may be reduced by an amount known as the Fresh Water Allowance (FWA) and this is calculated from the formula

$$\frac{W}{4\,T}\text{mm}$$

where *W* is the displacement in tonnes, in salt water at the summer loadline, and the symbol *T* represents the TPI (tonnes per cm immersion) in salt water at the same level. In the event of the displacement (*W*) being indeterminable, the Fresh Water Allowance is taken as one forty-eighth of the summer draught.

Fresh Water (*F*) is the summer fresh-water loadline. The distance between (S) and (F) is therefore equal to the FWA.

Tropical Fresh Water (*TF*) is, by a similar argument, situated above (T) by an amount equal to the FWA.

All the above distances are measured between the upper edges of the respective loadlines.

(2) Timber-carrying Vessels (Fig. 12.3). These loadlines are awarded to vessels engaged in the timber deck-cargo trade, excluding wood pulp, and are only to be used when the cargo is carried in accordance with the 1968 Deck Cargo Regulations. Such a vessel must have a

269

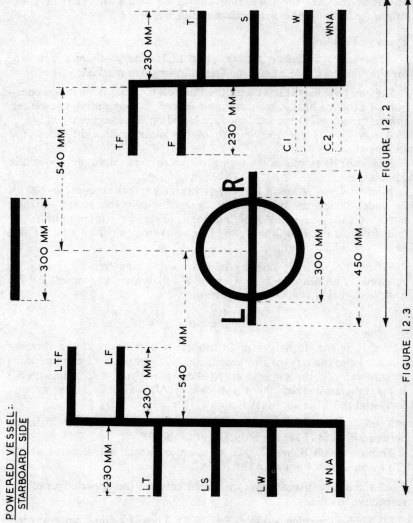

POWERED VESSEL: STARBOARD SIDE

FIGURE 12.2

FIGURE 12.3

forecastle extending at least 7% of the ship's length, and a poop or raised quarter-deck. Her double-bottom tanks within the midships half-length must be subdivided, and the ship must be fitted with efficient rails or bulwarks at least 1 m in height. Eyeplates for securing lashings must be riveted to the sheer strake not more than 3 m apart. Her steering-gears must be adequately protected from cargo damage.   39 in   10 ft

The vessel must fill her wells solidly with timber up to the standard height of her superstructures. In this way, she obtains greater reserve buoyancy and her summer freeboard may be reduced. This naturally reduces certain other loadline freeboards.

She will have a second set of loadlines situated 540 mm abaft the centre of the loadline disc, similarly marked for other loadlines, but with each letter prefixed by 'L' (Lumber).   21 in

Lumber Summer (*LS*) is at some computed level above the Plimsoll line, and its upper edge marks the summer salt-water timber loadline.

Lumber Winter (*LW*) is $\frac{1}{36}$ of the lumber summer draught below (LS). $\frac{1}{3}$ in /ft

Lumber Tropical (*LT*) is $\frac{1}{48}$ of the lumber summer draught above (LS). $\frac{1}{4}$ in/ft

Lumber Winter North Atlantic (*LWNA*) is on the same level as the (WNA) loadline, where marked. It therefore applies only to vessels of 100 m or under in length.   328 ft

The Loadline Certificate states a FWA for all freeboards, and hence the value is constant for both ordinary and lumber freeboards.

Lumber Fresh Water (*LF*) is therefore situated above (LS) by an amount equal to the FWA.

Lumber Tropical Fresh Water (*LTF*) is above (LT) by an amount equal to the FWA.

(3) **Sailing Ships** (Fig. 12.4). These ships have a deckline, a disc with an intersecting line, and two 230-mm loadlines situated 540-mm forward of the disc centre. The intersecting line marks the waterline for winter, summer, and tropical conditions. It is therefore an (S), (T), and (W) line.   9-in   21 in

The Fresh-water Loadline (*F*) is above the intersecting line by an amount equal to the FWA, computed as for steamers.

The Winter North Atlantic Line is below the intersecting line by an amount directed by the Assigning Authority.

Subdivision Loadlines

These may be assigned to a passenger vessel aboard which spaces exist which are used for the carriage of either passengers or cargo. She may have the usual loadline markings as shown in Fig. 12.2, and in addition a subdivision loadline (or loadlines, up to usually three in number), marked (C) to indicate Convention (Safety). Where there is more than one of these loadlines they are marked C1, C2, and C3, numbering them downwards towards the keel, so that C3 indicates the maximum freeboard. They are all situated below the Tropical (deepest salt water) loadline and often on the forward side of the vertical line. Two of these loadlines are shown pecked in Fig. 12.2.

Details of these loadlines are found in the Passenger and Safety Certificate, posted in a conspicuous position aboard the ship, and also in the Declaration of Survey (Survey 1 A), which is in the custody of the Master. The various spaces relating to each loadline are recorded in

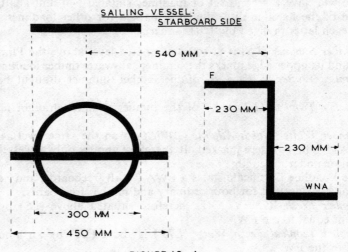

FIGURE 12.4

these forms. Whenever all the spaces are used for cargo carriage only the vessel loads to her usual loadlines. If, however, a space is used for the carriage of passengers, then the vessel must not submerge beyond the appropriate subdivision loadline.

These loadlines are not connected with the International Loadline Rules, but are provided under the terms of the Safety Convention and computed for British ships by the Department of Trade (D.o.T.) in the United Kingdom.

In the Far East, such as India, Ceylon, Hong Kong, and Singapore, vessels may be seen with additional subdivision loadlines marked D1, D2, etc., situated below the (C) lines. These provide an even greater freeboard, and are used in similar circumstances to the (C) lines but in bad weather seasons, such as the south-west monsoon in the Indian Ocean.

272

DRYDOCKING AND LOADLINES

The Calculation for the Dock Allowance

Considering, for the sake of convenience, the summer season, a vessel can load until she is submerged to the upper edge of the summer load-line provided she is in water of specific gravity 1·025. In water of specific gravity 1·000 she can submerge to the upper edge of the fresh-water loadline (F).

If the difference between these two levels is 125 mm (her fresh-water allowance), then it means that she can submerge her (S) line by 125 mm if she is loading in fresh water in summer.

If the water in the dock is of some intermediate S.G., then she may submerge her summer loadline by an amount (the dock allowance) calculated as a direct proportion.

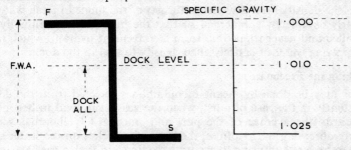

FIGURE 12.5

Suppose the vessel in the above case is loading in dock water of specific gravity 1·010. Fig. 12.5 shows the fresh and salt summer load-lines and the corresponding S.Gs. The dock allowance is shown by the distance D.A., extending upwards from the summer loadline, and level with 1·010 on the scale of S.Gs.

By simple direct proportion,

$$D.A. : F.W.A. : : 15 : 25$$

meaning that the dock allowance is the same fraction of the fresh-water allowance as 15 is of 25.

So,
$$\frac{D.A.}{F.W.A.} = \frac{15}{25}$$

And,
$$D.A. = \frac{15}{25} \times 125 \text{ mm}$$

$$= 75 \text{ mm}$$

So the summer loadline, or any other salt-water loadline when in season, can be submerged by 75 mm when the vessel is loading in dock water of this S.G.

273

The S.G. is measured by means of a hydrometer. A bucket of the dock water is obtained from overside, clear of all discharges, and not from the wash-deck line hydrants. The hydrometer is inserted into the water and spun between the fingers to break down surface tension, which may affect the reading. The S.G. is read from the scale adjacent to the water level. Some hydrometers show density, taken as roughly one thousand times the S.G., i.e. water of specific gravity 1·025 has a density of 1025 grams per litre.

The hydrometer may be made of brass; it has a long, thin stem on which are graduated the densities or specific gravities spaced in harmonic progression. The lower end of the stem joins a buoyancy chamber, below which there is a weighted sphere. The instrument is of constant volume and weight, and therefore varies its depth of immersion according to the density (and thus the upthrust) of the fluid. In fresh water it is nearly completely submerged so that the bucket should initially be well-filled and never topped up from a convenient hydrant, which may be supplying water of entirely alien density to that in the dock.

Checking the Freeboard

This may be done by means of plumblines lowered from the deck, particularly in the case of a list, when the vessel can load to her mean freeboard—the average of the port and starboard freeboards. When directly observing the loadlines, the lop and wavelets on the water surface can be very confusing to accurate readings. In such a case an open-ended glass tube may be held vertically against the loadlines with one end submerged. The water level will then remain fairly static within the tube. Such a method is equally useful when reading draughts.

CLEANSING OF FRESH-WATER TANKS

Although this may naturally be done at any time, it is quite likely to be carried out while in drydock, and for that reason is included in this chapter. In addition to cleansing, the tank may need to be cement-washed with a solution of cement in fresh water at a thin, creamy consistency. Attention should also be paid to the thick cement coating in the bottom of the water tanks, which just covers the rivet heads. Where cracked, this should be suitably keyed and refilled.

The following advice is from a Department of Trade Merchant Shipping Notice:

The attention of Shipowners and Masters is drawn to the need to ensure that the health of crews is not jeopardised by the use of fresh water from tanks which are not adequately and regularly cleansed, by the use of filters which are not periodically serviced and maintained, or by the use of sea water in the preparation of food.

DRYDOCKING AND LOADLINES

The Board's investigations suggest that insufficient attention is being paid to these matters, and Masters are, therefore, requested to ensure that the following precautions are taken:

1. Fresh Water Tanks

Drinking water tanks should be opened up, cleaned out, cement washed (or, if coated with a bituminous, plastic, or other proprietory composition, recoated where necessary) and aired at intervals not exceeding 12 months. In addition, it is recommended that tanks should be thoroughly pumped out and, where necessary, hosed prior to re-filling at approximately six-monthly intervals. During the cleaning process scrupulous attention should be paid to the hygiene and personal cleanliness of those engaged on the work.

2. Filters

When filters are fitted arrangements should be made for the maintenance and care of the apparatus, i.e. cleaning and where necessary changing the media to ensure that the apparatus does not become contaminated by bacteria and other foreign matter. It is recommended that the media, i.e. the carbon candles, should at intervals be removed and washed out in chlorinated water and lightly scrubbed with a brush to remove all traces of deposit on the surface of the filter. The frequency with which this should be carried out will, of course, depend on the amount of solid matter in the water, as water which gives a marked deposit on standing will soon clog up the pores of the filter, whereas pure water should allow the filter to work satisfactorily for a quite considerable time. In any case, filters should be cleaned out at least once a month, and more frequently if water containing an appreciable sediment is being passed through them.

It cannot be too strongly stressed that filters will not guarantee the bacteriological purity of the filtered water. Therefore, whenever there is any doubt as to the quality of the water, chlorination should be carried out in accordance with the instructions laid down in the Ship Captain's Medical Guide.

3. Use of Sea Water

The use of sea water in the preparation of food, washing up of dishes, cleaning of galley equipment or in installations such as potato peelers, should where possible be avoided. Where its use is unavoidable there should always be a final rinse through with fresh water. Under no circumstances should sea water be used for these purposes when the vessel is in, or in the vicinity of, port or coastal areas.

It is recommended that a warning on the above lines should be issued to Catering Department staffs.

PEST CONTROL IN SHIPS

There are two types of rat: the brown one, which is a shore dweller and tends to burrow, and the black one, which climbs, and frequents ships. The latter species is a plague carrier, transmitting the disease by means of its fleas.

275

Rats commence breeding at the age of two to three months, and up to ten may be born in a litter. The period of gestation is only three weeks, and it is therefore possible for a male and a female to cause the evolution of nearly 20000 rats in twelve months.

It is required that rats should be prevented from leaving a ship when in port. It is equally desirable of course, that rats from ashore should not join the ship. This prevention is carried out by means of circular alloy rat-guards which clip over the mooring lines, or by means of canvas parcelled around the moorings both at the shore and the ship (i.e. two parcellings on each line), well tarred, and each extending 2 ft 0·6 m in length.

The gangway should be hoisted clear of the quay when not in use, e.g. at night, or else well illuminated and/or whitewashed. Rats will avoid well-lighted places. Stores should be moved regularly to discover whether rats are harbouring, and refuse should not be allowed to accumulate on the ship.

Any rats caught alive should be drowned and then burned. They should not be taken ashore.

The International Sanitary Convention (Paris) 1926 requires that a Port Sanitary Authority shall be responsible for the issuing of Certificates of Deratisation and Certificates of Exemption from Deratisation. A ship calling at a port where the Convention applies, and having neither of these certificates, will most probably have to be fumigated.

Both Certificates are valid for six months, and whichever certificate is held should be presented on arrival at each port, to the Local Port Health Officer.

The Certificate of Deratisation is issued to the Master after fumigation has taken place. The Certificate of Deratisation Exemption is issued to a Master, if the Inspector is satisfied that there is no evidence of rats on the ship.

To this end, it is both politic and economic to ensure that the vessel is continuously kept rat-free.

United Kingdom vessels have an excellent reputation for being hygienic. In 1899 gas fumigation was first seriously attempted in the form of sulphur dioxide. In 1921 hydrocyanic acid gas (hydrogen cyanide or prussic acid gas) was used successfully, and continued in popularity until about 1952.

The use of hydrocyanic gas (HCN) involves great inconvenience and cost, for all work has to cease on board the ship, and it has to be completely evacuated except for the fumigating staff. Several deaths are recorded where personnel have been left aboard, sleeping in their cabins. However, in some ports, the use of HCN may still be necessary in order to obtain a Deratisation Certificate.

The most popular method employed in the United Kingdom at the present time is fumigation by means of sodium fluoracetate (1080), and this will deserve the issuing of a new Certificate.

The use of 'Biotrol' baits maintains a ship rat-free, for Biotrol is an anti-coagulant bait which is combined with a palatable fungicide in whole cereal grains. As a result, the bait stays fresh and attractive to rats for up to twelve months.

Only one-fortieth of a gram of bait per thousand grams of body weight, taken regularly, will kill a rat within a week. The rat feeds without suspicion, and is in no way bait-shy. The bait is practically harmless to domestic animals and humans.

The following is an M Notice, No. 115, cancelled but still relevant:

NOTICE TO SHIPMASTERS
FUMIGATION OF SHIPS WITH HYDROGEN CYANIDE

Fumigation with Hydrogen cyanide is a dangerous process which should be undertaken only by responsible persons with full knowledge of the nature of the gas and of the necessary precautions.

The Nature of the Gas

Hydrogen cyanide—which is also known as hydrocyanic acid gas or prussic acid gas—is an invisible and highly poisonous gas. It has a faint almond-like odour. Many people however cannot smell it, and in some cases the sense of smell becomes deadened. It is therefore highly dangerous to rely on the sense of smell for detecting the presence of the gas.

It is a fallacy to imagine that because the gas is a little lighter than air it can be induced to escape upwards merely by opening port holes or hatches of ships. When once mixed with air it cannot thus easily be got rid of. The whole atmosphere of a compartment or ship must be changed, and this can be done only by applying the well-known principles of ventilation. The circulation of air may be assisted by mechanical means, and special attention must be paid to places where ventilation is obviously difficult or slow, e.g., forepeaks, deep holds with small hatches, etc.

Warning Notices

Warning notices should be displayed on every gangway and other means of access to the ship before the fumigation is started, and they should be kept in position until the operation is over and ventilation is complete.

Preliminary Search for Unauthorised Persons

Before any part of a ship is put under gas steps should be taken to see that no unauthorised person is on board.

Clearance after Fumigation

The ship must be properly ventilated and the fumigant operators must ascertain by test that in no part of the risk area is the fumigant concentrated by more than one part by volume in one hundred-thousand parts of air.

Bedding, blankets, pillows, cushions, thick carpets, etc., must be thoroughly beaten in the open air.

Special attention should be paid to cabins and sleeping compartments. It is often advisable, after they are apparently free from gas, to close them for one hour and again test the air.

In cold weather ventilation is slow and repeated tests may be necessary. As the temperature rises gas may be liberated from materials which have retained it. In such circumstances it may be necessary to heat compartments and then re-test them before they are declared free of gas.

Special attention should be paid to cold storage chambers.

The crew's quarters or cabins must not be occupied during the night following a fumigation. If, however, this is unavoidable, all doors, port holes and other openings of spaces must be kept open and special attention must be paid to the previous beating—*in the open air*—of bedding, blankets, pillows, etc.

If the vessel has been fumigated with the cargo on board, special care is necessary, and the atmosphere should be kept under observation when unloading is in progress.

Symptoms of Poisoning

Hydrogen cyanide is extremely poisonous and poisoning may result from breathing the gas or absorbing it through the skin. The warning signs are irritation of the throat, dizziness, nausea, general weakness and headache, palpitation, a feeling of suffocation, pallor, deep breathing, sudden unconsciousness followed by a cessation of breathing, in that order.

A person showing these symptoms must be immediately removed to a pure atmosphere, laid down with his head into the wind and first aid must be given without delay, Speed is essential. A doctor must be summoned at once. The first aid procedure, if the patient is conscious, is as follows:

(1) Break a capsule of amyl nitrite on to a piece of cloth and allow the patient to inhale the vapour.
(2) Remove or cut away splashed clothing.

If the patient is unconscious, then in addition to (1) above, artificial respiration should be started simultaneously with (2) above. The patient should be kept warm and not walked about.

The reader's attention is drawn to the Hydrogen Cyanide (Fumigation of Ships) Regulations, 1951, in which precautions are laid down regarding the treatment of ships by this gas. Notice of the forthcoming fumigation must be given to the Medical Officer of Health; operators are required to be adequately trained and equipped with respirators. The Rules explain how unauthorised persons are permitted to enter the risk area in the event of emergency such as fire.

In the Port of London in 1959, 112 vessels were deratted by the use of sodium fluoracetate (1080) compared with only thirteen by the use of HCN. The use of 1080 has proved popular with shipowners as it presents no fire risk or danger to humans. It does not give off poisonous fumes and it cannot be absorbed through the unbroken skin. It is odourless and tasteless in use and presents no repellent effect. Rats drink a lot of water and will approach the solution confidently.

While deratting with 1080, the crew may remain on board and work can proceed in those parts of the ship not under treatment.

Article 52 of the International Sanitary Regulations requires that a vessel shall be kept in a condition such that the number of rodents on board is negligible. Such a ship can exist on Deratting Exemption.

This is achieved using the anti-coagulants baits, distributed through the ship in polythene sachets which are broken by the rats. These sachets help to keep the bait fresh. Ships with past records of rodent infestation have been kept completely clear by the use of these baits.

In the Port of London, 100 ships are deratted nearly every year. Over 2000 rats are destroyed on vessels in the port each year.

Methyl Bromide

This substance is a very effective fumigant, readily penetrating such commodities as soil and timber. It is highly toxic to man and should be used only by trained and competent operators. Symptoms of poisoning, which resemble drunkenness, may be delayed for several hours. A victim of poisoning may take years to recover. The gas is first smelled when in a concentration of 10000 ppm but by then it is far too late—poisoning having occurred at 35 ppm. A lachrymatory agent (producing tears) is usually added to the gas, to act as a warning.

Fumigated areas should be made gas-tight and operators should use halide detector lamps outside the area to detect leakage—they are basically blowlamps with a copper insert. When methyl bromide is present, the flame turns to a pale-green or bright-blue colour.

A ship should not be fumigated with methyl bromide until she has been searched and evacuated. Accommodation should be sealed and keys handed to the operator. On large vessels, total evacuation is not necessary, only of the areas adjacent to the fumigation. Ventilating systems should be watched for gas seepage.

279

CHAPTER XIII

THE OFFICER OF THE WATCH

TIME KEEPING

THE day at sea is divided into six 4-hour periods called watches. These extend, and are named as follows:

From 8 p.m. to midnight . . .	the first watch
From midnight to 4 a.m. . . .	the middle watch
From 4 a.m. to 8 a.m. . . .	the morning watch
From 8 a.m. to noon . . .	the forenoon watch
From noon to 4 p.m. . . .	the afternoon watch
From 4 p.m. to 8 p.m. . . .	the evening watch

In past days the evening watch was broken at 6 p.m. into two 2-hour periods called the first and second *dog watches*. This enabled two sets of watchkeepers (the watch-and-watch system) to alternate their routine day by day. Nowadays there are invariably three sets of watchkeepers, and the practice may only be used on small vessels manned by two watchkeeping officers.

The time is sounded by means of the ship's bell—usually the one fitted to the bridge-front bulkhead, the clapper of which is moved by means of a lanyard extending to the helmsman's position. The beginning of the watch is denoted by making 8 bells, the end of the first half-hour by 1 bell, the end of the first two half-hours by 2 bells, and so on, so that 3.30 a.m. and p.m., for example, is sounded by 7 bells. The number of bells made therefore never exceeds 8, except at midnight on the 31 December, when 16 bells are made, i.e. 8 for each year, often rung by the youngest member of the ship's company. The bells are made in pairs, followed by a single one if any, leaving a distinct pause between each pair and between a pair and an odd stroke. E.g. 3.30 is made as

$$1, 2, \ldots 3, 4, \ldots 5, 6, \ldots 7$$

At a quarter of an hour before the end of each watch, i.e. 3.45, 7.45, and 11.45, one bell is made to call the next watchkeepers.

The bell system in the dog watches (if kept) is unusual, unless it is treated as a full 4-hour watch. Even today in three-watch systems the dog-watch bells may be made, as follows:

1630 hrs. 1 bell	1700 hrs. 2 bells	1730 hrs. 3 bells
1800 hrs. 4 bells	1830 hrs. 1 bell	1900 hrs. 2 bells
1930 hrs. 3 bells	1945 hrs. 1 bell	2000 hrs. 8 bells

The bells are similar to those for other watches up to and including 1800 hrs. and also the watch-calling bell at 1945 hrs.

Many Masters today dismiss the use of the bells on the grounds that clocks are fitted throughout the ships. Others prefer to use them during the hours of daylight only, particularly when passengers are carried. It is perhaps a pity that such a well-known custom of the sea is tending to die out.

THE DUTIES OF THE OFFICER OF THE WATCH (O.O.W.)

A. At Sea

These are summarised as follows:

(1) Maintaining an efficient lookout, both ahead and astern, supplemented at night, and possibly by day as well, by one or more crew lookoutmen, posted where the O.O.W. thinks fit.

(2) Checking the vessel's position whenever possible and necessary. This does not imply a continuous sequence of sextant work. When coasting, many Masters require the ship's observed position to be plotted on the chart every 15–20 minutes. These fixes may be supplemented by the use of radar, according to the Master's Standing Orders. Whenever possible, radar ranges and bearings should be checked at least once a watch by means of visual bearings to ensure that this navigational aid is functioning properly. Radio direction-bearings and Consol counts may also be used by the O.O.W.

(3) Ensuring that the helmsman is maintaining a proper course, and steering to the best of his ability under the prevailing weather and sea conditions. A glance at the wake, by day, will provide a quick check on his accuracy.

(4) To keep a sharp lookout when men are working near the ship's side or when moving about the decks in heavy weather.

(5) To use the echo-sounding machine when instructed to do so.

(6) In fog, to ring the engine-room telegraphs to 'Stand-By', to commence sounding the Regulation fog-signal, to commence and organise a radar watch, to call the Master, to post extra lookouts forward and/or aloft, and to reduce to a moderate speed.

(7) To record all details of passing aircraft, in the Deck Logbook.

(8) To reply by visual signalling to any vessel or aircraft, particularly

Naval or Air Force craft, when it is convenient to do so; otherwise to visually signal the letter 'N' (Negative).

(9) To read the barometer regularly, particularly when in a hurricane zone in season.

(10) To make sure that lookoutmen are safe and that all watchkeepers are relieved on time.

(11) To make sure that suitable decklights are switched on and off at sunset and sunrise. This applies also to the navigation lights.

(12) To ensure that weather-deck doors and openings are closed when not in use.

(13) To ensure that flags are flying freely and that signal halliards are slackened in damp weather.

(14) To check the compass error regularly.

(15) To record in the Deck Logbook: engine movements and revolutions; log distances; wind directions and speeds; air and sea temperatures; barometer readings; weather conditions; courses steered; allowances made for current set or leeway; results of sextant observations; times of passing major navigational marks; names of pilots; details of action in fog or bad visibility; times when holds are ventilated; tank soundings; times when navigation lights are switched on and off; entries of heavy weather, and any soundings made together with the nature of the bottom, if known.

(16) To keep a meteorological logbook where arranged.

(17) To make sure that anchors are clear for use when approaching port.

(18) To frequently observe smoke-detecting apparatus cabinets.

(19) To bear in mind that awnings may be ripped by freshening winds and take action to prevent this.

(20) To ensure that men are clear of the fog-signalling apparatus before the O.O.W. uses it.

(21) To ensure that relieved helmsmen report the course to the O.O.W.

Duties which must take pride of place over others include numbers (1), (2), (3), (6), (11), and (14). It should be noted, however, that the execution of (1) will automatically include duties (4), (7), (10), (12), (13), (19), (20), and (21).

When taking over a watch, the O.O.W. will require to know: the course steered; allowances for leeway and set; the rudder carried, i.e. continuous port or starboard helm; the revolutions; ships or navigational marks in sight; the ship's position; whether sounding gear or radar is in use; whether extra lookouts are posted and where they are situated; details of any sound signals heard; the compass error. He will read and initial the Master's Night Order Book. It is customary to write the logbook entries for the watch after being relieved, and when the relieving officer has verbally agreed to take over the watch.

B. In Port, Berthed

(1) To ensure that a proper gangway watch is kept; that the gangway is adjusted for tidal range; that no unauthorised persons are allowed aboard and that the Officers' tally board is properly used. This latter indicates which Officers are aboard and which one is on duty.

(2) To ensure that all moorings are properly fitted with rat-guards.

(3) To ensure that decklights are switched on and off at dusk and dawn.

(4) To attend cargo operations, storing of the ship, and the supplying of fresh water to tanks.

(5) To ensure that watchmen are properly relieved and that when men are working overside or aloft their equipment is in a safe condition and that a man is employed to watch for their safety. The vessel should fly the two-flag signal 'RY', which means 'Reduce speed when passing me'.

(6) To frequently observe fire or smoke-detecting apparatus and to carry out fire patrols.

(7) To investigate disciplinary offences.

(8) To prevent smoking in appropriate parts of the ship.

(9) To be responsible for the custody of keys.

(10) To enter into the logbook: weather conditions; details of repair work; number of men employed on repairs; times when cargo is loaded or discharged and which holds are in use; the number of stevedore gangs employed; reasons for stoppages of cargo work; the ventilation of holds; tank soundings; the draught each day; details of heavy lift work; names of gangway watchmen.

(11) To regularly check moorings and fenders.

(12) To carry out sea duties (9), (12), (13), and (19).

C. In Port, at Anchor

(1) To ensure that the anchor lights are burning properly and at equal brilliancy.

(2) To ensure that the anchor ball is displayed by day.

(3) To make the appropriate sound signals in fog or poor visibility.

(4) To take all possible steps to detect a dragging anchor.

(5) To make sure a second anchor is ready for letting go.

(6) To lift the gangway when seas are breaking over it.

(7) To observe all boats arriving at and leaving the ship.

(8) To call the Master instantly should the vessel be in danger.

(9) To record in the logbook: the depth of water at the anchorage; the amount of cable veered; the nature of the bottom; the anchor bearings or transit bearings, i.e. those used to check the vessel's position;

any adjustments to the amount of cable veered; details of boats arriving at and leaving the ship; the arrival draught; any of the entries which are made at sea or when berthed in port and which are appropriate.

(10) To carry out sea duties (1), (4), (8), (9), (10), (11), (12), (13), (14), (16), (18), (19), and (20).

(11) To post extra lookouts in poor visibility, commence a radar watch, and call the Master.

(12) To ensure that the vessel is properly sheered (Chapter 1).

In all cases the O.O.W. should carefully attend to Standing Orders. He should report to the Master when:

(a) there is a deterioration of visibility, or
(b) the vessel sights certain navigational marks, or
(c) there is any unusual sighting of, or failure to sight, navigation marks, or
(d) any vessel fails in its duty to give way, or
(e) wrecks, unidentified objects, or survivors are observed, or
(f) the barometer falls sharply.

DUTIES OF OFFICERS PRIOR TO LEAVING PORT
(BERTHED)

The following duties will be shared among the Officers:

(1) To ensure that all hatchways are securely battened down and that booby (hold entrance) hatches are locked. All weather-deck doors should be closed where practical.

(2) All ship's side rails must be properly shipped and secured. Overside nets should be hauled aboard.

(3) Derricks will be stowed and securely lashed in their crutches. The decks are to be cleared of all running rigging.

(4) Standing rigging should be set tight—this applies when it has been cast off to facilitate the swinging out of derricks.

(5) To ensure that a proper exchange of documents has been made between the ship and the dock offices.

(6) All cargo should be securely tommed (shored) to prevent it shifting in a seaway.

(7) A thorough check must be made to ensure that no cargo for that port is being overcarried to the next destination.

(8) The Master will probably require a list to be made enumerating the spaces remaining within cargo compartments, particularly when the vessel is loading. Ideally, a copy of this should be sent to the next loading port.

(9) The draught is to be accurately read on both sides (in case the vessel is listed) and the density of the dock water determined. In some

localities where high temperatures prevail, such as the Persian Gulf, this may be as low as 996 grammes per litre, and a hydrometer suitable for oils will have to be used. The form FRE 13 (Notice of Draught and Freeboard) must be completed, signed by the Master and Chief Officer, and posted in a conspicuous place. The Master will enter the details listed in this form into the Official Logbook.

(10) To ensure that strong rooms and mail rooms are locked.

(11) To carry out a thorough search for stowaways in all parts of the ship, with particular reference to: lifeboats; funnel casings; large ventilators; crew accommodation; empty oil-cargo-tanks; engine-rooms; tunnel-escape trunkways and shaft tunnels (underneath the limbers); storerooms; coils of rope covered with canvas; holds, and the steering flat, etc. Stowaways may use the chain locker.

(12) To ensure that Muster Lists are posted throughout the ship listing the emergency duties of all crew members.

(13) To post a copy of the Articles of Agreement (ALC 6) in the crew accommodation.

(14) To ensure that a cabin, if required, is prepared for the Pilot.

(15) Late documents should be prepared ready for landing by means of the pilot cutter.

(16) To make preparations for the compass adjuster, if any.

(17) To obtain the latest weather-forecast chart, if required, and also the latest ice reports, in season.

(18) The whistle lanyards and main radio aerials should be erected.

(19) All necessary flags should be made ready. The Blue Peter (code flag 'P') should preferably be displayed for the final 12 hours.

(20) Telephones should be tested throughout the ship. Those provided by the shore Authorities should be disconnected and taken ashore. This applies to shore supplies of steam, gas, electricity, and water, etc.

(21) A check should be made to ensure that all passengers and crew members are aboard. This will normally be done by the Heads of the departments, who will report to the Chief Officer.

(22) The patent log, if of the towing type, should be made ready for streaming.

(23) The gyro compass should be running for about the final 6–12 hours. The gyro error should be checked and repeaters synchronised with the master compass. Some Masters prefer to adjust the repeaters so that they show no error. All clamps must be released on the master compass.

(24) The navigation bridge should be made ready with particular reference to: binoculars; telescopes; megaphones; chalk for course board; charts; chartwork instruments; sharp pencils; bridge notebook; signalling lamps; compass binnacle covers; azimuth mirrors (these should be tested for error by observing the bearings of an object with

the arrow both up and down); semaphore flags; torches; the chronometers should be checked for error; the radar, echo-sounding machine, engine-room telegraphs, steering-gear, whistles, and loud hailers should be tested; current Notices to Mariners must be obtained.

(25) Ratguards should be brought aboard.

(26) Fenders and gangways should be tended ready for shipping.

(27) All boats and lighters should be cast off. Propeller guards (floating spars, tangential to poop deck) should be shipped.

(28) To attend the moorings if the Engineers wish to test the engines.

When leaving an anchorage, particularly when cargo has been loaded or discharged, duties (23) and (24) may be dispensed with, assuming a proper anchor watch has been kept. Duty (25) will not apply.

DUTIES OF OFFICERS PRIOR TO ARRIVAL IN PORT

(1) Arrange for all necessary flags to be made ready, such as quarantine signals and the ship's signal letters group. Pyrotechnic pilot signals should be at hand.

(2) To prepare a list of cargo, together with its volume, carried in unregistered spaces, for declaration to the Customs Officers.

(3) To prepare derricks and cranes ready for immediate commencement of cargo work.

(4) To warn the Engineers at least 1 hour before the engines are to be stopped.

(5) To prepare a gangway and fenders ready for rigging overside.

(6) The patent towing log must be handed (brought aboard).

(7) A pilot ladder must be made ready.

(8) Mooring lines must be prepared for running. Heaving lines should be distributed fore and aft, and the springs should preferably have heaving lines already secured to them.

CONNING THE SHIP; HELM ORDERS

There is no single system of verbal helm orders, and the new seafarer is strongly advised to study the various methods and choose one for his own use, endeavouring to make sure that it will at all times be suitable for the prevailing conditions, e.g. conning among heavy traffic and also in narrow waters, etc., and that it is beyond misinterpretation.

The use of 'Hard a' starboard (or port)' is generally an emergency order when a rapid swing is required, and the order should be given in a calm voice to ensure that a flustered helmsman does not put the wheel over in the wrong direction. This latter action is likely to be a mistake made by any one of us, and may occur particularly when the helmsman is watching the events through the wheelhouse windows, instead of his instruments. The use of this order, however, may be quite regular and frequent in narrow channels when the ship is proceeding at slow speeds and carrying large rudder correction angles.

All orders to the helmsman must be repeated by him; when he reports a condition such as 'Wheel's amidships, Sir' this must be acknowledged by the O.O.W.

If the O.O.W. wishes to alter the vessel's course from, say, 270 to 330 degrees he may give the order, 'Alter course 60 degrees to starboard', or 'Steer 330 degrees', or else he may choose to control the swing of the ship himself, in which case he will watch the compass and say, 'Twenty degrees starboard wheel'. As the ship commences her swing the O.O.W. may say, 'Ease the wheel' or 'Ease to ten', in which case the wheel is rotated until the indicator shows a less value than 20 degrees, or else 10 degrees. The next order will be ''midships'. When the vessel reaches a heading of about 320 degrees (depending upon the rate of swing) the order will be 'Steady' or 'Meet her!', the wheel being rotated to provide port helm in order to check the swing. This must be done so that the ship stops swinging on a heading of 330 degrees, when the order is given 'Steady as she goes' or 'Steady on 330 degrees'.

This method of conning may be useful when the O.O.W. wishes to alter course to avoid another vessel. If he thinks an alteration of 15 degrees to port is sufficient, he may say simply 'Steer fifteen degrees to port', but if he prefers to swing the ship until a suitable alteration has been achieved, then he may use the sequence, 'Twenty degrees port wheel' . . . 'Ease to five' . . . ''midships' . . . 'Steady' . . . 'Steady as she goes'. The helmsman now reports the ship's heading.

Some Officers and Pilots use the expression 'Port twenty!', etc., but many helmsmen interpret this to mean 'You are to alter course twenty degrees to port' while others understand it to mean 'You are to carry twenty degrees of port wheel'. For this reason there must always be a clear understanding between the conning Officer and the helmsman. Assuming the latter interpretation, the above altering sequence can be changed to, 'Port twenty' . . . 'Port five' . . . ''midships' . . . 'Starboard fifteen' (to steady the swing) . . . ''midships' . . . 'Steady as she goes'.

The expression 'Port five' is used here instead of 'Ease to five'.

When instructing the helmsman to steer a certain course such as 330 degrees, it is always expressed as 'Three, three, Oh'. The helmsman must report courses in a similar manner.

If the O.O.W. wishes to be absolutely precise in his duties he may watch the wheel indicator as he gives an order. This enables him to detect instantly any mistaken helm application. The rudder indicator naturally shows a delayed action compared with that of the wheel, and a mistake is not instantly observed.

Whenever an order is rung on the engine-room telegraphs it will be answered by the Engineer, and the smaller pointer on the bridge tele-graph will align itself with the main control. It is most important that the Officer in charge of the telegraphs should observe this small pointer in order to detect errors.

When using the type of telegraphs controlled by chains, the handle should not be moved anywhere near a reverse-motion order when accelerating or decelerating. For example, if it is desired to change from 'Half astern' to 'Slow astern', the handle should be rotated only within the astern segments. Often it is whirled back and forth with the aim of obtaining a prolonged and stentorian ringing. This it achieves, but it is a sad occasion when the chains part while the handle is over, say, the 'Full ahead' segment! The aim should therefore be to ensure that should the chain break, the ship will not momentarily be reversed in motion when all that is intended is an increase or decrease in speed. A perfectly satis-factory ring may be produced by moving the handle within, say, three segments. The handle should never be allowed to rest on a line.

THE LOGBOOKS

Reference has been made in previous sections to a logbook. By this is meant the Chief Officer's logbook, which is virtually a diary of the ship's activities. The information contained therein is derived from the rough logbook, which is kept by the individual Officers-of-the-watch. The Chief Officer's log is written up daily, and each page is signed by the Chief Officer and witnessed by the Master. Both this book and the rough logbook may be produced in Courts of Law and also during Official Enquiries, such as are held by the Department of Trade (D.o.T.) in the U.K. subsequent to a collision, etc.

For this reason, pages should never be torn out of the book, and any alterations should be made by ruling a single line through the original entry, rewriting it as desired, and initialling the entry. It is preferable to have a witnessing signature. *In no circumstances should an erasure be made.*

At the end of the voyage the Chief Officer's log is often given into the custody of the shipowners while the rough copy is retained aboard for reference purposes. The Owners are then in a position to conduct de-fences even though the vessel is abroad. In this connection it is of the utmost importance to make a full entry in the logbook relating to all accidents which occur on the ship, no matter who the victim, e.g. visitor, stevedore, other shore employee, or crew member. In many cases the entry has been overlooked, and as many as five years later a claim for damages has been made, the claim relating to illness or incapacitance, etc., alleged to be a direct result of the original accident. Provided a full account, duly witnessed, and where possible signed by the victim, has been entered into the logbook, the Owners will be able to provide the maximum defence under conditions of litigation.

The Official Logbook (*O.L.B.*) is supplied by the Department of Trade in the United Kingdom when the Articles of Agreement have been completed to the satisfaction of the Mercantile Marine Office Superintendent, and before he issues the ship's certificate of outward clearance. It must be delivered to the Superintendent within 48 hours of arrival in the United Kingdom, or when the crew is discharged, whichever is the sooner.

This logbook is kept by the Master, and all entries are signed by him and witnessed by a crew member, usually the Chief Officer. The logbook contains entries relating to:

(1) Births, deaths, and marriages which occur on board.
(2) Wages due to a dead seaman, together with a list of his effects.
(3) Each case of sickness and the remedy used.
(4) A list of crew, with a report on their conduct and character. Also details of their qualifications.
(5) Offences, and the fines or forfeitures imposed. Convictions by a Court of Law.
(6) Details of crew changes and any promotions or disratings which occur.
(7) Beachings, strandings, and collisions.
(8) Orders of a Naval Court.
(9) Details of watertight doors, radio installations, deck line, and loadlines.
(10) Distress calls which resulted in no departure of the ship from her course. Full reasons for not going to the assistance of the distressed persons must be given.
(11) A list of documents within the Master's charge, e.g. Certificate of Registry, Certificate of Freeboard, copy of the crew's Agreement, charter-parties, Manifest, Bill of Health, radio logbook, etc.
(12) Refusal by any crew member to take anti-scorbutics (lime or citrus-fruit juices which are issued free to prevent scurvy).
(13) Wages and effects of any seaman who has been left behind, for any reason, at a previous port of call.
(14) Complaints regarding food and water.
(15) Tonnages of deck cargoes.
(16) The draught, dock allowance, and freeboard on leaving each port; these are copied from form FRE 13.
(17) Occasions on which the ship's life-saving appliances are inspected, including boat drills and fire drills.
(18) Wages due to a seaman who has deserted in order to join the Royal Navy.
(19) Inspections of the accommodation.

A copy of the entry should be furnished to a seaman who has been fined, suffered a forfeiture, or who has been disrated.

When the vessel has suffered heavy weather, stranded, or been beached, etc., i.e. any occurrence which might lead to damage to the vessel or her cargo, the Master 'notes protest' before a Notary Public within 24 hours of arrival in port. An entry to this effect should be made in the Chief Officer's logbook and also in the Official Logbook.

CHAPTER XIV

THE SAFETY OF NAVIGATION

NOTICES TO MARINERS

THESE are published for the correction of Admiralty charts, Sailing Directions, Light Lists, and other hydrographic publications, and are issued by the Admiralty for the use of both Royal and Merchant Navies.

For foreign-going vessels, the following Notices are issued:

(a) Daily notices to disseminate information of an urgent nature or of major importance.

(b) Weekly complete editions of notices, which contain all the information which has become available during the previous week and include any Daily Notices issued during that week.

(c) A quarterly edition containing, in a collated form, the hydrographic information published in the weekly complete editions during the previous quarter.

The first issue of the year contains roughly the first twenty notices, which are annual Regulations and on which candidates for D.T.I. examinations are closely questioned. The book also contains notices of a temporary character, preliminary notices in force on 1 January, reprint of navigational warnings still in force from the previous year, and corrections to NEMEDRI (North Europe, Eastern Mediterranean Routing Instructions, regarding mined areas). This book, which is some three-quarters of an inch thick, is often referred to simply as 'Notice No. 1'.

The weekly editions contain six parts:

Part 1. The index.

Part 2. Notices to Mariners.

Part 3. Navigational warnings.

Part 4. Amendments to NEMEDRI and areas dangerous due to the presence of mines.

Part 5. Corrections to Lights Lists, fog signals and visual time signals.

Part 6. Corrections to Lists of Radio Signals and Official Radio Messages to British Merchant ships.

291

THE SAFETY OF NAVIGATION

For home-trade and fishing vessels, daily notices are issued and also a weekly complete edition, but both refer only to the areas traversed by these vessels.

The Notices are issued gratis to Master's of ships, and all Officers should search them thoroughly, making all appropriate corrections to their hydrographic material. Navigational warnings should be initialled by each Officer. The Notices are obtainable at Mercantile Marine Offices throughout the United Kingdom. They may be inspected, and in many cases obtained, at important Commonwealth shipping offices and at important British Consulates. They are also obtainable from Admiralty Chart Agents.

THE AMVER SYSTEM

The Automated Mutual Assistance Rescue System, originated by the United States Coastguard, is a maritime mutual assistance organisation which provides important aid to the development and co-ordination of search and rescue (SAR) efforts in many offshore areas of the world.

Merchant vessels of all nations making offshore voyages are encouraged to send movement reports and periodic position reports to the AMVER centre at Coast Guard New York via selected radio stations. Information from these reports is fed into an electronic computer which supplies dead-reckoning positions for the vessels while they are within the plotting area.

Characteristics of vessels which are valuable for determining SAR capability are also entered into the computer from available sources of information.

The predicted location and SAR characteristics of each vessel known to be within the area of interest are made available upon request to recognised SAR agencies of any nation, or person in distress, for use in an emergency. The predicted locations are disclosed only for reasons connected with maritime safety.

Similar systems are now in operation in Madagascar, Australia, New Zealand and Denmark (Greenland area). All ships are urged to co-operate. AMVER messages are free to the ship.

Four types of report are in use. The nine-part report used to initiate a plot is sent before or soon after departure; it is virtually a sailing plan. There is also a deviation or delay report which is sent if the sailing plan is changed. A position report can be sent at random intervals to assist the computer (on long voyages). The fourth type of report is made on arrival at the vessel's destination.

THE SAFETY OF NAVIGATION
THE MARITIME BUOYAGE SYSTEM 'A'

The International Association of Lighthouse Authorities (I.A.L.A.) has approved one of the two systems of buoyage proposed for world-wide use. This system, known as system 'A'—the 'Combined Cardinal and Lateral System'—will be introduced into North-Western Europe commencing with the English Channel in April 1977.

Lateral marks (Fig. 14.2) are used for well-defined channels and show the port and starboard sides of the route to be followed. For example,

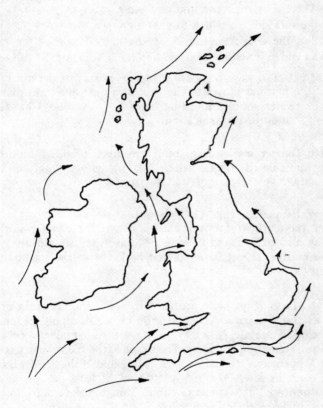

CONVENTIONAL DIRECTION OF BUOYAGE IN U.K.

FIGURE 14.1

port hand marks are to be left on the mariner's *port* hand when approaching a harbour, a river estuary or any other waterway from seaward, or when proceeding in the *conventional direction of buoyage*. The latter should, in general, follow a clockwise direction around land masses. The conventional direction of buoyage for the United Kingdom is shown in Fig. 14.1. The reader should note that lateral pillar buoys have coloured pillars.

Cardinal marks (Fig. 14.3) used in conjunction with the cardinal points of the compass, indicate

(*a*) where a mariner can find navigable water,

(*b*) the safe side on which to pass a danger,

(*c*) that the deepest water is on the named side of the mark, and

(*d*) a bend, a junction, a bifurcation (i.e. a fork) or the end of a shoal.

Cardinal marks are passed on the *named* side of the mark, in other words the mariner passes to the *west* of a *west* quadrant mark and so on. The reader should note that cardinal pillar buoys have coloured pillars for additional clarification.

Isolated Danger marks (Fig. 14.4) are erected on, or moored on or above an isolated danger which has navigable water all round it. They may have one or more red horizontal bands.

Safe Water marks (Fig. 14.4) show that there is navigable water all around the mark. It does not mark a hazard. Safe water marks can be used as mid-channel marks in which case they should always be left on the mariner's port hand so that he keeps to the starboard side of the fairway.

Special Marks (Fig. 14.5) are used to show special areas or features such as traffic separation, spoil grounds or dumping grounds where anchoring is unsafe, military exercise areas, underwater cables or pipelines, recreation zones etc. The shape of the special mark is optional. New Dangers are marked as soon as possible. If the danger is especially grave, such as a wreck across a channel, at least one of the marks is to be duplicated as soon as possible. This duplicate mark may carry a racon showing a signal one mile long on a radar display.

The I.A.L.A. consider that double-cone and double-sphere topmarks are features of major daytime importance and should therefore be as large as possible with the maximum separation.

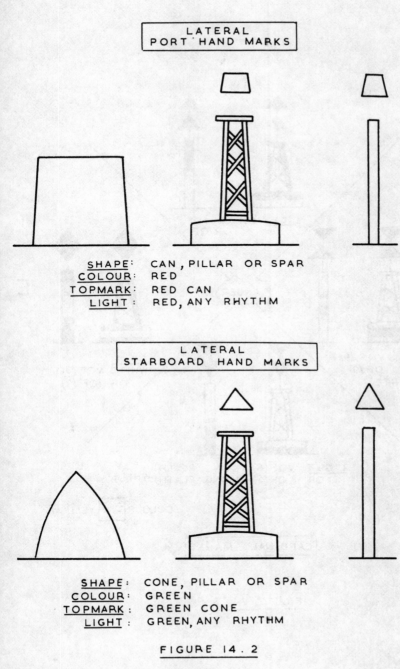

LATERAL PORT HAND MARKS

SHAPE: CAN, PILLAR OR SPAR
COLOUR: RED
TOPMARK: RED CAN
LIGHT: RED, ANY RHYTHM

LATERAL STARBOARD HAND MARKS

SHAPE: CONE, PILLAR OR SPAR
COLOUR: GREEN
TOPMARK: GREEN CONE
LIGHT: GREEN, ANY RHYTHM

FIGURE 14.2

295

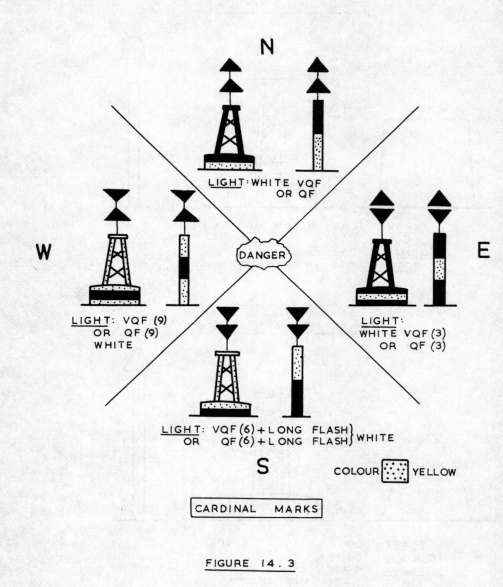

FIGURE 14.3

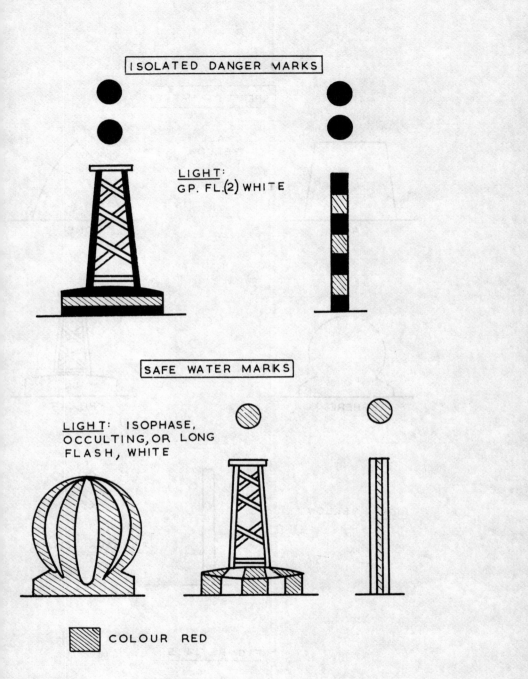

ISOLATED DANGER MARKS

LIGHT:
GP. FL.(2) WHITE

SAFE WATER MARKS

LIGHT: ISOPHASE,
OCCULTING, OR LONG
FLASH, WHITE

COLOUR RED

FIGURE 14.4

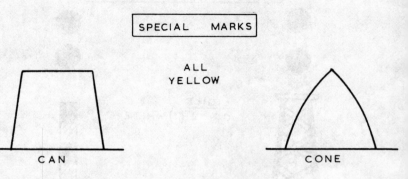

SPECIAL MARKS

ALL
YELLOW

CAN

CONE

SPHERE

PILLAR

LIGHT: YELLOW

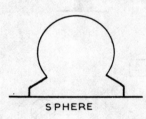

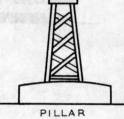

SPAR

TOPMARK: YELLOW

FIGURE 14.5

298

The lights used on System 'A' buoys are illustrated in Fig. 14.6 together with the usual abbreviations. A light graded as Very Quick Flashing flashes at the rate of 100 or 120 flashes per minute. A light graded as Quick Flashing will flash at half that rate, i.e. 50 or 60 flashes per minute.

Readers are advised to colour Fig 14.2 to 14.7 inclusive, preferably with crayons. Spirit inks or felt tip pens may produce seepage through to the other side of the paper. Where necessary, I have included a colour key and shading in the diagrams. This is obviously unnecessary in the case of lateral and special marks.

As an aid to memory, readers may like to observe that for cardinal marks, north quadrant topmarks point upwards or 'north', south quadrant topmarks point 'south', the western topmarks vaguely resemble a 'W' and the white separation cn the eastern topmarks resembles the middle bar of the letter 'E'.

As far as the complex light rhythms on the cardinal marks are concerned, the groups of 3, 6 or 9 flashes relate to the hands of a clock and can therefore be allied to East, South and West on a compass card.

THE REGULATIONS FOR PREVENTING COLLISIONS AT SEA, 1972.

Candidates for D.o.T. Examinations for Certificates of Competency will be expected to prove themselves thoroughly familiar with the Rules, and while an inability to recite them verbatim will not necessarily cause the candidate to fail, a poor knowledge of their context and application will surely do so. Candidates will not be placed in the position of handling a fully-rigged sailing ship (unless they are being examined for sail endorsement), but they will be expected to recognise the lights of these ships and to estimate the headings of such vessels.

It is pointless to dwell upon ambiguous wording within the Rules and to demonstrate certain minor instances of faulty wording, for this will

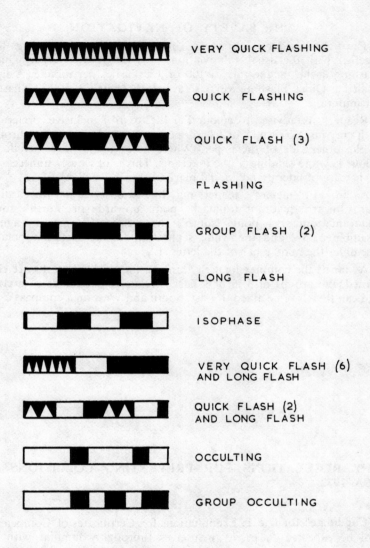

VERY QUICK FLASHING

QUICK FLASHING

QUICK FLASH (3)

FLASHING

GROUP FLASH (2)

LONG FLASH

ISOPHASE

VERY QUICK FLASH (6)
AND LONG FLASH

QUICK FLASH (2)
AND LONG FLASH

OCCULTING

GROUP OCCULTING

LIGHT CHARACTERISTICS

FIGURE 14.6

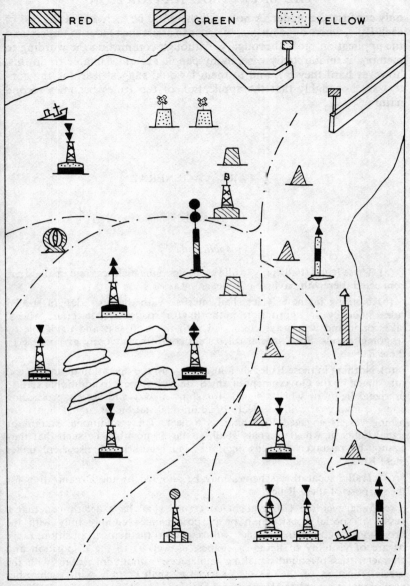

RED GREEN YELLOW

SYSTEM 'A' BUOYAGE SPECIMEN ROUTES — · — · —

FIGURE 14.7

only confuse the reader. A note will therefore be included at the end of each Rule, where appropriate, in order to assist the reader to understand the application more thoroughly. Although committing the wording to memory is undoubtedly wise, many people are quite unable to do this, however hard they try, and to them I would suggest learning the context so thoroughly that the application of the Rules becomes second nature.

PART A—GENERAL

RULE 1

Application

(a) These Rules shall apply to all vessels upon the high seas and in all waters connected therewith navigable by seagoing vessels.

(b) Nothing in these Rules shall interfere with the operation of special rules made by an appropriate authority for roadsteads, harbours, rivers, lakes or inland waterways connected with the high seas and navigable by seagoing vessels. Such special rules shall conform as closely as possible to these Rules.

(c) Nothing in these Rules shall interfere with the operation of any special rules made by the Government of any State with respect to additional station or signal lights or whistle signals for ships of war and vessels proceeding under convoy, or with respect to additional station or signal lights for fishing vessels engaged in fishing as a fleet. These additional station or signal lights or whistle signals shall, so far as possible, be such that they cannot be mistaken for any light or signal authorized elsewhere under these Rules.

(d) Traffic separation schemes may be adopted by the Organization for the purpose of these Rules.

(e) Whenever the Government concerned shall have determined that a vessel of special construction or purpose cannot comply fully with the provisions of any of these Rules with respect to the number, position, range or arc of visibility of lights or shapes, as well as to the disposition and characteristics of sound-signalling appliances, without interfering with the special function of the vessel, such vessel shall comply with such other provisions in regard to the number, position, range or arc of visibility of lights or shapes, as well as to the disposition and characteristics of sound-signalling appliances, as her Government shall have determined to be the closest possible compliance with these Rules in respect of that vessel.

THE SAFETY OF NAVIGATION

RULE 2

Responsibility

(a) Nothing in these Rules shall exonerate any vessel, or the owner, master or crew thereof, from the consequences of any neglect to comply with these Rules or of the neglect of any precaution which may be required by the ordinary practice of seamen, or by the special circumstances of the case.

(b) In construing and complying with these Rules due regard shall be had to all dangers of navigation and collision and to any special circumstances, including the limitations of the vessels involved, which may make a departure from these Rules necessary to avoid immediate danger.

Author's Note: This Rule is extremely important. '*Due regard to all dangers of navigation and collision*' refers among other things to cases where vessels are unable to take their stipulated avoiding action due to the proximity of other vessels, or the coast, reefs, etc. In such cases the privileged vessel should assist matters by taking (and indicating) early and substantial action to avoid collision. The Rule says a departure may be necessary and thus the privileged vessel should assess whether or not there is an onus upon her to keep clear. '*Limitations of the craft*' must surely draw attention to the vessels mentioned in Rules 24, 26 and 27. The inference in Rule 2 is, in my opinion, that literal observance of the Rules is certainly not intended when vessels are encountered which are hampered, disabled or encumbered in any way whatsoever.

RULE 3

General Definitions

For the purpose of these Rules, except where the context otherwise requires:

(a) The word 'vessel' includes every description of water craft, including nondisplacement craft and seaplanes, used or capable of being used as a means of transportation on water.

(b) The term 'power-driven vessel' means any vessel propelled by machinery.

(c) The term 'sailing vessel' means any vessel under sail provided that propelling machinery, if fitted, is not being used.

(d) The term 'vessel engaged in fishing' means any vessel fishing with nets, lines, trawls or other fishing apparatus which restrict manoeuvrability, but does not include a vessel fishing with trolling lines or other fishing apparatus which do not restrict manoeuvrability.

(e) The word 'seaplane' includes any aircraft designed to manoeuvre on the water.

(f) The term 'vessel not under command' means a vessel which through some exceptional circumstance is unable to manoeuvre as required by these Rules and is therefore unable to keep out of the way of another vessel.

(g) The term 'vessel restricted in her ability to manoeuvre' means a vessel which from the nature of her work is restricted in her ability to manoeuvre as required by these Rules and is therefore unable to keep out of the way of another vessel.

The following vessels shall be regarded as vessels restricted in their ability to manoeuvre:

(i) a vessel engaged in laying, servicing or picking up a navigation mark, submarine cable or pipeline;

(ii) a vessel engaged in dredging, surveying or underwater operations;

(iii) a vessel engaged in replenishment or transferring persons, provisions or cargo while underway;

(iv) a vessel engaged in the launching or recovery of aircraft;

(v) a vessel engaged in minesweeping operations;

(vi) a vessel engaged in a towing operation such as renders her unable to deviate from her course.

(h) The term 'vessel constrained by her draught' means a power-driven vessel which because of her draught in relation to the available depth of water is severely restricted in her ability to deviate from the course she is following.

(i) The word 'underway' means that a vessel is not at anchor, or made fast to the shore, or aground.

(j) The words 'length' and 'breadth' of a vessel mean her length overall and greatest breadth.

(k) Vessels shall be deemed to be in sight of one another only when one can be observed visually from the other.

(l) The term 'restricted visibility' means any condition in which visibility is restricted by fog, mist, falling snow, heavy rainstorms, sandstorms or any other similar causes.

Author's Note: Regarding section (i), it has been ruled that to be '*at anchor*', a vessel must be completely held by her anchor. The reader should distinguish carefully between the terms '*under way*' and '*making way*'. A vessel '*under way*' is not necessarily moving.

PART B—STEERING AND SAILING RULES

SECTION I—CONDUCT OF VESSELS IN ANY CONDITION OF VISIBILITY

RULE 4

Application

Rules in this Section apply in any condition of visibility.

THE SAFETY OF NAVIGATION

RULE 5

Look-out

Every vessel shall at all times maintain a proper look-out by sight and hearing as well as by all available means appropriate in the prevailing circumstances and conditions so as to make a full appraisal of the situation and of the risk of collision.

RULE 6

Safe Speed

Every vessel shall at all times proceed at a safe speed so that she can take proper and effective action to avoid collision and be stopped within a distance appropriate to the prevailing circumstances and conditions.

In determining a safe speed the following factors shall be among those taken into account:

(a) By all vessels:

   (i) the state of visibility;
   (ii) the traffic density including concentrations of fishing vessels or any other vessels;
   (iii) the manoeuvrability of the vessel with special reference to stopping distance and turning ability in the prevailing conditions;
   (iv) at night the presence of background light such as from shore lights or from back scatter of her own lights;
   (v) the state of wind, sea and current, and the proximity of navigational hazards;
   (vi) the draught in relation to the available depth of water.

(b) Additionally, by vessels with operational radar:

   (i) the characteristics, efficiency and limitations of the radar equipment;
   (ii) any constraints imposed by the radar range scale in use;
   (iii) the effect on radar detection of the sea state, weather and other sources of interference;
   (iv) the possibility that small vessels, ice and other floating objects may not be detected by radar at an adequate range;
   (v) the number, location and movement of vessels detected by radar;

(vi) the more exact assessment of the visilibity that may be possible when radar is used to determine the range of vessels or other objects in the vicinity.

RULE 7

Risk of Collision

(a) Every vessel shall use all available means appropriate to the prevailing circumstances and conditions to determine if risk of collision exists. If there is any doubt such risk shall be deemed to exist.

(b) Proper use shall be made of radar equipment if fitted and operational, including long-range scanning to obtain early warning of risk of collision and radar plotting or equivalent systematic observation of detected objects.

(c) Assumptions shall not be made on the basis of scanty information, especially scanty radar information.

(d) In determining if risk of collision exists the following considerations shall be among those taken into account:

(i) such risk shall be deemed to exist if the compass bearing of an approaching vessel does not appreciably change;

(ii) such risk may sometimes exist even when an appreciable bearing change is evident, particularly when approaching a very large vessel or a tow or when approaching a vessel at close range.

RULE 8

Action to avoid Collision

(a) Any action taken to avoid collision shall, if the circumstances of the case admit, be positive, made in ample time and with due regard to the observance of good seamanship.

(b) Any alteration of course and/or speed to avoid collision shall, if the circumstances of the case admit, be large enough to be readily apparent to another vessel observing visually or by radar; a succession of small alterations of course and/or speed should be avoided.

(c) If there is sufficient sea room, alteration of course alone may be the most effective action to avoid a close-quarters situation provided that it is made in good time, is substantial and does not result in another close-quarters situation.

(d) Action taken to avoid collision with another vessel shall be such as to result in passing at a safe distance. The effectiveness of the action shall be carefully checked until the other vessel is finally past and clear.

(e) If necessary to avoid collision or allow more time to assess the situation, a vessel shall slacken her speed or take all way off by stopping or reversing her means of propulsion.

THE SAFETY OF NAVIGATION
RULE 9
Narrow Channels

(a) A vessel proceeding along the course of a narrow channel or fairway shall keep as near to the outer limit of the channel or fairway which lies on her starboard side as is safe and practicable.

(b) A vessel of less than 20 metres in length or a sailing vessel shall not impede the passage of a vessel which can safely navigate only within a narrow channel or fairway.

(c) A vessel engaged in fishing shall not impede the passage of any other vessel navigating within a narrow channel or fairway.

(d) A vessel shall not cross a narrow channel or fairway if such crossing impedes the passage of a vessel which can safely navigate only within such channel or fairway. The latter vessel may use the sound signal prescribed in Rule 34(d) if in doubt as to the intention of the crossing vessel.

(e) (i) In a narrow channel or fairway when overtaking can take place only if the vessel to be overtaken has to take action to permit safe passing, the vessel intending to overtake shall indicate her intention by sounding the appropriate signal prescribed in Rule 34(c)(i). The vessel to be overtaken shall, if in agreement, sound the appropriate signal prescribed in Rule 34(c)(ii) and take steps to permit safe passing. If in doubt she may sound the signals prescribed in Rule 34(d).

    (ii) This Rule does not relieve the overtaking vessel of her obligation under Rule 13.

(f) A vessel nearing a bend or an area of a narrow channel or fairway where other vessels may be obscured by an intervening obstruction shall navigate with particular alertness and caution and shall sound the appropriate signal prescribed in Rule 34(e).

(g) Any vessel shall, if the circumstances of the case admit, avoid anchoring in a narrow channel.

RULE 10
Traffic Separation Schemes

(a) This Rule applies to traffic separation schemes adopted by the Organization.

(b) A vessel using a traffic separation scheme shall:

    (i) proceed in the appropriate traffic lane in the general direction of traffic flow for that lane;

    (ii) so far as practicable keep clear of a traffic separation line or separation zone;

    (iii) normally join or leave a traffic lane at the termination of the lane, but when joining or leaving from the side shall do so at as small an angle to the general direction of traffic flow as practicable.

(c) A vessel shall so far as practicable avoid crossing traffic lanes, but if obliged to do so shall cross as nearly as practicable at right angles to the general direction of traffic flow.

(d) Inshore traffic zones shall not normally be used by through traffic which can safely use the appropriate traffic lane within the adjacent traffic separation scheme.

(e) A vessel, other than a crossing vessel, shall not normally enter a separation zone or cross a separation line except:

(i) in cases of emergency to avoid immediate danger;
(ii) to engage in fishing within a separation zone.

(f) A vessel navigating in areas near the terminations of traffic separation schemes shall do so with particular caution.

(g) A vessel shall so far as practicable avoid anchoring in a traffic separation scheme or in areas near its terminations.

(h) A vessel not using a traffic separation scheme shall avoid it by as wide a margin as is practicable.

(i) A vessel engaged in fishing shall not impede the passage of any vessel following a traffic lane.

(j) A vessel of less than 20 metres in length or a sailing vessel shall not impede the safe passage of a power-driven vessel following a traffic lane.

SECTION II—CONDUCT OF VESSELS IN SIGHT OF ONE ANOTHER

RULE 11

Application

Rules in this Section apply to vessels in sight of one another.

RULE 12

Sailing Vessels

(a) When two sailing vessels are approaching one another, so as to involve risk of collision, one of them shall keep out of the way of the other as follows:

(i) when each has the wind on a different side, the vessel which has the wind on the port side shall keep out of the way of the other;
(ii) when both have the wind on the same side, the vessel which is to windward shall keep out of the way of the vessel which is to leeward;
(iii) if a vessel with the wind on the port side sees a vessel to windward and cannot determine with certainty whether the other vessel has the wind on the port or on the starboard side, she shall keep out of the way of the other.

308

(b) For the purposes of this Rule the windward side shall be deemed to be the side opposite to that on which the mainsail is carried or, in the case of a square-rigged vessel, the side opposite to that on which the largest fore-and-aft sail is carried.

Author's Note: A vessel with the wind dead aft has the wind on her *starboard* side for the purpose of this Rule when her mainsail or largest fore-and-aft sail lies to *port*, and vice versa.

RULE 13

Overtaking

(a) Notwithstanding anything contained in the Rules of this Section any vessel overtaking any other shall keep out of the way of the vessel being overtaken.

(b) A vessel shall be deemed to be overtaking when coming up with another vessel from a direction more than $22 \cdot 5$ degrees abaft her beam, that is, in such a position with reference to the vessel she is overtaking, that at night she would be able to see only the sternlight of that vessel but neither of her sidelights.

(c) When a vessel is in any doubt as to whether she is overtaking another, she shall assume that this is the case and act accordingly.

(d) Any subsequent alteration of the bearing between the two vessels shall not make the overtaking vessel a crossing vessel within the meaning of these Rules or relieve her of the duty of keeping clear of the overtaken vessel until she is finally past and clear.

RULE 14

Head-on Situation

(a) When two power-driven vessels are meeting on reciprocal or nearly reciprocal courses so as to involve risk of collision each shall alter her course to starboard so that each shall pass on the port side of the other.

(b) Such a situation shall be deemed to exist when a vessel sees the other ahead or nearly ahead and by night she could see the masthead lights of the other in a line or nearly in a line and/or both sidelights and by day she observes the corresponding aspect of the other vessel.

(c) When a vessel is in any doubt as to whether such a situation exists she shall assume that it does exist and act accordingly.

Author's Note: The phrase *'nearly ahead'* may confuse the reader. For this Rule to apply, both vessels must each see the sidelights of the other. If the lights are properly screened, this can only happen when each vessel is within the relative bearing arc of the other extending from two degrees on one bow to two degrees on the other.

THE SAFETY OF NAVIGATION

RULE 15

Crossing Situation

When two power-driven vessels are crossing so as to involve risk of collision, the vessel which has the other on her own starboard side shall keep out of the way and shall, if the circumstances of the case admit, avoid crossing ahead of the other vessel.

Author's Note: Vessels are occasionally encountered which do not obey this Rule, usually due to an improper lookout. Once the privileged vessel has ascertained that risk of collision exists, she should sound at least five short and rapid blasts by Rule 34, repeated if necessary and then take action under Rule 17. This is best achieved by altering to starboard *away from the other vessel and without reducing speed.* The degree of any impact will be proportional to the difference between the speeds of the two vessels, in other words the relative approach speed. A vessel which is crossing and overtaking at the same time comes under Rule 13.

RULE 16

Action by Give-way Vessel

Every vessel which is directed by these Rules to keep out of the way of another vessel shall, so far as possible, take early and substantial action to keep well clear.

RULE 17

Action by Stand-on Vessel

(a) (i) Where by any of these Rules one of two vessels is to keep out of the way the other shall keep her course and speed.

(ii) The latter vessel may however take action to avoid collision by her manoeuvre alone, as soon as it becomes apparent to her that the vessel required to keep out of the way is not taking appropriate action in compliance with these Rules.

(b) When, from any cause, the vessel required to keep her course and speed finds herself so close that collision cannot be avoided by the action of the give-way vessel alone, she shall take such action as will best aid to avoid collision.

(c) A power-driven vessel which takes action in a crossing situation in accordance with sub-paragraph (a)(ii) of this Rule to avoid collision with another power-driven vessel shall, if the circumstances of the case admit, not alter course to port for a vessel on her own port side.

(d) This Rule does not relieve the give-way vessel of her obligation to keep out of the way.

310

THE SAFETY OF NAVIGATION

RULE 18

Responsibilities between Vessels

Except where Rules 9, 10 and 13 otherwise require:

(a) A power-driven vessel underway shall keep out of the way of:

   (i) a vessel not under command;
   (ii) a vessel restricted in her ability to manoeuvre;
   (iii) a vessel engaged in fishing;
   (iv) a sailing vessel.

(b) A sailing vessel underway shall keep out of the way of:

   (i) a vessel not under command;
   (ii) a vessel restricted in her ability to manoeuvre;
   (iii) a vessel engaged in fishing.

(c) A vessel engaged in fishing when underway shall, so far as possible, keep out of the way of:

   (i) a vessel not under command;
   (ii) a vessel restricted in her ability to manoeuvre.

(d) (i) Any vessel other than a vessel not under command or a vessel restricted in her ability to manoeuvre shall, if the circumstances of the case admit, avoid impeding the safe passage of a vessel constrained by her draught, exhibiting the signals in Rule 28.

   (ii) A vessel constrained by her draught shall navigate with particular caution having full regard to her special condition.

(e) A seaplane on the water shall, in general, keep well clear of all vessels and avoid impeding their navigation. In circumstances, however, where risk of collision exists, she shall comply with the Rules of this Part.

Author's Note: A controversy has recently arisen over a situation where a Rule 27 vessel (hampered) is overtaking another vessel. It should be noted:

(a) In section (c) above, Rule 27 vessels are virtually being excused from giving way to fishing vessels, presumably in view of Rule 3 (f) and (g).
(b) Rule 3 (f) and (g) state that vessels which are hampered are *unable to get out of the way.*
(c) Rule 8(a) refers to the *observance of good seamanship.*
(d) Rule 2 refers to *departure from the Rules* in cases where dangers of navigation and collision, special circumstances and limitations of craft are involved. It also refers to precautions which may be required by these special circumstances.

If the reader refers to *Marsden's 'Law of Collision at Sea'* he will note:

(1) Literal observance of the Rules is not a defence where ordinary care might have avoided a collision.
(2) If it appears that another vessel is unable to comply with the Rules, the other vessel should watch her closely and *at once take steps to make a collision impossible.*

311

(3) The words *'Notwithstanding anything contained in the Rules'* were originally introduced into the 1880 Regulations so as to make it clear that Rule 13 superseded Rule 15.

(4) In the case of the Hawthornbank (1904) it was stated that a duty was cast upon a vessel, encountering another showing two red lights, *to keep out of her way.*

(5) The Rules do not apply, and a breach of them may be excused, when a vessel is disabled. *The Law does not require the impossible.*

I can only suggest, in addition to the above, that aircraft carriers working aircraft and travelling at 30 knots, or two vessels re-fuelling and travelling at up to 20 knots can hardly be expected to obey Rule 13. In view of (b), (3) and (4) above, I think that a vessel being overtaken by a Rule 27 vessel has a duty to keep clear. I fail to see why a hampered vessel is privileged when she encounters fishing craft and yet must avoid a perfectly manageable vessel which she happens to be overtaking. An argument against my reasoning has been that overtaking situations involve low relative approach speeds and hampered ships should therefore have time to take avoiding action. This may not be so nowadays with ships travelling at higher speeds.

SECTION III—CONDUCT OF VESSELS IN RESTRICTED VISIBILITY

RULE 19

Conduct of Vessels in Restricted Visibility

(a) This Rule applies to vessels not in sight of one another when navigating in or near an area of restricted visibility.

(b) Every vessel shall proceed at a safe speed adapted to the prevailing circumstances and conditions of restricted visibility. A power-driven vessel shall have her engines ready for immediate manoeuvre.

(c) Every vessel shall have due regard to the prevailing circumstances and conditions of restricted visibility when complying with the Rules of Section I of this Part.

(d) A vessel which detects by radar alone the presence of another vessel shall determine if a close-quarters situation is developing and/or risk of collision exists. If so, she shall take avoiding action in ample time, provided that when such action consists of an alteration of course, so far as possible the following shall be avoided:

(i) an alteration of course to port for a vessel forward of the beam, other than for a vessel being overtaken;

(ii) an alteration of course towards a vessel abeam or abaft the beam.

(e) Except where it has been determined that a risk of collision does not exist, every vessel which hears apparently forward of her beam the fog signal of another vessel, or which cannot avoid a close-quarters situation with another vessel forward of her beam, shall reduce her speed to the minimum at which she can be kept on her course. She shall if necessary take all her way off and in any event navigate with extreme caution until danger of collision is over.

PART C—LIGHTS AND SHAPES

RULE 20

Application

(a) Rules in this Part shall be complied with in all weathers.

(b) The Rules concerning lights shall be complied with from sunset to sunrise, and during such times no other lights shall be exhibited, except such lights as cannot be mistaken for the lights specified in these Rules or do not impair their visibility or distinctive character, or interfere with the keeping of a proper look-out.

(c) The lights prescribed by these Rules shall, if carried, also be exhibited from sunrise to sunset in restricted visibility and may be exhibited in all other circumstances when it is deemed necessary.

(d) The Rules concerning shapes shall be complied with by day.

(e) The lights and shapes specified in these Rules shall comply with the provisions of Annex I to these Regulations.

RULE 21

Definitions

(a) 'Masthead light' means a white light placed over the fore and aft centreline of the vessel showing an unbroken light over an arc of the horizon of 225 degrees and so fixed as to show the light from right ahead to 22·5 degrees abaft the beam on either side of the vessel.

(b) 'Sidelights' means a green light on the starboard side and a red light on the port side each showing an unbroken light over an arc of the horizon of 112·5 degrees and so fixed as to show the light from right ahead to 22·5 degrees abaft the beam on its respective side. In a vessel of less than 20 metres in length the sidelights may be combined in one lantern carried on the fore and aft centreline of the vessel.

(c) 'Sternlight' means a white light placed as nearly as practicable at the stern showing an unbroken light over an arc of the horizon of 135 degrees and so fixed as to show the light 67·5 degrees from right aft on each side of the vessel.

(d) 'Towing light' means a yellow light having the same characteristics as the 'sternlight' defined in paragraph (c) of this Rule.

(e) 'All-round light' means a light showing an unbroken light over an arc of the horizon of 360 degrees.

(f) 'Flashing light' means a light flashing at regular intervals at a frequency of 120 flashes or more per minute.

THE SAFETY OF NAVIGATION

Visibility of Lights

The lights prescribed in these Rules shall have an intensity as specified in Section 8 of Annex I to these Regulations so as to be visible at the following minimum ranges:

(a) In vessels of 50 metres or more in length:

— a masthead light, 6 miles;
— a sidelight, 3 miles;
— a sternlight, 3 miles;
— a towing light, 3 miles;
— a white, red, green or yellow all-round light, 3 miles.

(b) In vessels of 12 metres or more in length but less than 50 metres in length:

— a masthead light, 5 miles; except that where the length of the vessel is less than 20 metres, 3 miles;
— a sidelight, 2 miles;
— a sternlight, 2 miles;
— a towing light, 2 miles;
— a white, red, green or yellow all-round light, 2 miles.

(c) In vessels of less than 12 metres in length:

— a masthead light, 2 miles;
— a sidelight, 1 mile;
— a sternlight, 2 miles;
— a towing light, 2 miles;
— a white, red, green or yellow all-round light, 2 miles.

RULE 23

Power-driven Vessels underway

(a) A power-driven vessel underway shall exhibit:

(i) a masthead light forward;
(ii) a second masthead light abaft of and higher than the forward one; except that a vessel of less than 50 metres in length shall not be obliged to exhibit such light but may do so;
(iii) sidelights;
(iv) a sternlight.

(b) An air-cushion vessel when operating in the non-displacement mode shall, in addition to the lights prescribed in paragraph (a) of this Rule, exhibit an all-round flashing yellow light.

(c) A power-driven vessel of less than 7 metres in length and whose maximum speed does not exceed 7 knots may, in lieu of the lights prescribed in paragraph (a) of this Rule, exhibit an all-round white light. Such vessel shall, if practicable, also exhibit sidelights.

314

THE SAFETY OF NAVIGATION

Towing and Pushing

(a) A power-driven vessel when towing shall exhibit:

    (i) instead of the light prescribed in Rule 23(a)(i), two masthead lights forward in a vertical line. When the length of the tow, measuring from the stern of the towing vessel to the after end of the tow exceeds 200 metres, three such lights in a vertical line;

    (ii) sidelights;

    (iii) a sternlight;

    (iv) a towing light in a vertical line above the sternlight;

    (v) when the length of the tow exceeds 200 metres, a diamond shape where it can best be seen.

(*b*) When a pushing vessel and a vessel being pushed ahead are rigidly connected in a composite unit they shall be regarded as a power-driven vessel and exhibit the lights prescribed in Rule 23.

(c) A power-driven vessel when pushing ahead or towing alongside, except in the case of a composite unit, shall exhibit:

    (i) instead of the light prescribed in Rule 23(a)(i), two masthead lights forward in a vertical line;

    (ii) sidelights;

    (iii) a sternlight.

(d) A power-driven vessel to which paragraphs (a) and (c) of this Rule apply shall also comply with Rule 23(a)(ii)

(e) A vessel or object being towed shall exhibit:

    (i) sidelights;

    (ii) a sternlight;

    (iii) when the length of the tow exceeds 200 metres, a diamond shape where it can best be seen.

(f) Provided that any number of vessels being towed or pushed in a group shall be lighted as one vessel,

    (i) a vessel being pushed ahead, not being part of a composite unit, shall exhibit at the forward end, sidelights;

    (ii) a vessel being towed alongside shall exhibit a sternlight and at the forward end, sidelights.

(g) Where from any sufficient cause it is impracticable for a vessel or object being towed to exhibit the lights prescribed in paragraph (e) of this Rule, all possible measures shall be taken to light the vessel or object towed or at least to indicate the presence of the unlighted vessel or object.

RULE 25

Sailing Vessels underway and Vessels under Oars

(a) A sailing vessel underway shall exhibit:

    (i) sidelights;

    (ii) a sternlight.

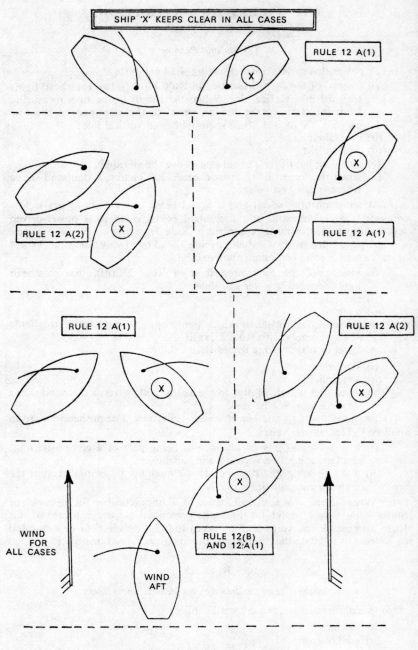

FIGURE 14.8 RULE 12

(b) In a sailing vessel of less than 12 metres in length the lights prescribed in paragraph (a) of this Rule may be combined in one lantern carried at or near the top of the mast where it can best be seen.

(c) A sailing vessel underway may, in addition to the lights prescribed in paragraph (a) of this Rule, exhibit at or near the top of the mast, where they can best be seen, two all-round lights in a vertical line, the upper being red and the lower green, but these lights shall not be exhibited in conjunction with the combined lantern permitted by paragraph (b) of this Rule.

(d) (i) A sailing vessel of less than 7 metres in length shall, if practicable, exhibit the lights prescribed in paragraph (a) or (b) of this Rule, but if she does not, she shall have ready at hand an electric torch or lighted lantern showing a white light which shall be exhibited in sufficient time to prevent collision.

(ii) A vessel under oars may exhibit the lights prescribed in this Rule for sailing vessels, but if she does not, she shall have ready at hand an electric torch or lighted lantern showing a white light which shall be exhibited in sufficient time to prevent collision.

(e) A vessel proceeding under sail when also being propelled by machinery shall exhibit forward where it can best be seen a conical shape, apex downwards.

RULE 26

Fishing Vessels

(a) A vessel engaged in fishing, whether underway or at anchor, shall exhibit only the lights and shapes prescribed in this Rule.

(b) A vessel when engaged in trawling, by which is meant the dragging through the water of a dredge net or other apparatus used as a fishing appliance, shall exhibit:

(i) two all-round lights in a vertical line, the upper being green and the lower white, or a shape consisting of two cones with their apexes together in a vertical line one above the other; a vessel of less than 20 metres in length may instead of this shape exhibit a basket;

(ii) a masthead light abaft of and higher than the all-round green light; a vessel of less than 50 metres in length shall not be obliged to exhibit such a light but may do so;

(iii) when making way through the water, in addition to the lights prescribed in this paragraph, sidelights and a sternlight.

(c) A vessel engaged in fishing, other than trawling, shall exhibit:

(i) two all-round lights in a vertical line, the upper being red and the lower white, or a shape consisting of two cones with apexes together in a vertical line one above the other; a vessel of less than 20 metres in length may instead of this shape exhibit a basket;

(ii) when there is outlying gear extending more than 150 metres horizontally from the vessel, an all-round white light or a cone apex upwards in the direction of the gear;

317

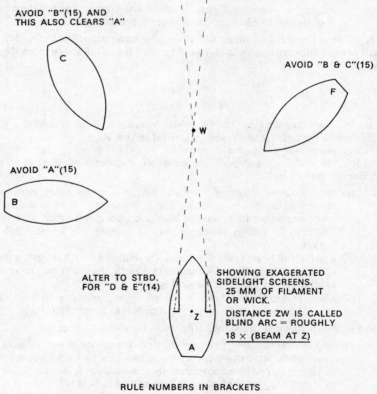

ALTER TO STBD. FOR "A"
(14) AVOID "C & F"(13)
AVOID "B" (15)

AVOID "B"(15) AND
THIS ALSO CLEARS "A"

AVOID "B & C"(15)

AVOID "A"(15)

ALTER TO STBD.
FOR "D & E"(14)

SHOWING EXAGGERATED
SIDELIGHT SCREENS.
25 MM OF FILAMENT
OR WICK.
DISTANCE ZW IS CALLED
BLIND ARC = ROUGHLY
$18 \times$ (BEAM AT Z)

RULE NUMBERS IN BRACKETS

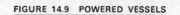

FIGURE 14.9   POWERED VESSELS

(iii) when making way through the water. in addition to the lights prescribed in this paragraph, sidelights and a sternlight.

(d) A vessel engaged in fishing in close proximity to other vessels may exhibit the additional signals described in Annex II to these Regulations.

(e) A vessel when not engaged in fishing shall not exhibit the lights or shapes prescribed in this Rule, but only those prescribed for a vessel of her length.

Author's Note: At night, vessels fishing at anchor will be indistinguishable from vessels fishing under way, but stopped. As in Rule 27, these craft show their sidelights *only when moving through the water*. Regarding section (c)(ii), the reader should note the similar inverted signal in Rule 25(e). For vessels with their gear fast to a rock etc., see the second Annex to the Rules.

RULE 27

*Vessels not under Command or Restricted in
their Ability to Manoeuvre*

(a) A vessel not under command shall exhibit:
(i) two all-round red lights in a vertical line where they can best be seen;
(ii) two balls or similar shapes in a vertical line where they can best be seen;
(iii) when making way through the water, in addition to the lights prescribed in this paragraph, sidelights and a sternlight.

(b) A vessel restricted in her ability to manoeuvre, except a vessel engaged in minesweeping operations, shall exhibit:
(i) three all-round lights in a vertical line where they can best be seen. The highest and lowest of these lights shall be red and the middle light shall be white;
(ii) three shapes in a vertical line where they can best be seen. The highest and lowest of these shapes shall be balls and the middle one a diamond;
(iii) when making way through the water, masthead lights, sidelights and a sternlight, in addition to the lights prescribed in sub-paragraph (i);
(iv) when at anchor, in addition to the lights or shapes prescribed in sub-paragraphs (i) and (ii), the light, lights or shape prescribed in Rule 30.

(c) A vessel engaged in a towing operation such as renders her unable to deviate from her course shall, in addition to the lights or shapes prescribed in sub-paragraphs (b)(i) and (ii) of this Rule, exhibit the lights or shape prescribed in Rule 24(a).

(d) A vessel engaged in dredging or underwater operations, when restricted in her ability to manoeuvre, shall exhibit the lights and shapes prescribed in paragraph (b) of this Rule and shall in addition, when an obstruction exists, exhibit:

   (i) two all-round red lights or two balls in a vertical line to indicate the side on which the obstruction exists;

  (ii) two all-round green lights or two diamonds in a vertical line to indicate the side on which another vessel may pass;

 (iii) when making way through the water, in addition to the lights prescribed in this paragraph, masthead lights, sidelights and a sternlight;

 (iv) a vessel to which this paragraph applies when at anchor shall exhibit the lights or shapes prescribed in sub-paragraphs (i) and (ii) instead of the lights or shape prescribed in Rule 30.

(e) Whenever the size of a vessel engaged in diving operations makes it impracticable to exhibit the shapes prescribed in paragraph (d) of this Rule, a rigid replica of the International Code flag "A" not less than 1 metre in height shall be exhibited. Measures shall be taken to ensure all-round visibility.

(f) A vessel engaged in minesweeping operations shall, in addition to the lights prescribed for a power-driven vessel in Rule 23, exhibit three all-round green lights or three balls. One of these lights or shapes shall be exhibited at or near the foremast head and one at each end of the fore yard. These lights or shapes indicate that it is dangerous for another vessel to approach closer than 1,000 metres astern or 500 metres on either side of the minesweeper.

(g) Vessels of less than 7 metres in length shall not be required to exhibit the lights prescribed in this Rule.

(h) The signals prescribed in this Rule are not signals of vessels in distress and requiring assistance. Such signals are contained in Annex IV to these Regulations.

Author's Note: This Rule covers a rare instance when ships switch off sidelights and sternlights though still under way, as in Rule 26 also. *Any other vessel showing sidelights and sternlights may be stopped or moving.*

Rule 28

Vessels constrained by their Draught

A vessel constrained by her draught may, in addition to the lights prescribed for power-driven vessels in Rule 23, exhibit where they can best be seen three all-round red lights in a vertical line, or a cylinder.

Rule 29

Pilot Vessels

(a) A vessel engaged on pilotage duty shall exhibit:

   (i) at or near the masthead, two all-round lights in a vertical line, the upper being white and the lower red;

  (ii) when underway, in addition, sidelights and a sternlight;

(iii) when at anchor, in addition to the lights prescribed in sub-paragraph (i), the anchor light, lights or shape.

(b) A pilot vessel when not engaged on pilotage duty shall exhibit the lights or shapes prescribed for a similar vessel of her length.

RULE 30

Anchored Vessels and Vessels aground

(a) A vessel at anchor shall exhibit where it can best be seen:

(i) in the fore part, an all-round white light or one ball;
(ii) at or near the stern and at a lower level than the light prescribed in sub-paragraph (i), an all-round white light.

(b) A vessel of less than 50 metres in length may exhibit an all-round white light where it can best be seen instead of the lights prescribed in paragraph (a) of this Rule.

(c) A vessel at anchor may, and a vessel of 100 metres and more in length shall, also use the available working or equivalent lights to illuminate her decks.

(d) A vessel aground shall exhibit the lights prescribed in paragraph (a) or (b) of this Rule and in addition, where they can best be seen:

(i) two all-round red lights in a vertical line;
(ii) three balls in a vertical line.

(e) A vessel of less than 7 metres in length, when at anchor or aground, not in or near a narrow channel, fairway or anchorage, or where other vessels normally navigate, shall not be required to exhibit the lights or shapes prescribed in paragraphs (a), (b) or (d) of this Rule.

RULE 31

Seaplanes

Where it is impracticable for a seaplane to exhibit lights and shapes of the characteristics or in the positions prescribed in the Rules of this Part she shall exhibit lights and shapes as closely similar in characteristics and position as is possible.

PART D—SOUND AND LIGHT SIGNALS

RULE 32

Definitions

(a) The word 'whistle' means any sound signalling appliance capable of producing the prescribed blasts and which complies with the specifications in Annex III to these Regulations.

(b) The term 'short blast' means a blast of about one second's duration.

THE SAFETY OF NAVIGATION

(c) The term 'prolonged blast' means a blast of from four to six seconds' duration.

RULE 33

Equipment for Sound Signals

(a) A vessel of 12 metres or more in length shall be provided with a whistle and a bell and a vessel of 100 metres or more in length shall, in addition, be provided with a gong, the tone and sound of which cannot be confused with that of the bell. The whistle, bell and gong shall comply with the specifications in Annex III to these Regulations. The bell or gong or both may be replaced by other equipment having the same respective sound characteristics, provided that manual sounding of the required signals shall always be possible.

(b) A vessel of less than 12 metres in length shall not be obliged to carry the sound signalling appliances prescribed in paragraph (a) of this Rule but if she does not, she shall be provided with some other means of making an efficient sound signal.

RULE 34

Manoeuvring and Warning Signals

(a) When vessels are in sight of one another, a power-driven vessel under way, when manoeuvring as authorized or required by these Rules, shall indicate that manoeuvre by the following signals on her whistle:
  —one short blast to mean 'I am altering my course to starboard';
  —two short blasts to mean 'I am altering my course to port';
  —three short blasts to mean 'I am operating astern propulsion'.

(b) Any vessel may supplement the whistle signals prescribed in paragraph (a) of this Rule by light signals, repeated as appropriate, whilst the manoeuvre is being carried out:
  (i) these light signals shall have the following significance:
    —one flash to mean 'I am altering my course to starboard';
    —two flashes to mean 'I am altering my course to port';
    —three flashes to mean 'I am operating astern propulsion';
  (ii) the duration of each flash shall be about one second, the interval between flashes shall be about one second, and the interval between successive signals shall be not less than ten seconds;
  (iii) the light used for this signal shall, if fitted, be an all-round white light, visible at a minimum range of 5 miles, and shall comply with the provisions of Annex I.

(c) When in sight of one another in a narrow channel or fairway:
  (i) a vessel intending to overtake another shall in compliance with Rule 9(e)(i) indicate her intention by the following signals on her whistle:
    —two prolonged blasts followed by one short blast to mean 'I intend to overtake you on your starboard side';

322

—two prolonged blasts followed by two short blasts to mean 'I intend to overtake you on your port side';

(ii) the vessel about to be overtaken when acting in accordance with Rule 9(e)(i) shall indicate her agreement by the following signal on her whistle:

—one prolonged, one short, one prolonged and one short blast, in that order.

(d) When vessels in sight of one another are approaching each other and from any cause either vessel fails to understand the intentions or actions of the other, or is in doubt whether sufficient action is being taken by the other to avoid collision, the vessel in doubt shall immediately indicate such doubt by giving at least five short and rapid blasts on the whistle. Such signal may be supplemented by a light signal of at least five short and rapid flashes.

(e) A vessel nearing a bend or an area of a channel or fairway where other vessels may be obscured by an intervening obstruction shall sound one prolonged blast. Such signal shall be answered with a prolonged blast by any approaching vessel that may be within hearing around the bend or behind the intervening obstruction.

(f) If whistles are fitted on a vessel at a distance apart of more than 100 metres, one whistle only shall be used for giving manoeuvring and warning signals.

RULE 35

Sound Signals in restricted Visibility

In or near an area of restricted visibility, whether by day or night, the signals prescribed in this Rule shall be used as follows:

(a) A power-driven vessel making way through the water shall sound at intervals of not more than 2 minutes one prolonged blast.

(b) A power-driven vessel underway but stopped and making no way through the water shall sound at intervals of not more than 2 minutes two prolonged blasts in succession with an interval of about 2 seconds between them.

(c) A vessel not under command, a vessel restricted in her ability to manoeuvre, a vessel constrained by her draught, a sailing vessel, a vessel engaged in fishing and a vessel engaged in towing or pushing another vessel shall, instead of the signals prescribed in paragraphs (a) or (b) of this Rule, sound at intervals of not more than 2 minutes three blasts in succession, namely one prolonged followed by two short blasts.

(d) A vessel towed or if more than one vessel is towed the last vessel of the tow, if manned, shall at intervals of not more than 2 minutes sound four blasts in succession, namely one prolonged followed by three short blasts. When practicable, this signal shall be made immediately after the signal made by the towing vessel.

(e) When a pushing vessel and a vessel being pushed ahead are rigidly connected in a composite unit they shall be regarded as a power-driven vessel and shall give the signals prescribed in paragraphs (a) or (b) of this Rule.

(f) A vessel at anchor shall at intervals of not more than one minute ring the bell rapidly for about 5 seconds. In a vessel of 100 metres or more in length the bell shall be sounded in the forepart of the vessel and immediately after the ringing of the bell the gong shall be sounded rapidly for about 5 seconds in the after part of the vessel. A vessel at anchor may in addition sound three blasts in succession, namely one short, one prolonged and one short blast, to give warning of her position and of the possibility of collision to an approaching vessel.

(g) A vessel aground shall give the bell signal and if required the gong signal prescribed in paragraph (f) of this Rule and shall, in addition, give three separate and distinct strokes on the bell immediately before and after the rapid ringing of the bell. A vessel aground may in addition sound an appropriate whistle signal.

(h) A vessel of less than 12 metres in length shall not be obliged to give the above-mentioned signals but, if she does not, shall make some other efficient sound signal at intervals of not more than 2 minutes.

(i) A pilot vessel when engaged on pilotage duty may in addition to the signals prescribed in paragraphs (a), (b) or (f) of this Rule sound an identity signal consisting of four short blasts.

Author's Note: Fishing vessels have no special anchor signal in fog, but they can use the short-long-short signal mentioned in section (f).

RULE 36

Signals to attract Attention

If necessary to attract the attention of another vessel any vessel may make light or sound signals that cannot be mistaken for any signal authorized elsewhere in these Rules, or may direct the beam of her searchlight in the direction of the danger, in such a way as not to embarrass any vessel.

RULE 37

Distress Signals

When a vessel is in distress and requires assistance she shall use or exhibit the signals prescribed in Annex IV to these Regulations.

PART E—EXEMPTIONS

RULE 38

Exemptions

Any vessel (of class of vessels) provided that she complies with the requirements of the International Regulations for Preventing Collisions at Sea, 1960, the keel of which is laid or which is at a corresponding stage of construction before the entry into force of these Regulations may be exempted from compliance therewith as follows:

(a) The installation of lights with ranges prescribed in Rule 22, until four years after the date of entry into force of these Regulations.

(b) The installation of lights with colour specifications as prescribed in Section 7 of Annex I to these Regulations, until four years after the date of entry into force of these Regulations.

(c) The repositioning of lights as a result of conversion from Imperial to metric units and rounding off measurement figures, permanent exemption.

(d) (i) The repositioning of masthead lights on vessels of less than 150 metres in length, resulting from the prescriptions of Section 3(a) of Annex I, permanent exemption.

(ii) The repositioning of masthead lights on vessels of 150 metres or more in length, resulting from the prescriptions of Section 3(a) of Annex I to these Regulations, until nine years after the date of entry into force of these Regulations.

(e) The repositioning of masthead lights resulting from the prescriptions of Section 2(b) of Annex I, until nine years after the date of entry into force of these Regulations.

(f) The repositioning of sidelights resulting from the prescriptions of Section 3(b) of Annex I, until nine years after the date of entry into force of these Regulations.

(g) The requirements for sound signal appliances prescribed in Annex III, until nine years after the date of entry into force of these Regulations.

The Annexes to the Rules are reproduced later in this chapter.

Court Verdicts

Some recent Court rulings have stated that:

(1) Vessels should not alter course in fog, when equipped with radar, until the course of the other vessel has been ascertained with accuracy, *preferably by plotting*.

(2) Any alteration so made should be substantial, so that it is instantly apparent to other vessels equipped with, and using, radar.

(3) Radar is an additional safeguard, and failure to use it might constitute negligence.

(4) A Master who relies on radar alone does so at his own risk.

(5) If a vessel carries proper functioning radar there is an affirmative duty to use it, in or approaching reduced-visibility areas.

(6) In certain circumstances of collision in fog the vessel which did not use her radar had to establish that this did not contribute to the collision.

(7) Undue reliance is often placed on the non-sighting of radar targets.

(8) The poor *interpretation* of the information displayed on the radar screen is deplorably frequent.

(9) Those who do not make use of their radar must ensure that a very effective lookout is kept.

Note: The student should study (9) and (4) together. (3) and (5) are a warning to the mariner that, far from wondering whether to switch the

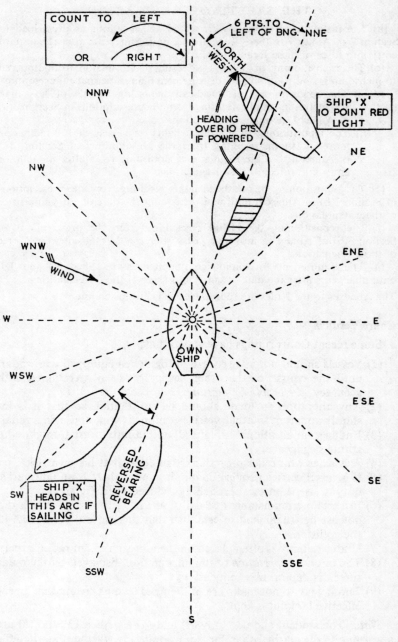

COUNT TO LEFT
OR RIGHT

6 PTS. TO
LEFT OF BNG. NNE

NORTH
WEST

SHIP 'X'
IO POINT RED
LIGHT

HEADING
OVER IO PTS.
IF POWERED

NNW

NW

NE

WNW
WIND

ENE

W

E

WSW

OWN
SHIP

ESE

SW

SHIP 'X'
HEADS IN
THIS ARC IF
SAILING

REVERSED BEARING

SE

SSW

SSE

S

FIGURE 14.10

radar on, he should always establish beyond reasonable doubt whether it is safe to switch it *off*.

THE DETERMINATION OF A VESSEL'S HEADING

Provided a sidelight is visible its arc of visibility is known, and it is a simple matter to estimate the arc of the compass through which that vessel may be navigating.

The principle involved is to determine, by means of the observed bearing of the light, the headings of the other vessel on which the sidelight is just about to 'shut out', i.e. the heading on which the other sidelight is just about to become discernible and the heading on which the sidelight eclipses in favour of the sternlight.

In Fig. 14.10 one's own ship is shown at the centre of a compass card. The mariner must always project himself to the bridge of this ship so that he appreciates what is meant by 'counting to the left (or right)', as shown in the top left-hand corner of the figure. This is particularly important when a candidate is being examined by means of a model ship, the stem of which is facing him; if he counts to his right it is the reverse of what he should do if he were on the bridge of that ship.

In the figure the red sidelight of ship 'X' is shown bearing NNE. If at that instant the ship 'X' is heading directly towards own ship, then it is heading on the reverse of the bearing, i.e. SSW. On this heading the red light is about to shut out in favour of the green light. The red light is visible over an arc of 10 points, so that the ship 'X' could be rotated through 10 points to the right of the reversed bearing before the red light shuts out in favour of the stern light, on a heading of NW. It should be noticed that this heading (NW) is also 6 points to the left of the bearing of the light. Two rules-of-thumb are thus possible:

When a ten-point red light is sighted reverse the bearing (1), and:

(a) count 10 points to the right of this reversed bearing to obtain another direction (2); or

(b) reverse the bearing (1) and count 6 points to the left of the original bearing to obtain another direction (2).

When a ten-point green light is sighted use rule (a) above, but count to the left; or use rule (b) above and count to the right.

In each case, (1) and (2) give the extreme headings. It should be noted that the vessel 'X' is sailing *nearly* on the reversed bearing, for if she were sailing directly on it both sidelights would be visible.

Some students prefer Rule (b), since they easily remember counting to the left for a left-hand (port) light, or to the right for a right-hand (starboard) light.

The reader should now attempt the following examples for power-driven vessels using 10-point sidelights. The answers are given in brackets:

(1) Red light bearing NW. (Between nearly SE and WSW.)
(2) Green light bearing E by S. (Between nearly W by N and S by E.)
(3) Red light bearing 6 points on the port bow; own ship heading north. (Between ESE nearly, and SW.)
(4) Green light abeam to starboard; own ship heading west. (Between nearly south and ENE.)
(5) Red light bearing ENE. (Between nearly WSW and N.)

Sailing Vessels

For all practical purposes, sailing ships are assumed to be able to sail
40 ft no closer than 6 points to the wind. Since (if of 12·19 m or over) their sidelights are visible over arcs of 10 points, the estimation of heading is initially identical to that for power-driven vessels, with the addition that the arc of heading so found (by the rules given above) must be modified so that the sailing ship is 6 or more points off the wind.

In Fig. 14.10 again, if ship 'X' is a sailing ship, then the estimated arc of SSW to NW must be modified because of the WNW wind which is blowing. It will be seen, in the bottom left-hand corner of the drawing, that SW is the closest that the ship can sail to the wind, so the vessel can only be heading between SW and SSW.

This, of course, assumes that the vessel is not in stays or in irons, i.e. she is not close to the wind's eye changing from one tack to the other. Naturally, in practice, the mariner must not dismiss this possibility, but for purposes of examinations it is safe for the candidate to assume that the ship is actually sailing.

In examination work the candidate may be required to give not only the headings of the sailing ship but also how she is sailing (i.e. close-hauled or running free, etc.).

The candidate should study the text above and then attempt the following examples:

(1) Wind north (i.e. blowing from the north); red light 6 points on port bow; own ship heading N.

    (Heading between nearly ESE and SW; running free to starboard or port, or wind dead aft.)

    Note: In this case the wind does not affect the first estimated headings.

(2) Own ship heading N; green light dead ahead; wind on the starboard beam.

(Heading between nearly S and SSE; sailing on the port tack.)

(3) Own ship heading W; wind 1 point before the port beam; red light 1 point before the starboard beam.

(Heading between West by North and West by South; sailing on the port tack.)

(4) Wind dead astern; green light dead ahead; own ship heading East.

(Heading between SSW and SSE; sailing on the starboard tack, or running free with the wind on the starboard quarter.) For fog signal, see Rule 35(c).

(5) Own ship heading N; wind 4 points on the port bow; red light 1 point before the starboard beam.

(When the headings are estimated by means of the rules it will be found that the extremities of the arc, N by E and W by S, are only 5 points away from the wind. The ship is therefore in stays and her fog signal will be the signal prescribed in Rule 35(c). Although such a vessel is not mentioned in Rule 3(g) she always gives the fog signal for a vessel with restricted manoeuvring ability.

(6) Own ship heading South; wind on the starboard beam; red light 6 points abaft the port beam.

(This ship can only be heading SSW; she is close-hauled on the starboard tack.)

(7) Own ship heading NE. Green light dead ahead. Wind south. How is the vessel sailing and what action should be taken?

(Heading ESE only. An alteration to port is advisable under Rule 18(a)(iv).) This vessel is crossing to starboard but her action should be watched closely in case she suddenly changes tack.

(8) Own ship heading South by West. Red light one point on the starboard bow. How is the vessel sailing if the wind is NNE?

(Heading between SE and E, closehauled or reaching to port, or wind on the port quarter.)

(9) Wind E $\frac{1}{2}$ S. Red light is bearing S $\frac{1}{2}$ E. How is she sailing?

(Between nearly N $\frac{1}{2}$ W and NE by N $\frac{1}{2}$ N. On the starboard tack or wind on the starboard quarter.)

(10) A stern light is observed bearing N. How is the vessel heading?

(Between WNW and ENE; in theory, on these headings the port and starboard sidelights respectively should be visible.)

329

KNOWLEDGE OF THE COMPASS CARD

By now the reader will undoubtedly have become aware of his ability to 'box' the compass card; he should be able to do it quite automatically.

In addition to the points of the compass card shown in Fig. 14.10, another sixteen exist. Each of these is placed midway between the points illustrated, and its name commences with the name of the nearest cardinal (N, E, S, W) or inter-cardinal point (NE, SE, SW, and NW). The latter part of its name, prefixed with the word 'by', is named after the other nearest cardinal point.

For example, between North and North-north-east, there is a point which will be named after the nearest cardinal point, i.e. NORTH. The second half of its name is that of the other nearest cardinal point, which in this case is EAST.

So, boxing these points from North to East we have: North by East; North-east by North; North-east by East, and East by North.

All the thirty-two points of the card are shown in Fig. 14.10 (*a*). In the same figure is shown the fact that each point of the compass is divided into quarters, known as quarter-points. A point is $11\frac{1}{4}$ degrees.

If we box the compass in quarter-points from South to East, we say:

S . . . S $\frac{1}{4}$ E . . . S $\frac{1}{2}$ E . . . S $\frac{3}{4}$ E . . . S by E . . . S by E $\frac{1}{4}$ E . . . S by E $\frac{1}{2}$ E . . . S by E $\frac{3}{4}$ E . . . SSE . . . SE by S $\frac{3}{4}$ S . . . SE by S $\frac{1}{2}$ S . . . SE by S $\frac{1}{4}$ S . . . SE by S . . . SE $\frac{3}{4}$ S . . . SE $\frac{1}{2}$ S . . . SE $\frac{1}{4}$ S . . . SE . . . SE $\frac{1}{4}$ E . . . SE $\frac{1}{2}$ E . . . SE $\frac{3}{4}$ E . . . SE by E . . . SE by E $\frac{1}{4}$ E . . . SE by E $\frac{1}{2}$ E . . . SE by E $\frac{3}{4}$ E . . . ESE . . . E by S $\frac{3}{4}$ S . . . E by S $\frac{1}{2}$ S . . . E by S $\frac{1}{4}$ S . . . E by S . . . E $\frac{3}{4}$ S . . . E $\frac{1}{2}$ S . . . E $\frac{1}{4}$ S . . . E.

The second, and most popular method of compass reference is by means of the three-figure notation in which the card is divided into 360 degrees, numbered clockwise from North, which is represented by 000°. The points of the compass are shown expressed in this notation in Fig. 14.10 (*a*).

The quadrantal system is generally dying out in favour of three-figure notation. In this system the card is divided into four quadrants, each of 90 degrees, and a course or bearing is expressed as North (or South), so many degrees East (or West), e.g. NORTHEAST is referred to as N 45° E.

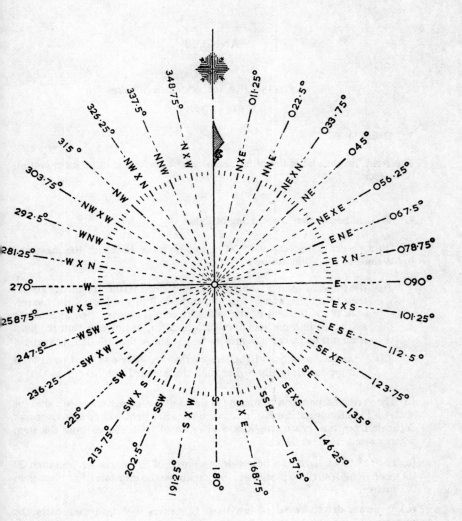

FIGURE 14.10 (A)

COMPASS POINTS IN THREE-FIGURE NOTATION

331

ANNEX I

1. Definition

The term 'height above the hull' means height above the uppermost continuous deck.

2. Vertical positioning and spacing of lights

(a) On a power-driven vessel of 20 metres or more in length the masthead lights shall be placed as follows:

    (i)   the forward masthead light, or if only one masthead light is carried, then that light, at a height above the hull of not less than 6 metres, and, if the breadth of the vessel exceeds 6 metres, then at a height above the hull not less than such breadth, so however that the light need not be placed at a greater height above the hull than 12 metres;

    (ii) when two masthead lights are carried the after one shall be at least 4·5 metres vertically higher than the forward one.

(b) The vertical separation of masthead lights of power-driven vessels shall be such that in all normal conditions of trim the after light will be seen over and separate from the forward light at a distance of 1000 metres from the stem when viewed from sea level.

(c) The masthead light of a power-driven vessel of 12 metres but less than 20 metres in length shall be placed at a height above the gunwale of not less than 2.5 metres.

(d) A power-driven vessel of less than 12 metres in length may carry the uppermost light at a height of less than 2·5 metres above the gunwale. When however a masthead light is carried in addition to sidelights and a sternlight, then such masthead light shall be carried at least 1 metre higher than the sidelights.

(e) One of the two or three masthead lights prescribed for a power-driven vessel when engaged in towing or pushing another vessel shall be placed in the same position as the forward masthead light of a power-driven vessel.

(f) In all circumstances the masthead light or lights shall be so placed as to be above and clear of all other lights and obstructions.

(g) The sidelights of a power-driven vessel shall be placed at a height above the hull not greater than three quarters of that of the forward masthead light. They shall not be so low as to be interfered with by deck lights.

(h) The sidelights, if in a combined lantern and carried on a power-driven vessel of less than 20 metres in length, shall be placed not less than 1 metre below the masthead light.

(i) When the Rules prescribe two or three lights to be carried in a vertical line, they shall be spaced as follows:

    (i) on a vessel of 20 metres in length or more such lights shall be spaced not less than 2 metres apart, and the lowest of these lights shall, except where a towing light is required, not be less than 4 metres above the hull;

    (ii) on a vessel of less than 20 metres in length such lights shall be spaced not less than 1 metre apart and the lowest of these lights shall, except where a towing light is required, not be less than 2 metres above the gunwale;

    (iii) when three lights are carried they shall be equally spaced.

(j) The lower of the two all-round lights prescribed for a fishing vessel when engaged in fishing shall be at a height above the sidelights not less than twice the distance between the two vertical lights.

(k) The forward anchor light, when two are carried, shall not be less than 4·5 metres above the after one. On a vessel of 50 metres or more in length this forward anchor light shall not be less than 6 metres above the hull.

3. Horizontal positioning and spacing of lights

(a) When two masthead lights are prescribed for a power-driven vessel, the horizontal distance between them shall not be less than one half of the length of the vessel but need not be more than 100 metres. The forward light shall be placed not more than one quarter of the length of the vessel from the stem.

(b) On a vessel of 20 metres or more in length the sidelights shall not be placed in front of the forward masthead lights. They shall be placed at or near the side of the vessel.

4.   Details of location of direction-indicating lights for fishing vessels, dredgers and vessels engaged in underwater operations

(a) The light indicating the direction of the outlying gear from a vessel engaged in fishing as prescribed in Rule 26(c)(ii) shall be placed at a horizontal distance of not less than 2 metres and not more than 6 metres away from the two all-round red and white lights. This light shall be placed not higher than the all-round white light prescribed in Rule 26(c)(i) and not lower than the sidelights.

(b) The lights and shapes on a vessel engaged in dredging or under-water operations to indicate the obstructed side and/or the side on which it is safe to pass, as prescribed in Rule 27(d)(i) and (ii), shall be placed at the maximum practical horizontal distance, but in no case less than 2 metres, from the lights or shapes prescribed in Rule 27(b)(i) and (ii). In no case shall the upper of these lights or shapes be at a greater height than the lower of the three lights or shapes prescribed in Rule 27(b)(i) and (ii).

5.   Screens for sidelights

The sidelights shall be fitted with inboard screens painted matt black, and meeting the requirements of Section 9 of this Annex. With a combined lantern, using a single vertical filament and a very narrow division between the green and red sections, external screens need not be fitted.

6.   Shapes

(a) Shapes shall be black and of the following sizes:

  (i) a ball shall have a diameter of not less than 0·6 metre;

  (ii) a cone shall have a base diameter of not less than 0·6 metre and a height equal to its diameter;

  (iii) a cylinder shall have a diameter of at least 0·6 metre and a height of twice its diameter;

  (iv) a diamond shape shall consist of two cones as defined in (ii) above having a common base.

(b) The vertical distance between shapes shall be at least 1·5 metres.

334

(c) In a vessel of less than 20 metres in length shapes of lesser dimensions but commensurate with the size of the vessel may be used and the distance apart may be correspondingly reduced.

7. Colour specification of lights

The chromaticity of all navigation lights shall conform to the following standards, which lie within the boundaries of the area of the diagram specified for each colour by the International Commission on Illumination (CIE).

The boundaries of the area for each colour are given by indicating the corner co-ordinates, which are as follows:

(i) *White*

x	0.525	0.525	0.452	0.310	0.310	0.443
y	0.382	0.440	0.440	0.348	0.283	0.382

(ii) *Green*

x	0.028	0.009	0.300	0.203
y	0.385	0.723	0.511	0.356

(iii) *Red*

x	0.680	0.660	0.735	0.721
y	0.320	0.320	0.265	0.259

(iv) *Yellow*

x	0.612	0.618	0.575	0.575
y	0.382	0.382	0.425	0.406

8. Intensity of lights

(a) The minimum luminous intensity of lights shall be calculated by using the formula:

$$I = 3 \cdot 43 \times 10^6 \times T \times D^2 \times K^{-D}$$

where I is luminous intensity in candelas under service conditions,

T is threshold factor 2×10^{-7} lux,

D is range of visibility (luminous range) of the light in nautical miles,

K is atmospheric transmissivity.

For prescribed lights the value of K shall be 0·8, corresponding to a meteorological visibility of approximately 13 nautical miles.

(b) A selection of figures derived from the formula is given in the following table:

Range of visibility (luminous range) of light in nautical miles	Luminous intensity of light in candelas for K = 0·8
D	I
1	0·9
2	4·3
3	12
4	27
5	52
6	94

NOTE: The maximum luminous intensity of navigation lights should be limited to avoid undue glare.

9. Horizontal sectors

(a) (i) In the forward direction, sidelights as fitted on the vessel must show the minimum required intensities. The intensities must decrease to reach practical cut-off between 1 degree and 3 degrees outside the prescribed sectors.

(ii) For sternlights and masthead lights and at 22·5 degrees abaft the beam for sidelights, the minimum required intensities shall be maintained over the arc of the horizon up to 5 degrees within the limits

336

of the sectors prescribed in Rule 21. From 5 degrees within the prescribed sectors the intensity may decrease by 50 per cent up to the prescribed limits; it shall decrease steadily to reach practical cut-off at not more than 5 degrees outside the prescribed limits.

(b) All-round lights shall be so located as not to be obscured by masts, topmasts or structures within angular sectors of more than 6 degrees, except anchor lights, which need not be placed at an impracticable height above the hull.

10. Vertical sectors

(a) The vertical sectors of electric lights, with the exception of lights on sailing vessels shall ensure that:
  (i) at least the required minimum intensity is maintained at all angles from 5 degrees above to 5 degrees below the horizontal;
  (ii) at least 60 per cent of the required minimum intensity is maintained from $7 \cdot 5$ degrees above to $7 \cdot 5$ degrees below the horizontal.

(b) In the case of sailing vessels the vertical sectors of electric lights shall ensure that:
  (i) at least the required minimum intensity is maintained at all angles from 5 degrees above to 5 degrees below the horizontal;
  (ii) at least 50 per cent of the required minimum intensity is maintained from 25 degrees above to 25 degrees below the horizontal.

(c) In the case of lights other than electric these specifications shall be met as closely as possible.

11. Intensity of non-electric lights

Non-electric lights shall so far as practicable comply with the minimum intensities, as specified in the Table given in Section 8 of this Annex.

12. Manoeuvring light

Notwithstanding the provisions of paragraph 2(f) of this Annex the manoeuvring light described in Rule 34(b) shall be placed in the same fore and aft vertical plane as the masthead light or lights and, where practicable, at a minimum height of 2 metres vertically above the forward masthead light, provided that it shall be carried not less than 2 metres vertically above or below the after masthead light. On a vessel where only one masthead light is carried the manoeuvring light, if fitted, shall be carried where it can best be seen, not less than 2 metres vertically apart from the masthead light.

13. Approval

The construction of lanterns and shapes and the installation of lanterns on board the vessel shall be to the satisfaction of the appropriate authority of the State where the vessel is registered.

ANNEX II

ADDITIONAL SIGNALS FOR FISHING VESSELS
FISHING IN CLOSE PROXIMITY

1. General

The lights mentioned herein shall, if exhibited in pursuance of Rule 26(d), be placed where they can best be seen. They shall be at least 0.9 metre apart but at a lower level than lights prescribed in Rule 26(b)(i) and (c)(i). The lights shall be visible all round the horizon at a distance of at least 1 mile but at a lesser distance than the lights prescribed by these Rules for fishing vessels.

2. Signals for trawlers

(a) Vessels when engaged in trawling, whether using demersal or pelagic gear, may exhibit:
    (i) when shooting their nets:
        two white lights in a vertical line;
    (ii) when hauling their nets:
        one white light over one red light in a vertical line;
    (iii) when the net has come fast upon an obstruction:
        two red lights in a vertical line.

(b) Each vessel engaged in pair trawling may exhibit:
    (i) by night, a searchlight directed forward and in the direction of the other vessel of the pair;
    (ii) when shooting or hauling their nets or when their nets have come fast upon an obstruction, the lights prescribed in 2(a) above.

3. Signals for purse seiners

Vessels engaged in fishing with purse seine gear may exhibit two yellow lights in a vertical line. These lights shall flash alternately every second and with equal light and occultation duration. These lights may be exhibited only when the vessel is hampered by its fishing gear.

ANNEX III

TECHNICAL DETAILS OF SOUND SIGNAL APPLIANCES

1. Whistles

(a) *Frequencies and range of audibility*

The fundamental frequency of the signal shall lie within the range 70–700 Hz.

The range of audibility of the signal from a whistle shall be determined by those frequencies, which may include the fundamental and/or one or more frequencies, which lie within the range 180–700 Hz ($\pm$ 1 per cent) and which provide the sound pressure levels specified in paragraph 1(c) below.

(b) *Limits of fundamental frequencies*

To ensure a wide variety of whistle characteristics, the fundamental frequency of a whistle shall be between the following limits:

(i) 70–200 Hz, for a vessel 200 metres or more in length;
(ii) 130–350 Hz, for a vessel 75 metres but less than 200 metres in length;
(iii) 250–700 Hz, for a vessel less than 75 metres in length.

(c) *Sound signal intensity and range of audibility*

A whistle fitted in a vessel shall provide, in the direction of maximum intensity of the whistle and at a distance of 1 metre from it, a sound pressure level in at least one 1/3rd-octave band within the range of frequencies 180–700 Hz ($\pm$ 1 per cent) of not less than the appropriate figure given in the table below.

Length of vessel in metres	1/3rd-octave band level at 1 metre in dB referred to 2×10^{-5} N/m^2	Audibility range in nautical miles
200 or more	143	2
75 but less than 200	138	1·5
20 but less than 75	130	1
Less than 20	120	0·5

The range of audibility in the table above is for information and is approximately the range at which a whistle may be heard on its forward axis with 90 per cent probability in conditions of still air on board a vessel having average background noise level at the listening posts (taken to be 68 dB in the octave band centred on 250 Hz and 63 dB in the octave band centred on 500 Hz).

In practice the range at which a whistle may be heard is extremely variable and depends critically on weather conditions; the values given can be regarded as typical but under conditions of strong wind or high ambient noise level at the listening post the range may be much reduced.

(d)   *Directional properties*

The sound pressure level of a directional whistle shall be not more than 4 dB below the sound pressure level on the axis at any direction in the horizontal plane within $\pm$ 45 degrees of the axis. The sound pressure level at any other direction in the horizontal plane shall be not more than 10 dB below the sound pressure level on the axis, so that the range in any direction will be at least half the range on the forward axis. The sound pressure level shall be measured in that 1/3rd-octave band which determines the audibility range.

(e)   *Positioning of whistles*

When a directional whistle is to be used as the only whistle on a vessel, it shall be installed with its maximum intensity directed straight ahead.

A whistle shall be placed as high as practicable on a vessel, in order to reduce interception of the emitted sound by obstructions and also to minimize hearing damage risk to personnel. The sound pressure level of the vessel's own signal at listening posts shall not exceed 110 dB (A) and so far as practicable should not exceed 100 dB (A).

(f)   *Fitting of more than one whistle*

If whistles are fitted at a distance apart of more than 100 metres, it shall be so arranged that they are not sounded simultaneously.

(g)   *Combined whistle systems*

If due to the presence of obstructions the sound field of a single whistle or of one of the whistles referred to in paragraph 1(f) above is likely to have a zone of greatly reduced signal level, it is recommended that a combined whistle system be fitted so as to overcome this reduction. For the purposes of the Rules a combined whistle system is to be regarded as a single whistle. The whistles of a combined system shall be located at a distance apart of not more than 100 metres and arranged to be sounded simultaneously. The frequency of any one whistle shall differ from those of the others by at least 10 Hz.

2. Bell or gong

(a) *Intensity of signal*

A bell or gong, or other device having similar sound characteristics shall produce a sound pressure level of not less than 110 dB at 1 metre.

(b) *Construction*

Bells and gongs shall be made of corrosion-resistant material and designed to give a clear tone. The diameter of the mouth of the bell shall be not less than 300 mm for vessels of more than 20 metres in length, and shall be not less than 200 mm for vessels of 12 to 20 metres in length. Where practicable, a power-driven bell striker is recommended to ensure constant force but manual operation shall be possible. The mass of the striker shall be not less than 3 per cent of the mass of the bell.

3. Approval

The construction of sound signal appliances, their performance and their installation on board the vessel shall be to the satisfaction of the appropriate authority of the State where the vessel is registered.

ANNEX IV

DISTRESS SIGNALS

1. The following signals, used or exhibited either together or separately, indicate distress and need of assistance:

(a) a gun or other explosive signal fired at intervals of about a minute;
(b) a continuous sounding with any fog-signalling apparatus;
(c) rockets or shells, throwing red stars fired one at a time at short intervals;

(d) a signal made by radiotelegraphy or by any other signalling method consisting of the group . . . ¯¯¯ . . . (SOS) in the Morse Code;

(e) a signal sent by radiotelephony consisting of the spoken word 'Mayday';

(f) the International Code Signal of distress indicated by N.C.;

(g) a signal consisting of a square flag having above or below it a ball or anything resembling a ball;

(h) flames on the vessel (as from a burning tar barrel, oil barrel, etc.);

(i) a rocket parachute flare or a hand flare showing a red light;

(j) a smoke signal giving off orange-coloured smoke;

(k) slowly and repeatedly raising and lowering arms outstretched to each side;

(l) the radiotelegraph alarm signal;

(m) the radiotelephone alarm signal;

(n) signals transmitted by emergency position-indicating radio beacons.

2. The use or exhibition of any of the foregoing signals except for the purpose of indicating distress and need of assistance and the use of other signals which may be confused with any of the above signals is prohibited.

3. Attention is drawn to the relevant sections of the International Code of Signals, the Merchant Ship Search and Rescue Manual and the following signals:

(a) a piece of orange-coloured canvas with either a black square and circle or other appropriate symbol (for identification from the air);

(b) a dye marker.

PILOT LADDERS

The Department of Trade and Industry's examination in seamanship requires that a candidate shall know how to rig a pilot ladder in a safe and proper manner. Every foreign-going cargo and passenger ship engaged on long international voyages is required to carry a ladder which is used only for the embarkation and disembarkation of pilots, officials or other persons while the vessel is arriving in or leaving port. The ladder must be rigged well clear of overboard discharges, so that each step rests firmly against the ship's side and so that the pilot can gain convenient access to the ship after climbing between 1·5 and 9 m.

The ladder must be a single length, capable of reaching the water from the access point at light draught, with normal trim and zero list. If the pilot has to climb more than 9 m, an accommodation ladder (or similar device) shall be used instead.

The treads of the ladder must be made of hardwood 48 cm long by 11·5 cm deep and 2·5 cm thick, spaced between 30 and 38 cm apart.

The steps must be horizontal. The two side-ropes, on each side, are to be of 18-mm manila rope. Two 20-mm manropes are to be fitted to enable the pilot to mount the ladder, together with a safety line if thought fit. Hardwood battens, 2 m long, must be fitted every so often to prevent the ladder from twisting. At night, both the ladder and the point of access are to be properly illuminated. A responsible officer must supervise the ladder when in use.

The Merchant Shipping (Pilot Ladders) Rules 1965, allow substitute materials if the D.o.T. is satisfied that they are of equal strength and suitability.

POLLUTION OF THE SEA BY OIL

The Prevention of Oil Pollution Act 1971 provides measures for controlling discharge of oil into the sea. New measures have been laid before the Safety Convention countries to tighten the Acts and remove several weaknesses. Regardless of the amount of jurisdiction, one fact remains: pollution of the sea can be finally prevented only by the integrity and diligence of the officers serving on oil-carriers.

The main points of the Acts are as follow:

(1) It is an offence for a British ship to discharge oil or oily mixtures (100 parts or more of oil in a million parts of mixture) into a prohibited area, at a rate exceeding 60 litres of oil per mile.
(2) If any oil or mixture, however small, is discharged into the territorial waters of the United Kingdom from a ship of any nationality, an offence is committed.
(3) In cases (2) and (3) it is a defence to show that the discharge or spillage was done for the safety of the ship, cargo, or lives, and that all steps were taken to prevent or stop accidental spillage.
(4) The maximum fine on summary conviction for offences under (1) and (2) is £50000.
(5) No oil is to be transferred between sunset and sunrise to or from a vessel in United Kingdom harbours, unless 3 to 96 hours notice has been given to the Harbourmaster. Penalty £100.
(6) Records are to be kept of oil discharges, oil leakages, ballasting of oil tanks, pumping of ballast from oil tanks, cleaning of oil tanks, separation of oil, disposal of oil or oily residues, and also the transfer of oil to and from vessels while in UK territorial waters.
(7) The penalty for failing to keep, or falsifying, records is £500 maximum on summary conviction.

The main exception to oil discharge or spillage into the sea is the pumping of oily mixture from bilges, containing only lubricating oil which has leaked or drained from machinery spaces. However, this is not permitted in United Kingdom territorial waters under any circumstances. A recent Notice from the Department of Trade explains that the use of separators may not allow the effluent to be entirely free of oil and a breach of the law may be committed if pumping oily bilge water or settled water is attempted in U.K. waters.

It should be noted that under this Act, the British Government has jurisdiction over foreign vessels only under (2). There are however sixty-one countries (1979) in the Convention, all with similar legislation. As far as British ships are concerned, the entire sea surface of the world is now a prohibited area.

MERCHANT SHIPPING NOTICES

From time to time, the Department of Trade in the U.K. issues Notices dealing with aspects of general safety aboard merchant ships, often based upon recent accidents and disasters. The notices are obtainable at Shipping Offices and are issued gratis to Masters.

The following section contains references to the more important 'M' Notices, relating to the work of this chapter. The notices have a great value provided they are produced as soon as possible after the event to which they relate. While it is fairly safe for a student to assume that, if there is a particular danger, there must be an 'M' notice about it, he should consult the full list of issues before presenting himself for examination.

Firefighting on Ships in Port

Fire fighting and prevention on board ships under construction is the builder's responsibility. It is the responsibility of the owners while the ship is under repair. When firefighting may endanger a ship's stability (i.e. flooding of the vessel) and a decision has to be made whether firefighting should cease, the decision of the Harbourmaster, or other Port Officer, is final, after consultation with interested parties. The Master, or Duty Officer, is not however relieved of his duty to inform the Fire Brigade Officer if he considers that dangerous circumstances are developing.

Emergency Medical Outfits

A fire on a tanker destroyed the amidships accommodation together with the medical outfit. It is recommended that tankers should carry a spare medical kit, aft, and preferably in the vicinity of the engine-room.

THE SAFETY OF NAVIGATION

Carriage of Air-dried Wood Pulp

Tests show that free expansion of wetted wood pulp can lead to a 50% increase in bale depth. Extreme care should be taken to see that this cargo is protected from the admission of water. Severe rupturing of compartment boundaries is otherwise likely to occur.

Direction-finding Apparatus

Serious errors have arisen in the use of this device owing to the proximity of domestic aerials to the D.F. loop. Domestic receivers in the vessel should either be connected to a communal aerial or have aerials rising no higher than the base of the loop, or at least 15 m from the base of the loop, measured horizontally. Random aerials can also affect R.T., W.T. equipment and radio-aids to navigation.

Prevention of Heat Illness

The health of officers on watch is of prime importance. Heatstroke can be very sudden and is always dangerous. It is due to a disturbance in the part of the brain which regulates body temperatures. It is characterised by a cessation of sweating, a burning dry skin, followed by delirium and unconsciousness. Cooling of the body becomes an urgent matter.

Heat exhaustion is less dramatic but may lead to collapse if neglected. Symptoms are fatigue, headache, nausea and faintness. It is caused by an inadequate intake of salt and water.

Heat illnesses may be prevented by drinking at least 4·5 litres of water per day in small but frequent quantities, taking extra salt, avoiding exposure to the sun around midday, and avoiding heavy meals and alcohol in the middle of the day. The body should be kept cool and well washed. Excessive consumption of alcohol under these conditions can lead to heatstroke and death.

Portable Radio Equipment

This must be regularly tested every 7 days and maintained in an efficient condition ready for instant use. One or more persons should be detailed on the Muster List to place the equipment in a lifeboat in an emergency.

Radio Telephone Procedure

This apparatus is required to have three cards displayed nearby. On vessels where the carriage of R.T. is not mandatory, the cards should still be carried if the equipment is fitted.

Card No. 1 explains the procedure for transmitting a distress call

e.g. 'MAYDAY MAYDAY MAYDAY. NONSUCH NONSUCH
NONSUCH. MAYDAY NONSUCH.
POSITION 54 25 NORTH 016 33 WEST
I AM ON FIRE AND REQUIRE IMMEDIATE ASSISTANCE.
OVER.'

(Where 'NONSUCH' is the name of the ship.)

Card No. 2 explains that the word 'MAYDAY' implies grave and imminent danger and a request for assistance. The word 'PAN' indicates a message of urgency and 'SECURITE' (pronounced SAY-CURITAY) preludes a navigational or meteorological warning.

Card No. 3 gives the phonetic alphabet and explains how to use R.T. for International Code signals when a language difficulty exists. This type of message uses the word 'INTERCO' to mean that International Code follows.

e.g. 'MAYDAY MAYDAY MAYDAY. NONSUCH NONSUCH
NONSUCH. MAYDAY NONSUCH.
INTERCO.
ALFA (A) NADAZERO (O) UNAONE (1) PANTAFIVE (5)
USHANT ROMEO (R) KARTEFOUR (4) NADAZERO (O)
DELTA X-RAY (DX)'

which means

Vessel NONSUCH requires immediate assistance. Position bearing 015 TRUE from USHANT, range 40 miles. I am sinking.

Lifeboat Launching Crews

These crews should include no more than two persons when launching a boat carried on a red-banded launching device.

Direction-finding an SOS Call

When not in use the D.F. set should be kept tuned to one of the international distress frequencies. This will enable rapid bearing location of the call. A suitable method is to link an automatic D.F. with the auto-alarm. In this way, while the radio officer is off watch, not only does the auto-alarm signal trigger off the warning bells but a direction is automatically taken.

Vessels Carrying Dangerous Goods

These vessels when under way at night in the open sea should not carry a red light visible all round the horizon. This light will constitute a breach of the Collision Regulations unless the vessel is leaking flammable spirit and is in distress with rockets likely to be fired towards her.

Magnetic Compasses

These can be seriously affected if portable radios, exposure meters, hand microphones or telephone handsets are placed within a distance of 4 m.

Polyurethane and other Organic Foams

These are highly dangerous when exposed to fire or other intense heat. Flames may spread at more than 30 m per minute. Temperatures of 1000°C may be generated together with large amounts of highly toxic gas and smoke.

Synthetic Mooring Lines

This type of material gives no audible warning when the breaking stress is approached. On parting, there is considerable recoil which can cause serious accidents. Surging and rendering these ropes around bitts or drums can cause the turns to fuse together and create binding. Only synthetic stoppers should be used on synthetic ropes. It is desirable that only one type of material should be used for mooring ropes in a particular ship. To expect the crew to handle alternately ropes of differing characteristics is to invite accidents.

THE NAVIGATIONAL WATCH

Several Merchant Shipping Notices have been published, following IMCO Resolutions, concerning safe navigation watchkeeping.
The basic recommendations are:

(1) The composition of the watch shall take into account the weather conditions, visibility, whether it is day or night, navigational hazards, use and condition of navigation equipment, automatic steering.
(2) Watchkeeping is not to be impaired by fatigue. The first watch of a voyage especially, shall be rested and fit.
(3) The Officer in charge of the watch shall not undertake duties which will interfere with safe navigation.
(4) At all times, there shall be an efficient and unimpaired visual and listening lookout. Ideally, the helmsman shall not also act as the lookout. By day, the Officer of the watch may act as the sole visual lookout but only after careful consideration of prevailing circumstances.

(5) The presence of a pilot shall not relieve the Master (or Officer in charge) of his duties and obligations regarding the safety of the ship.

(6) The Officer of the Watch shall under no circumstances leave the bridge until properly relieved. A proper lookout must be maintained during a visit to a separate chartroom. Such visits are to be brief.

(7) When the Officer is acting as sole lookout, he must not hesitate to summon assistance to the bridge if he needs it and such assistance is to be immediately available.

(8) The Officer should not hesitate to use engines and sound signalling apparatus.

(9) The Officer of the watch is responsible for the safe navigation of the ship **even when the Master is on the bridge, until the Master informs him that he has assumed full responsibility and this is mutually understood.**

(10) The automatic steering should be tested in manual at least once a watch. Manual steering should be adopted well before a close-quarters situation develops.

THE INTERNATIONAL CODE OF SIGNALS

It is beyond the size of this book to discuss flag signalling methods, and the reader is referred to the *International Code of Signals 1969* (*Revised*), where he will find the full procedure clearly discussed. At the same time he should thoroughly familiarise himself with the layout and use of this important book.

The flags themselves are included in Fig. 14.11 for reference purposes only; again, the reader is advised to colour them himself after carefully studying the colour key. The following are the meanings of the flags when used singly. The same meanings apply when used by any other method of signalling.

A   I have a diver down; keep well clear at slow speed.

*B   I am taking in, or discharging, or carrying, dangerous goods.

C   Yes (affirmative, or 'The significance of the previous group should be read in the affirmative').

*D   Keep clear of me; I am manœuvring with difficulty.

*E   I am altering my course to starboard.

F   I am disabled; communicate with me.

G   I require a pilot. (When made by fishing vessels operating in close proximity on the fishing grounds it means 'I am hauling nets'.)

*H I have a pilot on board.

*I I am altering my course to port.

J I am on fire and have dangerous cargo on board; keep well clear of me.

K I wish to communicate with you.

L You should stop your vessel instantly.

M My vessel is stopped and making no way through the water.

N No (negative, or 'The significance of the previous group should be read in the negative'). This signal may be given only visually or by sound. For voice or radio transmission the signal should be 'NO'.

O Man overboard.

P (In harbour) All persons should report on board as the vessel is about to proceed to sea. (At sea may be used by fishing vessels to mean 'My nets have come fast upon an obstruction'.)

Q My vessel is 'healthy' and I request free pratique.

R (No meaning given.)

*S My engines are going astern.

*T Keep clear of me; I am engaged in pair trawling.

U You are running into danger.

V I require assistance.

W I require medical assistance.

X Stop carrying out your intentions and watch for my signals.

Y I am dragging my anchor.

Z I require a tug (or, as in 'G' above, 'I am shooting nets').

Signals marked with an asterisk (*) may be made only by sound signalling according to Rules 34 and 35 of the Collision Regulations.

The code pennant is hoisted close-up to the halliard block to indicate that a flag message is understood. If it is kept at the dip, i.e. flying below the halliard block, it indicates that the message is not yet interpreted. The pennant is also used to indicate a decimal point.

Names in the text of a signal are to be spelt out using the alphabetical flags, preceded if necessary by the group 'YZ', meaning 'The words which follow are in plain language'.

Single-letter signals are usually of an urgent nature.

Two-letter signals are used for the general section.

Three-letter hoists begin with the letter 'M' and indicate medical signals.

Four-letter hoists will indicate signal letters of ships.

Latitude is expressed by four numerals preceded by 'L'. The first two indicate the degrees and the final two, the minutes. The letters 'N' or 'S' may follow if needed.

'L 3740 S' means Latitude 37°40' South

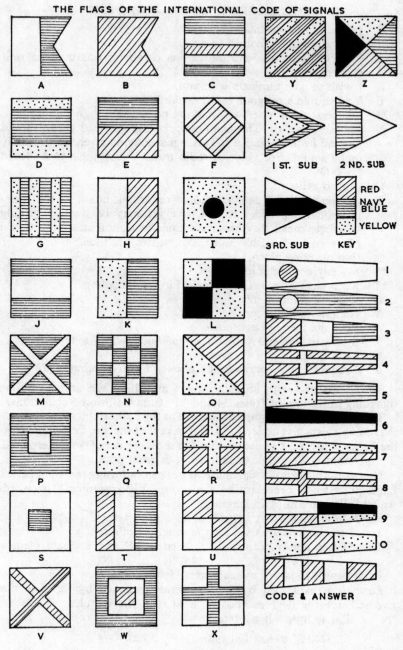

THE FLAGS OF THE INTERNATIONAL CODE OF SIGNALS

FIGURE 14.11

Longitude is expressed by four, or five, numerals preceded by the letter 'G'. When the longitude exceeds 99°, no confusion will normally arise if the figure indicating hundreds of degrees is omitted. In cases where confusion may occur, it should be used. The letters 'E' or 'W' may be used if necessary, thus

'G 13925 E' means Longitude 139°25′ East

Course is indicated by three numerals denoting degrees from 000 to 359, preferably preceded by the letter 'C'.

Speed in knots is indicated by numerals preceded by 'S'. The letter 'V' is used for kilometres per hour.

'C 240 S 18' means Course 240° Speed 18 knots.

Azimuth or bearing is expressed similarly to course, preferably preceded by 'A'. Bearings and courses are true unless otherwise stated in the context.

Distance is indicated in nautical miles by one or more numerals, preferably preceded by 'R'.

Date may be signalled by two, four or six numerals preceded by 'D'. The first two denote the day of the month. The next two indicate the month of the year and the final two the year itself.

'D 180763' indicates 18 July 1963.
'D 18' alone, indicates the 18th of the current month.

Time is denoted by the use of the 24-hour clock. Four numerals are used preceded by 'T' (local time) or 'Z' (G.M.T.). A time of 2359 is followed a minute later not by 2400 but by 0000.

The flag set of 40 contains three substitutes, used to repeat a flag in a group. Thus the group 'MMB' is sent as 'M', First substitute, 'B'. The group MBM would be sent as M, B, First substitute. The group number '1100' is sent as '1', First substitute, '0', Third substitute. But the group 'T 1100' would be sent in the same way, prefixed by 'T'. The prefix letter is not included when substitutes are made. Thus 'G 2444' would appear as 'G, 2, 4', Second substitute, Third substitute.

Sound signalling is a slow process. Its misuse may create serious confusion at sea and its use in fog should be kept to a minimum. Signals other than the single letters should be made only in extreme emergency and never in busy waters. The signals should be made slowly and clearly. If they are repeated, it should be at long intervals.

Flags Flown by British Merchant Ships

Section 74 of the Merchant Shipping Act 1894 states:

351

(1) A ship belonging to a British subject shall hoist the proper national colours—

   (*a*) On a signal being made to her by one of Her Majesty's ships, (including any vessel under the command of an officer of Her Majesty's Navy on full pay), and

   (*b*) on entering or leaving any foreign port, and

   (*c*) if of 50 tons *gross* tonnage or upwards, on entering or leaving any British port.

(2) If default is made on board any such ship in complying with this section the Master of the ship shall for each offence be liable to a fine not exceeding £100.

THE KNOWLEDGE OF THE OFFICER OF THE WATCH

The section which now follows is a comprehensive list of questions and answers relating to efficient watchkeeping. It cannot be stressed too much that these answers should come automatically to every Officer on watch, for in many cases lives may be at stake. A candidate for a D.o.T. certificate is likely to be questioned very closely in a similar fashion.

A space will be left after each answer so that from time to time the reader can insert any amendments which may be made by the Authorities. It is most important that the answers be kept up to date.

The letter 'M' will indicate that the information is promulgated by D.o.T. Notices, 'N.M.' will refer to Notices to Mariners, and 'S.R.' to Statutory Rules and Orders.

The questions are intended to cover work which has not already been dealt with in previous text, but a few may arise which refer to past reading, in order to emphasise an important point.

1. What is a Larsen trawl and what lights are shown by vessels thus fishing? (M).

It is a trawl towed between two trawlers; each vessel carries normal trawling lights, but a searchlight may be shone from each vessel towards the other.

Amendment

2. What is the visibility of sidelights carried on a 12·0 m sailing ship?

Two miles; the reduced range is permitted only on sailing ships of less than 12·0 m. (Rule 22.)

Amendment

3. A 50 m power-driven coaster runs aground. What signal must she show?

Anchor lights and two all-round red lights vertically disposed (Rule 30.)

Amendment

4. What signal is shown by a seaplane aground?

As far as possible, the signal mentioned in Question 3 above, and three balls by day (Rules 30, 31.)

Amendment

5. A pillar buoy is sighted in the North Sea coloured black over yellow. Topmark: two black cones points upwards. What action should be taken?

Pass to the north of this buoy. It is a north quadrant cardinal mark, system 'A'.

Amendment

6. What is an examination port? (N.M.)

It is a British or Commonwealth port where an Examination Service exists for the purpose of examining vessels desiring to enter the port or locality. It is often carried out in conjunction with Admiralty control or closure of the port.

Amendment

7. **Entrance to a port is prohibited. What signals are displayed?**
(N.M.)

Three flashing red lights (three red balls by day) vertically disposed in a conspicuous position in or near the port approach. The signals will also be shown by the Examination vessel or Traffic Control vessel.
Amendment

8. **What signals are used to indicate that a port or anchorage is under naval control and movement of shipping is prohibited? (N.M.)**

Three lights—red, green, red, vertically disposed by night; a blue flag by day.
Amendment

9. **What action should you take if the port is closed? (N.M.)**

Approach with the greatest caution and obey all instructions given by Traffic control and Examination vessels. Never enter a 'Dangerous Area' or remain anchored or stopped within such an area or a prohibited anchorage. Never approach boom defences without permission.
Amendment

10. **A fishing vessel is exhibiting two yellow lights, vertically disposed, and flashing alternately. What does this mean?**

The vessel is fishing with Seine nets. These are likely to cover one square mile. (2nd Annex to Rules.)
Amendment

11. Describe ODAS buoys. (N.M.)

These are Ocean Data Acquisition System buoys, collecting and recording ocean data. They are coloured in yellow and red vertical (moored) stripes or yellow and red horizontal (unmoored) stripes. The light is long-interrupted quick flashing of a bluish-white colour. A radar reflector is fitted.

Amendment

12. What signals are displayed by the Examination vessel? (N.M.)

The signals described in Question 7. Also three green lights vertically disposed at night to indicate that the port is open. All these lights are visible all round the horizon. The vessel will fly the Examination Service flag, which is rectangular and blue. In the centre is a rectangle divided horizontally into an upper white portion and a lower red portion.

Amendment

13. What day signal may be shown by vessels engaged in pair trawling?

International Code flag 'T' flown at the foremast.

Amendment

14. What actions are not permitted within an Examination anchorage? (N.M.)

To lower any boat; to communicate with the shore or other ships; to move the ship; to work cables, or to allow any person or thing to leave the ship. These actions are allowed only if they will prevent an accident or if the permission of the Examining Officer has been obtained.

Amendment

15. A fishing vessel displays two white lights, visible all round the horizon, vertically disposed, in addition to normal fishing lights. What does this indicate?

'I am shooting nets'. (2nd Annex to Rules.)

Amendment

16. Which vessels switch off their sidelights when stopped but under way?

All vessels mentioned in Rule 27, except minesweepers, and all fishing vessels.

Amendment

17. What lights are displayed by oil rigs? (N.M.)

Normally, an all-round white light visible for 10 miles. Also a red light at each 'corner' visible for 2 miles. All lights flash Morse 'U' every 15 seconds.

Amendment

18. In which direction do long nets lie by day, from a fishing vessel?

From the double cone (or basket) towards the single cone. (Rule 26.)

Amendment

19. What is the day signal for a trawler?

Two black cones, in a vertical line, points together. If under 20 m in length, she may show a basket instead. (Rule 26.)

Amendment

20. What is a telegraph buoy?

A black buoy, with the word 'Telegraph' painted on it in white. It marks a submarine cable and an area where anchoring should not be permitted.

Amendment

21. What fog signal is made by an oil rig? (N.M.)

Normally, a sound signal consisting of Morse 'U' every 30 seconds.

Amendment

22. What shapes are shown by a vessel servicing a buoy, by day, when also at anchor?

The three shapes prescribed in Rule 27, namely a ball, a diamond, and another ball, vertically disposed at least 1·5 m apart where they can best be seen. Also the anchor ball mentioned in Rule 30.

Amendment

23. What is a minehunter? (N.M.)

A small naval vessel locating mines with sonar devices or magnetic-anomaly detecting gear. Her lights are prescribed in Rule 27(*b*). Small vessels may operate nearby showing the lights prescribed in Rule 23 and also two red lights, horizontally disposed, 2 m apart.

Amendment

24. What signal is used to indicate that a vessel, at night, has not yet received free pratique to a port? (Int. Code of Signals.)

A red light over a white light, visible all round the horizon, 2·00 m apart, hoisted where they can best be seen.

Amendment

25. On which side of vessel will a disabled aircraft usually ditch? (M).

On her starboard side; this is due to the fact that the Captain of the aircraft usually sits on the port side. A lee should be made, therefore, on the starboard side.

Amendment

26. When a vessel finds herself in a firing practice area, what action should she take? (N.M.)

She should maintain her course and speed; if this is not possible due to the exigencies of navigation, she should clear the area as quickly as possible. All persons on board should take cover.

Amendment

27. What information is promulgated by Notices to Mariners with regard to aircraft carriers? (N.M.)

Their movements are uncertain and they must usually turn into the wind if aircraft are taking off or landing. Furthermore, Mariners are warned that by night aircraft carriers have their steaming lights placed permanently off the centre line of the ship. Alternative positions for their side lights:

(i) on either side of the hull,

(ii) on either side of the island structure, in which case the port bow light may be as much as 30 m from the port side of the ship.

100 ft

Certain aircraft carriers exhibit anchor lights as follows: four *white* lights located in the following manner:

5 ft   In the forward part of the vessel at a distance of not more than 1·5 m below the flight deck, two lights in the same horizontal plane, one on the port side and one on the starboard side.

15 ft   In the after part of the vessel at a height of not less than 4·5 m lower than the forward lights, two lights in the same horizontal plane, one on the port side and one on the starboard side.

Each light visible over an arc of at least 180 degrees. The forward lights visible over a minimum arc from 1 point on the opposite bow to 1 point from right astern on their own side, and the after lights from 1 point on the opposite quarter to 1 point from right ahead on their own side. (See also Rule 27(*b*).)

Amendment

28. What signal is exhibited by a submarine escort vessel? (N.M.)

The International Code group 'NE 2'. These vessels should be given a wide berth; if this is not possible, they should be approached at slow speed, until warning is received of the danger zone. A good lookout should be kept for submarines.

Amendment

29. How do submarines indicate their positions? (N.M.)

Either by their periscope, or in deeper water, by towing a red and white, or red and yellow float astern of them at the surface. A smoke candle may also be released, giving off a large quantity of smoke.

Amendment

30. What signals are used to indicate that a submarine is about to surface? (N.M.)

One red pyrotechnic light or smoke, repeated as often as necessary to indicate 'Keep clear. I am carrying out an emergency surfacing procedure. Do not stop propellers. Ships are to clear the area immediately and stand by to render assistance.' Two yellow pyrotechnic lights, or two white or yellow smokes, three minutes apart to indicate 'Keep clear. My position is as indicated. I intend to carry out surfacing procedure. Do not stop propellers. Ships are to clear the immediate vicinity.' It must not be inferred that submarines exercise only in the company of escort vessels.

Amendment

31. How may a sunken submarine indicate its plight? (N.M.)

By releasing an indicator buoy, yellow or white smoke and flame candles, or by pumping out air or oil.

Amendment

32. What action should the vessel take on sighting the buoy or any of these signals? (N.M.)

Inform the Navy, Coastguard, or Police; stand by downstream to pick up any escaping men; tap on the ship's side below the waterline, run the echo sounder, or explode small charges at least ¼ mile away, to warn the crew of the submarine that help is at hand.

Amendment

33. Describe the buoy. (N.M.)

It is of a highly visible orange colour, floats at a freeboard of 15 cm, 6 in has a white light flashing twice a second, visible to the naked eye in clear darkness for 1·75 miles. The light will flash for some 40 hours. There are cat's-eye reflectors around the upper surface, together with a whip aerial. (See Chapter VI.)

Amendment

34. What signals are displayed by vessels replenishing with fuel at sea?

British and Allied Warships in conjunction with auxiliaries frequently exercise Replenishment-at-Sea. While doing so the two or more ships taking part are connected by jackstays and hoses. They display the signals prescribed by Rule 27(*b*) of the International Regulations for Preventing Collisions at Sea, 1972.

Mariners are warned that while carrying out these exercises the ships are severely restricted both in manœuvrability and speed, and it is the duty of other vessels to keep well clear in accordance with Rule 3(*g*) of the above Regulations.

Amendment

35. Are there any peculiarities with regard to the navigation lights of submarines? (N.M.)

Submarines when at anchor, or moored to a buoy, may show a white light visible all round the horizon, from the conning tower. This is shown in addition to anchor lights prescribed in Rule 30.

Hitherto the navigation lights of submarines have been exhibited from the conning tower, which is near the centre of the vessel. The steaming light, bow lights, and overtaking light have been necessarily low down and closely spaced, with the result that they give no indication of the submarine's length nor of her exact course or change of course. Consequently they may be mistaken for the lights of a very much smaller vessel of the coaster type.

Special arrangements have now been made to fit H.M. Submarines with a second steaming light. The forward steaming light is placed on a
1 and 6 ft special fitting in the fore part of the vessel between 0·3 and 2 m above the hull. The main steaming light is fitted on the conning tower or fin. In submarines where the forward steaming light is appreciably less than
6 ft 2 m above the hull, and may in consequence be lower than the coloured side lights, the overall arrangement of lights as seen from other vessels may appear unusual. In addition, the vertical separation in some cases
15 ft is less than 4·5 m.

The overtaking light is placed on a special fitting near the stern of the vessel, but may be at a height considerably less than that of the side lights.
6 ft Some submarines carry a quick-flashing amber light 2 m above the steaming light, when on the surface at night.

360

36. What lights are carried by a seaplane engaged in towing?

The same as prescribed for other vessels in Rule 24. But see Rule 31 for special dispensation.

Amendment

37. What lights are carried by a seaplane not under command?

She may carry the lights prescribed in Rule 4 (*b*). She shows the side-lights only when she is moving.

Amendment

38. An aircraft fires white pyrotechnic lights or flashes its navigation lights. What does this mean? (N.M.)

The aircraft wishes to attract the attention of surface shipping.

Amendment

39. A tug is towing three vessels, the length of the tow being 180 m.   500 ft How many white masthead lights are shown?

Only two to indicate the fact that she is towing. (Rule 24.) She shall also show the light required by Rule 23(*a*)(ii).

Amendment

40. A light vessel signals the letter 'K' in Morse to a vessel. What does this mean? (Int. Code of Signals.)

She has something to communicate.

Amendment

41. If she hoists the two-flag signal 'NG', what does this mean?

'You are in a dangerous position'.

Amendment

42. What is the fog-signal for a minesweeper?

A long blast, followed by two short blasts, on the whistle, at intervals of not more than 2 minutes. She is unable to get out of the way. (Rules 27 and 35.)

Amendment

43. What signal is made by a sailing vessel before reaching a bend in a river?

One prolonged blast as prescribed in Rule 34(*e*).

Amendment

44. An aircraft flies over the vessel at sea, in open and unfrequented waters. What action should be taken? (N.M.)

Entries should be made in the logbook regarding the time, date, weather conditions, identification marks of aircraft, type of aircraft, its course, and estimated height.

Amendment

45. What are the limits of helicopter air–sea rescue? (M).

They will not operate at night, in reduced visibility, in winds over 45 knots, nor usually more than 90 miles from their base.

Amendment

46. What is a dracone? (N.M.)

200 ft   A tubular casing of nylon fabric and synthetic rubber, about 60 m long, used for the transportation of oil fuels and spirits. It is towed by a
200 yds   tug on a towline roughly 200 m in length. The dracone is almost sub-merged, since it floats at a draught commensurate with the specific

362

gravity of the casing and the liquid. It tows a float on which a black diamond flies by day, and an all-round white light shows by night. The tug exhibits a black diamond by day, and an all-round blue light at night visible 2 miles.

Amendment

47. What is a safe water mark?

A red and white buoy used to show that there is navigable water all around it.

Amendment

48. How should the O.O.W. indicate that he is unable to reply to signals received from warships or aircraft?

Signal 'N' in the Morse code or hoist flag 'N'.

Amendment

49. How may a pilot be summoned by day or by night?

Local signals should be used according to the Sailing Directions. The International Code flag 'G' may be flown. Morse 'G' may be made by any signalling method. Where language difficulties exist on R.T., the words 'INTERCO GOLF' may be used. Some ports may require the use of a blue pyrotechnic every 15 minutes, the pilot jack flown at the foremast or a bright white light shown above the rail at short intervals.

Amendment

50. When aground, 3 white star rockets are fired ashore. What does this mean? (M).

'You are seen: help will be given as soon as possible.'

Amendment

51. Approaching a disabled tanker in mist, you hear 'GU' sounded on the whistle. What does this mean? (M).

'It is not safe to fire a rocket.'

Amendment

52. A disabled tanker is flying flag B. By night it shows a red light at the masthead. What does this mean? (M).

'The vessel is leaking flammable liquid; it is dangerous to fire a rocket.'

Amendment

53. What is a range safety craft? (N.M.)

A vessel which patrols up to 8 miles away from a firing-area centre.
Amendment

54. What information is promulgated in Notices to Mariners with regard to these areas? (N.M.)

Firing and bombing practices, and defence exercises, take place in a number of areas off the coasts of British Commonwealth and Colonial Territories as well as in foreign waters.

In future, and in view of the responsibility of range authorities to avoid accidents, limits of practice areas will not as a rule be shown on charts and descriptions of areas will not appear in the Sailing Directions. Such range beacons, lights, and marking buoys as may be of assistance to the Mariner, or targets which might be a danger to navigation, will, however, be shown on charts and, when appropriate, mentioned in Sailing Directions.

Lights will be mentioned in the Admiralty List of Lights.

The principal types of practices carried out are:

(*a*) *Bombing Practice from Aircraft*
    Warning signals usually shown.

(*b*) *Air to Air, and Air to Sea, or Ground Firing*

The former is carried out by aircraft at a large white or red sleeve, a winged target, or flag towed by another aircraft moving on a steady course. The latter is carried out from aircraft at towed or stationary targets on sea or land, the firing taking place to seaward in the case of those on land.

As a general rule, warning signals are shown when the targets are stationary, but not when towed targets are used.

All marine craft operating as range safety craft, target towers or control launches for wireless controlled targets will display, for identification purposes, while in or in the vicinity of the danger area, the following markings:

(1) a large red flag at the masthead;
(2) a painted canvas strip, 2 m × 1 m, with red and white chequers   6 ft × 3 ft
in 0·3 m squares, on the fore deck or cabin roof.   1-ft

Anti-aircraft Firing

This may be from A.A. guns or machine guns at a target towed by aircraft as in (b) above, a pilotless target aircraft, or at balloons or kites. Practice may take place from shore batteries or ships.

Warning signals as a rule are shown from shore batteries. Ships fly a red flag.

Firing from Shore Batteries or Ships at Sea at Fixed or Floating Targets

Warning signals usually shown as above.

At Remote-controlled Craft

These craft are 21 m in length and carry 'not under control' shapes   68 ft and lights, which are prescribed in Rule 27(a). Exercises consisting of surface firing by ships, practice bombing, air to sea firing and rocket firing will be carried out against these craft or targets towed by them.

A control craft will keep visual and radar watch up to approximately 8 miles, and there will be cover from the air over a much greater range to ensure that other shipping will not be endangered.

Warning signals, when given, usually consist of red flags by day and *red fixed* or *red flashing* lights at night. The absence of any such signal cannot, however, be accepted as evidence that a practice area does not exist. Warning signals are shown from shortly before practice commences until it ceases.

Ships and aircraft carrying out night exercises may illuminate with bright *red* or *orange* flares.

Amendment

55. A man on a yacht is slowly moving his arms up and down. What does this mean?

It is a signal of distress. (4th Annex to Rules.)

Amendment

56. What shapes are shown by a vessel navigating stern-foremost? (M).

2 ft 8 ft 6 ft   Only when fitted with a bow rudder a vessel will show two black balls, each 0·6 m in diameter on a cross-yard 2·5 m apart and 2 m above the funnel top. The signal is shown aft.

Amendment

57. An aircraft fires a red flare. What does this mean? (N.M.)

The aircraft is threatened by grave and imminent danger and requires immediate assistance.

Amendment

58. An aircraft fires green flares every 10 to 15 minutes. What does this indicate? (N.M.)

The aircraft is searching for survivors. The signal should be answered by the survivors with the use of statutory distress signals—probably red hand flares or rockets.

Amendment

59. If a fishing vessel shows a white light over a red light, visible all round the horizon while fishing, in addition to her normal fishing lights, what does this mean? (2nd Annex to Rules.)

She is hauling her nets.

Amendment

60. A vessel of 100m or more is at anchor. What lights are shown?

Two anchor lights together with all available working lights to illuminate her decks. (Rule 30.)

Amendment

61. What signals are shown by deep-draught vessels?

The International Regulations for Preventing Collisions at Sea 1972 (Rule 28) suggests the following signals. In some ports they may be compulsory.

By day: A black cylinder where it can best be seen, measuring 0·6 m in diameter and 1·2 m high.
By night: Three red lights shown where they can best be seen. The lights should be equidistantly spaced, 2 m apart and visible all round the horizon for a distance of at least three miles.

The signals have already been adopted in many ports and may, in some areas, be applicable to vessels over a certain deadweight tonnage, or over a certain length, or over a certain draught. The signals do not absolve the vessels showing them from complying with the Regulations for Prevention of Collision at Sea, but if they are in any doubt as to whether another vessel is giving them sufficient searoom, they may give at least five short and rapid blasts under Rule 34. Other vessels, not showing such signals, should endeavour to keep clear and may indicate their intentions by making the Morse letter 'A' on the whistle or siren, in addition to manoeuvring signals prescribed in Rule 34.

Amendment

62. What may be indicated at sea when two all-round white lights are sighted, separated by a horizontal distance which greatly exceeds the vertical distance?

(i) A vessel at anchor of any length.
(ii) An aircraft at anchor of any length.
(iii) A power-driven vessel of any length, hull down, i.e. with side-lights not visible.
(iv) An aircraft carrier at anchor. (See Question 27.)

Amendment

63. What signal is displayed by a light-vessel which is out of position? (M).

The characteristic light is not shown, any daymark is struck, and the fog signal is not made. By day, she shows a large black ball at each end of the vessel and also the two-flag code group 'LO'. By night, she will display a red light, visible all round the horizon, at each end, together with a red flare and a white flare, shown amidships simultaneously every 15 minutes. If the use of flares is not possible, red and white lights may be displayed for about a minute at a time.

Amendment

64. If the light on a light-vessel is out of order, what signal is shown? (M).

6 ft   Only her riding light, which is exhibited about 2 m above the rail, on the forestay.

Amendment

65. At what speed would you navigate with caution?

At a speed commensurate with steerage way, or even stopped.

Amendment

66. What regulations apply to pilot ladders? (S.R.)

They must be capable of being used either side; they are only to be used for pilots' access. They are to have wide treads of adequate depth; a manrope each side of the ladder 20 mm in diameter; to be of adequate length and strength and to have anti-twisters fitted to them.

Amendment

67. What is the meaning of the International Code group 'ZW'?

'I require the Port Medical Officer'.

Amendment

68. What precautions would you take when approaching squadrons, convoys, aircraft carriers under way or at anchor, and other warships at sea? (N.M.)

Adopt early measures to keep out of the way.

Amendment

69. How far do some fishing gears extend, e.g. drift nets and Seine nets? (M), (N.M.)

Drift nets extend up to 2 miles from the craft. Seine nets may cover 1 square mile.

Amendment

70. You cannot avoid crossing nets. What action will you take? (M).

Stop engines and proceed across the nets with all speed. The propellers must be stopped revolving.

Amendment

71. Would you anchor near submarine cables? (N.M.)

No; if, however, I did this by accident, and fouled such a cable on my anchor, I would never cut the cable, which may be carrying high voltages. The anchor should be slipped if the cable cannot be cleared in the normal way. I would report to the shore Authorities.

Amendment

72. What provisions are made with regard to using radar in wartime or other emergency? (N.M.)

It must be used at sea only when imperative. In harbour or at anchor it should never be used except in the interests of safe navigation and when permitted to do so by the Naval Authorities.

Amendment

73. What precautions must you take regarding light-vessels? (M).

Always give them a very wide berth. Never 'home' on their radio direction-finding transmissions, as a collision may occur either with them or with other ships doing the same thing.

Amendment

74. What visual gale warnings are in use? (N.M.)

3 ft 3-ft
4 ft

A black cone, 1 m high with a 1 m-diameter base. A triangle of white or red lights, 1·2 m apart at the base. A flashing red light is used in some localities. When the triangle or cone is apex upwards a northerly gale is expected, or one commencing from the east or west, backing or veering to the north. If apex downwards, a southerly gale is expected. The signal is hauled down when a lull of at least 12 hours is anticipated.

Amendment

75. How many magnetic compasses must be carried on board ship? (S.R.)

At least two are recommended for Class 7 ships. Class 1 ships must carry at least three.

Amendment

76. What are the meanings of the International Code groups 'QQ' and 'ZV'?

'QQ' indicates 'I require health clearance'. 'ZV' indicates 'I believe I have been in an infected area during the last thirty days.'

Amendment

77. A buoy is sighted having white and green horizontal bands. What does it signify? (N.M.)

An area where practice minefields exist for the purpose of submarine exercises.

Amendment

78. What is a watch buoy?

A red can-buoy moored close to a light-vessel. It has the name of the lightship painted on it in white letters. Its purpose is to provide a mark so that the lightship can check its position.

Amendment

79. Distinguish between a barque, a barquentine, a brig, and a brigantine.

A barque is a three-masted vessel square-rigged on the forward two masts, while a barquentine also has three masts of which only the forward one is square-rigged.

A brig is a two-masted vessel, square-rigged on both masts.

A brigantine is a two-masted vessel, square-rigged on the forward mast only.

80. A buoy light is sighted in the Irish Sea. It is white, quick-flashing with nine flashes in a cycle. What action should be taken?

Pass to the west of this buoy. Nine flashes (i.e. nine o'clock) indicates that it is a west quadrant buoy.

Amendment

81. An isophase red buoy light is sighted in the English Channel. What action should be taken?

It is a port hand lateral mark to be left to port when following the conventional direction of buoyage.

Amendment

371

82. What is a schooner?

This is a vessel which may have from two to six masts, and she will be fore-and-aft rigged on all masts. A topsail schooner, however, will have her fore topmast rigged with square sails.

83. A buoy light is sighted in the North Sea, group flashing two, white. What action should be taken?

Pass either side. It is marking an isolated danger.

Amendment

84. Distinguish between a ketch and a yawl.

These are small sailing craft, each having a mainsail and a mizzen sail, with or without jibsails. The mizzen sail of the ketch is often the larger of the two mizzens, and the mizzen-mast is stepped forward of the rudder post. The mizzen-mast of the yawl is stepped much farther aft and the sail projects over the stern.

85. What information is promulgated with regard to Hovercraft? (N.M.)

These craft may be found operating anywhere on the United Kingdom coasts, where they will show a quick-flashing amber light visible all round the horizon for a distance of at least 5 miles, between sunset and sunrise. In poor conditions the light may be exhibited in daytime also.

At present these craft can proceed either fully waterborne, or partially airborne but with their keels or sidewalls remaining in the water, or fully airborne a few cm above water level.

In the first two cases they will behave similarly to shallow-draught vessels, but in the last case they are capable of speeds in excess of 80 knots over both land and sea, and are susceptible to wind drift. They can go astern, and can stop extremely quickly by simply alighting upon the water.

In general, they will keep clear of all vessels and avoid impeding their navigation. In circumstances where risk of collision exists they shall go at a moderate speed and behave as though they were power-driven vessels. Because of their noise level, they may not emit sound signals, neither may they hear those which are emitted by other vessels.

Amendment

CHAPTER XV

LIFTING GEAR

GENERAL

EVERY component of a lifting apparatus has an ultimate stress at which it will fracture and a safe stress at which it can normally be used. This latter is called the *safe working load* (S.W.L.). Every component has this S.W.L. stamped or painted upon it—in the case of wire or chain it is either stamped on a durable tablet attached to the material or else a notice is posted in a conspicuous place in the working vicinity where employees can refer to the safe working loads of all ropes, wires, and chains in use.

The ratio of ultimate stress to safe working load is called the *factor of safety*, and is usually between four and eight. For example, in the case of wire rope it is five, for fibre rope it is six, and again five for chains.

When assembling a lifting apparatus, every part is vital and must be adequately strong; a weak part may cause a disaster, and an over-strong part adds unnecessary weight.

Most gear is tested officially to find its ultimate stress, and also *proved* at a licensed Proving House to a load which will not produce weakness or injury to the part.

Gear should be proved at regular intervals after being put into initial use, to test for strength deterioration. After continuous use the metal may become brittle and fracture. This is expedited by ill-use. Before this state of affairs exists, the metal should be *annealed*, i.e. heated to a temperature depending upon the metal, say 600°–650° C, and then allowed to cool very slowly. This process removes the brittleness and restores the original grain to the metal. Many metal objects when loaded to beyond half their ultimate strength suffer a permanent *set* or distortion. In this case the *elastic limit* has been exceeded. Later as the load is increased the *yield point* will be reached, and at this stage *constriction* begins.

Safe loads should not be exceeded except where provided for under the Docks Regulations and in an emergency, such as the use of ground-tackle for ungrounding a vessel. This will restrict such overloading to isolated occasions, which may do no damage. The possibility of permanent distortion should be accepted, however.

373

BLOCKS AND PURCHASES

A purchase is said to be *used to advantage* when the effort or pull is being applied in the same direction as the achieved movement of the load. For example, if a weight were being hauled down a deck in an aft direction and the men on the fall were also pulling in an aft direction, then the purchase is used to advantage. Also there will be more parts of rope at the moving block than at the standing block.

A purchase is conversely *used to disadvantage* when the effort is being applied in the opposite direction to the achieved movement of the load, i.e. a forward pull to cause a weight to move aft. Also there will be more parts of rope at the standing block than at the moving block.

Now imagine a purchase suspended vertically, used to advantage and hoisting a weight W. The pull P is therefore also acting upwards, and the stress on the shackle securing the top or standing block must be $W - P$.

If the purchase is being used to disadvantage the pull P will be acting downwards in order to lift the weight, and the stress on the same top shackle becomes $W + P$.

Similarly, when a purchase is used to disadvantage the stresses in the fall when lowering or hoisting a given weight will be greater than when the purchase is used to advantage. This must be borne in mind when considering the S.W.L. of a purchase.

Within the purchase, each part of the fall bears a different proportion of the total load. When hoisting, the maximum stress is on the hauling part and the minimum on the standing part. When lowering, the reverse is true.

Blocks are usually stronger than their designed falls, hence the S.W.L. of a purchase is usually that of the fall.

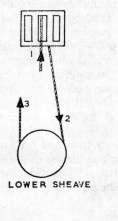 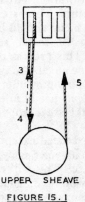 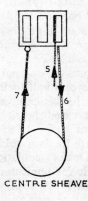

LOWER SHEAVE   UPPER SHEAVE   CENTRE SHEAVE

FIGURE 15.1

374

When a fall is under load the blocks tend to spin and produce turns in the purchase. One turn can increase the stress required (to continue lifting) by four-tenths. A long handspike placed through the parts of the fall close up to the standing block will prevent this, provided the ends of the handspike are stopped off at a nearby point.

A three-fold purchase can be prevented from twisting by reeving it as shown in Fig. 15.1—in addition, the hauling part coming away from the centre sheave prevents the block from canting.

MECHANICAL ADVANTAGE AND FRICTION

A purchase is a machine whereby a load or resistance can be overcome by means of an effort or applied force.

The mechanical advantage of any machine is found from the ratio

$$\frac{\text{load}}{\text{applied force}} \quad \text{or} \quad \frac{\text{resistance}}{\text{effort}}$$

The mechanical advantage of a machine is normally determined experimentally because it is only in this way that the frictional forces can be found.

Purchases are subject to friction, the amount depending upon the relative sizes of sheave and fall, the number of sheaves, and whether hoisting or lowering. For practical purposes, the total amount of friction within a purchase is assumed to be one-tenth (of the lifted weight) per sheave. In the case of heavy-derrick purchases, the amount of friction must be kept to a minimum. The design of these blocks is such that the friction is assumed to be one-twentieth of the lifted weight per sheave. The British Standards Institution adopts a figure of 2–6% of the load for each sheave depending upon the block type.

When heaving on the hauling part of a purchase, both the weight lifted and the friction have to be overcome.

VELOCITY RATIO

When a purchase is used to move a weight, the fall is hove through a greater distance than the weight, within a given period. The ratio of the larger distance to the smaller distance is the Velocity Ratio.

$$\text{V.R.} = \frac{\text{Velocity of effort}}{\text{Velocity of load}} = \frac{\text{Distance effort moves}}{\text{Distance load moves}}$$

In Figure 15.2 several purchases are illustrated together with the common names. Each name is followed by a number. This number represents the velocity ratio when using the purchase to advantage. In the single whip there is a velocity ratio of one. The double whip has a

375

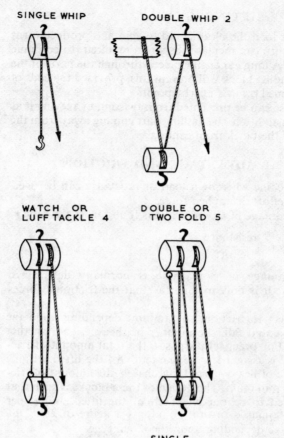

SINGLE WHIP   DOUBLE WHIP 2   GUN TACKLE 3

WATCH OR
LUFF TACKLE 4

DOUBLE OR
TWO FOLD 5

GYN TACKLE 6

THREE FOLD 7

SINGLE
SPANISH BURTON 3

DOUBLE
SPANISH BURTON 4

FIGURE 15.2

velocity ratio of two and there is only one way of using this whip. With the exception of these, and the Spanish Burtons, the velocity ratio will be reduced by one when the purchase is used to disadvantage.

It can be seen from the diagram that if a two-fold purchase is used to advantage to move a weight through 1 m, five parts of rope will each shorten by 1 m, so that 5 m of fall must be hove in, giving a velocity ratio of 5. If used to disadvantage, four parts of rope will shorten by 1 m, 4 m of fall will be hove in and the velocity ratio becomes 4.

EFFICIENCY

All machines have an efficiency, usually expressed as a percentage. Efficiency is the ratio of useful work done on the weight, to the work applied by the effort.

$$\text{Efficiency} = \left(\frac{\text{Useful work done on weight}}{\text{Work applied by effort}} \times 100 \right) \%$$

An efficiency of 100% will indicate that the machine is frictionless, because work done in overcoming friction is not useful work. Friction always exists and the efficiency is therefore always less than 100%.

In a perfect machine, the work done on the load would be equal to the work done by the effort. Let E be the effort, W the load, De the distance through which the effort moves and Dw the distance through which the load moves. Then in a perfect machine,

Work done by effort = Work done on load

or,
$$E \times De = W \times Dw$$

so that,
$$\frac{De}{Dw} = \frac{W}{E}$$

or,
$$V.R. = M.A.$$

In practice, there is an extra resistance to overcome in the form of friction, the weight of the pulleys and the weight of the fall. Call this quantity R and again use the principle of work,

$$E \times De = (W + R) \times Dw$$

so,
$$E \times V.R. = (W + R)$$

or,
$$E = \frac{(W + R)}{V.R.}$$

If we now substitute for R, ten per cent of the load for every sheave and call the number of sheaves n, we get

$$E = \frac{W + \dfrac{nW}{10}}{V.R.}$$

When a purchase is used to advantage $V.R. = (n + 1)$
When a purchase is used to disadvantage $V.R. = n$

The seaman, before putting a purchase into use, may use this expression to determine the approximate stress on the hauling part of the fall. The allowance for friction of 10% errs on the safe side.

Let us suppose that we are lifting 6 kg using a two-fold purchase used to disadvantage, with a V.R. of 4. Allowing 10% for friction, friction becomes 40% of 6 kg or 2·4 kg.

Total load to overcome is $6 + 2\cdot4 = 8\cdot4$ kg.

The applied effort is thus $\dfrac{8\cdot4}{4} = 2\cdot1$ kg.

In this case we need 2·1 kg to lift 6 kg and the Mechanical Advantage is therefore roughly 3.

Suppose the load now moves through 1 m.
Useful work done on load is 6 kg m.
The effort, of 2·1 kg, will have to move through 4 metres with a velocity ratio of 4.
So the work done by the effort is $2\cdot1 \times 4 = 8\cdot4$ kg m.

So the efficiency is $\dfrac{6}{8\cdot4} \times 100\% \qquad = 71\cdot4\%$,

This machine is therefore only about seven-tenths efficient owing to the fact that some of our effort is used in overcoming the 2·4 kg of friction. This is not useful work.
It should be noted also that

$$\text{Efficiency} = \frac{\text{Mechanical advantage}}{\text{Velocity Ratio}} \times 100\%.$$

PRACTICAL POINTS

ton   The seaman often refers to a derrick or block as being a '5-tonne
block' or a 'five-tonne derrick'. By this he means that the derrick or block
ton   has a S.W.L. of 5 tonnes and is not to be used for lifting weights
tons   greater than 5 tonnes.

A single-sheave block is proved to a proof load of four times its S.W.L. This S.W.L. must be stamped on it, together with the maker's name or trade mark, and the number of the block. If the S.W.L. is 5 tonnes and the block is used to lift a weight of 5 tonnes then the stress on the top eye of the block will slightly exceed 10 tonnes. The design of the eye in this block will be such that it has a S.W.L. in excess of 10 tonnes. A 10-tonne shackle would be used for securing the block.

tons tons
tons
tons
tons

Under the Docks Regulations a single-sheave block may be used to lift *twice* its normal S.W.L. provided the weight is attached directly *to the block* and is not attached to a rope passing around the sheave, i.e. the weight is attached to the eye of the block. For example, if a gun tackle is used to lift 5 tonnes, then the top block will be a 5-tonne block, but the lower one will be a 2½-tonne block and the weight will be either attached to the eye of the lower block or else attached to a hook which is integral with the block.

ton tons
ton

A multiple-sheave block will have an eye designed to withstand its S.W.L. together with the maximum stress liable to be applied to the hauling part. A 15-tonne purchase using multiple blocks will have two 15-tonne S.W.L. blocks.

ton
ton

Generally speaking, the size of wire rope to be used with a cargo-lifting block has a diameter which is one-fifteenth of the sheave diameter, i.e. with a 30 cm sheave a 20 mm wire rope will be used. For derricks of more than 15 tonnes S.W.L. the size of wire rope should be one-eighteenth of the sheave diameter in order to prolong rope life.

12-in 0·8-in
tons

Care of Blocks (Various types are illustrated in Plates 5 and 6)

Frequently check the swivel head for free movement by hand. Grease its shank and bearing. Examine the side plates for distortion or buckling; if they are buckled and the runner jams between the plates and the sheave, lives may be lost. Sheaves should turn freely when rotated by hand; examine them for cracks and bush-wear. The grooves must be frequently checked for wear, which will quickly ruin a new wire runner. Check that axle pins are secure and cannot work adrift. Carry out regular and adequate lubrication. It is better to oil the block surfaces rather than to use paint, which may clog oil holes, obliterate marks, and hide defects. Check wooden blocks for decay and splitting. Blocks should never be thrown on to the deck.

Weight of Purchases

A fully rove purchase complete with shackles, weighs approximately as follows:

¼ tonne: three-fold with 25-cm sheaves or a gun tackle with 42-cm sheaves.

ton 10-in 17-in

ton 12-in 18-in ½ tonne: four-fold with 30-cm sheaves or a double luff with 45-cm sheaves.

ton 16-in 1 tonne: five-fold with 40-cm sheaves.

tons 18-in 1½ tonne: six-fold with 45 cm sheaves.

Guys

A guy purchase including shackles and pennants, should have a S.W.L. as follows:

ton ton A 3-tonne S.W.L. Derrick should have 2-tonne S.W.L. guys.

ton ton A 5-tonne S.W.L. Derrick should have 3-tonne S.W.L. guys.

ton ton A 10–15-tonne S.W.L. Derrick should have 4-tonne S.W.L. guys.

ton A 16-tonne and over S.W.L. Derrick should have guys with S.W.L.'s

ton   equal to 25% of the derrick's S.W.L., e.g. a 60-tonne S.W.L.

ton   derrick should have 15-tonne guys.

Care of Ropes

Examine all ropes regularly and frequently for chafe, cutting, internal wear, deterioration of fibres, dryness (in a wire rope), and opening of the lay or *long-jawing*. All sheave grooves must be free from roughness and not deepened by wear. The grooves should be at least as wide as the diameter of the rope.

The diameter of sheaves should be at least five to six times the *diameter* of fibre ropes. Ropes, whether of fibre or wire, should not be used for pulling at an angle to the direction of load lift so that the ropes chafe on the block side-plates. Keep fibre ropes in store away from damp or heat. Hang them up if possible. Encourage good ventilation. Rope-rot often commences internally and is difficult to detect. Dry any wet ropes naturally and not with artificial heat. If ropes cannot be hung up, stow them on gratings. If they are to lie in store for long periods make sure there are no rats present, since they will use the rope fibres for their nests. Wire ropes must be condemned if the total visible number of broken wires (in any length of eight diameters) exceeds 10% of the total number of wires.

This last comment provides a good opportunity to discuss those parts of the *Docks Regulations* (1934) which relate to lifting gear and components.

Annealing of Wrought Iron which Has Become Brittle

This has already been referred to in a previous section. So far as the Regulations are concerned, the heating should be done within a furnace and not in a blacksmith's fire, which may cause uneven heating. The temperature of annealing (650° C) should be maintained for 30–60 minutes.

LIFTING GEAR

Chains, rings, hooks, shackles, and swivels *in general use* are to be annealed at least once every six months if of 12 mm and under in size. ½-in The period is twelve months for larger gear. Both periods may be doubled for gear which is used solely on hand-operated lifting machines. (A recommended practice is to halve all the periods in the case of gear which is being subjected to severe treatment.)

The above requirements are subject to the following exemptions:

Chains, rings, hooks, shackles, and swivels made of steel.

Pitched chains (i.e. chains used on gear wheels).

Rings, hooks, shackles, and swivels which are permanently attached to pitched chains, pulley blocks, or weighing devices.

Screw-threaded parts or specially hardened gear such as ball bearings.

Bordeaux connections (a device resembling a fattened thimble used for joining chain to wire. The wire is spliced round the groove while the chain passes through the thimble centre.).

These items of gear are exempted from annealing on the condition that they are thoroughly examined at least once a year.

Tests and Examinations

When test gear has been subjected to its specified proof load it must be thoroughly examined before being put into use. This, which must be done by a competent person, will enable detection of defects which have been brought to light by the proof load. Pulley blocks should be dismantled during this examination.

Blocks, chains (other than those permanently attached to a derrick), rings, hooks, shackles, and swivels should be tested before putting them into use and also after any repair. They shall also be examined each time before use, unless this has already been done within the preceding three months.

Wire rope is to be tested by breaking a sample—this ultimate stress must reach a required standard. It must be examined at least once every three months, but *every* month if any wire has broken. Wire rope is to be declared unfit if in any length of eight diameters the total number of visible broken wires exceeds 10% of the number of wires in the rope. (E.g., consider wire rope with a diameter of 24 mm. Suppose it is a six-stranded rope with 24 wires in each strand. The total number of wires is thus 144. Hence if in any length of roughly 19 cm the total number of visible broken wires exceeds 14, then the wire is condemned unfit.) The wire is also declared unfit for use if the corrosion, wear, etc., is considered excessive by the person inspecting.

Proof Loads

Chains, rings, hooks, shackles, swivels are proved to twice the S.W.L.
Single-sheave pulley blocks are proved to four times the S.W.L.

tons Multiple blocks up to 20 tonnes S.W.L. are proved to twice the S.W.L.
tons Multiple blocks 21–40 tonnes S.W.L. are proved to the S.W.L. plus
tons 20 tonnes.
tons Multiple blocks over 40 tonnes S.W.L. are proved to one and a half
times the S.W.L.

Pitched chains, their blocks and all permanently attached gear operated
by hand are proved to one and a half times the S.W.L.

Derricks and all permanent attachments relating to the derrick such
as mast lugs and deck eyebolts are to be inspected every year and
thoroughly examined at least once every four years.

All other lifting machinery (cranes, winches, and hoists) is to be
thoroughly examined at least every year.

A thorough examination is done visually, and may include hammer-
testing and dismantling. Derricks, winches, and cranes—completely
rigged for use—are tested before initial use and also after repair. (It is
the practice among some owners to test also at regular intervals, e.g.
every four years. Under the Regulations, if a derrick never needs repair
only one initial test is required in its life.)

Proof Loads

tons S.W.L. up to 20 tonnes—gear is proved to the S.W.L. plus 25%.
tons tons S.W.L. 20 to 50 tonnes—gear is proved to the S.W.L. plus 5 tonnes.
tons S.W.L. over 50 tonnes—gear is proved to the S.W.L. plus 10%.

The load is applied either by hoisting movable weights, or by using a
hydraulic or spring balance. The angle which the derrick makes with
the horizontal during the test is to be stated in the test certificate. If
movable weights are used the derrick is swung as far as possible in both
directions while under load. If the balance is used the pull should be
made at the limits of derrick swing. (This method has the disadvantage
in that the derrick is not *swung* under load and that the mast, rigging,
and other gear is not tested under working conditions.)

Before the test, all blocks and shackles, etc., are tested as laid down
previously, and the derrick is then fully rigged. It will usually be tested
while at its lowest working position—say 45 degrees to the horizontal.

After test, a final examination of all the gear is made and test certificates are issued for all components as required under the Regulations.

When testing heavy derricks the proof load is great, and the balance
should be anchored ashore to a strongpoint so as to avoid deck damage.
A suitable moving weight would be a loaded barge, using a test clock

attached to the lower purchase block to indicate the load. Great attention should be paid to examining the gooseneck after test.

Sometimes, in the case of hydraulic cranes, the available pressure will not cope with the specified proof load. In this case the maximum possible load will suffice.

Fibre Ropes require no test certificate. They should not, however, be used unless they are of suitable quality and free from defect.

Wire Splices are to have at least three tucks with whole strands followed by two tucks with halved strands.

Notice of S.W.L.

All lifting tackle, including derricks, must have its S.W.L. permanently and clearly marked upon it. In the case of chains it is either stamped upon a metal tab attached to the chain or else it is stamped, more usually, on the links. For wires, either a metal tab is used as before or else a notice is conspicuously posted showing sizes of wire and their S.W.L.s.

Exceeding S.W.L.

No gear is to be loaded beyond its S.W.L. except a crane, which can be overloaded as approved by the person in charge. It is done only in exceptional cases, and a record of the overload must be kept. The permission of the owner must first be obtained in writing. (With regard to this, remember that if a single-sheave pulley block has the weight directly attached to the block instead of to a rope passing around the sheave the actual load upon the block shall be considered as one-half of the actual load.)

The Register

Certificates of test, annealing, and all reports of inspections and examinations are to be entered in the Register before the gear concerned is put into use. The Register is to be kept on the vessel.

It is a buff-coloured book called 'Form 99', measuring 31 cm × 16 cm and is entitled on the front cover 'Register of Machinery, Chains, etc., and Wire ropes'. Entered on the front cover is the vessel's name, port of registry, and the owner's name and address. The book is often called simply the 'Chain Register'. $12\frac{1}{2}$ in $6\frac{1}{2}$ in

The inside front cover and page 1 contain instructions regarding examinations and annealing.

Part 1. Pages 2, 4, 6, are for entries concerning four yearly examinations.
Pages 3, 5, 7, are for entries concerning annual inspections.

Part 2. Pages 8–13 are for entries concerning annual thorough examinations of cranes, winches, and hoists and accessory gear, other than derricks.

383

Part 3. Pages 14–17 are for entries concerning the annual thorough examination of gear exempted from annealing.

Part 4. Pages 18–23 are for entries concerning the annealing of gear.

Page 24 contains some recommended minimum factors of safety namely:

tons
tons

Metal parts of lifting machinery: 5 for S.W.L. 10 tonnes or less; 4 for S.W.L. over 10 tonnes.
Wooden structures: 8.
Chains: $4\frac{1}{2}$.
Wire rope: 5.
Fibre rope: 7.

Test certificates, etc., are attached to the Register by means of gummed slips provided within the inside back cover. The Register is designed for eight years' service. When a new one is put into use the old one should be preserved for at least four years.

The following are arbitrary expressions for finding the breaking stresses of:

Fibre Rope

Manila $\dfrac{2D^2}{300}$ Polypropylene $\dfrac{3D^2}{300}$ Terylene $\dfrac{4D^2}{300}$ Nylon $\dfrac{5D^2}{300}$

(where D is the diameter in mm and the result is in tonnes).

Chain

Grade 2 Stud $\qquad \dfrac{30D^2}{600}$

(where D is the diameter of the bar forming the link in mm and the stress is in tonnes).

Wire Rope

(a) 6 strands, 12 wires per strand $\dfrac{15D^2}{500}$

(b) 6 strands, 24 wires per strand $\dfrac{20D^2}{500}$

(c) 6 strands, 37 wires per strand $\dfrac{21D^2}{500}$

(where D is the diameter in mm and the result is in tonnes).

In the foregoing expressions the result is approximate and usually errs on the safe side. In arriving at the safe working load, the breaking stresses are divided by 5 or 6, the safety factor. The results are a useful guide in the absence of more precise information. The same applies to the figure of 10% chosen for frictional effect in purchases. The figure applies more to fibre rope than wire rope. When employing wire or synthetic rope, a figure of 6% is more realistic.

In the past, a safety factor of about 2·5 has often been suggested for use with ropes which are used only occasionally. A wise seaman will reject this notion. Appreciating how rapidly a rope can deteriorate with misuse, the fact that a rope is used only occasionally is irrelevant. With so many materials being used for rope, with widely differing stresses, it is not surprising that one type of rope per ship is recommended for safety.

PATENT DERRICK SYSTEMS

When cargo is handled using one derrick only, the rig is known as a swinging derrick, shown in Fig. 15.16. For heavy loads, a more sophisticated rig is used, shown in Fig. 15.15. The swinging derrick requires four winches and it will be seen from the figures that heaving on the guys will not only increase the thrust at the heel of the derrick but also the stress in the span or topping lift For this reason, guys are sometimes secured to the load itself. The amount by which the derrick can be swung out of the centreline is limited, because the guy must not make too small an angle at the derrick head. If the angle is too small, then the guy loses control. All these disadvantages of the swinging derrick are partially overcome in the design of the Hallen derrick.

The Hallen Derrick (Fig. 15.3)

The boom is stepped on a mast, Y-mast or bipod mast, the basic requirement being a good spread of cross trees. The two guys are secured to the cross trees using swivel-outriggers which are stayed vertically and horizontally. These outriggers cannot swing inboard past the centreline and this maintains a good controlling angle between guy and derrick. In Fig. 15.3 the left-hand outrigger has moved to the right as far as it can and lies in the centreline. The other outrigger has swung outboard, following the derrick, and the outrigger stay—shown dashed—is slack. The plan view shows how the controlling angle is obtained, the derrick having been swung opposite to the direction in the perspective drawing. The guys also double as topping lifts; if both guys are hauled or slacked together, the derrick will top or lower. Three winches are used, two for the guys and one for the lifting wire or purchase, all operated by a joystick control. Limit switches are used to prevent over-topping and over-swinging but these may be adjusted to allow for alteration in the working range and for vertical stowage.

Fig. 15.3 shows only basic principles—in practice, the Hallen may be a heavy-lift derrick. Instead of using two gun tackles for the guys (as shown) the falls may be endless, running through further blocks on the centreline, which therefore gives a traditional topping lift. This type is known as the Hallen Universal derrick and superseded the **Hallen D-Frame** derrick which is also shown in plan view. A large steel bracket is welded to the mast in the centreline, making a D-shape to an observer facing athwartships. Here, the guys do not use outriggers but are attached to heavy, sprung pendants which bear against the D-frame when the derrick is swung, again maintaining a good controlling angle on the guys.

The Hallen derrick is best suited to cargoes such as containers, logs, steel rails, sawn timber and heavy lifts, and is not generally chosen for handling small, general cargo. The derrick can be made ready in a few minutes and employs only one winchman. The guys can carry 75% of the load, so there is good safety aloft. It does the job of a crane, with lower capital expenditure and a higher safe working load compared with current ship cranes. It will swing to 75 degrees from the centreline and work efficiently at only 15 degrees above the horizontal.

Where it is not desired to use outriggers or D-frames, a suitable system is the Velle derrick.

The Velle Derrick (Fig. 15.4)

This is shown in schematic form, with the derrick lowered to the horizontal and the lifting purchase hanging free. The reader is therefore looking along the derrick boom, which is shaded.

A yoke is fitted across the head of the boom, giving it a T-shape. The guys, which also act as topping and lowering units, are secured to the yoke with four short, steel-wire hanger ropes, one of which—for the sake of clarity—is shown dashed. The topping/lowering ends of the falls are made fast to half-barrels on one winch, being wound in the same direction so that the wires are run on or off the winch at uniform speed. The slewing ends are wound on to the half-barrels of another winch in opposite directions, for obvious reasons. A third winch is used for hoisting. The plan view shows how the yoke maintains the controlling angle of the guys at the head of the boom. The use of divergent cargo runners drastically reduces swing and rotation of the load. Winches are remotely controlled using a joystick duplex controller, all levers returning to neutral on being released.

The Stuelcken Derrick (Fig. 15.5)

This heavy-lift derrick is fitted to well over 200 ships. A safe working load of 275 tonnes is not uncommon. While a traditional heavy derrick may take eight hours to rig and require up to six winches, with extra stays on the masts, the Stuelcken is rapidly brought into use, affords easy sea stowage and employs only four winches. It is mounted on the centreline between two unstayed Samson posts in the shape of a V, and can therefore be swung through the posts to serve another hatch. One hoisting winch and one span winch are placed in each post, all four winches being operated by one man, using two levers—one for each post. Bearings, swivels, sheaves and the gooseneck are maintenance-free for up to four years, producing only about 2% friction. The winches have two ratios, using full or half loads. The span tackles are independent, the hoisting fall is endless. Revolving suspension heads are fitted on the posts and swinging-through takes about ten minutes. In the double-pendulum block type, half the cargo tackle may be anchored to the base of the boom. The fall still passes through the two purchases but because one end is anchored, the hook speed is doubled. The safe working load is naturally halved. Typical dimensions of a 275 tonne Stuelcken are: length 25·5 metres, diameter 0·97 metres, diameter of posts 3·4 to 1·5 metres, posts 18 metres apart (upper end) and 8·4 metres apart (lower end). Using full SWL of 275 tonnes, a hook speed of 2·3 metres per minute is obtained. With one end of the lifting purchase anchored, the figures become 137 tonnes and 4·6 metres per minute. By varying winch ratios, combinations of 100 tonnes (treble speed) and 68 tonnes (quadruple speed) can be used. The double-pendulum block type of Stuelcken is swung through by detaching the union table, allowing the lower blocks to swing free each side of the boom. The derrick is then slowly topped until nearly vertical. A bullrope is used to ease the derrick through the vertical until the span tackles have taken the weight on the other side. The union table is re-secured and the derrick is ready to work the other hatch.

Fig. 15.5 also shows a fork-type Stuelcken, using single-pendulum blocks. This is swung-through by detaching the cargo hook and hauling the lifting purchase until both blocks meet and seat in the fork. By the time this occurs, the lower block is above the top block, as shown. The derrick is topped and swung through as before and the lifting purchase extended to serve the other hatch.

tons

ton
83 ft 6 in 3 ft 2 in
11 ft 1 in 4 ft 11 in 58 ft 11 in
27 ft 6 in tons
7 ft 6 in
tons 15 ft
tons
tons

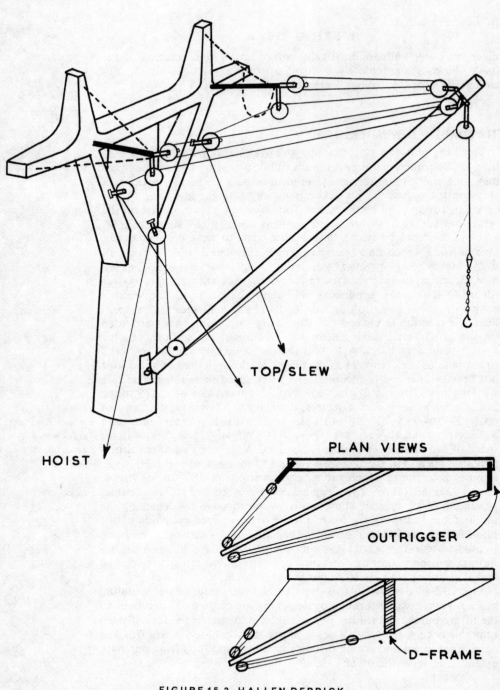

TOP/SLEW

HOIST

PLAN VIEWS

OUTRIGGER

D-FRAME

FIGURE 15.3 HALLEN DERRICK

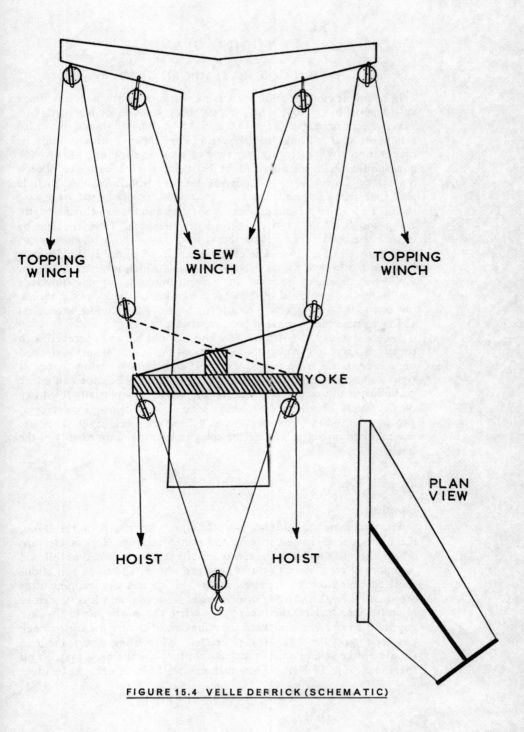

TOPPING
WINCH

SLEW
WINCH

TOPPING
WINCH

YOKE

HOIST

HOIST

PLAN
VIEW

FIGURE 15.4 VELLE DERRICK (SCHEMATIC)

RIGGING EXTEMPORE GEAR

In complete contrast to the foregoing work, the seaman is sometimes called upon to improvise lifting gear using wooden or steel spars to make sheers or a gyn (Figs 15.6 and 15.7). Why it should be called extempore gear is a mystery, since the word means 'without study or preparation'. When rigging this type of gear, the topping lift or back guy should make an angle of at least 45 degrees with the sheers, preferably between 60 and 90 degrees. Suitable woods for spars include teak, oak, elm, ash and beech. Spars can be strengthened by *fishing* them—i.e. securing stout timbers along the middle two-thirds length, using wire lashings or bolts. Strops are prevented from slipping by using rope collars just below the strops, or by fixing *thumb pieces*, shown inset in Fig. 15.6. The effective length of a spar is the distance between the heel of the spar and the *crutch*, which is where the spars are lashed together. *Splay tackles* prevent the heels slipping outwards and should be one-third of the effective length of the spars for sheers, but one-half of the effective length for a gyn. They should be secured as low as possible to prevent bending stresses.

Where lashings and strops cross, they should be well parcelled with canvas. To spread the weight of a spar and the load, the heel is stepped
3-in   on a shoe, made from two layers of 75-mm square-section timber at right angles to each other to form a lamination. The shoe can either be hollowed out or else the heel can be placed on a partially filled bag of wet sand. The deck may need to be shored below. Heel tackles provide multi-directional support and keep the heels rigid. They are not required on a gyn because the splay tackles maintain rigidity of the heels.

Sheerlegs

The two spars are laid flat, with their heels apart and on the shoes, the heads being crossed to take the crutch lashing. Heel tackles are set up, the splay tackle is tightened and the lashing is passed as follows. A timber hitch is placed on one spar just above the crutch and about fourteen round turns are passed around both spars. Six frapping turns are then made through the crutch, as in a seizing, and finally a clove hitch is made around the other spar. When the *martingale* (a forward guy used to prevent backward toppling) and the topping lift or back guy are rigged, the sheers can be erected. When using sheers, the load should not be swung out of the vertical otherwise the heels may lift off the shoes. Fig. 15.6 shows static sheers used like a derrick. In other

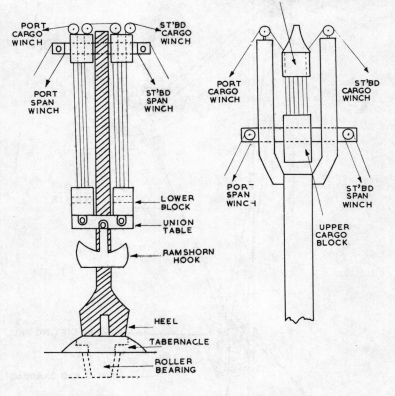

LOWER CARGO BLOCK

PORT CARGO WINCH

ST'BD CARGO WINCH

PORT SPAN WINCH

ST'BD SPAN WINCH

LOWER BLOCK

UNION TABLE

RAMSHORN HOOK

HEEL

TABERNACLE

ROLLER BEARING

PORT SPAN WINCH

ST'BD SPAN WINCH

UPPER CARGO BLOCK

DOUBLE-PENDULUM TYPE

FORK TYPE

FIGURE 15.5 STUELCKEN DERRICKS

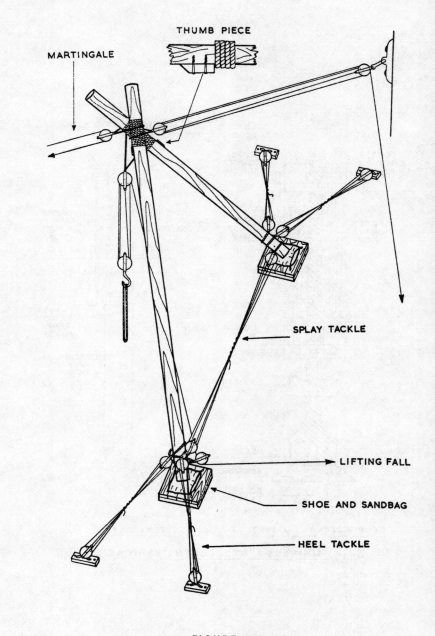

THUMB PIECE

MARTINGALE

SPLAY TACKLE

LIFTING FALL

SHOE AND SANDBAG

HEEL TACKLE

FIGURE 15.6

cases, on smooth ground or on a deck, the sheers can be rigged with very long forward and back guys, and equally long heel guys—two to each heel—leading in opposing directions along the line in which it is desired to shift the load. These are walking sheers and are used as follows. The sheers are tilted 20 degrees towards the load, which is lifted clear. The sheers are then tilted 40 degrees in the opposite direction and the load landed. By heaving on the heel tackles the sheers are moved to a new position and the process repeated. They are being swung-through rather like a Stuelcken derrick. If W is the load lifted, approximate stresses are $0 \cdot 6W$ in the back guy, $0 \cdot 3W$ in the heel tackles, $0 \cdot 5W$ in the splay and $0 \cdot 8W$ in the spar.

The Gyn

Here, three spars are set up as a tripod, two being crossed like sheers and known as *cheeks*. The third spar, or *prypole*, is lashed beneath the crutch of the cheeks. The only purchases required are three splay tackles and a lifting purchase. The lashing is passed as shown, using a timber hitch, half a dozen figure-of-eight turns and finally a clove hitch. The lashing is made not too tight, otherwise the cheeks cannot be opened out at their heels. Once opened, the cheek splay tackle is tightened and the gyn erected by heaving on the other two splays, using a fourth spar as a central lever.

The gyn is laterally unstable and the load must not be swung outside the base triangle. The gyn is primarily used for lifting an object and replacing it in the same position, for example the intermediate shaft of a windlass to enable re-bushing to be carried out. Estimated stress is roughly $0 \cdot 4W$ in the spars, $0 \cdot 6W$ in the spar used for the lifting purchase lead (if needed) and $0 \cdot 3W$ in the splays.

HANDLING TOPMASTS

Lowering a Telescopic Topmast (Fig. 15.8)

A telescopic topmast is one which is housed (in the lowered position) within the hollow lowermast. When erected, it is secured to the lowermast head by means of a steel fid passing through both masts.

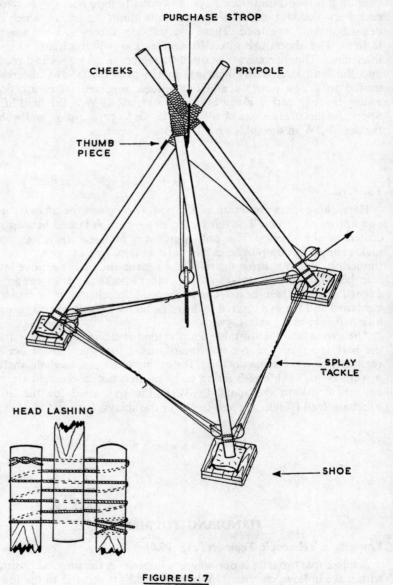

PURCHASE STROP

CHEEKS

PRYPOLE

THUMB PIECE

SPLAY TACKLE

SHOE

HEAD LASHING

FIGURE 15.7

A sheave is fitted in the topmast heel and a reeving rope of chain or wire is kept permanently rove through this sheave, each end being shackled to the lowermast head.

To lower the mast, a mastrope is bent on to the reeving rope, rove through the sheave by means of this, and shackled to the lowermast head. The rigging is slacked, the mastcoat and wedges are removed, the weight of the topmast is taken on the mastrope and the fid is removed.

The topmast is then housed by veering on the mastrope.

To erect the topmast, the procedure is reversed (the mastrope being kept rove while the topmast was housed). Before casting off the mastrope, its end is unshackled and used to pass the reeving rope ready for next time.

Lowering a Fitted Topmast (Fig. 15.8)

This mast is fitted on the fore side of the lowermast and passes through an eye on the lowermast head. Just below the cross trees is a steel gantry secured to the lowermast, containing a hinged pawl which engages in a ratchet plate on the topmast heel. The heel also contains a built-in sheave. A fid passes through the topmast and abuts either the gantry or the cross trees.

To lower, a mastrope is rove through a block on the lowermast head, through a lizard on the topmast, through the topmast sheave and is then led up to the lowermast head where it is secured (see figure). The standing rigging is backed with tackles so that it may be used to guy the topmast, a heel guy is secured to the topmast (not shown), and the standing rigging is slacked down.

The weight of the topmast may now be taken on the mastrope, and the fid removed. The pawl is knocked back clear of the ratchet and the topmast is lowered as desired, guying it carefully.

The standing rigging, or any other obstructions, must be cast off before the lowermast eye is reached. Notice that as long as the mastrope is taut, the lizard acts as a steadying guy on the topmast. The procedure for erecting the topmast will be apparent to the reader, having studied the text and sketches.

DERRICK RIGS

The Union Purchase (Fig. 15.9)

This is occasionally referred to as *married gear*, although its original title was the *yard and stay*. In the days of sailing ships the whips were rove through blocks secured to the yardarm and the mast stay. The name 'yard' is still used for the outboard derrick. In the figure the whips are connected to a union swivel. Although not shown, this unit has three swivels, one each for the whips, and a third for the hook. If only a swivel-

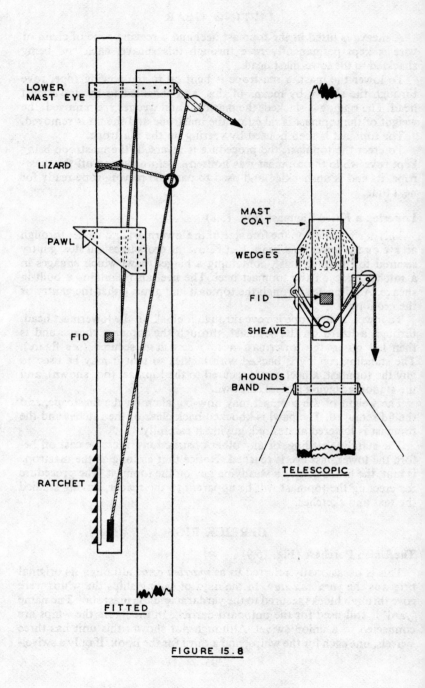

LOWER
MAST EYE

LIZARD

PAWL

FID

RATCHET

FITTED

MAST
COAT

WEDGES

FID

SHEAVE

HOUNDS
BAND

TELESCOPIC

FIGURE 15.8

lugged hook is available the runners are crossed through a shackle and then shackled to the swivel hook.

The rig is used for light loads of up to about 1½ tonnes. The derricks are secured in the plumbing positions, one over the quay and the other over the hatch, by means of standing guys. These guys are omitted from the drawing. Preventer, or lazy guys, are fitted to the outboard sides of the derricks to assist in absorbing the strong side-stresses. The load is lifted on one whip and hove across the deck on the other, slacking away on the first one. The angle between the whips should never exceed 120 degrees, since at this optimum angle the stress in each whip is equal to

tons

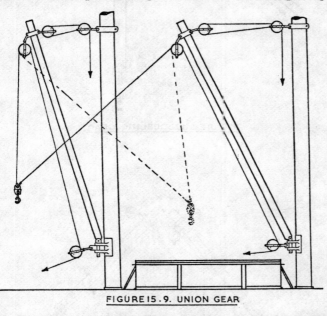

FIGURE 15.9. UNION GEAR

the load. Complete co-ordination between the two winchmen is essential. It is possible, through misjudgement and indifferent rigging, to overload the gear by *more than* 100%. For this reason the safe working loads of the derricks should be halved when *double-derricking*.

Doubling a Whip (Fig. 15.10)

This converts a single whip to a double whip and creates a mechanical advantage. Sufficient wire must be available to reach the farthest part of the worked compartment. If the second spider band shown in the drawing is not available the end of the whip is turned around the derrick just below the head block and shackled to the existing spider band. The derrick should be parcelled with canvas in way of the whip to prevent

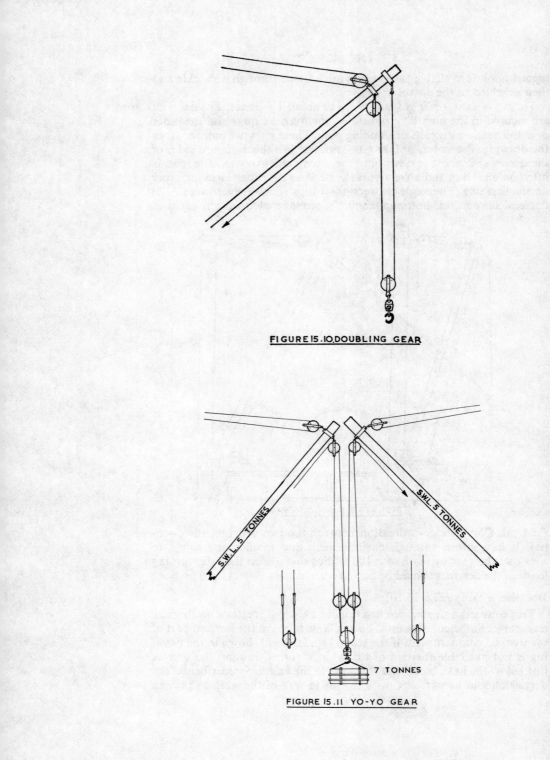

FIGURE 15.10, DOUBLING GEAR

S.W.L. 5 TONNES

S.W.L. 5 TONNES

7 TONNES

FIGURE 15.11 YO-YO GEAR

slipping and chafe. The method is used when it is desired to lift a weight greater than the safe working load of the fall.

The Yo-Yo Gear (Fig. 15.11)

This rig is used when it is desired to lift a weight in excess of the safe working load of the derricks. The heads are placed close together, and the whips shackled to each other via a strop which passes through a travelling block. In the figure, it has been assumed that the safe working load of the fall is insufficient, and gun tackles have been rigged as lifting purchases. Using the figures shown, each derrick will experience a stress of $3\frac{1}{2}$ tonnes. The advantage of the travelling block is apparent if   tons one winch suddenly fails when, without the travelling block, the full load would prevail on one derrick. It is not a popular rig among stevedores, because if the winches are worked at different speeds the travelling block is abutted by the lower block of one purchase, the slower-working one. To avoid using a strop on the whips, one whip is sometimes simply rove through the travelling block and shackled to the other whip. The angle between the whips or purchases should be kept as close to zero as possible. For this reason, the derricks must be very accurately guyed.

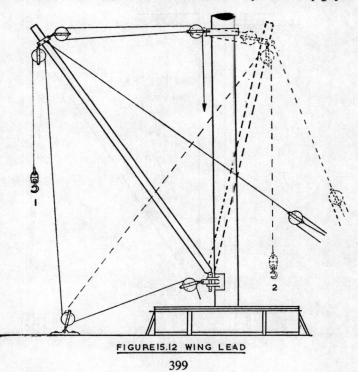

FIGURE 15.12 WING LEAD

The Wing-lead Derrick (Fig. 15.12)

This rarely-seen rig provides a very speedy method of working cargo. The whip is rove through the headblock from the hook, down to the deck, and through a block at the ship's side, and thence to the winch via the heel block. The load is lifted from below in the position (2) and raised clear of the coaming. The inboard guy is then slackened and the stress in the whip, together with its side lead, swings the derrick to (1). The derrick is then re-plumbed over the hatch by heaving on the inboard guy. The thrust in the derrick is increased in this rig compared with the traditionally-rove whip, and loads must therefore be light. The rig could be used for loading provided the wing-lead was shifted to the right-hand side of the coaming. The guy will then be rigged on the shore side of the derrick.

The Backweight or Deadman Rig (Fig. 15.13)

This is used to load or discharge with a single derrick. A lazy guy is led from the derrick head, through a block on the cross trees, and is

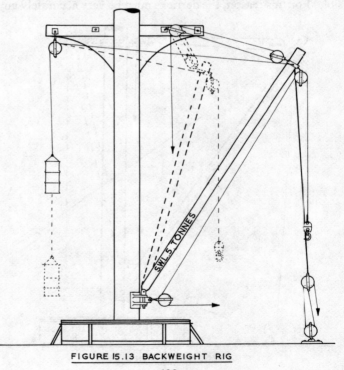

FIGURE 15.13 BACKWEIGHT RIG

then shackled to any suitable weight, such as a large drum of concrete or water. The derrick is plumbed overside by heaving on the *steam guy*, i.e. the one on the right-hand side of the drawing, which is led to a winch. The deadman is then rising. As soon as the steam guy is slacked the deadman descends and swings the derrick inboard, the swing being controlled by the steam guy. It provides a quick method of working light cargoes. It is popular in certain parts of the London docks for discharging timber cargoes. The backweight is a danger to persons on deck, and where another derrick is available it is plumbed overside and the lazy guy rove through its headblock. The deadman then operates overside.

The Liverpool Rig (Fig. 15.14)

This is used for light cargoes such as bagged goods and sacks of hides. A single derrick is plumbed overside and secured with standing guys

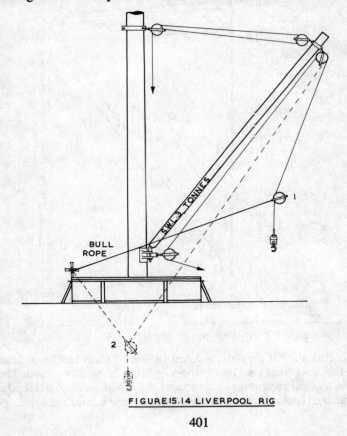

FIGURE 15.14 LIVERPOOL RIG

3–4-in

(not shown). The whip is led through a travelling block which is secured, by means of a 24–32-mm fibre bullrope, to a portable bollard clamped to the hatch coaming. When the whip is slack the bullrope-operator heaves on the rope and belays the line so that the block is in (2). The hook is lowered, the load lifted and raised. As it clears the coaming, the bullrope is slacked and the load is veered across the deck (1). When the load is plumb under the derrick head the bullrope is all slack. With an experienced man using the bullrope the method provides a very rapid discharge of cargo.

The Heavy or Jumbo Derrick (Fig. 15.15)

tons

These derricks have safe working loads often in excess of 100 tonnes. The basic principles are shown in the drawing. A sheave is built into the

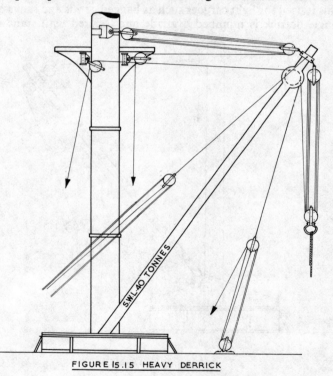

FIGURE 15.15 HEAVY DERRICK

derrick so that the lifting purchase can be used to advantage. A lead block on the cross trees enables the topping lift to be similarly used. The gain in mechanical advantage also reduces the thrust on the derrick, the head purchase block, the spider band, the gooseneck, and the topping-lift mast shackle. The stresses in the falls are also reduced. Both guys are winch controlled. During the use of this type of derrick the mast is rigged with extra stays.

When preparing the derrick for use all the wires and blocks should be carefully examined, particularly the sheaves for free rotation. The derrick is stowed against the mast and secured at its head either by chains and wedges, or a steel clamping-band, or both. Sometimes the top lifting-purchase block is left in position and a canvas hood shrouds the block and the derrick head.

A gantry, or a gallows, is usually fitted to the mast just above the derrick head. A block is hung off here and a gantline is rove through it to heave the topping lift blocks to their positions. With these secured in place, a heaving line is rove through the blocks. The topping-lift fall is bent on to the end and the heaving line is used to reeve the wire fall. The guy pendants are shackled to the spider band and their purchases are set up tight. The topping lift is then hove as tight as possible and a breaking-out wire passed round the derrick head above the spider band. The derrick is then detached from the securing band or chains, and the breaking-out wire stressed. The derrick then moves away from the mast, and very soon the topping lift becomes completely taut as it takes the weight of the derrick.

The derrick is then lowered to the horizontal position, controlling it with guys, when the lifting purchase is more conveniently secured and rove. The derrick is tested for free rotation at the gooseneck.

If, before the derrick is broken out, the topping-lift blocks abut each other so that the purchase cannot be hove tight, a wire will have to be rigged on the opposite side of the derrick to the breaking-out wire, so that the derrick can be eased away from the mast under control. Without this easing wire, the derrick may jump away from the mast to the extent of the slack topping-lift fall and damage the block shackles.

The Swinging Derrick (Fig. 15.16)

In this case a single derrick is used to load or discharge cargo, swinging it from hold to ship's side by means of two steam guys (winch controlled). The derrick can be used to the extent of its safe working load provided the whip is of sufficient strength. If a load of more than 3 tonnes is to be lifted the whip will normally require doubling.　　　　tons

Precautions when Handling Heavy Lifts

All gear involved, including strops and eyebolts, should be carefully examined beforehand. The stability of the ship must be checked so as to make sure that the rise in the centre of gravity of the ship will not produce a condition of negative metacentric height. In this connection, free-surface effects may have to be reduced.

The vessel should be on an initial even keel with moorings taut and manned. Barges not in immediate use must be cast off. Preventer stays will be rigged on the mast.

If loading the weight on deck the latter may require shoring from below. The guys should be rigged at 30 degrees to the deck and making a broad angle with the derrick. Winches will have to be checked and manned with reliable persons.

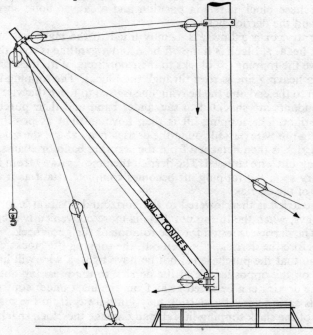

FIGURE 15.16 SWINGING DERRICK

The load must be plumbed by the derrick head and slung under the supervision of a competent person. Light lines are often secured to the load to act as steadying lines.

When discharging, the critical moment occurs when the load is just floated clear of the deck or tanktop, for the centre of gravity of the load is then virtually at the derrick head and the centre of gravity of the ship rises in proportion. If the stability of the ship becomes negative the vessel will fall over to an angle of loll. The load is then preferably landed, and the stability of the ship improved. If this is impossible lighters are sometimes secured to that side of the ship which will be the high side when the load is swung out of the fore-and-aft line.

404

As the load moves from the fore-and-aft line, the vessel will acquire an increasing list, whether or not her stability is negative.

When lowering the load into a truck on the jetty, due allowance must be made for the fact that at the instant when the load is landed the ship will rapidly right herself and cause a sudden lateral drag upon the truck. To prevent this, the offshore guy must be instantly slacked down together with a rapid veering of the lifting fall.

When loading the weight, the same reasoning applies. As soon as the weight is taken, the ship will heel due to a lateral movement of the ship's centre of gravity. This is also the critical moment of the operation as the centre of gravity of the load virtually rises to the derrick head. As the load is swung inboard, the heel decreases.

The following is an extract from a pamphlet issued by the Chain Testers' Association of Great Britain and is designed to be of help to all persons engaged in the use of lifting machinery:

DO

(1) Know the weight being lifted and allow for the purchase weight.

(2) Select lifting tackle of adequate strength and see that it is properly marked; no chain or rope should be used for any load exceeding the safe working load.

(3) See that end links, rings, or shackles are riding freely on any hook on which they hang.

(4) Use wood or other packing to protect the sling from any sharp edges on the load.

(5) Avoid shocks due to (a) the load slipping or (b) snatch in starting. The stress on all gear is much greater if the load is applied suddenly.

DO NOT

(1) Use an excessively pitted, corroded, or worn chain. (Condemn it and cut it up.)

(2) Use a chain in which links are locked, stretched, or do not move freely.

(3) Join chains by bolting or wiring links together.

(4) Shorten chains by tying knots in them (use an adjuster or keep an adequate supply of slings of suitable length).

(5) Drag a chain from under a load or drop it from a height.

(6) Hammer a link to straighten or force it into position.

(7) Carry idle slings on the hook at the same time as a loaded sling.

Multiple Leg Slings

The Association recommends a standard normal practice of marking and certifying these slings with the safe working load, at 90 degrees between legs. Above this angle the safe working load decreases rapidly.

If all the legs cannot be loaded equally, use a sling strong enough to support the load safely on those legs which may have to carry it.

Endless Chain Slings

These must be used with care to avoid possible overloading or damage to links by bending too sharply. The Association recommends as a standard normal practice the marking and certifying of these slings with a safe working load equal to $1\frac{1}{2}$ times the load on the single chain.

Wire Rope Slings

These should never be bent sharply, allowed to come into contact with hot metal, or to become rusty.

Fibre Ropes

These must be examined frequently for external chafe, cutting, internal wear between strands, and deterioration of fibre. Wet or damp ropes should be kept in a well-ventilated store and not dried rapidly in a boiler house, or left to dry out on the open ground.

CHAPTER XVI

ROPE AND CANVAS

FIBRE ROPE

THE process of manufacture entails combing selected fibre into long ribbons known as sliver, which are later twisted up into yarns. These yarns are then twisted into strands, three or four of the latter being finally laid up into the finished rope.

The primary object of twisting fibres together in a rope is that by mutual friction they may be held together when a stress is applied to the whole.

The essential features of a good rope are carefully selected and blended high-grade fibre, careful spinning into yarns of uniform size and strength, forming the yarns into solid circular strands with all yarns parallel, the strand being even, smooth, and having the correct degree of twist, and laying three or more of these strands into rope at the correct angle to suit the required working conditions.

Standard Lay implies a rope with that angle of lay which experience shows combines pliability, strength, and ability to withstand chafe to the best advantage for all general work.

Soft or *Long Lay* implies a rope in which the angle of lay is less than normal, the angle of lay being that between the axis of the strand and the axis of the rope. The pliability and, to some extent, the breaking stress are increased, but the elasticity is reduced. It is more liable to absorb water and lose its shape, but is very necessary for work such as sailmaking.

Hard, Firm, or *Short Lay* implies a rope in which the angle of lay is greater than normal. The effect is to increase the ability of the rope to retain its shape under load, and to reduce the absorption of water. Both the pliability and the breaking stress are, however, reduced, but the elasticity is increased.

Right-hand lay means the final laying up of the strands, regardless of the rope's construction, in the same as a screw-thread. In the trade it is described as a Z-*twist*. Left-hand lay is the reverse and is described as an S-*twist*. These are illustrated in Fig. 16.1 together with the construction of rope. It will be noticed that the fibres and the strands have the same twist, but the yarns have a reverse twist, i.e. in a right-handed rope the fibres are twisted together right-handed, the yarns are twisted left-handed, and the strands are laid up right-handed.

Three-stranded rope is referred to as *plain lay*. Seamen refer to it as a hawser-lay if it is right-handed, but the members of the rope trade find that it is frequently confused with cable lay so that when ordering it is preferable to use the term 'plain lay'.

Four-stranded rope is sometimes called *shroud lay*. It has a bigger bearing surface compared with plain lay. Its weight is greater and its strength less. The four strands are laid round a central fibre heart or core. Both three- and four-stranded ropes are normally laid up right-handed.

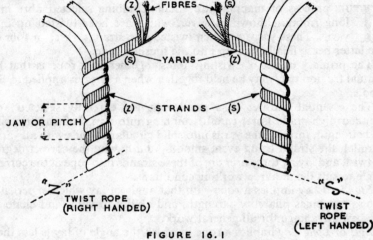

FIGURE 16.1

Cable or *Water Lay* is made by laying together three ropes each of three strands. The characteristic features are its greater pliability and elasticity compared with plain lay of equal size. The weight is slightly less and the strength is substantially reduced. Cable-lay rope has a good resistance to water penetration. If three 100-m ropes are laid into cable lay, the resulting rope would be about 83-m long. It is normally composed of three right-handed ropes laid up together left-handed. When required, however, it can be manufactured with a reverse lay. It is frequently used as a towing spring attached to a length of wire rope. It is essential that the two lines should have the same lay, otherwise the fibre line will tend to unlay itself. Since wire rope is invariably right-handed, it follows that most cable-laid towing springs also have a right-handed lay.

Warp-lay rope is the same as cable lay except that the first and final lays are very hard. Warps are often supplied twelve stranded, i.e. four

120 fathom
100 fathoms

primary ropes each having three strands are laid up together. For some work, the warp lay may even have fifteen strands.

Unkinkable Lay is not illustrated, since it appears the same as plain lay at first sight. This type of rope, specially made for lifeboat falls, has the yarns spun with the same twist as the strands instead of as in ordinary rope. This tends to eliminate the tendency of orthodox rope to kink and twist when working in multiple blocks.

Plaited mooring ropes of natural or synthetic fibre are highly flexible and almost undamaged by kinking. They have a lower stretch and ultimate extension than laid ropes of a similar size, but are nearly as strong.

This type of rope is found to develop an extremely good grip on winch drums and capstan barrels. Some plaited ropes consist of four left-handed strands and four right-handed strands laid up in pairs. In similar service, the life of a plaited rope may be double that of a plain-lay rope. It is particularly useful when the rope is liable to twist or turn in use. Natural-fibre plaited ropes are treated with water-repellent in manufacture.

Hard-fibre Ropes

1. Manila. This is made from *abaca* fibre, which comes from a plant belonging to the banana family. Its colour varies from ivory white to darkish brown. The production of this fibre constitutes the most important industry in the Philippines. It is available in various grades, the inner fibres of the leaf being much finer than those removed from the outer edge.

As a rope it is smooth, glossy, strong, flexible, very durable, easy to handle, and has a very high resistance to sea-water rotting. It is the most common natural fibre in use at sea. The following figures relate to the finest-quality manila rope:

Three-stranded, 48-mm diameter, weight 352 kg per 220 m coil:
Breaking stress 17·5 tonnes.
Four-stranded, 48-mm diameter, weight 349 kg per 220 m coil:
Breaking stress 15·6 tonnes.
Nine-stranded cable lay, 48-mm diameter, weight 309 kg per 220 m coil:
Breaking stress 10·5 tonnes. (If plaited, this size of rope has a breaking stress of 17 tonnes.)
Manila rope will stretch about 25% of its length.

2. Sisal. This fibre is taken from *aloe* leaves, in the pineapple family. East Africa and Java are the main producing centres. During the war, when manila was extremely scarce, sisal was in wide use in this country and at sea. Very few failures were reported, and in fact it is a fibre of very consistent strength, a very good sisal being of equal strength to medium-grade manila.

As a rope it is an attractive creamy-white colour, very brittle, glossy, and generally swells more than manila when wet. It is not a smooth rope, and its hairy surface promotes considerable discomfort after prolonged handling with the bare flesh. The following figures are for best-quality sisal:

Three-stranded, 48-mm diameter, weight as manila:
  Breaking stress 14·7 tonnes.
Four-stranded, 48-mm diameter, weight as manila:
  Breaking stress 13·2 tonnes.
Nine-stranded cable lay, 48-mm diameter, weight as manila:
  Breaking stress 8·9 tonnes. (If plaited, this size of rope has a breaking stress of 14 tonnes.)

Sisal rope is not generally considered suitable for marine work where manila is available.

3. Coir. This is the fibre of the *coconut* and is removed after the shell has been water-soaked for many months. It comes mainly from India and Ceylon, and is unique in that it is imported from there not as a fibre but as a yarn, already spun by the natives. It is very elastic, red in colour, rough to handle, floats very easily, and is extremely resistant to sea-water rotting. It is often called *grass* or *bass line*. It is principally

16 and 22 in circumference

used as towing and harbour springs, varying between 128 and 176 mm in diameter as a cable-laid rope. It is about one-half the weight of manila and roughly one-sixth as strong. The following figures are for best-quality coir:

Three-stranded, 48-mm diameter, weight 203 kg per 220 m coil:
  Breaking stress 3·05 tonnes.
Nine-stranded cable lay, 48-mm diameter, weight 153 kg per 220 m coil:
  Breaking stress 2·03 tonnes.

As a cable-laid rope, coir will stretch between 60 and 100%. As a three- or four-stranded rope, its elasticity is about 45%.

Soft-fibre Ropes

1. Hemp. Originally the bulk of this fibre came from Russia. Nowadays it is exported from India, Italy, the Balkans, and New Zealand. The hemp produced in New Zealand and St. Helena is not as strong as manila, and is mainly used for the cores of wire ropes.

Italian hemp is generally regarded as the best-quality hemp, having a strength one-fifth greater than top-grade manila. It has largely been superseded by manila, and is now found at sea as boltrope, small cordage, and high-grade twine.

Indian hemp is equally water-resistant as Italian hemp, and Bombay hemp is now of greatly improved quality as a result of strict Government grading.

Bolt-rope is spun from soft hemp and gives a special soft lay for easy handling and non-stretch qualities. It is a tarred rope. A 48 mm tarred bolt-rope made of soft hemp weighs 420 kg per 220-m coil and has a breaking stress of 12 tonnes (*three stranded*). If supplied untarred, the weight is reduced by 25% and the strength increased by 20%.

2. Jute. This is mainly used for hessian manufacture and the cores of wire rope. It is weaker than hemp.

3. Flax. This is used for sail and tarpaulin canvas. It is ideal for use as a sewing-twine due to its high resistance to abrasion.

4. Cotton. This fibre makes an excellent rope for use as a power drive. At sea it is generally found as an ornamental rope, particularly on gangways. It is very soft rope and easily soiled.

Synthetic-fibre Ropes

1. Polypropylene rope is the lightest synthetic rope, 60% stronger than manila. It stretches 40%, absorbs only 0·1% water and melts at 165°C. A 48 mm polypropylene rope will break at 27·5 tonnes.

2. Polythene is about twice as strong as cotton. As a rope, its strength lies midway between manila and nylon. It absorbs only 0·01% of water and will float almost indefinitely. It has made coir obsolescent for this reason. It melts at 135°C and shrinks about 4% at 60°C. It is unaffected by most industrial chemicals and micro-organisms. It offers good resistance to sunlight and abrasion. Size for size it is 7 times stronger than coir. A 48-mm polythene rope weighs 252 kg per 220-m coil and has a breaking stress of 22·4 tonnes.

3. Nylon and Terylene. Ropes made of these fibres are immensely strong, soft, and pliable. They are waterproof and their surfaces dry very quickly. They are equally flexible when at extremes of temperature and when wet or dry. They are pest- and corrosive-resistant. They are virtually impervious to rot and mildew and have a low fire risk. Due to their low melting-points, small cordage may have the ends of the strands sealed by momentarily holding them in a flame. This avoids whipping. nylon is generally more elastic than terylene, but both are good in this respect.

When splicing these ropes at least four tucks should be made, due to the slippery surface of the fibres. For this reason knots should be avoided, as they tend to slip. They are not so easy to handle, compared with, say, manila, due to their very smooth surface.

The resistance of these ropes to abrasion is extremely good. The outer

411

yarns, if abraded, form a *fuzz* of fibre which effectively prevents further abrasion. This means that the internal yarns of a used rope are not affected in strength, and there is no high inter-yarn and inter-strand abrasion, such as is often seen with sisal and manila.

The main danger points with these fibres are that nylon is attacked by strong acids and terylene by strong alkalis.

Nylon absorbs about one-third of the moisture taken in by a hemp rope, while terylene absorbs only a twentieth of this latter amount.

A 48-mm three-stranded nylon rope weighs about 330 kg per coil of 220 m and has a breaking stress of 42 tonnes. The reader should compare this with the stresses given for best-quality manila rope. Strength for strength, a nylon rope of about 30 mm may be substituted for a manila rope (best quality) of 48 mm diameter.

1-in

The following figures are of interest: Considering 8-mm ropes, each of three strands, terylene has a wet strength of 100%, Italian hemp has a wet strength of 80%, while the figure for best sisal is 90%. The com-

2000 lb   1340 lb
1030 lb

parable breaking loads are 1020 kg for terylene, 607 kg for Italian hemp, and 480 kg for sisal.

Nylon and terylene ropes are in wide use as *tails*, i.e. lengths of synthetic rope joined to mooring lines to act as shock absorbers. It is essential that both ropes have the same lay. The use of these tails effectively cushions the ropes to which they are attached and saves them from

6 fathoms

progressive damage. The tail will usually be about 12 m in length, fitted to the shore end of a mooring line, and its eye will be protected

6-in
4½–5 in
circumference

from bollard-chafe by means of a leather parcelling. A 48-mm mooring line will need a tail of 40 mm in diameter.

Waterproofing

This service is available from rope manufacturers at a small extra cost. It increases the life of the rope, prevents the entry of sea-water impurities, reduces kinking, hardening, and swelling. It affects neither the weight nor the breaking stress of the rope and provides an added advantage in that when the rope is discarded it may easily be sold to paper mills.

Preservation

Most fibre ropes are oil-spun, a small amount of lubricant being introduced at the time of manufacture to soften and oil the fibres. Excessive internal friction is thereby reduced, increasing the life of the rope. A dry-spun rope is stainless but non-waterproof.

The original methods of tarring a rope with Archangel tar increased the weight of the rope by 12½% and considerably decreased the breaking stress. Modern methods, using pure pine tars, Archangel tar, rot-proofing, and waterproofing compounds in conjunction, increase the weight

412

by only 5% and decrease the breaking stress by only 5%. The Gourock Ropework Company immersed three ropes into a tank which was bacterially rich. After two months of immersion, ordinary sisal showed a strength loss of 58%, old-fashioned tarred rope showed a loss of 23%, while the most-up-to-date tarring protected the rope to such a degree that only 5% strength loss was experienced.

Any strength losses due to tarring are more than offset by the prolonged life of continually submerged ropes.

If a very dry rope is required rot-proofing is possible by a process known as *tanning* or *barking* with 'Cutch Chrome'. It should be noted that straightforward tarring, used without a water-proofing compound, does not render a rope water-repellent.

The Care of Ropes

On an average-sized merchant ship there may be as much as 9 miles of fibre rope, weighing 15 tonnes. When one considers that a 220-m coil of high-grade manila rope, 72 mm in size, may cost £350, there is one very good reason for giving ropes every attention, quite apart from the safety aspect. [margin: tons 120-fathom 9 in]

The common causes of rope failure are excessive stress (which damages fibre more quickly than any other cause), abrasion or cutting on a sharp object, exposure to sulphur dioxide fumigation gas, and bad storage with inadequate ventilation, particularly in the case of ropes stored away in a wet condition.

Rotting very often commences on the inside of a rope and is difficult to detect unless the lay is open. If fibres are able to be rubbed loose or if there is much dust within the lay it is a sure sign of dry rot. If the interior of the rope is much darker than the outside it is a sign of dampness, while a grey powdery substance indicates mildew and poor ventilation.

The care of ropes has already been mentioned in Chapter XV; they must be stored away when *dry*, and either hung on wooden pegs, galvanised hooks, or stowed on gratings. They should be turned on these gratings every so often so that the weight of the coil is taken on a different part of the rope. The storeroom should be dry and airy, and away from weather. The ideal temperature is between 10° and 20°C, while the relative humidity most favourable to long life is between 40 and 65%. [margin: 50° 70°F]

Ropes, if dried artificially in extreme heat, will become dry (i.e. the lubricant will dry out) and brittle. On deck in port ropes should again be stowed on gratings and protected from sunlight, rain, and frost. The freezing of ropes is detrimental to their life, for the minute ice particles cut through the fibre.

After use, ropes should be cleaned and dried. After immersion in salt water they should ideally be hosed down with fresh water.

Kinks cause permanent injury to a rope. Knots cause kinks, and therefore splices are better. A short splice is stronger than a long splice. The safe stress on a rope should be regarded as about one-sixth of the breaking load. A sudden jerk may increase the stress up to eight times its value. Before making a splice it should be ascertained that there is no 'turn' left in the rope, which, when stressed, will continually pull at the splice.

A right-handed rope should always be uncoiled by taking away that end of the coil which enables the turns to be taken off anti-clockwise, i.e. the coil is unwound left-handed. The reverse applies to left-handed ropes. Naturally therefore, a right-handed rope is coiled down so that the turns *form* clockwise; the reverse is true for left-handed ropes.

Ropes should never be subjected to bad nips; if this is unavoidable the nip must be frequently freshened. The diameter of rollers should be ten to twelve times the diameter of the rope which is to be passed around them. The same figures apply to bollards and warping drums. A capstan or drum that will only revolve clockwise should be used only for a right-handed rope.

In Fig. 16.1 the term *jaw* is used. This refers to the pitch of the rope and is the distance along one complete spiral of a strand. A soft-lay rope will have a longer jaw than a hard-lay rope. When a rope is badly stretched so that it suffers permanent elongation the inside of the strands is quite clearly visible from the exterior of the rope, which is said to be *long-jawed*, for the pitch has extensively increased.

Whenever some line is cut from a coil, either the length removed or the length remaining should be marked up near by.

Miscellaneous Cords and Twines

Small Cordage is usually referred to at sea as small stuff. Some of the more common ones are listed below. The size of small stuff is often referred to by the number of threads or yarns. A three-stranded rope having three yarns in each strand would be known as nine-thread line. Generally, small cordage can be ordered by length in coils of 220, 110 or 55 m.

Houseline is made from Indian hemp and is 3-ply, i.e. three yarns twisted together. It is usually tarred and sold in balls by weight, usually of about 110 m to the kg.

Marline is similar to houseline but is 2-ply. Both marline and houseline are used for serving and whipping ropes.

Hambroline is a small tarred hemp used as a boltrope or very heavy servings. As a yacht lacing it is untarred Italian hemp. It is sold three-stranded in 55-m hanks, and runs at 6, 7 or 8 mm diameter.

Spunyarn is a tarred, soft hemp comprising two, three, or four threads twisted together. It is mainly used for serving and covering wire ropes and standing rigging. According to the number of threads it is sold either by weight or by length in coils.

Oakum is a mass of oily fibre made from tow or old ropes which have been picked to pieces. It is usually bought in small bales and ordered by weight. It is chiefly used for caulking deck seams, and is rolled into a long thread for this purpose. Three threads are necessary to caulk a new deck, while one or two threads are usually used to renovate an established wooden deck. The oakum is hardened down into the seams and then *payed* with molten pitch to seal the seam.

Tarred Cordage is made from soft hemp and used for general deck purposes, nine-thread line being popular as a heaving line. It is made in various sizes from nine to twenty-one threads, the corresponding cir-cumferences being 7–15 mm. It is often referred to as ratline.

Dressed hemp lines include 4- and 5-mm line for boat lacings, awning lacings and cod-line. It has a fine finish and is strong but light. It is obtained in 55- or 110-m coils and may also be sold in 8 or 10 mm sizes for signal halliards or plaited loglines.

Leadlines are made from high-grade cable-laid hemp. The final lay is usually left-handed. Hand leadlines are about 8–10 mm in diameter and supplied in 55-m coils. The heavier deep-sea leadlines are about 12 mm in diameter and supplied as 220-m coils.

Patent loglines are made of polythene (low absorption) or untarred Indian or European hemp, in coils varying from 73 to 220 m. The line is usually plaited and may have a copper-wire core. The size is from 10 to 12 mm.

Twine, 3-ply for seaming and 5-ply for roping, is made of flax or hemp. It is sold in 0·28 kg balls. Other twines made of polypropylene are used for general lacing work.

Signal halliards. Polythene is ideal, in 73-m coils, owing to its low water-absorption.

Bends, Hitches, and Knots

The use of these may locally reduce the strength of a rope by as much as 40–60%, and this should constantly be borne in mind when working with rope, upon which the safety of life may depend.

The terms used in this work are:

The *Bight*, which refers to the middle part of the rope between the ends, and also to a loop made from the rope. A rope suspended between two points is said to hang in a bight.

The *Standing Part* is the part of the bight nearest to the eye, bend, or hitch. It is also that part of a tackle fall which is secured to the block.

The *Running End* is that part of a rope which leads through a fairlead, which moves through pulleys, or which first comes away from a coil.

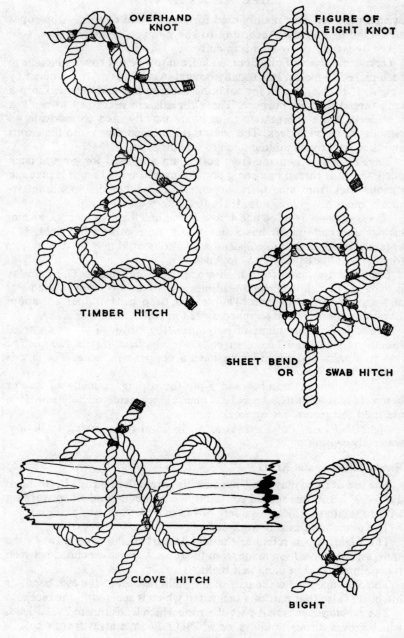

OVERHAND KNOT

FIGURE OF EIGHT KNOT

TIMBER HITCH

SHEET BEND OR SWAB HITCH

CLOVE HITCH

BIGHT

FIGURE 16.2

The *End* of a rope is the short length at the extremities of a rope. It also refers to the very short piece left after making a knot, bend, or hitch. The *Bare* or *Fag End* is the extreme end of a rope.

In Fig. 16.2 the following are illustrated:

The *Overhand Knot* which may be put into a rope so that a person can grip the line without his hands slipping. It is the basis of several bends and hitches, and is, in fact, a half-hitch.

The *Figure-of-eight Knot* is put into a rope to prevent it from unreeving through a block.

The *Timber Hitch* is often used to secure a line to a spar or a bale. If it is desired to tow or drag the object, or perhaps to hoist it, it is kept steady by passing a half-hitch round the object at a distance from the timber hitch and close to the forward or upper end.

The *Sheet Bend or Swab Hitch* is used for joining two ropes together or to secure an end to an eye. If it is made around both sides of a hook it is called a *Midshipman's Hitch*. If in the figure the end is again passed around the eye and finally tucked under the standing part, the result is a double sheet bend.

The *Clove Hitch* forms a quick means of securing a rope to a spar, rail, etc. It tends to slip under a side pull.

In Fig. 16.3 the following are illustrated:

The *Reef Knot*, which is used to join together two ropes of equal size. It consists of two overhand knots. The ends must be crossed opposite ways each time, i.e. left over right—right over left, or vice versa. If the overhand knots are made the same way each time a granny knot results, which usually either slips or, paradoxically, jams hard. If the lines are of unequal size, or if the reef shows signs of slipping, the ends may be stopped back on to the standing parts.

The *Bowline* forms an excellent method of introducing a temporary eye into the end of a rope. It is extremely reliable.

The *Rolling Hitch* has an extra turn compared with the clove hitch. This makes it suitable for withstanding side stresses, and it is therefore often used for stoppering-off a rope.

The *Half-hitch* is probably the most well-known hitch of all. It provides a very quick means of securing a line. It does not slip or jam, provided *two* half-hitches are made and preferably after passing a round turn around the spar, rail, etc. The end may be stopped back on to the standing part.

The *Marline-spike Hitch* is useful for securing a long object within the bight of a rope. It may be used to send gear aloft to men working in the rigging.

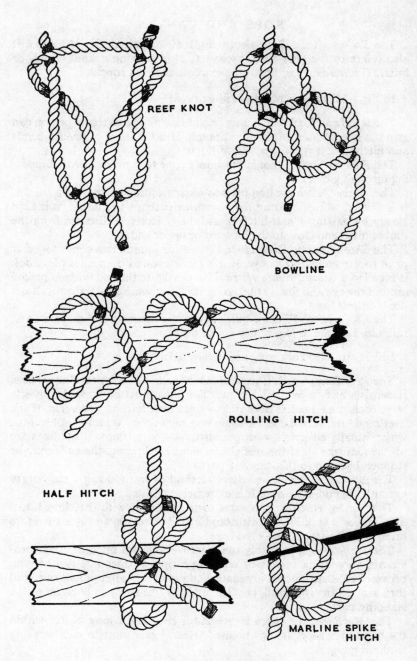

REEF KNOT

BOWLINE

ROLLING HITCH

HALF HITCH

MARLINE SPIKE
HITCH

FIGURE 16.3

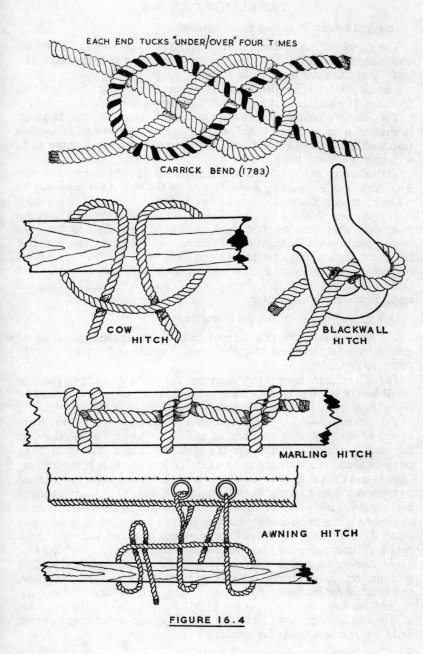

EACH END TUCKS "UNDER/OVER" FOUR TIMES

CARRICK BEND (1783)

COW HITCH

BLACKWALL HITCH

MARLING HITCH

AWNING HITCH

FIGURE 16.4

In Fig. 16.4 the following are illustrated.

The *Carrick Bend* makes a fairly long hitch when joining two ropes, and is therefore useful when passing the lines over a warping drum.The ends must be seized back to the standing parts.

The *Cow Hitch* again forms a quick means of securing a line to a rail, spar, etc. It becomes unstable if only one part of the rope is stressed.

The *Blackwall Hitch* secures a line to a hook. When the standing part is stressed it jams the bare end which is tucked beneath it. If another turn had been passed around the hook with the end it would have made a double blackwall hitch.

The *Marling Hitch* is used to lash bundles of sails, tarpaulins, etc. The work is called *marling down*. The eye in the end of the rope may be made by means of a bowline or timber hitch.

The *Awning Hitch* provides a quick means of unrigging awnings when the wind freshens. It should be noticed how the end has been tucked back so that a bight is left protruding. When the end is pulled the bight no longer exists and the hitch is cast off. This method of providing a quick-slipping hitch may be used on the sheet bend, clove hitch, bowline, rolling hitch, the last one of two or more half-hitches, and several others, not illustrated.

In Fig. 16.5 the following are illustrated:

The *Clove Hitch*, this time formed on the bight of the rope, using no end. A loop and a reverse loop are closed together and slipped over the object to be secured.

The *Sheepshank* temporarily shortens the bight of a rope. The two small bights, protruding from the half-hitches at each end, should be seized back on to the standing parts.

The *Bowline-on-the-bight*. This, as can be seen, is made on the bight of a doubled rope. It is commenced as for an ordinary bowline. When the 'end' is brought up through the bight, as shown, instead of being passed around the standing parts as in the bowline it is brought *away* from it and the entire hitch is passed through the end loop, as indicated by the arrows. As a result, the end loop finally runs up through the large bight and yet encircles the standing parts. It used to be a popular knot to give to a beginner, merely for the sport of seeing whether he could undo it, for at very first sight the beginner imagines that the entire length of the rope, not shown, has been passed through the end loop.

(A *Running Bowline* is made by passing the end around the standing part and making a bowline on its *own* part. It is a slip-knot or noose, and must never be used for lowering a man. The bowline-on-the-bight is used for this, and the two big bights hanging below the knot are adjusted to different sizes. The small bight is passed under a man's arms, and the larger one under his buttocks.)

420

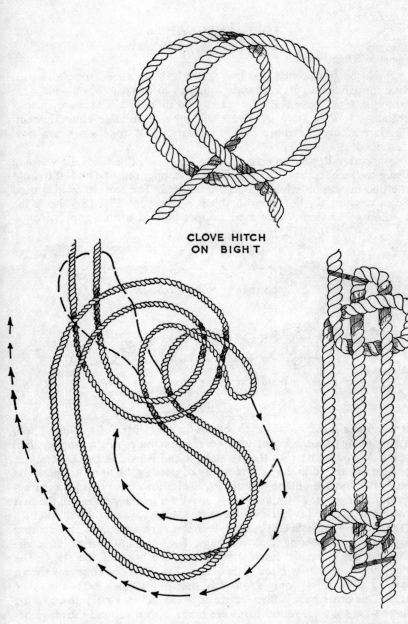

**CLOVE HITCH
ON BIGHT**

BOWLINE ON BIGHT

SHEEPSHANK

FIGURE 16.5

General Rope Work

It will be appreciated that knots, bends, hitches, and ropework provide enough text to fill a separate volume. For this reason, only the most common types have been illustrated and discussed. For more curious readers, *Ashley's Book of Knots* will provide suitable entertainment. Similarly, only the more important aspects of rope work are now described.

Stoppering Ropes. To transfer a taut mooring line from the warping drum to the bitts, or for similar work, a stopper must be passed to hold the line in tension while it is being belayed. The stopper is also used when working the line from the bitts to the drum. Fig. 16.6 shows the method of passing a fibre-rope stopper around a fibre rope which is

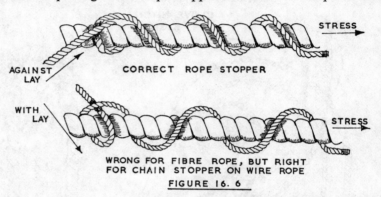

AGAINST LAY

STRESS

CORRECT ROPE STOPPER

WITH LAY

STRESS

WRONG FOR FIBRE ROPE, BUT RIGHT
FOR CHAIN STOPPER ON WIRE ROPE

FIGURE 16. 6

stressed as shown. A half-hitch, or the first two turns of a rolling hitch, are made against the lay of the line, the remainder of the stopper then being *dogged* round with the lay and the end is held in the hand.

Also illustrated is the incorrect way of passing the fibre stopper. The half-hitch has been made with the lay. This, however, provides a correct method for passing a *chain stopper* around a *wire rope*. Again, the first two turns of a rolling hitch will be more satisfactory than a half-hitch.

Stages and Bosun's Chairs. Fig. 16.7 shows two methods for securing a gantline (or lowering line) to a stage. The left-hand illustration is virtually a marline-spike hitch slipped over the horn of the stage. The right-hand method is more satisfactory. Two parts of rope are shown leading away; one is only about 2 m long and is bowlined to the other part. This other part is then led through the pulley block, down to the stage where several round turns are made with it around the stage between the horn and the end. These round turns are rendered (or slacked) when it is desired to lower the stage.

Also shown is a bosun's chair. Here, the running part is brought

6 ft

422

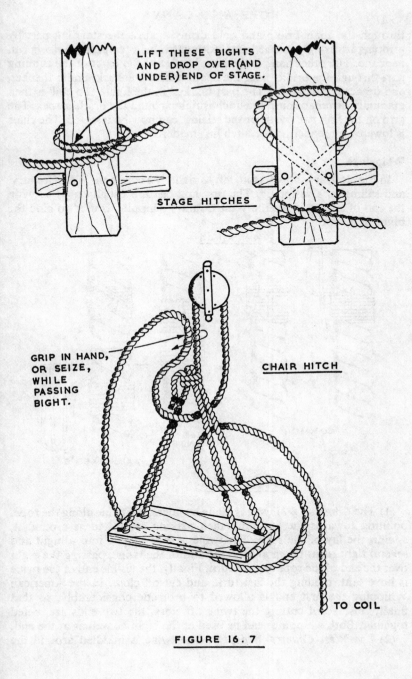

LIFT THESE BIGHTS
AND DROP OVER (AND
UNDER) END OF STAGE.

STAGE HITCHES

GRIP IN HAND,
OR SEIZE,
WHILE
PASSING
BIGHT.

CHAIR HITCH

TO COIL

FIGURE 16.7

through the chair bridle and held firmly against the standing part by gripping it strongly in one hand. Alternatively, a temporary seizing can be made. The other hand is then used to heave the bight of the running part through the bridle, over the head, behind the back, under the feet, and up across the knees. The part marked in the figure 'To coil' is then gradually hove taut until the hitch is tight around the bridle's apex. The grip on the first two parts, or the seizing, can now be released. The chair is lowered by rendering the hitch just made.

Whippings

In Fig. 16.8 are shown, from left to right, the common, West Country, and sailmaker's whipping. The first and last are usually used to whip the end of a rope, while the West Country whipping is used to bind the bight of a rope.

WHIPPINGS

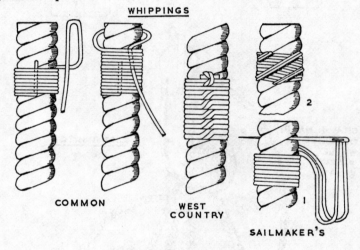

COMMON   WEST COUNTRY   SAILMAKER'S

FIGURE 16.8

(1) The *Common Whipping* is made by laying the twine along the rope, pointing towards the end, and then making several turns around it, *against* the lay of the rope. The twine is then looped into a bight and several tight turns taken around the end of the twine, passing the bight over the end of the rope at each turn. Finally, the visible end of the twine is hove taut, binding the last turn, and cut off close. In the American Whipping the first end is allowed to protrude considerably, so that finally, instead of cutting the twine off close, the two ends are reefed together. Both whippings can be used at the bight as well as at the end.

(2) The *West Country Whipping*. The twine is middled around the

424

rope, its ends brought up to the other side and half-knotted (overhand knot). The ends are then taken to the other side of the rope and again half-knotted. The process is repeated continuously and the ends are finally reef-knotted.

(3) The *Sailmaker's Whipping* is started by sewing into the heart of the rope, burying the end, and bringing the needle out on a long length of twine. The needle now hangs clear while several tight turns are passed *against* the lay. The needle is then finally used to sew the twine through strands so that the frapping turns are passed, as shown in the upper illustration. The end is then buried in the rope.

Serving a Rope

Fig. 16.9 demonstrates how a rope, fibre or wire, is bound with spunyarn (or any other small stuff) to protect it.

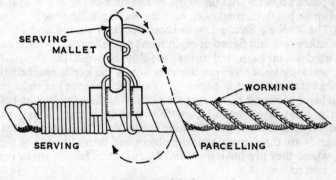

FIGURE 16.9

The strands are first filled by passing a *worming* (a very small cordage) with the lay. A long strip of tarred or oiled canvas is then wrapped or *parcelled* around the rope, again with the lay.

The binding, or serving, is then started, *against* the lay similarly to a common whipping, each turn being hove taut with a heaving mallet or by hand. When sufficient turns are on to prevent a slip occurring the serving mallet is used to finish the work. It is placed on the rope (its head being grooved to fit the line) and the spunyarn is brought up, passed round the handle, back down on the near side of the head, dipped under the rope, and is then dogged around the handle. The ball of spunyarn is then passed around the rope as the serving mallet makes each turn. The handle is gripped sufficiently loosely to allow the spunyarn to render. The process is easily recalled by the well-known doggerel: 'Worm and parcel with the lay, turn and serve the other way.' The serving is finished in the same way as a common whipping.

Seizings

Fig. 16.10 shows:

(1) The *Flat Seizing* to bind two ropes together, e.g. at the steps of a pilot ladder. The seizing is threaded through its eye as shown, and several round turns are made loosely around both ropes. The end is then passed back towards the eye under all the turns and rove again through the eye. It is then passed back, after all the turns have been hove taut, to make a pair of frapping turns around all parts. Finally, the end is clove-hitched around all parts. The end may either be buried, back-spliced, or knotted.

(2) The *Round Seizing* is commenced in the same way. Once the first layer of turns has been hauled taut, the end is used to make a second layer of round (riding) turns. At the right-hand side of the seizing the end is passed downwards through the last turn of the *lower layer* (which is shown in black throughout), and the seizing is finished as before.

(3) The *Racking Seizing* is more complex. It is started in the same way as the other two, but figure-of-eight turns are taken as shown. The end is then used to make round turns to fill-in between the figure-of-eight turns working back towards the eye. When the eye is reached the end is passed through it. It is again worked back towards the right, making a final layer of round turns over all parts. It is then finished as before.

Parbuckling is a method used for hoisting barrels, spars, or other round objects. Two ropes are used, with their similar ends fast. The other ends are then rove under the object and brought back to the other ends, where they are hove on. The object is thus hauled up in the bight of the two ropes.

Mousing a Hook is done to prevent an eye from slipping or jumping out of it. A flat seizing is passed around both parts of the hook, once the eye has been dropped over the bill of the hook.

Racking a Tackle is a term used to describe a method whereby a tackle may be held in tension while belaying or loosely handling the hauling part. All parts of the fall are merely gripped tightly together in the hands. If this is not possible the hauling part, where it leaves the sheave, may be jammed between the swallow of the block and the adjacent part of the fall. This is called *choking the luff*, and is detrimental to the rope.

Eyes may be made in hawsers either by splicing, in which case it is known as a *soft eye*, the outer curve of the eye most distant from the splice being known as the *crown* of the splice, or by passing the hawser around a thimble (a pear-shaped piece of galvanised steel, grooved to take the line), and seizing it to its own part. This makes a *hawser eye*. A thimbled eye, on the other hand, refers to an eye splice made around a thimble.

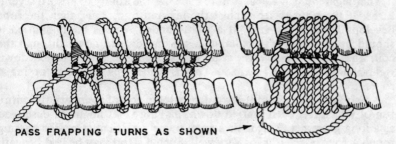

PASS FRAPPING TURNS AS SHOWN →

FLAT SEIZING

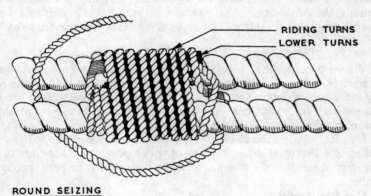

RIDING TURNS
LOWER TURNS

ROUND SEIZING

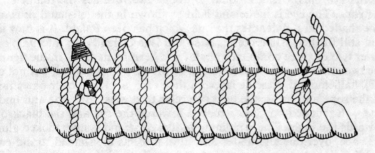

RACKING SEIZING

FIGURE 16.10

Thoroughfooting a Rope. A fibre rope has the ability to absorb several turns. If these turns are against the lay and numerous, then the rope develops kinks and *snarls*. If a right-handed rope is badly snarled it should be coiled down left-handed, the end dipped down through the coil, and used to heave the rope out straight. It is now coiled down right-handed, free from kinks. This is known as thoroughfooting a rope.

A Selvagee Strop comprises a dense, long, coil of spunyarn the entire run of which has been marled down, making what might be described as 'a long grommet. This makes an extremely efficient strop for passing round a rope, since it grips very well. Such a strop may be laid beneath a rope, brought up on both sides, one loop passed through the other, each loop taken underneath the rope again, and the process repeated. Finally, the two shortened loops are brought together and dropped over the bill of a hook. In this way a purchase may easily be secured to a rope.

Cordage Splicing

Where time permits, a splice is always preferable to a knot, but it should be assumed that the splice will reduce the safe load of the rope by about one-eighth. Only a few of the more common splices are discussed here, for, again, the space necessary to cover the subject would be out of proportion to the scope of this book.

Fig. 16.11 shows the *chain splice*, which is used when a rope has to be tailed to a length of chain, the size of which prevents the reeving of the full circumference of the rope, or when the chain is to pass through a pulley.

One strand of the rope is unlaid for a distance equal to the perimeter of the eye plus a length equal to about twelve times the diameter of the rope. The eye is made and held as shown in the left-hand drawing. The shaded strand denotes the one which has been unlaid. It is now unlaid still further, while the black strand is laid tightly up into its place. After two or three complete spirals have been made (two, in the figure), the two strands are halved (one half of the yarn is discarded, but not cut off), half-knotted with the lay, and then each is tucked over one strand of the rope and under the next (we refer to this as 'over one and under one'), the shaded one being tucked towards the eye and the black one towards the bight. The remaining untucked strand is now tucked along the rope, over one and under one, until it meets the shaded strand-end.

All five ends (the four half-strands and the full strand) are pulled tight and cut off. To make a neat splice, before the full strand is given its final tuck, it too may be halved, and the general result is a tapered splice. The ends of strands should really be dogged together, but this will be explained later.

The *cut splice* is also illustrated and forms a quick method of joining

428

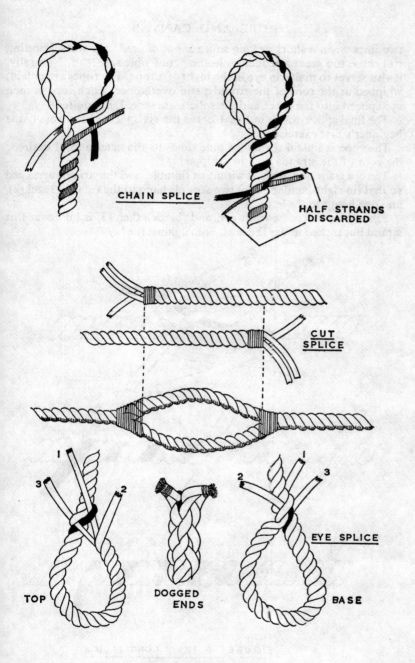

CHAIN SPLICE

HALF STRANDS
DISCARDED

CUT
SPLICE

EYE SPLICE

1
3
2
TOP

DOGGED
ENDS

2
1
3
BASE

FIGURE 16.11

two lines when a short or long splice is not desired, and when knotting will cause too great a reduction in the permissible safe load. Naturally, it also serves to make an eye in the bight of a rope. The ropes are unlaid, whipped at the root of the strands, and overlapped. Each rope is then eye-spliced into the other and the splices are served, if required.

The final splice drawn in Fig. 16.11 is the *eye splice*, and is usually the beginner's first exercise.

The rope is unlaid for about nine times its diameter and, if desired, the root of the strands may be whipped.

The eye is formed, with or without a thimble, and the strands arranged so that (in right-handed rope) two strands hang to the right, (1) and (2), and one hangs to the left, (3).

First, (1) is tucked beneath a strand (black), then (3) is laid over this strand but tucked under the next, both against the lay.

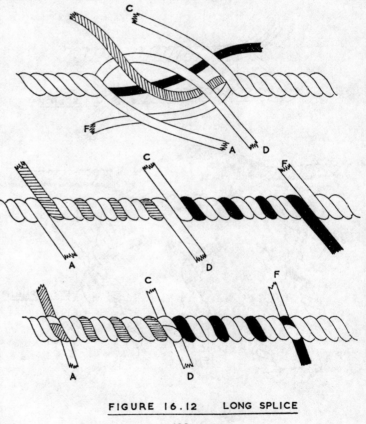

FIGURE 16.12   LONG SPLICE

430

The strands are pulled well through and into the 'lay' of the rope. The splice is then turned over and viewed from its base. One strand is clearly seen to be unoccupied, so (2) is tucked beneath it against the lay from right to left. All strands are then tucked over one and under one for about two or three full tucks. They are then halved and two further tucks made, after which the ends are dogged.

This is done, as shown in the figure, by halving each strand-end and whipping half of one strand to the half of the next adjacent strand.

Fig. 16.12 shows the *long splice* by which means two ropes are joined without in any way affecting the size of the join. The ropes are unlaid for about twelve to fifteen times the diameter, or even more if the splice is to suffer a considerable stress. The ends are married, that is, each strand of the right-hand rope is placed between a pair of strands from the left-hand rope, as shown in the upper part of the drawing.

(C) and (D) are then half-knotted with the lay.

(F) is now unlaid and the black strand is laid into its place for several complete spirals (three in the figure), in a similar manner to the chain splice.

(A) is also unlaid and the shaded strand laid into its place for three complete spirals. The strands are then situated in three pairs, equidistant. It should be noted that each strand of a pair meets the other end on, i.e. where they meet, they share one strand-groove; in the figure I have shown them side by side for the sake of clarity.

The half-knotting of (C) and (D) has been left until the last in the figure. To finish the splice, each strand is halved and the pairs are half-knotted together, the discarded halves having been omitted from the drawing. The ends are finished as for the chain splice, i.e. tucked over one and under one. The bare ends can either be cut off flush or else dogged together.

The *short splice* is not shown. It is stronger than the long splice, but more bulky. It is commenced by marrying the strands, as in the long splice, after which the strands are all tucked over one and under one for about three and a half tucks, a half-tuck being one executed with half strands. The ends are usually dogged.

STEEL WIRE ROPE

The first wire rope was produced in 1834, while fibre ropes have been in existence for over 5,000 years. The Admiralty authorised the use of steel wire ropes on naval ships in 1838, since which time the rope has developed almost bewilderingly in the diversity and complexity of its forms. Its terms of reference have been exactly reduced by science, metallurgy, and chemistry to a set of known values and characteristics.

A modern wire rope consists of a number of strands laid around a central *heart*, which may itself be a steel strand, steel wire rope, or be a strand or rope of vegetable or synthetic fibre. Each strand in turn is composed of a given number of individual wires again laid round a central wire or fibre *core*, the wire core in this case usually consisting of one single wire.

The steel is produced as cast ingots or billets, which are then reduced to rods by repeated rolling. The rods are then drawn, and progressively annealed and cold-worked until they become wires of the correct diameter.

Before the wires are laid into strands, and then the rope, ancilliary processes are undertaken to minimise corrosion. Most engineering ropes are *black*, i.e. they are ungalvanised, while except for certain classes of cargo runner, most shipping and fishing ropes are galvanised. Galvanising of the wire is always done before the strand is built and indeed, modern galvanising is so efficient that very often some of the wire-drawing stages are done after galvanising. The present-day electrolytic galvanising entails little or no loss of strength or ductility in the wire.

When a wire rope or strand has a fibre heart the latter must be adequately protected against penetration by moisture, which tends to lead to corrosion in the heart of the rope or strand, and this, in turn, could lead to a rapid breakdown in service. All hemp (or vegetable fibre) cores are immersed for long periods in baths of heated lubricants so as to give complete saturation of the fibre. When the strand (or the rope) is being formed, and the wires or strands laid over the core, the pressure is such that surplus lubricant is squeezed out, and this ensures lubrication of every part of the strand or rope at the completion of manufacture.

In the case of synthetic-fibre main hearts no lubrication is necessary to prevent water penetration so far as the hearts themselves are concerned, since nylon, terylene, polythene, etc., are all completely immune from micro-biological attack. In such a rope, however, the strand cores would still be of hemp and would be treated as described in the foregoing paragraph.

During the forming of the strand, and subsequently the rope, the wires are continually fed with heated lubricants so that the rope is finally wound on to its drum or reel in a fully lubricated condition.

Construction of the Rope

The number of wires in a strand is determined by the fact that 6 wires of equal size will just comfortably fit around a single wire core of the same size and that a further layer or *gallery* of wires of the same size laid on the 7-wire strand will naturally hold 12 wires. Such a strand would therefore have either 7 or 19 wires. A further gallery (which contains 18 wires) brings the total to 37 wires, and yet another (containing 24 wires) brings the total to 61 wires.

When a fibre strand-core is used the total number of wires does not follow a natural build-up system, but in practice usually totals either a single layer of 12 wires around the core or a total number of 24 wires laid as an outer gallery of 15 wires and an inner gallery of 9 wires.

It is possible to lay another gallery of 18 wires over the single layer of 12 wires and achieve a rope with 30 wires laid around a fibre core.

It can be seen then that there is a very wide variety of wire ropes available to the shipping industry alone, quite apart from mining and engineering projects.

The degree of flexibility of a steel wire rope is governed by the number of wires in the strand; the greater the number of wires, then generally the greater is the flexibility. Further, flexibility is increased by the introduction of a fibre strand-core at the expense of strength. On the other hand, both strength and flexibility are gained if the wire is built up from a very large number of small-gauge wires.

A wire which has each strand consisting of twelve wires laid over a fibre core may be more flexible than one which has twenty-four wires laid over a similar core in two galleries, assuming equal sizes of ropes. This is due to the fact that the core in the first rope is relatively larger than that of the second rope. So when we state that flexibility is directly proportional to the number of wires in each strand we are comparing ropes the strands of which have two or more galleries.

A wire rope is referred to by the use of two numbers: the first indicates the number of strands, and the second refers to the number of wires in each strand. Marine ropes invariably have six strands and may be summarised as follows:

Rope construction	Strand construction	Usual purpose
6 × 7	6/1	Standing rigging
6 × 12	12/Hemp	Deck ropes; running rigging
6 × 19	12/6/1	Cargo runners; topping lifts and pendants; towing lines; mooring lines
6 × 24	15/9/Hemp	
6 × 30	18/12/Hemp	As for 6 × 24
6 × 37 6 × 61	18/12/6/1 24/18/12/6/1	Where high flexibility is required

It should be noticed that strands having even numbers of wires are those fitted with fibre cores. The fibre heart of the rope not only forms a cushion for the strands so that under stress they can bed themselves into their natural positions but it also acts as a store for the lubricant (which should periodically be applied while in service), and squeezes this into the wires when the rope is flexed or stressed, thus minimising friction between the wires.

Other types of wire rope include flexible copper wire rope for use in the vicinity of magnetic compasses, e.g. as awning jackstays, seizing wire, which is usually between 6 and 10 mm in diameter consisting of one strand of 6/1 construction, and what are known as extra special flexible steel wire ropes (ESFSWR) in which the term 'extra special' refers to the quality of the steel.

The Lay of the Rope

There are five main types of lay in wire rope:

(1) *Right-hand ordinary lay*, in which the sfrands are laid up right-handed but the wires are twisted together left-handed.

(2) *Left-hand ordinary lay*, in which the strands are laid up left-handed but the wires are twisted together right-handed.

(Notice that these correspond to the plain lay of fibre ropes.)

(3) *Right-handed Lang's lay*, in which both wires and strands are laid up right-handed.

(4) *Left-handed Lang's lay*, in which both wires and strands are laid up left-handed.

(Notice that Lang's lay follows the principle of unkinkable fibre-rope lay. In a steel wire rope, Lang's lay gives wearing qualities far in excess of those of ordinary lay. When wear takes place in ordinary lay a flat is worn on the wires *across* their axes. The same wear applied to Lang's lay wears the wires *along* their axes, with the result that ordinary-laid ropes eventually have individual wires worn through and sticking up along their lengths, while Lang's laid ropes wear down evenly and eventually appear like bars of polished steel.

Unfortunately a Lang's laid rope tends to rotate much more in service, compared with the ordinary lay, and its use is therefore restricted to conditions where both ends of the rope are secure or where the rope travels in guides or on rails, such as in lifts, mines, excavating, etc. Were it not for this, then Lang's lay would undoubtedly be in universal use. It is rarely found in use on ships.)

(5) *Cable-laid wire rope*, which is very large and highly flexible. This is made in exactly the same way as cable-laid fibre rope, and a 36-strand wire rope composed of 6, 6-stranded ropes would be described as 6 × 6/19's or 6 × 6/24's, etc. The six ropes are invariably laid around a fibre heart.

Preformed Wire Rope

This used to be referred to as true-lay wire rope. Anyone who has handled an ordinary type of steel wire rope will know only too well its tendency to spring open and unlay itself when cut. A preformed rope has none of this tendency, and remains quite inert after being severed. The actual operation is performed merely by shaping each strand of the rope, before laying-up, into a helix of the same size and pitch that it would naturally have formed when laid into rope.

'Spring Lay' Wire Rope

This is an extremely flexible yet tough rope made of tarred sisal and galvanised wires. It has a great resistance to damage by sea-water and weather.

Its construction is $6 \times 3 \times 19$, i.e. 6 ropes each containing 3 sisal strands and 3 strands of 19 wires, the individual strands and the whole rope having central fibre cores. It is very easily handled and coiled. It is ideal for mooring ropes and towing springs. Its strength is about three times that of first-grade manila of equal size, and four times that of high-grade sisal of equal size. It resists shock loads.

General Remarks on Wire Rope

Wire rope resists bending and does not absorb turns so easily as fibre rope, with the result that it easily kinks and snarls. When this happens a kink which is about to develop should never be pulled out, otherwise the rope is long-jawed and permanently damaged. The kink, which appears as a loop or bight in the wire, of small diameter, is removed by grasping the rope on either side and pushing the hands together so that the diameter of the kink is enlarged. As soon as this is done, the kink—provided the wires are not permanently bent or damaged—will suddenly untwist itself.

Wire should never be subjected to sharp nips, such as altering its direction of lead by passing it through shackles, eye-bolts, or over plate edges. This will permanently damage the wire, the effect being known as *crippling*. When securing wire to a drum or bollard the diameter of the latter should be at least twelve times the rope diameter. The diameter of a roller around which a wire rope is to be passed should be at least ten times the rope diameter.

Wire rope should be stowed on reels or coiled down when not in use. When winding a new rope on to a drum it is best to start the first layer as follows:

If over-winding on to the upper side of the drum, anchor the wire on the left and run the wire on from left to right.

If underwinding on to the lower side of the drum, anchor it on the right-hand side of the drum and wind on from right to left.

This applies the same principle as that used with fibre ropes, i.e. that right-handed ropes must be uncoiled left-handed. These instructions are reversed if left-handed wire rope is being run on the barrel or drum. The directions are assumed to be for a person facing the drum and watching the wire fed towards him.

Ropes in store should be placed on gratings and turned every so often to alter the weight/contact point of the coil and also to stop drainage of lubricant.

Before putting a rope into service the grooves of drums and sheaves should be carefully examined to see that they are of the correct size for the rope in question, in proper alignment, and in good condition.

A wire rope should always be put into service by uncoiling it either from a drum or reel, under tension, or by unrolling the coil along the deck. If the rope is on a drum a spindle may be passed through the central hole, jacked up at both ends, or suspended from a cargo runner by means of a two-legged bridle, and the wire rope pulled carefully off. A drum without a central hole should be placed on a turntable and cross-battens lashed over the top of the wire to prevent turns jumping off. The rope should never be pulled from a coil loosely or thrown off a reel, otherwise serious kinks will form.

In service the wire should be frequently cleaned, examined, and lubricated. Many excellent rope lubricants are available, but the rope must be cleaned and dried before application of the oil. The rope should constantly be checked for internal corrosion, fractured wires, excessive wear, and rotting of cores. Several broken wires close together in one strand constitute a far greater danger than the same number distributed throughout the length of the rope.

Whenever possible wire rope should not be subjected to a bend and sudden reverse-bend. When it leads from a pulley to a drum the angle of lead should not exceed 5 degrees from the plane of the sheave.

The coiling of more than one layer of wire on a drum is detrimental to the rope, but is difficult to avoid. Dead layers which are never off the drum *should* be avoided. The higher the speed at which a wire rope, or any rope for that matter, is worked, the greater is the wear. It is more economical to increase load rather than speed.

The grooves of pulleys and drums should support one-third of the rope circumference in a true circle. The groove diameter should be 5% greater than the rope diameter. When a rope is placed on a grooved drum the laps should clear each other by about 1·5 mm. Worn grooves will prevent this.

When coiling a rope down, right-handed ropes are coiled right-handed; the free end should be able to revolve, because many turns may develop during coiling. If the end cannot be rotated the coil will have to be composed of several *Frenchmen*. These are occasional right-handed turns but with the uncoiled length emerging from *below* the last

$\frac{1}{16}$ in

436

turn instead of above it (see Fig. 16.13). They remove the twists quite effectively. When a right-handed rope has been belayed left-handed and strained it develops a left-hand set, i.e. it resists right-handed coiling, and only the use of 'Frenchmen' will enable it to be coiled down.

A coil should be stopped all round with yarns when not in use, to prevent the turns from jumping. A 'Frenchmen' coil will tend to throw off the turns more vigorously, if disturbed, compared with an ordinary coil.

Wire rope is about five times as strong as high-grade manila rope, depending upon the steel used. Greater comparison figures are possible of course. It stretches very little and may be considered non-elastic; it does in fact part very easily when subjected to a shock load. It should not be assumed that the wires in a rope are in one length—frequently, in a long rope, they are welded together to give the required length, but these joins are well staggered.

Cutting Wire Rope

Two whippings of marline or rope-yarn should be placed on the rope, each one commencing about 2·5 cm away from the point of sever and continuing for about 5 cm. It is most important to work *away* from the cutting point when whipping, so that the latter is not loosened when the rope is cut and the strands spring apart. 1 in 2 in

The 5 cm space left for cutting is now placed on a hard surface, such as the mooring bitts, and hammered once or twice to flatten the upper wires. This gives a good keying surface for the cold chisel which is finally used to sever the strands. Several designs of wire-cutter are available, and they give a neater finish than a cold chisel. 2 in

When cutting a length off a coil the length remaining or removed should be marked up locally.

Bulldog Grips

These are shown in Fig. 16.13. They are used to form an eye in a wire rope when splicing is not possible for any reason. They must never be used for joining two hawsers, simply by clamping the ropes together.

The base-plate of the grip must always be fitted under the working part of the rope, with the U-bolts over the dead end.

Three grips should be used on ropes up to 24 mm in size, four grips on ropes between 24 and 32 mm in size, and five or more on ropes over 32 mm in diameter. They should be spaced at distances equal to nine times the diameter of the rope. 3 in 3 and 4 in 4 in

They are extremely useful fittings, but they do, however, tend to crush and mark the rope.

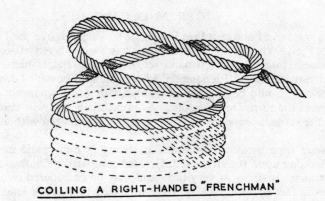

COILING A RIGHT-HANDED "FRENCHMAN"

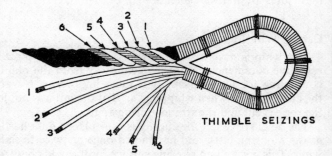

THIMBLE SEIZINGS

NUMBERING ENDS & STRANDS (WIRE EYE SPLICE)

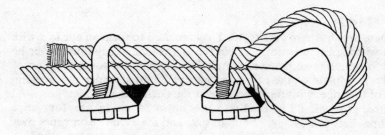

BULLDOG GRIPS

FIGURE 16.13

Inspection of the Rope

Distortion of the rope by kinking, crushing, crippling, etc., is likely to reduce the strength of the rope by as much as 30%. A rope in which the heart is protruding should be discarded.

Wearing of flats across the wires, giving them a bright appearance, does not affect the strength of the rope unless it is very pronounced. Sometimes the entire rope is seen to be flattened, such as a cargo runner continually being wound on to a drum in two or three laps. This indicates distortion of the strands, which is serious.

Broken wires should be examined to ascertain whether wear or corrosion has caused the breakdown. Reference should be made to Chapter XV to study the Docks Regulations stipulation on this point.

A wire rope should be frequently opened up with a marline spike; a dry, powdery heart or core indicates dry rot, and the rope should be either discarded or, if considered wise, lubricated.

At sub-zero temperatures the steel wires will become brittle and the rope may part without warning. Further, the flexibility is reduced. However, the wire will regain its normal characteristics under normal temperatures.

Splicing Wire Rope

This is done along the same lines as fibre-rope splicing, but greater skill is required due to the extreme resilience of the wires. The galvanising may be damaged during the process and before being parcelled and served, splices should be dipped in Stockholm tar or other preservative.

The strength of the rope may be considered to be reduced by about one-eighth by a good splice, but considerably more by a bad splice. Great care must be exercised to prevent tearing the strands or cores with the marline spike.

A long, tapered spike should be used and carefully inserted in the rope, avoiding the heart. The tucking end of a strand is inserted in the same direction as the spike, pulled beyond it, and then back into place. Strands should be tucked some distance away from where they last emerge, otherwise a bad nip is caused and the strands open, exposing the cores, quite apart from the fact that the wires are kinked. The marline spike can easily be worked back along the lay and the strand set carefully into place. It is far better to tuck too far away from the splice than too close to it.

In wire splicing a half-tuck may be either a tuck executed with halved strands or a tuck done with alternate strands, so that three ends emerge one tuck farther along the rope than the other three. Both types of half-tuck produce a tapered splice, which is highly desirable.

Short Splice

This is a bulky splice, and many seamen prefer to do a cut splice, in the belief that it is stronger and more easy to execute.

A whipping is put on each rope at a distance from its end equal to about thirty-six times the diameter. The end of the rope is already whipped presumably, close to the point where it was cut from a coil. Place another whipping about 15 cm away from the end one and cut the latter. The strands then unlay themselves for this distance of roughly 15 cm. Each end should be whipped with sail twine, bearing in mind that all whippings must work away from rope or strand ends. The wire rope can now be unlaid all the way to the main whipping (36 × D mm from the end).

The rope ends are married, so that a strand of one rope lies between two strands of the other and the ropes are hove together, so that the whippings nearly touch. Seize the strands of one rope on to the other rope, so that the other set of strands can be tucked without the operator being hampered by a dozen unruly strands.

We now see, therefore, two wire ropes butted together. The strands of the right-hand rope, say, are seized on to the left-hand rope. The strands of the left-hand rope are free to be tucked into the right-hand rope.

Cut the whipping on the right-hand rope and tuck the left-hand rope's strands into it as for a fibre-rope splice, i.e. each tucking end passes over the strand to its left and under the next strand.

After the first round of tucks pass a seizing round the splice to prevent the ends from easing back and becoming unspliced.

If the tucking ends have fibre cores, cut them out and lay up the strands again. Make three or four more rounds of tucks. Stopper back about a third of each strand and tuck the remaining two-thirds once again. Now halve each tucking end, stopper one-half back, and tuck the other.

With a mallet, flatten all tucks, working towards the bight of the rope, and finally cut off all ends.

Repeat the process on the other (left-hand) rope and finally serve the splice all over.

By reducing the tucking ends twice, a well-tapered splice is obtained.

Eye Splice (Fig. 16.13)

Many wire ropes nowadays are spliced by the 'Talurit' system, in which the eye is formed, with or without a thimble, and the dead end laid along the standing part, as in the case where grips are to be used. An alloy collar is slid over both parts, close up to the neck of the eye, and closed very tightly in a powerful press.

When splicing an eye the tucking ends should be of length equal to eighteen times the rope diameter, so that the strands are pliable to handle, do not kink easily, and can be pulled well tight.

The success of the splice depends upon the first round of tucks; if the ends are badly tucked initially the splice appears to be long-jawed.

Right-handed splicing merely involves laying each end around the same strand four or five times. The tucks are made with the lay; the splice is quick and easy, but is of no value if the rope is likely to rotate in service.

Left-handed splicing (over-and-under splicing) is more efficient, and the splice appears as though it is a plaited rope, giving very strong adhesion. It is a strong splice, three tucks of which are probably equivalent to about five right-handed tucks.

Locking splices, having possibly more than one lock in the splice, are always the strongest. Two ends are tucked under one strand so that they cross, i.e. they are tucked in opposite directions. Generally only one lock is made, and in the first round of tucks.

The Docks Regulations stipulate that eye splices shall consist of at least three full and two half tucks, all against the lay; any other splice may be used if it is equally or more efficient.

Before commencing the splice the length of the ends should be measured off and a serving put on the rope. If a thimble is to be used the serving is continued for the full length of the eye, measured by placing the thimble on the rope and turning it over once.

The thimble is then seized at the middle of the serving, the eye is formed, and the two parts seized at, and to, the neck of the thimble. A temporary whipping is put on the bare end, about 15 cm from it, and 6 in the extreme-end whipping is severed. The strands are whipped, the temporary whipping removed, and the strands unlaid to the thimble.

The first tuck is often made on a hard surface, such as the mooring bitts, after which the eye is hung up at chest-level for completion of the splice.

In the descriptions following the reader should imagine himself looking at the wire rope, from the crown of the eye towards the neck. The tucking ends are lying on his left hand and the standing part is to his right. The tucking ends, when allowed to lie in their natural lay, are numbered from 1 to 6, counting from the right-hand top end to the left-hand bottom end.

The strands of the rope are numbered from 1 to 6 along the rope away from the eye (Fig. 16.13).

The Left-handed Lock Splice (Boulevant)

Tuck No. 1 end through number one strand, towards the right.

Tuck No. 2 end through number two strand, towards the left. With

441

the spike still beneath number two strand, bring No. 6 end upwards, but beneath Nos. 3, 4, and 5 ends, and tuck it under number two strand towards the right; this forms a lock.

Tuck No. 3 end through number three strand, towards the left.

Tuck No. 5 end through numbers four and five strands, to the left.

Drop number five strand from the spike and tuck No. 4 end through number four strand, also to the left.

The splice is finished off as in fibre-rope, tucking over one and under one, i.e. left-handed.

The Naval Splice

Tuck No. 1 end through number one strand, to the left.
Tuck No. 2 end through number two strand, to the left.
Tuck No. 3 end through number three strand, to the left.
Tuck No. 4 end through number four strand, to the left.
Tuck No. 6 end through numbers five and six strands, to the left.
Tuck No. 5 end through number five strand, to the left.

The splice is finished off as before, and in both splices the strands may be reduced as described in the short splice to give a finely tapered result.

CANVAS

This is made from either hemp, cotton, jute or flax, or even a blended mixture of these materials. British canvas is predominantly manufactured from flax, while the bulk of American canvas is derived from cotton.

The threads running along the length of the roll or *bolt* of canvas are known as *warp* threads, while those running across the width of the bolt are called *weft* threads. The edge of the canvas does not fray due to the continuous weft, and is called the *selvedge*. Approximately 2·5 cm from each selvedge a coloured thread is woven parallel to the selvedge, and is called the *seam line* or *selvedge stripe*. This acts as a guide when sewing two cloths together.

1 in

If the canvas is cut, a *raw edge* is formed and fraying occurs.

2 to 3 ft

The width of the canvas varies from 0·6 to 1 m. It may be obtained flame-proofed and also waterproofed. This latter process is achieved either by means of wax impregnation or by chemicals. The former method does not give lasting protection, as the wax is affected by strong sunlight and cracks with continual folding. Tarpaulin canvas is often a coarser material, manufactured from second-grade flax, and is cheaper. It is available in the natural shade, or in brown or green.

Merchant Navy canvas is provided in seven grades numbered 0–6, the lower figure representing the stouter canvas. In the trade, canvas is referred to by weight, i.e. so many grammes per square metre. Duck canvas is a very light cotton material, and is used for fine work.

Canvas is liable to stretch considerably along the warp but very little across the weft. The same applies to shrinkage, and although a dyeing process initially shrinks the material, further shrinkage occurs continuously. To prevent this, canvas is often painted so that the paint fills in the spaces between the threads, and this also tends to prevent stretching. Naturally, the application of paint causes a certain amount of shrinkage. If it is desired to obtain a very taut canvas it is laced up tight, damped with fresh water, and painted while still moist.

Canvas Work

Sewing is done with flax sewing twine previously impregnated with beeswax to prevent kinking of the twine and to secure a more watertight seam. Some sailmakers prefer to run their twine through beeswax themselves, but it may be obtained already treated. The beginner tends to space his stitches too far apart, and they are then referred to as *Homeward Bound Stitches* or *Dog's Teeth*. For fine work, up to six stitches to 2·5 cm are used, but four to 2·5 cm is approved for normal work.

The sailmaker usually allows 2·5 cm in 30 cm run of cloth for shrinkage (boat covers, tarpaulins, etc.) and the same amount for stretch in the case of awnings. When sewing, the bottom cloth gradually shortens relative to the top cloth, and due allowance must be made for this.   1 in per ft

When sewing, a sailmaker's hook is used to hold the canvas firmly against the pull of the stitching, and acts as a sailmaker's third hand.

Fig. 16.14 shows the flat and round seams—the latter being the quicker of the two. The round seam is made on the inside of the work and then well rubbed down to make it flat. Both are shown joining two cloths. The sailmaker's hem is known as *tabling*, and strengthens the edge of a cloth when eyelets are to be inserted. It is always used when sewing rope to canvas, as shown. *Herringboning* is used to repair a cut or tear, and draws the two edges together. This method of stitching is also used when sewing canvas around rails; a normal stitch would cause the seam to spiral around the rail, giving an amateurish appearance.

Canvas is invariably sewn with doubled twine, but it is considered sharp practice to knot the twine when commencing. The professional method leaves the twine unknotted, and as the first stitch is made, about 4 cm of twine-end is left protruding. This is then tucked in the seam pointing in the sewing direction and is sewn over with the next few stitches. When a length of twine is used up the needle is cut away, leaving about 2·5 cm of twine protruding from the canvas. The last half-stitch is unpicked and the new length of twine passed through the

$1\frac{1}{2}$ in

1 in

443

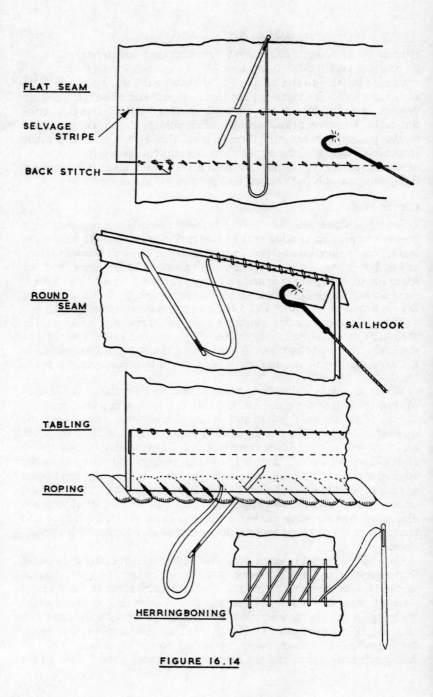

FLAT SEAM

SELVAGE STRIPE

BACK STITCH

ROUND SEAM

SAILHOOK

TABLING

ROPING

HERRINGBONING

FIGURE 16.14

vacant stitch-hole. The twine is drawn through so as to leave 4 cm 1½ in
protruding. There are now two twine-ends protruding inside the seam.
They are twisted together, laid along the sewing line and sewn over with
the next few stitches.

In the flat and tabling seams in the figure the end stitches are seen to
be doubled. This is because the seams have been finished with two or
three back-stitches, working the needle back along the seam, before
cutting off the twine.

A person sewing canvas uses a *palm*, which is a broad leather strap
secured across the palm of the hand by means of a thumb-hole. The
centre of the palm has a metal cup, which is used similarly to a lady's
thimble, i.e. to push the needle through the canvas. A roping palm has
a stouter cup and also a thumb guard. Sail needles are numbered, Nos.
10 and 11 being commonly used for roping, the finer No. 14 for sewing.
Nos. 15 and 16 are sufficiently fine for working duck canvas.

Brass eyelets are in two parts, a male and a female. A punch and die
are used, suitable for the size of eyelet. The hole is made in the canvas
by means of a piercing tool and widened with a fid. The male eyelet is
placed in the die, the canvas placed over the male, the female over the
canvas, and the punch is then used to tap down the protruding male
flange, locking the female part in place.

CHAPTER XVII

DECK APPLIANCES

CURRENT practice is to mark leadlines in fathoms, i.e. lengths of approximately 2 m. At the time of writing, metric marking is uncertain. Conversion is straightforward but the method of calling the depths will need revision.

(1) THE LEADLINE

A vessel of Class I is required by the Merchant Shipping (Construction) Rules 1965, to be equipped with an efficient mechanical depth-sounding device operated by a line, together with sufficient spare parts to enable it to be maintained in efficient working order. In addition, the ship is to be furnished with two hand leadlines, each not less than 45 m in length and weighted with a lead of at least 3·2 kg. Class 7 vessels are not included in the Rules, but there is little doubt that a cargo vessel engaged on long international voyages would, if she were not equally well equipped, be considered unseaworthy.

25 fathoms 7 lb

The hand leadline consists of a length of 8–10 mm diameter cable-laid rope, the final lay usually being left-handed. It is manufactured from dressed hemp. When making a leadline it must not be marked until the line has been stretched, and this is usually done by setting the line (well soaked in fresh water) tight by means of a light tackle. The slack is periodically taken up as the line lengthens.

An eye is then spliced in the end of the line, the eye being slipped through the lead-strop, passed over the base of the lead, and hove taut. The leadline is now carefully measured and marked. The markings for depth can either be made measuring from the base of the lead (known as 'lead-in') or from the strop of the lead ('lead-out'), which gives one the benefit of the lead, i.e. all soundings as read by the markings are actually *greater* by an amount equal to the length of the lead.

The markings are as follows:

2 fathoms: two tails of leather are inserted in the rope.
3 fathoms: three tails of leather are inserted in the rope.
5 fathoms: a piece of white linen is inserted in the rope.
7 fathoms: a piece of red bunting (flag material) is inserted.
10 fathoms: a piece of leather with a hole in it is inserted.

446

13 fathoms: a piece of blue serge is inserted in the rope.
15 fathoms: the mark is the same as used for 5 fathoms.
17 fathoms: the mark is the same as used for 7 fathoms.
20 fathoms: a piece of cord with two knots in it is inserted.

These markings are known as *marks*, while the remaining numbers up to 20 fathoms are called *deeps*, and are sometimes marked with a piece of cord having one knot in it. The materials used for 5, 7, 13, 15, and 17 fathoms are optional, but the colour is definite. As long as the leadsman is aware of the materials used, he can feel them in the dark (some seaman use their lips) and identify the mark.

The marks, or deeps, are always called by the leadsman in such a way that the whole number is cried last. For example:

5¼ fathoms is called as 'And a quarter *five*'.
8 fathoms is called as 'By the deep *eight*'.
10 fathoms is called as 'By the mark *ten*'.
12¾ fathoms is called as 'And a quarter less *thirteen*'.

The leadsman operates on a small platform projecting over the ship's side, called the *chains*. To take a sounding on the starboard side (the weather side normally being used so that the ship does not drift over the lead), he would stand facing forward holding the coil in his left hand and the last few metres of line, with the lead hanging down, in his right hand. A half turn is taken round the palm of the right hand. He then commences to *heave* the lead back and forth, finally releasing it on a forward swing so that it enters the water well ahead of him. He heaves in the slack after the coil has run away a few turns, and dumps the lead up and down on the bottom as the chains move over the line. He notes the mark on the line at the water's edge and gives the appropriate call.

Some seamen, when the lead is swinging forward with their arms straight, quickly bring their elbows into their sides and, provided the swing has been carefully judged, the lead describes a circle above their heads. It is spectacular and undoubtedly gives the lead a much greater cast ahead of the chains.

The base of the lead is hollowed out into a *score*, which is filled with tallow if a sample of the sea-bed is required. The tallow is then found to have sand, shells, gravel, or whatever the sea-bed consists of, adhering to it. This process is known as *arming* the lead.

(2) THE DEEP-SEA LEAD

This is made from larger line and uses a lead weighing about 13 kg.　28 lb
It is scored in a similar way and armed when desired. This line is at least
220 m long and is marked at every 5 fathoms with a cord having　120 fathoms

447

one knot in it. At 20, 30, 40 fathoms and so on, a piece of cord is used having one knot in it for every 10 fathoms, i.e. two, three, and four knots respectively. The lead is marked in this way to 120 fathoms, using a piece of leather with one hole in it at 10 fathoms, and a piece with two holes in it for 100 fathoms, i.e. a hole for each nought.

This lead is hove along the weather side by placing the lead forward and with several crew members ranged along the ship's side, each holding a few coils in his hands. In some cases the Officer in charge will stand where the lead is expected to touch bottom.

The lead is cast overboard and the coils run away, each man warning the one abaft him that the lead has not yet touched. The traditional warning is 'Watch there, watch'. The ship is stopped while heaving the deep-sea lead.

(3) THE SOUNDING MACHINE

The Kelvin Hughes sounding machine may be hand-driven or controlled by an electric motor. It is equipped with a drum on which is wound 550 m of seven-strand galvanised steel wire. This wire is secured at its outboard end to a 4-m length of hemp line. This line carries a brass sheath or tube which is perforated and fitted with a cap. Supplied with the machine are 100 sounding tubes, which are 60-cm hollow glass rods open at one end, and coated on their insides with silver chromate. The tubes therefore appear to be red.

One such tube is placed into the brass sheath, open end downwards, and the cap is placed on the sheath. The sounding wire is then allowed to run to the sea-bed under the influence of an 11-kg cast-iron sinker which has an arming score similar to sounding leads. While the sinker is descending a hooked metal rod called a feeler is held bearing very lightly upon the wire. Immediately it is felt that the wire no longer presents an upward resistance to the feeler the wire must be checked.

The sinker is now hove-in, the glass sounding tube is removed and held against a boxwood scale graduated in metres. Sea-water will have been forced into the glass tube to an extent which is dependent upon the depth to which the tube was lowered. Further, the action of the salt water will have changed the coating in the tube to white silver chloride. With the tube held in the boxwood scale therefore the dividing line between red and white coatings enables the depth of water to be read.

It is most important to check the wire as soon as the sinker touches the sea-bed; if the tube is allowed to fall from the vertical the sea-water already in it will be able to move farther up the tube and a false reading will be made.

The wire can either be lowered using a sheave built on to the rail aft or by means of a sounding boom which is swung out perpendicular to

300 fathoms
2-fathom

24-in

24-lb

the ship's side. In this latter case the wire runs through a travelling sheave which may be hove out to the end of the boom. The speed of the ship should be reduced when making a sounding.

The following are the maker's instructions for operating a motor-driven machine:

'Attach sinker and stray line to machine. Place glass tube in guard sheath and replace cap. Place the sinker over the ship's side and let wire out gently by easing the handwheel in the running-out direction with the bolt in the lower position. Snatch the wire into the block of the carrier. Run the carrier out to the end of the boom and belay. Lower sinker until nearly touching surface and hold in this position. Set pointer to zero.

'Place the loop of the feeler pin over the right wrist and gently press the feeler pin on to the wire. Smartly rotate the handwheel one half-turn only in the running-out direction and watch the pointer as the wire runs out. Release the handwheel and catch the starting switch handle in the eft hand.

'At the instant the wire slackens off, read the number of metres of wire out as indicated by the pointer. At the same time put the starting switch handle over about half-way and then gradually over to the "on" position to heave in at full speed. When the pointer shows 20 m   10 fathoms the switch handle should be eased back gradually so that the motor stops before the swivel reaches the carrier block. Read off the exact depth on the glass tube with the scale provided.

'Use a pad of oiled canvas to guide the wire on to the drum while heaving in.'

In later models, the tube was plain glass but constricted, and worked on the principle of a clinical thermometer. Water was forced into the tube at depth but could not get out until the tube was shaken. It did not, therefore, matter if the tube fell on its side because there was no internal coating to be affected.

The sounding machine is now obsolete but is included here, together with Plate 24, for interest's sake. Many ships which were fitted with the machine have now had it replaced with a second echo-sounder. The success of the sounding machine operation was perhaps too dependent upon human factors.

(4) THE SHIP LOG

From the earliest days when man ventured to sea in wooden boats, navigation, however crude, has been necessary.

Probably the earliest known attempt to estimate distance or speed at sea was made by the Romans, who used a type of waterwheel fixed to the hull of the galley which carried a drum inboard filled with pebbles. Every time the wheel revolved one pebble fell out into a tally box. By counting the number of pebbles in the box, an estimate of distance travelled could be obtained.

Of the early methods of estimating speed and distance, the best known are the Dutchman's Log and the Common Log. Both methods have been in use since the fifteenth century, and even today there is reason to believe that these methods are still practised.

The Dutchman's Log gives an accurate method of finding a ship's speed. Two points are chosen on the ship and the distance between them measured accurately. A small float or similar object is then thrown as far ahead of the ship as possible and timed accurately between the two marks. The success of the results depends on the accuracy of observation and timing.

The Common Log or Ship Log was first invented or used about 1578, and consisted of a piece of wood attached to a line and thrown overboard to lie like a 'log' on the water. The Common Log consists of a wooden quadrant called the log ship, weighted at the base to keep it upright. In the log ship are two or three holes; to one or two of the holes the log line is made fast, while in the other is a bone peg attached by a cord to the log line. When heaving the log, the log ship at the end of the line is thrown overboard, well clear and to windward of the ship, and the line paid out from the log reel on which is it wound. The first 20 or 30 metres of the log line are called stray-line, and this is allowed to carry the log beyond the disturbed wake of the vessel. Where the stray-line joins the log line, a piece of bunting is inserted, called the *turnmark*. Beyond this mark, the line is marked with pieces of cord, each having a certain number of knots in it. Between these marks there is situated a piece of cord having one knot in it.

10 or 20 fathoms

The distance apart of the marks is in the same proportion to the number of metres in a nautical mile (1 854) as the duration of the sand-glass used is to the number of seconds in an hour (3600).

feet 6 080

The sandglass is inverted as soon as the turnmark runs over the rail. This glass is usually a 14- or 28-second timer. At the instant the sand-glass is run-out the cord nearest the rail is noted. The number of knots in the cord represent the number of knots of ship's speed, for they increase in number from the log-ship towards the vessel. The one-knot marks indicate half-knot speeds.

The line has to be quickly nipped as the sandglass runs out, and this is simplified by the use of a 'Burt's nipper', which is a device consisting of a handle and rollers through which the line is allowed to run. The operation of the handle causes the rollers to jam the line. This nipping action pulls the bone peg from the log-ship, allowing it to be easily hove-in.

The marking of this logline provides an excellent explanation for the use of knots as ship-speed units.

DECK APPLIANCES

There are now three basic types of ship log:

(a) The Towing Log

In this design a streamlined gunmetal rotator having four pitched fins is towed by means of a patent logline having a wire heart. The rotator revolves at a speed proportional to the speed of the ship through the water and induces a constant twist into the line. The latter is connected to the register, which dissipates the twist within its mechanism, which in turn converts the number of rotations into nautical miles, indicated on the dial of the register.

The towing log has been in use for over 150 years—it is simple to use, and provided reasonable care is taken to see that the line is of the correct length and the rotator is not damaged, accurate results may be obtained. A damaged rotator should be discarded, for its pitch will undoubtedly be affected.

The most modern towing log is the Walker's 'Commodore' (see Plate 7), which was introduced in 1956 to replace the Walker's 'Trident' electric log. The register provides mechanical indication of distance run on the dial, remote indication of distance run on the chart-room receiver dial, a speed feed to true-motion radar installations, speed indication, and speed and distance recording.

The register, fitted with 4 m of five-core electric cable, requires no internal lubrication except at very long intervals of about 100,000 miles. The dial movement is grease-packed and requires no attention. The contact movement is a complete assembly providing reduction gears and electrical contacts. It causes an electrical pulse every tenth of a mile for distance-repeating on the chart-room receiver, and a pulse every 10 m which is used either for speed feed to radar, or speed indication, or both. [15 ft] [yd]

The register employs the 'Cherub' rotator, which makes 900 turns to the nautical mile. The register is connected to a socket by means of a four-pin plug having an earth connection. The socket has a spring-loaded cap which must always be kept closed when the log is not in use, and it must never be painted, otherwise the cap may not seat properly.

Installation. The usual causes of error are either that the rotator is damaged, the line is of incorrect length, or that the rotator is towed in the propeller slipstream.

Both port and starboard mountings should be provided for the register and preferably with an outrigger bracket so that not only does the rotator clear the wake but also that the iron governor wheel, just abaft the register, does not foul the ship when the helm is hard over.

In a vessel over 120 m in length, with long, straight sides from the bridge position to the runaway aft, the log may be towed from a side boom, using a terylene logline. In this case a 'Viking' connector is [400 ft]

451

fitted at the outer end of the boom and transmits the turns from the line, through a fine copper aerial wire, to the register mounted in the wing of the bridge.

Before streaming the log the hands of the register and the chart-room receiver should be synchronised, by turning the hands in the opposite direction to that in which they normally revolve.

Speed Indication. For this the register is wired to the 'Commodore' switchcase, which provides feed for the radar, the bridge speed-indicator, and for the combined speed and distance recorder. This speed indication is accurate to within 2% if speeds are above 3 knots. The chart on the recorder, showing speeds from 3 to 23 knots, will suffice for about 4,000 miles.

Speed feed to radar from the log is much more efficient than a feed taken from the main propeller shafting, because no adjustments are necessary when varying engine revolutions in foggy or crowded traffic waters.

The Logline. The length used depends upon the ship's speed and the height of the register above the water level. The following lengths are recommended when streaming the log from astern:

40–50 fathoms	For a maximum speed of 12 knots use 73–90 m.
60–65 fathoms	For a maximum speed of 15 knots use 110–120 m.
70–80 fathoms	For a maximum speed of 18 knots use 130–150 m.

New lines stretch considerably, and their length should be carefully checked after a short initial period of service. It is always preferable to use the maximum length of line, for the rotator, being deeper in the water, is less affected by rough weather.

When the length has been decided one end is rove through the shell of the rotator (a streamlined connector secured to the rotator by about 1 fathom 2 m of line), a figure-of-eight knot is made in the end of the line, and this is hauled tightly back inside the shell. The other end of the line is secured to a hook by means of a round turn, seizing the end back on to the standing part several times.

When using a new line, or one which has been stowed away for a considerable period, the hook end should be paid out astern until all kinks are removed. It can then be hauled in and coiled down ready for use.

When streaming the log the line is hooked into the eye of the register and the rotator passed overboard. When the line is nearly paid out the load must be gradually transferred to the register spindle. Some seamen prefer to pay out the bight of the line, fling the rotator astern, and then grip the line to the rail, finally transferring the load to the register. There is the possibility here that the line may part as it jerks tight astern; on the other hand, by streaming the rotator first the line tends to run overboard with a rush, and may prove difficult to control. The former method is recommended by the manufacturers.

When *handing* the log, i.e. bringing it aboard, it is necessary to pass the hook end overboard and pay it out as the rotator is hauled in. When the rotator comes aboard the line may be hove-in free of turns.

If the log is streamed from abeam it can be handed without the line becoming badly snarled with undissipated twist by using one of the following methods: a grapnel may be cast across the line and slid down until it nearly touches the rotator. The latter can then be quickly plucked from the water. The other method uses a line having a thimbled eye in it through which the logline runs. The tripping line, as it is called, is made fast inboard. When it is desired to hand the log the tripping line is cast off inboard and passed aft along the ship's side until the thimbled eye touches the rotator, which may again be quickly withdrawn from the water. The use of such a tripping line tends to promote wear in the log-line in way of the thimble.

(b) The Electromagnetic Log

This device uses electromagnetism as its operating principle. The log transducer or sensor contains an energised winding which is supplied from a power transformer. This power, which is of the order of 50 volts at 0·7 amp, is used to produce an alternating magnetic field which is projected into the sea. An electric voltage gradient is therefore induced in the water as it flows through the magnetic field.

The voltage is then detected by electrodes on the outer face of the sensor and passed to the electronic unit for measurement. Since its value is only a few millivolts, even at full steaming speeds, it has to be processed to provide a suitable speed signal. It is also integrated with respect to time to provide pulses for recording distance travelled and for feeding to radar, satellite navigators, etc.

The log sensor. This protrudes through the ship's bottom plating by a distance of 28 mm, its face being flush with a bronze capping welded to the shell plating. The siting of the sensor will be governed to a large extent by the availability of suitable space in the forward part of the ship. Because the sensor electrodes are so close to the shell plating, it is vital that the siting is chosen where a clear flow of water exists. It should be positioned within the first 15 metres of the ship's length and in a dry space. There must be 1·15 metres vertical clearance for removal of the sensor. If a bow thrust unit is fitted, the sensor is sited below the thruster tube or well clear of the thruster and as near the centre line as possible, bearing in mind that it should be well clear of lines of docking blocks. The situation becomes even more critical because the siting must not allow the sensor to leave the water in heavy seas or when at light draught.

1 in

50 ft
3·8 ft

453

The sensor should be accessible in case a fault develops. Under no circumstances should grease or paint be allowed to cover the electrodes. Should this occur it will be found impossible to zero the log correctly.

7 in   Having chosen a suitable site, a 178 mm diameter hole is cut into the shell plating. Two sensors are provided with each log, one should remain boxed up as a spare.

To change a sensor it is only necessary to switch off the power, retract the sensor by means of the handle and lead screw and then close the sea valve completely. The removal of two bolts then enables the sensor to be replaced.

The electronic unit. This carries out all the electronic processing necessary to obtain speed and distance indication. It is intended for bulkhead mounting and should be placed where it will be accessible for servicing and calibration. It could be mounted on the bridge for ease of calibration but this will be costly due to the long run of cable between the unit and the sensor. This is special cable and for reasons of economy, it is preferable to keep the electronic unit near the sensor. The length of cable joining the unit to the bridge is not critical in any way.

Speed and distance repeaters. These can be located where required but are not watertight. An engine-room repeater is normally also supplied.

Electrical requirements. The log operates from 100/120 to 200/250 volts A.C. 50/60 Hz.

(The above information together with the diagram of the sensor assembly in Figure 17.1 was kindly provided by Thomas Walker and Son Limited.)

(c) The pitot log

This device makes use of a log tube measuring the static pressure of water and also the impact pressure as the ship moves. Differences in these two pressures cause a small beam to move. This movement is counteracted by an electromagnet. The current required to energise this magnet is therefore proportional to the ship's speed and may be used by the speed indicators and also the integrator for distance run. The log tube is raised by motor power in 20 seconds. Provision is also made for hand operation.

The tube is easily replaced at sea and provision is made for blowing silt out of the tube either with water at a pressure of $2 \cdot 8$ kg/ cm^2 (30–50 lb/in^2) or by using air.

Speed and distance indicators are fitted in the wheelhouse, chartroom and engine-room.

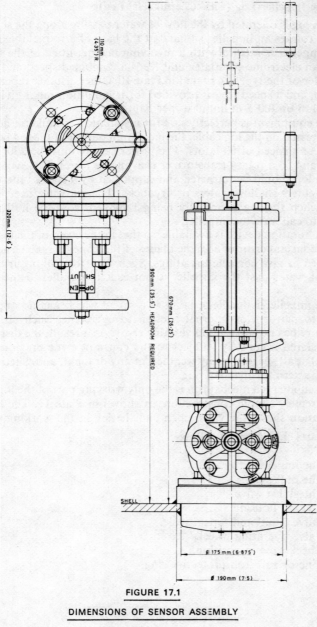

110 mm (4·35") R

320mm (12·6")

OPEN SHUT

900mm (35·5") HEADROOM REQUIRED

670mm (26·25")

SHELL

Ø 175 mm (6·875")

Ø 190mm (7·5")

FIGURE 17.1

DIMENSIONS OF SENSOR ASSEMBLY

(c) The Impeller Log (The 'Chernikeeff' Log)

This log is operated by the flow of water passing along the ship's hull, which rotates an impeller situated at the base of a retractable log tube. The impeller is integral with a revolving magnet fitted at the base of a coil. An electronic computer unit feeds a combined speed and distance recorder of the type illustrated in Plate 10. Other distance repeaters may be run, and a speed feed is provided for true-motion radar giving either 200 10-m or 400 5-m impulses per nautical mile.

The equipment is perfectly safe for installation in tankers; no current is impressed on the log cable, the maximum output of the log being only 1 volt at a speed of 60 knots. The power supply must be 230/240 volts A.C., and so a rotary transformer is available for all D.C. voltages.

The log should be retracted and supported by a check tube when the vessel enters shallow waters or drydocks. The sea valve need be closed only when the log is actually being removed from the hull fitting in order to calibrate the impeller.

A calibration device is available, so that in the event of the log having, say, a constant error of 5 %, the blades of the impeller may be accurately adjusted to give corrected readings. Such an error will occur when the flow of water past the impeller is not exactly parallel to the impeller shaft.

The impeller is loadless, i.e. it is a screw which has no appreciable work to perform or internal friction to overcome. Such an impeller therefore has no slip and no variable error. As a result, the distance run is registered accurately (subject to the constant error previously mentioned) at all speeds, in any weather, at any draught, and whether going ahead, astern, or manœuvring.

The submerged mechanism is the only working part of the log, having an extremely simple construction, as shown in Plate 11. The left-hand illustration shows the valve open and the log in the working position.

The parts shown are as follows:

 (1) The impeller.
(14) The hull plate.
(15) The sluice valve.
(16) The log housing.
(17) Valve 'shut' and 'open' scale.
(18) Valve operating wheel.
(19) Check tube in position.
(20) Zinc or soft iron protective ring.

The right-hand side of the plate shows the log withdrawn into its housing with the valve shut. In each diagram there will be noticed a valve at the top of the log. This provides oil injection to the working part of previous-model logs. The electronic log under discussion has a water-lubricated impeller bearing.

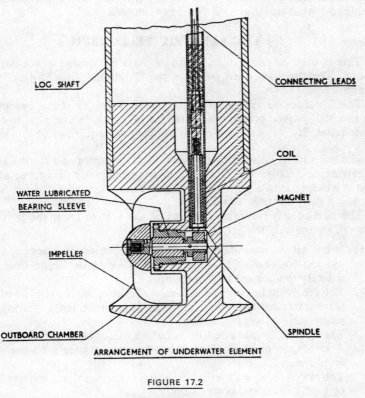

ARRANGEMENT OF UNDERWATER ELEMENT

FIGURE 17.2

CHERNIKEEFF LOG

The arrangement of the underwater element is shown in Fig. 17.2, while the revolving parts are shown in Plate 9, compared with the size of a matchbox. The components are, from top to bottom, the magnet, the housing, the water-lubricated bearing, the impeller spindle, and the impeller screw. The impeller is shown on the right. The components are shown in section in Fig. 17.2.

The log incorporates a tide control, whereby the speed indicator can be reset to record the speed over the ground. This assumes a known current, and of course the instrument must be reset when the current changes. The distance recorded is always that through the water.

Remote control is available for raising and lowering the log from the bridge or chart room, either for electric or manual operation.

14-in 30-in
49-in

The impeller is 35 cm below the plating when in use; 75-cm clearance is required within the ship while the log is in use; 125-cm clearance is required within the ship while the log is stowed.

(5) THE ELECTRIC TELEGRAPH

This is used to communicate orders from the bridge to the engine-room. The type described below is the Chadburn 'Synchrostep' telegraph.

The Synchrostep system of order transmission has been developed from a well-proven principle and has the inherent feature, vital to complete reliability, of being essentially simple and requiring the minimum of working parts.

The transmitter consists of a face-plate commutator and brush carrier revolving co-axially. The receiver consists principally of a three-phase stator winding with a permanent-magnet rotor (wound rotor for A.C.) to which the pointer is attached.

The particularly desirable features of the system from the point of view of its use as a telegraph system are:

(1) It has all the instantaneous and positive action of a normal step-by-step transmission system while being at the same time absolutely self- or auto-synchronous.
(2) The receiving instrument accurately follows the movement of the transmitter without the use of rotating components, gearing, or parts liable to wear in service.
(3) The system is unaffected by variation of supply voltage.
(4) A minimum number of cable conductors between instruments is employed.
(5) The system is equally suitable for operation on ships' mains (A.C. or D.C.) or on low-power supply.
(6) Transmitters can be mechanically or electrically interconnected, and any number of repeaters can be included in the system.

Operation

The Synchrostep Telegraph operates in the same manner as the orthodox mechanical installation, with the notable exception of the bridge and engine-room alarms. These are arranged to sound continuously from the time an order is given until that particular order is acknowledged. Such an arrangement has two advantages—for the bridge the immediate operation of their alarm confirms that their order has been transmitted, and for the engine-room the fact that their bell operates continuously ensures that attention must be drawn to the telegraph, even if the Engineer is not on the starting platform at the time.

The operation of pointers is positive and instantaneous, and the power of the motors operating them is such as to ensure accurate location, even under conditions of severe vibration.

Instruments

Instruments are supplied in high-quality corrosion-resistant aluminium castings, stove-enamelled grey, hammer finish. Brass instruments are available where required.

Transmitters are of quadrant form, the dial occupying a sector of some 160 degrees. This design, while maintaining true directional characteristics of a lever and pointer which do not move below the horizontal, gives the largest possible width of order.

The transmitter provides an unusual feature in that the instrument has both a peripheral and a side dial, with reply pointers working over each, and this design is of great benefit to the operator, particularly in the case of vessels which use their telegraphs frequently.

Receiver dials are of quadrant form, or can be supplied for panel mounting in circular form, for incorporation in starting-platform panels and consoles, etc.

The instruments are of robust construction, fully watertight, and the transmitter is provided with double night illumination lamps and dimmer. The electrical components and dials are effectively sealed from the mechanical linkage by means of a watertight compartment. This prevents condensation and moisture settling on any electrical component, and so obviates the possibility of short-circuits and corrosion damage.

In all cases the electrical equipment is chassis mounted and can be readily and easily withdrawn for servicing purposes or for replacement of interchangeable units.

Supplementary Equipment

A *Wrong-way Alarm* may be fitted, which is a warning device to sound should the propeller shaft or manœuvring gear (as applicable) be operated in a direction contrary to the transmitted order. A lamp and bell indicator is mounted in a convenient position on the starting platform and, by means of a directional switch working in conjunction with directional contacts in the receiver, the audible and visible alarms are put into operation if the engine is manœuvred in a direction contrary to the transmitted order, and they remain so until the mistake is rectified.

The directional switch may be operated by a friction clutch from any engine member whose direction of rotation is that of the propeller shaft or by linkage from the manœuvring gear.

A *Current-failure Alarm* automatically indicates, both visibly and audibly, that there is a supply failure to the telegraphs. It is normally fed from an independent battery supply. Arrangements can be made whereby as soon as the supply fails, an auxilliary supply is automatically established.

The *Isolator–Selector System* enables any number of instruments, wherever they may be located, to be electrically connected. In this way, one instrument can take charge of the whole installation. The reply-back, however, is shown on each instrument whether it is in charge or not. The one instrument remains in charge until a different transmitter is operated. The system is useful where instruments are remotely located, such as in the wings of bridges, etc.

Remote control is possible with the Synchrostep Telegraph, so that the engines can be controlled directly from the bridge.

The servicing of these telegraphs will not concern the Deck Officer. Should he find himself on a vessel fitted with mechanical telegraphs operated throughout by wire and chain, the only servicing necessary will be adjustment of the chain-lengths, which is provided for with tightening screws, and adjustment of the bronze pulleys to compensate for wear. All metal parts are bronze, galvanised steel, or brass. The mechanical telegraph may be fitted with electric illumination in addition to oil lamps, wrong-way alarms, and a supplementary alarm whereby a klaxon sounds if an order is made after long periods of 'Full ahead'. The wire-and-chain telegraphs, of which Chadburns were the patentees and original manufacturers, are also available for transmitting docking, steering, anchoring, and warping orders.

Plate 12 shows desk-mounted Chadburn 'Synchrostep' electric transmitters, as fitted to the *Oriana*.

(6) THE WELIN–MACLACHLAN QUADRANT BOAT DAVIT

This is an extremely reliable luffing davit, the design of which has remained virtually unaltered since its introduction in 1901.

The fundamental feature of the quadrant davit is a toothed quadrant at the lower end of the arm engaging and rolling upon a rack on the davit deck frame, which has the effect of moving the pivoting point of the davit progressively outwards as the davit arm is swung outboard, thus levelling the path of the davit head and making the davit easily operated.

The movement of the arm is controlled by a non-ferrous screw some distance above and parallel with the base of the deck frame, the arm being located by a guide rod immediately above the screw.

1. Firing 'Speedline' with buoyant head on rocket. *Above:* 'Speedline' self-contained line-throwing apparatus.

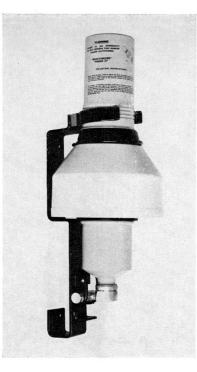 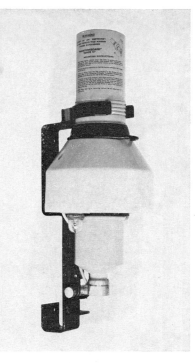

Pains-Wessex 'Buoysmoke'.   Pains-Wessex 'Manoverboard'.

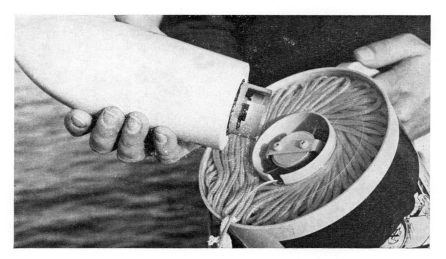

2. Buoyant Head for 'Speedline' unit.

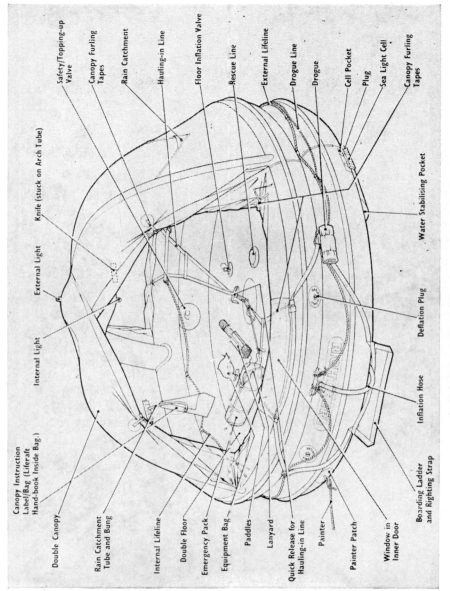

Safety/Topping-up Valve

Canopy Furling Tapes

Rain Catchment

Hauling-in Line

Floor Inflation Valve

Rescue Line

External Lifeline

Drogue Line

Drogue

Cell Pocket

Plug

Sea Light Cell

Canopy Furling Tapes

Knife (stuck on Arch Tube)

External Light

Internal Light

Canopy Instruction
Label/Bag (Liferaft
Hand-book Inside Bag.)

Double Canopy

Rain Catchment
Tube and Bung

Internal Lifeline

Double Floor

Emergency Pack

Equipment Bag

Paddles

Lanyard

Quick Release for
Hauling-in Line

Painter

Painter Patch

Window in
Inner Door

Boarding Ladder
and Righting Strap

Inflation Hose

Deflation Plug

Water Stabilising Pocket

3. Inflatable rubber liferaft—sectional view.

4. R.F.D. 20-person liferaft for single-point suspension. *Below*, Fully laden lowering. Note black trip lanyard on hook.

Streamlined block with swivel eye.

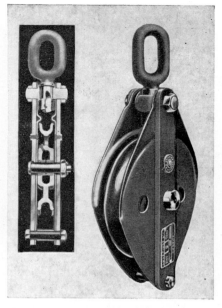

Single derrick block with section view.

Standard wire rope snatch block with
swivel oval eye.

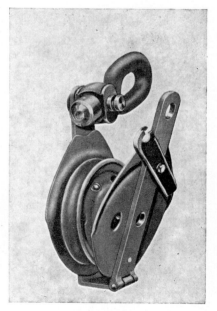

Special purpose snatch block opened
only when eye is horizontal.

5. Single-sheave cargo blocks.

Two-fold with swivel
oval eye and becket.

Three-fold with swivel
oval eye.

Six-fold with plate
crosshead and becket.

Swivel duckbill eye.

Swivel drilled eye.

Swivel jaw.

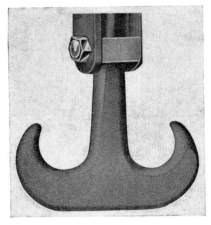

Ramshorn hook.

Flemish hook with saucer.

6. Multiple blocks and fittings.

Commodore Register.

Chart House Receiver.

Speed Recorder.

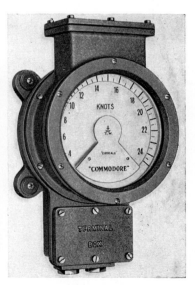

Speed Indicator.

7. Commodore Log equipment.

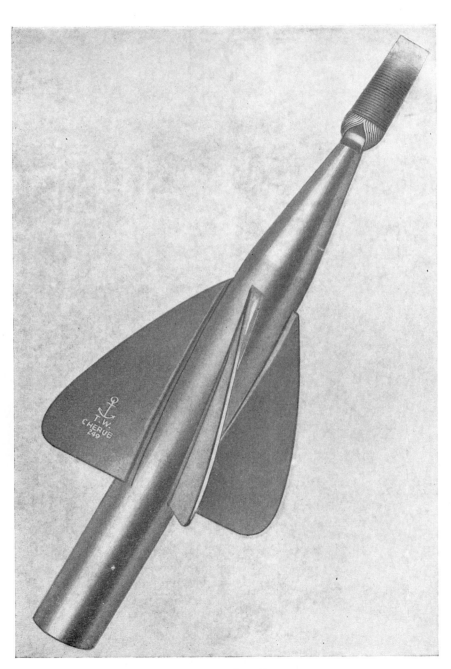

8. Commodore Log Rotator.

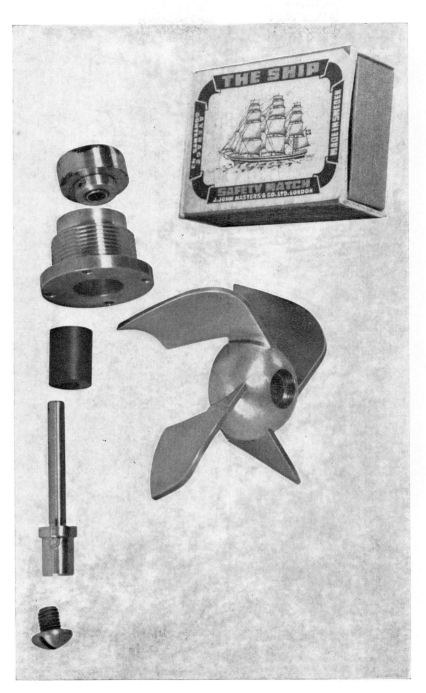

9. Chernikeeff Log—Impeller assembly.

10. Chernikeeff Log—Indicator.

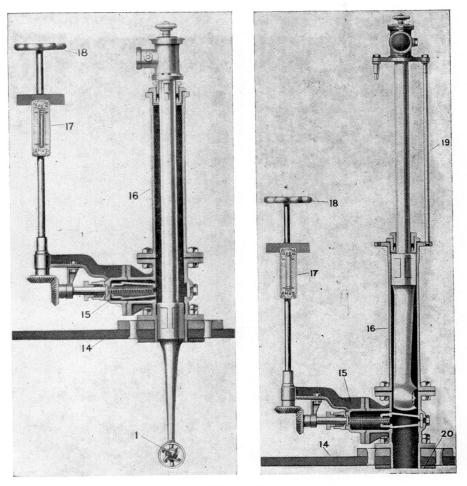

11. Chernikeeff Log—Tube assembly.

12. Desk-mounted 'Synchrostep' telegraphs.

13. Single-speed quadrantal davits.

14. Overhead-type quadrant davits.

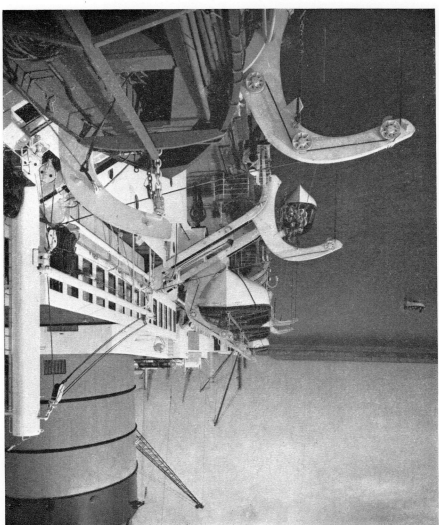

15. Welin gravity davits (*Saxonia*).

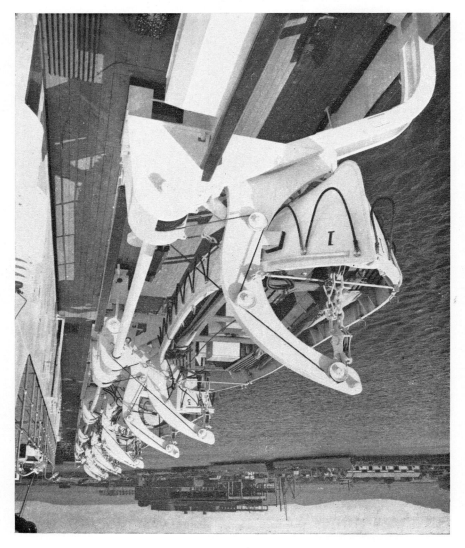

16. Welin gravity davits (B.T.C. Vessel).

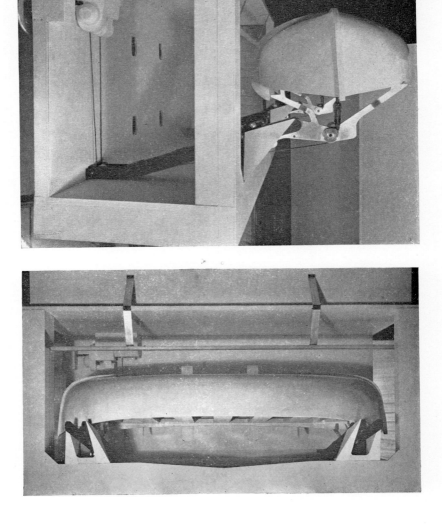

17. Underdeck davits. *Above*, boat stowed. *Below*, boat swung out.

18. Underdeck davits handling fibre glass lifeboats.

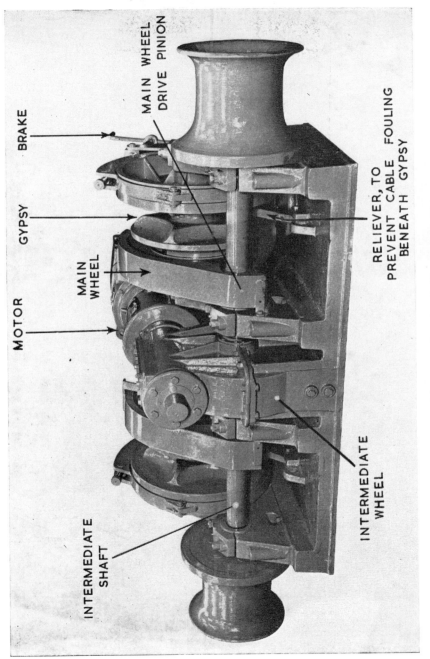

BRAKE

GYPSY

MOTOR

MAIN WHEEL DRIVE PINION

MAIN WHEEL

RELIEVER, TO PREVENT CABLE FOULING BENEATH GYPSY

INTERMEDIATE WHEEL

INTERMEDIATE SHAFT

19. Clarke Chapman electric windlass—fore side.

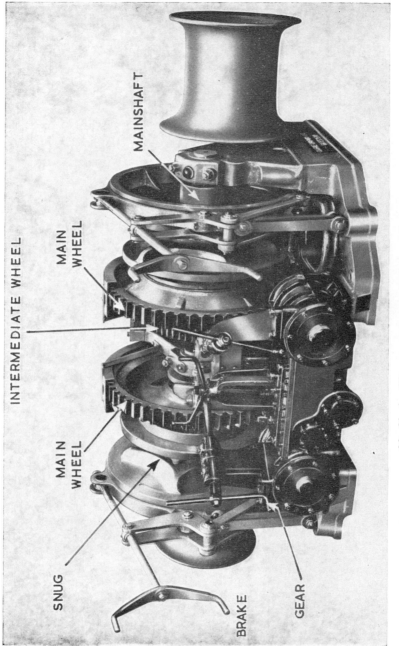

20. Clarke Chapman steam windlass—aft side.

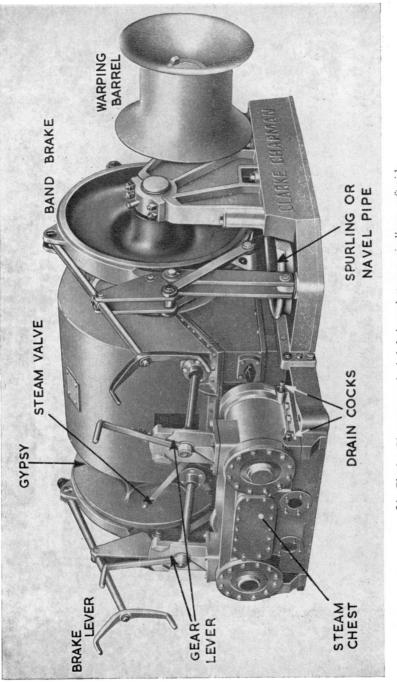

BRAKE LEVER

GYPSY

STEAM VALVE

BAND BRAKE

WARPING BARREL

GEAR LEVER

STEAM CHEST

DRAIN COCKS

SPURLING OR NAVEL PIPE

CLARKE CHAPMAN

21. Clarke Chapman splash-lubricated steam windlass—aft side.

22. Clarke Chapman electric mooring capstan.

23. Clarke Chapman splash-lubricated electric cargo winch.

24. Kelvin electrically-driven sounding machine.

A winding handle is provided at the end of the screw for operating the davit, and a two-speed gear is available on the larger sizes.

Hitherto, this type of davit has been made in cast steel. It is now available fabricated and welded entirely from wrought mild steel.

This construction, while retaining all the strength of the cast steel, is considerably lighter and has other important advantages. The quadrant and teeth of the arm are of such construction as to be less liable to be affected by ice and the two-speed gear (when fitted) is totally enclosed and operates in an oil bath.

The davit arm is of rectangular box form, fabricated and welded together to form a very strong and light member, the inside being hermetically sealed and airtight.

The davit is made in the same variety of sizes and types as those previously associated with the cast-steel quadrant davit, namely, the ordinary type for use outside the end of the boats; the long-arm type for use with superimposed boats; and the overhead type for use within the length of the boat, the boat being stowed in the davit arm with the keel some distance above the deck.

The davit is suitable for use with either manila falls and bollards or wire falls and winches, using any normal purchase of block and tackle.

Plate 13 shows the earlier type of quadrant davit, and the reader should note the operating handle on the left-hand davit, which is not fitted with two-speed gear. A stag-horn bollard is clearly shown at the base of the davit, with the fall leading to the winding reel. When operating this davit in the turning-out condition it is very easy for the davit to take charge, and for this reason the handle should always be firmly held. If it is released by a novice marvelling at the way the davit runs out by itself (with rapidly rotating handle) the davit will be brought to a halt at its outermost plumbing position with considerable force.

Plate 14 shows the Welin overhead type quadrant davit fitted with wire-rope falls and an electric winch. At the extreme left-hand side of the photograph the long-arm type is just visible, together with two nested boats. On the overhead davit the two-speed gear is visible on the right hand side of the photograph, just above the operating handle.

(7) THE WELIN–MACLACHLAN GRAVITY DAVIT

The outstanding feature of the Welin–Maclachlan gravity davit is its extreme simplicity and reliability. Its construction, which is well known, consists of a pair of trackways, and a pair of cradles. The inner flange of the channel trackways forms the path along which the rollers of the cradles run; the inclination of the trackways is 30 degrees, consequently the davits will operate under extreme conditions of list.

The outboard end of the inclined trackways is bent downwards until

461

it is vertical, the lower end being rigidly connected to the deck. The radius around which the two front rollers of the cradles run swings the head of the davit outboard, and gives the outreach necessary to lower the boat clear of the ship's side.

The use of these davits leaves the boat deck completely clear of obstructions and provides a clear promenade, not only fore and aft but also up to the ship's rails.

The channel trackways are made up from standard sections, and the bent portion is fabricated in a special manner, ensuring that the section remains constant, allowing the rollers to be a close fit in the channel trackways and preventing side sway and slogger (judder).

The cradles are of a fabricated box section, hermetically sealed to prevent internal corrosion. They carry four rollers which run in the trackways, and the simplicity of the design gives accessibility to all parts, there being no links or other complications to screen portions of the davits and cause corrosion. This simplicity of design makes inspection and maintenance very easy.

The cradles in the stowed position are held rigidly with the trackways by a trigger operated by the lifeboat gripes, the pressure exerted by the gripes being multiplied by the trigger lever, thus ensuring complete rigidity when the gripe wires are tightened. In the stowed position the lifeboats are entirely prevented from any fore-and-aft surge in a seaway, as the boat under these conditions is not suspended by the falls at the davit head, but is resting its full weight on the keel support of the cradle. This has the effect of lowering the suspension point of the boat in the stowed position, which makes it easier to control; in those cases where nested boats are in use, an arrangement such as this is vital.

The four rollers of each cradle are carried on pins with gunmetal bushes and grease lubricant, the various sheaves on the cradle being similarly supported. The floating blocks are fitted with roller bearings, giving smooth operation and reducing friction to a minimum. All the bearings are packed with grease at the maker's works, and further grease can be added at intervals by means of a high-pressure grease gun supplied with the equipment.

The general layout and disposition of the various components of these gravity davits is generally arranged to suit the particular ship to which they are being fitted. The inboard end of the trackway is supported either on a deck house or on an 'A' frame, preferably of tubular construction. Winches are available both in the vertical and horizontal types. The vertical winch (with one drum above the other) may be placed adjacent to one of the trackways, at the edge of the boat deck, making a very simple and convenient arrangement, and ensuring a good lead for the wire falls, which are all carried overhead. Drip trays under the wire-rope falls are easily arranged, and ensure a clear and clean boat deck.

On the other hand, where a deck house is available, a very neat arrangement can be provided by a horizontal winch placed on the deck house, mid-way between the inner attachments of the two trackways, with the wire ropes leading fore and aft from the winch. An objection often raised to this arrangement is that the winch operator cannot see the boat as it is being lowered down the ship's side, but this difficulty can be overcome by a remote-control arrangement, enabling the main brake to be operated from the edge of the deck despite the winch being placed some little distance away on an upper deck. The remote control does not rely upon rods, links, etc., and is extremely simple and reliable.

These davits are capable of launching a lifeboat within 20 seconds from the time when the gripes are cast off.

Plate 15 shows the davits in use on board the *Saxonia* (Cunard Line). Among the features which the reader should study are:

(1) The boat-gripes, and one of these is visible just to the right of the Officer who is standing at the ship's rail. It is hanging in a bight from the base of the trackway to the trigger-mechanism, mounted just below the fall at the top of the trackway.
(2) The method whereby the block of the nearest boat fall is hooked to the davit cradle.
(3) The tricing pendants referred to in Chapter XVIII. The left-hand nearest davit has one suspended from the cradle just below the centre sheave. It is fitted with a patent slip at its lower end. The boat at the bottom of the plate has its tricing pendant slip made fast to the link on the block. These pendants are fully discussed in Chapter XVIII.

Plate 16 shows gravity davits fitted to a British Transport Commission vessel. The tricing pendants are again visible.

The canvas-covered gripes can be seen extending across the boat forward and aft, and if their lead is followed inboard they will be observed secured to the cradle trigger-mechanisms. At the after end of the boat it is possible to see the hand-linkage ring for quick release of the after hook.

(8) THE WELIN–MACLACHLAN UNDERDECK GRAVITY DAVIT

In recent times Naval Architects have again been giving considerable thought to the desirability of entirely removing boats and davits from exposed upper decks and installing them on a lower covered deck with the object of keeping upper decks clear, reducing top weight, and reducing deterioration and maintenance to a minimum.

This problem was complicated by the need for gravity davits, which by Regulation require either a trackway inclination of 30 degrees or a continuous positive turning-out moment with the vessel listed 25 degrees either way.

The new boat deck consists of a bay occupying the height of *two* decks and running the requisite length of the vessel to accommodate the necessary number of boat stations; trackways are connected to the underside of the deck above, and the winches are mounted on the cabin bulkhead to give full headroom on the operational deck, which will also be the embarkation deck. The lifeboats will be suspended at a sufficient height to. permit of full headroom for promenade purposes on the bay deck; and the height and angle of the lifeboats has been carefully adjusted to permit an unobstructed view from the windows of the two decks inboard of the lifeboat bay deck.

The necessary gravitational operation of the davits has been obtained by a combination of trackway inclination and a counterweight; and the positive turning-out moment stipulated by the Regulations has thus been ensured.

The trackway is in mild steel, but the cradle and the gunwale steadying arms are made of aluminium alloy. The light weight of the cradle reduces the size of the counterweight, and it is interesting to note that this new davit complete with counterweight is approximately 15% lighter than the standard trackway-type overhead gravity davit. Another novel feature is the tusk, which holds the floating block in position on the cradles; this tusk is controlled by the movement of the cradle, and can release the floating block (which carries the lifeboat) only when the davit reaches the fully outboard position.

This davit can therefore release and lower a lifeboat against a 25 degrees adverse list and a 10 degrees trim, and this has been confirmed by tests carried out by the British Department of Trade and Industry.

Among the many benefits obtained are the following:

(1) The Davit can actually launch a lifeboat at 25 degrees adverse list.
(2) Clear upper decks.
(3) Reduction of top weight.
(4) Protection of boats and davits from deterioration.
(5) Easier maintenance.

Plate 17 includes two photographs of a working-model of the new davits, while Plate 18 shows them in actual use on board the Orient liner *Oriana*, used in conjunction with polyester glass-fibre lifeboats.

(9) THE CLARKE–CHAPMAN ELECTRIC WINDLASS
(Plate 18)

A watertight electric motor mounted on the after side of the windlass bedplate drives, by means of worm and spur gearing, two five-snug cable lifters suitable for steel stud link anchor cable having either bolt or lugless shackles. These are fixed to, and revolve with, the mainshafts when letting go or when heaving up. They are fitted with large sheaves to take powerful screw band brakes.

When heaving anchor the appropriate main wheel is engaged with the gypsy by means of screw gear (the operating handle being on the after side of the windlass), which slides the mainwheel outboard and along the mainshaft until the jaws on its outboard face engage the jaws on the inboard face of the gypsy. The main wheels are always engaged with the pinions on the intermediate shaft.

The basic principle of the windlass is that the engine or motor driving pinion is forward and in the centreline. This drives the large intermediate wheel, which is mounted on the intermediate shaft. This shaft has warping ends and also a small pinion on either side of the intermediate wheel. For this reason, whenever the windlass is working the intermediate shaft, warping ends, and main wheels always revolve.

The main wheels are in no way fixed to the mainshafts, and the latter (which are independent so that one gypsy may be used even though the other may be damaged) revolve only with the gypsies.

The warping drums are of high-duty iron and are secured to the intermediate shaft by gib keys. When using the warping ends the cable lifters are held on the band brakes, the main wheels are taken out of gear with the gypsies, and they then revolve freely on the stationary mainshafts.

Hand crank gear is available if required.

All bearing and working parts are lubricated by means of grease gun and 'Tecalemit' nipples. The motor may be mounted, if desired, either on deck integral with the windlass, or below decks, or in a separate deckhouse.

A windlass having a 64-kilowatt motor will have a cable duty of 27·5 tonnes at 7·5 m per minute and will be able to warp 9 tonnes at 25 m per minute or slack rope at 49 m per minute.

(10) THE CLARKE–CHAPMAN STEAM WINDLASS
(Plate 20)

The layout and operation of this windlass is identical to the electric type, except that the motive power is derived from a powerful twin-cylinder double-acting reversible steam engine. In the most recent design all engine and gearing parts are totally enclosed in an oil-tight casing providing splash-lubrication throughout. The outer frame bearings are lubricated by grease cups. The machine is extremely silent in operation.

A drain cock is fitted to each end of each cylinder. When about to heave anchor the drain cocks are opened and the steam turned on gradually, the engine being run both ways to clear the cylinders and lines of water. The drain cocks are then closed, the main wheels slid into gear, and the windlass is fully operational.

When letting go (in steam or electric windlasses) the band brakes are screwed tight, the main wheels slid out of gear, and the cable is controlled by the brake only.

Regarding maintenance, the cylinder draincocks should be kept open when not in use to prevent corrosion in the cylinders and steam chest, and frost damage. Both the cylinders and the steam chest should be opened periodically to ensure that the bores, valves, and chest faces are in good condition. The underside of the cylinders and steam chest require particular attention, and should be frequently painted. Greasing is by 'Tecalemit' grease gun. Unless splash-lubricated, the spur gearing should be smeared with grease at regular intervals.

(11) THE CLARKE–CHAPMAN ELECTRIC MOORING CAPSTAN
(Plate 22)

A watertight A.C. electric motor, three-phase and two-speed with built-in magnetic disc braking, is mounted vertically inside the capstan head. The baseplate houses the gears and also grease nipples in an oil-tight case. The master controller is visible on the right of the photograph with a deadman handle feature and a speed control for heave and veer. This capstan may be bolted directly to the deck.

50 ft   A 48 kilowatt motor in this capstan provides a duty of about 14
100 ft   tonnes at a rate of 15 metres per minute or slack rope heaving at 30 metres per minute.

(12) THE CLARKE–CHAPMAN TOTALLY ENCLOSED SPLASH-LUBRICATED CAPSTAN

This is very quiet-running and employs a powerful twin-cylinder, double-acting, reversible steam engine. Draincocks are again fitted to the cylinders, and should be used as in the windlass. One such capstan
100 lb/in^2 can, provided 7 kg/cm^2 pressure is maintained at the cylinders, exert a pull of 10 tonnes at 30 metres per minute. Such an engine consumes
7 000 lb roughly 3 200 kg of steam per running hour.

(13) THE CLARKE–CHAPMAN WARD–LEONARD ELECTRIC WINCH

This is suitable for either A.C. or D.C. supply, employs a horizontal electric motor, and is entirely self-contained, with no outlying contactor gear. The motor drives a single shaft carrying a cargo runner barrel and two warping ends. Grease-nipple lubrication is provided, and the winch is controlled at remote-control pedestals adjacent to the hatch coamings. A 41-kilowatt motor provides a lifting capacity of 5 tonnes at 40 m per minute on full load, reaching this speed in a few seconds. A light hook can be worked at 100 m per minute.

(14) THE CLARKE–CHAPMAN SPLASH-LUBRICATED CARGO WINCH (Plate 23)

The standard A.C. cargo winch comprises one wire rope drum and one warping end. Both are cast iron and both are keyed to the shaft. Options include two warping ends, a secondary drum for heavy derrick operation and portable controllers. In Plate 23 the warping end is out of view on the left side of the rectangular gearcase.

The gearing is totally enclosed and oil splash-lubricated. Two fans are used to cool the motor. The master controller is fixed to the deck and has the same features as the electric capstan mentioned in section (11). The motor is a marine watertight unit, of three-phase squirrel-cage type with built-in disc-type magnetic braking.

Using high gear, this winch will hoist 5 tonnes at between 4 and 40 metres per minute depending upon the control step. Low gear will lift 2·5 tonnes at between 8 and 80 metres per minute.

13 ft   130 ft

26 ft   260 ft

As with all splash-lubricated meachines, the casing must be regularly dipped to ensure that the correct oil level is maintained.

(15) STEERING-GEAR (TELEMOTOR AND HYDRAULIC)

Deck officers are required to understand the basic principles of their steering-gear, and the following short discussion will suffice.

The wheelhouse telemotor transmitter consists basically of two vertical cylinders, each containing a piston. The pistons are driven in alternate vertical directions by means of a single central pinion mounted on the wheel shaft. The telemotor gear is filled with oil or a mixture of glycerine and distilled water. When the wheel is turned one piston moves down, compressing the fluid in that cylinder. This pressure is transmitted through small-bore copper piping to the receiver or telemotor mounted in the steering flat aft.

Here, the pressure is used to cause two floating cylinders to move over four fixed, hollow pistons, the cylinders being bridged and connected by means of a cross-head. The cross-head carries a rod which is connected by a floating link to the steering-pump motor.

The electric-pump motor rotates at constant speed and direction, the controls merely altering the discharge and suction outlets of the pump.

One end of the floating link operates the pump, and the other end is secured to the tiller. The tiller is keyed to the rudder stock. The end of the tiller is secured to the centre of a sliding ram, which moves to port or starboard under the action of the pump fluid.

When the cross-head rod is caused to move, then the floating link operates the pump and the ram slides to one side, carrying the tiller with it, thus rotating the rudder. As the tiller turns, the fulcrum of the floating link moves from the tiller head to the end of the telemotor rod. This eventually causes the pump to cease driving the ram. The rudder therefore comes to rest at the desired angle. This 'switch-off' of the power is known as the hunting gear.

By now, the telemotor rod has caused a spring to be in either tension or compression. As soon as the steering-wheel is released the spring relaxes, the rod, cross-head, and floating cylinders move back to their original positions, and the wheel and rudder are centralised.

Variations of this method of steering may be found.

The telemotor may also be used to control a steam engine driving a floating quadrant. This quadrant, though free to revolve on the rudder stock, is secured by springs to a tiller which is keyed to the stock. In the event of tiller fracture, arrangements are sometimes incorporated whereby the floating quadrant can be keyed to the stock and become a fixed quadrant.

Emergency transmission sometimes consists of a wheel aft which is directly connected to the telemotor rod. This is used in the event of failure in the bridge transmission.

Auxiliary steering-gear consists, in the case of a quadrant, of two double or three-fold purchases rove with a wire fall. The purchases are secured to each side of the quadrant, the falls are led to the deck winches, and the steering engine is slid clear of the quadrant.

In cases where no quadrant is employed, such as in the hydraulic gear, a second pump having an independent circuit is fitted. Arrangements are often made for the second pump to automatically cut-in as the first pump fails.

CHAPTER XVIII

THE SHIP'S BOAT

REQUIREMENTS BY LAW

A PASSENGER ship engaged on voyages, any of which are long international voyages is required to be equipped as follows:

(a) Sufficient boats to carry the entire ship's complement, evenly distributed on both sides or,

(b) Lifeboats and liferafts to carry the entire ship's complement, including enough boats to carry at least 75% of the people, evenly distributed on both sides.

(c) One lifeboat on each side to act as an emergency boat. It shall not exceed 8·5 m in length and may be a motor boat. It need not   28 ft
be fitted with skates.

(d) At least one motor boat on each side. (Powered emergency boats may be counted.) Each motor boat shall carry a searchlight.

(e) A radio installation, radio cabin and dynamo shall be fitted in each motor boat. If less than 1,500 persons are carried only one motor boat need be so equipped, but a portable radio shall also be provided on the ship.

(f) Lifeboats shall be at least 7·3 m long, and each shall be attached   24 ft
to a set of gravity davits, unless the turning-out weight does not
exceed 2¼ tonnes, when luffing davits may be used.   tons

(g) At least one launching appliance on each side for the liferafts mentioned in (b).

(h) Liferafts for 25% of the complement and buoyant apparatus for 3% of the complement. The rafts shall be capable of being used with launching appliances if rafts are carried in compliance with (b).

(j) Eight to thirty lifebuoys, depending upon the vessel's length.

(k) One lifejacket for every person plus lifejackets for 5% of the complement, the latter to be stowed on deck.

(l) Twelve parachute rockets and one line-throwing appliance.

These ships are known as Class 1 ships.

Steamers engaged on voyages, any of which are long international voyages shall be equipped as follows:

24 ft

tons

(a) On each side of the ship sufficient lifeboats to carry all persons on board. The boats shall be at least 7·3 m long, and each shall be attached to a separate set of gravity davits, except that in ships other than tankers, davits may be of the luffing type if the turning-out weight of the boats does not exceed $2\frac{1}{4}$ tonnes.

(b) Except in tankers, there shall be liferafts for 50% of the ship's complement.

(c) In tankers over 3000 tons gross there shall be at least two boats on each side, two carried aft and two carried amidships. If there is no amidships structure all boats may be carried aft. *If only two boats can be carried aft in the latter case the following extra provisions apply—*

26 ft

(i) *Lifeboats shall not exceed 8 m in length.*

(ii) *The boats shall be stowed as far forward as possible and each shall be clear of the propeller by at least $1\frac{1}{2}$ boat lengths.*

(iii) *Each boat shall be carried as near sea level as possible.*

(iv) *There shall be liferafts for 50% of the ship's complement.*

(d) One lifeboat shall be a motor boat except in tankers, when at least one motor boat shall be carried on each side.

(e) There shall also be carried one portable radio, one lifejacket per person, at least eight lifebuoys, twelve parachute rockets and one line-throwing appliance.

These ships are known as Class 7 ships.

General Requirements

Lifeboats. These shall be sufficiently strong to be lowered with the full complement of persons and equipment. The total weight when thus

tons

ft³/10

laden shall not exceed 20 tonnes. The carrying capacity of the boat shall be the greatest whole number obtained by dividing the volume in cubic metres by 0·283. No boat shall carry more than 150 persons. If more than 100 persons are carried the boat must be a motor lifeboat. If more than 60 persons are carried it shall be either a motor boat or mechanically propelled.

Motor Boats. These shall have diesel engines, be capable of going astern, and have sufficient fuel for 24 hours continuous operation at a speed of 6 knots (4 knots in dry-cargo ships) in smooth water when fully laden.

Mechanically Propelled Boats. The mechanism should be capable of being operated by persons of differing stature, by untrained persons, and when the boat is flooded. It should be capable of producing a speed of 3½ knots in smooth water for a quarter of a mile when fully laden. The helmsman shall have a device capable of causing the boat to go astern.

Liferafts. Inflatable liferafts shall be surveyed at an approved service station every 12 months. They shall be fit to withstand a drop of 18 m. 60 ft (See also page 133.) The carrying capacity shall be 6 to 25 persons. The maximum weight in the container shall be 180 kg. They shall be 400 lb capable of at least 30 days exposure in all sea conditions.

Marking. Lifeboats, rafts, and buoyant apparatus shall be marked to show the carrying capacity. Lifeboats shall also be marked with the dimensions, and the name of the ship and her port of registry shall be marked on each bow.

Lifebuoys. These shall be capable of providing 14·5 kg of buoyancy 32 lb in fresh water for at least 24 hours. The diameters shall be 46 and 18 92 cm (inside and outside respectively). They shall be of a highly visible 30 in colour. The maximum weight is 6·1 kg. 13½ lb

Lifebuoy Lights, Signals, and Lines. Self-igniting lights shall be fitted to at least half the number of lifebuoys. The electric type is to be used on tankers. They shall burn for at least 45 minutes. One lifebuoy on each side shall have a 27·5 m buoyant line attached, but no self-igniting 15 fathom light. At least two of the buoys fitted with lights shall also have self-activating, 15-minute smoke signals nearby. Two of these shall be carried on the bridge, and ready for quick release. Lifebuoys shall weigh at least 4·3 kg when their weight is used to release lights or smoke 9½ lb signals.

Handling of Appliances. All appliances on Class 1 ships are to be capable of being launched overall within 30 minutes. Boats shall be capable of being launched against a list of 15 degrees. They shall only be stowed on more than one deck if there is no risk of fouling. They are not to be stowed in the bows. They shall be served by wire-rope falls together with winches and hand gear. Two lifelines, long enough to reach the water when the ship is at light draught and listed 15 degrees adversely, shall be fitted to a span between davits, so that two lines serve each boat. Emergency boats shall be equipped with pendants (between hook and fall block) to enable easy recovery in heavy weather. If a davit is not strong enough to lower a boat fully laden it shall be marked with a 15-cm red band on a white background. A ladder shall be pro- 6-in vided at each set of davits, which, like the falls, shall be as long as the lifelines.

Manning. A deck officer or lifeboatman shall be in charge of each boat. A trained person shall be assigned to each liferaft in Class 1 ships. A capable person shall be assigned to each motor boat to look after the motor. A person able to operate the radio and searchlight shall be assigned to each motor boat on Class 1 ships.

Lifejackets. These are capable of being worn inside-out, and of turning the wearer within 5 seconds to a position inclined backwards, with the mouth 15 cm above the water. They shall be impervious to oil, highly visible in colour, fitted with a whistle, and able to allow the wearer to jump 6 m vertically without injury. For persons of 32 kg and over, they shall be so marked and shall provide 16 kg of buoyancy in fresh water for 24 hours. For persons of less than 32 kg they shall be so marked and able to give 6·8 kg of buoyancy in fresh water for 24 hours. Inflatable types are allowed in Class 7 ships; they are to be marked "CREW ONLY" and shall contain two buoyancy compartments providing either 9 kg of buoyancy in each from air, or 6·8 kg of air of buoyancy in one and 9 kg of solid-material buoyancy in the other. The spare lifejackets on Class 1 ships for 5% of the complement shall be the type for persons over 32 kg.

Equipment in Lifeboats

(1) A single-banked complement of oars, two spare oars and a steering oar. A set and a half of crutches on lanyards and a boathook.
(2) Two plugs for each hole, attached on chains or lanyards; a bailer and two buckets.
(3) A rudder and a tiller.
(4) A lifeline becketed around the boat; bilge keels or keel rails, and grablines from gunwale to gunwale under the keel.
(5) A locker for small items.
(6) Two hatchets, one at each end of the boat.
(7) A lamp, with oil for 12 hours burning.
(8) A watertight box containing matches not easily extinguished by wind.
(9) A mast or masts with galvanised rigging; orange sails marked with the first and last letters of the ship's name.
(10) A compass in a binnacle.
(11) A sea anchor with a warp three times as long as the boat and a tripping line 4 m longer than the warp.
(12) Two painters of sufficient size and length; one shall be secured to the stem and the other fitted with a strop and toggle for easy slipping.
(13) 4½ litres of fish, vegetable or animal oil; and oil bag capable of being attached to the sea anchor.
(14) Four parachute distress rockets and six red hand flares.
(15) Two buoyant orange-smoke signals.
(16) A first-aid outfit.
(17) An electric torch suitable for Morse-signalling with one spare set of cells and a spare bulb.
(18) A heliograph.
(19) A jack-knife fitted with a tin opener, secured to the boat on a lanyard.
(20) Two light buoyant heaving lines.

472

(21) A manual pump.
(22) A whistle.
(23) A fishing line and six hooks.
(24) A highly visible cover capable of protecting the occupants from exposure.
(25) Means to enable persons in the water to climb into the boat.
(26) A list of the Rescue Signals used by Coastguards.

No motor boat or mechanically propelled boat need carry masts or sails nor more than half the complement of oars. These boats shall carry two boathooks. Motor boats must carry two portable fire extinguishers, a receptacle containing sand together with a scoop.

Rations in Lifeboats. There shall be at least:

450 grammes of biscuits per person;	16 oz
450 grammes barley sugar per person;	16 oz
450 grammes of sweetened condensed milk per person; and	16 oz
3 litres of fresh water for every person the boat is certified to carry.	6 pints

There shall be at least one water-dipper and three rust-proof drinking vessels, one graduated.

All the food and water must be labelled and secured in watertight containers. The water must be frequently charged.

Equipment in Liferafts

(1) A buoyant rescue quoit on 30 m of line.   100 ft
(2) One safety knife and one bailer for up to 12 persons. If more than 12 are carried, two knives and two bailers shall be carried.
(3) Two sponges and two paddles.
(4) Two sea anchors, one attached to the raft and one spare.
(5) One puncture-repair outfit and one topping-up pump or bellows.
(6) Three safety tin openers and one graduated rustproof drinking vessel.
(7) Two parachute distress rockets and six red hand flares.
(8) 340 grammes of non-thirst-provoking food and 170 grammes of barley sugar or other suitable sweet, per person. 1·5 litres of fresh water per person.   12 oz 6 oz 3 pints
(9) Six anti-seasickness tablets per person.
(10) English instructions on how to survive in the raft.
    Also items (16), (17), (18), (22), (23), and (26) of the lifeboat equipment.

In both rafts and boats one-third of the minimum fresh water ration may be produced by desalting apparatus.

(Author's Note: Readers should observe that passenger ships have boats, rafts, and buoyant apparatus for 128% of the ship's complement. Non-passenger ships, however, carry boats and rafts for 250% of the complement. These are minimum requirements.)

Boat Drills

In the Merchant Shipping (Musters) Rules, 1965, the term 'muster' indicates a boat drill and a fire drill.

In Class 1 ships a muster of the crew shall be held before the vessel finally leaves the United Kingdom, and a muster of the passengers shall be held within 24 hours of embarkation. Thereafter, a muster of the crew shall take place at intervals of not more than seven days.

In Class 7 ships crew musters shall take place at intervals of not more than fourteen days, and within 24 hours of leaving port if more than 25% of the crew have been changed.

The emergency signal for summoning passengers to the embarkation assembly stations shall be a succession of seven or more short blasts followed by one long blast, on the whistle or siren. This signal is usually referred to as the *general emergency signal*. It is the only one which is statutory, that is to say a signal to indicate an outbreak of fire is up to the discretion of the Master. Often, however, it takes the form of a continuous ringing of alarm bells. There is no statutory signal for abandoning ship, for example; such a serious order will undoubtedly be given verbally.

COMPONENTS OF LIFEBOATS

A side elevation of the stem, and a half-midship section of a wooden lifeboat are illustrated in Fig. 18.1, so that the reader may become familiar with the terms used to identify the various parts.

A side elevation of the stern has been omitted for the reason that no unusually-named parts exist there; there is a deadwood, an apron, crutches instead of breasthooks, and a sternband, in the after position.

Nowadays, metal lifeboats are in common use, being made of pressed steel or aluminium. Fibre-glass lifeboats are gradually being introduced. With regard to aluminium boats, care should be taken to avoid the use of mercury or lead-based paints being applied directly to the bare metal, otherwise intense and rapid corrosion will ensue. A steel lifeboat will still be fitted with wooden thwarts, sidebenches, gangboards, stretchers, bow and sternsheets, tank cleadings, and bottom boards. The hooks for lifting the boat always face towards amidships.

The *Bilge* is the rounded part of the hull adjacent to the bilge keelsons.

The *Block Span* is a light wire often stretched between the lower fall blocks, at the hooks, to prevent the blocks from rotating on their swivels as the boat is hoisted.

Buoyancy Tanks are omitted from Fig. 18.1, but are placed under the sidebenches and held in place by a fore-and-aft wooden framework called the *tank cleading*. They may be varnished or coated with boiled linseed oil as a protective measure.

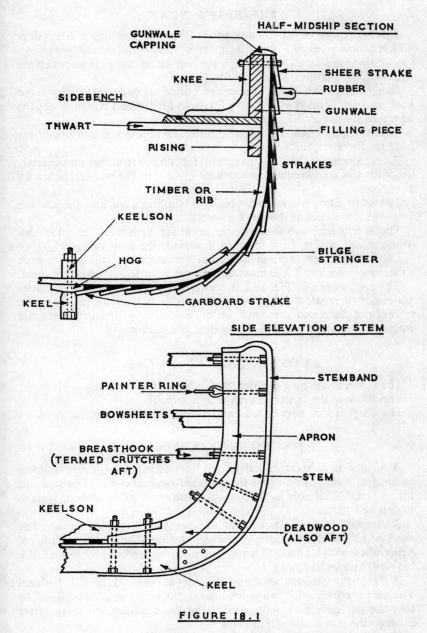

HALF-MIDSHIP SECTION

GUNWALE
CAPPING

KNEE

SIDEBENCH

THWART

RISING

TIMBER OR
RIB

KEELSON

HOG

KEEL

SHEER STRAKE

RUBBER

GUNWALE

FILLING PIECE

STRAKES

BILGE
STRINGER

GARBOARD STRAKE

SIDE ELEVATION OF STEM

PAINTER RING

BOWSHEETS

BREASTHOOK
(TERMED CRUTCHES
AFT)

KEELSON

STEMBAND

APRON

STEM

DEADWOOD
(ALSO AFT)

KEEL

FIGURE 18.1

COMPONENTS OF WOOD BOAT

Pintles are pins projecting downwards from the fore side of the rudder which fit into eyes projecting from the sternpost, called *Gudgeons*.

Life-rings are small metal rings secured along the hull, to which are becketed the lifelines, shown in Fig. 18.3.

Gangboards. The lifting hooks are bolted through the keelson and keel, and are bedded into strong fore-and-aft timbers which bisect the bow and sternsheets. These are gangboards.

Stretchers are flexible pieces of timber extending from one side of the boat to the other, underneath the thwarts.

Each oarsman is thus able to rest his feet on the stretcher immediately abaft his thwart. Stretchers contribute greatly to the power exerted by oarsmen.

The *Mast Step*, is a socket, usually metal-lined, cut into the keelson into which the heel of the mast is seated.

The *Mast Clamp* is a semicircular steel band secured to the after edge of the second thwart from forward. It clamps the mast upright.

Chain Plates have eyes in them and are secured to the gunwale on either side of the boat. The mast shrouds are shackled, or lashed to them.

The boat shown in Fig. 18.1 is *clinker*-built. The overlapping strakes are easier to repair than those in a *carvel*-built boat. In this type the strakes are flush and the construction is generally stronger, since the whole of the strake width bears against the timbers.

COMPONENTS OF AN OAR

The *Loom* is the part grasped by the hands when rowing.
The *Blade* is the flattened area which grips the water.
The *Shaft* is that part of the oar between the blade and the loom.

ROWING TERMS

A *Crutch* is a brass or galvanised-iron fitting, comprising a lower cylindrical stem with a horse-shoe-shaped piece above it. The stem fits into a metal-lined hole in the gunwale, and the shaft of the oar rests in the curved part.

A *Rowlock* is merely a rectangular piece *cut out of the gunwale*. The shaft of the oar rests in the gap when rowing. The gap is capable of being filled with a piece of wood (attached to the boat by means of a lanyard) known as a *poppet*.

A *Thole Pin* projects up from the gunwale into which it is bedded. The oars used with this fitting are drilled, the hole being metal-lined, so that the oar may be lowered on to the thole pin, which then passes through the oar, holding it in place.

'*Out oars*'—an order at which the crew fit their oars into the crutches, rowlocks, or thole pins, and sit on their thwarts, hands grasping the looms of the oars. The oars should be horizontal.

'*Give way together*'—an order at which both port and starboard oarsmen commence rowing. The stroke oar, i.e. the man rowing adjacent to the coxswain, sets the stroke and timing, and the others each watch the back of the man immediately in front, and not their individual oars. In this way the men are able to keep in step.

'*Oars*'—an order at which one more stroke is made, the oars are raised from the water, and allowed to rest horizontally projecting from the boat.

'*Hold water*'—an order at which the blades are placed in the water and the oars held rigidly at right angles to the gunwale. This assists in taking the way off the boat.

'*Back water*'—an order at which the oars are used in the reverse direction in order to gather sternway, i.e. the looms are pushed aft instead of being pulled forward.

'*Bow*'—an order at which the bowman boats his oar and stands by in the bow sheets with boathook or painter, ready for going alongside.

'*Way enough*'—an order at which one more stroke is made and the oars are then placed as for the command 'Oars'.

'*In oars*'—this follows 'Way enough' almost at once. Each loom is swung forward and towards the gunwale. The oars are then lifted from their fittings and laid on the side benches.

'*Toss and boat the oars*' is an order frequently used in double-banked boats (two oarsmen on each thwart), where the oars are to be boated and laid down the fore-and-aft midships line of the boat. A port oarsman, for example, will place his left hand on top of the loom at the extreme end of the oar and his right hand underneath the shaft close to the crutch or rowlock. In one movement he bears down with his left hand and lifts with his right, so that the oar swings up through a right angle. It should come to rest in a vertical position with the end of the loom resting on the bottom boards between the oarsman's feet, and at the same time being given a twist so that the blade plane is fore and aft. All oars are then simultaneously lowered, blades forward in this case, and laid on the middles of the thwarts, again twisting the oar so that the blade lies flat. It is extremely spectacular, but not greatly favoured by inexperienced lifeboat crews. Before a boat leaves a ship's side it is often very useful to toss the inside oars and use the blade tips to bear away the boat.

GENERAL REMARKS ON BOAT HANDLING (see also Chapter IX)

A boat should preferably be on an even keel with no list. A slight trim by the stern, however, is favourable when running before a heavy sea, since this prevents the bows from being driven under.

When unhooking the falls, particularly when the ship has way on her or, what amounts to the same thing, the boat is fast alongside head-to a stream current, the after fall should be unhooked first. When berthing heading into a current the forward block should be hooked *on* first. In both cases the boat is then prevented from being swung athwart the tide.

Once clear of the ship or quay, all fenders and loose ends of rope should be brought inboard. Needless to say, when lowering a lifeboat from davits the plug should be checked well before the boat is launched. At night the plug is often difficult to find, and many boats have a mark or arrow cut into the gunwale or side benches abreast of it. If such a mark is brightly painted it serves a useful purpose by day and prevents burrowing under the bottom boards.

Careful allowance should be made for all currents in the vicinity, remembering that, generally speaking, they are weakest close inshore. A wide berth should be given to all anchored ships, and in a stream current it is advisable to pass astern of them. It is surprising otherwise how quickly a boat may be swept towards the anchor cables. When handling a rowing-boat, it should be borne in mind that large rudder angles retard the boat and put an added stress on the oarsmen.

In a moderate or heavy sea, rather than running to a destination beam-on to the waves, it is better to zig-zag, i.e. steer a *dog's-leg* course. Survivors in boats should use the oars only for heading towards a rainstorm (when short of water), for exercise in freezing conditions, and for avoiding navigational dangers. They will initially be used for clearing the abandoned ship, although it must be emphasised here that one of the prime duties of a motor-boat is to muster the rowing-boats together and tow them until such time as the fuel supply is exhausted. This is particularly important when rowing-boats are desperately trying to clear a ship which is rolling heavily, on fire, or liable to capsize over the boats.

Breaking waves, and the wash of other craft, should be met bows-on, the oars possibly being temporarily feathered, i.e. rested horizontally with blade planes parallel to the water.

The wind or stream, whichever has the stronger effect, should always be stemmed when going alongside, and as soon as possible, in a tideway, a painter should be led well ahead from the inside bow. If this is kept tight the boat can be sheered either way while riding alongside, and is thus under the control of her rudder. Only one fairlead is usually fitted to lifeboats, on the forward gunwale, and this is primarily for passing the sea-anchor warp.

If the lifeboat is to anchor the bitter end of the anchor line should be well secured, the stock of a common anchor well locked in place, and sufficient line streamed to reach the bottom before the anchor is let go. It is as well to have a little sternway on the boat when paying out the anchor warp. A scope of at least four should be used, calculated on high-water depths. If the lifeboat continually snatches at her anchor warp more line should be veered. As a last resort, a heavy object should be slid down the warp until it lands on the sea-bed. If the boat is to be anchored on a rocky bottom it is as well to secure the warp to the crown of the anchor, stopping it lightly to the anchor ring. If the anchor is later found to be fouled a sharp tug on the warp will carry away the stopping, the anchor then being hove up crown first.

HOISTING A BOAT INBOARD

A long boat-rope should be passed along the hull and secured fore and aft. The falls should be slacked down until the blocks are just at the right height for hooking-on, and if within reach they should be tended to make sure that they do not become twisted or that the lower blocks become thorough-footed, i.e. capsized upside-down. In very heavy weather scrambling (cargo) nets should be rigged overside, together with mattresses to act as fenders.

The vessel should form a lee, and spread oil if necessary, to reduce the breaking of waves.

As the lifeboat rises to a wave the forward block should be secured and the after one hooked-on almost immediately following this. The only advantage of this procedure is that since the boat will undoubtedly have approached heading into the waves, if the after block fails to hook-on, when the boat is virtually jerked bows out of the water in the next wave trough, the more buoyant end is still waterborne. Further, the boat is in a better position to meet advancing cross-seas. If a cross-sea met the boat while it was stern out of the water the bows would undoubtedly be swamped.

If time permits the blocks should be turned to remove any twists in the falls.

The boat should immediately be hoisted clear of the sea and raised to the davit heads. The plug may be removed to drain the bilge water, and the crew should hold on to the lifelines, in case the falls should part. The boat-rope, which should by now be secured in the boat fore and aft, is tended by the crew to prevent the boat from surging back and forth along the hull. If the surging becomes excessive the hoisting should be checked until the crew are able to control this movement. It cannot be emphasised too strongly that *no person should be allowed to stand abaft the after block, or forward of the stem block, either when hoisting or lowering*. The reader should visualise himself standing almost at the stem post when the *after* fall parts. He will be crushed between the bow sheets and the forward fall, which now takes the whole weight of the laden boat.

A flooded boat should be hoisted clear of the water and the plug removed. If possible, in the case of independent falls, the boat should be trimmed so that the water flows out over the stem or stern. If this is not possible, then the boat should be left to drain before attempting to hoist it the full distance.

Before leaving a boat, the crew should make sure that the oars and mast are stowed so as to be well supported throughout their length. If this is overlooked these components will quickly warp and become virtually useless.

LOWERING A LIFEBOAT

The crew should be wearing life-jackets. The plug must be checked and fenders rigged over the inboard side. The boat-rope should preferably be passed as before, to prevent surging, together with a painter, which must be kept tight. No one should stand between the falls and the boat ends. All crew members should grasp the lifelines, in addition to working the boat-rope if necessary.

The after block is cast-off first in a tideway to prevent the boat from broaching to. In a heavy sea the boat may be lowered on to a wave crest. As she slides into the succeeding trough, her falls are automatically overhauled (slacked) by the boat's weight. On rising to the next crest they are amply slack for rapid unhooking.

The painter should be kept tight in order to keep the boat fore-and-aft when launched. If the ship is making way, or if a stream is running down from ahead, a tight painter enables the boat to be sheered clear using her rudder. It also means that as soon as the boat is launched, no matter whether the ship is making way or a stream is running, the boat is virtually towed alongside and is kept vertically below the davit heads, facilitating unhooking.

On gravity davits a chain pendant is secured to the lower blocks by means of a patent slip. The other end is shackled to a point roughly two-thirds of the way up the davit. As the boat is lowered from the davit heads, the pendant tightens and the boat swings in to the embarkation deck-level, virtually on a union purchase.

If this pendant is later slipped, when the boat is ready for further lowering, the lifeboat will swing violently outboard as the fall seeks the vertical. This has been the cause of many serious accidents, for the swing is sufficiently sudden and rapid to hurl a crew member over the side. Again, these accidents are prevented if the lifelines are held and the crew keep low down in the boat.

3-in Once the boat has been triced in to the ship's side by these pendants, a length of 24-mm manila rope, provided for the purpose, is passed between the boat sheets and the cleat on the lower davit body. The two or three parts are then held taut in the hands by gripping them together. The chain pendant may now easily be slipped, the manila jerks slightly as it grows bar-tight, and the boat is readily for easing out fore and aft on both manilas. A better arrangement is to use two small tackles and ease the boat out on these.

When time permits both of these remedies may be dispensed with: once the boat is ready for lowering to the water, it is hoisted on the winch, moves away from the ship's side and the pendant grows slack. The latter is cast off and the boat launched in the normal way. One advantage, however, of passing the tricing lines or tackles is that they act as preventers in case the chain pendant should part.

Some davits fitted with fibre rope falls provide for the boat to be lowered by hand control. A stag's head bollard is usually provided in way of each davit. A suitable method of passing the fall around such a bollard is shown in Fig. 18.2, where it is rigged ready for lowering.

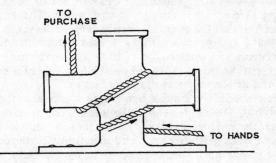

FIGURE 18.2

LOWERING TURNS ON STAGHORN BOLLARD

BEACHING A LIFEBOAT

There is little that can be used here except man-power. As soon as the boat grounds, the crew should jump out and evenly distribute themselves along the sides of the boat. They should then make a combined effort as the next wave breaks, taking care that the boat does not broach-to and injure them. It should be hauled up the beach above the high-water mark, and for this reason, beaching at high water is ideal. The painter may be passed round the hull of the boat, led up the beach, and hove-on by the crew. The yard, mast, and any other short pieces of round timber will act as useful rollers to relieve the stresses.

When it is desired to beach the boat in an area of surf great care must be exercised, wrong judgement quite easily resulting in substantial damage to the boat and possible serious injury to the crew members.

The greatest danger exists within an area of breaking waves. On a

481

gently shelving beach this area may extend well out to seaward. The coxswain should preferably be experienced in this type of boat handling, and the crew must obey all orders implicitly.

A rowing-boat is preferable to a motor-boat when beaching through surf, because not only does the propeller of a power boat race a great deal when pitching, contributing nothing to the boat's way, but there will also usually be poor manœuvring qualities when the boat is running astern. A diesel-engined lifeboat usually has poor acceleration properties, particularly when reversed. A major consideration is that within an area of surf, there is a great deal of white, aerated water, upon which the propeller develops a poor grip. A pulling boat, on the other hand, is more manœuvrable, since the oars can be adjusted for inclination in order to grip the deeper water.

The boat should have sufficient freeboard not to be swamped when proceeding through the unbuoyant surf water. The ends should be lightly laden so that the boat rides easily over the waves, but not to such a degree that it is dangerously lively. A boat fitted with a transom stern, as distinct from the whaler-type of lifeboat, is extremely buoyant aft, and is liable to be carried forward on the fore side of a breaking wave (surfing) and driven under as the wave breaks.

The crew should be double-banked so as to give the boat better manœvrability. The rudder should be unshipped, since it will be of no value when the boat is pitching. The steering oar should be shipped in the after crutch or grommet strop and held firmly by the coxswain, who preferably stands up in the boat so as to have a clear view over the heads of the oarsmen.

While beaching, there is a very great danger of being broached-to, swamped, or hurled shorewards on the fore side of a breaking wave, completely out of control.

Both when beaching and launching in a heavy surf the boat should be headed bows out to sea. Although the crew will have to back water while beaching, a tiring process, the boat will be in a much safer attitude. One consolation is that the surf itself will assist the boat's motion shorewards. In this way the coxswain has a clear view of the dangerous seas advancing towards the boat, and further, the crew are *not* in a position to see them. This serves a dual purpose, reducing any fears, and also enabling them to concentrate entirely on the coxswain's orders, which should be curt and instantly obeyed.

If the boat is capsized it is better for the crew to momentarily strike clear of it, so that they are not hurled against it by succeeding waves.

The boat should meet each advancing wave at right angles to the line of the wave. During the beaching process the stroke oarsmen should keep a sharp lookout for rocks and other dangers.

30-ft   Given a good crew and coxswain, a 9-m lifeboat should be able to

negotiate waves up to 4·5 m in height, by day. At night waves higher 15 ft
than about 2 m should not be attempted. The relationships hold good 7 ft
for other lengths of boats.

It must be remembered that waves have a cycle of development and deterioration, there being from five to seven waves in a cycle. At the end of each cycle there is a period of relatively quiet sea. This period must be chosen for the commencement of the run ashore, and for the actual grounding. Ideally, the boat should ground on the heels of the last wave of a cycle.

Once the area has been selected, then the end of a wave cycle should be awaited and the boat turned head-out to sea. The oars are then used to back the boat shorewards. Ideally, the boat should be kept at least two boat-lengths ahead of a breaker. As a wave reaches the boat, whether breaking or not, the oars should be used to hold water, keeping them inclined well downwards so that they are not snatched from the oarsmen's grasps. If the waves are slow-moving it will be preferable to give way together strongly as a wave reaches the boat so that it is traversed as quickly as possible.

When the boat grounds, say on a shallow beach in a light surf, the steering oar should be boated and the stroke oarsmen ordered out of the boat. They will cling to the stern and hold it against the beach as best they can while the rest of the crew keep backing in such a way that the boat is kept bows-on to the surf. The crew are then ordered out in pairs, starting from aft and leaving the bowmen until last of all. These two men continue the task of keeping the boat head to sea, until they too are ordered out. The entire crew then rapidly heave the boat on to the shore.

In a very heavy surf there is a great danger presented by the undertow, which may sweep the men out to sea and hurl them on to the sea-bed in the inshore breakers. As soon as the boat touches therefore, the whole crew should leap out and heave the boat rapidly on to the shore. Precise timing is needed for this operation, otherwise the boat will broach-to and the men be sucked out and into the breakers.

LAUNCHING A LIFEBOAT FROM A BEACH THROUGH SURF

In a light surf the oars should be fitted into the crutches and laid across the gunwales ready for immediate use. The crew station themselves around the hull and stand abreast their respective thwarts. The boat is quickly launched and the bowmen immediately board the boat and keep her bows-on to the seas. The others then jump in quickly, in pairs, working from forward to aft. As each pair boards, they use their oars to hold the boat in attitude. Last of all, the coxswain boards and the crew pull strongly out to sea.

The boat should continue at speed through the surf, the oarsmen holding water only when a wave is breaking well ahead. The steering oar is again used to keep the boat at right angles to the wave-line.

In a very heavy surf the procedure is similar, except that as soon as the boat is waterborne the crew jump in together and give way strongly. Again, precise timing is necessary to prevent the boat from being broached-to. In each case the end of a wave cycle should be chosen as the instant for launching.

APPROACHING A ROCKY SHORE

Here the boat is used either to land the crew, who then dispense with the boat, or else to embark people from the shore.

The boat should approach the beach heading bows-out. The anchor should be let go when well outside the limit of the breakers, and the boat then backs in towards the beach, streaming the anchor warp. When about half-way inshore from the anchorage the hold of the anchor should be tested. If it breaks out the procedure will have to be repeated until a suitable holding ground is found. The stroke oarsmen again keep a sharp lookout for rocks, and when these are in sight the anchor warp is secured. The crew continue to gently back water, thus holding the boat in position, while the persons ashore enter the boat, carefully watching its motion before they choose their instant of boarding. The task will be made easier if an oarsman jumps out and holds the stern steady by means of a painter. Once the boat is loaded it can be hove out to the anchor, and the latter weighed.

If using a motor-boat there is no reason why the approach should not be made bows-on to the shore, provided there are good securing arrangements aft for the anchor warp.

MANŒUVRING ALONGSIDE A SHIP AT SEA

If the vessel is a wreck or derelict the approach should be made as described in Chapter IX.

For a normal approach the bows and stern of the ship should be avoided, since there will be excessive swirl at these localities. The best place for the landing will be roughly amidships on the lee side. Great care should be taken to avoid the propeller area of a twin-screw ship, since the vessel may be using her engines even as the boat moves close in.

A boat-rope will be rigged overside together with ample fenders and a ladder. If the ship is pitching this motion will be felt least alongside the midships section. Should the vessel have a projecting rubbing strake or band, close to the water level, an oar may be held vertically against this and the boat's gunwale while alongside. This will prevent any chance of the gunwale catching underneath the rubber.

TOWING OTHER LIFEBOATS

This will usually be done by means of a painter. It should be made fast in the sternsheets of the towing boat, either to a towing bollard or to the after two thwarts. A useful method of distributing the stress of the towline is to make an eye in the end which is aboard the towing boat. The eye is then rove beneath the after thwart and held up forward of it. An oar is passed through the eye and laid flat along the thwarts, fore and aft. The oar then acts as a toggle. The eye should be slid down the oar until it is hard up against the forward edge of the after thwart. This will avoid excessive bending stresses in the oar.

The towed boat should stream a sea-anchor when running before a heavy following sea to prevent surfing ahead and on to the towing craft. The length of the towline should be adjusted so that both boats are in step with the waves. (See Chapter X.)

Any number of boats may be towed, but the painter of each should be secured into the sternsheets of the next in line ahead, preferably by means of the 'toggle oar'.

In breaking seas each boat should stream oil from the bows.

LIFEBOAT SAILING

Terms in General Use

Close-hauled, By the wind, On the wind, are expressions used to denote that a boat is sailing as closely as possible in the direction from which the wind is blowing. In a lifeboat about five points is the closest possible angle to the wind. The boat is only free to alter course away from the wind, i.e. to pay off.

Reaching refers to a boat which is sailing with the wind on the beam (a broad reach), or forward of the beam (a close reach), but not so as to be close-hauled. She is free to alter her course in either direction, but more so down-wind.

Tack: a boat is on the port or starboard tack when the wind is on the port or starboard bows. For the purpose of fog-signals, it extends as far as the beam.

Tacking or *Going about* occurs when the boat changes from one tack to the other by sailing through the wind's eye (wind direction). It is preceded by the order '*Ready about*' or '*Stand by to tack*'.

Beating refers to a boat which is sailing to windward, close-hauled on a series of alternate tacks, i.e. she steers a zig-zag or dog's-leg course. If she can sail to her destination on one tack, and back on another, she is said to have a *Soldier's wind*.

Running or *Running free* refers to a boat which has the wind abaft the beam.

485

Sailing free refers to a boat which is able to alter her course either way; it does not therefore include boats which are close-hauled.

Gybing. This occurs when the wind is from aft and, due to yaw or gusting, the wind catches the sail on the wrong side. The sail is then flung violently across the boat, and if not loose-footed, i.e. if it has a boom attached to the foot, it may do serious injury to the crew. In addition to this, the violence of a gybe can often carry away the mast and/or rigging. The danger is most prevalent when sailing with the wind dead astern. Gybes are often executed purposely, but in this case they are controlled.

Wearing is a means of changing tack by moving the boat's stern through the wind's eye. The boat is headed away from the wind, her stern runs into the wind, a controlled gybe is carried out, and she is slowly brought round on to the other tack.

On the port (or starboard) gybe refers to a boat which is running with the wind on the port (or starboard) quarter.

Brought by the lee refers to a condition where the wind catches the sail on the lee side; an example of this occurs when the boat gybes accidentally.

No higher is a term used to indicate that the boat must not be brought any closer to the wind.

Nothing off is the reverse of 'No higher', and therefore means that the boat is not to pay off any more.

To miss stays refers to a boat which has tried to go about but which has paid off again on the original tack.

In irons or *In stays* refers to a boat which has tried to go about, has headed into the wind's eye, but which has failed to pay off on *either* tack. It may be remedied by holding the clew of the jib out to the original lee side, i.e. the jib is *backed*.

Helm. The tiller is usually referred to as the helm. The lee and weather sides of the boat are respectively called the *down* and *up* sides for the purpose of helm orders, so that when the order '*Down helm*' is given the tiller is put a-lee and the boat runs up into the wind. Similarly, '*Up helm*' results in the boat paying off. Other terms are '*Up-wind*' and '*Down-wind*'. '*Bear up*' means the same as 'Up helm'.

Carrying lee helm indicates that if the tiller is left amidships the boat tends to pay off. In this condition she is likely to broach-to in squally conditions, and *carrying weather helm* is a preferable state of affairs, for the boat is constantly seeking the wind.

One point on the sail surface is considered to be the centre of effort, where all the wind force may be considered to act. One point on the underwater hull surface, at or near the pivoting point, is considered to be the centre of lateral resistance. If the two points, centres of effort, and lateral resistance are not in line the boat will carry lee or weather helm, for a couple exists between these two points.

Luff, or *Luff-up* means to steer closer to the wind.

Weathering an object means to pass to windward of it.

Flat aft refers to sails, the sheets of which have been hauled as tightly aft as possible.

A boat is *Taken-aback* when the sails fill suddenly from the wrong direction, due to a yaw or a sudden change in wind direction. *Hugging* means sailing as close to the wind as possible, while *Pinching* refers to a boat which is sailing too close for efficiency. *To reef* or *Shorten sail* means to reduce the sail area. A boat *Lies to* when she is in the wind's eye with a small sail area hoisted. She is *Hove-to* when she is stopped in the water; it is achieved by backing the sails in the wind's eye. A boat is *Goosewinged* when running dead before the wind with the sails set on both sides of the boat.

SAILING THE LIFEBOAT

Generally, this is an unsatisfactory procedure, the best that is achieved being a trend in the desired direction. The boat has no drop-keel and only a small lateral resistance, as a result of which she will invariably make considerable leeway.

The lifeboat is fitted with a lugsail, the one illustrated in Fig. 18.3 being a standing lugsail, since once it is hoisted, no further manœuvring of the yard or gaff boom is necessary, unless of course the wind freshens. The dipping lugsail, however, extends considerably farther forward from the mast, and its tack is secured at the stem head. This lugsail must always lie on the lee side of the mast, so that the yard must be lowered and dipped around the mast each time the boat changes tack. In the case of the standing lug it is left permanently rigged on one side of the boat.

The sail is made of terylene or flax canvas and is loose footed, i.e. has no roping at the foot. The roping extends along the head, the luff, and around the clew as far as the reef band. This sail roping may be manila or boltrope, which is a tarred soft hemp. It is always sewn on the port side of a sail.

The reader should study the various parts of the sail and learn the names. The letters MV on the sails represent the first and last letters of the ship's name, e.g. S.S. *Mativ*. The jib may be secured to a forestay by means of jib clips, but usually the lifeboat has no forestay, and so the jib is hoisted free on the halliards. If the jib halliards are set up tight the roping on the jib luff acts in the same way as a forestay.

The mast traveller is simply a metal ring sliding on the mast. Forged in to the ring is a hook projecting downwards and an eye projecting

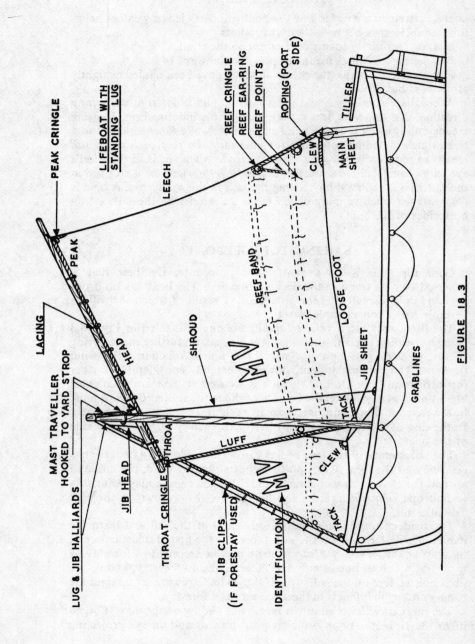

PEAK CRINGLE

LIFEBOAT WITH STANDING LUG

REEF CRINGLE
REEF EAR-RING
REEF POINTS

ROPING (PORT SIDE)

LEECH

PEAK

MAIN SHEET

CLEW

TILLER

LACING

REEF BAND

HEAD

SHROUD

LOOSE FOOT

MAST TRAVELLER HOOKED TO YARD STROP

JIB HEAD

JIB SHEET

LUG & JIB HALLIARDS

THROAT

TACK

GRABLINES

THROAT CRINGLE

LUFF

CLEW

JIB CLIPS (IF FORESTAY USED)

IDENTIFICATION

TACK

FIGURE 18.3

upwards. The eye is secured to the main halliards and the hook is passed through the strop on the yard, leaving the lugsail ready for hoisting.

The head of the mainsail is bent on to the yard by means of peak and throat lashings or ear-rings, passed through the peak and throat cringles. The remainder of the head may be secured by means of a spiral lacing passed around the yard and through the eyelets worked into the sail. This has the disadvantage of carrying away the majority of the sail head if one part of the lacing chafes through. A preferable arrangement is to use separate stops for each eyelet, as shown in the illustration.

The sails must always be carefully handled and maintained; periodically at sea, they should be unrolled and hung up to air, making sure that they are sufficiently secure to prevent them flapping about. They should never be stowed away wet, and all traces of salt must be washed off with fresh water, before they are dried and stowed. A close watch must be kept for signs of mildew.

New cotton duck or canvas sails should be run-in at an early opportunity, since they stretch considerably when new. The boat should be sailed on a bright, sunny day, reaching in a gentle or light breeze. Beating should not be attempted on this first run. After about three or four hours of figure-of-eight reaching, the sails should be sufficiently stretched for close-hauling. Neither the halliards nor the tack lashing should be too tight, otherwise the luff will stretch more than the leech. The peak lashing should be continually adjusted to take up the slack forming in the head. The sail should never be reefed until it has been properly stretched.

Dirty sails may be lightly scrubbed with fresh, soapy water, endeavouring always to keep such a solution off tarred roping. When dry, the sails should be folded away in their covers; the best way of doing this is to lay the sail flat and fully extended, but not on a sandy or gritty surface, place the luff and leech along the yard, gather up the bight of the sail in a roll, and lightly stop it to the yard with rope yarns.

Setting the Sails

The standing lugsail should be hoisted with the yard strop situated about one-third of the length of the yard abaft the throat. The luff should be set tight and the tack lashing hove taut until a crease just begins to run down from the peak, the crease later disappearing when the sail fills with wind.

The lugsail should preferably be hoisted on the lee side of the mast, heaving the halliards taut on the *windward* side so as to provide extra support to the mast. The jib should be hoisted with the luff tight, and the lead of the sheets should be such that a continuation of the line of the sheet will bisect the angle at the clew. When the mast is later stowed it is surprising how tangled the rigging can become, and it is as well to lay all the lines, shrouds, and halliards along the full length of the mast in the reverse order to that in which they are set up. They are then lightly stopped to the mast with rope yarns, which can easily be cut.

The jibsheet should be adjusted so that the wind can pass freely between it and the lee side of the mainsail, thus creating a pressure drop behind the mainsail. The jibsheet may be belayed at times, but it is unwise to do this with the mainsheet unless a jambing cleat is provided.

Manœuvring the Boat

Fig. 18.4 shows the action of a wind on the sail of a boat. In the upper illustration the boat is close-hauled, ST represents the thrust of the wind

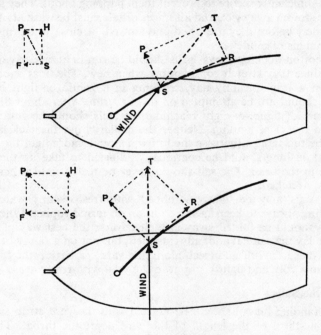

FIGURE 18.4

at the centre of effort, and SR a component of this force acting along the surface of the sail. The other component SP, acting perpendicularly to the surface of the sail, may be resolved into two components, SH heeling the boat and producing leeway, and SF causing forward motion. It will be noticed that the heeling force is greater than the forward propelling force.

In the lower illustration the same boat is reaching. SF is considerably increased, and a boat sailing in this way does so at a greater speed than when she is beating.

Heeling may be corrected by seating the crew to windward, and leeway by the use of a drop-keel, the use of which is not provided for in a lifeboat. The rudder suffers a loss in efficiency when the boat is heeled, so that the boat should be trimmed slightly by the stern under this condition.

It will be noticed that the sheet must be eased when the wind is brought broader on the bow, otherwise there will be a danger of capsizing. The more the sail can be eased out, the less is the active heeling force; this becomes obvious after careful study of the lower illustration. As the heeling force decreases, so the propelling force increases.

This state of affairs does not hold good, however, when the sheet is eased right out, as when running with the wind dead aft, for then the effective wind on the sail consists of the true wind less the speed of the boat. Although the heel will be zero, the propelling force will not be so great as when reaching, for in this latter manœuvre the effective wind is the same as the true wind and a greater speed is attained. The reader should distinguish between the effective wind on a sail, and the apparent wind felt by the crew. In the reaching position, although the crew will feel a breeze from a direction forward of the beam, the full speed and effect of the prevailing true wind is able to act on the sail.

Summarising, then, the boat's speed is greater when reaching than when close-hauled. Similarly, the speed is greater with the wind on the quarter or gybe, rather than dead astern.

The trim of a boat must vary constantly. Beating, reaching, and running all require different conditions of trim for maximum efficiency. Generally, heavy weights should be kept away from the ends of a boat, otherwise she is likely to ship a lot of water fore and aft. When running, an even keel is desirable, for a trim by the stern causes her to be pooped, while a trim by the head tends to make her continually luff-up.

In this way, it will be seen that a trim by the stern will correct a tendency to carry weather helm, and vice versa in the case of lee helm.

Beating

Here the sheet is drawn aft as tightly as possible and the boat sailed as close to the wind as can be achieved without the luff shaking. If the luff is shaking the sail is not holding the wind and the boat is pinching.

When it is decided to go about, pay off a little in order to gather headway, and then ease the helm down. As the boat comes up into the wind's eye let fly the sheets and stand by to tack the jib if it looks as though she may get into irons. As she casts off on the new tack, haul aft the lee jibsheets and the mainsheet, setting her close to the wind.

If the boat gets in stays trim the crew aft, to increase the forward hull wind-area, and back the jib out on to the original lee bow. If she gathers sternway reverse the helm. An oar should be made ready to row the bow through the wind's eye.

Reaching

The boat should be on an even keel with preferably no heel. If any existing heel increases the mainsheet may need easing. Heel which develops suddenly through a gust of wind striking a sail which is sheeted home too tightly may be corrected by putting the helm down. When easing the sheet on a reach, do so until the luff starts to shiver and then heave it in just sufficiently to check this effect.

Running

The sails should be at right angles to the direction of the wind. In addition to sailing more slowly when the wind is dead aft rather than on the quarter, the boat tends to yaw continually, particularly in a rough sea. Further, there is the risk of an accidental gybe. For this reason, it is better to sail a zig-zag course to a downwind destination, sailing on the port and starboard gybes alternately. When running before a heavy sea, a drogue should be streamed from aft, using either the sea-anchor or a bucket. This prevents, to some extent, the risk of surfing and broaching-to.

Wearing

Ease the sheets and put the helm up. The boat then pays off, gathering way. Just before the wind comes astern, give the order 'Stand by to gybe' and heave the mainsheet hard aft. Turn the stern through the wind's eye and the sail will fling across to the other quarter, but the violence of its movement is checked by the tight sheet. The latter must be eased away rapidly as the wind broadens on the quarter. The boat is then luffed-up close to the wind, heaving home the mainsheet. Generally speaking, it is better to avoid a gybe in a lifeboat, whether accidental or otherwise, and the yard is often lowered while passing through the wind's eye astern.

Squalls

If the boat is struck by a squall the sheets should be let fly, the helm put hard down, and the boat allowed to luff-up into the wind, spilling it from her sails. When running with the wind dead aft a gybe must be avoided, and this is done by putting the helm, or tiller, hard over towards the sail clew.

When water is being shipped on the lee side it may be time to take a reef. The boat is run up into the wind and the main halliards are eased. The tack lashing and sheet are secured at the reef cringles and the foot loosely gathered to the reef points, which are stopped around the folds. A rolled sail will tend to hold spray rather more than one which is loosely folded. A reef is shaken out only after the boat has run into the wind's eye.

If capsized, cast off all the rigging, sails and spars, and unship the mast. This gear is then allowed to float clear on a buoyant line. The crew can then place their feet on the keel and heave on the righting lines. Once the boat is righted, it should be quickly baled out.

Berthing and Unberthing

The berth should always be approached head to wind, lowering the sails in ample time. Over-running can be prevented by using full rudder or backing the foresail. When berthing with the wind aft, it is better to run in on the jib alone.

Unberthing is usually done head to wind, backing the jib so as to cast off on the first tack, clear of the berth.

Accidents

If a crew member falls overside, when reaching or beating, put the helm up and wear the boat round to leeward of the man. The boat should then beat up towards him, coming into the wind's eye at the last moment. If the boat is already running she should be luffed up on the same tack and brought into the wind's eye close to the man.

The Use of the Sea-anchor

This is used mainly to keep the boat head to wind and sea by streaming it from the bows, lowering the sails. It may also prove valuable when running before a very heavy sea, since its drag effect will prevent the boat from surfing and broaching-to.

The sea-anchor is a conical canvas bag, open at both ends. Its larger end, or mouth, faces the boat and is kept open either by means of a galvanised-iron hoop or by iron spreaders. The use of these spreaders enables the sea-anchor to be folded flat when not in use. A bridle runs from the mouth to the sea-anchor warp, which is a heavy manila line of length equal to three times the boat's length. A light tripping line, 4 m longer than the warp, is secured to the tail of the sea-anchor. 12 ft The tripping line is used to turn the canvas bag so that it may easily be towed back to the boat.

It is important to realise that in a gale of wind the boat may still make a considerable lee drift, perhaps up to 2 knots.

From the statutory specifications for a sea-anchor, it may be seen that the mouth diameter is approximately equal to $\frac{1}{12}$ of the length of the boat's waterline. The length of the bag is roughly one and a half times

493

the mouth diameter, while the tail and mouth diameters are nearly in the ratio of one to eight.

A drogue can also be provided by towing a bucket, or a jib having a 6-in bridle rigged from its corners, the clew weighted, and a 15-cm hole cut in the centre of the surface.

MOTOR-BOATS

These should generally be handled as described in Chapter 3, for large vessels. Their engines should be frequently overhauled, for they are called upon to run at full power for long periods, idle alongside gangways for several minutes at a time, and are usually given little time to warm through.

When starting the engine the maker's recommendations should be followed closely. The oil level should be checked, the circulating-water system ventilated and flooded, and the engine allowed to warm up at half revolutions for a little while before using full power. It is most important to check the flow of oil and circulating water before leaving the berth. The correct grade of sump oil must be used, otherwise extremely difficult starting, not to mention excessive wear, may be experienced in cold conditions.

When leaving the motor-boat, all valves and controls should be left in the maker's recommended positions, otherwise an emergency start may be impossible. If anything unusual is noticed regarding the controls, of if they are not left in the starting positions, a note should be left attached to the throttle lever.

Never race the engine in neutral. In the case of Diesel engines, the maximum power and revolutions are controlled by governors, and adjustments to these should never be made without the permission of the Duty Engineer. Any extra power so gained will usually be at the expense of wear and possible breakdown.

The crew should be trained to watch for: overheating; darkening exhaust; labouring; alterations in engine note not due to throttle adjustments; excessive vibration; strong smells from a *clean* engine; leakage of oil or fuel; an increase in the oil level, which may be caused by water in the sump; a smell of petrol vapour in the bilges, and clutch slip—which should be repaired immediately. All these are warning signs and must not be ignored.

The boat should avoid sandy or muddy water, the particles suspended therein tending to choke the circulating system. Fire extinguishers should be tested regularly and the engine cover kept on at all times, except when repairs or adjustments are made. It is most important to keep salt water from entering the electrical ignition system of a petrol engine.

CHAPTER XIX

THE DEPARTMENT OF TRADE ORAL
EXAMINATION—FOREIGN-GOING

THE three following sections include the seamanship syllabuses for oral examination which forms a part of each Certificate of Competency. It should be noted that candidates for Class One and Class Two Certificates are likely to be questioned, in addition, on the work of previous examinations; in other words an Officer who presents himself for a Class One Certificate of Competency is expected to be thoroughly familiar with all previous syllabuses.

Classes 3, 4, 5

The rigging of ships. Methods of ascertaining the proof and safe working loads of ropes, including synthetic fibre and wire ropes. Rigging purchases and a knowledge of the power gained by their use. Knots, bends and hitches in common use. Seizings, rackings, rope and chain stoppers. Splicing plaited and multi-stranded manila and synthetic fibre ropes and wire rope, with strict reference to current practice. Slinging a stage. Rigging a bosun's chair and pilot ladder.

Preparations for getting under way; duties prior to proceeding to sea, making harbour and entering a dock. Berthing alongside quays, jetties or other ships and securing to buoys, with special reference to the after end of the ship. Duties of officers in port.

Helm orders. Conning the ship. Effect of propellers on the steering of a ship. Stopping, going astern and manoeuvring. Turning a power-driven vessel short round. Emergency manoeuvres. Man overboard.

Anchors and cables and their use and stowage. Bringing a ship to a single anchor in an emergency.

Knowledge of the use of all deck appliances including emergency steering gear. I.M.C.O. watch-keeping principles. Use and upkeep of mechanical logs and sounding appliances.

Use and care of rocket and line-throwing apparatus.

Use and care of life-saving appliances.

Bending, setting and taking in lifeboat sails. Starting a compression-ignition engine. Management of boats under oars, sail and power and in heavy weather. Recovering boats at sea. Beaching or landing.

Survival procedure in liferafts or lifeboats.

Use and care of fire appliances including the smoke helmet and self-contained breathing apparatus.

A full knowledge of the content and application of the Collision Regulations and the Annexe to the Rules. (Candidates will not be placed in the position of handling a sailing vessel, but will be expected to recognise a sailing ship's lights and to have a knowledge of her possible manoeuvres according to the direction of the wind.)

Distress and pilot signals; penalties for their misuse.

Knowledge of D.o.T. Merchant Shipping Notices and Admiralty Notices to Mariners. British and I.A.L.A. Buoyage systems. Wreck marking. Code of Safe Working Practices.

Class 2

The handling of heavy weights with special reference to the type and strength of gear used.

The use and care of all deck and above-deck appliances and fittings including winches, capstans, windlasses, davits, fairleads, emergency steering gear and fittings used between anchor and cable locker.

Different types of anchors. Their advantages and disadvantages. Cables and their care. Preparations for anchoring. Anchoring with a single anchor and the use of the second anchor. Clearing foul anchor and foul hawse. Anchoring in a tideway and confined space. Mooring. Hanging off anchors. Breaking and slipping cables.

Getting under way.

Carrying out anchors in boats.

Effect of current, wind, shallows and draught on manoeuvring. Manoeuvring in rivers and harbours. Berthing alongside and leaving quays and oil terminals, with or without the use of tugs.

Management of ships in heavy weather. Means to employ to keep a disabled or unmanageable vessel out of the trough of the sea and to lessen the lee drift. Handling a disabled ship. Extra precautions to be taken before the onset of bad weather.

Outline knowledge of the regulations concerning life-saving and fire appliances.

Measures to be taken following accidental damage, including collision and grounding. Heavy-weather damage and leaks. Methods of dealing with shipboard fires. Organisation and direction of firefighting, liferaft and lifeboat preparation parties.

Practical knowledge of the screening of ships' navigation lights.

Preparations for drydocking and undocking. Use of shores, bilge blocks and bilge shores.

D.o.T. ORAL EXAM.—FOREIGN-GOING

Measures to be taken to prevent the spillage of oil during cargo work, bunkering or transferring. The keeping of records under the Prevention of Oil Pollution Act.

The Collision Regulations and buoyage systems as for Class 3.

Class 1

Exceptional circumstances. Loss of rudder and/or propeller. Jury steering. Action following collision or sustaining damage of any kind. Action following grounding. Methods of refloating. Surveys subsequent to refloating. Beaching a ship.

Steps to be taken when disabled or in distress. Preservation of passengers and crew. Abandoning ship. Survival procedure. Abandoning a wrecked ship. Communication with the shore. Use of rockets and rocket apparatus. Assisting a ship or aircraft in distress. Use of direction for homing on to a casualty.

Rescuing crew of a disabled ship or ditched aircraft. Launching accident boats.

Bad weather manoeuvres. Precautions at anchor and at sea. The use of oil for smoothing the sea. Anchoring, and working anchors and cables in all circumstances. Approaching rivers and harbours and manoeuvring therein. Approaching off-shore loading points under open-sea conditions. Towing and being towed.

Drydocking. General procedure and precautions to be observed. Distribution of weight. Drydocking with full cargo for inspection of propellers and shafting. Bilge blocks. Leaving the vessel waterborne. Putting into port with damage to ship and/or cargo from both business and technical points of view. Safeguarding of cargo.

Prevention of fire at sea and in port. Methods used and action taken to prevent fire spread. Full knowledge of the use, and precautions in use, of fire appliances.

Methods of pest control and fumigation of holds and living spaces. Safeguards in use of these methods.

The Collision Regulations and buoyage as for Class 3.

Radio-telephony. Knowledge of distress and safety communication procedure on R/T distress- and calling-frequencies as indicated in the International Code of Signals and the Post Office Handbook for Radio Officers.

Portable radio equipment. Preparation and use of portable radio equipment as used in lifeboats and liferafts, including the erection of aerials. Knowledge of facilities and frequencies provided.

Port radio information. Knowledge of the type of service to aid vessels entering ports and assist in berthing as indicated in the Admiralty List of Radio Signals 'Port Radio Stations and Pilot Vessels'.

INDEX

Abandoning ship, 143, 182, 474
  clothing for, 183
  diving overboard, 182
  use of boats, 182
Abbreviations, chart, 299
A'cockbill, *see* Anchor
Acts
  Anchors & Chain Cables (1967), 9, 10
  Merchant Shipping, 142
  Oil in Navigable Waters, 343
Admiralty Pattern, *see* Anchor
Advance of turning, 59
Aft, anchoring from, 32
Agents, Lloyd's, 171, 173
Aggregate for concrete, 148
Agreement
  Crew's, ALC 6, 285
  Lloyd's Salvage, 169, 213, 214
Air
  compressed, use of, 148
  search, 122
  starvation of, 236
  traffic control centres, 119
Aircraft
  assistance from, 122
  carriers, 358, 367, 369
  distress signals, 123
  ditching of, 125, 357
  general remarks, 122, 125
  lights, 304
  low flying, 125
  rubber dinghy, 125
  sighted at sea, 281, 362
  survivors' signals, 125, 366
  urgency signals, 124, 366
  see also Seaplanes
Alarms, 459–60
Altering course in ice, 114
AMVER system, 292
Anchor
  a'cockbill, 15
  Admiralty pattern, 1
  angle of rotation of head, 2
  backing-up, 160

Anchor (*con'd.*)
  bad weather at, 20, 22
  ball, 19, 23
  bell, 18, 23
  bower, 2, 4, 14, 160, 181
  broken out, 2, 21
  care of, 12, 261
  carrying out, 160, 164
  cast Type A.C.14, 4, 181
  changing an, 33
  clearing an, 15, 23, 28
  common, 1
  cross-bearings at, 19, 20
  depth of water at, 19
  dimensions, 1, 2
  disadvantages of types, 1, 2
  drag on vessel at, 20
  dragging, 19, 20, 22
  duties at, 20
  foul, 15, 23, 28, 368
  gravity band, 2
  hammer test, 10
  hanging of, 29
  heat treatment, 9, 12
  holding ground, 4
  holding power, 1, 2, 4
  hurricane at, 22
  kedge, 1, 2, 14, 27, 153, 161
  lee, 37
  lifeboat, 1, 220
  lights, 19, 23, 33
  Lord Nelson's, 1
  loss in weight in water, 33
  manufacturers, 2
  markings, 11
  materials, 9
  parts, 1, 3
  patent stockless, 2
  percussive test, 9
  pitching at, 18
  pointing ship at, 25
  proof load of, 10
  retesting, 12
  riding, 37
  sea, *see* Sea anchor

Anchor (*contd.*)
  second, 22, 37
  securing, 18
  shackle, 6, 8, 9, 11
  sheer at, 20
  sheet, 2
  size, 1, 2
  sleeping, 37
  spare bower, 2
  spheres, 1
  spreading oil at, 193
  stability of, 1, 2, 4
  stocked, 1, 9
  Stokes, 4–6, 181
  stream, *see* kedge
  survey of, 24, 261
  swinging room at, 19, 37
  test certificate, 9
  tests, 9
  throat, *see* trend
  towing, 160
  transit bearings at, 20
  trend of, 3, 10
  turning on, 27, 89, 105
  types, 1, 2, 4
  use as sea anchor, 208
  use as second, 22, 37
  use in manoeuvring, 27, 69, 88 *et seq.*
  use in tandem, 160
  use in ungrounding, 160
  various parts, 1, 3
  veering cable at, 22
  walking back, 14
  washing, 2, 13
  watches, 20
  weighing, 2, 22, 30
    without windlass, 30
  weights of, 1, 2, 10
  yawing at, 20
Anchoring
  at high speed, 24
  casting when, 17
  from aft, 32
  in a current, 17
  in a wind, 17
  in deep water, 16, 17
  in ice, 116
  near a danger, 24
  near a steep beach, 26
  on a shoal, 24
  terms, 14
  to single anchor, 16
  use of bell, 18
    of windlass, 30

Annealing
  lifting gear, 373, 380
Angle
  drift, 59
  rotation of anchor head, 2
Anti-
  aircraft firing, 365
  fouling paint, 261–2
  freeze, 112
  scorbutics, 289
Areas, practice or firing, 364
Arming leadline, 445
Artificial horizon, 115
Ashore, running, 171
Assistance
  from aircraft, 122
  rendering, 126, 188
Association, Salvage, 171
Auto-alarm, 119, 323, 346
Automatic release hooks, 136
Awning(s), 186, 206, 240, 282
  spars, 194, 206
Axe, felling, 32

Back
  angle, 115
  -weight gear, 400
Backing, *see* Anchor
Bad weather
  at anchor, 20, 22
  at sea, 204
Ball, *see* Anchor
Ballast condition, 152
Baltic moor, 43
Band, gravity, 2
Bank
  cushion, 67, 69
  suction, 67, 69
Barque, 371
Barquentine, 371
Beach
  for beaching, 177
  steep, anchoring near, 26
Beaching
  a lifeboat, 481
  a vessel, 142, 177
  bow on, 178
  holdfasts, 179
  stern on, 178
Bearings
  cross, 19, 20
  transit, 20
Beaufort, hydrostatic release, 140

Behaviour of vessel in heavy sea, 200, 201
Bell
  anchoring, 18, 23
  for indicating, 141
  for time-keeping, 280
  signalling apparatus, 341
Bends
  in river, 68, 69
  in rope, 415
Berthing
  in a wind, 78, 90 et seq.
  in calms, 76, 87 et seq.
  in currents, 66, 77, 86
  to stern moorings, 45
  see also Practical ship handling
Beset in ice, 110
Bias, propeller, 52
Bight of rope, 415
Bilge
  blocks, 258
  limbers, 209
  shores, 258–9
Birds near ice, 112
Bitter end, 13
Bitts, 168, 222
Blocks
  care of, 379
  choice of, 379
Boarding nets, 125
Boat
  drill, 183, 289
  see also Lifeboat
Bolster, canvas, 146
Bolt
  hook, 146
  -type shackle, 7
Bordeaux connection, 381
Boring in ice, 110
Bos'un's chair hitch, 421
Bow
  -on beaching, 178
  stopper, 16, 19, 218
  wave, 61, 67
Box
  cement, 148
  -ing compass, 330
Brake linings, windlass, 17
Breaking
  cable, 29, 30, 32
  sheer, 21
  stresses of gear, 6, 10, 347, 383
Breakwater, 33
Breathing apparatus, 243, 244

Breeches buoy, 130
Brig, 371
Brigantine, 371
Brittle cable, 12
Broaching to, 202
Brought-up, 14
Build-up of ice, 117
Bulkhead
  collapse, 143, 147
  collision, 142
  shoring up, 142, 150
Bulldog grips, 437
Bullrope, 33, 401
Buoyage
  cardinal marks, 294
  direction of, 294
  lateral marks, 293
  safe water marks, 294
  special marks, 294
  types of buoys, 294
Buoyancy
  estimating loss of, 172
  reserve, 194
  restoring, 144, 148
  tanks, 474
Buoyant rockets, 132
Buoys
  anchor, 18
  breeches, use of, 130
  clearing in currents, 81
  clearing in a wind, 81
  lying at, 83
  manoeuvring to, 76 et seq.
  ODAS, 355
  securing to with cable, 85
  submarine indicator, 126, 356
Bureau Veritas, 268
Burns, 245

Cable
  amount to use, 19
  bitter end of, 13
  breaking, 18, 29, 30, 32
  breaking stress, 6
  brittle, 12
  care of, 12, 261
  carrying in boats, 173
  clench, 13
  cross in, 38
  elbow in, 39
  growth of, 14, 18
  half-turn in, 28

Cable (*contd.*)
heat treatment, 12
laying out, 173
lee, 37
lengths, 6
links, 6, 10
locker, 13, 261
loose studs, 12
manufacturers, 10
markings, 11
materials, 6
minimum weight, 6
nipped, 16
officer's duties, 18
parting, 18
proof stress, 6
ranging, 12, 14, 261
re-marking, 12, 261
rendering, 16
resistance of, 19
riding, 37
scope of, 19
securing, 13
securing to buoys, 85
shackles, 6, 10, 11, 261
shortening, 14
shots, 6
size of, 6
  links, 7
sleeping, 37
slipping, 21, 30
snubbing, 14
springs on, 18
stones in, 18
stress in, 6
studs, 6, 12
submarine, 28, 369
surging, 14
survey of, 24, 261
taking charge, 17
tests, 10
use in towing, 216
veering, 14
wear in, 12, 261
weight of, 6, 10
Calling the master, 281, 284
Calms
berthing in, 87 *et seq.*
securing to buoys in, 76
unberthing in, 100
Calving of bergs, 108, 110
Canals
effect on handling, 66, 68
speed in, 67

Candles, smoke, 127
Canvas
bolsters, 146
colours of, 442
duck, 443
eyelets in, 445
fibre used for, 442
flame-proofing, 442
grading of, 442
herringboning, 443
needles, 444
painting, 443
raw edge, 442
seam line, 442
selvedge, 442
sewing, 443
shrinkage, 443
stitch size, 443
stretch, 443
tabling, 443
tarpaulin, 442
types of seam, 443
warp threads, 442
waterproofing, 442
weft threads, 442
Capsizing, 202
Capstan
electric, use of, 466
steam, use of, 466
Carbon
dioxide, use in fire, 235
monoxide, in fire zone, 244
tetrachloride, use of, 237, 246
Cardinal marks, 294
Careening, 264
Cargo
dangerous, 346
drydocking with, 258, 267
permeability of, 147
shifting, 201
wet grain, 205, 235
wet wood pulp, 205, 235, 345
Carpenter's
adze, 111
stopper, 168
Casting off
tugs, 72
ship's head, 17
Catenary of towline, 216
Caulking decks, 414
Caution, navigating with, 378
Cavitation, 55
Cement
box, 148

Cement (*contd.*)
  mixing, 148
  use of, 111, 148
Centre of pressure, 150
Certificate
  anchor test, 9
  cable test, 10
  deratisation, 276
  deratisation exemption, 276
  loadline, 268
  safety, 272, 332
  safety equipment, 331
  seaworthiness, 145, 173
Chafe in lifting gear, 387
Chain
  cable, 6, 12
  check stopper, 163
  locker, 13, 261
  open link, 6
  plates, 475
  Register, 383
  size, 6
  splice, 428
  stopper, 422
  stresses in, 6, 384
Chains for heaving lead, 446
Channel centre
  true, 68
  visual, 68
Chart abbreviations, 299
Cheeks of gyn, 393
Chock, sidelights, 332
Claws, devil's, 15, 218
Cleaning
  tanks, 274
  vessel in drydock, 259, 263
Clear
  anchor, 23
  hawse, 15
Clearing
  anchors, 15
  foul anchor, 28
  foul hawse, 45
  see also Handling
Clench, cable, 13
Clothing, abandoning ship, 183
Coast radio stations, 119
Coiling
  ropes, 414
  wires, 436
Collision
  abandoning ship, 143
  action in, 141
  at anchor, 141

Collision (*contd.*)
  at moorings, 141
  bulkhead, 142
  damage due to, 142
  flooding in, 142
  mats, 111, 143
  Master's duty in, 142, 213
  pad or patch, 144
  procedure in, 141
  pumping compartments, 142
  rate of flooding, 142
  Regulations, 299, 359; Annex, 324
  sheared rivets, 144
  shoring after, 142, 150
  temporary repairs, 144
  use of compressed air, 148
  use of concrete, 148
Combustion, spontaneous, 231, 238, 241
Compass
  card, 330
  interference, 347
  magnetic, 347, 370
  number carried, 369
Compressed air, use of, 148
Concrete, mixing, 148
Conning the ship, 113, 286
Containers, liferaft, 135
Copper wire rope, 434
Coral, 176
Cordage, small, *see* Rope
Course alterations in ice, 114
Court rulings on radar, 325
Cradle, floating, 267
Crew
  preservation of, 183
  rescue from wreck, 188
Cross
  bearings at anchor, 19
  in cables, 38
Crossing, fishing nets, 368
Crutch of spars, 390
Current
  anchoring in, 17
  berthing in, 66, 86
  clearing buoys in, 81
  drift, 208
  effect on handling, 65
  securing to buoys in, 77
  strength in rivers, 65, 69
  unberthing in, 66, 86
  wake, 55
Cut splice, 428
Cycles, wave, 200, 482

Damage
  control gear, 111, 143 *et seq.*
  due to collision, 142
  heavy weather, 151
  pounding, 152
  to hatches, 151
  to plating, 144, 152
  to ventilators, 152
Danger
  anchoring near, 24
  during fumigation, 276
  mooring near, 39
  signals, 127
  to navigation, 211
  use of distress signals, 118, 120
Davits
  gravity, 461, 469, 470
  luffing, 460, 469, 470
  quadrantal, 460
  single arm suspension, 138
  underdeck, 463
Deadman
  derrick gear, 400
  in ice, 116
Deceleration, during turn, 59
Deck line, 268
Declaration of Survey, 272
Deep
  draught, vessels, 367
  -sea leadline, 447
  water, anchoring, 16, 17
Dehydration, 185, 345
Deicing a vessel, 117
Department of Trade and Industry
  recommendations, 120, 121, 274, 277,
    310
  syllabus, 495
Derelict, 211
Derrick
  deadman, 400
  doubling up, 397
  Hallen, 385
  heavy, 402
  rigging a, 390, 395, 402
  rigs, 395
  Stuelcken, 387
  swinging, 403
  tests, 382
  Velle, 386
  wing-lead, 400
Determining vessel's heading, 327
Devil's claws, 15, 218
Diameter
  of turning circle, 59

Diameter (*contd.*)
  tactical, 59
Diesel, engines, 51
Dimensions
  of anchor, 1, 2
  of liferafts, 136
  of loadlines, 268
  of waves, 200
Dinghy, aircraft, 125
Dioptric lens, 338, 340
Direction of a vessel, 325
Direction-finding apparatus, 345, 346
Disabled
  seaplane, 125
  ship, 201, 206
    handling a, 206
    rescuing crew of, 188
  tanker, 130, 362
Disc, loadline, 268
Discharge
  of cargo, 170
  of fuel oil at sea, 172
Disintegration, of ice, 108
Dispersal vessel, wreck, 364
Distant signal, 121, 127
Distress
  aircraft signals, 123
  call, 123, 289, 346
  duties of Master, 120
  flares, 121
  frequencies, 118
  in lighthouses, 127
  in lightvessels, 127
  message, 120
  parachute rocket, 121
  procedure, 121
  public services, 119
  revoking a call, 121
  rockets, 121
  silent periods, 118
  signals, private, 119
    smoke, 120, 121, 127, 133
    survivors, 125
    use of, 121
Ditching of aircraft, 125, 357
Divers, 145, 177, 357
Divisions, statutory, *see* Fire
Dock
  allowance, 273
  entering, 71, 105
  entrances, handling in, 71
  floating, 265
  graving, 265
  leaving a, 106

Dock (*contd.*)
  Regulations 1934, 380, 441
Dog watch, 280
Doors, watertight, 141
Doubling gear, 397
Dracone, 362
Drag
  of ship at anchor, 20
  steering by, 158
Draught
  before entering dock, 257
  marks, 260
Dredging
  craft, 169
  down, 23
Drift
  angle, 59
  currents, 21, 208
  lee, 190, 203, 204, 208
  nets, crossing, 369
    extent, 369
  relative, 189, 220
Drill
  boat, 183, 289, 474
  fire, 289, 474
Drinking sea water, 185
Drive, friction, 30
Drogue rockets, 132
Dropping
  down, 23
  moor, 39
Drydock
  action before entering, 257
  bilge blocks, 258
    shores, 258–9
  cargo aboard in, 258, 267
  cleaning vessel in, 259, 263
  draught and trim for, 257
  fire in, 234
  flame-cleaning in, 263
  floating, 265
  graving, 265
  inspecting the, 258
  painting in, 261
  procedure in, 257
  ranging cables in, 261
  repairs in, 257, 261
  routine, 259
  sand-blasting, 263
  shot-blasting, 263
  stability aspects, 256
  ultra-sonic cleaning, 263
  use of anti-fouling, 261–2
  use of shores, 258, 259

Drying ropes, 406, 413
Duck canvas, 443
Duty
  of Master, collision, 142, 213
    distress, 120
  of Officers, at anchor, 20
    at sea, 141, 281, 348
    berthed, 283
    in fire, 242
    in heavy weather, 206
    leaving port, 284
    prior to arrival, 286
Dyes, surface, 125

Echo
  false in ice, 112
  sounder, 20, 281
Efficiency of purchases, 377
Elastic limit, 373
Elbow in cables, 39
Electric(al)
  capstan, 466
  fires, 239, 246
  navigation lights, 332
  telegraph, 458
  winch, 456
  windlass, 464
Emergency
  signal, general, 474
  stations, 141, 241
  steering, 468
Encounter, period of, 201
End link, 7
Enemy of State, 120
Engine
  diesel, 51
  main, 51
  racing, 202, 210
  -room, telegraph, 458, 460
  steam, 51
  turbine, 51
Ensign, when used, 351
Entering
  a dock, 71, 105
  pack ice, 113
Entries in logbooks, 118, 120, 264, 268,
    281 *et seq.*
Equipment
  anchors and cables, 14
  of lifeboat, 472
  of liferaft, 473
Erratic steering, 61
Escort vessel, submarine, 358

Establishing contact between ships, 189, 220

Examination
of lifting gear, 380
port, 353, 355
ship-handling in, 75
syllabus, 495
vessel, 354, 355

Explosive signals, 120
Extempore gear, 390
Eye
in rope, 426
splice, *see* Rope; Wire rope

False echoes in ice, 112
Fast ice, 110
Faying surface, 152
Felling axe, 32
Fenders, use of, 71, 105, 141
Fetch of wind, 200
Fibre-glass lifeboats, 474
Field ice, 110
Fire
axe, 32
Brigade, 236, 242, 245
controlled, 237, 244
dangers of using water, 232
dispersal of gear, 241
divisions, 254
drill, 289, 473
duties of officers, 242
electrical, 239, 246
extinguishers, 236
fatal gases, 238, 244
-fighting gear, 241, 243, 247
fighting in port, 344
flash point, 231
floating fuels, 233, 239
flooding the vessel, 233
general action, 241
hoses, care of, 235
ignition, spontaneous, 231
in drydock, 234, 260
Kidde
Smoke detector, 250, 253
Zone system, 247
Kidde Lucas plant, 253
main, 234
oil, 232, 237, 238, 245
oxidation, 231
patrols, 241
re-ignition, 237
removal of heat, 232

Fire (*contd.*)
of material, 237
smoking as cause, 238, 240
smothering, 235
sources, 237
spontaneous combustion, 231, 241, 238
starvation of air, 236
statutory fire protection, 254
triangle, 231
types, 245
use of
blankets, 236
breathing gear, 243
carbon dioxide, 235, 245
carbon tetrachloride, 237, 246
foam, 236, 246
liquid nitrogen, 246
pumps, 233, 234
solids, 236
steam, 235, 245, 246
water, 232
Firing area, 357, 364
Fish bolt, 149
Fishery inspector, 119
Fishing
nets, crossing, 368
extent of, 368
spars, 390
vessels, 267, 308, 309, 310, 352, 354, 355, 366
Fitting, shackles, 9
Fixing position in ice, 115
Flags
flown by ships, 351
International Code, 348–51
National, 351
Flame cleaning, 263
Flare
hand, 121, 133
of bow, 29
Flash point, 231
Flat
seam, 442
seizing, 426
Floating
cradle, 267
dock, 265
Floats, smoke, 133
Floe, 110
-berg, 110
Flooding
a hold, 209
dealing with, 143

Flooding (*contd.*)
  in collision, 142
  in fire, 233
  rate, of, 142
Flotsam, 212
Flying moor, 41
Foam
  polyurethane, 347
  use in fire, 236, 246
Fog
  action in, 281
  horn, 342
  lookouts in, 141, 281
  man overboard in, 199
  -signalling gear, 206, 282, 341
  signals, 356, 362, 372
  use of radar, 281, 325
Food, in lifeboat, 184, 185, 473
Forelock, 13
Forfeitures, 289
Foul, *see* Anchor; Hawse
Free, surface, effect, 205, 209
Freeboard
  checking in rough sea, 274
  see also Loadlines
Frenchman, coiling a, 436
Friction
  drive, 30
  in purchase, 375
Frictional wake, 53
Frost
  bite, 185, 188
  glazed, 117
Fuel oil
  discharge at sea, 172
  on skin, 188
  swiming through, 183
Fumigation, *see* Pest control

Gale warning signals, 370
Galvanising wire rope, 432
Gangboard, 475
Gangway, as jury rudder, 155
General
  average, 173
  behaviour of ships, 200, 201
  emergency signal, 474
Girding (girting) a tug, 73
Glaciers, 108
Gobline, 73
Gong, signalling, 341
Grapnel rockets, 132
Graving dock, 265

Gravity
  band, 2
  davit, 461, 469, 470
Ground
  holding, 4, 19
  tackle, heaving on, 167
    laying, 159
    stresses in, 174
    use of, 159
Grounding. *see* Stranding, *see also* Purchase
Growler, 110
Guillotine, 16, 218
Gyn, 393
Gypsy, windlass, 29, 30

Half
  hitch, 417
  turn in cable, 28
Hallen, 385
Halon, 255
Hambroline, 414
Hammer test of anchor, 10
Hand
  flares, 121, 133
  leadline, 446
Handing a log, 452
Handling
  a heavy lift, 403
  a lifeboat, 477
  clearing buoys and berths, 66, 81, 86, 99, 100
  disabled ships, 201, 206
  effect of
    bends, 68, 69
    canals, 66, 68
    cavitation, 55
    currents, 65, 66
    engines, 51
    free surface, 205, 209
    list, 60
    loading, 59
    moored ships, 74
    narrow entrances, 71
    propeller, 52 *et seq.*
    rivers, 66, 69
    rudder, 57
    screw race, 55
    shallows, 61, 66
    sideslip, 58
    skid, 58
    sternway, 57, 62
    trim, 60
    tugs, 71

Handling (*contd.*)
    twin screws, 28, 52, 54, 57, 59, 62, 154
    wake current, 55
    wind, 62
  entering a dock, 71, 105
  in examination, 75
  in heavy weather, 203
  leaving a dock, 106
  man overboard, 196
  practical ship, 76 *et seq.*
  principles of, 51 *et seq.*
  securing to berths, 45, 66, 76, 86, 90
  securing to buoys, 76 *et seq.*, 85
  towing, 116, 214 *et seq.*
  turning the vessel, 27, 65, 89, 104, 106, 203, 209
Harbour, hurricane in, 22
Hatches, damage to, 151
Hawse
  clear, 15
  foul, 15, 21, 37, 45
  open, 15, 38
  pipe, 2, 12, 205
Heat illness, 345
Heat treatment
  anchor, 9, 12
  cable, 12
  shackles, 380
Heaving
  down, 264
  the lead, 446
  to, 114, 204
Heavy weather
  at anchor, 22
  behaviour in, 200, 201
  damage, 151
  handling in, 203
  heaving to in, 204
  preparing for, 204
  towing in, 223
  use of lifeboats in, 189, 478
Heel tackles, 386
Helicopters
  limits of, 122, 362
  recovering survivors, 123
  ship procedure with, 123
  use of, 122
Helm orders, 286
Her Majesty's Coastguard, 119, 126, 129, 213
Herringboning, 443
Hitches
  in chair, 421

Hitches (*contd.*)
  in rope, 415, 417
  in stage, 421
Hoisting lifeboats, 479
Hold, flooding a, 209
Holdfasts, 179
Holding
  ground, 4, 19
  power of anchor, 12, 20, 160
Hook
  auto-release, 136
  bolts, 146
  union, 394
Horizon, artificial, 115
Hose
  fire, 235
  steam, 117, 235
Houseline, 414
Hove to, 204
  in ice, 114
Hovercraft, 372
How's she heading, 327
Hurricane, action in harbour, 22
Hydrogen cyanide, *see* Pest control
Hygiene
  fumigation, 275, 277
  Sanitary Convention 1926, 276
    see also Pest control

Ice
  accretion, 116, 211
  action when beset, 115
  action when nipped, 115
  anchoring in, 116
  Antarctic, 109
  Arctic, 108, 110
  barrier, 109
  beset in, 110
  berg, 108
  birds and seals near, 112
  blink, 112
  boring in, 110
  breaker, 114
  calving bergs, 108, 110
  caps, 108
  care of propeller, 113
  concentration of, 110
  conning in, 113
  course alterations in, 114
  crack, 110
  crust, 110
  deck machinery in, 111, 116
  disintegration of, 108
  dock, 116

Ice (*contd.*)
  entering pack, 113
  fast, 110
  field, 110
  fixing position in, 115
  floe, 110
  floeberg, 110
  freezing tail shaft, 114
  freezing of sea-water, 117
  glaciers, 108
  growler, 110
  heavy, 110
  hove-to in, 114
  hummocky, 110
  indications of, 112
  International Patrol, 109
  islands, 109
  lead in, 110
  lilypad, 110
  line of motion of, 113
  lookout in, 113
  mattock, 111
  mooring in, 116
  navigating in, 111
  nipped in, 110
  pack, 111
  pancake, 111
  polar, 108
  preparing vessel, 111
  rafted, 111
  rate of growth, accretion, 116
  rigging in, 111
  rotten, 111
  screwing pack, 111
  shore, 111
  sighting of, 112, 113
  slewing in, 111
  slob, 111
  sludge, 111
  slush, 111
  smoke fog in, 112
  specific gravity of, 109
  survival of bergs, 109
  tabular, 109
  terminology, 110
  towing in, 116
  Track Agreement, 109
  track of bergs, 108
  use of whistle in, 112
  vulnerability of screws, 114
  walking on, 115
  water sky, 112
  working in, 111
  young, 111

Indicating
  distress, 120, 126
  growth of cable, 14, 18
  surface wind, 123
  urgency, 121, 124
Inert gas, 253 *et seq.*
Intelligence, Lloyd's, 119
Intermediate
  link, 7
  shaft, 50
International
  Code of Signals, 348
  distress signals, 120
  Ice Patrol, 109, 117
  loadline ships, 268
  Sanitary Regulations, 276, 279
Inward-turning screws, 54, 57

Jaw
  long, 379, 413
  of rope, 408, 414
Jetsam 212
Jettisoning
  cargo, 212
  rafts, 194
Joining shackles
  bolt, 7
  lead pellet, 7, 261
  lugless, 8
  marks on, 11, 12
  position, 21
  spile pin, 7
Joggle shackle, 33
Jury rudder
  rigging, 154
  types, 154
  use of, 112, 153

Kedge, *see* Anchor
Kelvin sounding machine 448
Ketch, 372
Keying device, radio, 119
Kidde
  fire-fighting gear, 247, 253
  smoke detectors, 250, 263
Kinks in wire rope, 435
Kite, survivors', 125
Knots
  in rope, 414 *et seq.*
  speed unit, 450

Landing
  aircraft lights, 124

Landing (*contd.*)
  signals, 128
Larsen trawl, 352
Lateral marks, 293
Lay
  of ropes, 407
  of wires, 434
Laying out
  cable, 16, 18
  ground tackle, 161
Lead
  in ice, 110
  pellet, 7
Leadlines, 446
Leaks, 149
  stopping equipment, 111, 149
Leaving
  berths, 66, 81
  buoys, 81
  docks, 106
  moorings, 44, 37
Lee
  anchor, 37
  cable, 37
  drift, 190, 203, 208
  making a, 125
  shore, 208
  tide, 14
Legal aspects
  salvage, 212
  towing, 214
  wreck, 173, 212
Length
  of cable, 6
  of towline, 218
Lifeboat
  abandoning ship in, 182, 474
  accidents in, 493
  action in squall, 492
  anchor, 1, 220
  approaching rocky shore, 484
  beaching, 481
  beating in a wind, 485, 491
  berthing, 493
  buoyancy tanks, 474
  cargo ship requirements, 470
  components of, 474
  conduct in, 184
  davits, 460
  drills, 183, 474
  emergency signal, 474
  equipment, 472
  establishing contact by, 189, 220
  flooded, hoisting, 479

Lifeboat (*contd.*)
  general specification, 470
  handling, 477
  hoisting, 479
  launching, 189, 346, 471, 483
  laying out anchors in, 161 *et seq.*, 173
  lowering, 189, 480
  lowering turns, 481
  manoeuvring alongside, 484
  material used for, 474
  mechanically propelled, 470
  motor, care of, 494
  motor, handling, 494
  motor, specification, 470
  musters, 474
  oar, parts of, 476
  painter, 472, 485
  parts of, 474
  passenger ship requirements, 469
  radio, 119, 186, 469
  rations, 184, 185, 473
  reaching, 485, 492
  rowing, 475–6
  running in a wind, 485, 492
  sails, 487–90
  sailing, 485 *et seq.*
  sea anchor, 472, 485, 491–2
  setting sails, 489
  stowage, 471
  survival in, 185
  towing other boats, 485
  tricing lines, 480
  wearing, 486, 491
Lifebuoy
  dimensions, 471
  inflatable rocket, 132
  number carried, 469, 470
  tests, 471
Lifejacket
  kapok, 192
  number carried, 469, 470
  specification, 472
  tests for, 472
  when diving overside, 182
Lifelines, 205, 471, 472
Liferaft, inflatable
  dimensions, 136
  equipment, 473
  hydrostatic release, 135, 140
  laden launching, 136
  operating procedure, 134
  release gear, 136
  rockets, 133, 473
  safety factor, 134

Liferaft (*contd.*)
  servicing, 135, 471
  single point suspension, 136
  stowage, 135
Life-saving
  appliances, 128, 131, 469 *et seq.*
  by R/T, 118
  by rocket apparatus, 128
  by W/T, 118
  services, 118
  signals, 128
Lifting gear
  annealing, 373, 380
  backweight, 400
  Bordeaux connection, 381
  care of blocks, 379
  care of ropes, 380, 406, 412
  care of wires, 381
  chafe, 387
  Chain Testers Association, 404
  cheeks, 393
  choice of blocks, 379
  crutch, 386
  derrick, 390, 395, 402
  Docks Regulations 1934, 380
  doubling gear, 397
  efficiency, 377
  elastic limit, 373
  factor of safety, 373
  fishing spars, 386
  friction, 375
  heel tackles, 386
  Liverpool rig, 401
  martingale, 387
  mechanical advantage, 375
  proving, 373, 382
  prypole, 393
  purchases, 374
  reeving purchase, 375
  rigging extempore gear, 385
  rigging a gyn, 393
  rigging sheers, 387
  safe thrust in spars, 385
  shoes, 386
  splay tackles, 387
  stresses on parts, 390, 393
  tests and examinations, 381
  thumb pieces, 386
  types of purchases, 376
  union purchase, 395
  velocity ratio, 377
  weight of purchases, 379
  yield point, 373
  Yo-yo gear, 34, 399

Lifts, heavy, 402
  see also Safe working load
Ligan, 212
Lighters, use of, 170
Lighthouses
  communication with ships, 128
  distress calls, 127
Light-vessels, 370
  communication with ships, 128
  distress calls, 127
  light faulty, 368
  out of position, 367
Lights
  anchor, 19, 23, 366
  landing, 124
  masthead, 332 *et seq.*
  navigation, 352–72
  not under command, 361
  screening of, 332, 334 *et seq.*
  side, 332 *et seq.*
  stern, 332 *et seq.*
Lilypad ice, 110
Limbers, bilge, 209
Limit
  elastic, 372
  of helicopters, 122, 361
Line-throwing rocket appliances, 128
Linings, windlass brake, 17
Link
  common, 6
  dimensions of, 7
  end, 7
  intermediate, 7
  open, chain, 6
List, effect on handling, 60
Liverpool rig, 401
Lloyd's
  Agent, 171, 173
  Intelligence Dept., 119
  salvage agreement, 169, 213, 214
  surveys, 145
Load
  proof, 6, 10
  safe working, 373, 384
Loading, effect on handling, 59
Load line
  certificate, 268
  checking freeboard, 274
  deck line, 268
  dimensions, 268
  disc, 268

Load line (*contd.*)
  dock allowance, 273
  for lumber ships, 269
  for sailing ships, 271
  marks, 268
  ships, International, 268
  subdivision, 271
  types, 269
Lock entrances, effect of, 71
Locking splice, 441
Log
  boom, 451
  common, 449
  electromagnetic, 453
  handing the, 453
  impeller, Chernikeeff, 257, 456
  lines, 415, 452
  speed feed from, 452
  streaming the, 452
  towing, Commodore, 451
Logbook
  deck, or rough, 173, 188, 264, 281,
    282, 283, 288
  official, 120, 142, 173, 188, 268, 285,
    288, 289
  radio, 118, 289
Long
  splice, 431
  stay, 14
Lookout
  at sea, 141
  in ice, 113
Loose studs in cable, 12
Loss of
  buoyancy, 172
  propeller, 206
  rudder, 153
Lowering
  lifeboats, 189, 480
  turns, 481
Lubrication of deck machinery, 112
Lugless shackels, 8
Lumber loadlines, 269
Lying
  at anchor, 20
  at buoys, 83
  at moorings, 37, 98

Main engines
  diesel, 51
  steam, 51
  turbine, 51
Main
  shaft, windlass, 30
  wheel, windlass, 30
Man overboard
  missing persons, 199
  procedure, 195, 492
  ship handling, 196
  signals, 133, 195
Manoeuvring
  lifeboats, 477, 484
  liferafts, 134
  ships, *see* Handling
Manufacture of ropes and wires, 407,
  432
Marks
  draught, 260
  loadline, 268
  on anchor, 10
  on cable, 11
  on leadlines, 446–7
  on shackles, 11
Marline, 414
Master
  duty in collision, 142, 213
  dity in distress, 120
  standing orders, 281, 284
  when to call, 281, 284
Masthead lights, screening, 334
Materials
  of anchors, 9
  of cables, 6
  of ropes, 408 *et seq.*
Mattock, ice, 111
Mechanical advantage, 375, 378
Mediterranean moor, 45
Medical outfits, 344
Merchant Shipping
  Notices, 118, 344
Methyl bromide, 279
Mildew in rope, 413
Minefields, 370
Minehunters, 306, 357
Minesweepers, 305, 362
Misdemeanour, 120
Mixing
  cement, 148
  concrete, 148
Mizzen sail, 64, 153
Moor
  Baltic, 43
  dropping, 39
  flying, 41
  Mediterranean, 45
  open, 35
  ordinary, 39
  running, 41

Moor (contd.)
  standing, 39
  straight, 39
Moored ship, passing a, 74
Mooring
  advantages, 37
  buoys, 85
  disadvantages, 37
  in ice, 116
  lines, 85, 347, 412
  near a danger, 39
  stern to, 45, 89 et seq., 96
  stress in cables, 35
  to buoys, 76 et seq.
Motor boat, see Lifeboat
Mousing a hook, 426
Musters, 474

Narrow entrances, 71
Natural sheer, 20
Naval
  control, 354
  splice, 442
Navigation
  dangers to, 211
  safe, 348
  stern-foremost, 366
  with caution, 368
  see also Ice
Needles for canvas, 445
Nets
  boarding, 125
  crossing, 369
  drift, 369
  scrambling, 126, 187
  seine, 369
Nip, freshing the, 216
Nipped
  cable, 16
  in ice, 110
North Atlantic, Track Agreement, 109
Not under command lights, 336
Notices
  Draught and Freeboard FRE 13, 285
  to Marines, 118, 291
  Merchant Shipping, 118, 344
Noting protest, 173, 289

Oakum, 8, 415
Oar
  parts of, 476
  rowing terms, 476
  steering, 155

Oar (contd.)
  use of, 186, 476
Occulting light, 299
Ocean Data (ODAS) buoys, 355
Officer
  cable, duties of, 18
  of the watch, at anchor, 21
    at sea, 141, 281, 348, 352–72
    in fire, 242
    in heavy weather, 206
    in port, 283
    leaving port, 284
    prior to arrival, 286
Offset effect of screws, 53
Oil
  for quelling seas, 189, 192
  fires, 232, 237, 238, 245
  lights, 332, 334
  pollution, 343
  Prevention of Pollution Act, 343
  rigs, 356
  slick, 189, 192
  see also Fuel oil
Open
  hawse, 38
  link chain, 6
  moor, 35
Orders, standing, 281
Ordinary moor, 39
Outward-turning screws, 53
Overboard, man, 133, 195
Overhauling purchases, 30
Oxidation in fire, 231

Pack ice, entering, 113
Pad
  collision, 144
  pieces, 149
Paint
  antifouling, 261
  covering power, 262
Painter, lifeboat, 472
Painting
  canvas, 443
  in drydock, 261
Panama Canal, handling in, 68
Parachute rockets, 121, 133
Parbuckling, 187, 426
Parting of cable, 18, 29, 30, 32
Passenger
  preservation of, 183, 188
  ship, 254
Patch, collision, 144

Patent
  rivet-stopper, 111, 149
  slip, 15, 161
Patrol
  fire, 241
  International Ice, 109
Pellet, lead, 7, 8
Pendant
  anchor buoy, 18
  tricing, 462, 479
Percussive test, 9
Period
  of encounter, 201
  of pitch, 201
  of roll, 201
  of waves, 200
  silent, 118
Permeability, 147
Pest control
  anti-coagulant bait, 279
  Biotrol bait, 277
  Cert. of Deratisation, 276
    exemption, 276
  dangers during, 276
  first aid, 278
  fumigation, 277
  hydrogen cyanide, 276–9
  pests, 277
  rats, 275
  Sanitary Convention 1926, 276
  sodium fluoracetate, 277
Pierheads, effect on handling, 71
Pilot
  ladders, 342, 368
  signals, 286, 363
  vessels, 307, 367
Pipe, see Hawse; Spurling
Pistol, Schermuly, 131
Pitching
  at anchor, 18
  period of, 201
  synchronous, 201
Pivoting point, 58
Plating, damaged, 144, 152
Pointing ship, 25
Pollution, oil, 343
Pooping, 202
Posts, samson, 183
Pounding damage, 152
Power-driven boat, see Lifeboat
Practical ship handling
  in exams, 75
  to berths, 66, 76 et seq.
  to buoys, 76 et seq.

Practical ship handling (contd.)
  towing, 225
Practique signals, 357
Preservation of
  crew, 183
  passengers, 183
  rope and wire, 380, 406, 413, 435
Pressure
  centre of, 150
  water, 150, 265
Principles of ship handling, 51 et seq.
    see also Handling
Proof stress
  anchors, 10
  cable, 6
Propellers
  bias, 52
  bow, 55
  controllable pitch, 53
  inturning, 54
  left-handed, 52, 53
  offset effect, 53
  out-turning, 52
  quadruple, 52
  right-handed, 52, 53
  screw effect, 52
  transverse thrust, 52
  triple, 52
  vibration, 55, 61
Protest, noting, 173, 290
Proving lifting gear, 373, 382
Prypole, 393
Public distress services, 119
Puddings, canvas, 146
Pumping compartments, 143
Pumps, capabilities, 143, 233
Purchase
  choking the luff, 425
  efficiency of, 377
  for heaving ground tackle, 174
  friction in, 375
  heel, 386
  mechnical advantage, 375
  racking, 425
  reeving, 375
  securing a heavy, 167
  splay, 387
  stresses in, 174
  types of, 376
  use of, 31, 33, 174, 373
  velocity ratio, 375
Putty, 152
Pyrotechnics, 121, 124, 188

Quadrantal
  davits, 460
  notation, 330
Quadruple screws, 52
Quarantine signals, 286, 357, 368, 370
Quarter
  points, 330
  trough at, 61
Quelling seas, 189, 192
Questioning survivors, 125
Questions and answers, 352

Racing engine, 202, 210
Racking
  seizing, 426
  tackle, 426
Radaflare rocket, 133
Radar
  Court verdicts, 325
  in fog, 325
  use of, 20, 112, 369
Radio
  auto-alarm, 119
  controlled target, 364
  direction-finding, 346
  keying device, 119
  lifeboat, 119, 186, 469
  portable, 119, 186, 345, 469, 470
  Rules, 118
  stations, coast, 119
  telegraphy, 118
  telephony, 118, 345
  VHF, 119, 123
Raft, making, 193
  see also Liferaft
Range safety craft, 364
Ranging cable, 14, 261
Rate of
  drift, 122, 203, 204, 208
    currents, 208
  flooding, 142
Rations
  lifeboat, 184, 185, 473
  minimum issues, 185
Receiver of Wreck, 211–13
Reciprocating steam engine, 51
Reefs, 492
Reeving purchases, 375
Refuelling at sea, 360
Register of machinery (form 99), 383
Relative drift, 189, 220
Release hook, automatic, 136
Remote-controlled target, 364

Repairs
  in drydock, 257, 261
  temporary, 144
  to hatches, 152
  to ship, 144
Requirements
  for lifeboat, 470
  for lifebuoys, 471
  for lifejackets, 192, 472
  for liferafts, 133, 473
Requisitioning ships, 120
Rescue
  air-sea, 45
  by boat in heavy sea, 189
  of crew of wreck, 188
  of man overboard, 195
  of submarine crew, 126
  of survivors, 123, 125, 187
Reserve buoyancy, 194
Resistance of cable, 19
Revoking distress calls, 121
Riding
  anchor, 37
  cable, 37
Rivers
  effect on handling, 66
  speed in, 69
  strength of currents, 65, 69
  turning in, 65, 70
Rivet
  sheered, 144, 149
  stopper, 111, 149
Rocket
  and mortar gear, 129
  buoyant, 132
  distress, 121
  drogue, 132
  firing a, 130, 131, 220, 245
  grapnel, 132
  inflatable lifebuoy, 132, 198
  line-throwing, 128
  parachute, 121, 133, 473
  Radaflare, 133
  Schermuly pistol, 131
  use on tankers, 130
Rolling
  factors causing, 201
  period of, 201
  synchronous, 153, 201
Room, swinging, 19, 37
Rope
  bass, 410
  bends in, 415 et seq.
  bight of, 415

Rope (*contd.*)
bosun's chair hitch, 422
bull, 33, 401
care of, 380, 406, 413
chain splice, 428
choking the luff, 426
coiling, 414
coir, 410
construction of, 407
cotton, 411
cut splice, 428
dressed hemp, 415
dry spun, 412
drying, 406, 413
end of, 417
essential features, 407
eye splice, 430, 440
fibre, 383, 387, 406, 407
flax, 411
four-stranded, 409
grass, 410
hambroline, 414
hemp, 410, 415
hitches in, 415 *et seq.*
houseline, 414
jute, 411
knots in, 414, 415, 417
leadlines, 415, 446
loglines, 415
long-jawed, 380, 414
long splice, 431
making eyes, 426
manila, 384, 409, 412, 413
manufacture of, 407
marline, 414
mildew, 413
mousing a hook, 426
nine-stranded, 409
nylon, 217, 412
oakum, 8, 415
oil-spun, 412
parbuckling, 187, 426
parcelling, 425
plaited, 409
polypropylene, 411
polythene, 411
preserving, 412
racking tackle, 426
rotting of, 379, 406, 413
running end, 415
S-twist, 407
seizings, 426
selvagee strop, 167, 428
serving, 425

Rope (*contd.*)
short splice, 431, 440
signal halliards, 415
sisal, 409
sliver, 407
small cordage, 414
spunyarn, 414
stage hitch, 422
standing part, 415
stopper, 422
stresses, 384, 410 *et seq.*
tarred, 412, 414, 415
terylene, 411, 412
thoroughfooting, 428
three-stranded, 408, 409
twine, 415
types, 407
unkinkable lays, 409, 434
waterproofing, 412
wear in, 380, 406, 413
whippings, 424
wire, *see* Wire rope
worming, 425
Z-twist, 407
Round
seam, 442
seizing, 426
Routine
at anchor, 20
in drydock, 259
in port, 283
leaving port, 284
Rowing a lifeboat, 186, 475–6
Royal
Air Force, 119
National Lifeboat Institution, 119, 213
Navy, 119, 213
Rudder
active, 55
jury, 153–4
loss of, 153
turning properties, 57
types, 57
use of, 57, 69, 112
Running
ashore, 171
before the sea, 202
moor, 41
on a lee shore, 208

Safe working load
exceeding, 373, 383
in rope, 384
lifting gear, 373 *et seq.*

Safe working load (*contd.*)
  meaning, 373
  of spars, 385
  wire, 384
Safety factor
  liferaft, 134
  lifting gear, 373
Sail
  lifeboat, 487
  mizzen, 64, 153
  parts of, 488
  setting, 489
Sailing
  a lifeboat, 485, 487
  terms, 485
  theory of, 490
Salt water, drinking, 185
Salvage
  agreement, 169, 213, 214
  Association, 171
  legal aspects, 212
  operators, 149, 160
  personnel, 144
Samson posts, 183
Schermuly
  buoyant, rocket, 132
  drogue rocket, 132
  grapnel rocket, 132
  inflatable lifebuoy rocket, 132, 198
  man-overboard signal, 133
  pistol apparatus, 131
  quick-release link, 199
  Radaflare rocket, 133
Schooner, 372
Scope of cable, 19
Scouring, 169
Scrambling nets, 126, 187
Screening navigation lights, 332, 334
Screwing pack ice, 111
Screw
  effect, 52
  in-turning, 54, 57
  left-handed, 52
  offset effect, 53
  out-turning, 52
  quadruple, 52
  right-handed, 52
  transverse thrust, 52
  triple, 52
  twin, 28, 52, 62, 154
  vibration, 55, 61
Sea
  anchor
    lifeboat, 493

Sea (*contd.*)
  types, 207
  use of, 153, 207, 209
  smoke 112
  water, drinking, 185
    freezing of, 117
Seals in ice, 112
Seaplanes, 352
  disabled, 125
  not under command, 361
  signals from, 123, 124
  towing, 361
Search
  air, 122
  and rescue (SAR), 292
Seaworthiness, Certificate of, 145,
  173
Securing
  anchor, 18
  cable, 13
  heavy purchase to wire, 167
  stern moorings, 98
  to berths, 86 *et seq.*
  to buoys, 76 *et seq.*
  to buoys with cable, 85
Seine nets, 354, 369
Seizing
  flat, 425
  racking, 425
  round, 425
  wire, 434
Selvagee strop, 167, 428
Serving a rope, 425
Sewing canvas, 443
Shackle
  anchor, 6, 8, 9, 11
  bolt, 7
  fitting to cable, 6
  fitting to gypsy, 9
  joggle, 33
  joining, 7, 12
  lugless, 8
  marks on, 11
  of cable, 6
  position of, 21
  spile pin, 7
Shaft
  intermediate, 30
  main, 30
  tail-end in ice, 114
Shallows
  effect of, 61, 66
  squat in, 61
Sheared rivets, 144, 149

Sheer
  breaking, 21
  of vessel at anchor, 20
  under way, 61, 69
Sheerlegs, 390
Sheet anchor, *see* Anchor
Ship
  bell, indicating on, 18, 23, 141, 280
  handling principles, 51 *et seq.*
  practical handling, 75 *et seq.*
Shoal, anchoring near, 24
Shoes, extempore gear, 386
Shores
  length of, 150
  use of, 111, 150
Shoring bulkheads, 142, 150
Short
  splice, 431, 439
  stay, 14
  turning round, 104, 105
Side lights, screening, 332 *et seq.*
Sideslip, 58
Signals
  abandon ship, 474
  aircraft, 124
  code of, 348
  danger, 127
  distant, 121, 127
  distress, 118, 120, 121
  explosive, 120
  fire alarm, 241, 250, 474
  fog, 356
  gale warning, 370
  general emergency, 474
  landing, 128
  lifesaving, 128
  man overboard, 133
  parachute, 121, 133
  pilot, 286, 362
  private, 119
  pyrotechnic, 121, 124, 286
  quarantine, 286, 357, 368, 370
  safety, 211
  smoke, 121, 127, 133
  sound, 123
  survivors, 125
  urgency, 121, 124
  visual, 123
Silent periods, 118
Single
  anchor, coming to, 16
  -point suspension liferafts, 136
  screw ships, 52, 57, 62

Siren
  ship, 339
  use in ice, 112
Skid, 58
Slamming, 202
Sleeping, *see* Anchor; Cable
Slewing in ice, 111
Slip, patent, 15, 161
Slipway, 267
Small cordage, 413
Smelling the ground, 61, 68
Smoke
  candles, 127
  detectors, 250, 263
  fog. 112
  making, 125
  signals, 120, 121, 127, 133
Snubbing cable, 14
Soda, 148
Sound signals
  bells, 341
  gongs, 341
  sirens, 339
  whistles, 339
Sounding devices
  deep-sea lead, 447
  hand lead, 446
  Kelvin machine, 448
Soundings, 16, 258
Spars
  fishing, 390
  safe thrust of, 385
Specification
  lifeboat, 470
  lifebuoys, 471
  lifejacket, 192, 472
Specimen equipment, anchors, cables,
  14
Speed
  anchoring at high, 24
  in rivers and canals, 67, 69
Spheres, on anchor stock, 1
Spile pin, 7–8
Splay tackles, 390
Splicing, 428, 439
Spontaneous
  combustion, 231, 238, 241
  ignition, 231
Spreading oil, 189, 192
Springs, 18
Spunyarn, 414
Spurling pipe, 205
Squalls, sailing in, 492

Squatting, 61
Stability
  during fire, 233
  free surfaces, 205, 209
  in drydock, 256, 266
  range of, 202
Stage hitch, 422
Standing
  moor, 39
  orders, 281, 284
Stations, emergency, 141, 241, 473
Stay
  long, 14
  short, 14
Steam
  capstan, 466
  hose, 117, 235
  in firefighting, 235, 245
  main engines, 51
  winch, 466
  windlass, 30, 116, 465
Steel wire rope, see Wire rope
Steep beach, anchoring on, 26
Steering
  by drags, 158
  erratic, 61
  faulty gear, 153
  gear, 153, 467
  in heavy seas, 202
  in shallows, 61
  jury rudder, 153
  oar, 155, 471
  under sternway, 62
Stern
  -beaching, 178
  -board, 80
  -bore, 64
  -foremost navigating, 366
  lights, screening, 336
  mooring, 45, 89, 96, 98
  wave, 61, 67
  -way, 57, 62
Stock of anchor, 1
Stones in cable, 18
Stopper
  bow, 16, 19
  carpenter's, 168
  chain, 422
  chain-check, 163
  rivet, 111, 149
  rope, 422
Stopping leaks, 149
Storm oil, 189, 192
Storms, 211

Stowage
  lifeboats, 471
  liferafts, 135
  rope, 413
  wire rope, 435
Stowaways, 285
Straight moor, 39
Stranding
  action on, 171, 363
  anchors in tandem, 160
  discharge of cargo, 170
  general procedure on, 171
  laying ground tackle, 159, 373
  stresses in tackle, 174
  use of manpower, 174
    of other ships, 170, 176
    of tugs, 168
    of swell, 169
Stream anchor, see Anchor, kedge
Streaming
  anchor buoy, 18
  log, 452
Stresses
  in chain, 6, 384
  in ground tackle, 174
  in purchases, 174
  in ropes, 384, 410 et seq.
Strong
  back, 146
  point, 217
Strop and toggle, 167
  selvagee, 167, 427
Studs in cable, 6
Stuelcken derrick, 387
Subdivision loadlines, 271
Sublimation, 117
Submarine
  action when sunk, 126
  cables, 28, 356, 369
  escort vessel, 358
  indicating position, 126, 358
  indicator buoy, 126, 359
  peculiarities of, 360
  sunken, 126, 359
  surfacing signals, 359
Surface dyes, 125
Surfing, of ship, 202
Surging, cables, 14
Survey of anchors and cables, 24
Survey 1A, 272
Survival in boat, 185
Survivors
  aircraft, 125, 366
  distress signals, 125

Survivors (*contd.*)
  questioning, 125
  recovery by helicopter, 123
  rescue of, 123, 187
  swimming, 182, 187
Swimming
  bath, 206
  through oil, 183
Swinging
  derrick, 402
  room at anchor, 19, 37
Synchronous
  pitching, 201
  rolling, 153, 201

Tabular icebergs, 109
Tactical diameter, 59
Tail-end shaft in ice, 114
Taking charge
  cable, 17
  davits, 460
Tally board, 129
Talurit splice, 440
Tandem, anchors in, 160
Tanker
  behaviour in wind, 64
  disabled, 130, 363
  leaking, 130
  using rockets, 130, 363
Tanks
  buoyancy, 474
  cleaning, 274
Target vessels, 365
Tarpaulins, 152, 204
  canvas, 442
Telegraph
  buoys, 356
  cables, 356
  electric, 458
  engine-room, 458, 460
Temperature
  freezing, salt water, 117
  sub-zero, 117
Temporary repairs, 144
Tests
  anchors, 9
  cable, 10
  for lifting gear, 382
  lifebuoy, 471
  lifejacket, 472
  percussive, 9
Thoroughfooting, *see* Rope
Throat of anchor, 10

Thrumbs, 143
Thrust of propeller, 52
Thruster unit, 55
Thumb pieces, 390
Tide
  anchoring in, 17
  berthing in, 66, 86
  clearing buoys in, 81
  lee, 14
  mooring in, 39, 41
  -rode, 14
  securing to buoys in, 77
  unberthing in, 66, 68
  weather, 14
Timber loadlines, 269
Timekeeping at sea, 280
Titanic, 108
Topmasts, fitted, 395
  telescopic, 393
Towing
  commencing, 222
  connecting up, 177, 218
  considerations, 214
  fittings, strength of, 217
  illuminating a tow, 223
  in ice, 116
  legal aspects, 214
  lifeboats, 485
  lights, 223, 361
  log, 451
  making contact, 220
  methods of, 177
  recent case of, 225
  required pull, 176, 218
  slipping the tow, 224
  supplying power to tow, 219
  voyage, 223
  yaw of tow, 224
Towline
  belaying, 222
  composite, 216
  length of, 218
  securing, 73
  types, 215
  use of cables, 215
  wear of, 219
Track of icebergs, 108
Transfer, 59
Transit bearings, 20
Transverse thrust, 52
Treatment, heat, 9
Trend of anchor, 10
Tricing lines, 463, 480

Trim, effect on handling, 60
Tropical storm, 211
Tropics, survival in, 184
Trough, 61
Tugs
  casting off, 72
  force of, 72, 169, 218
  girding, 73
  gobline, 73
  lights, 304, 361
  scouring, 169
  use of, 71, 72, 106, 168, 218
Turbine engines, 51
Turning
  short round, 104
  twin-screw ship, 28, 55, 59, 62
Turning circle,
    advance, 59
    deceleration in, 59
    diameter of, 59
    drift angle, 59
    effect of current, 65
    effect of list, 60
    effect of loading, 59
    effect of trim, 60
    for twin-screw ship, 58
    path of, 58
    tactical diameter, 59
    time to complete, 59
    transfer, 59
Twin-screw ships, 28, 52, 54, 57, 59, 62
  turning circle, 59
Twine, 415, 443

UHF radio, 123
Unberthing
  in a current, 66, 81, 86
  in a wind, 81, 99, 101
  in calms, 100 et seq.
Underdeck davits, 462
Ungrounding, see Stranding
Union purchase, 395
Unkinkable lays, see Rope
Urgency signals, 121, 124
Urination, 185

Veering cable, 14
Velle derrick, 386
Velocity ratio, 375
Ventilators, damage to, 152
Venturi effect, 67
Vessels
  aground, 311

Vessels (contd.)
  cable-laying, 305
  disabled handling, 206
  examination, 354
  in distress, 120
  in tow, 116, 360
  missing, 119
  not under command, 305, 336
  overdue, 119
  overtaking, 319
  pilot, 308
  quadruple screws, 52
  range safety, 363
  single screw, 52, 57, 62
  triple screw, 52
  twin screw, 28, 52, 54, 59, 62
  see also Handling
VHF radio, 119, 123
Vibration, 55, 61
Visual signals, 121, 123

Wake
  current, 55
  frictional, 53
Walker's log, 451
Warp threads, 442
Warping barrel, 30, 32
Warships, 267, 363, 369
Washing anchor, 2, 13
Washplate, 33
Watch
  buoy, 371
  dog, 280
  officer of the, 21, 141, 281, 348, 352
Watches, anchor, 20, 283
Water
  deep, anchoring in, 16, 17
  shallow effects, 61, 66
  sky in ice, 112
  use in firefighting, 232
Waterproofing
  canvas, 442
  rope, 412
Wave
  bow, 61, 67
  cycles, 200, 483
  dimensions, 200
  making, 69
  period of, 200
  quelling, 189, 192
  stern, 61, 67
Way
  carrying, 50
  losing, 60

Weather tide, 14
Wedges for shoring, 150
Weft threads, 442
Weighing
  anchor, 2, 22
  rate of, 23
  with no windlass power, 30
Welin davits
  gravity, 461
  liferaft, 136
  quadrantal, 460
  underdeck, 463
Whip, rocket apparatus, 129
Whipping ropes, 424
Whistle
  ship's, 339
  use in ice, 112
Williamson turn, 196
Winch
  electric, description, 466
  steam, description, 467
Wind
  anchoring in, 17
  berthing in, 90 *et seq.*
  clearing buoys in, 81
  effect of handling, 62
  fetch of, 200
  -rode, 14
  securing to buoys in, 78 *et seq.*
  turning in, 64, 106
  unberthing in, 81, 99, 101
Windlass
  brake linings, 17
  electric, description, 464
  friction drive on, 30
  power of, 23
  steam, description, 465
  use of, 30, 116, 465
Wing-lead derrick, 399
Wipers, electric, 117
Wire
  on anchor buoy, 18
  insurance, 218
  towing, 216
Wire rope, bulldog grips, 437
  cable-laid, 434
  care of, 381, 435
  coiling, 436
  construction of, 432

Wire rope (*contd.*)
  copper, 434
  cutting, 437
  eye splice, 438, 440
  flexibility, 433
  Frenchman, 436
  galvanising, 432
  general remarks, 435
  inspecting, 439
  kinks, 435
  Lang's lay, 434
  lay of, 434
  lock splice, 441
  lubrication of, 432
  manufacture of, 432
  Naval splice, 442
  preformed, 434
  preserving, 435
  rot in, 436, 439
  seizing wire, 434
  short splice, 440
  splicing, 439
  spring lay, 435
  stowage of, 435
  strength of, 384, 437
  stresses, 384
  Talurit splice, 440
  unkinkable, 434
  wear of, 434, 439
Wireless telegraphy, *see* Radio
Wood
  for extempore gear, 386
  pulp cargo, 205, 235, 345
Working in ice, 111
Worming a rope, 425
Wreck
  dispersal vessel, 365
  legal aspects, 173, 212
  marking systems, 294
  Receiver of, 211
  rescuing crew of, 189

Yachts, 267, 365
Yaw
  at anchor, 20
  of towed vessel, 224
Yawl, 372
Yield point, 373
Yo-yo derrick gear, 34, 399